Uses of Artificial Intelligence in STEM Education

Uses of Artificial Intelligence in STEM Education

Edited by

XIAOMING ZHAI
AI4STEM Education Center, University of Georgia

JOSEPH KRAJCIK
CREATE for STEM Institute, Michigan State University

Great Clarendon Street, Oxford, OX2 6DP,
United Kingdom

Oxford University Press is a department of the University of Oxford.
It furthers the University's objective of excellence in research, scholarship,
and education by publishing worldwide. Oxford is a registered trade mark of
Oxford University Press in the UK and in certain other countries

Published in the United States of America by Oxford University Press
198 Madison Avenue, New York, NY 10016, United States of America

British Library Cataloguing in Publication Data

Data available

Library of Congress Control Number: 2024932940

ISBN 9780198882077

DOI: 10.1093/oso/9780198882077.001.0001

Printed and bound by
CPI Group (UK) Ltd, Croydon, CR0 4YY

Contents

PART II AI TOOLS FOR TRANSFORMING STEM LEARNING

PART III AI-BASED STEM INSTRUCTION AND TEACHER PROFESSIONAL DEVELOPMENT

Foreword

Artificial intelligence (AI), a term not so long ago still reserved for computer scientists and engineers despite the fact that AI was conceived more than sixty years, is now part of everyday language. From White House summits to congressional hearings, from business meetings to academic conferences, and from news to social media, AI has become a focus of policymaking, economic planning, national security, and social debate, thanks to the release of ChatGPT, a large language model-based chatbot developed by OpenAI, in November 2022. The age of AI has arrived.

The U.S. National Science Foundation (NSF) is an independent federal agency that has supported science and engineering in the US since 1950. NSF has been supporting research and development of AI since AI's early conception. Specifically, NSF has provided grants to support research and development in all domains of STEM education, ranging from cognitive and noncognitive tutoring to development of science and engineering practices, teacher learning, and assessment. NSF's investment in AI has accelerated in recent years with the publication of *NSF's 10 Big Ideas* in 2017 and the launch of a multifederal agency and federal–private partnership annual funding program, the National Artificial Intelligence (AI) Research Institutes, in 2019.

Uses of Artificial Intelligence in STEM Education, edited by Xiaoming Zhai and Joseph Krajcik, is a product of the International Conference on Artificial Intelligence in STEM Education sponsored by NSF. As the cognizant program officer of this conference grant, I attended the three-day conference held at the University of Georgia in May 2022. Conference attendees led scholars in applications of AI in STEM education from around the world; many US attendees were NSF grant recipients for their reported work. Many young scholars (i.e., doctoral students and postdoc researchers) were also in attendance. Through keynote and breakout session presentations, as well as stimulating discussions inside and outside of sessions, I witnessed the excitement about the potential of AI in STEM education. I was also pleased to learn of many advances in applications of AI in STEM education, where it was evident that significant progress has been made, particularly in such areas as intelligent tutoring, automated scoring, and feedback giving. I thank Professors Zhai and Krajcik for their vision and hard work in organizing the conference, and for their continued hard work in editing the conference presentations into this book.

Uses of Artificial Intelligence in STEM Education includes twenty-six chapters; it covers the challenges and opportunities of AI-based STEM education; applications of AI in automated scoring systems in biology, chemistry, physics, mathematics, and engineering; intelligent tutors and adaptive learning systems in STEM; AI-enabled inclusive STEM learning for all students; and the ethical considerations of AI applications in STEM education. Along with the Introduction and Conclusion chapters by Professors Zhai and Krajcik, the chapters provide readers with a snapshot of the cutting-edge research and development in AI applications in STEM education; it also demonstrates the potential of AI in transforming STEM education today and for the future.

Congratulations to Professors Zhai and Krajcik and the chapter authors for publishing this timely and important book; it is a major contribution to the field. This book should be a valuable guide for educators, researchers, and policymakers in learning, planning, and implementing AI applications in STEM education. I am sure that this book will stimulate further advances in applications of AI in STEM education in the US and around the world!

Xiufeng Liu, PhD
NSF Program Director, 2020–2
SUNY Distinguished Professor
University at Buffalo, State University of New York

Preface

We proudly introduce this book, *Uses of Artificial Intelligence in STEM Education*, a collaborative effort that encapsulates the groundbreaking work of sixty-five experts from around the globe. Comprising twenty-six chapters, this book serves as a testament to the transformative power of interdisciplinary research, marking the emergence of a new interdisciplinary field focused on the integration of artificial intelligence (AI) into science, technology, engineering, and mathematics (STEM) education.

This burgeoning field gained momentum with the establishment of the Research Interest Group of NARST—RAISE (Research in AI-based Science Education) in 2022. RAISE has become a pivotal platform for scholars, educators, and policymakers, facilitating interdisciplinary dialogues and collaborative research. As the editors of this book, we initiated and witnessed the emergence of this new field. We are delighted to see that this initiative not only underscores the growing recognition of AI's transformative potential in STEM education but also legitimizes it as a distinct and vital area of inquiry within the broader educational landscape.

The inspiration for this book was sparked during the NSF-funded International Conference of AI-based STEM Education in Athens, Georgia, in 2022, which we had the honor of chairing. The conference followed the establishment of RAISE, acting as a catalyst, igniting cross-disciplinary conversations, and highlighting the need for a comprehensive resource in this rapidly evolving domain.

The themes and questions addressed in this book were inspired by a special issue, "Applying Machine Learning in Science Education," published in the *Journal of Science Education and Technology* (Volume 30(2), 2021), and the insights gained from our current AI-related projects and our colleagues'. Even though AI has been sparsely applied in STEM education for more than a decade, the four practical and theoretical gaps recognized in the special issues have yet to be filled. Endeavors such as our PASTA project, UC Berkeley's WISE project, and MSU's ACCR project have explored opportunities to use AI to support STEM learning and instruction but also realized challenges. Therefore, a collective effort like this book can be timely and useful for scholars in the field to further this endeavor.

The book is organized into four themes, each focusing on a critical aspect of AI for STEM education—from assessment and learning tools to teacher development and ethical considerations. Leading experts in the field have penned the chapters, offering a rich tapestry of research findings, practical frameworks, and thoughtful analyses. We believe that the challenges and opportunities presented in this book will benefit our broad audience—STEM educators, researchers, policymakers, and AI scholars.

As we look toward the future, the intersection of AI and STEM education offers exciting possibilities. We acknowledged that the complexity of AI for STEM education presents challenges that require multiple vantage points. We hope this volume will serve as a foundational resource that inspires collaborative, interdisciplinary efforts to navigate the intricate landscape of AI-based STEM education. Meanwhile, we are also acutely aware of the ethical and practical challenges that accompany these technological advancements. We believe this book will equip readers with the knowledge, tools, and inspiration to engage in this critical discourse and contribute to shaping an equitable and effective educational landscape.

We extend our heartfelt gratitude to the contributors for their invaluable insights and rigorous scholarship. We anticipate this volume will serve as a guide and an inspiration for future endeavors in the exciting intersection of AI and STEM education. We also thank the National Science Foundation for their support, without which this work would not have been possible.

Best,
Xiaoming & Joe

List of Contributors

Scott T. Acton is the Lawrence Quarles Professor and Chair of Electrical & Computer Engineering at the University of Virginia. He was Program Director at the National Science Foundation. He is a graduate of the University of Texas at Austin and Virginia Tech. He is a Fellow of the IEEE.

Selin Akgün is a Ph.D. candidate in Curriculum, Instruction, and Teacher Education at Michigan State University. Selin's research focuses on teacher identity and promoting elementary students' sensemaking in science. She also studies the applications of artificial intelligence in education by centering how to teach societal and ethical implications of AI in K-12 STEM settings.

Holly Amerman is a Ph.D. student at the University of Georgia interested in the impact of AI and machine learning educational technologies on teaching pedagogies. Holly has more than 15 years of experience in the classroom and is passionate about helping teachers improve their instruction through research and professional development.

Andreas Borowski is a Professor of physics education at the University of Potsdam in Germany. His research interests are focused on the professional knowledge of pre-service and in-service physics teachers, as well as the competencies of upper secondary school students and university-level physics students.

Lydia Bradford is a graduate student in Measurement and Quantitative Methods at Michigan State University. Lydia was a former high school chemistry and economics teacher. Her current research interest lies in statistical modeling, analysis, research design, mediation and moderation effects, and causal inference in educational research.

David Buschhüter is a Senior Researcher at the German Research Centre for Artificial Intelligence. His research interests include university-level physics education, physics teacher training, and the integration of machine learning and artificial intelligence into the educational sciences.

Mei-Hung Chiu is a Professor Emerita of Science Education at National Taiwan Normal University. Her research areas include conceptual change, modeling competence, assessments and automated scoring, and finding optimal moments of learning via facial recognition systems. She was the first President of the NARST from a non-English speaking country.

Ikseon Choi , Ph.D., Professor and Assistant Dean of Education Systems Science in Nell Hodgson Woodruff School of Nursing at Emory University, applies virtual reality, machine learning, and biosensing technologies to innovate pedagogical solutions that enhance human learning and performance in real-world, ill-defined problems, collaborating with health science and engineering scholars.

Dante Cisterna is a research scientist in ETS's research division. His interests include research on design and use of assessment tasks in classrooms, teachers' development of formative assessment practices, and assessment of student learning of science topics with social and civic implications.

Rachel Dickler is Community Research and Evaluation Manager at the Denver Zoo, where she conducts social science research. Rachel has an interdisciplinary research background spanning Artificial Intelligence in Education, Collaborative Learning Technologies, and Formal/Informal Science Education.

Jennifer Doherty is an Assistant Professor in Lyman Briggs College and the Department of Physiology at Michigan State University. She earned her Ph.D. in Biology from the University of Pennsylvania. She is a biology education researcher and investigates how undergraduate students develop principle-based reasoning in physiology, ecology, and evolution.

Hendrik Drachsler is the head of Educational Technologies at DIPF – the German Leibniz Institute for International Educational Research. His research interests include Learning Analytics, Personalisation technologies, Recommender Systems, Educational data, mobile devices, and their applications in the fields of Technology-Enhanced Learning and Health 2.0.

Jonathan K. Foster is an Assistant Professor of Mathematics Education at the University at Albany. He was a former Postdoctoral Research Associate at the University of Virginia. His research brings together teacher education, artificial intelligence, and argumentation in STEM education.

Libby Gerard is a Research Professor in the University of California, Berkeley School of Education. Her research examines how learning technologies can capture student ideas and help teachers use those ideas to make decisions about classroom instruction. Her recent projects explore the use of machine learning to provide personalized guidance.

Janice D. Gobert is a Professor of Learning Sciences at Rutgers Graduate School of Education and CEO of Apprendis, which is productizing Inq-ITS (inqits.com). She specializes in the use of AI to assess and scaffold students' science learning in real time and to support teachers' instruction in real time.

Adrian Grimm , is a PhD student at the Leibniz Institute for Science and Mathematics Education in Kiel, Germany. His work focuses on equitable Learning Analytics in physics education.

Gey-Hong Gweon is an experimental condensed matter physicist who taught physics extensively at college and graduate levels. He is the founder/CEO of Physics Front LLC and specializes in characterizing the epistemology of physical and virtual experimental inquiry, developing learning analytics, and educating emerging technologies in physics.

Kevin C. Haudek , an associate professor in the department of Biochemistry and Molecular Biology and CREATE for STEM Institute at Michigan State University, is a discipline-based education researcher and utilizes approaches from artificial intelligence to develop science assessments and evaluate student writing.

Peng He is an Assistant Research Professor of science education at Michigan State University, CREATE For STEM Institute. His research interests include designing and testing learning environment with innovative technologies (e.g., Artificial Intelligence), learning progression, classroom assessment, science measurement, and teacher knowledge and practices.

Xinyu He is a Ph.D. student of Science Education at the University of Georgia. She has experience in developing and applying models of automatic scoring for teachers' formative assessment practices in the classroom.

Anna Herdliska is an Ed.D. student of Science Education at the University of Georgia. She is interested in developing AI-based learning tools for K-12 educational settings and measuring the impacts of such tools.

Anett Hoppe is a Senior Researcher at the Leibniz Information Centre for Science and Technology (TIB) in Hannover, Germany. She focuses on interdisciplinary research questions around improving technological support of human learning and scientific workflows.

Devon Kinsey , a Research Associate at ETS, focuses his research on examining the use of teaching simulations within the pre-service teacher population and the development of a career interests situational judgment test.

Matthew Korban is a Postdoctoral Research Associate at the University of Virginia, working with Prof. Scott T. Acton. His research interests include human action recognition, motion synthesis, and human geometric modeling.

Joseph Krajcik directs the CREATE for STEM Institute and is a University Distinguished Professor at Michigan State University. Joe research focuses on designing and testing project-based learning environments to reform science and learning teaching practices.

Marcus Kubsch is a professor of Physics Education at Freie Universität Berlin, Germany. His work focuses on using AI to support individualized learning for all, epistemic cognition in inquiry learning, and human-AI collaboration in research methodologies.

Ehsan Latif is a postdoctoral researcher at AI4STEM Education Center at the University of Georgia. His research focuses on advancing STEM education with the use of AI and designing solutions for automatic performance evaluation.

Hee-Sun Lee is a Senior Research Scientist at the Concord Consortium. Her research addresses the design and implementation of technology-enhanced science curriculum materials, the design and validation of learning theory-based science assessment frameworks and instruments, and the design and validation of AI-enabled formative assessment systems.

Chenglu Li is an Assistant Professor of Educational Psychology at the University of Utah. His research interests include fair AI for educational use, learning engineering with large language models, learning analytics, educational software development, and educational games.

Haiying Li is a former Post-Doctoral Associate with the Inq-ITS group at Rutgers Graduate School of Education. Currently, Haiying is a Program Manager and instructor at the UPenn Graduate School of Education. Her main research addresses conversational/pedagogical agents in ITSs and games for learning.

Xijuan Li is an Assistant Researcher at the College of Chemistry, Beijing Normal University. Her primary research interests encompass learning science, scientific attitudes, and preservice science teacher education.

Marcia C. Linn is the Evelyn Lois Corey Professor of Instructional Science in the Berkeley School of Education, specializing in science and technology. She is a member of the National Academy of Education and a fellow of several prestigious organizations.

Jiutong Luo is an Assistant Professor at Faculty of Education, Shenzhen University and previously a Postdoc at Beijing Normal University. He received his PhD in Education from the University of Hong Kong. His main research interests are educational technology and psychology, ICTs in Education, learning science and educational neuroscience.

James H. Martin is a Professor of Computer Science and a fellow in the Institute of Cognitive Science at the University of Colorado Boulder. His research involves Natural Language Processing with a focus on computational semantics and its application to problems in medical informatics, crisis informatics, and personalized learning.

Ross H. Nehm is Professor of Ecology & Evolution and PI of the Biology Education Research Lab at Stony Brook University. His lab pioneered the use of open-source Natural Language Processing and Machine Learning technologies in biology assessment.

Andreas Nehring is a Professor of Science Education with a focus on chemistry education at the Leibniz University Hannover, Germany. He uses machine learning as tool for learning analytics and learning support toward inclusion. Being involved in numerous STEM research and development activities, he publishes in internationally visible journals and books.

Knut Neumann is the head of the Department of Physics education at the Leibniz Institute for Science and Mathematics Education in Kiel, Germany. His research interests include learning progressions (of the energy concept), science teachers' professional competence, and science assessment.

Amy Pallant is a senior Research Scientist at the Concord Consortium. She has directed numerous high-impact Earth and Environmental science research and development projects that produced evidence-based digital curriculum modules integrated with computer simulation and data visualization technologies for secondary school students.

Sahrish Panjwani-Charania is a PhD student of science education at the University of Georgia. She is also an instructional coach supporting high school teachers working with students with learning disabilities. Her research interests are in supporting science teachers who teach students with learning disabilities.

James W. Pellegrino , a Distinguished Professor Emeritus of Liberal Arts and Sciences, and Education at the University of Illinois at Chicago, focuses his research and development on children's and adult's thinking and learning and the implications of cognitive research and theory for assessment and instructional practice.

William R. Penuel is a Distinguished Professor in the Institute of Cognitive Science and School of Education at the University of Colorado Boulder. His research focuses on interest-related learning across settings, classroom assessment in science, teacher learning, and promoting the equitable implementation of reforms in STEM education.

Marisa Pfläging is a PhD student at the University of Potsdam in Germany. Her research focuses on the Nature of Science and science understanding within the context of teacher trainings for science educators and on criteria of effectiveness of teacher development programs.

Yi Qi , a Senior Research Project Manager in ETS's Research Division, completed her Master's degree at the University of Missouri-Columbia. Yi's work centers around policy issues related to teacher education and development, and managing research projects in student learning and assessment.

Ali Raza , a Research Scientist at the University of Colorado Boulder in the Institute of Cognitive Science, focuses his research on using a design-based research approach to create novel learning environments that can disrupt inequitable structures in STEM, support teacher orchestration in classrooms as well as understand educators' individual sensemaking.

Marvin Roski is a Ph.D. student at the Institute of Science Education (IDN) at the Leibniz University Hannover, Germany. His research focuses on integrating learning analytics and machine learning in (inclusive) chemistry education.

Nikol Rummel is a professor of educational psychology and technology at Ruhr-Universität Bochum. One of her main research interests is on adaptive support for computer-supported collaborative learning (CSCL). Another focus of her work is on developing methods for automated analyses of process data combining multiple data sources.

Ji Shen is Professor of STEM education in the Department of Teaching and Learning at the University of Miami. His scholarly work focuses on developing innovative, technology-enhanced learning environments, interdisciplinary and integrated STEM learning and assessment, and modeling-based teaching and learning.

Lehong Shi is an Assistant Research Scientist at the University of Georgia, centers research on the engagement of educators with advanced technologies like AI, machine learning, and social robots, particularly focusing on the influences of the interaction on teachers' perceptions, competency, and literacy, and the dynamic evolution of their rapport with emergent technologies.

Namsoo Shin , an Associate Research Professor at Michigan State University, is interested in the research and development of individualized learning environments for diverse learners. Her research focuses on learning progressions and innovative learning technologies that enhance teaching and learning.

Megan Shiroda is Assistant Professor for the Human Biology Program at Michigan State University (MSU). She earned her PhD in Microbiology and Molecular Genetics at MSU and is a discipline-based education researcher who uses constructed response assessments to better understand student thinking in STEM undergraduate courses.

Kenneth Steimel is an Associate AI Engineer at Educational Testing Service (ETS). He received his Master of Arts in Computational Linguistics from Indiana University and is currently a PhD candidate in Linguistics, with an emphasis on Computational Linguistics. His research interests lie at the intersection of Natural Language Processing and education.

Tamara Sumner , a Professor at the University of Colorado Boulder, holds a joint appointment between the Institute of Cognitive Science and the Department of Computer Science. Her research interests include personalized learning, learning analytics, cyberlearning environments, educational digital libraries, scholarly communications, and human-centered computing.

Changzhao Wang is a postdoctoral scholar at University of Southern California. She received her Ph.D. in STEM Education from the University of Miami, and bachelor's degree in physics. She has K – 12 teaching experience in both China and USA. Her research interests include AI education for adolescents, integrated STEM learning and assessment, and gender equity in STEM education.

Abhijit Suresh , a machine learning Engineer at Reddit, received his Ph.D. from the University of Colorado Boulder. Dr. Suresh's research focuses on applying machine-learning techniques spanning different domains, including K-12 education and AdTech.

Cong Wang is an Assistant Researcher at the Beijing Academy of Educational Sciences. He received his doctoral degree from Beijing Normal University. His primary research interests encompass science education measurement and assessment, scientific argumentation, and the application of machine learning in science education.

Lei Wang is a Professor at Beijing Normal University and the Director of the Discipline Committee for Chemistry Education. She has led the development and revision of chemistry curriculum standards, commissioned by China's Ministry of Education. Her research spans across chemistry education, project-based learning, learning progression, and the application of machine learning.

Quan Wang is Ph.D. student at the College of Chemistry, Beijing Normal University. His research interests lie in the fields of chemistry education and science education measurement and assessment.

Ginger S. Watson is director of the Instructional Training Systems division and the Learning and Performance Research Laboratory in the Virginia Modeling, Analysis, and Simulation Center at Old Dominion University. Her research focuses on the design, development, implementation, and evaluation of technology-enhanced learning environments for the purposes of professional preparation.

Wanli Xing is the Informatics for Education Associate Professor of Educational Technology at the University of Florida. His research interests are artificial intelligence, learning analytics, STEM education, and online learning.

Peter Youngs , a professor and chair of the Department of Curriculum, Instruction, and Special Education at University of Virginia, focuses his research on how educational policies influence teacher outcomes. He led a longitudinal, multi-institution study of elementary teacher preparation and novice teachers' enactment of mathematics and reading instruction.

Mao-Ren Zeng is a Ph.D. candidate at the Graduate Institute of Science Education, National Taiwan Normal University. His research interest is in developing curriculum for modeling practice in middle schools. He visited Michigan State University as a visiting scholar sponsored by the National Science and Technology Council from August 2022 to June 2023.

Xiaoming Zhai is Associate Professor of Science Education and Artificial Intelligence and Director of the AI4STEM Education Center at the University of Georgia. He is interested in applying cutting-edge technology, such as AI, in assessment practices to facilitate science teaching and learning.

INTRODUCTION

1
Artificial Intelligence-Based STEM Education

Xiaoming Zhai and Joseph Krajcik

Introduction

As the twenty-first century unfolds, the educational landscape is incontrovertibly influenced by the pervasive advent of artificial intelligence (AI), machine learning, and large language models (LLMs), particularly within the domains of science, technology, engineering, and mathematics (STEM) education. STEM education holds a pivotal role in shaping the future of society and humanity at large. As the bedrock of innovation and technological advancement, STEM disciplines are not merely academic subjects but the driving force that fuels economic growth, helping to solve complex problems and enhancing the quality of life. From addressing climate change and advancing medical research to developing sustainable energy solutions and improving cybersecurity, the applications of STEM are manifold and far-reaching. By equipping students with the skills and knowledge they need to excel in science, technology, engineering, and mathematics, STEM education serves as a foundational pillar for creating informed citizens capable of making thoughtful decisions in an increasingly complex world. In essence, investing in STEM education and considering the growing needs of individuals to survive in the AI era is necessary to create a more sustainable, equitable, and prosperous future for all.

Although STEM education is indispensable for critical thinking, creativity, and innovation, it is confronted with challenges that obstruct its effectiveness and accessibility. One of the paramount challenges is engaging students in using scientific knowledge to solve complex natural and social problems, a critical competency in the contemporary, technology-driven world. The traditional frameworks of STEM education often fall short in fostering such goals and creating environments where students can seamlessly transition from theoretical knowledge acquisition to practical, applied problem-solving and solution design. This gap impedes students' understanding of STEM subjects. It hinders their ability to effectively utilize their knowledge in real-world scenarios, which is imperative for their future careers and for addressing the complex challenges of the twenty-first century. Engaging students in this manner requires a dynamic, interactive, and responsive educational approach with intelligent technologies that impart knowledge and cultivate inquiry, analysis, and application skills.

Xiaoming Zhai and Joseph Krajcik, *Artificial Intelligence-Based STEM Education*. In: *Uses of Artificial Intelligence in STEM Education*. Edited by: Xiaoming Zhai and Joseph Krajcik, Oxford University Press.
 DOI: 10.1093/oso/9780198882077.003.0001

The intersection between AI and STEM education heralds a transformative epoch characterized by a recalibration of instructional paradigms and the emergence of innovative learning methodologies. The field has explored using AI in STEM education for more than a decade, but the recent summit of research and applications emerged due to the expansive advances of machine learning and LLMs (Latif et al. 2023). Advanced AI offers a unique set of tools to help resolve these challenges by creating highly personalized learning environments wherein instructional content and assessment methodologies are tailored to accommodate individual students' learning needs and preferences (Zhai et al. 2020b). The advent of automated scoring systems, intelligent tutoring mechanisms, and adaptive learning platforms, all underpinned by AI, facilitates the provision of immediate feedback, the identification of learning deficits, and the delivery of targeted instructional support. This confluence of factors contributes to creating a learning environment that is engaging and productive.

With its capacity for adaptability and personalization, AI supports the development of students' problem-solving skills by providing instant feedback, enabling them to iteratively refine their approaches and solutions. It also allows for incorporating experiential learning and project-based assignments into the curriculum, providing students with opportunities to tackle real-world problems and develop practical solutions (Zhai et al. 2023). AI-powered platforms can deliver dynamic and interactive content, simulations, and virtual labs that demystify complex STEM concepts and allow students to experiment, explore, and apply their knowledge in various contexts. This approach enhances students' understanding of STEM concepts. It fosters a deeper engagement with the material, promoting the development of critical thinking and problem-solving skills essential for success in STEM fields and beyond.

Moreover, AI offers invaluable support to diverse learners, including those with learning disabilities. By deploying assistive technologies and developing personalized learning trajectories, AI ensures that all students, irrespective of their learning challenges, can access and succeed in STEM education (Zhai and Nehm 2023). This inclusive approach democratizes education and cultivates a diverse and inclusive talent pipeline, which is indispensable for fostering innovation and progress within the STEM disciplines.

Conversely, the challenges encompass technical, pedagogical, ethical, and accessibility dimensions (Zhai 2021). Technically, the infusion of AI into educational environments necessitates the deployment of sophisticated infrastructure, consistent and reliable connectivity, and state-of-the-art hardware. These prerequisites often impose substantial financial burdens and maintenance responsibilities upon educational institutions, creating significant operational challenges. From a pedagogical perspective, educators must integrate AI tools into their instructional repertoire that neither diminishes the quality of education nor erodes the essential human elements intrinsic to the educational process. The ethical dimension introduces additional complexities, with issues pertaining to data privacy, algorithmic bias, and the potential worsening of the digital divide. Addressing these concerns requires a concerted effort from educators, technologists, and policymakers alike to ensure that AI-driven educational practices are equitable, inclusive, and respectful of students' rights and dignity.

The ensuing chapters of this volume include four themes and twenty-six chapters in total, which will engage in a more granular exploration of the multifaceted relationship between AI and STEM education, elucidating the opportunities and challenges inherent to this dynamic. This volume provides a comprehensive and insightful narrative by examining innovative applications, ethical considerations, practical implications, and future trajectories of AI in STEM education. Each chapter, authored by experts in the field, contributes to constructing a holistic understanding of how AI is reconfiguring the contours of STEM education, offering invaluable insights for educators, researchers, and policymakers engaged in this field. The chapters present a rich tapestry of ideas, practices, and reflections. Through the expert contributions of educators, researchers, and policymakers, this volume illuminates the transformative potential and practical applications of AI within and beyond the classroom, providing a roadmap for navigating the future of education in an increasingly AI-centric global landscape. In the following, we introduce each section of the volume.

AI in STEM Assessment

Part I, "AI in STEM Assessment," offers a meticulous exploration of the role of AI in the complex landscape of STEM education assessment. This section aligns closely with the overarching theme of the book, contributing a specialized discourse on the assessment dimension of STEM education in the era of AI. Assessment, a cornerstone in the educational process, is particularly complex in STEM disciplines, which require evaluating students' conceptual understanding, problem-solving skills, and practical application of knowledge. The advent of AI introduces transformative possibilities for addressing these complexities. Research can now use machine learning to automatically assess explanations, arguments, and paper–pencil-drawn models. As such, AI can achieve automation in areas traditionally considered labor-intensive, thereby alleviating the assessment burden on educators. Furthermore, AI-driven assessments can offer invaluable insights into students' reasoning patterns, learning trajectories, and understanding, informing instructional design and facilitating more targeted and effective teaching approaches. AI as a tool for supporting assessment heralds a new era of efficiency and precision.

The integration of AI into STEM assessment, however, is not without challenges. Various authors critically examine issues related to the accuracy of AI-driven assessments, the potential for bias and inequity, and the challenges associated with the development and validation of AI tools. The chapters in this section addressed concrete issues in AI-based assessment.

Chapter 2 inaugurates the section by providing a panoramic view of STEM assessment, underscoring its multifaceted nature that extends from classroom evaluations to international standardized tests, and the potential of AI to transform assessment practices. The chapter meticulously delineates the continuum of assessment practices, emphasizing the imperative alignment with curriculum, orientation, and temporal frameworks. It introduces readers to the nuanced process of reasoning from evidence, a process that intricately intertwines student cognition, observational evidence, and interpretation mechanisms. While highlighting the transformative potential of technology and AI in STEM assessment, the chapter does not shy away from addressing the inherent challenges related to design, equity, and validity in technology-driven assessments. It advocates for a collective, multidisciplinary endeavor to harness intellectual, fiscal, and political capital to advance AI-based STEM assessment practices for equitable education.

Chapter 3 delves into the specific domain of biology education assessment, providing a retrospective analysis of a decade's worth of research on the AI-based EvoGrader assessment system and the associated ACORNS instrument. The chapter elucidates the complex consequences emanating from the development of technological tools designed to replicate human tasks, with a focus on the automated scoring of biological explanations. It highlights the intricate relationship between automation efforts and the educational systems within which they are embedded, revealing how AI scoring performance is influenced by a myriad of factors, including instructor discourse practices, disciplinary language, writing fatigue, implementation conditions, and attributes of English learners. This chapter exemplifies how AI can offer more accurate, efficient, and nuanced understandings of student performance, a theme that is central to this section.

In Chapter 4, the focus shifts to the application of NLP tools in scoring students' written explanations, thereby opening new vistas for science education. The chapter reports on research informed by the knowledge integration (KI) pedagogical framework, using online Authorable and Customizable Environments (ACEs) to promote a deep understanding of complex scientific topics. It explores how personalized guidance can be aligned with tested pedagogical frameworks to enable students to make productive revisions to their written explanations during instruction.

Chapter 5 introduces readers to the application of machine learning and neural networks in assessing paper–pencil-drawn models of optics, a critical practice in promoting students' knowledge-in-use in science learning. The chapter reports on the application of 2D convolutional neural networks to assess models drawn by students to explain the refraction phenomenon, highlighting the variations in scoring accuracy among groups with different proficiency levels of modeling.

Chapter 6 explores the challenges and possibilities of automated scoring in the Chinese language for science assessments. The chapter reports on tests conducted with students in Taiwan, revealing the accuracy levels of automated scoring for explanations of phenomena and factual knowledge. It concludes that automated scoring is a viable approach for science assessment in the Chinese language, with analytic scoring outperforming holistic scoring in terms of accuracy and kappa value.

Chapter 7 examines the attributes of successful machine-learning assessments for scoring undergraduate constructed response assessment items. The chapter explores the relationship between scoring accuracy and different assessment items, computer scoring models (CSM), and training set features, providing insights into the factors that influence CSM accuracy and aiding decision-making during CSM development.

Finally, Chapter 8 discusses a project exploring the use of machine learning to identify student reasoning patterns related to the three dimensions of the Next Generation Science Standards. The chapter describes the development and validation of an AI tool to automate the classification of reasoning patterns and provide feedback to students, concluding with a discussion on validity issues, potential uses and limitations, and future research directions.

Collectively, the chapters within this section offer invaluable insights into the opportunities and challenges associated with the integration of AI into STEM assessment practices. They illuminate the transformative potential of AI in redefining assessment practices while also highlighting the need for careful consideration of the challenges and complexities that characterize this dynamic intersection between AI and STEM assessment (Zhai et al. 2020a). Through the exploration of various domains within STEM assessment, the chapters contribute to a deeper understanding of the ways in which AI can be harnessed to enhance the accuracy and efficiency of assessment practices while also promoting equity and inclusion within STEM education. Chapters in Part I serve as a lighthouse, guiding educators, researchers, and policymakers through the complex yet promising landscape of AI-driven assessment in STEM education, thereby making a significant contribution to the field and the broader discourse on AI in education. This part lays the groundwork for future research, development, and implementation of AI-driven assessment practices that are equitable, reliable, and conducive to enhanced learning and understanding in STEM disciplines.

AI Tools for Transforming STEM Learning

Part II, "AI Tools for Transforming STEM Learning," serves as a critical juncture in this volume, focusing on the transformative potential of AI in enhancing various facets of STEM learning. This part is particularly salient given the inherent challenges in STEM education, which include not only the imparting of complex theoretical knowledge but also the crucial need for students to apply this knowledge in problem-solving and the design of solutions. Traditional educational paradigms often struggle to seamlessly integrate these two aspects, leaving a gap between conceptual understanding and science and engineering practices. The chapters in Part II collectively address this gap, showcasing how AI tools can revolutionize STEM learning.

One of the recurring themes across these chapters is the role of AI in facilitating scientific inquiry and problem-solving, which are foundational elements of STEM education. Automated feedback is highlighted for its potential to improve students' simulation-mediated scientific argumentation practice. However, challenges such as equity concerns and the need for teacher buy-ins are also emphasized, thereby providing a nuanced understanding of the complexities involved.

Part II also delves into the intricacies of individualized student assessment and support, a critical need given the diverse learning styles and paces found in any classroom. Moreover, the chapters explore the practicalities of implementing AI tools in classroom settings. However, the part does not shy away from discussing the challenges and limitations associated with the deployment of AI tools in STEM learning. These range from questions of validity and bias in AI tools to the technical and pedagogical challenges in developing effective automated feedback systems. Equity concerns are also raised, emphasizing the need for these AI tools to be accessible and beneficial for all students, regardless of their socioeconomic backgrounds. Following is an overview of these chapters:

Chapter 9 focuses on the transformative potential of AI in science education, particularly through the lens of AI-based scientific inquiry. The chapter categorizes students into three distinct archetypes—*pragmatic innovators*, *foundational explorers*, and *holistic visionaries*—to explore diverse learning trajectories. It emphasizes the need for adaptive pedagogical strategies that can cater to the multifaceted learning needs of students in an AI-centric educational landscape. The chapter serves as a seminal contribution, setting the stage for a new, responsive, and forward-thinking era in science education.

Chapter 10 delves into the complexities of designing an effective AI-enabled automated feedback system, known as HASbot, for science education. The chapter outlines the design research process and examines how automated feedback on scientific argument artifacts can enhance students' simulation-mediated scientific inquiry. It also discusses the challenges in developing AI-afforded automated feedback systems, such as improving diagnostic models and addressing equity concerns. The chapter provides a comprehensive view of the potential and limitations of AI in enhancing feedback mechanisms in science education.

Chapter 11 explores the role of AI in providing individualized support to students in physics learning within a digital environment. Utilizing evidence-centered design, the chapter presents a framework for building an AI-based approach that can continuously evaluate students' learning at a granular level. It discusses questions related to the validity and bias of such instruments, offering insights into the complexities of implementing AI tools for individualized educational support.

Chapter 12 provides a historical overview of intelligent tutoring systems (ITSs) and introduces Inq-ITS, an ITS designed for science education currently in use across the United States. The chapter offers an in-depth description of a classroom study testing the efficacy of AI-based scaffolding in supporting students' science competencies. It outlines the patented AI approach used in Inq-ITS for real-time, automated, scalable assessment and scaffolding of inquiry practices, contributing to the discourse on the role of AI in enhancing authentic science practices.

Chapter 13 introduces AI-Scorer, an AI-augmented assessment and instruction system designed to revolutionize formative learning in STEM education. The chapter highlights the designing principles for the system's capabilities in providing immediate, accurate scoring of complex student responses and offering real-time insights into student performance. Developed in collaboration with experienced teachers, AI-Scorer emphasizes usability and adaptability, making it a significant step forward in leveraging AI to support ongoing instructional decision-making.

Chapter 14 presents the Smart Learning Partner (SLP), an innovative AI-based system, aimed at enhancing students' subject competency development. The chapter introduces a comprehensive subject competency framework that integrates core knowledge, cognitive modes, research contexts, and tasks. SLP leverages this framework to provide personalized recommendations and support, aiding independent learning and classroom teaching. The chapter proposes a holistic model that aligns assessment, learning, and teaching strategies, contributing to effective subject competency development in education.

Collectively, these chapters offer a nuanced understanding of the transformative potential and challenges of integrating AI tools into STEM learning. They examine various facets of STEM education, from scientific inquiry and individualized support to formative assessment and competency development, showcasing how AI tools can be harnessed to make STEM education more engaging, personalized, and effective. The chapters also highlight the design principles of AI tools, as well as the complexities and ethical considerations that educators and policymakers must navigate. This section thus stands as a significant contribution to the ongoing discourse on the future of STEM education in an increasingly AI-driven world.

AI-Based STEM Instruction and Teacher Professional Development

Part III, "AI-Based STEM Instruction and Teacher Professional Development," serves as a pivotal component of this volume, addressing the transformative role of AI in enhancing teaching practices and professional development within the realm of STEM education. This part is particularly timely given the increasing complexity of STEM curricula and the need for dynamic, responsive teaching methods that not only impart knowledge but also facilitate its application from the teachers' perspective. Significantly, the chapters in this section contribute to both the academic literature and practical applications by offering a multidimensional analysis of AI's capabilities and limitations in instructional settings. They introduce novel frameworks, methodologies, and tools that have the potential to reshape pedagogical strategies, thereby filling existing gaps in the literature. Furthermore, these chapters provide actionable insights for educators, administrators, and policymakers, offering a nuanced understanding of how teachers can integrate AI effectively into STEM education to improve both teaching efficacy and student outcomes. This dual contribution to theory and practice makes this section an indispensable resource for those interested in the future of STEM education in an AI-augmented landscape.

Conceptually, the chapters in this section contribute to the burgeoning literature on the integration of AI in educational settings by offering frameworks and models that elucidate the roles AI can play in teaching and assessment. Practically, the chapters offer actionable insights and tools that can be directly applied in educational settings. Moreover, the chapters address the critical issue of scalability and automation in teacher assessments and classroom observations. We next present a brief overview of the chapters in this part.

Chapter 15 offers a systematic review of the literature on AI's role in supporting teaching practices. It categorizes AI applications into five types and identifies three salient pedagogical roles that AI can play: as an instructional partner, an evaluative partner, and a pedagogical decision partner. The chapter provides a comprehensive overview of the technological characteristics of AI in teaching, thereby shaping the discourse on AI's transformative impact on instructional paradigms and pedagogical innovations.

Chapter 16 introduces a conceptual framework designed to guide teachers in utilizing AI-based classroom assessments to improve instructional decisions. The chapter addresses the challenges teachers face in interpreting and applying data generated by AI technologies, particularly in the context of Next Generation Science Standards. It outlines a four-stage framework that includes engagement with the AI system, evaluation of assessment reports, consideration of AI-suggested instructional strategies, and determination of instructional decisions and actions.

Chapter 17 explores the use of AI tools like the TalkMoves application to provide teachers with automated, personalized feedback on their classroom discourse patterns. The chapter highlights the potential of AI tools to foster student-driven conversations and rigorous learning environments, while also acknowledging the challenges posed by disruptions such as the shift to remote learning due to COVID-19.

Chapter 18 delves into the innovative use of machine learning in scoring teacher observations, both as a tool for studying interventions and as an intervention itself. The chapter provides an example that employs machine learning to transform observation field notes into mediator variables and treatment fidelity indicators, showcasing how machine learning can be meaningfully incorporated into research design.

Chapter 19 focuses on the use of structural topic models (STMs), a form of unsupervised machine learning, to broaden the focus of science assessments. The chapter illustrates how STMs can inductively identify potential learning gains, thereby addressing the limitations of traditional assessment methods that often miss the learners' strengths.

Chapter 20 examines the potential of deep learning neural networks in automating the classification of instructional activities in classroom videos. The chapter discusses the moderate degree of accuracy achieved by neural networks in detecting instructional activities and explores the opportunities and challenges in automating classroom observations for educational research and teaching practice.

In aggregate, the chapters in this part furnish a multifaceted and exhaustive examination of both the prospects and impediments tied to the incorporation of AI in STEM pedagogy and educator career advancement. They yield critical perspectives on the potential of AI to refine the efficacy, customization, and adaptability of STEM instruction. Concurrently, they underscore the intricate and ethical dilemmas that educational stakeholders and decision-makers are compelled to confront. Therefore, this section serves as a pivotal addition to the extant dialogue concerning the trajectory of STEM education in a world progressively influenced by AI.

Ethics, Fairness, and Inclusiveness of AI-Based STEM Education

Part IV, "Ethics, Fairness, and Inclusiveness of AI-Based STEM Education," serves as an indispensable intellectual fulcrum in this volume, bridging technological innovation with ethical imperatives. The chapters within this part make conceptual and practical contributions to the field, thereby enriching the discourse on the ethical dimensions of AI in STEM education. Conceptually, the chapters contribute to a burgeoning yet underexplored area of research that interrogates the ethical underpinnings of AI applications in educational settings. In addition, the chapters in this part offer actionable strategies and frameworks that can be directly applied in educational settings.

The chapters collectively offer a nuanced and multidimensional exploration of the ethical considerations inherent in the integration of AI into STEM education. They provide both conceptual scaffolding and practical tools for navigating the ethical complexities, thereby making a significant contribution to the ongoing discourse on the ethical implications of AI in educational settings. This dual focus on conceptual understanding and practical application ensures that the benefits of AI in STEM education can be realized in an ethically responsible manner. Specifically, the following introduces each chapter.

Chapter 21 serves as an eye-opener by revealing the limited scope of existing AI applications for students with learning disabilities. While AI has shown promise in areas like adaptive learning and intelligent tutoring, the study uncovers that the focus has been disproportionately on dyslexia, leaving other learning disabilities underexplored. The use of the SAMR-LD model adds a nuanced understanding of how AI can be more effectively integrated at different levels of educational support. This chapter is crucial because it not only identifies gaps but also sets the stage for future research, urging the educational technology community to develop AI tools that are more inclusive and tailored to a broader range of learning disabilities.

Chapter 22 goes beyond the surface-level benefits of AI in K–12 STEM classrooms to interrogate the ethical and power dynamics at play. It raises important questions about who gets to define what constitutes an "ethical" AI system and how power imbalances can manifest in educational settings. By advocating for critical pedagogical approaches, the chapter contributes a valuable framework for educators to engage students in discussions about the ethical dimensions of technology. This is a seminal contribution, as it fills the void in current discourse by integrating ethical considerations into the practical application of AI in STEM education.

Chapter 23 is groundbreaking in its focus on the fairness of AI applications in STEM education. While many studies tout the benefits of AI, this chapter takes a step back to scrutinize the ethical pitfalls, particularly biases that can adversely affect students. By offering a guide to building fair and ethical AI systems and discussing state-of-the-art cases, the chapter serves as a practical handbook for researchers and practitioners. It moves the conversation from merely acknowledging bias to actively seeking solutions, making it a must-read for anyone committed to equitable education.

Chapter 24 introduces the innovative AIISE framework, which aims to marry AI, science education, and inclusive pedagogy. By extending the NinU-framework, it provides a comprehensive roadmap for creating inclusive, AI-supported learning environments. This is a significant leap forward in the field, as it not only identifies the criteria for inclusivity but also offers actionable strategies for avoiding discrimination in machine learning-enhanced learning. The chapter is a cornerstone for researchers and educators looking to navigate the complex landscape of inclusivity in AI-based STEM education.

Chapter 25 tackles the often-overlooked issue of pseudo artificial intelligence bias (PAIB), which can perpetuate existing inequities and create unwarranted fears around AI. By categorizing PAIB into three types—misunderstandings, pseudo-mechanical bias, and overexpectations—the chapter provides a structured approach to understanding and mitigating these biases. This is a pioneering contribution, as it not only identifies the problem but also offers concrete solutions, such as user certification and customized guidance, to combat PAIB effectively.

The ethical, fairness, and inclusiveness considerations of AI-based STEM education are complex and multifaceted. While AI offers promising avenues for enhancing educational outcomes, it also poses challenges that educators, policymakers, and technologists must address collaboratively before we can fully implement AI tools in STEM classrooms. These chapters collectively emphasize the need for more research, critical pedagogical approaches, and ethical frameworks to ensure that AI serves as an equitable and inclusive tool in STEM education.

Future Directions

The integration of AI into STEM education has been the focal point of this book, offering a complex and multifaceted exploration of both opportunities and challenges. While the contributions within this volume provide a comprehensive understanding of the current state of the field, they also highlight the nascent and evolving nature of this interdisciplinary domain. As we look toward the future, several critical avenues for both research and practice emerge as particularly pressing.

Empirically, one of the most urgent needs is to broaden the scope of research to include diverse learner populations. For example, this book offers a glimpse into the transformative potential of AI in supporting students with learning disabilities. However, it also reveals a significant gap in empirical studies that move beyond merely diagnosing learning disabilities to actively intervening in the educational experiences of these students. This gap is not just a lacuna in the research; it is a missed opportunity for educational equity. As AI technologies become increasingly sophisticated, there is a compelling need for empirical studies that investigate how to design and deploy these technologies to offer personalized, adaptive learning experiences that cater to a broad demographic spectrum, providing equitable opportunities to learn for all students. This includes students with various disabilities and extends to those from diverse cultural, linguistic, and socioeconomic backgrounds. Such research would contribute to the literature and significantly impact educational practice by making inclusive education a tangible reality.

The ethical dimensions of AI in education, particularly concerning fairness and bias, present another area that requires rigorous empirical scrutiny. This volume, for instance, raises critical questions about the potential for algorithmic bias in educational settings. This is not merely a technical issue to resolve but an ethical imperative that demands immediate attention. The potential for AI to perpetuate existing social and educational inequities makes it crucial for future research to scrutinize AI algorithms' fairness. This involves not just the de-biasing of algorithms but also the development of methodologies that can assess the impact of these technologies on various student populations. Such empirical work is essential for ensuring that AI is an equitable tool in educational settings, aligning with broader societal values and ethical norms.

Regarding the role of teachers in an AI-integrated educational landscape, there is a notable gap in empirical research. The authors of this book introduce a promising framework for facilitating teachers' utilization of AI-based assessments. However, the effectiveness of such frameworks in educational settings remains largely untested. Future empirical studies investigating the impact of professional development programs focused on AI in STEM education could provide invaluable insights. These could range from identifying best practices, understanding potential pitfalls, and informing policy and practice. The role of the teacher is especially critical as educational systems worldwide grapple with integrating AI technologies. Understanding how to best support teachers in this transition could have far-reaching implications for AI's successful and ethical deployment in classrooms.

Conceptually, the field is ripe for developing robust ethical frameworks that can guide the responsible deployment of AI in educational settings. This work underscores the absence of such frameworks, particularly at the K–12 level, and highlights the need for conceptual work to inform policy and practice. Moreover, as AI's role as a pedagogical tool gains recognition, there is a conspicuous absence of conceptual models that integrate AI into existing pedagogical frameworks. Such integrative models could guide future empirical work and offer a more holistic understanding of AI's educational potential. This is not merely an academic exercise but a practical necessity. As AI technologies become increasingly integrated into educational settings, the absence of guiding ethical and pedagogical frameworks could lead to a range of unintended consequences, from the perpetuation of educational inequities to the erosion of educational quality.

On a practical level, the issue of scalability remains a significant challenge. While several chapters introduce AI systems that have shown promise in specific educational settings, the broader applicability of these systems remains an open question. Efforts to adapt and scale these solutions across diverse educational contexts could offer a more comprehensive understanding of their utility and limitations. This is not just a question of technical feasibility but also of educational impact. As AI technologies are scaled, it is crucial to understand how they interact with different educational ecosystems, each with its own unique set of challenges and opportunities.

Finally, as AI technologies become increasingly pervasive in educational settings, there is an emergent need for policy guidelines that govern their ethical and equitable use. This concern resonates with the discourse in several chapters, which call for a more nuanced understanding of the potential biases and ethical implications associated with AI in education. Developing such policy guidelines is not just a bureaucratic necessity but a critical step in ensuring that deploying AI technologies aligns with broader educational goals and societal values.

In conclusion, integrating AI into STEM education is a dynamic and rapidly evolving field that offers unprecedented opportunities and complex challenges. The academic community and educational practitioners must engage in collaborative, interdisciplinary efforts to realize the full potential of AI-based STEM education while conscientiously mitigating its risks. The future directions outlined herein serve as a roadmap for these endeavors, seeking to advance the scholarly literature and practical applications in this pivotal study area.

Acknowledgments

This material is based upon work supported by the National Science Foundation (NSF) under Grant 2138854. Any opinions, findings, and conclusions or recommendations expressed in this material are those of the author(s) and do not necessarily reflect the views of the NSF.

References

Latif, E., Mai, G., Nyaaba, M., Wu, X., Liu, N., Lu, G., Li, S., Liu, T., and Zhai, X. 2023, April 01. "Artificial General Intelligence (AGI) for Education." arXiv:2304.12479. https://arxiv.org/abs/2304.12479

Zhai, X. 2021. "Practices and Theories: How Can Machine Learning Assist in Innovative Assessment Practices in Science Education." *Journal of Science Education and Technology* 30, no. 2: 139–49. https://link.springer.com/article/10.1007/s10956-021-09901-8

Zhai, X., Haudek, K. C., Shi, L., Nehm, R., and Urban-Lurain, M. 2020a. "From Substitution to Redefinition: A Framework of Machine Learning-Based Science Assessment." *Journal of Research in Science Teaching* 57, no. 9: 1430–59.

Zhai, X., and Nehm, R. 2023. "AI and Formative Assessment: The Train Has Left the Station." *Journal of Research in Science Teaching* 60, no. 6: 1390–98.

Zhai, X., Neumann, K., and Krajcik, J. 2023. "AI for Tackling STEM Education Challenges." *Frontiers in Education* 8, no. 1183030. https://www.frontiersin.org/articles/10.3389/feduc.2023.1183030/full

Zhai, X., Yin, Y., Pellegrino, J. W., Haudek, K. C., and Shi, L. 2020b. "Applying Machine Learning in Science Assessment: A Systematic Review." *Studies in Science Education* 56, no. 1: 111–51.

PART I
AI IN STEM ASSESSMENT

2
A New Era for STEM Assessment
Considerations of Assessment, Technology, and Artificial Intelligence

James W. Pellegrino

Introduction and Overview

This volume is the product of a 2022 convening of a diverse group of scientists, science educators, computer scientists, policymakers, and educational practitioners, representing different states, countries, and even continents, all of whom have a deep interest in science, technology, engineering, and mathematics (STEM) education.[1] The participants at that convening at the University of Georgia, many of whom are contributors to this volume, represent diverse areas of knowledge and expertise including STEM education, educational assessment, classroom teaching and learning, curriculum design, artificial intelligence (AI), and data analytics as well as various intersections of those areas of expertise. What binds this group together is concern about the current state of STEM education, locally, nationally, and globally, and the wish to contribute to the improvement of student learning in the STEM disciplines. What further binds this group together is a firm belief that contemporary advances in technology, data analytics, and artificial intelligence can advance STEM education by significantly improving research and practice in the field of STEM assessment across the K–16+ educational span. The chapters in this volume are proof positive of that belief and commitment.

One of the great benefits of bringing together scholars such as those who attended the original convening and contributed to this volume is the breadth of expertise and the opportunities to learn from each other. One of the challenges that can simultaneously exist is a lack of common ground and shared background knowledge regarding several of the foundational issues related to STEM knowledge and assessment. That may also be true for readers of this volume since its focus should be of interest to individuals representing multiple communities who, like the authors of the work in this volume, have diverse interests and background knowledge. Thus, one of the goals for this chapter is to provide some common ground regarding STEM proficiency and assessment so that those interested in STEM assessment can appreciate some of

[1] Several of the topics discussed in this chapter draw upon ideas and text from the author's prior publications on teaching, learning, and assessment. These prior publications include Pellegrino, Chudowsky, and Glaser (2001); Pellegrino and Hilton (2012); Pellegrino (2013); Pellegrino, DiBello, and Goldman (2016); and Pellegrino, Foster, and Piacentini (2023).

James W. Pellegrino, *A New Era for STEM Assessment.* In: *Uses of Artificial Intelligence in STEM Education.*
Edited by: Xiaoming Zhai and Joseph Krajcik, Oxford University Press.
 DOI: 10.1093/oso/9780198882077.003.0002

the history behind how we reached the present situation, the challenges we face and need to overcome, and the opportunities that exist for advancing STEM education and assessment by harnessing multiple intellectual communities who can appreciate the capabilities and affordances of contemporary information technologies and advancements in artificial intelligence and help solve an important educational problem—producing valid and valuable STEM assessments for use across multiple contexts in the educational system. As argued at the end of this chapter, it will take a diverse and committed "intellectual village" to achieve our collective STEM assessment educational goals.

By way of the topics to be covered, we begin with a bit of relevant history as related to theory, research, and practice regarding STEM education and assessment as they have evolved over the past twenty-plus years, touching briefly on the appearance of "national" standards in the STEM disciplines of mathematics and science in the decade before the start of the twenty-first century and the evolution of ideas since then. The goal is to establish a common understanding of the current state of expectations about what students are supposed to know and be able to do in STEM, with a specific focus on science.

The remainder of the chapter is focused on five key topics in the literature on STEM assessment, each of which provides a context for examining and evaluating the contributions of the work presented in this volume. For each topic, a summary is presented of key ideas and its importance for STEM assessment. Each topic discussion closes with questions the reader should be asking about how the work reported in the volume contributes to addressing that topic. The five topics are:

1. Grand challenges in STEM assessment
   - Three major challenges for assessment of contemporary views of science proficiency and why addressing them is important to STEM education.
2. Positioning assessment along a continuum
   - Locating an assessment in terms of its relationship in time and space to teaching and learning and determining its purpose and intended interpretive use.
3. Assessment as a process of reasoning from evidence
   - The cognition, observation, and interpretation elements of the reasoning-from-evidence process that characterizes all assessment activities and the role of learning research in achieving coherence.
4. The affordances of technology and artificial intelligence (AI) for impacting STEM assessment
   - Aspects of the reasoning-from-evidence process that technology and AI can impact to enhance the scope and quality of STEM assessment.
5. Validity, fairness, and equity in STEM assessment
   - Establishing the validity of an assessment as an evidence-based argument and establishing its equity and fairness as part of the validity argument.

The final section of this chapter speaks to the forms of intellectual, fiscal, and political capital needed to advance the field of STEM assessment and how they need to come together to significantly impact STEM education and assessment.

STEM Education and Assessment in Context: Benchmarks along a Long and Winding Road

There is a long history of theory and research on the nature of STEM teaching, learning, and assessment and it is well beyond the capacity of this chapter to fully discuss major trends and developments from that vast literature. Rather, the goal of this section is to try to summarize key developments and put into perspective what we now expect students to know and be able to do in STEM disciplines and the implications for instruction and assessment. This discussion opens by highlighting major publications from the U.S. National Research Council on learning, assessment, and STEM education since 2000. Figure 2.1 captures some of the many landmark publications that have impacted the STEM education and STEM assessment landscape.

The path traced in Figure 2.1 begins with two of the most influential publications regarding learning, instruction, and assessment—*How People Learn: Brain, Mind, Experience and School* (Bransford et al. 2000) and *Knowing What Students Know: The Science and Design of Educational Assessment* (Pellegrino, Chudowsky, and Glaser 2001). Each has been cited thousands of times and together they have influenced many other major publications of theory and research on STEM teaching, learning, and assessment. Among the latter are two NRC science education reports published in the early 2000s—*Systems for State Science Assessment* (Wilson and Bertenthal 2006) and *Taking Science to School: Learning and Teaching Science in Grades K-8* (Duschl, Schweingruber, and Shouse 2007). These two science education reports, along with the NRC report *Adding it Up: Helping Children Learn Mathematics* (Kilpatrick, Swafford, and Findell 2001), highlighted an ongoing evolution in conceptions of the knowing, learning, teaching, and assessment of mathematics and science. Each drew upon and went beyond STEM standards documents from the 1990s. The latter included the AAAS Benchmarks for Science Literacy (AAAS 1993), the NRC Science Education Standards (NRC 1996), and the NCTM Principles and Standards for Mathematics Education (NCTM 1989). Further developments and refinements in conceptions of STEM knowing, learning, and assessment were reflected in the *Common Core State Standards for Mathematics* (NGA 2010), and the NRC *Framework for K-12 Science Education* (NRC 2012). The latter in turn led to the *Next Generation Science Standards* (NGSS 2013) and the NRC report *Developing Assessments for the Next Generation Science Standards* (Pellegrino et al. 2014). The path shown in Figure 2.1 takes us to the present volume on AI and STEM assessment.

An important trend in the collective body of work noted above are changing expectations regarding what students are expected to know and be able to do in the STEM disciplines. These expectations are reflected in contemporary frameworks and standards documents and have substantial implications for instruction and assessment. To consider these implications we juxtapose the evolution of STEM standards and frameworks with another major trend with implications for STEM instruction and assessment—deeper learning and twenty-first-century skills.

The past two decades have seen substantial interest in changing the landscape of education through ideas labeled as "deeper learning" and "twenty-first-century skills." This global trend is indicative of a long-standing concern in education about the difficult task of equipping individuals with transferable knowledge and skills

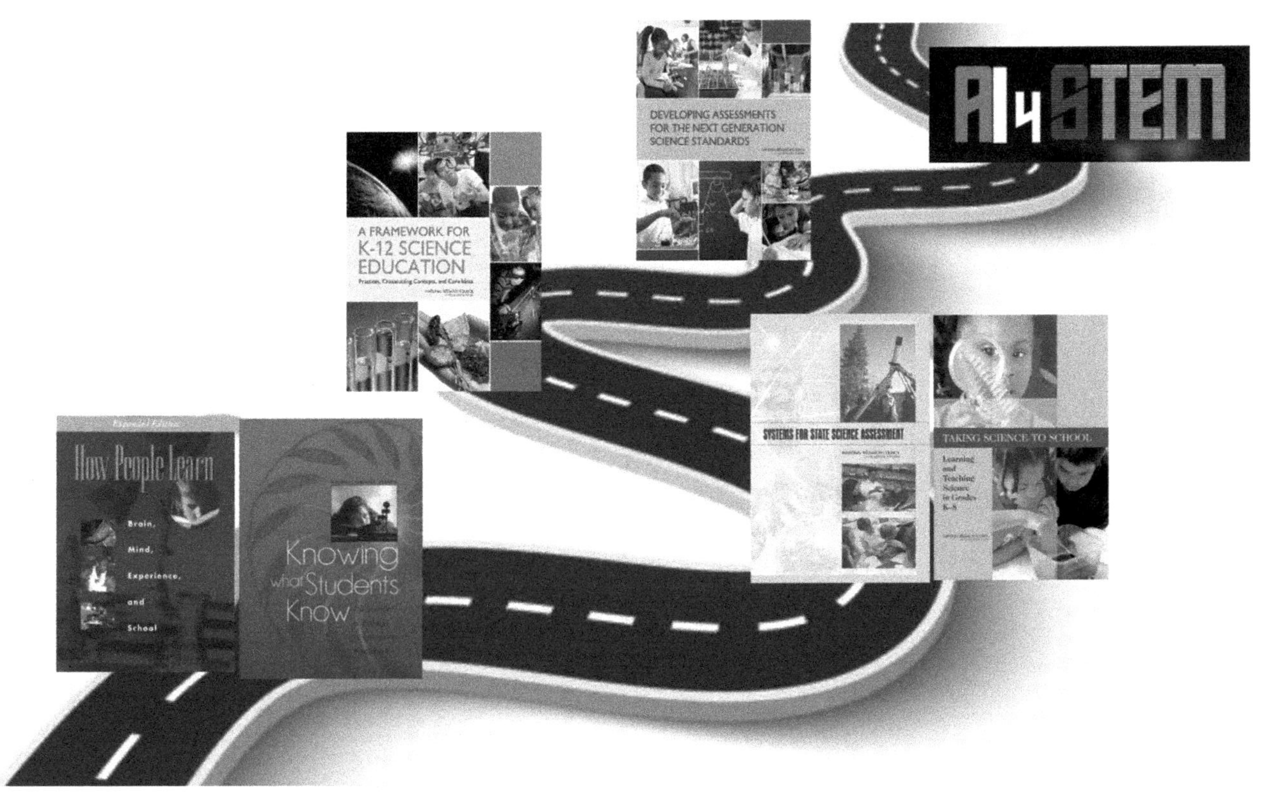

Figure 2.1 STEM education and assessment in context: some markers along a long and winding road.

(e.g., Bellanca 2014). As argued in the NRC report *Education for Life and Work: Developing Transferable Knowledge and Skills in the 21st* Century (Pellegrino and Hilton 2012), deeper learning is the product of interconnected cognitive, interpersonal, and intrapersonal processes that enable students to thoroughly understand academic content and recognize when, how, and why to apply that knowledge to solve new problems and engage in processes of critical thinking.

Concepts related to deeper learning and twenty-first-century skills are reflected in the disciplinary frameworks and standards for mathematics and science education mentioned earlier (see, e.g., Pellegrino and Hilton 2012). For example, contemporary mathematics standards emphasize learning with understanding and the development of usable, transferable mathematics competencies. They do so by identifying critical mathematical content knowledge to be mastered over time as well as the integration of that content with practices of mathematical thinking and reasoning. The theme of argumentation/reasoning is explicitly stated in two of the standards for mathematical practice: "Reason abstractly and quantitatively" and "construct viable arguments and critique the reasoning of others." The standards also deal explicitly with problem solving; the first standard in the category of mathematical practice is "make sense of problems and persevere in solving them." In addition, the standards for mathematical practice give attention to competencies such as self-regulation, persistence, and the development of an identity as someone who can do mathematics.

In science, the integration of scientific content and reasoning and the focus on depth rather than breadth of knowledge was most clearly articulated by the National Research Council's *Framework for K-12 Science Education* (NRC 2012). The framework explains in detail what all students should know and be able to do in science by the end of high school. An overarching goal expressed in the framework is to ensure that all students—whether or not they pursue careers in the fields of science, technology, engineering, and mathematics—have "sufficient knowledge of science and engineering to engage in public discussions on related issues, are careful consumers of scientific and technological information related to their everyday lives and are able to continue to learn about science outside of school" (NRC 2012, 14).

The science framework and derivative Next Generation Science Standards (NGSS 2013) include three dimensions which are conceptually distinct but are integrated in practice in the teaching, learning, assessment, and doing of science and engineering. Disciplinary core ideas reflect a small set of core ideas in each discipline, reducing the long and often disconnected catalogue of factual knowledge that students historically had to learn. Students are supposed to encounter these core ideas over the course of their school years at increasing levels of sophistication, deepening their knowledge over time. The NRC Framework and NGSS include seven cross-cutting concepts that have importance across many disciplines, such as patterns, cause and effect, and stability and change. Eight key science and engineering practices are identified, such as asking questions (for science) and defining problems (for engineering); planning and carrying out investigations; and engaging in argument from evidence. The framework emphasizes that disciplinary knowledge and scientific practices are intertwined and must be coordinated in science and engineering education. By engaging in the practices of science and engineering, students gain new knowledge about the disciplinary core ideas and come to understand the nature of how scientific knowledge develops.

As with the mathematics standards, there are several areas of overlap between the science framework and enumerations of twenty-first-century skills. Critical thinking, nonroutine problem solving, and constructing and evaluating evidence-based arguments are all strongly supported in the framework, as is complex communication. In the domain of interpersonal skills, the framework provides strong support for collaboration and teamwork; a prominent theme is the importance of understanding science and engineering as a social enterprise conducted in a community, requiring well-developed skills for collaborating and communicating. The framework also supports adaptability, in the form of the ability and inclination to revise one's thinking or strategy in response to evidence and review by one's peers. The framework also gives explicit support to metacognitive reasoning about one's own thinking and working processes, as well as the capacity to engage in self-directed learning about science and engineering throughout one's lifetime.

The foregoing summary highlights the fact that contemporary mathematics and science standards focus on the integration of key disciplinary ideas and practices in ways designed to promote deeper learning and transfer. The challenge with both sets of standards since their introduction during the past decade has been how to design curricular and instructional materials to support acquisition of these important competencies and how to organize classroom instruction, including the design and use of assessment, to promote student attainment of the complex disciplinary objectives embodied by contemporary STEM standards (see, e.g., Pellegrino et al. 2014). The remainder of this chapter involves discussion of five critical topics relevant to addressing the challenge of improving STEM assessment by bringing to bear ideas and capabilities associated with technology and AI. Each of these topics is important for considering the individual and collective contributions made by this volume of research and development work.

Grand Challenges in STEM Assessment

Over ten years ago Bruce Alberts, former President of the U.S. National Academy of Sciences and then editor of *Science*, asked me to write an article about the challenges and opportunities that existed for the assessment of proficiency in science (Pellegrino 2013). The timing of his request aligned with several of the developments noted earlier in "STEM Education and Assessment in Context," including the evolution of theory and research on science learning and instruction and the appearance of significant K-12 science education position pieces including the *Framework for K-12 Science Education* (NRC 2012) and the *Next Generation Science Standards* (NGSS 2013). Although the article was published a decade ago, the three grand challenges identified at the time remain current.

1. Design valid and reliable assessments reflecting the integration of practices, crosscutting concepts, and core ideas in science.
2. Use assessment results to establish an empirical evidence base regarding progressions in science proficiency across K-12.

3. Build and test support tools and information systems which teachers can use to effectively implement assessment for learning in the classroom.

The first challenge reflects the fact that the performance expectations of the NGSS pose significant assessment design challenges. It was argued that considerable research and development would be needed to create and evaluate assessment tasks and situations that can provide adequate evidence of the proficiencies implied in the NGSS. Those arguments were further expanded in a 2014 NRC report *Developing Assessments for the Next Generation Science Standards* (Pellegrino et al. 2014). It was further argued in both the 2013 article and 2014 NRC report that such work needed to be conducted in instructional settings where students had adequate opportunity to construct the integrated knowledge envisioned by the NRC framework and the NGSS. While work of this type has proceeded forward over the ensuing decade (e.g., Harris et al. 2019), much still needs to be done across the K-12 grade span and for multiple content domains.

The 2013 *Science* article also argued that much of what is assumed in the *Framework* and NGSS regarding learning progressions needs to be validated through empirical research. The latter requires assessment tasks and situations that can be used across multiple age/grade bands so that we can determine how proficiency changes over time and with appropriate instruction. The empirical results can be used to support the design of more effective curriculum materials and instructional practices. While such work has ensued in the intervening decade, there is still much to do regarding the integration of curriculum, instruction, and assessment based on empirically validated progressions of learning (e.g., Duncan and Rivet 2018). This holds for multiple aspects of science proficiency and includes both the separate and integrated development of disciplinary core ideas and science and engineering practices.

The 2013 *Science* article argued that for teachers to effectively implement assessment as part of their pedagogy they would need instructionally informative assessment tasks as well as tools for presenting tasks and collecting and scoring student performance. They would also need smart systems that could provide actionable information about the meaning and implications of student performance relative to instruction and student learning. It was argued that such systems would need to be designed in collaboration with learning scientists and teachers to ensure their validity, usability, and utility. While some progress has been made in this area, much remains to be done (see Zhai and Wiebe 2023, for an excellent summary and evaluation of work to date). It is here that recent developments in technology, data analytics, and AI can make significant contributions to the myriad issues associated with meeting this challenge.

Critical questions to consider as you read the contributions in this volume:

- *Which of the* ***three grand challenges*** *in STEM assessment are being addressed by the work reported in this volume?*
- *What is the* ***nature and scope*** *of the contribution?*
- *What* ***evidence of progress*** *has been provided with respect to addressing conceptual issues and/or providing pragmatic solutions to the* ***challenges*** *posed?*

Positioning Assessment along a Continuum: Variation in Orientation, Time, Space, and Purpose

Assessment occurs in multiple educational contexts (e.g., classrooms and school districts, as well as state, national, and international assessment programs) and is intended to serve multiple purposes such as assessment for learning (formative assessment), assessment of learning (summative assessment), and program evaluation (see the discussion of contexts and purposes in Pellegrino, Chudowsky, and Glaser 2001). Often the public, policymakers, and educators express confusion about results obtained from these different contexts of use, often leading to inappropriate and incorrect interpretations of the meaning of outcomes obtained in and across these varying assessment contexts.

The literature on educational assessment often draws a dichotomy between *internal* classroom assessments administered by teachers and *external* large-scale tests administered by districts, states, nations, or international consortia. Ruiz-Primo et al. (2002) argue that these two very different assessment contexts are better understood as two points on a continuum defined by their distance from the enactment of specific instructional activities which has important consequences for their instructional sensitivity. As illustrated in Table 2.1, Ruiz-Primo et al. identify five discrete points or levels on a continuum of assessment distance and practice: *immediate* (e.g., observations or artifacts from the enactment of a specific activity), *close* (e.g., embedded assessments and semiformal quizzes of learning from one or more activities), *proximal* (e.g., formal classroom exams of learning from a specific curriculum), *distal* (e.g., criterion-referenced achievement tests such as required by the U.S. ESSA legislation), and *remote* (broader outcomes measured over time, including norm-referenced achievement tests and some national (e.g., NAEP) and international achievement measures (e.g., TIMSS, PISA)). Different assessments can be understood as different points on this continuum, especially with respect to their orientation and their alignment with curriculum and instruction. The timescales for the five levels can be characterized as *minutes, days, weeks, months,* and *years,* respectively. Timescale is important because of the different competencies that various assessments along the continuum focus on and, therefore, their capacity for contributing information to fulfill timescale-relevant formative or summative functions of assessment, including their sensitivity to variations in the quality of instruction and the impact on student learning.

A second pervasive dichotomy in the assessment literature is between the practices of formative assessment to advance learning and summative assessment to provide evidence of prior learning. Consistent with the discussion above, it is often assumed that classroom assessment is synonymous with the formative purpose of assessment and that external, large-scale assessment is synonymous with the summative and/or program evaluation purpose assessment. The summative and formative functions of assessment can be identified for most assessment activities regardless of context of use or where they fall on the time-space continuum. While it is beyond this chapter to discuss the nuances of the formative versus summative distinction as applied to the continuum discussed above, suffice it to say that much still needs to be done in the area of assessment literacy so that the public, policymakers, and educators at multiple levels of the system can understand the formative–summative distinction

Table 2.1 Representation of the assessment continuum from Ruiz-Primo et al. (2002).

Level (Example)	Primary Orientation	Time Scale Relationship to Curriculum & Instruction
IMMEDIATE (artifacts from the enactments of the curriculum)	Specific Events	Minutes
CLOSE (semi-formal classroom assessment)	Specific Activities	Days
PROXIMAL (formal classroom assessment)	Partial or Entire Curricula	Weeks
DISTAL (criterion-refrenced external tests)	Regional or National Content Standards	Months
REMOTE (norm-referenced external tests)	(Inter) National Achievement	Years

and properly interpret results obtained from assessments designed to support these different functions and purposes. It is particularly important that teachers understand the formative–summative distinction regarding assessment function and use in the classroom and can appropriately and effectively implement both sets of assessment practices as part of their pedagogy.

Critical questions to consider as you read the contributions in this volume:

- *Where is the work reported in this volume situated with respect to the* ***assessment continuum****?*
- *What specific* ***functions and uses*** *of assessment results are targeted by the work?*
- *What evidence of progress has been provided with respect to addressing conceptual and/or pragmatic solutions regarding* ***assessment function and interpretive use*** *for cases located along the continuum?*

Assessment as a Process of Reasoning from Evidence

As noted in "Positioning Assessment along a Continuum," assessments can take several forms, are deployed in multiple contexts, and are intended to serve many purposes in the educational system. But regardless of these variations, the goal in assessing students is to learn about what they know and can do and to use it productively. Assessment is a tool designed to elicit students' behavior to produce evidence that can be used to draw reasonable inferences about what students know. The process of collecting evidence to support inferences about what students know represents a chain of reasoning from evidence about student learning that characterizes all assessments from classroom quizzes to standardized achievement tests, computerized tutoring programs, and the conversation a student has with her teacher as they work through a math or science problem.

In the 2001 report *Knowing What Students Know: The Science and Design of Educational Assessment*, issued by the National Research Council, the process of reasoning from evidence is portrayed as the *assessment triangle* (Pellegrino, Chudowsky, and Glaser 2001). The vertices of the assessment triangle represent the three key elements underlying any assessment: a model of student *cognition* and learning in the domain of the assessment; a set of assumptions and principles about the kinds of *observations* that will provide evidence of students' competencies; and an *interpretation* process for making sense of the evidence. The three are represented as vertices of a triangle because each is connected to and dependent on the other two. A major tenet of the *Knowing What Students Know* report is that for an assessment to be effective and valid, the three elements must be in synchrony given the intended interpretive purpose.

The *cognition* corner of the triangle refers to theory, data, and sets of assumptions about how students represent knowledge and develop competence in a subject matter domain (e.g., fractions or chemical reactions). In any particular assessment application, a model of learning in the domain is needed to identify the set of knowledge and skills that is important in assessing for the context of use, whether that be characterizing the competencies students have acquired at some point in time to make a summative judgment, or for making a formative judgment to guide subsequent instruction so as to maximize learning. A central premise is that the model should represent the most scientifically credible understanding of typical ways in which learners represent knowledge and develop expertise in domain.

Every assessment is also based on a set of assumptions and principles about the kinds of tasks or situations that will prompt students to say, do, or create something that demonstrates important knowledge and skills. The tasks to which students are asked to respond on an assessment are not arbitrary. They must be carefully chosen to provide evidence linked to the model of learning and to support the kinds of inferences and decisions that will be made based on the assessment results. The *observation* vertex of the assessment triangle represents a description or set of specifications for assessment tasks that will elicit illuminating responses from students.

Every assessment is also based on certain assumptions and models for interpreting the evidence collected from observations. The *interpretation* vertex of the triangle encompasses all the methods and tools used to reason from fallible observations. It expresses how the observations derived from a set of assessment tasks constitute evidence about the knowledge and skills that are targeted. In the context of large-scale assessment, the interpretation method is usually a statistical model, which is a characterization or summarization of patterns one would expect to see in the data given varying levels of student competency. In the context of classroom assessment, the interpretation is often made less formally by the teacher and is often based on an intuitive or qualitative model rather than a formal statistical one.

A crucial point is that each of the three elements of the assessment triangle not only must make sense on its own, but also must connect to each of the other two elements in a meaningful way to lead to an effective assessment and sound inferences. Thus, to have a valid and effective assessment, all three vertices of the triangle must work together in synchrony. Central to this entire process are theories, models, and data on how students learn and what students know as they develop competence for important aspects of the curriculum.

Critical questions to consider as you read the contributions in this volume:

- *What assumptions have been made about the* ***cognition, observation, and interpretation*** *components of the reasoning-from-evidence process in the work reported in this volume?*
- *To what extent are those* ***assumptions justifiable*** *given current theory and research?*
- *Is there evidence of* ***coordination and coherence*** *among cognition–observation–interpretation in the assessment examples provided by the work reported in this volume?*

Affordances of Technology and AI to Advance and Enhance STEM Assessment

Much has been written and speculated about the power of technology and AI to both improve and transform assessment across a range of assessment contexts and purposes (see e.g., Behrens, DiCerbo, and Foltz 2019; Gane, Zaidi, and Pellegrino 2018; Pellegrino, Chudowsky, and Glaser 2001; Pellegrino and Quellmalz 2010). For present purposes two things are most salient regarding applications of technologies and AI to issues of STEM assessment: (a) what can be validly and reliably assessed, and (b) using the results of assessment to inform instruction and guide student learning.

Regarding what can be assessed, what matters is what we are trying to reason about—contemporary conceptions of student cognition in a STEM domain like mathematics or science. As noted earlier, contemporary views of proficiency in STEM disciplines include the expectation that learners should be able to use their disciplinary knowledge to engage in a variety of domain-specific practices in the service of solving domain-related problems (NGA 2010; NRC 2012). Given that the concept of student cognition in STEM disciplines has expanded in terms of what students are supposed to know and be able to do, technology affords opportunities for substantially changing and extending the observation and interpretation components of the assessment triangle to validly assess key aspects of those competencies. Doing so enhances the entire evidentiary reasoning process and the validity of any science assessment given its intended interpretive use, whether that be at the classroom level for supporting learning and instruction or at district, state, national, or international level for supporting system monitoring and policy purposes.

With respect to observation, technology provides opportunities for presenting dynamic assessment stimuli (videos, graphics, 2- and 3-D simulations, etc.) that can be interacted with to elicit relevant sets of responses from students. Simultaneously, technology allows for the generation and capture of a variety of response products, including situations in which students generate responses using multiple modalities (e.g., drawing and writing). In general, technology-enhanced assessments open the door to interactive, adaptive stimulus environments and response formats that better match the intended reasoning and response processes that form the basis for desired claims about student proficiency in STEM (e.g., Gorin and Mislevy 2013).

Students' interactions with technology-enhanced assessments can be logged to provide fine-grained data on how they engage in thinking and reasoning processes. Understanding the operations that students performed in the process of creating a final product may be critical to evaluating students' proficiency. Log data offer the opportunity to reveal these actions, including where and how students spend their time, and what choices they make in situations like using a simulation (see, e.g., Ercikan and Pellegrino 2017). However, such data can be complex, and an ongoing challenge is identifying how to take massive volumes of log data and distill it into actionable information to make judgments about students' knowledge, skills, and abilities (see, e.g., Bergner and von Davier 2019).

With respect to the interpretation vertex, technology and AI offer significant opportunities for enhancement of the reasoning-from-evidence process given the types of observations described earlier. It makes little sense to collect the types of data just mentioned unless we have ways of interpreting them reliably and meaningfully. This can come about through mechanisms such as automated scoring of responses and application of complex parsing, statistical and inferential models for response process data. The potential exists for examining the global and local strategies students use while solving assessment problems and the implications, including how such strategies relate to the accuracy or appropriateness of final responses. While capturing such data in a digital environment is "easy," making sense of it is far more complicated. The same can be said for capturing data to constructed response questions where students may express in written and/or graphical form an argument or explanation about the solution of some mathematical or scientific problem or investigation.

The data capture contexts described above are challenging with respect to scoring and interpretation. It is here that AI and machine learning can play a significant role in STEM assessment with regards to triangulating and processing rich, fine-grained multimodal data. Advances have been made in the automated scoring of short written constructed responses for various topics and content in science and other subjects (see, e.g., Beggrow et al. 2014). Developments in machine learning may also allow researchers to analyze complex response process data of the type described above (see, e.g., Zhai 2021; Zhai et al. 2020a,b; Zhai, Krajcik, and Pellegrino 2021). Such data may prove to be especially informative about student thinking and reasoning and thus add greatly to the validity arguments for STEM assessments and the knowledge we can gain about student competence.

There is one more very important way that technology and AI can impact STEM assessment and student learning. One might argue that addressing this challenge transcends all others. It concerns the productive use of assessment in the STEM classroom. As noted earlier, teachers often face conceptual issues in understanding and implementing the formative assessment process and distinguishing it from summative assessment. Even when they understand and embrace formative assessment as an important part of their classroom assessment practice, they still encounter operational challenges in implementing the process. A major operational obstacle is the burden of managing a complex process which includes: (a) selecting and then administering assessment tasks, (b) capturing student responses, (c) evaluating student responses for strengths and weaknesses, (d) interpreting student outcomes relative to trajectories of learning, and (e) considering the implications for instruction. Technology-based assessment applications could significantly impact the feasibility and implementation of formative assessment practices to enhance student learning in the STEM classroom if support can be provided for as many of the operational elements of the formative assessment process as possible. Doing so would very directly begin to address the third of the grand challenges mentioned earlier.

While technology and AI possess many affordances for advancing STEM assessment and use, there are two important caveats that cannot be ignored regarding its application. The first is related to issues of design and is considered next. The second is related to issues of equity and fairness which is considered subsequently in the discussion of validity.

For technology and AI to be of greatest benefit, a very deliberate and principled design process needs to be used for task design and data capture—a process that takes into consideration the relevant forms of evidence and the means for interpretation of that evidence. Recognizing that assessment is an evidentiary reasoning process, it has proven useful to be systematic in framing the process of assessment design as an evidence-centered design process (e.g., Mislevy and Haertel 2006; Mislevy and Riconscente 2006). The process starts by defining the claims that one wants to be able to make about student knowledge and competence including the ways in which students are supposed to know and understand particular aspects of a content domain. Examples might include aspects of algebraic thinking, ratio and proportion, force and motion, heat and temperature, etc. The most critical aspect of defining the claims one wants to make for purposes of assessment is to be as precise as possible about the elements that matter and express these in the form of verbs of cognition that are more precise and less vague than high-level cognitive, superordinate verbs such as *know* and *understand*. Example verbs might include compare, describe, analyze, compute, elaborate, explain, predict, and justify. Guiding this process of specifying the claims is theory and research on the nature of domain-specific knowing and learning.

While the claims one wishes to make or verify are about the student, they are linked to the forms of evidence that would provide support for those claims—the warrants in support of each claim. The evidence statements associated with given sets of claims capture the features of work products or performances that would give substance to the claims. This includes which features need to be present and how they are weighted in any evidentiary scheme, i.e., what matters most and what matters least, or not at all. For example, if the evidence in support of a claim about a student's knowledge of the laws of motion is that the student can analyze a physical situation in terms of the forces acting on all the bodies, then the evidence might be a free body diagram that is drawn with all the forces labeled including their magnitudes and directions.

The precision that comes from elaborating the claims and evidence statements associated with a domain of STEM knowledge and skill pays off when one turns to the design of tasks or situations that can provide the requisite evidence. In essence, tasks are not designed or selected until it is clear what forms of evidence are needed to support the range of claims associated with a given assessment situation. The tasks need to provide all the necessary evidence and they should allow students to "show what they know" in ways that are as unambiguous as possible with respect to what the task performance implies about student knowledge and skill, i.e., the inferences about student cognition that are permissible and sustainable from a given set of assessment tasks or items. This evidence-centered design thinking is required throughout the task design, task refinement, task tryout, and task validation process. It is a mistake to try to graft technology and AI onto assessment tasks and assessment data after the fact since doing so seldom works efficiently or well. Technology and AI cannot solve problems of inference and interpretation associated with data obtained from poorly designed tasks that yield limited forms of evidence.

Critical questions to consider as you read the contributions in this volume:

- *Which aspects of the* ***cognition–observation–interpretation*** *reasoning from evidence process are being addressed by the work reported in this volume?*
- *What is the nature of the innovation proposed,* ***where is it focused****, and how well does it represent application of a principled,* ***evidence-centered design*** *process?*
- *What evidence of progress has been provided with respect to applications of* ***technology and AI*** *for addressing important conceptual issues and/or pragmatic challenges in* ***assessment design, interpretation, and/or use****?*

Validity, Fairness, and Equity in STEM Assessment

While much is made about evidence of an assessment's reliability, the most important characteristic of an assessment is evidence of its validity. It is well established that an assessment is not valid in and of itself. Rather, judgment about an assessment's validity is based upon evidence related to its intended interpretive use. An assessment that might be highly valid for diagnostic use in the math classroom might not be valid for use on a large-scale state achievement test and vice versa. In Messick's construct-centered view of validity, the theoretical construct the test score is purported to represent is the foundation for interpreting the validity of any given assessment (Messick 1994). For Messick, validity is "an integrated evaluative judgment of the degree to which empirical evidence and theoretical rationales support the adequacy and appropriateness of inferences and actions based on test scores" (Messick 1989). Important work has been done to refine and advance views of validity in educational measurement and contemporary perspectives call for an interpretive validity argument that "specifies the proposed interpretations and uses of test results by laying out the network of inferences and assumptions leading from the observed performances to the conclusions and decisions based on the performances" (Kane 2006).

Kane (2006) and others (Haertel and Lorie 2004; Kane 1992, 2001, 2013; Mislevy, Steinberg, and Almond 2003) distinguish between the interpretive argument, i.e., the propositions that underpin an assessment's interpretation, and the evidence and arguments that provide the necessary warrants for the propositions or claims of the interpretive argument. In essence this view identifies as the two essential components of a validity argument the claims being made about the focus of an assessment and how the results can be used (interpretive argument), together with the evidence and arguments in support of those claims. Appropriating this approach, contemporary educational measurement theorists have framed test validity as a reasoned argument backed by evidence (e.g., Kane 2006). An argument and evidence framing of validity supports investigations for a broad scope of assessment designs and purposes, including many that go beyond typical large-scale tests of academic achievement and move into the arena of innovative and instructionally supportive assessments (e.g., see Pellegrino, DiBello, and Goldman 2016).

Given the nature of the STEM constructs of current interest, including their inherent complexity and multidimensionality, we must acknowledge from the outset the challenges that exist in establishing validity arguments for innovative assessments of contemporary STEM competencies, including the reporting of results for various intended use cases. Validity arguments will depend on well-developed interpretive arguments that include (1) clear specifications of the constructs of interest and their associated conceptual backing; (2) the forms of evidence associated with those constructs; and (3) the methods for interpretation and reporting of that evidence. Such interpretive arguments are essential for guiding the assessment design processes, including carefully thought-out applications of technology, data analytics, and AI to support the observational and inferential aspects of the overall reasoning-from-evidence process. As noted above, carefully articulated claims about what is being assessed and reported need to be supported by empirical evidence. Such evidence can be derived from multiple forms of data involving variations in human performance and are essential to establishing an assessment's validity argument. Validity of an assessment should not be assumed a priori nor should it be something miraculous as illustrated by Figure 2.2. Rather, we must strive to make explicit our claims and evidence related to an assessment's validity and that encompass the equity and fairness issues noted in the following.

In pursuing innovative assessment of twenty-first-century competencies, of paramount concern are issues of equity and fairness as part of the validity argument. Of particular concern is comparability of results and validity of inferences derived from performance obtained across different modes of assessment and types of tasks, especially for varying groups of students (see Berman, Haertel, and Pellegrino 2020). As assessment has moved from paper-and-pencil formats to digitally based assessment, the general focus has been on mode comparability with concerns about student

Validity of an assessment is not something miraculous -- we must strive to make **explicit** *our claims and evidence related to* **assessment validity**

Figure 2.2 Being explicit in developing the validity argument for an assessment.

familiarity and differential access to the hardware and software used (see Way and Strain-Seymour 2021). However, as the digital assessment world advances, a significant issue for innovative assessment is determining how student background characteristics including language, culture, and educational experience influence performance on different types of tasks and innovative assessment designs that leverage the power of technology. As the assessment environments and tasks become more innovative, equity and fairness concerns become of paramount importance. Thus, a key part of the validity argument for any innovative assessment will be establishing the sociocultural boundaries related to equitable and fair interpretations and uses of the assessment results.

Critical questions to consider as you read the contributions in this volume.

- *What is the* ***validity argument*** *for the work reported in this volume and what* ***evidence*** *has been provided in support of the* ***interpretive argument*** *for the specific assessment cases?*
- *What* ***evidence of progress*** *has been provided with respect to addressing conceptual and/or pragmatic* ***issues of validity*** *for STEM assessments?*
- *How is the work helping to* ***promote*** *and/or* ***support equity and fairness*** *in STEM assessment and STEM education?*

Why Progress in STEM Assessment Demands a Village

No single assessment can evaluate all the forms of STEM knowledge and competency that we value for students, nor can a single instrument meet all the goals and information needs held by parents, practitioners, and policymakers. Ultimately, we need coordinated systems of assessments in which different tools are used for different inferential and reporting purposes—for example, formative and summative, diagnostic versus large-scale monitoring. Such assessment tools would operate at different levels of the educational system from the classroom on up to school, district, state, national, and/or international levels of application. Within and across these levels, all assessments should faithfully represent the STEM constructs of interest and reflect and reinforce desired outcomes that arise from good instructional practices and effective learning processes.

Innovation in STEM assessment of the type envisioned by this volume's body of work cannot be undertaken nor will it succeed without an investment of multiple forms of capital. The discussion that follows considers the three forms of capital needed and expands on why each is critical to the success of such an endeavor. They include intellectual capital, fiscal capital, and political capital. Each is necessary, but insufficient on its own—yet collectively they provide what is needed to advance the theory and practice of STEM educational assessment and maximize its educational and societal benefit in the twenty-first century (see Pellegrino, Foster, and Piacentini 2023, for an expanded discussion of these issues).

Intellectual Capital

The collective work described in this volume illustrates that no single discipline or area of expertise will be sufficient to accomplish what needs to be done to innovate STEM assessment. Advances to date reveal that next generation STEM assessment development is inherently a multidisciplinary enterprise: different communities of experts need to work together collaboratively to find solutions to the many conceptual and technical challenges noted by the chapters in this volume, as well as those yet to be uncovered. Enlisting creative people from multiple backgrounds and perspectives to the enterprise of assessment design and use, and facilitating collaboration among them, is critical. Synergies need to be fostered between assessment designers, technology developers, learning scientists, domain experts, measurement experts, data scientists, educational practitioners, and policymakers.

There are multiple intellectual and pragmatic challenges in merging learning science, data science, and measurement science to understand how the sources of evidence we can obtain from complex STEM tasks can best be analyzed and interpreted using models and methods from artificial intelligence, machine learning, statistics, and psychometrics. Collaborative engagement with these concerns by learning scientists, data scientists, measurement experts, assessment designers, technology experts, experts in user interfaces, and educational practitioners could yield significant insights for STEM Assessment Engineering.

Fiscal Capital

Development of assessments for application and use at any reasonable level of scale is a time-consuming and costly enterprise, especially for innovative STEM assessment of the types envisioned in this volume. The bulk of the substantial funds currently expended on assessment programs is for the design and execution of large-scale assessments focused on traditional disciplinary domains like mathematics, literacy, and science (e.g., state achievement tests, the U.S. NAEP program, and OECD's PISA program). Most such assessments fall within conventional parameters for task development, delivery, data capture, scoring and reporting. This has been true for quite some time even though most large-scale assessment programs have moved to technology-based task presentation, data capture, and reporting. However, capitalizing on many of the affordances of technology as discussed earlier has not been a distinct feature of those assessment programs.

Developing and validating technology-rich assessment tasks and environments of the type advocated for in this volume is a much more costly activity than updating current assessments by generating traditional items using standard task designs and specifications and presenting them via technology rather than paper and pencil. Such new instruments require considerable research and development regarding task design, implementation, data analysis, scoring, reporting, and validation. As noted above, that scope of work needs to be executed by interdisciplinary groups representing domain experts, problem developers, psychometricians, interface designers, and programmers. Sustained funding for the type of research and development needed is a key element in advancing next generation STEM assessment.

Substantial fiscal capital is required to assemble and support the multidisciplinary teams needed to conduct research and development supporting the creation of innovative next generation assessments. The dollars currently invested in multidisciplinary assessment R&D are but a tiny fraction of what is spent on more conventional assessment development and implementation. Government funding agencies, private foundations, testing companies, and governmental assessment agencies must be willing to make the systematic and sustained investments required. Funding at fiscal levels representing a small percentage of the total fiscal expenditures on typical large-scale educational assessment would make a significant difference in what could be done and the time to do so. Without sustained and increased investments in the types of work required it will prove difficult, if not impossible, to accumulate the knowledge required to solve the conceptual and technical problems that remain and generate the solutions required for valid and useful assessment of challenging STEM constructs at any reasonable level of implementation and scale.

Political Capital

As currently practiced, educational assessment is a highly entrenched enterprise, particularly the use of large-scale standardized assessments for educational monitoring and policy decisions. Standardization includes what is assessed, how it is assessed, how the data are collected and then analyzed, and how the results are interpreted and then reported. This is not an accident but the product of many years of operating within a particular perspective on what we want and need to know about the knowledge, skills, and abilities of individuals, coupled with a highly refined technology of test development and administration that is further coupled with an epistemology of interpretation about the mental world rooted in a measurement metaphor derived from the physical world.

It is hard to make major changes within existing systems when there are well-established operational programs entrenched in practice and policy. Change of the type needed requires strong political will and vision to encourage people to think beyond what is possible now or even in the next decade. Without political will, it will be impossible to generate sufficient fiscal capital to assemble the intellectual capital required to pursue next generation STEM assessment development and implementation and thus achieve meaningful change in STEM educational assessment.

The political capital needed is not limited to policymakers. It encompasses multiple segments of the educational assessment development community, the measurement and psychometric community, and the educational practice community. Each of these communities has entrenched assumptions and practices when it comes to assessment. Thus, each community needs to buy into a vision of transformation and, regardless of where the process may lead, these communities must work together to generate the amount of political will and capital needed to organize, support, and sustain a transformation process for STEM educational assessment in ways envisioned in this volume.

Final Comment

This volume's collective work serves as a marker for what is possible as well as a stimulus for assembling the multiple forms of capital needed to move ahead. We need to transform and harness STEM assessment to serve as a powerful vehicle that can positively impact equity and fairness in the teaching and learning of science in ways envisioned by contemporary STEM education frameworks and standards. While much remains to be done, bringing this diverse intellectual community together and sharing their work illustrates the substantial opportunity that exists for significant advancement in STEM assessment and argues that further pursuit of this R&D agenda is both necessary and feasible.

References

American Association for the Advancement of Science (AAAS). 1993. *Benchmarks for Science Literacy*. Oxford: Oxford University Press.

Beggrow, E. P., Ha, M., Nehm, R. H., Pearl, D., and Boone, W. J. 2014. "Assessing Scientific Practices Using Machine-Learning Methods: How Closely Do They Match Clinical Interview Performance?" *Journal of Science education and Technology* 23: 160–82.

Behrens, J. T., DiCerbo, K. E., and Foltz, P. W. 2019. "Assessment of Complex Performances in Digital Environments." *Annals of the American Academy of Political and Social Science* 683, no. 1: 217–32.

Bellanca, J. 2014. *Deeper Learning: Beyond 21st Century Skills*. Bloomington, IN: Solution Tree Press.

Bergner, Y., and von Davier, A. A. 2019. "Process Data in NAEP: Past, Present, and Future." *Journal of Educational and Behavioral Statistics* 44, no. 6: 706–32.

Berman, A. I., Haertel, E. H., and Pellegrino, J. W., eds. 2020. *Comparability of Large-Scale Educational Assessments: Issues and Recommendations.* Washington, DC: National Academy of Education.

Bransford, J., Brown, A., Cocking, R., Donovan, S., and Pellegrino, J. W., eds. 2000. *How People Learn: Brain, Mind, Experience, and School* (expanded edition). Washington, DC: National Academies Press.

Duncan, R. G., and Rivet, A. E. 2018. "Learning progressions." In *International Handbook of the Learning Sciences,* edited by F. Fischer, C. E. Hmelo-Silver, S. R. Goldman, and P. Reimann, 422–32. London: Routledge.

Duschl, R. A., Schweingruber, H. A., and Shouse, A. W., eds. 2007. *Taking Science to School: Learning and Teaching Science in Grades K-8.* Washington, DC: National Academies Press.

Ercikan, K., and Pellegrino, J: W., eds. 2017. *Validation of Score Meaning for the Next Generation of Assessments: The Use of Response Processes.* London: Taylor & Francis.

Gane, B. D., Zaidi, S. Z., and Pellegrino, J. W. 2018. "Measuring What Matters: Using Technology to Assess Multidimensional Learning." *European Journal of Education* 53, no. 2: 176–87.

Gorin, J. S., and Mislevy, R. J. 2013, September. "Inherent Measurement Challenges in the Next Generation Science Standards for Both Formative and Summative Assessment." In *Invitational Research Symposium on Science Assessment.*

Harris, C. J., Krajcik, J. S., Pellegrino, J. W., and DeBarger, A. H. 2019. "Designing Knowledge-in-Use Assessments to Promote Deeper Learning." *Educational Measurement: Issues and Practice* 38, no. 2: 53–67.

Haertel, E. H. and Lorié, W. A. 2004. "Validating Standards-Based Test Score Interpretations." *Measurement* 2, no. 2: 61–103.

Kane, M. T. 1992. "An Argument-Based Approach to Validity." *Psychological Bulletin* 112, no. 3: 527.

Kane, M. T. 2001. "Current Concerns in Validity Theory." *Journal of Educational Measurement* 38, no. 4: 319–42.

Kane, M. T. 2006. "Validation." In *Educational Measurement* (4th ed.), edited by R.L. Brennan, 17–64. Washington, DC: American Council on Education and Praeger.

Kane, M. T. 2013. "Validating the Interpretations and Uses of Test Scores." *Journal of Educational Measurement* 50: 1–73.

Kilpatrick, J., Swafford, J., and Findell, B., eds. 2001. *Adding It Up: Helping Children Learn Mathematics.* Washington, DC: National Academies Press.

Messick, S. 1989. "Meaning and Values in Test Validation: The Science and Ethics of Assessment." *Educational Researcher* 18, no. 2: 5–11.

Messick, S. 1994. "The Interplay of Evidence and Consequences in the Validation of Performance Assessments." *Educational Researcher* 23: 13–23.

Mislevy, R. J. 1993. "Foundations of a New Test Theory." In *Test Theory for a New Generation of Tests,* edited by N. Fredericksen, R. J. Mislevy, and I. I. Bejar, 19–39. Mahwah, NJ: Erlbaum.

Mislevy, R., and Haertel, G. 2006. "Implications of Evidence-Centered Design for Educational Testing." *Educational Measurement: Issues and Practice* 25, no. 4: 6–20.

Mislevy, R. J., and Riconscente, M. M. 2006. "Evidence-Centered Assessment Design: Layers, Concepts, and Terminology." In *Handbook of Test Development,* edited by S. Downing and T. Haladyna, 61–90. Mahwah, NJ: Erlbaum.

Mislevy, R. J., Steinberg, L. S., and Almond, R. G. 2003. "On the Structure of Educational Assessments." *Measurement: Interdisciplinary Research and Perspectives* 1, no. 1: 3–62.

National Council of Teachers of Mathematics (NCTM). 1989. *Curriculum and Evaluation Standards for School Mathematics.* Reston, VA: National Council of Teachers of Mathematics.

National Governors Association (NGA). 2010. *Common Core State Standards.* Washington, DC.

National Research Council. 1996. *National Science Education Standards.* Washington, DC: National Academies Press.

National Research Council. 2012. *A Framework for K-12 Science Education: Practices, Crosscutting Concepts, and Core Ideas.* Washington, DC: National Academies Press.

NGSS Lead States. 2013. *Next Generation Science Standards: For States, by States.* Washington, DC: National Academies Press.

Pellegrino, J. W. 2013. "Proficiency in Science: Assessment Challenges and Opportunities." *Science* 340, no. 6130: 320–23.
Pellegrino, J. W., Chudowsky, N., and Glaser, R., eds. 2001. *Knowing What Students Know: The Science and Design of Educational Assessment*. Washington, DC: National Academies Press.
Pellegrino, J. W., DiBello, L. V., and Goldman, S. R. 2016. "A Framework for Conceptualizing and Evaluating the Validity of Instructionally Relevant Assessments." *Educational Psychologist* 51, no. 1: 59–81.
Pellegrino, J. W., Foster, N., and Piacentini, M. 2023. "Conclusions and Implications." In *Innovating Assessments to Measure and Support Complex Skills*, edited by N. Foster and M. Piacentini, 239–51. Paris: OECD Publishing.
Pellegrino, J. W., and Hilton, M., eds. 2012. *Education for Life and Work: Developing Transferable Knowledge and Skills in the 21st Century*. Washington, DC: National Academies Press.
Pellegrino, J. W., and Quellmalz, E. S. 2010. "Perspectives on the Integration of Technology and Assessment." *Journal of Research on Technology in Education* 43, no. 2: 119–34.
Pellegrino, J. W., Wilson, M. R., Koenig, J. A., and Beatty, A. S., eds. 2014. *Developing Assessments for the Next Generation Science Standards*. Washington, DC: National Academies Press.
Ruiz-Primo, M. A., Shavelson, R. J., Hamilton, L., and Klein, S. 2002. "On the Evaluation of Systemic Science Education Reform: Searching for Instructional Sensitivity." *Journal of Research in Science Teaching* 39, no. 5: 369–93.
Way, D., and Strain-Seymour, E. 2021. *A Framework for Considering Device and Interface Features That May Affect Student Performance on the National Assessment of Educational Progress*. https://www.air.org/sites/default/files/Framework-for-Considering-Device-and-Interface-Features-NAEP-NVS-Panel-March-2021.pdf
Wilson, M. R., and Bertenthal, M. W., eds. 2006. *Systems for State Science Assessments*. Washington, DC: National Academies Press.
Zhai, X. 2021. "Practices and Theories: How Can Machine Learning Assist in Innovative Assessment Practices in Science Education." *Journal of Science Education and Technology* 30, no. 2: 1–11.
Zhai, X., Haudek, K. C., Shi, L., Nehm, R., and Urban-Lurain, M. 2020a. "From Substitution to Redefinition: A Framework of Machine Learning-Based Science Assessment." *Journal of Research in Science Teaching 57*, no. 9: 1430–59.
Zhai, X., Yin, Y., Pellegrino, J. W., Haudek, K. C., and Shi, L. 2020b. "Applying Machine Learning in Science Assessment: A Systematic Review." *Studies in Science Education* 56, no. 1: 111–51.
Zhai, X., Krajcik, J., and Pellegrino, J. 2021. "On the Validity of Machine Learning-Based Next Generation Science Assessments: A Validity Inferential Network." *Journal of Science Education and Technology* 30, no. 2: 298–312.
Zhai, X., and Wiebe, E. 2023. "Technology-Based Innovative Assessment." In *Classroom-Based STEM Assessment: Contemporary Issues and Perspectives*, edited by C. Harris, E. Wiebe, S. Grover, and J. W. Pellegrino, 99–126. Community for Advancing Discovery Research in Education (CADRE). Boston: Education Development Center.

3

AI in Biology Education Assessment

How Automation Can Drive Educational Transformation

Ross H. Nehm

Introduction

Biology education research (BER), like other areas of science education, has increasingly leveraged artificial intelligence (AI) tools (e.g., data mining, machine learning, natural language processing) to investigate a range of topics in assessment, cognition, and learning (Linn et al. 2014; Zhai et al. 2020a, b). In this chapter I will review the past decade of research on AI in biology education using the Assessment of COntextual Reasoning about Natural Selection (ACORNS) instrument and the associated machine learning (ML)-based EvoGrader automated scoring system as a case example (Moharreri et al. 2014; Nehm et al. 2012). I begin the chapter with a brief overview of the development of these systems, go on to illustrate key findings and insights relevant to automated assessment more broadly, and end by situating this body of work within broader discussions of the role of AI in teaching and learning. I conclude the chapter by arguing that the role of a single tool or approach (like AI) cannot be cleanly disentangled from the field's epistemic aims, conceptual frameworks, and educational practices. Indeed, the examples in this chapter demonstrate that a systems perspective is needed to fully understand and appreciate AI's growing and often unanticipated impacts on science education research and practice.

Development of the ACORNS Assessment and the EvoGrader System

In the early to mid-2000s, large-scale deployment of constructed response assessments in undergraduate biology education generated data that matched findings from K–12 science education: students had great difficulty explaining basic biological phenomena using normative scientific frameworks (cf. Driver et al. 1994). Idiosyncratic and naive responses like those of much younger age cohorts were quite common (e.g., Nehm and Reilly 2007; Wilson et al. 2006). Although during this time scholarly enthusiasm and federal funding for multiple-choice concept inventory (CI) development and deployment were growing (see Libarkin 2008), empirical work had

Ross H. Nehm, *AI in Biology Education Assessment.* In: *Uses of Artificial Intelligence in STEM Education.*
Edited by: Xiaoming Zhai and Joseph Krajcik, Oxford University Press.
© Oxford University Press (2024). DOI: 10.1093/oso/9780198882077.003.0003

already begun to demonstrate the limits of CIs compared to constructed response assessments (see Nehm and Schonfeld 2008).

In addition to the rich insights that constructed response assessments offer about student thinking (Haudek et al. 2011), an advantage of using this format in undergraduate education is the large sample sizes (hundreds of students enrolled in introductory biology courses taught by the same instructor). These sample sizes enabled sufficient statistical power to investigate the diversity of student ideas and to explore whether seemingly idiosyncratic reasoning patterns might in fact be accounted for by specific aspects of the natural phenomena used in assessment items. Previous small-scale evolution assessment work missed predictable reasoning patterns tied to task phenomena and item features revealed in large samples (Nehm and Ha 2011; Nehm and Ridgway 2011; although see Weston et al. 2015). Reasoning about the evolutionary addition of traits was found to be easier than the loss of traits, and plant evolution was found to be more difficult than animal evolution. These and many other reasoning biases (e.g., trait function, familiarity) were found to generalize beyond the United States and to occur in students from China, Indonesia, Korea, and Germany (reviewed in Nehm 2018).[1] These findings were essential to developing an "evidence and task space" for assessment development (Evidence Centered Design, Mislevy, Steinberg, and Almond 2002). Claims about whether a student possessed desired knowledge about natural selection required evidence about student reasoning across different evolutionary polarities and patterns in the tree of life.

The richness of findings from constructed response assessments, coupled with predictable phenomenological reasoning biases, motivated the development and evaluation of a constructed response instrument (the ACORNS, a standardized and updated version of Bishop and Anderson's [1990] assessment). The ACORNS leveraged basic cognitive principles to make productive use of these phenomena-based reasoning biases and to quantify student learning performances (Opfer, Nehm, and Ha 2012; Figure 3.1). In line with "preparation for future learning" perspectives (Harris et al. 2019), the instrument was designed to measure students' competencies relating to evolutionary causation across many past and yet-to-occur biological phenomena (e.g., COV-19 evolution; Nehm et al. 2012). Phenomena-based reasoning biases, while essential to the ACORNS validity argument, were significant challenges in the development of EvoGrader's ML-based scoring models (see the section "Automation Efforts Prompt New Questions, Research Areas, and Epistemic Aims").

In biology education research, the value of using the ACORNS to measure student learning performances was counterbalanced by the burdens of scoring student responses. Six distinct burdens were noted by Nehm and Haertig (2012, 58): "(1) grading time and cost; (2) scorer training costs; (3) the complexity of rubric development and evaluation; (4) inconsistent scores among raters due to differences in scorer expertise and subjectivity; (5) grading fatigue; and (6) responses that may be difficult to interpret with consistency and accuracy." The cost of scoring was substantial by academic standards (see Nehm and Haertig 2012 for early attempts at cost estimation), and this greatly limited faculty use of constructed response assessments. To reduce barriers for using the ACORNS, to allow faculty to gain deeper insights

[1] The use of AI in translation and scoring responses from different countries is discussed in Ha and Nehm (2023).

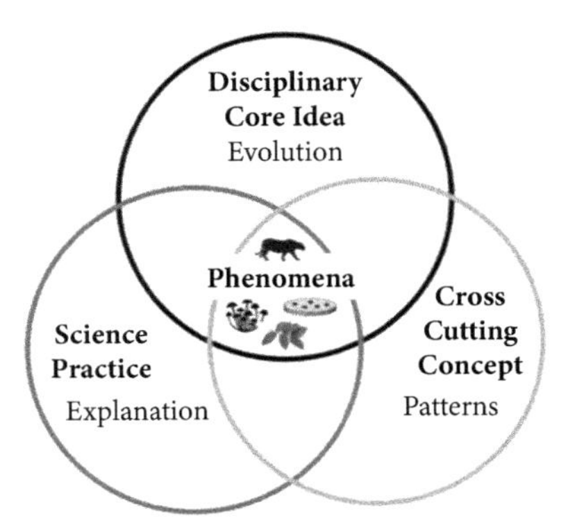

Figure 3.1 The ACORNS assessment aligns with the US Next Generation Science Standards perspective on three-dimensional learning. ACORNS tasks are anchored in a variety of specified phenomenological patterns (a cross-cutting concept) that are used to elicit evidence about student knowledge of the disciplinary core idea of evolution through the scientific practice of explanation. Students are asked to write a scientific explanation, which is then analyzed in the EvoGrader system.

into their students' learning challenges, and to modify instruction accordingly, digital tools for categorizing and scoring student responses were explored.

From today's perspective, it is difficult to appreciate how far AI in biology education (and society in general) has come. Fifteen years ago, computing power was low and expensive, and digital tools such as Google translate, Siri, and Alexa had yet to become integrated into the lives of millions. Large, digital text corpora in biology education were hard to come by because most assessments in higher education remained paper- and pencil-based, although digital learning management systems (e.g., Blackboard) had started to offer more convenient data capture tools. At colloquium talks at research universities and conferences during this time, a common claim by academics was that computers could never score text-based student answers as well as a faculty member or produce useful insights into student thinking. In the face of evidence to the contrary, it was not uncommon to be told that computer scoring success results had to be wrong, the interpretations were wrong, or the findings were a fluke and could not be replicated. Similar criticisms were raised in grant and manuscript reviews. These reactions occurred even though much larger studies from other fields had already demonstrated robust efficacy. Examples included Intelligent Essay Assessor (Landauer et al. 2003), PEG (Page 2003), E-rater (Burstein 2003), and C-rater (Sukkarieh and Bolge 2008). From the perspective of developing the EvoGrader scoring portal, proof of concept was an early and significant barrier to be broken. In summary, in the early to mid-2000s many biology educators and biologists expressed deep skepticism about AI-based assessment.

During this time two different AI methods were explored for biology assessment: text analysis (TA) and ML. TA was first used in undergraduate biology assessment by Urban-Lurain and colleagues at Michigan State University (e.g., Moscarella et al. 2008). One TA program, SPSSTA (SPSS Inc.), used linguistic-based techniques to identify, extract, and classify text using semantic networks, text libraries, and text co-occurrence patterns. Analyses of text were based on a combination of statistical and linguistic extraction methods, such as identifying equivalent classes of terms and their synonyms, indexing, and clustering terms, and detecting distribution patterns relative to pre-populated term libraries (SPSS Inc. 2006).

In science assessment contexts, automated extraction and classification alterations were typically dependent upon the burdensome process of manual (i) specification of categories, types, and terms and (ii) development of programming rules for classifying text using categories, types, and terms (see Nehm and Haertig 2012 for more details). Limitations aside, TA was able to produce robust correspondences with expert human scoring of students' knowledge regardless of "grain size" (e.g., holistic vs. concept-specific scales) or variations in how the construct was theorized (see Nehm and Haertig 2012). Applying the human-generated libraries and rule-based algorithms to larger scales was nevertheless challenging, primarily because of the proprietary and prohibitively expensive commercial software (see Nehm et al. 2012 for a discussion of other limitations).

The burdensome nature of TA and the financial costs of using commercial software in a Web portal led to the exploration of alternative methods for TA. In 2010, collaborations with the developers of the open-source ML programs SIDE and lightSIDE (Summarization Integrated Development Environment; Mayfield and Rose 2010) at Carnegie Mellon University began. SIDE (and later, the nimbler LightSIDE) was used to explore whether ML-based scoring models offered a better alternative to TA (Nehm et al. 2012). One difference between TA and SIDE was that SIDE was developed for confirmatory text analyses (identifying patterns that differentiate sets of previously categorized text responses) and for analyzing features from categorized text to develop scoring algorithms or models. In contrast, TA was often used for exploratory purposes (situations where categories and dimensions of text were less established or understood). TA was useful for identifying possible terms, categories, themes, and rule classifications. LightSIDE, on the other hand, used the scores generated by expert raters to build models that accounted for scoring patterns (see Moharreri et al. 2014 for details). LightSIDE was subsequently used to build and test ML-based scoring models on new corpora. Numerous challenges arose during feature engineering and model building that spurred additional research questions and new epistemic aims (discussed in the section "Automation Efforts Prompt New Questions, Research Areas, and Epistemic Aims").

EvoGrader (see http://www.evograder.org) was the eventual result of using the open-source SIDE program within Amazon's elastic cloud, and in 2012 it debuted as one of the first non-commercial machine-learning assessment tools designed for use in undergraduate biology education (Moharreri et al. 2014). EvoGrader was last updated in 2014. In the past decade, numerous advances in open-source software ecosystems have occurred that make EvoGrader's infrastructure antiquated. Nevertheless, this "living fossil" continues to persist as a free, online, on-demand ML-based scoring system for ACORNS item responses. EvoGrader contains an on-demand query box prompting the upload of typed explanations in .csv format. After upload and "one-click" analysis, EvoGrader generates faculty-friendly scoring reports illustrating the presence or absence of accurate scientific ideas (key concepts), non-normative concepts (naïve ideas or "misconceptions"), and holistic reasoning models (pure scientific, "mixed," and pure non-normative). About eighty items (essentially different surface feature arrangements) are available, combinations of which facilitate quantification of students' learning performances across biological phenomena (Opfer et al. 2012).

It is important to emphasize that the shift to envisioning large educational text corpora (in this case graded student work) as highly valuable data was facilitated in part by the growth of ML perspectives outside of computer science. Given that thousands of ACORNS-type responses had already been graded in prior classroom settings, a large, tagged corpus was available for assembly and application in ML model building and testing. Re-envisioning the scored responses as data facilitated rapid development of AI tools. Yet even today many faculty do not preserve or concatenate scored datasets into corpora, essentially discarding valuable data for future ML projects. Initiatives by the science education community to collect and store these valuable resources are needed.

Automation Efforts Prompt New Questions, Research Areas, and Epistemic Aims

The quest for replicating human actions in assessment (Zhai et al. 2020a,b) was a fundamental epistemic aim of the TA and ML research that resulted in the EvoGrader system. Iterative feature engineering, model building, model testing, and score generalization testing (e.g., new demographic samples) often resulted in failures that were at the time difficult to understand. Making sense of scoring failures and fine tuning of scoring models stimulated new questions and lines of research. Figure 3.2 highlights some of the unanticipated research areas that emerged from trying to understand automation failures (for brevity, numerous smaller topics are omitted). Reviewing the lines of research stimulated by the ACORNS and EvoGrader illustrates how AI research often extends beyond automating human tasks; new questions, research areas, and epistemic aims emerge as natural outgrowths of new findings. Such holistic perspectives raise questions about how best to characterize ML-based work in science assessment (Zhai et al. 2020a, b). This will be addressed after a review of some of the key areas of inquiry motivated by automation challenges using the ACORNS and EvoGrader (see Appendix).

Teacher Talk, Student Language, and Corpus Effects

Given that ML applications in biology assessment rely on natural language processing of text corpora, seeking to understand where text corpus variation originates and what the language contained in a corpus means is important. In many science domains, much remains to be understood about scientific language use. Rector, Nehm, and Pearl (2012) provided a simple model that included four factors relevant to interpreting text in biology education: "word meanings, discourse communities and contexts, intended meaning(s) of the speaker/instructor, and interpretation(s) of the term/language by the student." A few of these factors are worth discussing given their relevance to text corpus composition, interpretation, and AI analyses.

Helping students differentiate everyday and formal scientific meaning-making often involves connecting students' "real world" experiences with scientific concepts

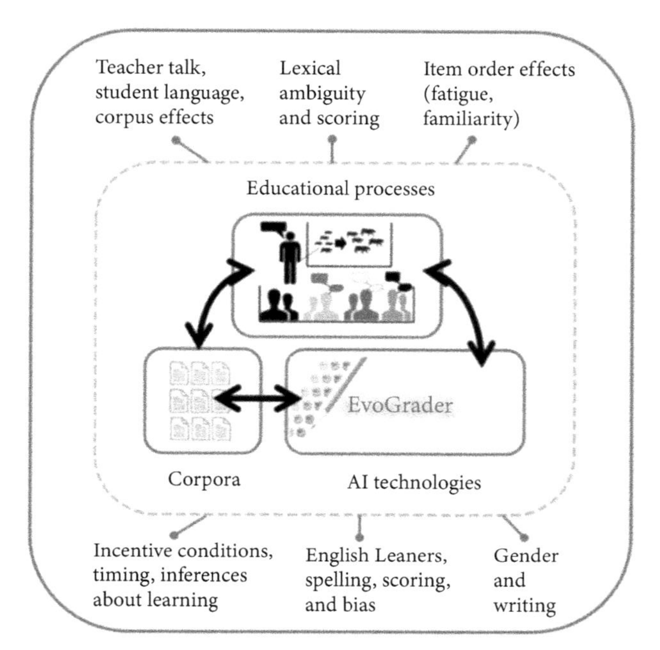

Figure 3.2 The role of AI technologies may be viewed from many vantage points, necessitating a systems perspective to appreciate its impact on biology education. In this chapter, the aims of AI research are envisioned as embedded within a complex network of educational processes and interactions (thick arrows) that in turn require a broad vantage point for understanding their impact. (Note that the ACORNS assessment is part of the EvoGrader assessment system.)

discussed in class (NRC 2001). In so doing, teachers often provide their own (spontaneous and idiosyncratic) examples based on what they think will be helpful to students as they engage with a concept or respond to questions. These discourse practices often find their way into assessment text corpora because "teacher talk" is often mimicked or parroted back by students (Nehm, Rector, and Ha 2010; Ha et al. 2011). As a result, different populations of students—such as biology majors and nonmajors, or students in instructor A's versus those in instructor B's class—often employ subtly different linguistic expressions to represent the same idea or concept. Signatures of teacher talk are a source of variation in assessment text corpora.

As an example, Ha et al.'s (2011) study using a version of the ACORNS and an iteration of EvoGrader found that scoring success for some concepts was sensitive to corpus sample source (different universities and classes with different instructors) and sample sizes (number of student responses). For example, although large percentages of students used the concept of "differential survival" (according to human scoring), computer scoring performed modestly because of sample-specific linguistic features. Differences in expressions and concept use patterns were also apparent because of institution (and corresponding differences in student background variables). However, this may not always be the case. In two studies of primarily underrepresented biology students from a minority-serving institution,

Nehm and Reilly (2007) and Nehm and Schonfeld (2008) used early versions of the ACORNS to document students' explanations of evolutionary change. They found that the types of student misconceptions were very similar to those previously documented in primarily white samples from the science education literature.

Biology teachers often switch between everyday and formal discourse practices in the classroom yet do not consistently or explicitly differentiate them to students (Clough and Wood-Robinson 1985; Dagher and Crossman 1992; Jungwirth 1975). This can muddle student understanding of the circumstances under which particular discourse practices are appropriate (or sought in assessment tasks). For example, tasks that prompt students to explain how they think a phenomenon works versus how teachers or scientists would explain how it works produce differences in the forms of language generated. This has relevance for task design. The intentional design of the ACORNS to cue scientific perspectives produced more valid inferences in terms of normative understanding than an unspecified discourse frame (that is, students choose the discourse frame they viewed as appropriate for the task; Nehm et al. 2012). Cueing formal scientific discourse can be helpful for scoring efforts because students' personal experiences/examples—often used in their scientific explanations (see Nehm and Schonfeld 2008)—will vary to a greater extent than normative scientific perspectives. Nevertheless, class examples and teacher talk inevitably find their way into text corpora.

Corpus variation is the raw material of many AI-based approaches, and making sense of such variation should be considered in both supervised and unsupervised ML. Much is known about student and teacher discourse practices in science education, and this knowledge should be leveraged to improve constructed response task design, rubric design, and scoring model evaluation. Overall, this strand of work on language and corpus variation helped to shed light on the contributions that teacher talk, task framing effects, and sample sources had on corpus composition, which in turn helped to explain (and ultimately reduce) ML-based scoring failures in EvoGrader. The broader point is that AI-based automation efforts cannot be divorced from broader educational considerations like science discourse practices and teacher talk; replication failures spurred deeper thinking about instructors and classrooms.

Lexical Ambiguity of Terms and Score Inferences

In addition to large-scale corpus variation patterns, individual words can play central roles in natural language processing and human scoring. Yet many core terms and concepts in science have intrinsically ambiguous meanings even when considered within the context of their use (Clerk and Rutherford 2000). Prior work on biological language, for example, has documented a large diversity of meanings that individual words represent (Abrams, Southerland, and Cummins 2001; Mead and Scott 2010a,b; Nehm, Rector, and Ha 2010). In a study of scientific explanations of evolutionary change, Rector, Nehm, and Pearl (2012) found that 81% of 1282 student explanations contained at least one important but lexically ambiguous term. One example relates to the term "pressure" in evolutionary contexts.

When evolutionary biologists use the term "pressure" (or "evolutionary pressure," "selective pressure"), they are using a metaphor that typically refers to a biotic or abiotic variable causing variation in the magnitude of differential survival/reproduction in a population. When students read or hear the word "pressure" in evolutionary contexts in science classrooms, they in contrast have been shown to use their prior knowledge to construct a variety of models about what this term means (Nehm, Rector, and Ha 2010). One common student model envisions pressure as a causal force *producing* biological variation (vs. *sorting* variation). Large numbers of students have been found to adopt meanings of "pressures" that are at odds with the instructor's intended meaning (even though the same term is used by both groups; Rector, Nehm, and Pearl 2012). "Pressure" represents an example of the general phenomenon of students incorporating and reciting scientific terms and phrases with little understanding of them (so-called mimicry or naming practices) or harboring alternative models of what the terms mean (lexical ambiguity). Many other biological terms have been found to pose similar challenges (e.g., "adaptation," "fitness," "random").

Employing supervised or unsupervised ML methods on text corpora requires some consideration of the challenges lexical ambiguity poses and quantification of its putative effects. It is worth emphasizing that perfect computer–human scoring agreement on a text response needs not indicate that valid inferences have been drawn regarding learning performances; independent data sources are necessary to test inferred correspondence. But the standard procedure in science education is to statistically compare human scores to computer scores alone and conclude that high correspondence values (above some benchmark) are evidence of scoring "success" (Lee et al. 2019; Liu et al. 2016). Clinical interviews can, of course, be used to test the inferred meaning of score correspondences. Beggrow et al. (2014) conducted clinical interviews with a hundred students and compared performance patterns to corresponding EvoGrader scores and a widely used multiple-choice (MC) assessment of the same construct. The EvoGrader scores were found to have greater correspondence with clinical interviews than the widely used MC test. Yet in most AI studies, clinical interviews remain limited (e.g., ten students per item) and/or unrepresentative of the larger sample. Developing more robust quality control standards for automated scoring would be beneficial to the field.

One attempt to investigate the impact of lexical ambiguity on scoring involved developing a simple technological tool known as the Assessment Cascade System (ACS). This system was used to conduct a large-scale study to quantify how often scoring misinterpretations of lexically ambiguous terms occurred (thereby quantifying inference errors; Rector, Nehm, and Pearl 2012). The ACS worked in the following way: After a student's explanation was submitted in response to a specific ACORNS item, the system automatically scanned the response to determine whether it contained lexically ambiguous terms important to scoring. If present, then a follow-up question was immediately posed to the student: "Please explain what you meant by the term ________ and how it fits into your explanation."

The responses generated by the computer system were scored in two different ways. First, *without* the follow-up information, expert scorers determined whether the term evolutionary "pressure" was used accurately, inaccurately, or ambiguously (i.e., not possible to determine). Second, after initial scoring was complete, the initial response *along with* the follow-up text was scored by the experts (without having access to their original scores). Figure 3.3 illustrates the impact of the term clarification on scoring. As the figure shows, most scores (approximately 80%, see middle bars) thankfully did *not* change, but up to 20% did. Two other patterns were notable. First, text reinterpretation differed among isomorphic tasks (1–4, left) despite trivial differences in their "cover stories," and second, most responses overall were inaccurate or ambiguous even though the normative term was employed.

Importantly, most scores did *not* change because of further clarification with the automated system ("% no change"; see Figure 3.3). However, a sizable number of reinterpretations produced score decreases ("% score decreases") or score increases ("% score increased"). Generally similar patterns of score stability and change occurred across the four tasks.

The process of analyzing student discourse patterns and language to improve scoring models ultimately led to faculty conversations about "shorthand" language, teacher talk, mimicry, and term meanings. These discussions, in turn, led to the realization that students' struggles and confusion about scientific language issues necessitated the development and deployment of curriculum materials about scientific language itself. The resulting teaching materials ("The Language of Science") are now a standard part of introductory biology instruction (delivered to more than 1200 students annually). These materials include learning objectives and assessments to gauge science language mastery (e.g., When a biologist uses the term fitness, what do they mean?). The transformation of educational goals and practices in this case was the direct result of engaging with AI. More work in other science domains is needed given that generally robust scoring models can at times produce false inferences (e.g., misclassification) about substantial numbers of students. The epistemic aim of scoring automation can lead to significant changes in educational practices,

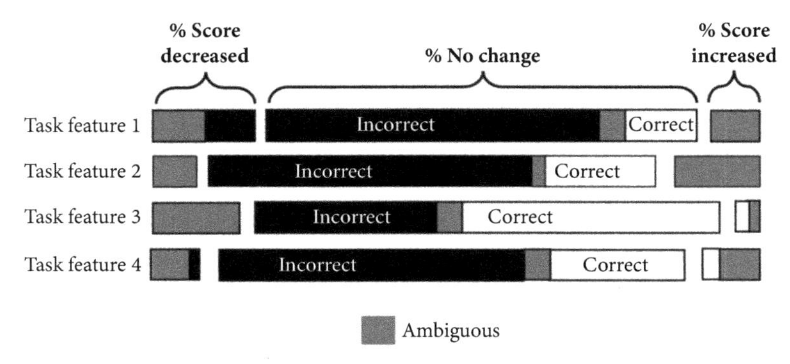

Figure 3.3 Illustration of the impact of the follow-up information on expert scoring of explanations containing the term evolutionary "pressure." As shown, most student responses were judged to be inaccurate or ambiguous even though the term *evolutionary pressure* itself is a normative concept, illustrating the dangers of taking the presence of scientific language as an indicator of understanding. Modified from Rector, Nehm, and Pearl (2012).

which serves to illustrate how AI work is embedded in interconnected educational systems (Figure 3.2).

Item Order Effects and Item Features

Although automatically scored constructed-response assessment tasks have the potential to offer rich and informative insights about student proficiencies, oftentimes an empirical rationale for the structure of the instrument or task battery in terms of item numbers, features, and sequencing/order is lacking (e.g., see Gotwals and Songer 2010; Lee et al. 2019; McNeill et al. 2006; Peker and Wallace 2011; Songer, Kelcey, and Gotwals 2009). In order to better understand how these factors impact inferences derived from ACORNS items and EvoGrader scores, studies of four items in different orders and varying in surface features or contexts were conducted. Such work has implications for how AI-based assessment tools should be implemented in real-world settings.

Measuring the extent to which students can reason beyond an anchoring phenomenon typically requires the presentation of different phenomena, scenarios, or contexts across tasks within instruments. Many studies about the disciplinary core idea of evolution have demonstrated that items about one phenomenon rarely provide valid indicators of evolutionary thinking more broadly (reviewed in Nehm 2018). Given that the ACORNS assessment was designed to employ different task features across phenomena to measure conceptual abstraction (Nehm et al. 2012), several questions about the use of these explanation tasks arose: How many items should be employed in an assessment battery? How different should the item "cover stories" be? Would the order of presentation of these items (considering the number and features of the items) impact inferences about student reasoning? An inherent challenge to this effort was that the items needed to include features that differed from the target phenomenon to some extent, but they could not differ by too much or too little given the sensitivity of evolutionary reasoning to such contexts (Nehm and Ha 2011). Limiting the range of scenarios or contexts also has implications for automation efforts given that ML-based methods have been shown to be negatively impacted by contextual diversity (Nehm, Ha, and Mayfield 2012; for a more expansive analysis of features that impact scoring success, see Zhai, Shi, and Nehm 2021).

Several experiments on these topics indicated that both item sequencing and the diversity of item features impacted student performance (Federer et al. 2014). Specifically, item order interacted with item features when students perceived the item features as being too similar. For example, when employing items prompting reasoning about the evolutionary gain of traits alone but using different taxa, many (but by no means all) students viewed the items as too similar. In such cases, response verbosity was found to significantly decrease as item number increased (i.e., less text later in the sequence; Federer et al. 2014). Verbosity in turn significantly impacted the number of concepts detected by humans and EvoGrader. Items with a mixture of evolutionary polarities (some gain of trait items, some loss of trait items, both of which were mixed with different taxa) minimized verbosity effects. This was found to be the result of the items being perceived as different by students (even though from an expert perspective they were not; Nehm and Ridgway 2011). The extreme similarity of the structure of the ACORNS items in these studies was also a likely contributor, as more recent work has added extraneous information to the tasks to make them appear less identical to students, which in turn minimizes downstream verbosity effects (unpublished data).

Counterbalanced designs are a common solution to order effects (e.g., latin square or other randomization methods during task administration). However, item feature effects and student fatigue remain as factors to consider. Many years of classroom-based observations of university students have shown that two explanation tasks (rather than four) for measuring reasoning across contexts tend to produce more valid indicators of understanding because they minimize fatigue and frustration at being asked similar questions multiple times. Students would often complain that there was "too much writing" required on assessments given their proclivities for selected-response formats. These real-world considerations must be studied to ensure robust measures of learning performances.

Too few studies of automated scoring of constructed response items have explored a wide array of phenomena and the extent to which student reasoning transcends these instances (Moscarella et al. 2016). Domain-specific models of learning must align with cognitive principles relating to conceptual abstraction, as should assessment developers' claim, evidence, and task spaces (Mislevy et al. 2002; see also NRC 2001). If preparation for future learning is considered an important educational outcome, then these issues should rise to greater prominence in AI research on constructed response assessments. As the research discussed earlier suggests, measuring reasoning generalizability requires careful consideration of topics beyond automation. In summary, much more work is needed on feature effects, order effects, fatigue, and effort in practice-based science assessments. In the case of the ACORNS, such studies have helped to find an effective balance between the number of items and the features of items to measure abstraction while minimizing student fatigue and frustration.

Incentive Conditions, Timing, and Inferences about Student Understanding and Learning

Constructed response tasks involving scientific practices such as explanation, communication, model building, and argumentation are necessary for measuring performance expectations related to the *Next Generation Science Standards* (NGSS Lead States 2013) and *Vision and Change* (AAAS 2011). AI-based tools are essential for evaluating these assessment products, yet significant gaps exist in the literature on the impact of administration conditions on both static measures of understanding and longitudinal measures of learning derived from constructed response formats. Prior work on multiple-choice and true–false assessments have documented measurement biases associated with administration conditions (Couch and Knight 2015; DeMars 2000; Ding et al. 2008; Duckworth et al. 2011; Smith, Thomas, and Dunham.

2012; Wolf, Smith, and DiPaolo 1996; Wolf and Smith 1995). It seems reasonable to anticipate that some of these biases will apply to constructed response assessments, or that unique factors caused by the more cognitively demanding effort (e.g., cognitive load) required of science practice-based tasks may impact score inferences. Even though educators have called for the widespread adoption of practice-based science assessments (and three-dimensional learning in general), remarkably little evidence-based guidance is available to help inform assessment administration decisions for constructed-response instruments (Sbeglia and Nehm 2022). Given that the ACORNS has been used for formative and summative assessment purposes, it was used to empirically investigate this topic.

Sbeglia and Nehm (2022) used the ACORNS and EvoGrader to examine potential biases introduced by different student incentive conditions and assessment timings that undergraduate instructors routinely employ. Participation incentive was the first factor examined, which refers to whether completing the assessment was a required or "regular credit" part of the course grade or whether completing the assessment was not required but offered as "extra credit" or points in addition to the standard grade. The second factor investigated was the end-of-course time point or when the post-test was administered (for example, during the final exam or later). A quasi-experimental design was used to examine these effects.

Using ACORNS explanations and three EvoGrader scores, Sbeglia and Nehm (2022) reported that the variations in these two administration conditions did not meaningfully impact score inferences at single time points (how much students understood at a particular stage of the class) or over time (how much students learned). There were significant differences in some cases, but the effect sizes of these differences were small. The findings were also compared across race/ethnicity and gender groups and no significant differences were noted. These results were welcomed because oftentimes faculty cannot control the administration context of CR assessments but nevertheless need to compare performance patterns derived from low- and high stakes assessments.

Similar work using three-dimensional assessments deserves greater focus in K–12 contexts given that remarkably little is known about how assessment administration contexts impact inferences about student reasoning and learning. Models of learning performances increasingly rely on knowledge integration perspectives, which themselves require sufficient text to detect such integration. But understanding how administration conditions impact the amount of information generated (e.g., verbosity) is a prerequisite to evaluating text. Researchers and teachers may wish to compare student models from an assignment to models generated on a quiz, and knowing whether such comparisons are meaningful is crucial. Similar comparisons may be sought between lower stakes quizzes and higher stakes tests. The investigation of background effects for race/ethnicity and gender, while not significant in the studies noted above, remain potentially relevant topics for K–12 contexts. Administration conditions may impact motivation or appeal to students in different ways (e.g., those with poor grades vs. those with higher grades). Science educators rely upon "change over time" measures to examine which instructional approaches facilitate conceptual growth, but it remains unclear whether studies of the impact of test administration conditions from static datasets translate to longitudinal contexts. Overall, work with the ACORNS and EvoGrader has established evidence-based guidelines for administration conditions that remain uninvestigated for many other areas of science education.

English Learners, Spelling, Scoring, and Score Inferences

Language plays a foundational role in most science performance assessments, yet limited work has explored the extent to which ML-based scoring approaches may bias inferences about English learners (ELs) in jargon-rich domains like biology. Although there are many possible biases, one of the easiest to investigate is the role of misspelled words (MSW) on score patterns. As anyone who has graded student work knows, MSW are ubiquitous, and research has confirmed this common observation (Connors and Lunsford 1988). MSW, spacing errors, and other common text features can cause problems for AI-based assessments. For example, if a student response contains the text "fedunctity [*sic*]" or "geneticmutation [*sic*]" instead of "fecundity" and "genetic mutation," human graders will in most cases identify these cases as MSW and score them appropriately; computer algorithms may not (Ha and Nehm 2016).

Spell check and text suggestion programs are far from perfect—as anyone using them can attest—and they may be particularly problematic for term-laden fields like biology. Common biology terms continue to be inappropriately highlighted as errors in many word processing programs (e.g., Microsoft Word). Technology is improving and reducing MSW, but questions also arise about whether such tools should be provided along with digitally based performance assessments. Such technology systems could be used to suggest terms or concepts in addition to fixing spelling errors. However, providing such a tool doesn't mean that students will actually use it, as Ha and Nehm (2016) reported. More work in disciplinary domains is needed, particularly given that prior studies have shown that MSW may differ among student groups. English learners in particular have been shown to produce almost twice as many MSW in biology contexts (Ha and Nehm 2016).

In a study of the ACORNS and EvoGrader, Ha and Nehm (2016) empirically examined the impact of MSW using a corpus of biological explanations. They found that spelling errors were rare overall (~2%), although 29% of the MSW were important in the rubrics used to accurately score biological explanations and for the associated ML-based scoring algorithms. The positive result from the Ha and Nehm study was that MSW in most cases did *not* impact scores because a wide range of text features were typically used to model the presence of a concept in a student response. The overall scoring error rates associated with EvoGrader scoring of MSW were therefore quite small (< 3%; Ha and Nehm 2016). However, it remains an open question whether these findings will generalize to other domains (e.g., physics), assessment formats (e.g., student models, arguments), and data capture systems (e.g., voice recognition). Science education research would benefit from reporting MSW percentages among student groups along with whether language scaffolds (e.g., spell check, text suggestions) were used.

Gender and Writing

AI-based assessments must consider the role of gender given that more than fifty years of educational research has documented patterns of gender performance disparities. Studies in science education in particular have shown that females tend to outperform males on written assessments (reviewed in Federer, Nehm, and Pearl 2016). This work highlights the importance of considering how background variables interact with assessment formats to influence constructed response score inferences.

Investigations of the roles that gender might play in the ACORNS assessment were studied by Federer, Nehm, and Pearl (2016). Quantitative analyses were conducted using the normative and non-normative ideas contained within twelve different ACORNS explanation tasks ($n > 1000$). Clinical interviews were also conducted to corroborate interpretations. Differential test function and differential item function were used to quantify performance patterns on the ACORNS instrument (DTF) and on individual items (DIF). Gender-based DTF/DIF patterns were then used to explore potential assessment biases.

In general, Federer et al. found that the twelve ACORNS items (arranged into different assessments) did not function differently across genders. However, gender DTF was found to relate to the degree of taxon familiarity (e.g., prosimian vs. penguin) in the tasks, suggesting that item contexts were a salient factor for explanation performance. Specifically, when the item sequence consisted of familiar and unfamiliar ACORNS items, males tended to incorporate fewer normative ideas when explaining evolutionary change in unfamiliar taxa, whereas females tended to incorporate fewer non-normative ideas when explaining evolutionary change in familiar taxa. When the instrument consisted of exclusively familiar items, however, the pattern reversed; females used fewer normative ideas than males. These findings suggest that in biological situations, taxon familiarity may interact with gender to produce performance differences in unexpected ways. Fortunately, these complications were the exception across the twelve items. Similar studies are needed for many other science domains, practices, and task types given extensive evidence of gender differences. Like the other examples discussed earlier, AI-based efforts require engagement with science education research because automation efforts are never divorced from educational contexts and processes (Figure 3.2).

Situating AI-Based Assessment within Broader Educational Contexts and Processes

As the prior review illustrates, many studies of the ACORNS and EvoGrader have been completed (see Appendix). Most of the studies discussed in this chapter evaluated AI tools through the wider lens of educational processes and practices (Figure 3.2). That is, these studies did not simply seek to replicate and automate human scoring without consideration of the broader milieu in which these tools were operating. The work collectively illustrates that AI automation aims cannot be easily disentangled from a slew of factors potentially impacting inferences about student outcomes more broadly. Indeed, understanding the meaning of language use patterns by teachers and students, uncovering student reasoning processes to inform assessment task space design, ensuring that implementation conditions do not meaningfully impact student effort and downstream inferences about their magnitudes of knowledge integration, and scrutinizing whether disadvantaged groups such as English learners are impacted by mundane issues like spelling errors collectively illustrate that AI approaches are interwoven with existing institutional practices and disciplinary frameworks. As is the case for many complex systems, the role of a single tool or approach (like AI) cannot be cleanly disentangled from other epistemic aims, conceptual frameworks, and disciplinary practices. Because of this, AI research should be envisioned and modeled from a systems perspective in order to fully understand and appreciate its growing impact—for better or worse—on many aspects of science education research and practice.

Although research efforts focused on replicating human actions may have been the starting point for science educators' engagement with AI (Kubsch, Krist, and Rosenberg 2022), in some cases they were certainly not the planned end point. The National Science Foundation proposals that requested funding for the work described in this chapter did focus on the need for replication of human efforts; yet they also emphasized how such replication could generate large-scale datasets capable of revealing novel patterns of human thinking and learning. This is, in fact, what happened. For example, the ability to replicate scoring and analysis of student explanations on a massive scale using EvoGrader generated foundational insights into how students think about evolution. This work, in turn, altered ideas about how undergraduate instructional environments should be engineered (Nehm, Sbeglia, and Finch 2022). Literally thousands of students per year are currently taught in new ways because of the rich insights into thinking produced by AI tools. Further examples include the use of these large corpora to predict student performance and thereby effectively engineer student groups during collaborative learning (e.g., Bertolini, Finch, and Nehm 2022, 2023). Despite painstaking planning in research, nearly every pursuit produces surprising and unintentional insights and outcomes. The same may be said of the development and use of AI in biology assessment.

Maintaining AI Systems in an Ever-Changing Educational Environment

Like many non-commercial educational technologies, EvoGrader now exists as a "living fossil" doomed to extinction in an evolving digital ecosystem. Because EvoGrader is a kluge of multiple software systems, data corpora, algorithms, servers, and GUIs, system malfunction is inevitable because of myriad factors. It is remarkable that EvoGrader is functional after ten years (and eight years since it was last updated). Other tools have not fared as well, in part because funding agencies (e.g., NSF) too rarely support the maintenance, transformation, or preservation of educational technology systems. All AI systems will eventually become obsolete, but the same cannot be said of their constituent parts. For example, funds are needed to salvage, curate, and store the unique data corpora and training sets generated in science education research (e.g., written explanations, trace data, student interfaces). Online platforms (e.g., GITHUB) can be used to preserve open-source code for various components of an AI system. But there is no systematic framework or approach for deciding which components are worth preserving (e.g., corpora, algorithms, user dashboards, combinations thereof), risking the loss of potentially useful infrastructure. The research community and funding agencies would benefit from the development of preservation frameworks and decision-making tools when confronting questions about whether to maintain or salvage features of non-commercial educational AI systems (like EvoGrader).

Conclusion

In this chapter I used the past decade of research on the ACORNS instrument and AI-based EvoGrader automated scoring system to illustrate the complex consequences of trying to replicate simple human actions (in this case, scoring explanations). As many of the examples in this review show, it is challenging to cleanly isolate these replication efforts from the educational systems in which they are used. Replication failures (and successes) raised questions about the broader research contexts in which the work was occurring (implementation conditions, instructor discourse practices, disciplinary language, assessment fatigue, English learner attributes; see Figure 3.2) and led to new questions and actions. These findings suggest that future studies of the impact of AI on science education assessment would benefit from the adoption of a systems perspective that embraces the possibility that small and seemingly trivial insights could impact science education in large, unintentional, and emergent ways. Simply put, all scientific innovations, however small, can end up having large impacts. In the case of EvoGrader, the simple goal of replicating human scoring of evolutionary explanations ended up transforming the ways in which the disciplinary core idea of evolution was envisioned and taught. The impact has been significant, as the learning gains of thousands of students demonstrates (e.g., Nehm et al. 2022).

Acknowledgments

Sincere thanks to Professor Xiaoming Zhai and the organizers of the AI education conference at the University of Georgia for the opportunity to contribute; former students Drs. Liz Beggrow, Roberto Bertollini, Megan Federer, Minsu Ha, and Kayhan Moharreri for productive collaborations on this work; and colleagues Bill Boone, Stephen Finch, John Opfer, Dennis Pearl, and Mark-Urban Lurain for essential insights, perspectives, and guidance on the research discussed in this chapter. Support by National Science Foundation DUE 1322872 DRL 0909999 and a HHMI Science Education Inclusive Excellence Award was essential to this work. Any opinions, findings, conclusions, or recommendations expressed in this publication are those of the author and do not necessarily reflect the views of the National Science Foundation or HHMI.

References

American Association for the Advancement of Science (AAAS). 2011. *Vision and Change in Undergraduate Biology Education.* Washington, DC: AAAS.

Abrams, E., Southerland, S., and Cummins, C. 2001. "The How's and Why's of Biological Change: How Learners Neglect Physical Mechanisms in Their Search for Meaning." *International Journal of Science Education* 23, no. 12: 1271–81.

Beggrow, E. P., Ha, M., Nehm, R. H., Pearl, D., and Boone, W. J. 2014. "Assessing Scientific Practices Using Machine-Learning Methods: How Closely Do They Match Clinical Interview Performance?" *Journal of Science Education and Technology* 23, no. 1: 160–82.

Bertolini, R., Finch, S. J., and Nehm, R. H. 2021. "Enhancing Data Pipelines for Forecasting Student Performance: Integrating Feature Selection with Cross-validation." *International Journal of Educational Technology in Higher Education* 18: 44. https://doi.org/10.1186/s41239-021-00279-6

Bertolini, R., Finch, S. J., and Nehm, R. H. 2022. "Quantifying Variability in Predictions of Student Performance: Examining the Impact of Bootstrap Resampling in Data Pipelines." *Computers and Education: Artificial Intelligence* 3: 100067.

Bertolini, R., Finch, S. J., and Nehm, R. H. 2023. "An Application of Bayesian Inference to Examine Student Retention and Attrition in the STEM Classroom." *Frontiers in Education* 8: 1073829. https://doi.org/10.3389/feduc.2023.1073829

Bishop, B. A., and Anderson, C. W. 1990. "Student Conceptions of Natural Selection and its Role in Evolution." *Journal of Research is Science Teaching* 27: 415–27. https://doi.org/10.1002/tea.3660270503

Burstein, J. 2003. "The e-Rater Scoring Engine: Automated Essay Scoring with Natural Language Processing." In *Automated Essay Scoring: a Cross-disciplinary Perspective*, edited by M. D. Shermis and J. Burstein, 113–22. Mahwah, NJ: Lawrence Erlbaum Associates.

Connors, R. J., and Lunsford, A. A. 1988. "Frequency of Formal Errors in Current College Writing, or Ma and Pa Kettle Do Research." *College Composition and Communication* 39, no. 4: 395–409.

Clerk, D., and Rutherford, M. 2000. "Language as a Confounding Variable in the Diagnosis of Misconceptions." *International Journal of Science Education* 22, no. 7: 703–17.

Clough, E. E., and Wood-Robinson, C. 1985. "How Secondary Students Interpret Instances of Biological Adaptation." *Journal of Biological Education* 19: 125–30.

Couch, B., and Knight, J. 2015. "A Comparison of Two Low-Stakes Methods for Administering a Program-Level Biology Concept Assessment." *Journal of Microbiology and Biology Education* 16: 178–85.

Dagher, Z., and Crossman, G. 1992. "Verbal Explanations Given by Science Teachers: Their Nature and Implications." *Journal of Research in Science Teaching* 29, no. 4: 361–74.

DeMars, C. E. 2000. "Test Stakes and Item Format Interactions." *Applied Measurement in Education* 13: 55–77.

Ding, L., Reay, N. W., Lee, A., and Bao, L. 2008. "Effects of Testing Conditions on Conceptual Survey Results." *Physical Review Spec Top Physics Education Research* 4: 010112.

Driver, R., Squires, A., Rushworth, P., and Wood-Robinson, V. 1994. *Making Sense of Secondary Science: Research into Children's Ideas.* New York: Routledge.

Duckworth, A. L., Quinn, P. D., Lynam, D. R., Loeber, R., and Stouthamer-Loeber, M. 2011. "Role of Test Motivation in Intelligence Testing." *Proceedings of the National Academy of Sciences USA* 108: 7716–20.

Federer, M. R., Nehm, R. H., Opfer, J. E., and Pearl, D. 2014. "Using a Constructed-Response Instrument to Explore the Effects of Item Position and Item Features on the Assessment of Students' Written Scientific Explanations." *Research in Science Education* 45, no. 4: 527–53.

Federer, M. R., Nehm, R. H., and Pearl, D. 2016. "Examining Gender Differences in Written Assessment Tasks in Biology: A Case Study of Evolutionary Explanations." *CBE—Life Sciences Education.* https://doi.org/10.1187/cbe.14-01-0018

Gotwals, A. W., and Songer, N. B. 2010. "Reasoning up and down a Food Chain: Using an Assessment Framework to Investigate Students' Middle Knowledge." *Science Education* 94: 259–81.

Ha, M., and Nehm, R. H. 2016. "The Impact of Misspelled Words on Automated Computer Scoring: A Case Study of Scientific Explanations." *Journal of Science Education and Technology* 25, no. 3: 358–74. https://doi.org/10.1007/s10956-015-9598-9

Ha, M., and Nehm, R. H. 2023. "Measuring Scientific Understanding Across International Samples: The Promise of Machine Translation and NLP-Based Machine Learning Technologies." In *Advancing Natural Language Processing in Educational Assessment*, edited by V. Yaneva and M. von Davier, 200–16. NCME Educational Measurement and Assessment Book Series. Taylor & Francis.

Ha, M., Nehm, R., Urban-Lurain, M., and Merrill, J. 2011. "Applying Computerized Scoring Models of Written Biological Explanations across Courses and Colleges: Prospects and Limitations." CBE-Life Sciences Education 10, no. 4: 379–93.

Harris, C. J., Krajcik, J. S., Pellegrino, J. W., and DeBarger, A. H. 2019. "Designing Knowledge-In-Use Assessments to Promote Deeper Learning." *Educational Measurement: Issues and Practice* 38, no. 2: 53–67. https://doi.org/10.1111/emip.12253

Haudek, K. C., Kaplan, J. J., Knight, J., Long, T., Merrill, J., Munn, A., Nehm, R. H., Smith, M., and Urban-Lurain, M. 2011. "Harnessing Technology to Improve Formative Assessment of Student Conceptions in STEM: Forging a National Network." *CBE Life Sciences Education* 10, no. 2: 149–55.

Jungwirth, E. 1975. "The Problem of Teleology in Biology as a Problem of Biology-Teacher Education." *Journal of Biological Education* 9: 243–46.

Kubsch, M., Krist, C., and Rosenberg, J. 2022. "Distributing Epistemic Functions and Tasks—A Framework for Augmenting Human Analytic Power with Machine Learning in Science Education Research" [preprint]. *Open Science Framework*. https://doi.org/10.31219/osf.io/sg9jk

Landauer, T. K., Laham, D., and Foltz, P. W. 2003. "Automated Scoring and Annotation of Essays with the Intelligent Essay Assessor." In *Automated Essay Scoring: a Cross-disciplinary Perspective*, edited by M. D. Shermis and J. Burstein, 87–112. Mahwah, NJ: Lawrence Erlbaum Associates.

Lee, H., Pallant, A., Pryputniewicz, S., Lord, T., Mulholland, M., and Liu, O. L. 2019. "Automated Text Scoring and Real-Time Adjustable Feedback: Supporting Revision of Scientific Arguments Involving Uncertainty." *Science Education* 103, no. 3: 590–622. https://doi.org/10.1002/sce.21504

Libarkin, J. 2008. *Concept Inventories in Higher Education Science. A manuscript prepared for the National Research Council Promising Practices in Undergraduate STEM Education Workshop.* Washington, DC, Oct. 13–14, 2008

Linn, M. C., Gerard, L., Ryoo, K., McElhaney, K., Liu, O. L., and Rafferty, A. N. 2014. "Computer-Guided Inquiry to Improve Science Learning." *Science* 344, no. 6180: 155–56.

Liu, O. L., Rios, J. A., Heilman, M., Gerard, L., and Linn, M. C. 2016. "Validation of Automated Scoring of Science Assessments." *Journal of Research in Science Teaching* 53, no. 2: 215–33. https://doi.org/10.1002/tea.21299

Mayfield, E., and Rosé, C. 2010. LightSIDE: Researcher's User Manual. Unpublished.

McNeill, K. L., Lizotte, D. J., Krajcik, J., and Marx, R. W. 2006. "Supporting Students' Construction of Scientific Explanations by Fading Scaffolds in Instructional Materials." *Journal of the Learning Sciences* 15, no. 2: 153–91.

Mead, L. S., and Scott, E. C. 2010a. "Problem Concepts in Evolution Part I: Purpose and Design." *Evolution Education and Outreach* 3: 78–81.

Mead, L. S., and Scott, E. C. 2010b. "Problem Concepts in Evolution Part II: Cause and Chance." *Evolution Education and Outreach* 3: 261–64.

Mislevy, R. J., Steinberg, L. S., and Almond, R. G. 2002. "Design and Analysis in Task-Based Language Assessment." *Language Test* 19, no. 4: 477–96.

Moharreri, K., Ha, M., and Nehm, R. H. 2014. "EvoGrader: An Online Formative Assessment Tool for Automatically Evaluating Written Evolutionary Explanations." *Evolution: Education and Outreach* 7, no. 1: 15. https://doi.org/10.1186/s12052-014-0015-2

Moscarella, R. A., Haudek, K. C., Knight, J. K., Mazur, A., Pelletreau, K. N., Prevost, L. B., Smith, M., Urban-Lurain, M., and Merrill, J. 2016. "Automated Analysis Provides Insights into Students' Challenges Understanding the Processes Underlying the Flow of Genetic Information." Presented at the NARST 2016 Annual Conference, Baltimore, MD.

Moscarella, R. A., Urban-Lurain, M., Merritt, B., Long, T., Richmond, G., Merrill, J., Parker, J., Patterson, R., and Wilson, C. 2008, March 30–April 2. "Understanding Undergraduate Students' Conceptions in Science: Using Lexical Analysis Software to Analyze Students' Constructed Responses in Biology." Paper presented at the NARST 2008 Annual International Conference, Baltimore, MD.
National Research Council (NRC). 2001. *Knowing What Students Know*. Washington, DC: National Academies Press.
Nehm, R. H. 2018. "Evolution." In *Teaching Biology In Schools*, edited by K. Kampourakis and M. Reiss. London: Routledge.
Nehm, R. H., Beggrow, E., Opfer, J., and Ha, M. 2012. "Reasoning about Natural Selection: Diagnosing Contextual Competency Using the ACORNS Instrument." *The American Biology Teacher* 74: 92–98.
Nehm, R. H., and Ha, M. 2011. "Item Feature Effects in Evolution Assessment." *Journal of Research in Science Teaching* 48, no. 3: 237–56.
Nehm, R. H., Ha, M., and Mayfield, E. 2012. "Transforming Biology Assessment with Machine Learning: Automated Scoring of Written Evolutionary Explanations." *Journal of Science Education and Technology* 21, no. 1: 183–96.
Nehm, R. H., and Haertig, H. 2012. "Human vs. Computer Diagnosis of Students' Natural Selection Knowledge: Testing the Efficacy of Text Analytic Software." *Journal of Science Education and Technology* 21, no. 1: 56–73.
Nehm, R. H., Rector, M., and Ha, M. 2010. "'Force Talk' in Evolutionary Explanation: Metaphors and Misconceptions." *Evolution Education and Outreach* 3: 605–13.
Nehm, R. H., and Reilly, L. 2007. "Biology Majors' Knowledge and Misconceptions of Natural Selection." *BioScience* 57: 263–72.
Nehm, R. H., and Ridgway, J. 2011. "What Do Experts and Novices 'See' in Evolutionary Problems?" *Evolution: Education and Outreach* 4: 666–79. https://doi.org/10.1007/s12052-011-0369-7
Nehm, R. H., Sbeglia, G. C., and Finch, S. 2022. "Is Active Learning Enough? The Contributions of Misconception-Focused Instruction and Active Learning Dosage on Student Learning of Evolution." *BioScience* 72, no. 11: 1105–17.
Nehm, R. H., and Schonfeld, I. 2008. "Measuring Knowledge of Natural Selection: A Comparison of the CINS, an Open-Response Instrument, and Oral Interview." *Journal of Research in Science Teaching* 45: 1131–60.
NGSS Lead States. 2013. *Next Generation Science Standards: For States, by States*. Washington, DC: National Academies Press.
Opfer, J. E., Nehm, R. H., and Ha, M. 2012. "Cognitive Foundations for Science Assessment Design: Knowing What Students Know about Evolution." *Journal of Research in Science Teaching* 49: 744–77. https://doi.org/10.1002/tea.21028/
Page, E. B. 2003. "Project Essay Grade: PEG." In *Automated Essay Scoring: a Cross-disciplinary Perspective*, edited by M. D. Shermis and J. Burstein, 43–54. Mahwah, NJ: Lawrence Erlbaum Associates.
Peker, D., and Wallace, C. S. 2011. "Characterizing High School Students' Written Explanations in Biology Laboratories." *Research in Science Education* 41: 169–91.
Rector, M., Nehm, R. H., and Pearl, D. 2012. "Learning the Language of Evolution: Lexical Ambiguity and Word Meaning in Student Explanations." *Research in Science Education* 43: 1107–33. https://doi.org/10.1007/s11165-012-9296-z
Sbeglia, G. S., and Nehm, R. H. 2022. "Measuring Evolution Learning: Impacts of Student Participation Incentives and Test Timing." *Evolution: Education and Outreach* 15: 9. https://doi.org/10.1186/s12052-022-00166-2
Smith, M., Thomas, K., and Dunham, M. 2012. "In-class Incentives That Encourage Students to Take Concept Assessments Seriously." *Journal of College Science Teaching* 42, no. 2: 57–61.
Songer, N. B., Kelcey, B., and Gotwals, A. W. 2009. "How and When Does Complex Reasoning Occur? Empirically Driven Development of a Learning Progression Focused on Complex Reasoning about Biodiversity." *Journal of Research in Science Teaching* 46, no. 6: 610–31.
SPSS Inc. 2006. *SPSS Text Analysis for SurveysTM 2.0 User's Guide*. Chicago: SPSS Inc.

Sukkarieh, J., and Bolge, E. 2008. "Leveraging c-Rater's Automated Scoring Capability for Providing Instructional Feedback for Short Constructed Responses." In *Proceedings of the 9th International Conference on Intelligent Tutoring Systems, ITS 2008*, Montreal, Canada, June 23–27, 2008, Lecture Notes in Computer Science, vol. 5091, edited B. P. Woolf, E. Aimeur, R. Nkambou, and S. Lajoie, 779–83. New York: Springer-Verlag.
Weston, M., Haudek, K. C., Prevost, L., Urban-Lurain, M., and Merrill, J. 2015. "Examining the Impact of Question Surface Features on Students' Answers to Constructed-Response Questions on Photosynthesis." *CBE—Life Sciences Education* 14: 2.
Wilson, C. D., Anderson, C. W., Heidemann, M., Merrill, J. E., Merritt, B. W., Richmond, G., Sibley, D. F., and Parker, J. M. 2006. "Assessing Students' Ability to Trace Matter in Dynamic Systems in Cell Biology." *CBE—Life Sciences Education* 5: 323–31.
Wolf, L. F., and Smith, J. K. 1995. "The Consequence of Consequence: Motivation, Anxiety, and Test Performance." *Applied Measurement in Education* 8: 227–42.
Wolf, L. F., Smith, J. K., and DiPaolo, T. 1996. "The Effects of Test-Specific Motivation and Anxiety on Test Performance." Paper presented at the annual meeting of the National Council on Measurement in Education, New York.
Zhai, X., Haudek, K., Shi, L., Nehm, R., and Urban-Lurain, M. 2020a. "From Substitution to Redefinition: A Framework of Machine Learning-Based Science Assessment." *Journal of Research in Science Teaching* 57, no. 9: 1430–59. https://doi.org/10.1002/tea.21658
Zhai, X., Shi, L., & Nehm, R. 2021. "A Meta-analysis of Machine Learning-Based Science Assessments: Factors Impacting Machine–Human Score Agreements." *Journal of Science Education and Technology* 30, no. 3: 361–79. https://doi.org/10.1007/s10956-020-09875-z
Zhai, X., Yin, Y., Pellegrino, J. W., Haudek, K. C., and Shi, L. 2020b. "Applying Machine Learning in Science Assessment: A Systematic Review." *Studies in Science Education* 56, no. 1: 111–51. https://doi.org/10.1080/03057267.2020.1735757

Appendix

Table A.1 Brief summary of selected journal articles relating to the ACORNS and/or EvoGrader

ACORNS and/or EvoGrader study	Journal article	Key findings
Grounding of ACORNS in cognitive principles (assessment triangle) and validity evidence	Opfer et al. (2012)	The ACORNS aligns with three core cognitive principles central to scientific reasoning following NRC (2001) recommendations.
Instrument items, properties, and validity evidence	Nehm et al. (2012)	ACORNS task design and validity evidence
Correspondence of ML-based scores to 100 clinical oral interviews	Beggrow et al. (2014)	100 students' interview scores were compared to EvoGrader scores and found to have greater correspondence than to a widely used multiple-choice concept inventory (CI).

Continued

Table A.1 *Continued*

ACORNS and/or EvoGrader study	Journal article	Key findings
English learner (EL) biases	Ha and Nehm (2016)	EvoGrader scoring of EL ACORNS responses with and without MisSpelled Words did not show bias even though ELs used twice as many MSW.
Gender biases	Federer, Nehm, and Pearl (2016)	DIF analyses found minimal gender bias in ACORNS written tasks although familiarity of task features did interact with gender in some items.
Item order effects	Federer et al. (2014)	Two ACORNS items differing in surface features can minimize documented order effects and verbosity patterns.
Lexical ambiguity and explanation interpretation	Rector, Nehm, and Pearl (2012)	The vast majority of scoring interpretations were corroborated after follow-up questioning, although misinterpretation errors remained.
Corpus comparisons across institutions	Ha et al. (2011)	Corpus variations occur because of teacher talk, student backgrounds, and discourse variation.
EvoGrader system design and performance compared to trained raters	Moharreri et al. (2014)	The EvoGrader automated scoring tool provides accurate and consistent scoring of answers, eliminating human-rater inconsistencies across individuals and through time.
Impacts of testing incentives and timing	Sbeglia and Nehm (2022)	Inferences about evolution learning were in most cases robust to variations in participation incentives and end-of-course timing. Findings were not impacted by race/ethnicity or gender.
ACORNS and EvoGrader score utility in predictive learning analytics	Bertollini et al. (2021)	Scores enhance predictive accuracy above university-level variables; scores are useful in predictive analytics.

4
Assessing and Guiding Student Science Learning with Pedagogically Informed Natural Language Processing

Marcia C. Linn and Libby Gerard

Introduction

Advances in natural language processing (NLP) tools enable the scoring of students' written explanations with pedagogically inspired rubrics (e.g., Kubsch, Krist, and Rosenberg 2022; Linn et al. 2014; Zhai et al. 2020). Few studies have tested these tools in classroom research and explored their usefulness for teachers and students (Zhai et al. 2020). We investigate ways to design instruction aligned with the knowledge integration (KI) pedagogy. The KI pedagogy focuses on four key processes central to constructing knowledge: students analyze their own ideas, discover new insights into the phenomena, distinguish among these ideas, and reflect on their investigations (Linn and Eylon 2011). We report on ways to promote KI using NLP-based scores for student explanations. Instruction elicits students' explanations for complex scientific phenomena and accurately scores these explanations using NLP. We test ways to design guidance based on the scores to motivate each student to analyze the connections among their ideas, distinguish gaps or inaccuracies, and integrate new evidence-based ideas with the ideas they expressed initially to strengthen their argument. We report on how we iteratively refined the web-based instruction, informed by the KI pedagogy, to motivate students to explain nuanced scientific situations and to deepen their understanding of target science concepts. We describe how our recent investigations using NLP scores in units designed using an authorable and customizable environment (ACE) can amplify teacher guidance and improve student ability to revise their scientific explanations.

Transforming Education with Technology

Starting in the 1970s, with the advent of the personal computer, there were widespread claims that technology would transform education (e.g., Darrach 1970). However, most initial uses of technology in education mimicked the functionality of existing educational materials, often implementing a transmission model of education, rather than exploiting the affordances of emerging technologies (Linn

Marcia C. Linn and Libby Gerard, *Assessing and Guiding Student Science Learning with Pedagogically Informed Natural Language Processing*. In: *Uses of Artificial Intelligence in STEM Education*. Edited by: Xiaoming Zhai and Joseph Krajcik, Oxford University Press. © Oxford University Press (2024). DOI: 10.1093/oso/9780198882077.003.0004

2003). The first computers available in schools supported programming in BASIC or LOGO and offered designers limited resources for creating applications (Friedler, Nachmias, and Linn 1990; Mandinach et al. 1986). In 1980 Seymour Papert laid out a perspective on constructivism and described the potential of teaching students to program in LOGO in Mindstorms (Papert 1980). Many warned about the widening digital divide in educational opportunities as computers became available to students whose families could afford them (e.g., Linn 2003; Lockheed and Frakt 1984).

With increased access to more powerful computers for education, designers extended efforts to align innovations with psychological frameworks. Anderson (1996) and his collaborators created cognitive tutors primarily for mathematics and computer science guided by ACT∗ theory. ACT∗ is a general theory of cognition focusing on memory processes. Subsequently Koedinger and collaborators incorporated the knowledge, learning, and instruction (KLI) pedagogy summarizing the psychological literature on instruction to refine the design of the tutors (Koedinger, Corbett, and Perfetti 2012; Van Lehn 2011). These tutors sought to achieve the same level of proficiency as typical instruction, in topics such as algebra, geometry, and LISP programming, while shortening the instructional time needed, drawing on an architecture organized in production-rule units (Anderson et al. 1995). The cognitive tutors detect student errors and provide immediate feedback consisting of short error messages while students solve problems; they are currently commercial products (Koedinger and Aleven 2016).

In science, many investigators built on constructivist pedagogy (e.g., Cognition and Technology Group 1991; Gerard et al. 2015a; Inhelder 1987) with the goal of supporting inquiry learning. Constructivism views learning as an active process in which students build knowledge by connecting new ideas to their initial ideas, reconcile contradictions, and reformulate ideas into a coherent perspective. These groups designed technology-enhanced environments designed to develop metacognitive learners who could direct their own learning (e.g., Azevedo 2005).

In this chapter we illustrate how the constructivist pedagogy, knowledge integration, informed our use of NLP to design instruction, assessments, and guidance. The KI pedagogy emerged from longitudinal and experimental studies of science and computer science instruction, designed to use innovative technologies to improve student outcomes and teacher success (Clancy and Linn 1999; Linn 1995; Linn and Clancy 1992; Linn and Hsi 2000; Mokros and Tinker 1987). It draws on research showing that students typically have multiple, incomplete, and fragmented ideas about scientific phenomena (diSessa 2000; Smith, diSessa, and Roschelle 1994).

Authorable and Customizable Environments for Inquiry Science

Authorable and customizable environments that supported students to construct understanding emerged in the 1990s and enabled designers to scaffold science learning (Quintana et al. 2004). ACEs are web-based learning environments that provide interactive instruction to students and include easy-to-use authoring tools that allow users to create and modify content. Rather than emulating typical textbooks, ACE design is informed by constructivist frameworks that emphasize inquiry learning (e.g., Linn and Eylon 2011). ACEs are designed by partnerships of teachers, computer scientists, discipline experts, and learning scientists (e.g., Könings, Seidel, and van Merriënboer 2014; Kyza and Agesilaou 2022; Shear et al. 2004; Slotta and Linn 2009). ACE partnerships include Concord Consortium (https://concord.org, Molros and Tinker 1987), Go-Lab (https://www.golabz.eu/; de Jong et al. 2021), PhET (https://phet.colorado.edu/; Wieman, Adams, and Perkins 2008), STOCHASMOS (Kyza, Michael, and Constantinou 2007), and the Web-based Interactive Science Environment (WISE, https://wise.berkeley.edu; Linn and Eylon 2011). Many ACEs are free and open source, encouraging teachers and researchers to create experimental activities.

ACEs log student work and include scaffolds to guide students, making them potentially ideal for leveraging NLP tools. Further, ACEs take advantage of interactive visualizations of scientific phenomena, including models or simulations and real-time data collection, as well as creating ways to support hands-on investigations (Smetana and Bell 2012). Studies of designs using inquiry to illustrate complex ideas in specific disciplines showed the value of using visualizations in varied science disciplines (Linn, Donnelly-Hermosillo, and Gerard 2023; McElhaney et al. 2015). Many advocated combining virtual and hands-on activities to capitalize on the strengths of each format (de Jong, Linn, and Zacharia 2013). Many ACEs also feature collaborative tools (Ke and Hoadley 2009; Matuk and Linn 2018) and aspects of learning management systems (LMS). ACEs can incorporate varied assessments, including engineering designs (McBride et al. 2016), concept maps (Ryoo and Linn 2012), and written explanations for complex questions (Tansomboon et al. 2017).

Researchers have been investigating ways to personalize guidance in ACEs, taking advantage of logs of student interactions and responses to assessments (e.g., Gerard et al. 2015a; Puntambekar and Hübscher 2005). Materials delivered by ACEs are often easy to use in experimental designs. They can support personalized instruction for each student as well as random assignment of students to conditions. Partnerships have built and tested multiple activities that are used by thousands of teachers today. The major finding from a wide range of studies using ACEs is that inquiry learning is facilitated by personalized guidance and that teachers benefit from tools to amplify their efforts to guide their students (reviewed in Furtak et al. 2012).

Most ACEs are supported by systems such as WISE that are themselves open source and available on GitHub (https://github.com/WISE-Community). Materials delivered by ACEs are often easy to use in experimental designs. They can support personalized instruction for each student as well as random assignment of students to conditions. Embedded assessments enable teachers to monitor student progress during learning and to use student work when planning customizations (e.g., Wiley et al. 2023).

As NLP tools have been incorporated into ACEs, the field has also begun to address issues of privacy, algorithmic bias, ethics, and equity (e.g., Vakil and Higgs 2019). For example, it is essential to develop NLP scoring algorithms with students who have the same cultural background as the students who will use the materials

(Liu et al. 2016). The advances in ACEs support the possibility of transforming education with seamless school-to-home solutions.

The WISE ACE and KI Pedagogy

Reviews show the advantage of using pedagogies such as KI to guide the design of ACEs, assessments, guidance, and tools for teachers (Donnelly, Linn, and Ludvigsen 2014; Krajcik and Mun 2014; Linn, Donnelly-Hermosillo, and Gerard 2023; Reiser et al. 2021). The WISE ACE offers tools that support designers to implement the four KI processes. For example, WISE elicits student ideas in multiple ways, often by posing dilemmas such as "How do animals get energy from the sun?" or by asking students to make predictions about a complex situation such as predicting the temperature within a car sitting in the sun on a snow-covered road. To support students to discover ideas, students often use models, virtual experiments, or hands-on investigations, such as using a temperature probe to measure the temperature of objects in the room and comparing the measured temperature to how the object feels. To help students distinguish ideas, students might conduct virtual experiments by varying the amount of CO_2 in the atmosphere, conduct hands-on experiments with temperature probes to compare the insulating properties of cups made of different materials, or use the idea basket to compare their explanations to those of their peers (e.g., Matuk and Linn 2018). To encourage students to reflect on their ideas, students might write essays, make concept maps, or sort materials by some property. The WISE ACE logs all the students' activities and can provide real-time personalized guidance based on student responses.

KI Assessments

KI assessments are embedded in WISE instruction, including as pretests and posttests. They may feature designing experiments using a virtual system (McBride et al. 2016), making a concept map (Ryoo and Linn 2012), or writing explanations of complex situations where they link ideas with evidence (e.g., Tansomboon et al. 2017; Vitale, Appleaum, and Linn 2019). KI rubrics analyze student explanations for promising ideas, links between ideas justified by evidence, and multiple links between ideas (see example question and rubric in Table 4.1). Rather than rewarding only the right answer, KI rubrics reward students for sorting out their disparate ideas and using evidence to justify the ideas they incorporate into their explanations. Alignment of the design of the explanation prompt and the criteria in the rubric used to evaluate responses has shown to be a significant moderator to the benefits of NLP (Zhai et al. 2020).

WISE units have always featured explanation items, due to their value in developing understanding. Generating explanations is more effective than answering multiple-choice questions during learning (Richland, Linn, and Bjork 2007). Research shows that generation items are also better predictors of long-term retention

Table 4.1 KI Rubric and Automated Guidance for "Cancer" Explanation in a Mitosis Unit

Item Prompt: Humans have a control mechanism that regulates cell division. When that control mechanism is broken, cells are allowed to divide out of control. As we have seen, this can lead to cancer. Now that we have successfully completed our investigation, let's use what we know to design a new drug to treat cancer. Which phase of mitosis would you have your drug target to stop cancer growth? [MC—NOT scored]. *Explain the effect your drug would have on the different parts of the cell in that phase, and how this would help keep cancer growth under control.*

Key Ideas

Describes a cell organelle or phase to be affected by the medicine

- Ways students might say this: "My drug would make the spindle fibers not be able to grow."

Explains how the medicine will disrupt the function of/action related to the organelle

- Function of OR action for an organelle (e.g., chromosomes carry genetic info (function) OR chromosomes are pulled apart (related action)
- Ways students might say this: "keeping cancer cells' chromosomes from being pulled into equal portions of each new cell."

Mentions need for medicine to stop cell division/cancer growth

- Controlling cancer cell growth; stopping cell division; stopping cells from splitting; stopping X from making new cells
- Ways students might say this: "If you stop the chromosomes from dividing, then there wouldn't be any new cells."

Side effects of drug treatment and their cause.

- Brings together ideas "stops cell division" + "but will stop good and bad cells (or cancerous and non-cancerous or normal and bad)."
- Ways students might say this: "cancer drugs target any cell that is dividing, which means cuts heal slower, and hair may not grow back."

Score	Criteria	Student examples	KI guidance
1	**Off task** Writes text, does not answer question	IDK	Think about mitosis. What phase of mitosis will your drug target and WHY? Look at the phases in Step 2.5. Then, write a new description of your drug below.
2	**Irrelevant/incorrect** Incorrect/ nonnormative ideas Vague response	It would help the cancer cells stop growing because the cells would die.	Think about mitosis. What phase of mitosis will your drug target, and WHY? Look at the phases in Step 2.5. Then, write a new description of your drug below.

Continued

Table 4.1 *Continued*

3	**Partial link** Any ONE of the three key ideas is correctly explained. OK to mention additional, incorrect ideas.	My drug would either freeze or burn the cell at the point where the cell multiplies.	Good start—you are moving in the right direction. Now, add details about what function of the cell is important to stop and WHY. Watch the phases in Step 2.6 to gather ideas. Then, write a new description of your drug below.
4	**Full Link** Any TWO of the three key ideas are correctly explained and linked.	I would stop this phase because if you stop the spindle fibers, the chromosomes just float around and the cell can't reproduce.	Great work! Now, think about side effects—how will your drug affect the body? Check out Step 3.2 to gather some ideas. Then, write a more detailed description of your drug below.
5	**Complex Links** All THREE key ideas are correctly explained and linked.	This phase is the beginning of cell division. If you stop the cell from duplicating the chromosomes, the cell will not divide.	Nice thinking! Now, think about the rate of cell division in different parts of the body. Where in the body will your drug have the greatest impact? Check out Step 1.4 to gather some ideas. Then, write a more detailed description of your drug below.

than recall items, even for straightforward material (Bertsch et al. 2007). Further, a comparison of multiple choice and KI items covering the same material showed that KI items were better than multiple choice at discriminating between high and low scorers; they also captured nuances of progress more effectively (Lee, Liu, and Linn 2011).

Nevertheless, most science assessments use multiple-choice questions that require recall of details and some form of problem-solving (e.g., PISA assessment), often informed by an information processing pedagogy (e.g., Anderson 1996). This has led to extensive classroom practice on multiple-choice factual questions that are often embedded in textbooks. It sends a message to teachers that recall is a major component of science learning. Yet, little of this information is retained as indicated by many assessments of adults. Further, investigations of public understanding of science consistently reveal a weak and fragmented understanding of crucial science concepts (e.g., Weber and Stern 2011).

Although teachers would like to score each student's work, this is difficult in middle school when teachers often have six science classes per day, each with thirty students. Teachers report spending up to ten minutes per student writing personalized guidance when teaching an online inquiry unit—or five hours per class (Gerard et al. 2015b). Developing NLP to score student written responses initially involves a big commitment to collect and annotate the data and build the model. Once developed, the NLP models can be used for many students as long as the new students resemble the students whose responses were used for training (Liu et al. 2016).

NLP Scoring

Our partnership uses c-raterML, a NLP tool developed by our collaborators at the Educational Testing Service (ETS) to score explanations for KI. The system scores each student essay based on a five-point KI rubric that rewards students for using evidence to make links among scientifically normative ideas. For example, as shown in Table 4.1, c-raterML assesses the degree to which students link ideas about cell organelle functions, the phases of mitosis, and health impacts from interrupting cell division, to explain how a drug they have designed will slow the spread of cancer.

C-raterML works by building a model of the linguistic features evident in human-scored student explanations at each KI score level. To build the human-scored data set, we collect over one thousand student responses to the prompt from students in schools with demographics similar to those who will use the NLP-based guidance. This is done by working in sustained partnership with teachers who are using web-based curriculum units in which the explanation prompts are embedded. Two humans use the KI rubric to reach inter-rater reliability. They then score at least one thousand student written explanations to the prompt. C-raterML forms a statistical model based on its analysis of the given human scored data set. The c-raterML scoring has demonstrated satisfactory agreement with human scoring for constructed response items in inquiry science, meaning they demonstrated a sufficient quadratic-weighted kappa (K_{QW}; Liu et al. 2014; Liu et al. 2016; Riordan et al. 2020). Models that result in a coefficient above 0.75 in testing on a novel data set of student responses are deemed sufficient for use in instruction. This level of agreement is equivalent to rater agreement between typical trained humans.

The resulting NLP models can be deployed in the WISE units. They enabled our partnership to score KI explanation items that ask students to generate their ideas instead of using multiple-choice items that often rely heavily on recall of information and knowledge of advanced vocabulary to differentiate among responses. Establishing the automated KI scores is the first step. A big open question is how best to use the automated scores to guide students' engagement in KI processes as they revise scientific explanations. In the next section, "Design Research on Personalized Guidance for Revision," we illustrate how our partnership has iteratively refined NLP-based personalized guidance for student written explanations about science phenomena such as thermodynamics, photosynthesis, and plate tectonics.

Design Research on Personalized Guidance for Revision

We report on the results from the design research conducted by our partnership to find effective ways to use NLP scores to promote productive revision of scientific explanations. We conducted multiple iterations of the guidance across many WISE units on varied topics in middle school classrooms (see Table 4.2). We use mixed methods including quantitative methods to analyze both comparison studies and pretest/post-test studies and qualitative methods in observational and interview studies. This work is both informed by and intended to strengthen the KI pedagogy.

Specifically, these studies have enabled us to refine our KI assessments, rubrics, instructional frameworks, professional learning tools, and the WISE ACE.

Design Research Methods

The series of design studies (see Table 4.2) follows design research methods (Sandoval and Bell 2004). This work is conducted by a partnership using qualitative and quantitative methods.

Partnership

Our work is conducted using a partnership model. Each partner conducts design research with the goal of using NLP tools to personalize guidance for students and to help teachers guide their students to revise their explanations (e.g., Linn et al. 2023; Wiley et al. 2023). Partners included teachers and their students in over twelve participating middle schools, computer scientists and software designers who created the WISE ACE, learning science researchers, psychometricians, professional developers, and experts in NLP at ETS. Each partner contributed to the outcomes and respected the expertise of the others.

Our partnership had many participants who met regularly at school site meetings, professional development workshops, and on-campus seminars. In partnership meetings, we analyzed the results of each study and discussed ways to improve the personalized guidance, drawing on the KI pedagogy and related research. We focused on guiding students to revise their explanations based on research showing that generating explanations is a powerful way to build student understanding of their experimental investigations (e.g., Krist 2020), and that productive revision can deepen student understanding (Berland et al. 2016; Hayes and Flower 1986). This also aligns with the reported value of explanation in laboratory science as supported by ethnographic studies of scientific communities (e.g., Latour 1987). We recognized that revision is difficult to motivate and often superficial (Crawford, Lloyd, and Knoth 2008; Freedman et al. 2016). Ultimately, the partnership incorporated NLP scoring into a set of twelve units on topics including mitosis, photosynthesis, chemical reactions, thermodynamics, plate tectonics, and global climate change, to guide student engagement in KI processes as they revise scientific explanations.

Assessments of Revision

We used embedded explanations requiring knowledge integration scored by KI rubrics that reward students for linking ideas with evidence, reinforcing self-directed learning and knowledge building (e.g., Scardamalia and Bereiter 2006). We scored the initial response using NLP and assigned guidance. We then scored the resulting revision in several ways. First, we noted whether the student revised their response.

Table 4.2 Classroom Studies of NLP-Based KI Guidance for Student Written Explanations.

Citation	Study design and topic	Impact on item revision	Impact on revision pretest/post-test	Prior knowledge interaction
A: Tansomboon et al. (2015). AERA	KI vs. simulated teacher guidance, 1 round—global climate change (GCC)	KI is more effective.	No difference in KI gains between conditions. Students who integrated an idea (normative or non-normative) when revising during instruction made greater pretest–post-test gains than students who made superficial revisions	No interaction detected.
B: Gerard et al., (2015b). Ed Psych Study 1	Teacher-assigned KI vs. teacher-assigned generic, 1 round—mitosis, chemical reactions	KI is more effective than generic guidance across contexts. No effect on the accuracy of NLP.	No difference between conditions.	N/a
C: Gerard et al. (2015b). Ed Psych Study 2	KI Automated vs. KI teacher assigned, 1 round—cell respiration	No difference in KI gains. No effect on the accuracy of NLP. Took teachers 1–2 minutes to assign guidance to each student.	No difference between conditions.	N/a
D: Gerard and Linn. (2016c). ESERA	KI vs. simulated teacher guidance, 1 round—photosynthesis	No difference in KI gains between conditions. With KI guidance, more likely to integrate ideas when revising.	Greater pretest to post-test gains for low prior knowledge with KI guidance. Low prior knowledge students who integrated an idea (normative or non-normative) when revising made greater pretest–post-test gains than students who did not integrate when revising.	KI is more effective for low prior knowledge on pretest–post-test gains.

Continued

Table 4.2 *Continued*

Citation	Study design and topic	Impact on item revision	Impact on revision pretest/post-test	Prior knowledge interaction
E: Vitale, McBride, and Linn (2016).	KI vs. specific guidance, 2 rounds—GCC	Slight advantage for specific guidance during instruction, but not significant.	Advantage of KI guidance for pretest to post-test gains on essay item, and delayed post-test; correlation between time spent revisiting visualization and pretest–post-test gains	No interaction detected.
F: Gerard and Linn. (2016b). AERA	KI Guidance—revision rubric categories, 1 round—photosynthesis	Significant gains with KI guidance. High prior knowledge students are more likely to integrate ideas when revising—low prior likely to add disconnected ideas.	Students who integrated ideas when revising made greater pretest–post-test gains in school A. No difference in school B (73% in school B did not revise at all).	High prior knowledge students were more likely to integrate ideas when revising.
G: Tansomboon et al. (2017). IJAIED—Study 1	Student name + transparent KI vs. typical KI guidance, 2 rounds—thermodynamics	Transparent was more effective. [No difference between students who engaged in 1 vs. 2 rounds of revision, suggesting indication of progress did not impact outcomes.	No difference between conditions. Transparent is more effective for low prior knowledge, significant higher scores at post-test	No interaction was detected on embedded. Transparent was more effective for low prior on pretest–post-test
H: Tansomboon et al. (2017). IJAIED—Study 2	KI planning vs. KI revisiting guidance, 2 rounds—thermodynamics	No significant gains in revision. Students in revisiting more likely to revisit evidence; students in planning are more likely to make substantial revisions.	No difference between conditions.	No interaction detected
I: Gerard and Linn (2016a). JSTE	KI + teacher alerts vs. KI, 2 rounds—Photosynthesis	KI + Teacher alerts are more effective for low prior knowledge in school A [no difference in school B].	Greater gains for KI + teacher alerts for low prior knowledge in school A, than 2 rounds KI guidance [no difference in School B].	KI + teacher alerts more effective for low prior knowledge.

J: Gerard et al. (2019). IJCSCL	Teacher adaptive KI + teacher alerts vs. 2 rounds of KI guidance for low prior [conditions did not hold in classroom study—only 2 pairs received a teacher alert]—plate tectonics	Significant revision gains. Teacher gave different guidance to low vs. high, built on adaptive KI guidance. Teacher checked in with each group, high rate of revision	Significant pretest–post-test gains	N/a
K: Gerard et al. (2016c). ICLS	Annotator + KI vs. KI, 2 rounds—photosynthesis	Annotator + KI made greater revision gains	Annotator + KI made greater revision gains on post-test revision essay. Students who made integrated revisions when revising made greater pretest to post-test gains	High prior knowledge students more likely to integrate ideas when revising on KI revision item.
L: Gerard and Linn (2022). Computers & Education	KI 2 rounds vs. Annotator + KI—photosynthesis, plate tectonics	Annotator + KI more effective on revision gains; Annotator + KI resulted in more integrated revisions.	Annotator + KI greater revisions on post-test KI revision item	Annotator + KI is more effective for low prior on embedded and KI revision item
M: Linn and Gerard (2024). This chapter.	Annotator + KI, 2 rounds	Annotate own explanation vs. annotate fictitious student explanation	Both conditions revise, gain on KI revision item; annotate fictitious student greater revisions.	Fictitious student conditions created more unique labels.

Note: A–D, initial studies in italics; E–H, refinement of guidance; I, J, teacher alerts; K–M, modeling revision with the Annotator.

Then we scored the revised response using the KI rubric. In addition, in later studies we analyzed the nature of the revisions students made, including noting whether students tacked on ideas, paraphrased their initial ideas, made grammatical improvements, or revised their reasoning.

In some studies we use a pretest/post-test KI revision item to assess student progress in revision across the unit. The KI revision items asked students to write an explanation, gave the student guidance, and asked the student to revise their response. Since most five- to twelve-day units had one NLP item, we did not expect the limited opportunity for revision during the unit to have a big impact on the KI revision items between pretest and post-test.

Sequence of Guidance Designs

We designed NLP-based guidance to encourage students to build on their insights and observations in conjunction with new information, following the KI pedagogy. Students responding to KI guidance can use resources in the unit to find the evidence they need to determine which ideas are most useful and valid. As shown in Table 4.1, the guidance included a prompt with a link to visit relevant evidence within the unit. Rather than relying on authorities, the guidance encourages students to gain appreciation for relying on evidence to refine their knowledge. Ultimately KI guidance promotes cumulative understanding. Students who become better at KI become able to evaluate new arguments and see whether they align with the evidence available to them.

In this paper we synthesize our design research studies to illustrate how taking advantage of emerging NLP technology and analyzing the impact of each revision is strengthening our understanding of personalized guidance. Each iteration of the instruction led to insights into the factors contributing to productive revision and to ways that personalized guidance can amplify the impact of teachers during inquiry instruction.

Initial Studies: Comparing Guidance Designs for Knowledge Integration

In our initial studies, we developed adaptive knowledge integration guidance for students' written arguments using c-raterML (Linn et al. 2014; see Table 4.1). The goal of the guidance was to prompt productive revision of student ideas. We designed the adaptive KI guidance to align with the KI pedagogy. It built on the current student answer and was intended to enable the student to move to the next level of the KI rubric. It included four parts: (1) acknowledgment of the students' current ideas, (2) a question about the key missing or non-normative idea, (3) a suggestion to revisit related evidence in a dynamic visualization, and (4) a prompt asking the student to use the evidence they've gathered to generate an improved response (see Figure 4.1).

In our four initial studies, we found that the adaptive KI guidance was more effective in improving students' knowledge integration abilities, relative to other types of guidance typically used in middle school classrooms (Table 4.2, rows A–D). We compared KI guidance to simulated teacher guidance (e.g., Redo. What does

Description	Initial Response	Revised Response [**bold** italics is the revised idea]
No Revision		
Integrated New Connects new idea(s) to initial ideas. The new idea builds on what was stated in the initial response, by elaborating, extending, or contrasting.	Heat goes up into the atmosphere then cools down then goes back down into earths core and repeats the process.	Heat goes up into the atmosphere ***where the density is higher*** then cools down then goes back down into earths core ***where it is less dense*** and repeats the process.
	The heat makes it less dense, as it flows away from the heat source it becomes less dense. It comes back down to the heat source after being in circulation.	The heat makes it less dense, as it flows away from the heat source it becomes less dense. It comes back down to the heat source after being in circulation. ***The reason it goes from top to bottom is because it looses its density as it goes to the bottom. When it looses its density it gets lighter and floats to the top. When it gets heavier it sinks to the bottom. The process is ongoing.***
Integrated Redundant Adds an idea that repeats initial idea or paraphrases; does not add new science idea.	The bottom of the lamp is hot like the core. The blob is like the convection currents. At the bottom the blob is heated becoming less dense floating to the top. At the top it becomes less dense and goes back down.	The bottom of the lamp is hot like the core. The blob is like the convection currents. At the bottom the blob is heated becoming less dense floating to the top. At the top it becomes less dense and goes back down. ***Like the convection current in goes up and goes back down.***
	I think a lava lamp works by the heat in the lamp causing the blobs to go up word and then it gets more dense and then when the blobs go down it gets less dense.	I think a lava lamp works by the heat in the lamp causing the blobs to go up word and then the ***density increases*** and then when the blobs go down it gets less dense.
Disconnected New Writes an entirely new response. Or, adds a new idea with no edit to the initial response, that does not connect to the initial idea(s).	The heat from the lava lamp makes the blobs less and causes them to move easily. It's similar bc in earth's mantle it slowly comes out like a lava lamp	***When it's too hot at the bottom, it goes up, gets too cold, and goes back down, like a cycle.***
	We think that the blob of colored fluid goes up because of heat and density. Heat makes density less dense and density is what brings up the fluid.	***We think that, the blob of colored fluid goes up because of heat and density. Heat makes density less dense and density is what brings up the fluid. There is also more density on the top with low heat and less density on the bottom and high heat on the bottom.***

Figure 4.1 Type of revision response to KI guidance (Gerard and Linn 2022).

increased carbon dioxide do to global temperature?), generic guidance (e.g., Go back and review the visualization to improve your answer), and specific guidance (e.g., Light energy transformed into __ kind of energy). Studies of the logged revisions and student navigation indicated that in comparison to the other forms of guidance, the KI guidance was more likely to support students to revisit specific evidence in the unit when revising and to integrate a new idea into their initial response.

Refinement of Guidance Designs

The initial studies established that our KI guidance was as effective as guidance from experienced teachers and more effective than generic guidance or specific guidance. In our refinement studies we sought to improve on the initial designs (Table 4.2, rows E–H).

Specific Guidance

We built on these studies to explore the role of KI versus specific guidance. In specific guidance, students were explicitly directed to the right answer, whereas the KI guidance directed the student to use evidence to distinguish the correct idea (Vitale, McBride, and Linn 2016). Consistent with other research on learning, we found that specific guidance was as effective as KI guidance during instruction. The KI guidance was more effective than specific guidance for promoting durable understanding as measured by a delayed post-test (Richland, Linn, and Bjork 2007).

Transparency about Guidance

Some students did not recognize that the guidance was personalized and dismissed it (Tansomboon et al. 2017). Students' uncertainty about whether the guidance was personalized is consistent with beliefs about computers when the study was conducted. To help students appreciate that the guidance was personalized to their ideas, we made the NLP process more transparent. We added student names to the guidance. We explained how the computer read their response, compared their response to the responses from thousands of other students of the same grade level, and then selected guidance to address their distinct science ideas. We found that the transparent guidance condition led to greater rates of revision particularly for students who initially displayed low prior knowledge (Tansomboon et al. 2017). This extended prior research suggests that when students are challenged, they are more likely to engage and persist if they perceive the guidance they receive as connected to their reasoning (Shute 2008). We altered the KI guidance interface to always provide transparent guidance.

Reflection on Refinements

Analyzing the overall effectiveness of guidance in these refinement studies, we noted that although the KI guidance helped many students to integrate new evidence into their explanations and strengthen the links among their ideas, there were limitations. Many students still struggled to use the guidance to revise their arguments. Only about half of the students were able to make productive revisions (Gerard, Linn, and Madhok 2016). In one study, over 50% of students who received automated guidance either did not revise their answers or only made surface-level changes without adding a new idea (Tansomboon et al. 2015). In addition, integrating new ideas when revising was most challenging for students who initially displayed low prior knowledge (Gerard and Linn 2016b). Further, in student interviews conducted during guidance studies, some students reported that they preferred their teacher's guidance over the automated KI guidance because their teacher gave feedback that was specific to their response.

This resonates with prior research findings that when confronted with contrasting evidence, students tend to ignore the evidence and restate their own perspective, consistent with confirmation bias (Clark and Chase 1972; Höttecke and Allchin 2020). Further, when given feedback from teachers or peers, using technology tools such as collaborative Google Docs, students most often make minimal or superfluous changes to their science explanations (Freedman et al. 2016; Sun et al. 2017; Zheng et al. 2015; Zhu, Liu, and Lee 2020). Learners tend to make changes to spelling and grammar rather than to revise for meaning (Bridwell 1980; Fitzgerald 1987; Strobl et al. 2019; Zhu, Liu, and Lee 2020).

Combining Teacher and Personalized Guidance

To address the revision challenges faced by low prior knowledge students we tried alerting teachers to guide students who were stuck (Table 4.2, rows I, J). The partners decided on the conditions under which they wanted alerts. Typically, teachers wanted alerts when students made two attempts at revision without any progress or continued to express vague ideas (level 2 on KI rubric). We designed alerts which showed up on the students' computer screen. Teachers could see the alert as they circled the classroom. Students could keep working while the alert showed on their screen, and the teacher could come to talk with the student about the item (Gerard and Linn 2016a). We found that the alerts led to gains in one school and not in the other school, suggesting that the process needed fine-tuning.

Analyzing Students' Revision Strategies

Our initial analysis of the nature of student revisions suggested the need for deeper understanding of how students were envisioning revision. We noticed qualitatively different patterns in the kinds of revisions students were making after they received KI guidance. Specifically, some students made integrated revisions while others tacked on ideas or did not revise at all. Those who integrated ideas when revising during instruction, were also making greater pretest to post-test gains (Gerard and Linn 2016b; Tansomboon, Gerard, and Linn 2015). We then systematically investigated how students were revising their science writing based on the KI guidance, and what kinds of revisions to science arguments led to building coherent, long-term science understanding (see Table 4.2, rows K, L).

To characterize how students revised their science writing based on the KI guidance, we analyzed students' writing in their initial and revised explanations and identified what changes, if any, students made to their writing. We developed an emergent coding scheme: those who integrated new ideas when revising their writing, those who integrated redundant ideas or paraphrased what they had said initially, those who added new but discrete ideas, and those who made no changes at all (see Figure 4.1; Gerard and Linn 2022). In coding students' writing revision strategies, we evaluated only the changes in the students' science writing, not the scientific accuracy of the change. Consistent with the KI pedagogy, we hypothesized that making connections among ideas would be a more productive learning strategy than accumulating more discrete ideas or not refining the ideas at all.

We found that the type of revision strategy impacted learning outcomes (Tansomboon et al. 2017; Gerard and Linn 2016b). For example, in one study students wrote a short essay in a photosynthesis unit and received one round of KI guidance. We coded students' initial and final (after receiving the guidance) short essays in the unit, and student responses on pretest–post-test short essay items using KI rubrics. We found that students who integrated ideas when revising their essay during instruction made greater pretest to post-test gains on the short essay items than those students who added ideas when revising during instruction or those who chose to make no changes at all. The difference in pretest–post-test gains between those who integrated ideas and those who did not was significant on the energy story pretest–post-test item (Integrated $n = 181$, M = 0.81, SD = 1.16; Did Not Integrate $n = 159$, M = 0.43, SD = 0.96; $t(338) = 3.19$, $p = 0.002$). These results suggested that the students who made no attempt to integrate ideas lacked a model of the revision process.

Designing Guidance to Model Explanation Revision: The Annotator

The challenge that integrating ideas posed for students suggested that some students were not sure what revision looks like. We designed the Annotator (see Figure 4.2) to provide students with an interactive model of integrated argument revision. The Annotator asks students to help a fictitious student make decisions about revision by placing premade labels on the students' response. The student also has the opportunity to author their own labels to guide the revision. Studies of the Annotator showed that combining one round of adaptive KI guidance with one round of the Annotator was more effective in promoting integrated revision, especially for students who initially expressed "unintegrated ideas" and hence had received low KI scores (1 to 2), than providing multiple rounds of adaptive KI guidance (see Table 4.2, rows K–M).

These findings documented the importance of providing a model of the revision process, especially for low prior knowledge students. When learners had the opportunity to select and place labels on the response of another student, they were more likely to revise their own response. Indeed, students often remarked that they were using the same strategy they used to choose a label when revising their own explanation. For example, one student reflected on their use of the Annotator in the plate tectonics unit: "This way [the Annotator] gets your brain on what you need, like what she [fictional peer in Annotator] does not have . . . Placing the labels was useful [to revising in the next step] bc it had many things i didn't think about." Another student reflected on their use of the Annotator in the photosynthesis unit: "I realized I needed to expand more what I wrote." Another student expressed: "It helped set up a structure for my writing. I went back to our writing and thought about those questions." Across the student interviews, across unit contexts, students reported how their experience using the Annotator helped them to notice gaps in their explanation, or to recognize a new idea they held to strengthen the links in their explanation (Gerard and Linn 2022).

A Recent Experiment: Peer versus Self Annotator

We report here on a recent study that clarified the mechanisms underlying the benefit of the Annotator. This study tested a refinement of the Annotator with a focus on fostering self-directed learning in revision. We designed a version where students annotated their own responses. We hypothesized that placing the pre-authored labels onto the explanation was the central mechanism promoting integrated revision. It (a) modeled for the student the process of distinguishing which key ideas in an

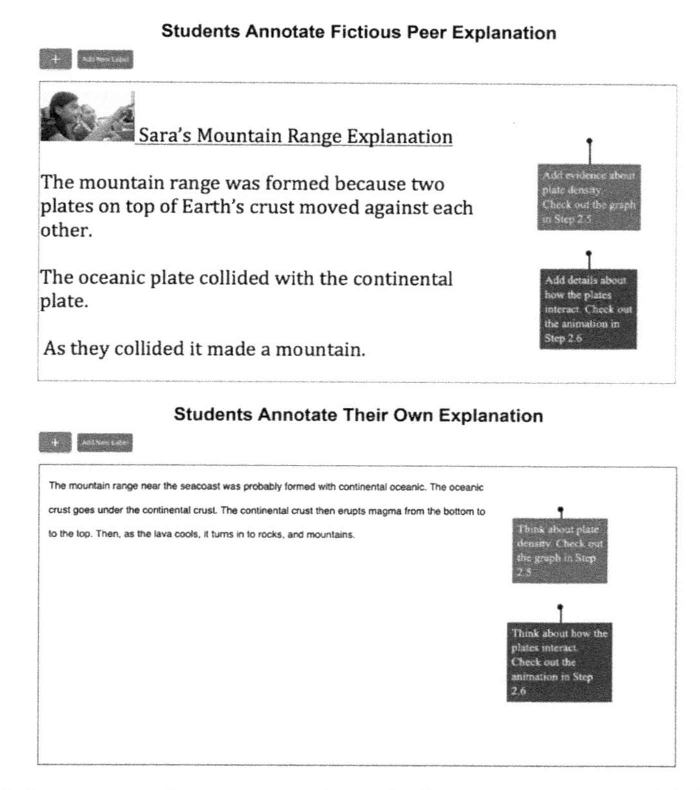

Figure 4.2 Annotator tool to support revision. Students move prewritten labels to suggest ways an explanation can be improved. Students can also create their own labels.

explanation are missing by evaluating the response using the ideas in the labels and (b) modeled how to link new ideas with existing ideas by determining where to place the labels onto the written response. It appeared that students could then apply this approach to their own explanation when using the KI guidance. To test this idea, we designed an iteration of the Annotator to support the student to annotate their own explanation—rather than a fictional peer's—with pre-authored labels. We conjectured that this may increase students' sense of autonomy and hence self-directed learning in the revision process while also promoting integrated revision.

We studied the impact of the self- and peer-annotations in an unpublished study. Students were asked to place prewritten labels on sections of an explanation to suggest areas for change or improvement. They were also given the opportunity to make self-constructed labels. The prewritten labels were designed to elicit evidence central to explaining the phenomenon most often missing in student explanations.

For example, an explanation prompt embedded in a unit on plate tectonics asks students to explain how Mt. Hood was formed (given a photograph of Mt. Hood on the Pacific coast). A prewritten label in the Annotator for a fictional peer's response to the Mt. Hood explanation says "Think about plate density. Check out the graph in Step 2.5." Many students leave out this idea and it is central to understanding how the plates interact. Selecting the relevant labels and placing them in the written response encourages students to distinguish ideas in the response and in the labels, and to link new knowledge suggested by the labels with prior knowledge in the initial explanation. This stands in contrast to the novice revision practices of tacking on disconnected information to the end of a response. We compared this new version of the Annotator intended to strengthen student agency in revision to the initial Annotator design involving peer annotation. We hypothesized that instantiating the student's own essay in the Annotator would encourage students to view their essay as a scientific product and attend more carefully to each expressed idea, the connections among them, and possible gaps. Flower and Hayes (1981) showed that when students succeeded in analyzing the structure and argument of their essay, they were capable of making valuable revisions to their reasoning (see Figure 4.2).

Methods

Five teachers from three schools and their 678 seventh-grade students participated in this study. All students used the WISE plate tectonics unit. For two activities embedded in the plate tectonics unit, all students wrote an explanation. Each prompt called for students to connect ideas about plate boundary interactions and convection to explain a land formation. After writing their argument, when students moved to the next step, they were randomly assigned using the WISE branching technology to one of two conditions: (a) annotate their own argument or (b) annotate a peer's argument.

In the *peer-annotator* version, an explanation by a fictitious peer named Sara was preloaded in the Annotator (Table 4.3). A peer explanation was selected at a KI level 3, to reflect a common student idea and missing evidence, making it generative for critique. The labels were predesigned to be personalized to Sara's explanation, meaning that they elicited evidence which would link to an existing idea in the explanation. The predesigned labels stated: (a) "Add evidence about plate density. Check out the graph in Step 2.5," and (b) "Add details about how the plates interact. Check out the animation in Step 2.6." The instructions also encouraged students to write their own label if they have another comment.

In the *self-annotator* version, the student's written explanation was automatically imported into the Annotator (Table 4.4). The same predesigned labels as in the "peer-annotator" version appeared to the right of their explanation. While the labels were personalized to Sara's explanation, the labels raised key concepts that were general enough that we hypothesized one or both of the labels could likely be applied to improve most student written explanations.

In both conditions, students used labels to address gaps or inaccuracies in the explanation, revised their own work, and then had one opportunity to receive personalized KI guidance for their explanation and revise again. Students completed a pretest and a post-test before and after the unit with an item that called for students to write and revise.

Data Analysis

We analyzed students' initial and revised explanations on the embedded lava lamp short essay revision activity and students' written explanations on the pretest–post-test. All students' written explanations were automatically scored for KI by c-raterML based on a 5-point rubric for the specific item. Each of the rubrics rewards students for making scientifically accurate links among ideas. For each item, a researcher who

Table 4.3 Peer-Annotate Condition, Example of Student Writing, Annotation and Revision

Event	Student work
Initial explanation	**Initial**: The mountain range was probably formed by the Oceanic crust and Continental crust push against sediment that goes up. That sediment then turns into a mountain.
They place the labels where Sara should add the suggested ideas. They also add their own label encouraging the student to distinguish how this type of plate interaction is different from the interactions that occur at a transform boundary and divergent boundary, as explored in Step 2.1	 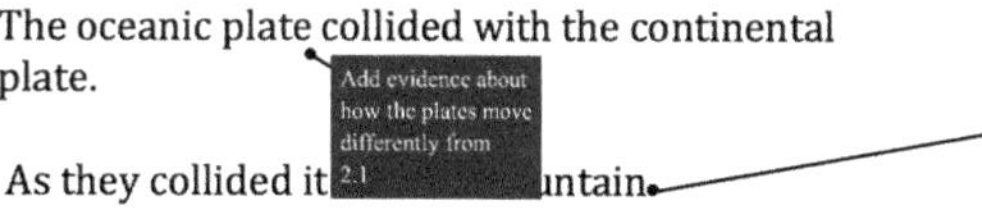
After annotating Sarah's explanation, they revised their explanation. They added a new idea to their explanation that they had previously recognized was missing in Sara's explanation, based on their placement of the labels.	Revised 1: The mountain range was probably formed by the Oceanic crust and Continental crust pushing against sediment that goes up. **They push because one is more dense than the other; one goes under the continental crust**. That sediment then turns into a mountain.
The student then received **adaptive KI guidance** for their explanation.	**Adaptive KI Guidance**: *Elliott, add details to your explanation. How does the density of the two plates affect their movement? Check out for a hint. Then, expand your explanation.*
They further revise their explanation, clarifying the plate interactions due to their differing densities.	**Final explanation**: The mountain range was probably formed by the Oceanic crust and Continental crust push against sediment that goes up. They push because one is more dense, t**he oceanic crust goes under the continental crust, pushing the continental crust up. The crust then forms a mountain.**

Table 4.4 Self-Annotate Condition, Example of Student Writing, Annotation and Revision

Event	Student work
Writes explanation mid-way through the plate tectonics unit	**Initial Explanation**: This mountain range near the seacoast was probably formed with continental oceanic. The oceanic crust goes under the continental crust. The continental crust then erupts magma from the bottom to the top. Then, as the lava cools, it turns into rocks and mountains.
The student's explanation is imported into the Annotator, with pre-authored labels on the side. In this case the labels hence are well aligned to gaps in the student's explanation. They place the labels in their explanation to indicate where to make a link to evidence.	This mountain range near the seacoast was probably formed with continental oceanic. The oceanic crust goes under the continental crust. The continental crust then erupts magma from the bottom to the top. Then, as the lava cools, it turns into rocks, and mountains. Think about plate density. Check out the graph in Step 2.5 Think about how the plates interact. Check out the animation in Step 2.6
After the student annotated their own explanation, they incorporated a new idea to strengthen the link between plate density and subduction.	**Revised explanation after using the annotator**. "This mountain range near the seacoast was probably formed with continental oceanic. **The crust push into each other.** The oceanic crust goes under the continental crust**. This is because the oceanic crust is denser than the continental crust, so the oceanic crust subducts under the continental crust.** The continental crust then erupts magma from the bottom to the top. Then, as the lava cools, it turns into rocks, and mountains."
The student then received automated KI Guidance level 5	*Sam, nice thinking! Look over your explanation to be sure it addresses the density of the plates and how they interact. Revise your explanation as much as you think is needed.*
The student continued to clarify the role of density in plate movement.	**Final explanation**. This mountain range near the seacoast was probably formed with continental oceanic. The crust push into each other, **causing** the oceanic crust goes under the continental crust. **The oceanic crust is denser than the continental crust. Denser things sink, so that's why the oceanic crust went under the continental crust.** The continental crust then erupts magma from the bottom to the top. Then, as the lava cools, it turns into rocks, and mountains.

was previously trained with the rubric sorted the explanations by the automated c-raterML KI score, read each response, checked the accuracy of the automated KI score, and then corrected errors (corrected approximately 20%).

We also coded the annotations students made on the lava lamp revision activity, for the students from one teacher in each of the three schools. We scored the annotations two ways. First, we scored the annotations for their accuracy in critiquing the provided explanation. A 0–3 rubric was developed by two researchers: 3 = student placed two labels correctly. This means each label identified a correct scientific gap in the explanation that could be filled correctly with the idea called for by the label; 2 = placed at least one label correctly or created one correct label; 1 = placed both labels incorrectly; = did not place labels. We also scored the labels that were generated by students, for the focus of their critique. Second, we coded the new labels that students created for the nature of their critique. We coded these as: (a) general (e.g., add more), (b) add a new idea (e.g., what about convection currents?), or (c) fill a gap to clarify the mechanism (e.g., why does heat cause molecules to become less dense?).

Findings

Use of the Annotator to Critique Arguments

Students using the Annotator were better able to identify and remedy gaps with scientifically accurate suggestions when annotating a fictional peer's explanation than when annotating their own. A two-sample *t*-test revealed that student annotations in the peer-annotator condition were scored significantly higher than those in the self-annotator condition (peer annotator, M = 2.03, SD = 1.03; self annotator, M = 1.33, SD = 1.15; $t(282) = 5.47$, $p < 0.0001$).

Students reported that the peer annotator enabled them to gather new ideas. As one student stated: "I like revising the classmates and ours was hard to revise because we're the ones who made them." Another student commented, "I reviewed Sara's and so then I just added a sentence [to mine] because it gave me more information and then I put that into my own words." As seen in Table 4.3, the student added a new idea to their explanation about plate density after prompting the fictional peer Sara to consider this same idea. Teachers echoed the student perspective, noting that students were more likely to critique a peer's explanation than their own as they presume their own response is correct, and particularly for students with initially vague ideas, they may also be uncertain of what criteria to use to evaluate their own explanation.

Creating New Annotator Labels to Critique Arguments

In both Annotator conditions, students were given two pre-authored labels to use in annotating the argument, and they were also instructed to create their own new label if they identified an additional gap in the argument. A chi-square analysis indicated that the number of students who created new labels differed by condition. Students in the peer-annotator condition were significantly more likely to create new labels during annotation (36% of students, $n = 185$) than students in the self-annotator condition (22%, $n = 144$) ($\chi^2(1) = 8.35$, $p = 0.005$).

For example, in Table 4.3, the student created a new label "add evidence about how the plates move differently from in 2.1," prompting the fictional peer to consider how oceanic and continental plates interact differently than two continental plates colliding. In both conditions, students primarily generated labels focused on filling a gap to clarify the mechanism in the explanation (peer annotator: 72% of student generated labels; self annotator: 68%). Taken together, the analyses suggest that annotating a fictional peer's explanation may lead to greater student engagement in evaluating the ideas in a scientific argument, and in generating new mechanistic ideas to strengthen the argument.

Embedded Revision KI Gains

A paired-samples *t*-test was used to compare students' initial KI score to their revised KI score (after engaging with the Annotator + KI guidance). The analysis indicated that students used the guidance to significantly improve their explanations in the revision activity in each guidance condition (AnnotatePeer Gain, M = 0.40, SD = 0.67, $t(216) = 8.76$, $p < 0.0001$; AnnotateOwn, M = 0.37, SD = 0.68, $t(218) = 7.95$, $p < 0.0001$]. Students made larger revision gains after using the Annotator in the first round of revision, and smaller gains in the second round of revision after receiving the KI guidance (AnnotatePeer (1st round) M = 0.27, SD = 0.65; (2nd) M = 0.13, SD = 0.61; AnnotateOwn (1st) M = 0.30, SD = 0.65; (2nd) M = 0.07, SD = 0.57). We ran a regression using the students' revision gain score (initial to final revised) as the dependent variable and condition as the independent variable. There was no main effect for the condition, suggesting that both critiquing a peer and one's own argument can strengthen student explanation writing and revising.

Pretest to Post-test Gains

Students in both conditions made significant pretest to post-test gains (gains: AnnotatePeer M = 0.56, SD = 0.88; AnnotateOwn M = 0.47, SD = 0.80) with no significant difference between conditions.

Discussion

Revising explanations is central to the iterative process of knowledge building in science, yet it is unfamiliar and challenging to most learners (Berland et al. 2016; Mercier and Sperber 2011). We created the peer annotator to model the process of revising. We designed labels personalized to the response and also enabled students to write their own labels. We created the self annotator to directly allow students to annotate their own response by using the labels or writing their own.

Our findings suggest that students benefit from a model of revision that helps them discern key science practice such as distinguishing criteria to critique a scientific argument. Students wrote more labels in the peer than in the self condition, suggesting that the personalized labels in the peer annotator modeled revision. The peer annotator was more effective than the self condition for promoting revision of students' initial response. Students reported that they were more likely to gather new ideas that they could then apply to their own explanation.

This also suggests that students in the self-annotator condition did not see the pre-authored labels as helping them to identify new ideas to incorporate into their responses. An important difference between the conditions was the design of personalized pre-authored labels for the fictional peer's explanation. The labels for the self-annotation condition were the same as in the peer-annotator condition and hence not personalized to the student's response.

This raises opportunities for personalizing the self-annotation condition. Would students benefit from labels personalized to the response they are annotating? How would NLP designed personalized labels for students' own responses or labels for the students' own explanations enhance the self-annotator condition? For example, personalizing the labels may support students to (a) see how the model of revision is aligned to their ideas and hence elicit greater engagement in the revision process, thus building on Tansomboon et al (2017), and (b) help the student distinguish between the ideas they expressed in their explanation and those suggested by the personalized labels to determine what evidence to pursue fill a gap or clarify a link. How would these efforts to use NLP designed labels lead to more coherent revisions?

These results also suggest the value of improving the model of revision in the Annotator. To promote agency, do students need a model of the metacognitive processes of considering alternatives for revision? How could we design an annotator or another tool that enables students to diagnose when they need to distinguish among their ideas rather than tack another idea on to the explanation? Could a Metacognitive Annotator engage students in distinguishing among possible revisions, including some that tack on ideas and others that integrate evidence?

Summary and Future Directions: Using NLP to Improve Personalized Guidance

Advances in NLP along with advances in ACEs offer designers new opportunities to improve instruction. In our work, we were guided by the KI pedagogy as well as the insights of expert teachers to test and refine personalized guidance for KI items. We initially focused on capturing the guidance of expert teachers to move students to the next level of the KI rubric. We found that, like expert teachers, the personalized automated guidance had impacts and limitations. The guidance significantly improved responses to the KI items, was more effective than specific guidance, and led to durable understanding as measured by a delayed post-test.

Limitations resulted from the automated nature of the guidance. Students prefer the guidance of their teachers, often saying that their teachers were more likely to provide the right answer. They suspected the automated guidance was not personalized. By being transparent about how automated guidance was designed, we were able to reduce distrust and increase the impact of automated guidance. In addition, the automated guidance often resulted in the same superficial revisions, or lack of revision, common when teachers give guidance.

We sought to combine the impacts of automated and teacher guidance by alerting teachers about students who were struggling. This process has promise. We have initiated a line of work involving teacher dashboards that responds to teacher interest in more nuanced information about their students than simply an alert. They would like information about the whole class as well as about the needs of individual students so they can target their guidance to the needs of each student (Wiley et al. 2023).

During this series of design studies, we did a detailed analysis of the types of revisions students made and identified additional opportunities to improve personalized guidance. Some students did not have a clear understanding of the nature of revision. We designed the Annotator to model revision. The Annotator was helpful, especially for students who started with low prior knowledge and therefore were likely to lack a model of revision. To explore ways to improve the Annotator, we compared the situation where students annotated the response of a peer to a condition where they annotated their own explanation. We found that students, as anticipated, had difficulty annotating their own responses, consistent with work on the limitations of metacognition. An important difference between the conditions was that students placed a personalized pre-authored label to annotate the peer explanation. We identified some directions for future work on a self annotator. For example, we hypothesize that an NLP model for identifying pre-authored labels for the students' own explanation would enhance the self-annotator condition. We will also explore ways to design a MetaCognitive Annotator.

Design Research: Reflection

Emergent technologies offer educators opportunities to improve instruction. Finding optimal uses of these technologies often takes many design iterations. In our work, the iterations are informed by deliberations of the design research partners; by analysis of the logged data that provides detailed insights into the interaction between student thinking, guidance, and revision; and by reflection on the way results align with the underlying pedagogy. This paper reports on ways that NLP tools have been refined to improve student learning. The results show that personalized guidance aligned with the KI pedagogy emphasizing rewarding students to integrate their ideas has advantages for long-term retention as well as for the development of self-directed learners. This aligns with other work on self-directed learning (e.g., Azevedo 2005; Scardamalia and Bereiter 2006).

This design research illustrates how partnership refinement of guidance can improve student learning. By combining the expertise of each partner, we were able to gain insight into ways to promote revision. We were inspired by the excellent guidance provided by expert teachers. We benefited from the insights of psychometricians to design KI items that require students to generate arguments and that measure how students respond to personalized guidance with KI revision items. We refined the adaptive guidance that both promotes revision and encourages self-directed exploration of scientific evidence by conducting whole partnership reflections at professional development workshops (e.g., Gerard et al. 2022b). We were able to realize often nascent ideas when the software designers brought prototypes of the Annotator, new designs for discussion tools, and refinements to the interactive models to partnership meetings. We worked closely with the NLP designers to clarify the strengths and limitations of early models and improve accuracy (e.g., Riordan et al. 2020).

This design research tested forms of personalized guidance informed by KI pedagogy and strengthened our understanding of KI pedagogy as a result. By analyzing the ways that students respond to requests to integrate their ideas, this research revealed opportunities for refining KI design recommendations. We found that students often had no experience evaluating and revising science explanations, emphasizing the need for engaging students in finding gaps in their arguments. This resonates with earlier work on metacognitive reasoning and KI (e.g., Linn, Davis, and Eylon 2004). We found that students often chose to tack on an idea rather than to distinguish it from their other ideas. This finding resonates with other studies of KI that revealed the need for more emphasis on distinguishing ideas (e.g., Gerard et al. 2020; Ryoo and Linn 2012; Vitale, Appelbaum, and Linn 2019).

NLP technology has the potential to amplify the role of the teacher by providing automated guidance to students, revealing to teachers how students use the automated guidance, and identifying the learners who would most benefit from teacher guidance. Building on the ways that successful teachers guide students, we show how NLP tools implemented in ACEs can strengthen science instruction. Initially, we diagnosed student performance using a KI rubric and designed guidance intended to enable the student to revise their explanation and achieve the next level of the rubric. This was helpful but many students floundered or did not revise at all. Based on observations of how teachers interact with individual students, we can envision the potential of hybrid models of personalized guidance that combine NLP scoring with opportunities for teachers to continue the conversation. Guidance embedded in the unit can encourage the student to strengthen the links between different pieces of evidence to explain a phenomenon. The guidance may also serve as a conversation starter between teacher and student or student and peer, thus combining automated and human guidance. Building on the findings from studies combining adaptive KI guidance with a teacher dashboard that alerts the teacher in real time to students whose explanation was scored by the NLP below a set threshold, we are also exploring hybrid models that optimize referrals to peers, teachers, or an alternative approach such as a computer–student dialogue. Our current work takes advantage of new NLP models designed to identify specific ideas rather than KI levels and could support these types of dialogues (Gerard et al. 2022a).

This design research program illustrates the process of iterative design and the ways it has benefitted student learning. However, many challenges remain. As we noted initially, NLP can provide scores for student work, but the challenge is figuring out what to do with the scores to guide revision and ultimately promote student integrated understanding.

Acknowledgments

Funding for this research was provided by the National Science Foundation awards NLP-TIPS: Natural Language Processing Technologies to Inform Practice in Science (NSF Project 2101669), STRIDES: Supporting Teachers in Responsive Instruction for Developing Expertise in Science (NSF Project 1813713), and GRIDS: Graphing

Research on Inquiry with Data in Science (NSF Project DRL-1418423). Any opinions, findings, conclusions, or recommendations expressed in this material are those of the author(s) and do not necessarily reflect the views of the National Science Foundation.

References

Anderson, J. R. 1996. "ACT: A Simple Theory of Complex Cognition." *American Psychologist* 51, no. 4: 355–65. https://doi.org/10.1037/0003-066X.51.4.355

Anderson, J. R., Corbett, A. T., Koedinger, K. R., and Pelletier, R. 1995. "Cognitive Tutors: Lessons Learned." *Journal of the Learning Sciences* 4, no. 2: 167–207. https://doi.org/10.1207/s15327809jls0402_2

Azevedo, R. 2005. "Computers Environments as Metacognitive Tools for Enhancing Learning." *Educational Psychologist* 40, no. 4: 193–97.

Berland, L. K., Schwarz, C. V., Krist, C., Kenyon, L., Lo, A. S., and Reiser, B. J. 2016. "Epistemologies in Practice: Making Scientific Practices Meaningful for Students." *Journal of Research in Science Teaching* 53, no. 7: 1082–112. https://doi.org/10.1002/tea.21257

Bertsch, S., Pesta, B. J., Wiscott, R., and McDaniel, M. A. 2007. "The Generation Effect: A Meta-analytic Review." *Memory & Cognition* 35, no. 2: 201–10. https://doi.org/10.3758/BF03193441

Bridwell, L. 1980. "Revising Strategies in Twelfth Grade Students' Transactional Writing." *Research in the Teaching of English 14*, no. 3: 197–222.

Clancy, M. J., and Linn, M. C. 1999. "Patterns and Pedagogy." *SIGCSE Bulletin* 31, no. 1: 37–42.

Clark, H. H., and Chase, W. G. 1972. "On the Process of Comparing Sentences against Pictures." *Cognitive Psychology* 3, no. 3: 472–517. https://doi.org/10.1016/0010-0285(72)90019-9

Cognition and Technology Group. 1991. "Technology and the Design of Generative Learning Environments." *Educational Technology* 31, no. 5: 34–40.

Crawford, L., Lloyd, S., and Knoth, K. 2008. "Analysis of Student Revisions on a State Writing Test." *Assessment for Effective Intervention* 33, no. 2: 108–19. https://doi.org/10.1177/1534508407311403

Darrach, B. 1970, November 20. "Meet Shaky, the First Electronic Person." *LIFE Magazine* 69, no. 21: 58B–68B.

de Jong, T., Gillet, D., Rodríguez-Triana, M. J., Hovardas, T., Dikke, D., Doran, R., Dziabenko, O., Koslowsky, J., Korventausta, M., Law, E., Pedaste, M., Tasiopoulou, E., Vidal, G., and Zacharia, Z. C. 2021. "Understanding Teacher Design Practices for Digital Inquiry-Based Science Learning: The case of Go-Lab." *Educational Technology Research and Development* 69, no. 2: 417–44. https://doi.org/10.1007/s11423-020-09904-z

de Jong, T., Linn, M. C., and Zacharia, Z. C. 2013. "Physical and Virtual Laboratories in Science and Engineering Education." *Science* 340, no. 6130: 305–8. https://doi.org/10.1126/science.1230579

diSessa, A. A. 2000. *Changing minds: Computers, learning and literacy*. Cambridge, MA: MIT Press.

Donnelly, D. F., Linn, M. C., and Ludvigsen, S. 2014. "Impacts and Characteristics of Computer-Based Science Inquiry Learning Environments for Precollege Students." *Review of Educational Research* 84, no. 4: 572–608. https://doi.org/10.3102/0034654314546954

Fitzgerald, J. 1987. "Research on Revision in Writing." *Review of Educational Research* 57, no. 4: 481–506.

Flower, L., and Hayes, J. R. 1981. "A Cognitive Process Theory of Writing." *College Composition and Communication* 32, no. 4: 365–87. https://doi.org/10.2307/356600

Freedman, S., Hull, G., Higgs, J., and Booten, K. 2016. "Teaching Writing in a Digital and Global Age: Toward Access, Learning, and Development for All." In *Handbook of Research on Teaching*, edited by D. H. Gitomer and C. A. Bell, 5th ed., 1389–449. Washington, DC: American Educational Research Association.

Friedler, Y., Nachmias, R., and Linn, M. C. 1990. "Learning Scientific Reasoning Skills in Microcomputer-Based Laboratories." *Journal of Research in Science Teaching* 27, no. 2: 173–91.

Furtak, E. M., Seidel, T., Iverson, H., and Briggs, D. C. 2012. "Experimental and Quasi-Experimental Studies of Inquiry-Based Science Teaching: A Meta-Analysis." *Review of Educational Research* 82, no. 3: 300–29. https://doi.org/10.3102/0034654312457206

Gerard, L., Bichler, S., Bradford, A., Linn, M. C., Steimel, K., and Riordan, B. 2022a. "Designing an Adaptive Dialogue to Promote Science Understanding." In *Proceedings of the 16th International Conference of the Learning Sciences—ICLS 2022,* edited by C. Chinn, E. Tan, C. Chan, and Y. Kali, 1653–56. International Society of the Learning Sciences.

Gerard, L., Kidron, A., and Linn, M. C. 2019. "Guiding Collaborative Revision of Science Explanations." *International Journal of Computer-Supported Collaborative Learning* 14: 291–324. https://doi.org/10.1007/s11412-019-09298-y

Gerard, L. F., and Linn, M. C. 2016a. "Using Automated Scores of Student Essays to Support Teacher Guidance in Classroom Inquiry." *Journal of Science Teacher Education* 27, no. 1: 111–29. https://doi.org/10.1007/s10972-016-9455-6

Gerard, L. F., and Linn, M. 2016b, April 10. "Writing and Revising in Science." Paper presented at the Annual Meeting of the American Educational Research Association.

Gerard, L., and Linn, M. C. 2016c. "How Do You Design Automated Guidance for Students' Writing in Inquiry Science?" In *Electronic Proceedings of the ESERA 2016 Conference.* Annual Meeting of the European Science Education Research Association (ESERA). Helsinki, Finland.

Gerard, L., and Linn, M. C. 2022. "Computer-Based Guidance to Support Students' Revision of Their Science Explanations." *Computers & Education* 176: 104351. https://doi.org/10.1016/j.compedu.2021.104351

Gerard, L., Linn, M. C., and Madhok, J. 2016. "Examining the Impacts of Annotation and Automated Guidance on Essay Revision and Science Learning." In *Transforming Learning, Empowering Learners: The International Conference of the Learning Sciences (ICLS) 2016*, Vol. 1, edited by C. K. Looi, J. L. Polman, U. Cress, and P. Reimann, 394–401. International Society of the Learning Sciences. https://repository.isls.org//handle/1/141

Gerard, L., Matuk, C., McElhaney, K., and Linn, M. C. 2015a. "Automated, Adaptive Guidance for K–12 Education." *Educational Research Review* 15: 41–58. https://doi.org/10.1016/j.edurev.2015.04.001

Gerard, L. F., Ryoo, K., McElhaney, K., Liu, L., Rafferty, A. N., and Linn, M. C. 2015b. "Automated Guidance for Student Inquiry." *Journal of Educational Psychology* 108, no. 1: 60–81. https://doi.org/10.1037/edu0000052

Gerard, L. F., Vitale, J., and Linn, M. C. 2017. "Argument Construction to Drive Inquiry." Paper presented at the 12th Conference of the European Science Education Research Association (ESERA), Dublin, Ireland.

Gerard, L., Wiley, K., Bradford, A., King Chen, J., Breitbart, J., and Linn, M. C. 2020. "Impact of a Teacher Action Planner Capturing Student Ideas on Customization Decisions." In *The Interdisciplinarity of the Learning Sciences, 14th International Conference of the Learning Sciences (ICLS) 2020,* Vol. 4, edited by M. Gresalfi and I. S. Horn, 2077–84. International Society of the Learning Sciences.

Gerard, L., Wiley, K., Debarger, A. H., Bichler, S., Bradford, A., and Linn, M. C. 2022b. "Self-directed Science Learning During COVID-19 and Beyond." *Journal of Science Education and Technology* 31, no. 2: 258–71. https://doi.org/10.1007/s10956-021-09953-w

Graesser, A. G., McNamara, D. S., and VanLehn, K. 2005. "Scaffolding Deep Comprehension Strategies through Point&Query, AutoTutor, and iSTART." *Educational Psychologist* 40, no. 4: 225–34.

Hayes, J. R., and Flower, L. S. 1986. "Writing Research and the Writer." *American Psychologist* 41, no. 10: 1106–13.

Höttecke, D., and Allchin, D. 2020. "Reconceptualizing Nature-of-Science Education in the Age of Social Media." *Science Education* 104, no. 4: 641–66. https://doi.org/10.1002/sce.21575

Inhelder, B. 1987. *Piaget Today.* Hillsdale, NJ: Erlbaum.

Ke, F., and Hoadley, C. 2009. "Evaluating Online Learning Communities." *Educational Technology Research and Development 57*, no. 4: 487–510. https://doi.org/10.1007/s11423-009-9120-2

Koedinger, K. R., and Aleven, V. 2016. "An Interview Reflection on 'Intelligent Tutoring Goes to School in the Big City.'" *International Journal of Artificial Intelligence in Education* 26, no. 1: 13–24. https://doi.org/10.1007/s40593-015-0082-8

Koedinger, K. R., Corbett, A. C., and Perfetti, C. 2012. "The Knowledge-Learning-Instruction (KLI) Framework: Bridging the Science-Practice Chasm to Enhance Robust Student Learning." *Cognitive Science* 36, no. 5: 757–98.

Könings, K. D., Seidel, T., and van Merriënboer, J. J. G. 2014. "Participatory Design of Learning Environments: Integrating Perspectives of Students, Teachers, and Designers." *Instructional Science* 42, no. 1: 1–9.

Krajcik, J. S., and Mun, K. 2014. "Promises and Challenges of Using Learning Technologies to Promote Student Learning of Science." In *Handbook of Research on Science Education*, Volume II, edited by N. G. Lederman and S. K. Abell, 337–60. London: Routledge.

Krist, C. 2020. "Examining How Classroom Communities Developed Practice-Based Epistemologies for Science through Analysis of Longitudinal Video Data." *Journal of Educational Psychology* 112, no. 3: 420–43. https://doi.org/10.1037/edu0000417

Kubsch, M., Krist, C., and Rosenberg, J. M. 2022. "Distributing Epistemic Functions and Tasks—A Framework for Augmenting Human Analytic Power with Machine Learning in Science Education Research." *Journal of Research in Science Teaching* 60, no. 2: 1–25. https://doi.org/10.1002/tea.21803

Kyza, E. A., and Agesilaou, A. 2022. "Investigating the Processes of Teacher and Researcher Empowerment and Learning in Co-design Settings." *Cognition and Instruction* 40, no. 1: 100–25. https://doi.org/10.1080/07370008.2021.2010213

Kyza, E. A., Michael, G., and Constantinou, C. P. 2007. "The Rationale, Design, and Implementation of a Web-Based Inquiry Learning Environment." In *CBLIS Conference Proceedings 2007 Contemporary Perspective on New Technologies in Science and Education*. https://gnosis.library.ucy.ac.cy/handle/7/64727

Latour, B. 1987. *Science in Action: How to Follow Scientists and Engineers through Society*. Cambridge, MA: Harvard University Press.

Lee, H.-S., Liu, O. L., and Linn, M. C. 2011. "Validating Measurement of Knowledge Integration in Science Using Multiple-Choice and Explanation Items." *Applied Measurement in Education* 24, no. 2: 115–36.

Linn, M. C. 1995. "Designing Computer Learning Environments for Engineering and Computer Science: The Scaffolded Knowledge Integration Framework." *Journal of Science Education and Technology* 4, no. 2: 103–26.

Linn, M. C. 2003. "Technology and Science Education: Starting Points, Research Programs, and Trends." *International Journal of Science Education* 25, no. 6: 727–58. https://doi.org/10.1080/09500690305017

Linn, M. C., and Clancy, M. J. 1992. "The Case for Case Studies of Programming Problems." *Communications of the ACM* 35, no. 3: 121–32.

Linn, M. C., Davis, E. A., and Eylon, B.-S. 2004. "The Scaffolded Knowledge Integration Framework for Instruction." In *Internet Environments for Science Education*, edited by M. C. Linn, E. A. Davis, and P. Bell, 47–72. London: Routledge.

Linn, M. C., Donnelly-Hermosillo, D., and Gerard, L. F. 2023. "Synergies between Learning Technologies and Learning Sciences: Promoting Equitable Secondary Science Education." In *Handbook of Research on Science Education*, Vol. III, edited by N. Lederman, D. Zeidler, and J. Lederman, 447–98. London: Routledge Press.

Linn, M. C., and Eylon, B.-S. 2011. *Science Learning and Instruction: Taking Advantage of Technology to Promote Knowledge Integration*. New York: Routledge.

Linn, M. C., Gerard, L., Ryoo, K., McElhaney, K., Liu, O. L., and Rafferty, A. N. 2014. "Computer-Guided Inquiry to Improve Science Learning." *Science* 344, no. 6180: 155–56. https://doi.org/10.1126/science.1245980

Linn, M. C., and Hsi, S. 2000. *Computers, Teachers, Peers: Science Learning Partners*. Mahwah, NJ: Lawrence Erlbaum Associates.

Liu, O. L., Brew, C., Blackmore, J., Gerard, L., Madhok, J., and Linn, M. C. 2014. "Automated Scoring of Constructed-Response Science Items: Prospects and Obstacles." *Educational Measurement: Issues and Practice* 33, no. 2: 19–28. https://doi.org/10.1111/emip.12028

Liu, O. L., Rios, J. A., Heilman, M., Gerard, L., and Linn, M. C. 2016. "Validation of Automated Scoring of Science Assessments." *Journal of Research in Science Teaching* 53, no. 2: 215–33. https://doi.org/10.1002/tea.21299

Lockheed, M. E., and Frakt, S. B. 1984. "Sex Equity: Increasing Girls' Use of Computers." *Computing Teacher* 11, no. 8: 16–18.

McBride, E. A., Vitale, J. M., Applebaum, L., and Linn, M. C. 2016. "Use of Interactive Computer Models to Promote Integration of Science Concepts through the Engineering Design Process." In *Transforming Learning, Empowering Learners: The International Conference of the Learning Sciences (ICLS) 2016*, Vol. 2, edited by C. K. Looi, J. L. Polman, U. Cress, and P. Reimann, 799–802. International Society of the Learning Sciences. https://repository.isls.org//handle/1/313

McElhaney, K. W., Chang, H.-Y., Chiu, J. L., and Linn, M. C. 2015. "Evidence for Effective Uses of Dynamic Visualisations in Science Curriculum Materials." *Studies in Science Education* 51, no. 1: 49–85. https://doi.org/10.1080/03057267.2014.984506

Mandinach, E., Linn, M., Pea, R., and Kurland, M. 1986. "The Cognitive Effects of Computer Learning Environments." *Journal of Educational Computing Research* 2: 409–10. https://doi.org/10.2190/GQ23-EA33-51BM-5HCT/

Matuk, C., and Linn, M. C. 2018. "Why and How Do Middle School Students Exchange Ideas during Science Inquiry?" *International Journal of Computer-Supported Collaborative Learning* 13, no. 3: 263–99. https://doi.org/10.1007/s11412-018-9282-1

Mercier, H., and Sperber, D. 2011. "Why Do Humans Reason? Arguments for an Argumentative Theory." *Behavioral and Brain Sciences* 34, no. 2: 57–74. https://doi.org/10.1017/S0140525X10000968

Mokros, J. R., and Tinker, R. F. 1987. "The Impact of Microcomputer-Based Labs on Children's Ability to Interpret Graphs." *Journal of Research in Science Teaching* 24, no. 4: 369–83. https://doi.org/10.1002/tea.3660240408

Papert, S. 1980. *Mindstorms: Children, Computers, and Powerful Ideas.* New York: Basic Books.

Puntambekar, S., and Hübscher, R. 2005. "Tools for Scaffolding Students in a Complex Learning Environment: What Have We Gained and What Have We Missed?" *Educational Psychologist*, 40, no. 1: 1–12.

Quintana, C., Reiser, B. J., Davis, E. A., Krajcik, J., Fretz, E., Duncan, R. G., Kyza, E., Edelson, D., and Soloway, E. 2004. "A Scaffolding Design Framework for Software to Support Science Inquiry." *Journal of the Learning Sciences* 13, no. 3: 337–86.

Reiser, B. J., Novak, M., McGill, T. A. W., and Penuel, W. R. 2021. "Storyline Units: An Instructional Model to Support Coherence from the Students' Perspective." *Journal of Science Teacher Education* 32, no. 7: 805–29. https://doi.org/10.1080/1046560X.2021.1884784

Richland, L. E., Linn, M. C., and Bjork, R. A. 2007. "Instruction." In *Handbook of Applied Cognition*, 2nd ed., edited by F. T. Durso, 555–83. Chichester: Wiley.

Riordan, B., Bichler, S., Bradford, A., King Chen, J., Wiley, K., Gerard, L., and Linn, M. C. 2020. "An Empirical Investigation of Neural Methods for Content Scoring of Science Explanations." In *Proceedings of the Fifteenth Workshop on Innovative Use of NLP for Building Educational Applications*, 135–44. https://doi.org/10.18653/v1/2020.bea-1.13

Ryoo, K., and Linn, M. C. 2012. "Can Dynamic Visualizations Improve Middle School Students' Understanding of Energy in Photosynthesis?" *Journal of Research in Science Teaching* 49, no. 2: 218–43. https://doi.org/10.1002/tea.21003

Sandoval, W. A., and Bell, P. 2004. "Design-Based Research Methods for Studying Learning in Context: Introduction." *Educational Psychologist* 39, no. 4: 199–201.

Scardamalia, M., and Bereiter, C. 2006. "Knowledge Building: Theory, Pedagogy, and Technology." In *Cambridge Handbook of the Learning Sciences*, edited by K. Sawyer, 97–118. Cambridge: Cambridge University Press.

Shear, L., Bell, P., and Linn, M. C. 2004. "Partnership Models: The Case of the Deformed Frogs." In *Internet Environments for Science Education*, edited by M. C. Linn, E. A. Davis, and P. Bell, 289–314. London: Routledge.

Shute, V. J. 2008. "Focus on Formative Feedback." *Review of Educational Research* 78, no. 1: 153–89.

Slotta, J. D., and Linn, M. C. 2009. *WISE Science: Web-Based Inquiry in the Classroom*. New York: Teachers College Press.

Smetana, L. K., and Bell, R. L. 2012. "Computer Simulations to Support Science Instruction and Learning: A Critical Review of the Literature." *International Journal of Science Education* 34, no. 9: 1337–70. https://doi.org/10.1080/09500693.2011.605182

Smith, J. P., III, diSessa, A. A., and Roschelle, J. 1994. "Misconceptions Reconceived: A Constructivist Analysis of Knowledge in Transition." *Journal of the Learning Sciences* 3, no. 2: 115–63. https://doi.org/10.1207/s15327809jls0302_1

Strobl, C., Ailhaud, E., Benetos, K., Devitt, A., Kruse, O., Proske, A., and Rapp, C. 2019. "Digital Support for Academic Writing: A Review of Technologies and Pedagogies." Computers and Education 131: 33–48. https://doi.org/10.1016/j.compedu.2018.12.005

Sun, D., Looi, C.-K., and Xie, W. 2017. "Learning with Collaborative Inquiry: A Science Learning Environment for Secondary Students." *Technology, Pedagogy and Education* 26, no. 3: 241–63. https://doi.org/10.1080/1475939X.2016.1205509

Tansomboon, C., Gerard, L., and Linn, M. C. 2015. "Impact of Knowledge Integration and Teacher Simulated Guidance on Student Learning." Paper presented at the Annual Meeting of the American Education Research Association, Chicago, IL.

Tansomboon, C., Gerard, L. F., Vitale, J. M., and Linn, M. C. 2017. "Designing Automated Guidance to Promote Productive Revision of Science Explanations." *International Journal of Artificial Intelligence in Education* 27, no. 4: 729–57. https://doi.org/10.1007/s40593-017-0145-0

Vakil, S., and Higgs, J. 2019. "It's about Power." *Communications of the ACM* 62, no. 3: 31–33.

Van Lehn, K. 2011. "The Relative Effectiveness of Human Tutoring, Intelligent Tutoring Systems, and Other Tutoring Systems." *Educational Psychologist* 46, no. 4: 197–221. http://dx.doi.org/10.1080/00461520.2011.611369

Vitale, J. M., Applebaum, L., and Linn, M. C. (2019). "Coordinating between Graphs and Science Concepts: Density and Buoyancy." Cognition and Instruction 37, no. 1: 38–72.

Vitale, J. M., McBride, E., and Linn, M. C. 2016. "Distinguishing Complex Ideas about Climate Change: Knowledge Integration vs. Specific Guidance." *International Journal of Science Education* 38, no. 9: 1548–69. https://doi.org/10.1080/09500693.2016.1198969

Weber, E. U., and Stern, P. C. 2011. "Public Understanding of Climate Change in the United States." *The American Psychologist* 66, no. 4: 315–28. https://doi.org/10.1037/a0023253

Wieman, C. E., Adams, W. K., and Perkins, K. K. 2008. "PhET: Simulations That Enhance Learning." *Science* 322, no. 5902: 682–83.

Wiley, K., Gerard, L., Bradford, A., and Linn, M. C. 2023. "Teaching with Technology: Empowering Teachers and Promoting Equity in Science." In *Oxford Handbook of Educational Psychology*, edited by A. M. O'Donnell, J. Reeve, and N. Barnes, C52S1–C52S34. Oxford, UK: Oxford University Press. https://doi.org/10.1093/oxfordhb/9780199841332.013.52

Zhai, X., Haudek, K. C., Shi, L., Nehm, R. H., and Urban-Lurain, M. 2020. "From Substitution to Redefinition: A Framework of Machine Learning-Based Science Assessment." *Journal of Research in Science Teaching* 57: 1430–59.

Zhai, X., Yin, Y., Pellegrino, J. W., Haudek, K. C., and Shi, L. 2020. "Applying Machine Learning in Science Assessment: A Systematic Review." *Studies in Science Education* 56, no. 1: 111–51. https://doi.org/10.1080/03057267.2020.1735757

Zheng, B., Lawrence, J., Warschauer, M., and Lin, C.-H. 2015. "Middle School Students' Writing and Feedback in a Cloud-Based Classroom Environment." *Technology, Knowledge and Learning* 20, no. 2: 201–29. https://doi.org/10.1007/s10758-014-9239-z

Zhu, M., Liu, O. L., and Lee, H.-S. 2020. "The Effect of Automated Feedback on Revision Behavior and Learning Gains in Formative Assessment of Scientific Argument Writing." *Computers & Education* 143: 103668. https://doi.org/10.1016/j.compedu.2019.103668

5

Applying Machine Learning to Assess Paper–Pencil-Drawn Models of Optics

Changzhao Wang, Xiaoming Zhai and Ji Shen

Introduction

Machine learning (ML) is being applied to achieve automation in education. Despite the dramatic development of learning technologies, it remains challenging for teachers to attend to multiple students at the same time in classroom settings. Customized and instant feedback is not always available for all students, which is especially needed when students are engaged in complex practices such as scientific modeling. The application of ML can make a difference through automated assessment[1] and intelligent agents, which have been proven to be able to facilitate customized learning and/or group collaboration (Wang and Shen 2023; Zhai et al. 2020a). Automated assessment can free teachers from repetitive and time-consuming scoring tasks so that they will have time for more constructive activities. Automated assessment has been applied to written responses (e.g., Nehm, Ha, and Mayfield 2012; Sung et al. 2021) and programming assignments (e.g., Mohan 2017).

ML is making a difference in science education. ML can contribute to resolving the challenges in the assessment of science learning (Zhai 2021), such as the difficulties in analyzing complex data for evidentiary inference of students' science learning and satisfying the multiple purposes of the assessment (Zhai et al. 2020b). It helps to overcome these challenges by enriching the assessment functionality, supplementing statistics for data interpretation, and targeting complex science constructs (Zhai et al. 2020b). Scientific practices (e.g., modeling, argumentation) usually involve students' understanding and application of complex science concepts, so ML can greatly benefit the assessment of these scientific practices.

However, most of the current ML applications for automated assessments focus on text-based responses (Zhai et al. 2020b). Very few attempts have been made to assess paper–pencil drawing responses, a form that is critical to evaluate students' modeling abilities because the complexity involved in paper–pencil drawings adds to the difficulty for the computer to learn their patterns. Therefore, this study aims to fill the gap by applying ML to automatically score paper-based drawings of refraction in optics, guided by the following two research questions (RQs): (1) How accurately does

[1] The automated assessment throughout this article refers to automated analyzing, grading, and/or scoring students' responses, rather than assessments that are automatically generated or assigned.

Changzhao Wang, Xiaoming Zhai, and Ji Shen, *Applying Machine Learning to Assess Paper–Pencil-Drawn Models of Optics*. In: *Uses of Artificial Intelligence in STEM Education*. Edited by: Xiaoming Zhai and Joseph Krajcik, Oxford University Press.
 DOI: 10.1093/oso/9780198882077.003.0005

the ML algorithm score drawn models of refractions compared to human scores? (2) Does the accuracy of ML scoring vary by student proficiency level of modeling? If so, how?

Theoretical Perspectives

Models and Modeling in Optics

Scientists build models to help explain and understand the natural world. Scientific models are simplified representations that extract essential features from real-world systems (Schwarz et al. 2009). There are various scientific models to explain different phenomena that are not easily observable for humans, such as atomic models to illustrate the structure inside atoms, cosmological models to show the evolvement of cosmological bodies, and light ray models to visualize and explain the propagation of light. Taking the light ray model as an example, it uses a straight line to represent the path of light when it travels in a homogeneous medium, with an arrow to show the traveling direction. It makes it easier for people to understand light propagation by abstracting and visualizing the mechanism of the invisible propagation of light. The Next Generation Science Standards (NGSS Leads States 2013) lists modeling, the process of constructing, evaluating, using, and revising models (Schwarz et al. 2009), as one of the core scientific practices that students need to learn in science classrooms.

Models can be represented by mathematical formulae, 2D drawings, 3D computer animations, and other types of formats (Lehrer and Schauble 2006). Despite the popularity of computer-based modeling platforms (Shen et al. 2014), hand-drawing remains an important process of constructing a model in a classroom setting (Glynn 1997; Glynn and Duit 1995). Hand-drawing not only provides students (and teachers) with flexibility and access to modeling when a computer or software is not readily available, but also facilitates students' active transformation of a mental entity to a materialized model (Latour 1990; Shen and Confrey 2007).

Drawing has been widely used in assessing students' models and modeling ability. They may also help teachers identify students' alternative conceptions that are not present in texts or verbal communications (Karlberg, Henriques, and Colburn 2021). National Research Council (2014) described a drawing task that assesses how students construct a model of volcano formation. Quillin and Thomas (2015) created a framework called Drawing-to-Learn that categorizes the reasons for using drawing in science classrooms. They also delineated specific scaffolding strategies instructors could use to help students practice model-based reasoning when using drawings. For instance, they laid out how experts attend to aspects of models (e.g., relationship to reality, salient features, the purpose of modeling) in the drawing.

Understanding Refraction Using Ray Models

Light and optics is an important topic of high school science learning and is required in many curriculum standards, such as the Next Generation Science Standards

(NGSS Lead States 2013) and the High School Physics Curriculum Standards in China (Department of Education 2017). This topic is essential for students to develop an understanding of phenomena related to light and optics. However, students have difficulty understanding light and optics due to the high level of obscurity and abstraction in conceptualizing light (Galili and Hazan 2000). A simple ray model is a crucial part of geometric optics and includes the following key principles:

- A point light source emits light rays in all directions;
- A light ray travels in one medium in a straight line;
- A light ray travels in one medium to infinity unless it is absorbed by an object, reflected by an object, or refracted when entering a different medium;
- When a light ray reflects off a surface, the angle of reflection is equal to the angle of incidence (Figure 5.1a); and
- When a light ray travels from one medium to another, the light ray refracts following the law of refraction (Figure 5.1b).

The law of refraction, commonly known as Snell's Law, refers to the change in the direction of light rays passing from one medium to another (Nofziger 1995). Figure 5.1b shows how an incident ray entering from one medium (e.g., air) to a denser one (e.g., water) bends toward the normal line (the line perpendicular to the intersection of the two media). While teaching refraction, teachers often spend little time addressing the modeling of geometric optics but focus more on mathematical calculations.

Consequently, many students have a difficult time conceptualizing refraction (Ashmaann, Anderson, and Boeckman 2016). For example, it is difficult for students to correctly demonstrate the direction of refracted light and the position of a virtual image in a diagram. When labeling or drawing diagrams, students often do not demonstrate that light refracts/bends when traveling through media. Students may show the virtual image as being directly above the object, rather than at a correct refracted position (Kaewkhong et al. 2010). These mistakes result from a lack of connection between the computation and the deep conceptual understanding

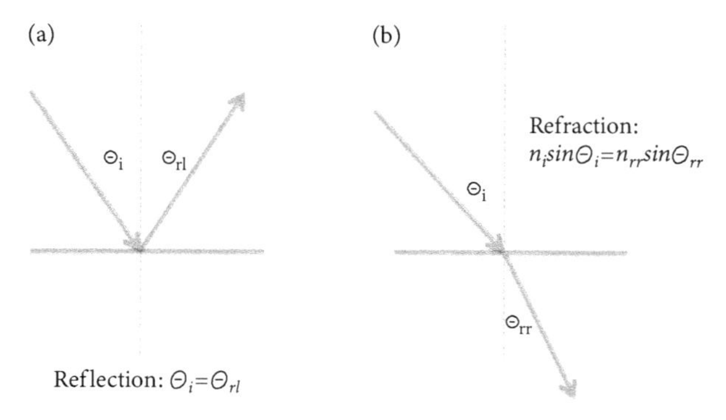

Figure 5.1 Illustration of the reflection and refraction laws for light rays.

of optics principles (Favale and Bondani 2013; John, Molepo, and Chirwa 2018; Pompea et al. 2007).

Automatic Scoring of Student-Drawn Models

Having students draw scientific models is an efficient and equitable approach for assessing their scientific thinking. Models reflect how students conceptualize phenomena and utilize scientific knowledge to construct explanations and represent their ideas (Zhai 2022), yet different types of models may function differently when used as assessment instruments. Based on our non-exhaustive literature search in this field till July 2023, we have found a limited number of existing literatures that documented research applying ML to automatically score computer-based and paper–pencil-drawn models.

Smith et al. (2018) compared students' scores on computer-based drawn models and written explanations using the same rubrics and found that student-drawn models outperformed their written responses. Consistent results were reported in Zhai, He, and Krajcik (2022), who compared middle school student's computer-based drawn models for the Next Generation Science Assessments and their written descriptions of the models. Their findings suggest that drawn models may provide an additional avenue for students with low writing proficiency to express their ideas, thus being more equitable than writing. Moreover, both studies reported low correlation coefficients between students' scores on written responses and drawn models. Based on the evidence, Zhai, He, and Krajcik (2022) argued that although both drawing and writing can be used to represent the mechanisms that students identified to account for phenomena, the low correlations might imply that drawing and writing are different information-processing channels for students. Written descriptions reflect one's sequential thinking that usually includes more procedural information, while drawn models can express more structural information. In addition, Stenning, Cox, and Oberlander (1995) found that drawings included less ambiguity than written descriptions in representing ideas. For example, "the particle is subjected to a force" does not entail the magnitude nor the direction of the force, while a model using an arrow can show the magnitude and direction of the force. Despite these promises of drawn models, they are not frequently used in the classroom for assessing student thinking due to the intensive need of time and labor to score them.

To meet this challenge, researchers have employed ML to automatically score student-drawn models. For example, Smith et al. (2018) automatically scored middle school students' computer-based drawings about magnetics. Their items were structured, and students were required to use the components provided to develop a model. Students could drag the components and change their positions (see Figure 5.2). Smith et al. (2018) applied a topology-based approach to score student-drawn models. This approach first defines a set of possible relations between objects as near, far, and contains. Rules were also applied to limit the relations between certain components, so that the resulting outputs would be limited. Smith et al.'s (2018)

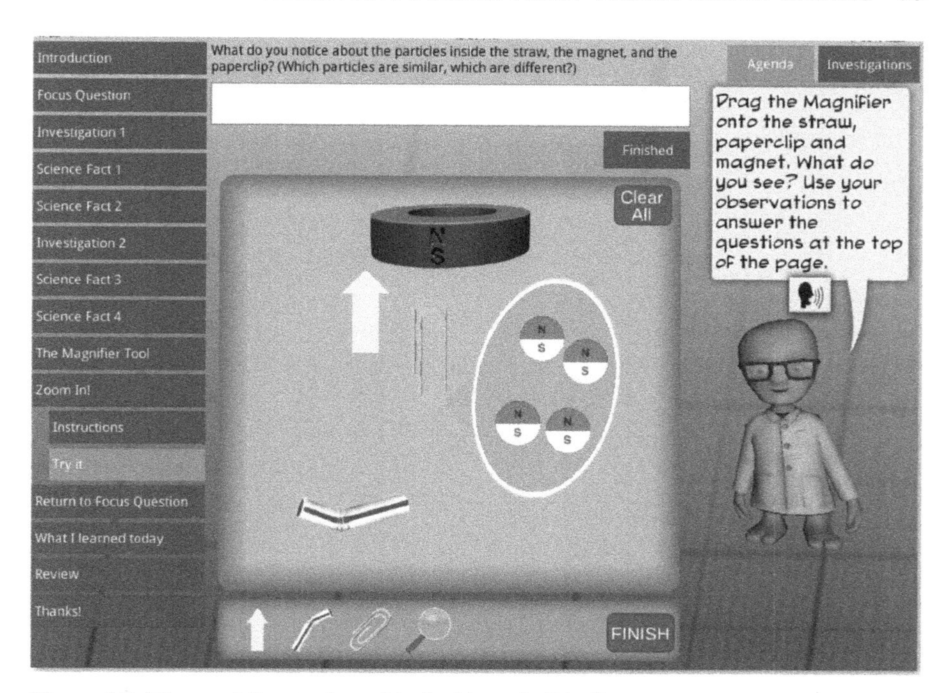

Figure 5.2 The modeling tool used in Smith et al. (2018).

method can handle cases in which the outputs are limited yet is not capable if cases are unpredictable like free drawing.

To deal with free drawings, von Davier, Tyack, and Khorramdel (2022) applied deep learning to automatically score one item from the Trends in International Mathematics and Science Study (TIMSS). This item provides a grid space and asks students to draw models to represent their thinking about the phenomena. Though students could draw models, they could only draw using the given grids, which limited the variability of drawn models (see Figure 5.3). In this study, von Davier, Tyack, and Khorramdel (2022) employed convolutional neural networks (CNNs) and feed-forward neural networks (FFNs) to automatically score students' drawn responses. CNNs and FNNs are two different types of artificial neural networks, and they differ mainly in how they process input data and how they learn from data. Using the two approaches, von Davier, Tyack, and Khorramdel (2022) found that CNNs outperformed FFNs. They also realized that CNN models outperformed humans, evidenced by the fact that some human-incorrectly-labeled cases were correctly labeled by computer.

Recent work by Zhai, He, and Krajcik (2022) has provided evidence of automatic scoring free-drawn models. Zhai, He, and Krajcik (2022) reported on six modeling assessments for middle school students and used a thousand student responses for algorithmic model development. Their assessment tasks do not add constraints for drawing; thus, students could draw models as freely as they would like to. However, basic drawing tools (e.g., circles) were provided (see Figure 5.4).

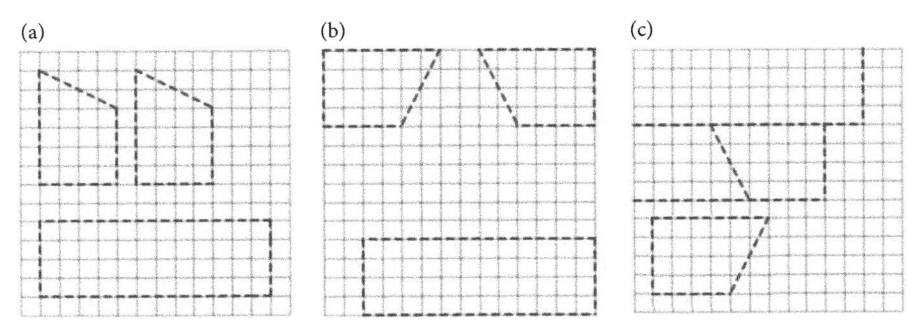

Figure 5.3 The grid space for modeling in von Davier, Tyack, and Khorramdel (2022).

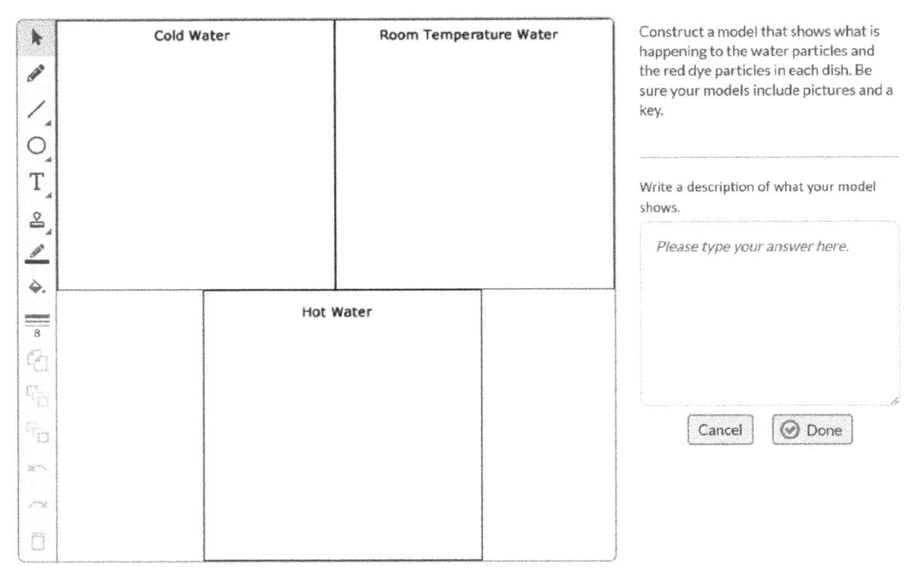

Figure 5.4 The modeling interface for the red dye diffusion activity in the Next Generation Science Assessment Project (Harris, Kracjik, and Pellegrino 2024).

Zhai, He, and Krajcik (2022) applied the ResNet-50 V2 CNNs to automatically score the drawn models. As one of the most popular CNNs, RestNet-50 includes a function of skip connections (i.e., residuals) to avoid prediction accuracy becoming saturated as layers increase using a residual block. Therefore, the identified block can learn from the residual (i.e., ResNet) which significantly improved the accuracy.

More recently, two studies reported the automatic scoring of students' paper–pencil-drawn models. Li, Liu, and Krajcik (2023) applied CNNs to assess elementary students' paper–pencil-drawn models: one model of ecology and two models of mechanics. Based on 2076 student models, they achieved the testing accuracies of 62.32% (±1.63%), 73.25% (±1.47%), and 53.29% (±1.21%) for the three different models. Lee, Lee, and Hong (2023) also used CNNs, specifically a pre-trained Inception-v3 model, to score 1028 students' (grades 2–11) hand-drawn models of gas particles in two different situations. Their testing accuracies of automatic scoring fell in the range between 82.0% and 94.2%.

Overall, it is much more challenging to achieve automatic scoring of paper–pencil-drawn models than computer-based-drawn models. First, paper–pencil drawing allows students more freedom to draw what they want and where they would like to draw, which can significantly increase the variability of the models compared to drawing with computer-based structural tools as in von Davier, Tyack, and Khorramdel (2022). Second, paper–pencil drawing needs to be scanned and cropped before computers can identify them. This process could generate additional variability that would impact scoring accuracy. Moreover, we found that some students contaminated the drawing spot occasionally using pencil. These types of variability added to the image could worsen the algorithm development and, more importantly, are inevitable. Therefore, researching how to automatically score paper–pencil-drawn models is critical and challenging.

Methods

Participants and Data Collection

A total of 767 eleventh-grade students, recruited from a high school in China, participated in this study. The students aged from 16 to 18 and came from 17 classes. They studied a unit on optics before taking the test for this study. Researchers were blocked from students' identifiable information for this study.

The test on optics was written in Chinese. The test consisted of three items that targeted refraction and/or total internal reflection. For this study, we focused on the second item that asked students to draw a model to explain a refraction phenomenon. As shown in Figure 5.5, the item presents a context of a boy and his father spearing fish in a river. The question asked students to draw a model to explain why the boy should aim somewhere below the fish rather than right at the fish in order to spear it (see Figure 5.5).

Data Preparation

Data Cleaning

Students' responses were scanned as image files. Since the three items are presented on one page, we cropped each image to keep the area for the focused item—including the printed question, the printed background image, and the student's drawing. Nine of the responses were excluded from analysis because (1) the drawings were presented on a different paper from the printed paper that every student received; (2) the

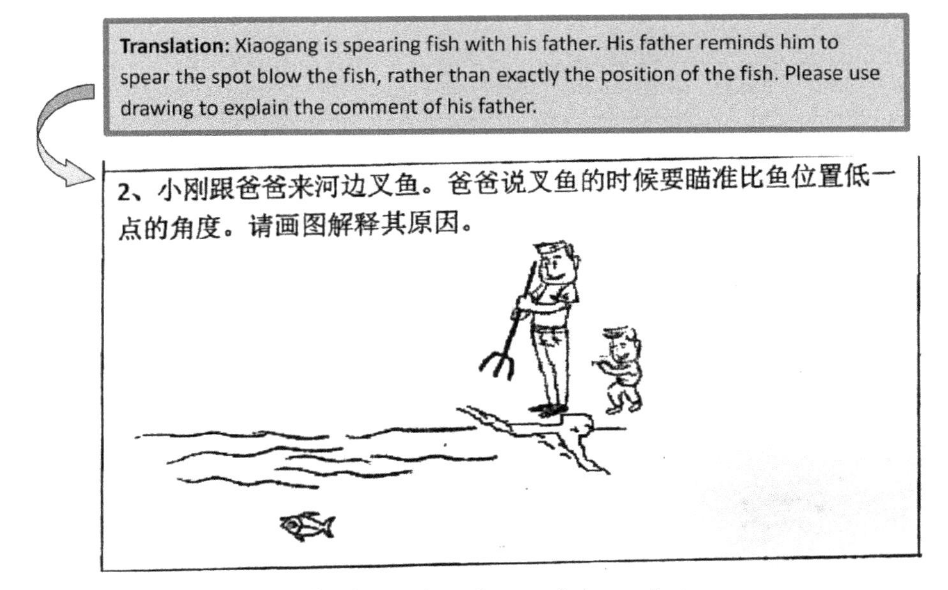

Figure 5.5 The focus item for this study and its English translation.

drawings were presented on the correct paper but not in the specified area for responses; or (3) the drawings contained irrelevant information from teachers (i.e., teachers' correction marks). In addition, we manually cleaned students' correction marks, irrelevant scratches, and written words for some images (about 30) to avoid interfering with ML classifications. Finally, the remaining 758 images were binary processed (i.e., transformed into black and white images) and used for analysis. Figure 5.6 shows three example responses after these data-cleaning steps.

Human Scoring

The authors, with expertise in physics education, collaboratively developed a rubric to classify drawn models into three levels: 0—beginning, 1—developing, and 2—proficient, based on the quality of how well the overall drawn model explained the phenomenon. The scoring rubric is shown in Table 5.1. It focuses on two relevant aspects of how the drawings demonstrate students' modeling ability (Quillin and Thomas 2015): the *salience of model features* and their *relationship to reality*. The salience of model features refers to the key (conventional) representational features of a ray model, such as using solid lines to represent light rays, how many critical rays one typically draws, and whether the drawn light rays follow the refraction law. Relationship to reality refers to whether the drawings include the virtual image of the fish (so that the drawn model can be used to explain what a person observes in this case). Figures 5.6a, 5.6b, and 5.6c show examples of levels 0, 1, and 2, respectively. Two authors independently scored a small set (n = 30) of drawings that were randomly sampled. The weighted Cohen's kappa of the two raters'

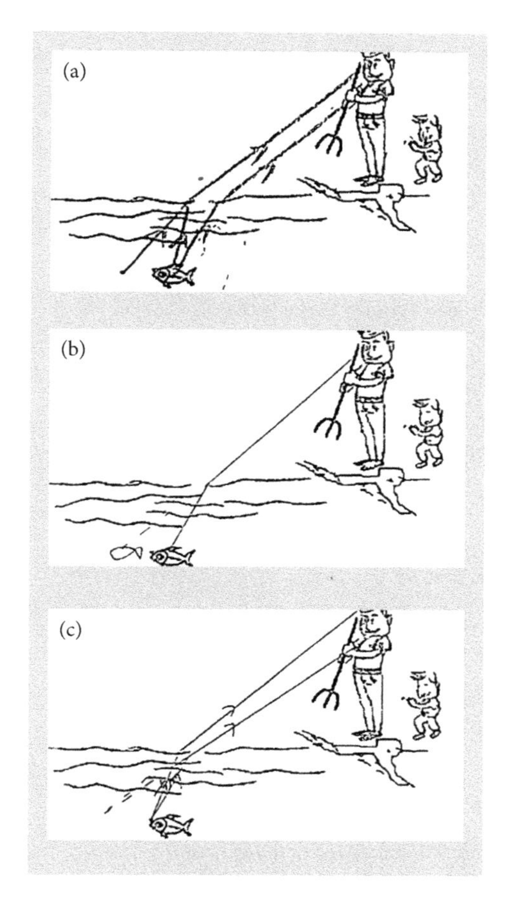

Figure 5.6 Examples of images after data cleaning.

scores reached 0.89, indicating strong inter-rater reliability (Altman 1991; Cohen 1968; Pedregosa et al. 2011). All the discrepancies were resolved through discussion, then one rater scored the remaining images in about an hour. Eventually, 134 models were classified as beginning (score = 0), 316 as developing (score = 1), and 308 as proficient (score = 2). These scores were used as labels of images to train the ML model.

Dataset Creation

Since the inputs of neural networks should be of the same size, cropped images were resized to 100×100 pixels. A dataset was created to store the pixels of each image and their corresponding labels (the labels refer to the scores of images).

Dataset Split

The dataset was randomly split into testing and training sets at a ratio of 1:9. The training set was further randomly split into a validation (developing) and a real training set at a ratio of 1:4.

Table 5.1 Scoring Rubric

Score	Modeling criteria	Example
0	If any of the following criteria is satisfied, the drawing is scored as 0: 1. There is no drawing, or the drawing is too messy to tell its pattern. [salience of model features] 2. The light path does not follow the law of refraction. [relationship to reality] 3. (For the situation when there is only one light ray from the fish) There is no representation (a point or a sketch of fish) of the virtual image of fish or the opposite extension of the refraction light, or there is the virtual image of fish but it's not on the extended line of the refraction light.	Figure 5.6a
1	If there is only one light ray from one point on the fish, and all the following four points are satisfied: [salience of model features] 1. The light path is in a solid line. 2. The extended line of the refraction light is in a dashed line. 3. The light path follows the refraction law. [relationship to reality] 4. The virtual image of the fish is represented as a point or a sketch of the fish, somewhere along the extended line of the refraction light. If there are two light rays from the fish, and all the following three points are satisfied: [salience of model features] 1. The light paths are in solid lines. 2. The light paths follow the refraction law. [relationship to reality] 3. There may be no representation of the virtual image of the fish, or the virtual image of the fish is not along the extended line of the refraction light.	Figure 5.6b
2	If all the following criteria are met: [salience of model features] There is one pair of light rays coming from one point on the fish. Their traveling paths follow the law of refraction. The refraction lights point at the facial area of the human. There may be arrows towards the human or there may be no arrows. [relationship to reality] The virtual image is at the intersection of the extended lines of the two refraction lights. Note: • The extended lines (drawn in dashed lines) of refraction lights are not necessary. • If there are more than one pair of light rays that satisfy the above criteria, the drawing still deserves 2 points.	Figure 5.6c

Algorithmic Model Development

We developed and trained the algorithmic models[2] from scratch (see Figure 5.7). We employed a sequential model composed of four convolutional layers, along with four dropout layers (to prevent overfitting), followed by a flattening layer (to convert the output of convolutional layers into a one-dimensional feature vector), three fully connected layers (for classification), and an output layer.

The model was compiled with the following parameters: loss = "sparse_ categorical_crossentropy," optimizer = "adam," metrics = "accuracy" (these parameters are used to configure the way the model works during training and evaluation, with the goal of minimizing the loss and maximizing the accuracy of the model's predictions). The CNN algorithm was trained using gradient descent. Each iteration began with computing the output of each layer and then passed forward, then the gradient of the loss function "sparse categorical cross entropy" with regard to the weight of the model and passing them backward, and lastly updating the weight based on the derivatives to minimize the loss. The Adam optimizer is a stochastic gradient descent method that supports the adaptive learning rate.

Convolutional Neural Networks

Neural networks, in particular artificial ones, are computational models designed in a structure similar to human neural networks with several connected artificial neurons (also called nodes) to process information. Neurons transmit the information to adjunct neurons through the many connections (i.e., edges) while assigning weight to increase or decrease the strength of the signal. The neurons are usually aggregated in multiple layers, in which information transmits or traverses between layers (Hastie, Tibshirani, and Friedman 2009). Convolutional neural networks are a special kind that use convolution or cross-correlation in one or more layers (Goodfellow,

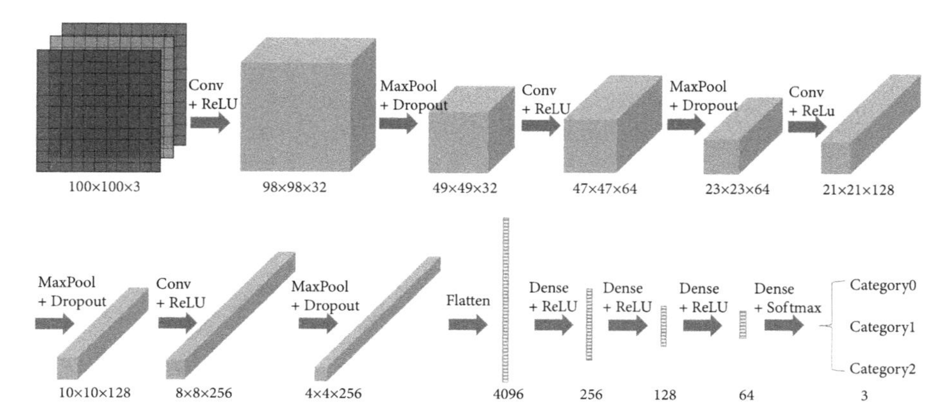

Figure 5.7 Architecture of the sequential CNN model.

[2] ML models refer to the computational models for the ML training process, which is a different concept from scientific model/modeling.

Bengio, and Courville 2016). Cross-correlation is used by many ML libraries, which are collections of prewritten functions and ML methods ready for use (e.g., Keras, PyTorch). CNNs are mainly used for signal- (1D CNNs) and image- (2D CNNs) related applications, such as electrocardiogram (ECG) signal analysis, image-based medical diagnosis, and face recognition. A typical convolutional layer comprises three stages in a linear sequence: convolution, detector (activation function), and pooling (Goodfellow, Bengio, and Courville 2016). CNN has been successful in the automated scoring of students' computer-based drawings of water molecules (Zhai, Krajcik, and Pellegrino 2021).

Data Analysis

To investigate the two RQs, different steps and research methods were applied. To answer RQ 1, we followed the following steps and methods:

- Repeated the one-time process ten times. Each time it generated the best model and a result of testing accuracy based on the model.
- Conducted nested cross-validation to obtain mean accuracy.

Testing Accuracy. Weighted accuracy is used to compute the testing accuracy of the model (obtained from the training process) on the testing set. It is the average of the prediction accuracy within each class. More specifically, it is computed by the formula $\frac{1}{3}\left(\frac{a}{A}+\frac{b}{B}+\frac{c}{C}\right)$, where A, B, C are the number of samples in each class; a, b, c are the number of correct predictions in each class; 3 is the total number of classes. It can avoid underweighting the classes that include less samples, compared with the unweighted accuracy, which is computed by $\frac{a+b+c}{A+B+C}$.

Nested Cross-Validation. For this study, the dataset of 758 images is less than the common data size for CNN classifications. To avoid an overly optimistic or pessimistic result, nested (double) cross-validation was applied (Brownlee 2021). It consists of two layers of k-fold cross-validation. In the outer layer, the dataset was divided into $k = m$ non-overlapping folds/parts. One of the m folds was used as a testing set, and the remaining $m - 1$ folds were used as a training set. The testing process was repeated m times, with a different combination of testing and training sets each time (so-called cross-validation). Within each training process (the inner layer), the $m - 1$ folds of data were divided into $k = n$ non-overlapping folds. One of the n folds was used as a validation set, and the other $n - 1$ folds were used as the real training set. Thus, each training process for the outer layer implies n training processes in the inner layer. In each training process in the inner layer, each of the n folds took turns to be the validation set. The n training processes (in the inner layer) produced the best model to be tested on the testing set. Each test returned a score of the accuracy of the model. The m tests generated m scores of accuracies. The final average accuracy was represented by the mean of the m scores, along with their standard deviation. To remain consistent with the ratio of dataset split, m was set as 10 and n was set as 5 in this study.

To answer RQ 2 we used the following steps and methods:

- Scored all images ten times, based on the ten best models from the ten one-time processes for RQ 1.
- Documented how many times the ML scoring was incorrect for each image.
- Conducted one-way ANOVA to examine whether the accuracy of ML scoring varied among different drawing levels, and if yes, which specific levels differed from each other.

One-Way ANOVA. One-way ANOVA was conducted to examine whether there was a significant overall difference in the accuracy of ML scoring among three different proficiency levels (in terms of modeling). It is a between-subjects design, as each image belongs to one of the three levels. The only independent variable is the proficiency level of modeling, and the dependent variable is the number of times when each image is given an incorrect score by the machine. Therefore, one-way ANOVA was identified as the appropriate statistical method.

Post Hoc Comparisons. If one-way ANOVA shows significant overall differences, post hoc tests need to be performed to find between-group differences in the models. Since our data did not meet the homogeneity of variance assumption, the Games-Howell test was selected for the post hoc comparisons (Field 2018).

Results

Machine Scoring Accuracy of Paper-Pencil Drawn Models

Before conducting nested cross-validation, the training algorithm followed by a one-time validation and a one-time testing was executed several times, and each time the dataset was split randomly with the specified ratio. This one-time process was repeated ten times and generated the following results of testing accuracy: 0.990, 0.922, 0.915, 0.955, 0.711, 0.861, 0.742, 0.969, 0.928, 0.912 (mean = 0.891, SD = 0.09). Among the ten times, the average scoring accuracy on the testing datasets reached 89.1% (SD = 9%). Then nested cross-validation was performed. The result of the average testing accuracy is 61.9% (SD = 5.2%).

Variations of Machine Scoring Accuracy by Proficiency Level of Modeling

All images were scored ten times based on the ML models generated in the ten one-time processes. Table 5.2 presents the descriptive statistics from the analysis. As a result, the level-0 images were given incorrect scores (either 1 or 2) for an average of 2.60 times with a standard deviation of 1.82; the level-1 images were given incorrect scores (either 0 or 2) for an average of 1.04 with a standard deviation of 1.57; and the level-2 images were given incorrect scores (either 0 or 1) for an average of 0.35 times with a standard deviation of 0.90.

Table 5.2 Descriptive Statistics of How Many Times the Machine Scored Incorrectly within Each Level

Modeling level	Number of images	Minimum	Maximum	Mean	Std. deviation
0	134	0	6	2.60	1.82
1	316	0	7	1.04	1.57
2	308	0	6	0.35	0.90
Total	758	0	7	1.04	1.60

The results of one-way ANOVA showed that there was a significant difference in terms of the accuracy of ML scoring among different drawing levels ($F(2, 755) = 122.2$, $p < 0.001$), where 24.4% of the variation in ML scoring accuracy can be explained by the factor of drawing level among the three groups of images ($\eta^2 = 0.244$). A Games-Howell post hoc test revealed that there were significant differences (in how many times the image was given an incorrect score by the machine) between any two groups of images in terms of their modeling levels (Table 5.3): The level-2 images (0.4 ± 0.9 times, $p < 0.001$) and level-1 images (1.0 ± 1.6 times, $p < 0.001$) include significantly fewer times of incorrect scoring than the level-0 images (2.6 ± 1.8 times), and the level-2 images include significantly fewer times of incorrect scoring than the level-1 images as well ($p < 0.001$).

Discussion

Deep Learning Has Great Potential to Score Paper–Pencil-Drawn Models

This study makes a contribution to the field by examining the potential of applying deep learning to automatically score paper–pencil-drawn models. While prior research has applied AI in scoring students' drawn models (e.g., Smith et al. 2018; Zhai, He, and Krajcik 2022), few studies have automatically scored paper–pencil-drawn models. We did not provide any computer-based drawing tools to students

Table 5.3 Results of Games-Howell Post Hoc Comparisons

Modeling level (I)	Modeling level (J)	Mean difference (I – J)[a]	Std. error	p
0	1	1.57	0.18	0.000
	2	2.25	0.17	0.000
1	0	−1.57	0.18	0.000
	2	0.69	0.10	0.000
2	0	−2.25	0.17	0.000
	1	−0.69	0.10	0.000

[a] The mean difference is significant at the 0.05 level.

to draw the models. Paper–pencil drawing includes more variations than computer-based drawing due to the complexity of hand drawing, thus increasing the challenges of developing accurate scoring models. Additionally, scanning and processing paper–pencil images may have further introduced more distractors than the digital images generated by computer tools. Despite these challenges, the scoring accuracy from the ten one-time processes of training, validation, and testing reached the mean value of 89.1% (SD = 9%). The overall high values of accuracy show the great potential of the algorithm to produce a high-performing model for the automatic scoring of paper–pencil-drawn models. However, the large variation among the ten results needs to be taken cautiously when applying the model to new datasets. These variations may be due to the small sample size for training.

The result of nested cross-validation—average testing accuracy of 61.9% (SD = 5.2%)—further suggests the limitation of our small sample size. During the one-time process, when the testing dataset was similar to the training dataset by chance, the training process generated models that could predict more accurately on the testing dataset; if not, the testing accuracy may be relatively low. Nested cross-validation reduced the chance effect by including fifty different combinations of the training, validation, and testing sets, and therefore, produced a lower accuracy result than the one-time processes.

While a sample size limitation exists, our future work in this research field may be improved through multiple approaches. First, the current study only focuses on students' drawing responses to one item. Future research could try to improve machine scoring accuracy by including students' responses to the other two items in the analysis. The representations used in these drawings of optical models are highly relevant, so students' drawings for the other optics items are useful data sources for ML algorithms to learn the patterns in their modeling. Including data from more items can potentially help to develop a generic algorithmic model that would perform better on a specific item. On the other hand, adding more items to the analysis can help to triangulate findings from each of the assessment items, thus providing a more accurate measurement of each student's modeling ability. Moreover, future research could explore other ML algorithms, such as (1) transfer learning (i.e., to incorporate part of the ML model that has been well trained with large, open-source dataset) to further improve the performance of the machine scoring, and (2) clustering (i.e., a type of unsupervised ML, which is to group students' drawn models without human labeling in advance) to see whether the patterns learned by unsupervised ML on its own will reveal any of the students' alternative mental models.

Lower Performing Students' Drawn Models Are More Challenging to Automatically Score

Based on the one-way ANOVA, the accuracy of machine scoring for students with higher modeling proficiency is significantly higher than for those with lower proficiency. After reviewing the models at each proficiency level, we found that less proficient students' drawn models involved more errors, which significantly increased the variability of the models. This is reasonable as the closer a student-drawn model is to the ideal model, the less likely it involves variability. On the other hand, a poorly drawn model might include a range of different errors, which would add to the difficulty of automatic scoring. Specifically, with an increase in errors (i.e., distractors) occur, the variability increases, causing machine scoring to have difficulty classifying them into correct categories. We found that the current classifier could not recognize the details critical for determining students' modeling proficiency. To illustrate this, we employed Zhai, He, and Krajcik's (2022) manual match approach by identifying models that look similar, yet some of which were correctly labeled, and the remaining were mislabeled (see Figure 5.8).

Figure 5.8a represents a close-to-ideal modeling of this phenomenon and received the correct score from the machine for all ten times. Figures 5.8b and 5.8c look similar to 5.8a at first glance but are frequently scored incorrectly as level-2 by the machine. All three models employ two lines to represent the light rays from the fish to human eyes, with arrows indicating the correct direction. However, the latter two models contain incorrect representation components. In Figure 5.8b, the left light ray that travels vertically from the fish to the surface of the water should continue its vertical path instead of changing direction to the human eye, which violates the refraction law. Figure 5.8c only includes obscure connections between the fish and the light rays above water, without clear illustration of how light travels from the fish and refracts at the interface between water and air.

Figure 5.8d is scored as level-1 by both humans and the machine, in which there are two solid lines to represent the light paths from the fish to the human eye, no arrows to show the direction of light, and dashed lines to represent the opposite extension

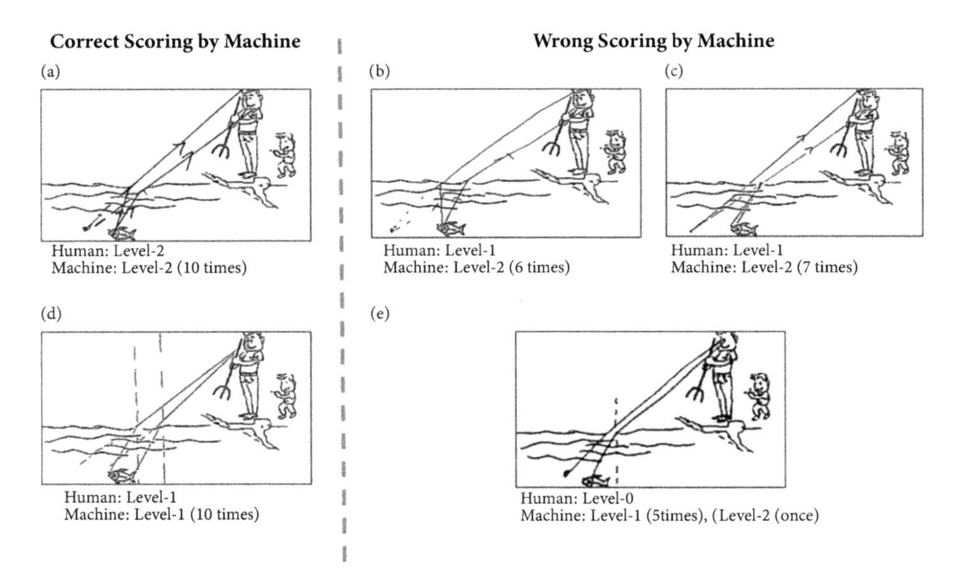

Figure 5.8 Comparison of images that received correct and incorrect scores from the machine.

of the lights above water to show the position of fish in human eyes. Figure 5.8e is similar to 5.8d and received incorrect scores from the machine six times. Yet, the two light paths in Figure 5.8e are independent of each other, and Figure 5.8e does not include the dashed lines as Figure 5.8d does to indicate the position of the fish in human eyes. This model thus cannot explain why the fish in human eyes is above the actual position of the fish.

Since paper–pencil drawing may include unexpected errors, the assessment tasks should be designed and presented in a way that can avoid introducing extra variations without sacrificing the benefits of paper–pencil drawing for assessment. For example, the item can explicitly require students to draw straight lines with a ruler, so that the light rays can be represented more uniformly, making it easier for the machine to recognize them. The printed backgrounds (e.g., two people, and the representation of the river) can also be simplified to reduce the variations introduced by them.

Conclusion

This study is one of the first studies that apply image classification with 2D CNN to automatically score students' paper–pencil-drawn models. Though the average testing accuracy needs improvements, the high accuracy from random dataset split shows the great potential of the approach to score drawn models. Given the additional challenges of scoring paper–pencil-drawn models compared to computer-based drawn models, this study fills in the gap of applying ML to automatically score paper–pencil-drawn models in science education. Our findings suggest that lower-performing students' drawn models introduced more variations, positioning additional challenges for automatic scoring. Future work needs to study further how the drawn model features impact machine scoring accuracy. Research should also investigate how to better design and present assessment tasks to reduce potential variabilities of drawn models to increase the scoring accuracy.

Limitation

Because of the technical challenges, we included images of only one item and no text information as supplementary data, and we trained the automatic assessing system based on a simple categorization into three levels. As ML algorithms learn patterns from data, so typically, a bigger size of dataset will contribute to the scoring accuracy and the generalizability to assessing other kinds of paper–pencil-drawn models. The small sample size in this study (758 images included in the final dataset for training ML model) was a big constraint for the ML algorithm to reach a possibly higher scoring accuracy or to become more generalizable to other models.

References

Altman, D. G. 1991. *Practical statistics for medical research*. London: Chapman and Hall.

Ashmann, S., Anderson, C. W., and Boeckman, H. 2016. "Helping Secondary School Students Develop a Conceptual Understanding of Refraction." *Physics Education* 51, no. 4: 045009.

Brownlee, J. 2021. "Nested Cross-Validation for Machine Learning with Python." Machine Learning Mastery: Making Developers Awesome at Machine Learning. https://machinelearningmastery.com/nested-cross-validation-for-machine-learning-with-python/

Cohen, J. 1968. "Weighted Kappa: Nominal Scale Agreement Provision for Scaled Disagreement or Partial Credit." *Psychological Bulletin* 70, no. 4: 213–20. https://doi.org/10.1037/h0026256

Department of Education. 2017. *High School Physics Curriculum Standards*. Beijing: People's Education Press.

Favale, F., and Bondani, M. 2013, July. "Misconceptions about Optics: An Effect of Misleading Explanations?" In *Education and Training in Optics and Photonics*, EthI4. Washington, DC: Optical Society of America.

Field, A. 2018. *Discovering Statistics Using SPSS*, 5th ed. London: Sage.

Galili, I., and Hazan, A. 2000. "Learners' Knowledge in Optics: Interpretation, Structure and Analysis." *International Journal of Science Education* 22, no. 1: 57–88.

Glynn, S. 1997. "Drawing Mental Models." *The Science Teacher* 64, no. 1: 30–32.

Glynn, S., and Duit, R. 1995. "Learning Science Meaning-Fully: Constructing Conceptual Models." In *Learning Science in the Schools*, edited by S. M. Glynn and R. Duit, 3–34. Mahwah, NJ: Lawrence Erlbaum Associates.

Goodfellow, I., Bengio, Y., and Courville, A. 2016. *Deep Learning*. Cambridge, MA: MIT Press. https://www.deeplearningbook.org/

Hastie, T., Tibshirani, R., and Friedman, J. 2009. *The Elements of Statistical Learning: Data Mining, Inference, and Prediction*. New York: Springer.

John, M., Molepo, J. M., and Chirwa, M. 2018. "Secondary School Learners' Contextualized Knowledge about Reflection and Refraction: A Case Study from South Africa." *Research in Science & Technological Education* 36, no. 2: 131–46.

Kaewkhong, K., Mazzolini, A., Emarat, N., and Arayathanitkul, K. 2010. "Thai High-School Students' Misconceptions about and Models of Light Refraction through a Planar Surface." *Physics Education* 45, no. 1: 97.

Karlberg, C., Henriques, L., and Colburn, A. 2021. "Drawing to Learn to Draw Out Student Understanding." *Science Scope* 44, no. 6: 32–38.

Latour, B. 1990. "Drawing Things Together. In *Representation in Scientific Practice*, edited by M. Lynch and S. Woolgar, 19–68. Cambridge, MA: MIT Press.

Lee, J., Lee, G.-G. and Hong, H.-G. 2023. "Automated Assessment of Student Hand Drawings in Free-Response Items on the Particulate Nature of Matter." *Journal of Science Education and Technology* 32: 549–66. https://doi.org/10.1007/s10956-023-10042-3

Lehrer, R., and Schauble, L. 2006. "Cultivating Model-Based Reasoning in Science Education." In *The Cambridge Handbook of the Learning Sciences*, edited by R. K. Sawyer, 371–88. New York: Cambridge University Press.

Li, T., Liu, F., and Krajcik, J. 2023, June. "Automatically Assess Elementary Students' Hand-Drawn Scientific Models Using Deep Learning of Artificial Intelligence." Presented at the 2023 annual meeting of International Society of Learning Sciences (ISLS), Montreal, Canada.

Mohan, A. 2017. "A Web-Based Application for Automatic Evaluation of Programming Assignments." Master's thesis, University of Nevada, Reno. ScholarWorks, Electronic Theses and Dissertations. http://hdl.handle.net/11714/2079

National Research Council. 2014. "Developing Assessments for the Next Generation Science Standards. Committee on Developing Assessments of Science Proficiency in K-12. Board on Testing and Assessment and Board on Science Education." In *Division of Behavioral and Social Sciences and Education*, edited by J. W. Pellegrino, M. R. Wilson, J. A. Koenig, and A. S. Beatty., pp. 167–70. Washington, DC: The National Academies Press.

Nehm, R. H., Ha, M., and Mayfield, E. 2012. "Transforming Biology Assessment with Machine Learning: Automated Scoring of Written Evolutionary Explanations." *Journal of Science Education and Technology* 21, no. 1: 183–96.

NGSS Lead States. 2013. *Next Generation Science Standards: For States, By States*. Washington, DC: National Academies Press.

Nofziger, M. J. 1995, October. "Optics Curriculum for Middle School Students." In *1995* International Conference on Education in Optics, Vol. 2525, 213–24. Bellingham, WA: International Society for Optics and Photonics.

Pedregosa, F., Varoquaux, G., Gramfort, A., Michel, V., Thirion, B., Grisel, O., Blondel, M., et al. 2011. "Scikit-learn: Machine Learning in Python." *Journal of Machine Learning Research* 12: 2825–30.

Pompea, S. M., Dokter, E. F., Walker, C. E., and Sparks, R. T. 2007, June. "Using Misconceptions Research in the Design of Optics Instructional Materials and Teacher Professional Development Programs." In *Education and Training in Optics and Photonics*, EMC2. Washington, DC: Optical Society of America.

Quillin, K., and Thomas, S. 2015. "Drawing-to-Learn: A Framework for Using Drawings to Promote Model-Based Reasoning in Biology." *CBE Life Sciences Education* 14, no. 1: 1–16. https://doi.org/10.1187/cbe.14-08-0128.

Schwarz, C. V., Reiser, B. J., Davis, E. A., Kenyon, L., Achér, A., Fortus, D., Shwartz, Y., Hug, B., and Krajcik, J. 2009. "Developing a Learning Progression for Scientific Modeling: Making Scientific Modeling Accessible and Meaningful for Learners." *Journal of Research in Science Teaching* 46, no. 6: 632–54. https://doi.org/10.1002/tea.20311

Shen, J., Lei, J., Chang, H., and Namdar, B. 2014. "Technology-Enhanced, Modeling-Based Instruction (TMBI) in Science Education." In *Handbook of Research on Educational Communication and Technology*, edited by J. M. Spector, M. D. Merrill, J. Elen, and M. J. Bishop, 4th ed., 529–40. New York: Springer.

Shen, J., and Confrey, J. 2007. "From Conceptual Change to Transformative Modeling: A Case Study of an Elementary Teacher in Learning Astronomy." *Science Education* 91: 948–66. https://doi.org/10.1002/sce.20224

Smith, A., Leeman-Munk, S., Shelton, A., Mott, B., Wiebe, E., and Lester, J. 2018. "A Multimodal Assessment Framework for Integrating Student Writing and Drawing in Elementary Science Learning." *IEEE Transactions on Learning Technologies* 12, no. 1: 3–15.

Stenning, K., Cox, R., and Oberlander, J. 1995. "Contrasting the Cognitive Effects of Graphical and Sentential Logic Teaching: Reasoning, Representation and Individual Differences." *Language and Cognitive Processes* 10, nos. 3–4: 333–54. https://doi.org/10.1080/01690969508407099

Sung, S. H., Li, C., Chen, G., Huang, X., Xie, C., Massicotte, J., and Shen, J. 2021. "How Does Augmented Observation Facilitate Multimodal Representational Thinking? Applying Deep Learning to Decode Complex Student Construct." *Journal of Science Education and Technology* 30, no. 2: 210–26.

von Davier, M., Tyack, L., and Khorramdel, L. 2022. "Scoring Graphical Responses in TIMSS 2019 Using Artificial Neural Networks." *Educational and Psychological Measurement* 83, no. 3: 556–85.

Wang, C., and Shen, J. 2023. "Technology-Enhanced Collaborative Learning in STEM." In *International Encyclopedia of Education*, 4th ed., edited by R. J. Tierney, F. Rizvi, and K. Ercikan, 207–14. Oxford: Elsevier.

Zhai, X. 2021. "Practices and Theories: How Can Machine Learning Assist in Innovative Assessment Practices in Science Education." *Journal of Science Education and Technology* 30, no. 2: 139–49. https://doi.org/10.1007/s10956-021-09901-8

Zhai, X. 2022. "Assessing High-School Students' Modeling Performance on Newtonian Mechanics." *Journal of Research in Science Teaching* 59, no. 8: 1313–53.

Zhai, X., Haudek, K. C., Shi, L., Nehm, R., and Urban-Lurain, M. 2020b. "From Substitution to Redefinition: A Framework of Machine Learning-Based Science Assessment." *Journal of Research in Science Teaching* 57, no. 9: 1430–59. https://doi.org/10.1002/tea.21658.

Zhai, X., He, P., and Krajcik, J. 2022. "Applying Machine Learning to Automatically Assess Scientific Models." *Journal of Research in Science Teaching* 59, no. 10: 1765–94. https://doi.org/10.1002/tea.21773

Zhai, X., Krajcik, J., and Pellegrino, J. 2021. "On the Validity of Machine Learning-Based Next Generation Science Assessments: A Validity Inferential Network." *Journal of Science Education and Technology* 30, no. 2: 298–312.

Zhai, X., Yin, Y., Pellegrino, J. W., Haudek, K. C., and Shi, L. 2020a. "Applying Machine Learning in Science Assessment: A Systematic Review." *Studies in Science Education* 56, no. 1: 111–51. https://doi.org/10.1080/03057267.2020.1735757.

6
Automated Scoring in Chinese Language for Science Assessments

Mei-Hung Chiu and Mao-Ren Zeng

Introduction

With science learning focusing on integrating disciplinary core ideas, crosscutting concepts, and scientific practice (Ministry of Education in Taiwan 2018; NGSS Lead States 2013), and the assessment paradigm having shifted from summative to formative assessment, there is a need to support such a transformation to match the needs and goals of instruction and curriculum standards in science education (NRC 2014; Zhai et al. 2020b). As science and technology has developed rapidly, one of the artificial intelligence (AI) fields, machine learning (ML), has shown its potential and the impact of its power in various areas, including science education. In particular, there is an increasing number of studies deploying ML in science assessment to monitor, track, and support students' learning in science (Gobert et al. 2013; Lee et al. 2021; Liu et al. 2016; Wang et al. 2021; Zhai et al. 2020a; Zhai, Haudek, and Ma 2022; Zhai, Shi, and Nehm 2021). For instance, Zhai et al. (2020b) reviewed forty-nine articles and found that the majority of the studies used supervised ML to extract attributes from student-written responses and focused on the validity feature that is the examination of the accuracy of ML. The studies include text recognition, classification, and scoring, with an emphasis on the construction of scientific explanations in science. It was evident that many studies reported on human–machine agreements and tried to ensure the accuracy of the analyses. In another systematic meta-analysis of ML-based science assessment, Zhai, Shi, and Nehm (2021) identified the factors contributing to scoring success on 110 studies: algorithm, subject domain, assessment format, construct, school level, and machine supervision type. They found that, for the magnitudes of machine–human score agreements (MHAs), all six factors have significant moderator effects on scoring success magnitudes. Among them, the algorithm and subject domain had more significant effects than the other factors (i.e., type of assessment, construct, school level, and supervision).

Meanwhile, the supervision factor had a minor moderator effect on MHAs, which had always been thought to generate higher MHAs than factors of unsupervised and semi-supervised ML (Zhai et al. 2020b). Based on the supervision ML, Maestrales et al. (2021) state that machine scoring algorithms achieved a scoring accuracy comparable to human raters on the same items. However, the use of formal scientific terminology in student responses would likely reduce machine–human agreements. For instance, students were unfamiliar with formal scientific terminology (e.g.,velocity).

Mei-Hung Chiu and Mao-Ren Zeng, *Automated Scoring in Chinese Language for Science Assessments*. In: *Uses of Artificial Intelligence in STEM Education*. Edited by: Xiaoming Zhai and Joseph Krajcik, Oxford University Press.
 DOI: 10.1093/oso/9780198882077.003.0006

Instead, they used everyday terms (e.g., speed) to express their understanding of phenomena (Maestrales et al. 2021). Thus, well-defined concepts, such as a small number of concepts, narrowly describing concepts, or eliciting distinct concepts in the item, contribute to MHAs (Lottridge, Wood, and Shaw 2018; Zhai, Shi, and Nehm 2021).

Research Purposes and Questions

To be admitted into universities in Taiwan, high school students have to attend national entrance examinations. The examinations are held in January and May, twice a year. Both are high stake events. However, the main format of the examination is multiple-choice questions, which cannot fully discern what students really know and whether they can use the knowledge to explain phenomena or solve science problems. Other forms of assessment, such as open-ended questions, might be a better option for students to express their understanding of science (in a logically sound manner). Yet, it is difficult to analyze Chinese response words automatically due to their implicit expressions and sentence patterns. Consequently, it remains unclear whether automated scoring can grade students' written responses in Chinese as accurately as human graders (Kuo, Li, and Huang 2021; Wang et al. 2021). Moreover, there are different resources of corpus in traditional Chinese and potential differences of common use of terms in simplified and traditional Chinese that might prevent them from accurate scoring when they were used in different scoring systems.

Therefore, the purpose of this study is to explore the possibility of adopting ML in traditional Chinese text-based constructed responses and provide an alternative approach for assessing students' competence in science. Moreover, the realization of assessing students' performance in science learning in Chinese characters will allow school teachers to assess their students and provide feedback based on each individual's needs.

The research purpose of this study is to explore the possibility of automated scoring of Taiwan students' scientific explanations for the phenomena. There are four research questions:

1. What are the accuracies and kappa values of scoring agreements between human and machine scoring?
2. How do ML scoring accuracy and kappa values differ by the ratio between training and testing samples?
3. What are the accuracies and kappa values of scoring in terms of CER?
4. Is there a difference in accuracies of automated scoring between scores based on holistic and analytic rubrics?

Machine Learning-Based Assessment in Science Education

ML-based assessment research has dramatically bloomed over the past decade (Jordan and Mitchell 2015; Krajcik 2021; Luan and Tsai 2021; Maestrales et al. 2021; Zhai 2021; Zhai et al. 2020a). ML has been adopted in the following areas:learning progression (Jescovitch et al. 2021), argumentation and evidence (Lamb, Hand, and Kavner 2021; Lee et al. 2021; Wang et al. 2021; Zhai, Haudek, and Ma 2022), scientific explanations (Huang et al. 2011; Mao et al. 2018), modeling competence (Rosenberg and Krist 2021; Zhai et al. 2020a; Zhai, He, and Krajcik 2022), relations between dropping out from the course and student examination performance prediction (Tomasevic, Gvozdenovic, and Vranes 2020). Among them, eleven of the forty-nine studies examined the effect of using ML in classrooms, and twenty-four studies embedded ML in learning activities, including web-based inquiry, argumentation, and online games. However, only five studies showed the potential of ML as a learning guide for students to revise their scientific explanations (Zhai, Shi, and Nehm 2021). In addition, there is much more research in the area of presenting the effectiveness of automated feedback to support students in revising their scientific arguments and for teachers to compose the instructional guidelines for school practice (Lee et al. 2021; Linn et al. 2014).

With respect to the use of ML in assessing students' performance in the Chinese language, only limited research has been carried out. Wang et al. (2021) scored students' written responses on interpreting data, generating arguments, and making claims in Chinese under an ecological topic developed by the Stanford NGSS Assessment Project. They used LightSIDE, a free platform designed by Carnegie-Mellon University (Mayfield, Adamson, and Rosé 2014), to analyze 4,000 grades 8–10 students' responses. They found that at least 800 human-scored student responses were needed for the training sample to accurately build scoring models. They also found that automated scoring accuracy did not differ substantially by length of response. This claim was consistent with Nehm and Haertig (2012)'s study. However, the languages used in these studies were different. Kuo et al. (2021) used Bidirectional Encoder Representation from Transformers (BERT) developed by Google to diagnose and establish the model of automated scoring for students' Chinese writing. The study investigated Chinese language literacy tests on a total of 1,185 students' writing. The results show that compared to the traditional automated scoring method of latent semantic analysis (LSA; whose overall accuracy rate of expert scoring is 64.73%), using the fine-tuned Google BERT model had better results since the overall accuracy rate (Accuracy) of the ML system and human expert scoring reached 92.07%. Both studies showed the promising potential of automated scoring for students' performance in Chinese despite the fact that the platforms were different.

Scientific Explanations

Encouraging students to apply their understanding of science in authentic contexts, otherwise known as knowledge-in-use, has received ample attention in the past decades. Engaging students in knowledge-in-use learning and providing students with opportunities of generating scientific explanations in science activities have been documented in Framework for K–12 Science Education (NRC 2014) and Next Generation Science Standards (NGSS) (NGSS Lead States 2013; Pellegrino 2014; Zhai, Krajcik, and Pellegrino 2021). In PISA 2015, it examined students' scientific literacy in three aspects (OECD 2017), namely:

(1) Explaining scientific phenomena that requires students to be able to use scientific theories to explain ideas, information, and facts (core content knowledge) and to recognize, offer, and evaluate explanations for a range of natural and technological phenomena;
(2) Interpreting data and evidence scientifically, which requires students to be able to analyze and evaluate data, claims, and arguments in a variety of representations (such as pie charts, bar graphs, scatter plots, or Venn diagrams) and draw appropriate scientific conclusions; and
(3) Evaluating and designing scientific inquiry, which requires students to be able to describe and appraise scientific investigations and propose ways of addressing questions scientifically.

Developing such scientific competence not only encourages students to use scientific evidence to interpret the observed phenomenon (e.g., Jiménez-Aleixandre and Crujeiras (2017)) but also encourages teachers to elicit students' epistemic knowledge and epistemic practice to allow students to build and use their knowledge in decision-making and for creativity and innovation (Cunningham and Kelly 2017; Duschl 2008).

In a series of studies on promoting students' competence in generating explanations in authentic science practices, a group of researchers promoted an educational approach for students to engage in science tasks, which include the use of evidence (E) to support their claims (C) and to generate reasoning (R), components of scientific explanations (with CER as its acronym, McNeill and Krajcik 2008; McNeill et al. 2006; McNeill and Martin 2011). Promising results of students' performance on CER were found. It is a global trend to emphasize cultivating students' competence in generating evidence-based explanations in science curriculum standards (NGSS 2013; Schwarz, Passmore, and Reiser 2017). Therefore, we are investigating students' responses to a scenario in science in terms of their performance on CER.

Methods

Participants

The tests were conducted with 896 students of grades 10–12 in northern Taiwan who had learned some chemistry since grade 8. All the participants were informed about the research purposes and compensated with an honorarium after participation. They were free to withdraw from the tests at any time.

Constructed Response Items

There were three topics tested in this study, namely, solution layers in a test tube, aluminum–air battery, and acid rain. According to the response format of the items and the quality of students' responses, we analyzed and reported on the topic of

Xiao-Min (小明) put two kinds of liquids into a test tube. The two liquids can mix fully with each other. Then, Xiao-Min heated the test tube to observe whether the liquids can react with each other. After heating the liquids, two layers of liquids can be seen in the test tube.

Xiao-Min measured the properties of the liquids and the layers, calculated the densities of the matter, and recorded the data in Table 1.

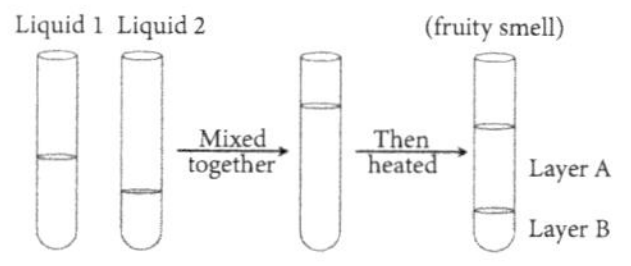

Table 1: Data of sample **before** and **after** heating

State	Sample	Volume	Whether dissolved in water	Smell	Boiling point	Density	Temperature
Before heating	Solution 1	0.45 cm^3	Yes	Alcohol	78.4 °C	0.79 g/L	25 °C
	Solution 2	0.35 cm^3	Yes	Vinegar	118.5 °C	1.05 g/L	25 °C
After heating	Layer 1	0.40 cm^3	No	None	77.1 °C	0.90 g/L	48 °C
	Layer 2	0.30 cm^3	Yes	Fruit	100.0 °C	1.00 g/L	48 °C

Use the data in Table 1 to answer the following two questions:

Question 1: Please illustrate the relationship between whether the reaction occurred or not when Solution 1 and Solution 2 mixed together and the phenomena of the liquids turned into two layers before and after heating.

Question 2: Please illustrate which data in the table can be used as evidence to support your claim and illustrate why you use those data.

Figure 6.1 The NGSA item.

"solution layers in a test tube" taken from the Next Generation Science Assessment (NGSA) (see Figure 6.1). The test item was translated from English into Chinese by a middle school science teacher with a master's degree in science education and back translated by a postdoctoral researcher in science education. Finally, the completeness and correctness of the translation were confirmed by a professor in science education. We also conducted a pilot test with 104 participants in the ninth and twelfth grades to affirm the readability and reliability (the inter-rater reliability, $\alpha > 0.9$) of the item. The items were then inserted into a Google form to allow students to provide their answers to the questions. It was easier to collect and assess hundreds of students' responses digitally than if it were in a paper-and-pencil format.

Procedures

To answer our research questions, we selected an item from NGSA to assess students' competence in providing explanations for a scientific experiment and followed a seven-step framework of ML-based science assessment practice proposed by Zhai, Krajcik, and Pellegrino (2021). The seven steps ranged from identifying target performance expectations, domain analysis, domain modeling, and task and rubric development, to constructing algorithmic models, performance classification, and instructional decision-making. In this study, we used a modified version of the procedure to illustrate how the study was carried out (see Figure 6.2). However, it did not imply that we did not identify the target performance expectations.

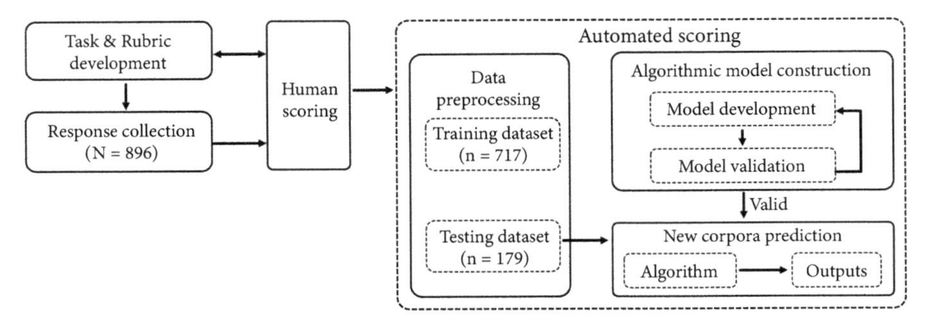

Figure 6.2 A simple modified version of the procedures of this study.

Take the group of training and testing dataset at the ratio of 8:2 as an example; the procedure indicated that we developed task and rubric tools and collected responses from 896 secondary students. Human scoring with three raters was then developed and validated by an algorithmic model with 717 students. The process was iterated until the model was validated. Lastly, 179 students' responses were scored by the validated algorithmic model to test the accuracy of the ML scoring model.

Rubric Development

Two layers of analyses were conducted on students' written responses, namely the holistic analysis and the analytic analysis. The holistic analysis was to consider the overall performance on the test items in relation to chemical reactions. Scores ranging from 0 to 2 were given based upon students' performance responses: for complete responses, including the descriptions of properties of the substances and drawing relevant evidence to support the claim they made, two points were given; for partially correct responses, whether it is providing irrelevant evidence or incomplete claim, one point was given; and for a completely incorrect claim or insufficient evidence, zero points were given (see Table 6.1).

As for the analytic rubric, we adopted CER, proposed by McNeill and Krajcik (2008), as the categories of analysis. For each category, we scored the responses in three levels, similar to the holistic analysis in terms of the correctness of the responses. For instance, for the claim aspect, a student would be scored two points if his/her responses in relation to claim and the claim about chemical reactions were explicitly stated. However, s/he would be scored one point if his/her claim was not explicitly stated but could be inferred from the texts (see Table 6.1).

Human Scoring

The students' responses were scored by three independent coders. The coders are not only science teachers in middle schools but also graduate students in science education. To ensure the coherence and consistency of human scoring, the raters went through iterated rounds of training for calibration. In addition, we used Kendall's *W* to measure the agreement between two or more raters (Corder and Foreman 2009). At the beginning of the training rounds, the first raters introduced the item rubrics

Table 6.1 Rubrics for Holistic and Analytic Analyses

Rubrics	**Level**		
	2	**1**	**0**
Holistic analysis	Response includes ALL of the following criteria: (a) Makes a claim clearly stating that a chemical reaction occurs when the dissolved Liquid 1 and Liquid 2 (the reactants) are mixed to make Layer A and Layer B (products) because they are **different substances.** (b) The **properties of the compounds** can be used to determine whether it is a chemical reaction according to the description of the problem. (c) Provides **evidence by stating patterns in the data** that indicate differences in at least one of the characteristic properties of the reactants and the products (i.e., solubility, odor, boiling point, and density).	Response includes **ONE of the following criteria:** (a) Response includes criteria (a), (b), or (c) listed under "Level 2." (b) Presents **irrelevant evidence** of compound properties. (i.e., volume, temperature, weight)	Response does NOT include any criteria listed under "Level 1."
Analytic analysis			
Claim	The response **clearly indicates** that the reaction is a chemical reaction.	The response does not directly indicate that this reaction is a chemical reaction, but in the following explanation, it can be **inferred** that a chemical reaction has occurred.	The response indicates that the reaction is **not a** chemical reaction
Evidence	Provides the **correct evidence**.	Provides **irrelevant** evidence (e.g., volume, temperature, mass, weight).	With no supporting evidence.
Reasoning	Presents a complete **generalized narrative:** (a) Chemical reactions can produce new compounds. (b) Different compounds have different properties.	**Repeatedly** mentions that changes in solubility, odor, boiling point, or density are indicative of chemical reactions.	**No reasoning statements** are provided

to the other raters. Next, the raters were trained with a random subset of thirty students' responses. Based on the scores assigned to the students' responses, the raters discussed and slightly revised the rubrics to reach a consensual score. Lastly, they scored an additional subset of sixty students' responses until Kendall's $W > 0.8$. After the training rounds, the raters independently scored students' responses. In other words, each student received one score for the holistic analysis and three scores for the analytic analysis. The inter-rater reliability was as follows: $W = 0.83$ for the holistic rubric, $W = 0.81$ for the analytic rubric of claim, $W = 0.93$ for the analytic rubric of evidence, and $W = 0.87$ for the analytic rubric of reasoning.

The Process of Automated Scoring

We conducted the data analysis with LightSIDE, an open-source platform, including the machine-learning and feature-extraction core as well as the researcher's workbench, which has been and continues to be funded in part through Carnegie Mellon University, in particular by grants from the National Science Foundation and the Office of Naval Research (Mayfield, Adamson, and Rosé 2014). However, we ran into challenges in extracting Chinese features in LightSIDE, and then we used the local developers' Chinese Knowledge and Information Processing (CKIP) system to segment and find the appropriate synonyms recorded in the database. For instance, the following example shows the differences between the two systems, suggesting that CKIP fits our needs much better than LightSIDE (see Figure 6.3). Moreover, we followed the user manual of LightSIDE (Mayfield, Adamson, and Rosé 2014), and the options from related research using LightSIDE (Jescovitch et al. 2021; Wang et al. 2021) to apply automated scoring in the Chinese language for science assessments. Therefore, we divided the process into three stages, namely data preprocessing, algorithmic model construction, and new corpora prediction.

Data Preprocessing

The first stage is data preprocessing. We had to organize the students' responses into Excel files for ML. For instance, we checked the response for typos and arranged the synonyms of keywords (e.g., smell, odor, and flavor). To improve the problem of Chinese word segmenting, we used the CKIP Tagger to segment all the responses in the tokens and checked whether those tokens were meaningful. In accordance with the research purpose, we split the training and testing datasets by different ratios (9:1, 8:2, 7:3, etc.) on a random basis to explore the possibility and the sample size of automated scoring.

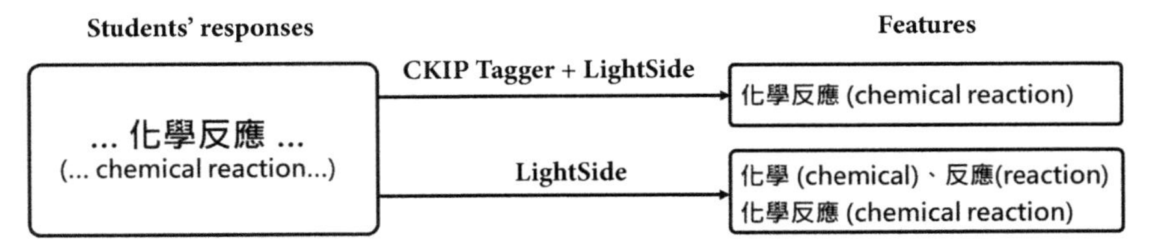

Figure 6.3 The comparison of features between CKIP and LightSIDE.

Constructing Algorithmic Model

We imported the training dataset into LightSIDE to extract features in the build model stage. Then we filtered the meaningless words, numbers, and punctuations. After extracting features, we used the decision tree algorithm (Wang et al. 2021) and the tenfold cross-validation process (Jescovitch et al. 2021) to build the algorithm model. Furthermore, we calculated the machine–human scoring agreement of the training dataset and used accuracy as the major indicator for model evaluation. If the accuracy is ≥ 0.80, we would keep the applicable algorithmic model and carry on to the next stage. In other words, we would revise the features if the accuracy is < 0.80. Based on the user manual of LightSIDE, we could reserve the particular features which were the keywords in the rubrics or combine similar meaning features as new features. To explore the possibility of automated scoring, we would revise and accept the highest accuracy of the algorithmic model ten times when the accuracy was still less than 0.80. However, we would also pay special attention to the overfitting of the training dataset when we revised the features.

Predicting New Corpora

Lastly, we imported the testing dataset into LightSIDE and used the applicable algorithmic model to predict labels. In addition to exporting the file with the predicted labels, we computed the accuracy, Cohen's kappa, and the 95% confidence interval of the testing dataset. To reduce potential problems with sampling (Zhai, He, and Krajcik 2022), we repeated the process five times for each group of the training and testing datasets.

Machine–Human Scoring Agreement

Zhai, Shi, and Nehm (2021) consider that the machine–human scoring agreement (MHA) presents the validity of the ML. In other words, we can compare the difference in scoring between machine and human consent scores to measure the quality of the machine algorithmic model. Therefore, there are many statistical methods to calculate MHA in science assessments, and each statistical method presents different properties and limitations (Zhai et al. 2020). We used the accuracy and the weighted Cohen's kappa as the MHA in this study. The accuracy indicated the percentage of correct predictions among all responses by the machine algorithmic model. Take the groups of training and testing datasets at the ratio of 8:2; for example, the accuracy of the training dataset was 0.83. After that, we used the machine algorithmic model to predict the testing dataset, and the accuracy was 0.83. The result showed that the training and testing datasets were similar and the machine algorithmic model presents good quality accuracy.

However, the accuracy only focuses on the correct prediction that includes guessing (i.e., chance agreements between machine and humans) but does not provide the complete performance among classifiers, especially in polytomous scoring (Zhai, Shi, and Nehm 2021). Cohen's kappa compares the observed accuracy with an expected accuracy to exclude chance agreement. Therefore, Cohen's kappa not only presents the complete performance among classifiers but also reduces misleading accuracy. In addition, we interpret Cohen's kappa of MHA as follows: 0.41–0.60 as moderate agreement, 0.61–0.80 as strong agreement, and 0.81–1.00 as almost perfect agreement (Nehm, Ha, and Mayfield 2012).

Results

According to Zhai, Shi, and Nehm (2021), MHA indicates the effect of automated scoring among different factors such as rubrics and training sample size. In the results that follow, we provide the accuracy and the weighted Cohen's kappa to present the MHA and address each of our research questions. First, we computed the MHA of holistic rubrics to confirm the possibility of applying the automated scoring of science assessment in the Chinese language. Second, we ensured the threshold for the ratio of training to testing datasets with the holistic rubric. Last, we compared the effectiveness of automated scoring between holistic and analytic rubrics.

The Effect of Holistic Rubric on Machine–Human Scoring Agreement

To address research question 1, we divided the data into ten groups to develop the algorithmic model. The ratios between training and testing datasets were 9:1, 8:2, 7:3, 6:4, 5:5, 4:6, 3:7, 2:8, and 1:9. Table 6.2 presents the accuracies that range from 0.74 to 0.84 for the training dataset and from 0.76 to 0.83 for the testing dataset. The results indicate that most of the groups performed well with accuracies above 0.8, but there are three groups (group G, H, and I) with less than 0.8 in the training dataset. Although the accuracies of the testing dataset are greater than the training dataset in

Table 6.2 The Accuracy and Weighted Cohen's Kappa of Holistic Rubric

Group	The ratio of dataset[a]	Training dataset		Testing dataset	
		Accuracy[b]	k^c	Accuracy[b]	k^c
A	9:1	0.84 (0.83–0.84)	0.73 (0.71–0.74)	0.82 (0.78–0.85)	0.72 (0.66–0.79)
B	8:2	0.83 (0.83–0.84)	0.72 (0.70–0.73)	0.83 (0.79–0.87)	0.72 (0.63–0.80)
C	7:3	0.83 (0.82–0.84)	0.71 (0.69–0.73)	0.83 (0.81–0.86)	0.73 (0.68–0.77)
D	6:4	0.81 (0.79–0.83)	0.68 (0.63–0.73)	0.83 (0.80–0.86)	0.71 (0.66–0.76)
E	5:5	0.82 (0.79–0.84)	0.70 (0.65–0.74)	0.83 (0.81–0.85)	0.72 (0.68–0.75)
F	4:6	0.81 (0.78–0.83)	0.68 (0.64–0.73)	0.82 (0.81–0.83)	0.70 (0.67–0.72)
G	3:7	0.79 (0.75–0.82)	0.65 (0.59–0.71)	0.81 (0.79–0.83)	0.68 (0.64–0.72)
H	2:8	0.75 (0.72–0.79)	0.58 (0.51–0.65)	0.77 (0.76–0.79)	0.62 (0.59–0.65)
I	1:9	0.74 (0.70–0.77)	0.56 (0.50–0.63)	0.76 (0.75–0.77)	0.60 (0.58–0.62)

[a] The ratio of training dataset to testing dataset.
[b] Accuracy (95% CI).
[c] Weighted Cohen's kappa (95% CI).

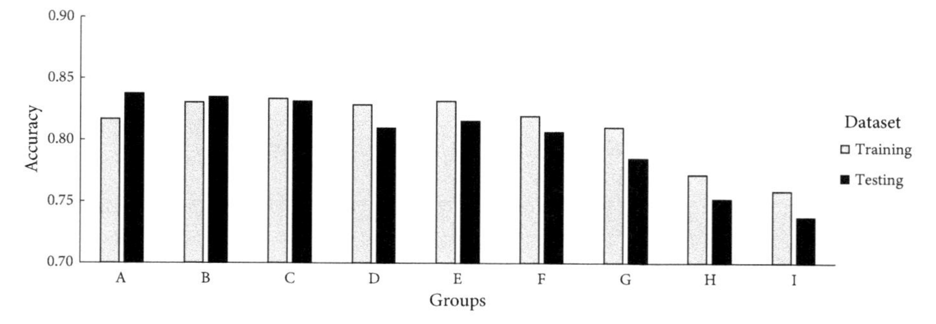

Figure 6.4 The accuracies of holistic rubric among the groups.

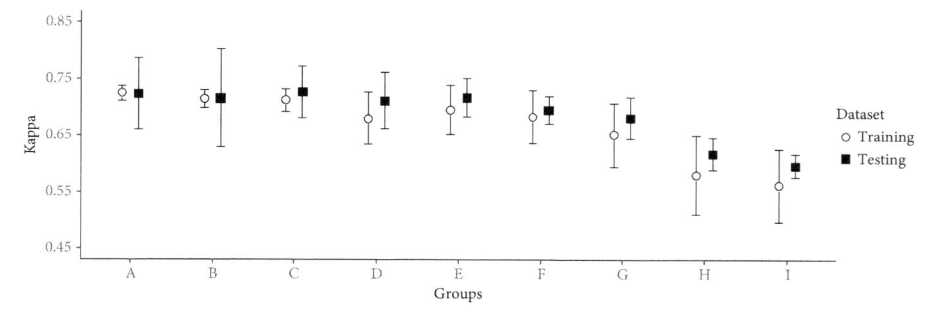

Figure 6.5 The weight Cohen's kappa of holistic rubric among the groups.

several groups (from groups C to I), there is no significant difference between the training and testing datasets (see Figure 6.4).

On the other hand, we compute the weighted Cohen's kappa from the confusion matrix. Except for groups I and H (1:9 and 2:8), the weighted Cohen's kappa for most of the groups is above 0.6, which is a strong agreement based on Nehm, Ha, and Mayfield (2012) (see Figure 6.5). Overall, the results suggest that automated scoring can apply to the holistic rubric of science assessment in the Chinese language.

The Ratio of Dataset Training to Testing Dataset with Holistic Rubric

As mentioned earlier, we split the responses into ten sub-datasets and reorganized them randomly. Taking group B as an example, eight of the ten sub-datasets were used as the training dataset to construct and validate the algorithmic model. After that, the remaining two sub-datasets were used as the testing dataset to predict the scores using the validated algorithmic model. In this way, we computed the accuracy and the weighted Cohen's kappa to ensure the threshold for the ratio of a dataset.

In Table 6.2, we found the pattern of the accuracy and the weighted Cohen's kappa that the smaller the size of the training dataset, the weaker the MHA of the testing dataset performed. Moreover, the training and testing data presented similar accuracy as the weighted Cohen's kappa in the group. According to the criteria and the stability of MHA, the results showed that three ratios of datasets were acceptable (9:1, 8:2, and 7:3). In other words, we can confidently use the automated scoring in the Chinese language for science assessments when we train the applicable algorithmic model by the training dataset.

The Effectiveness of Automated Scoring between Holistic and Analytic Rubrics

To compare the effectiveness of automated scoring with holistic and analytic rubrics, we asked the raters to score the students' responses with the two rubrics, and constructed the algorithmic models with the same procedure. Therefore, we also used MHA as an indicator to present the quality of the analytic rubric and showed the effectiveness of the two rubrics.

The Effect of Analytic Rubric on Machine–Human Scoring Agreement

To address research question 3, we coded the responses based on the three aspects of CER mentioned previously. Table 6.3 presents the MHAs of claim, evidence, and reasoning by group. Among the analytic categories, the accuracies perform well on the claim (0.88–0.90) and evidence (0.87–0.91). According to the content of analytic rubrics, there are precise keywords in the claim and evidence, such as weight, boiling point, and flavor. However, students need to provide a complete statement; e.g., the chemical reactions can produce new compounds. The semantics-based features may cause slight differences among the analytic categories.

Furthermore, we also computed the weighted Cohen's kappa and presented it in Table 6.3. The results indicate that all of the weighted Cohen's kappa were not only above 0.6 in the training and testing dataset but also close to 0.8. Therefore, the results suggest that we use the analytic rubric to construct the algorithmic model and have a strong agreement between machines and humans. Overall, automated scoring for each category fits well with the model, and it is evident that ML could be applied to analyzing analytic scoring of science assessments in the Chinese language (see Figure 6.6 and Figure 6.7).

The Effectiveness of Automated Scoring between Holistic and Analytic Rubrics

According to the MHA of the holistic and analytic rubrics, we would say that automated scoring can be applied in the Chinese language for science assessments. Furthermore, we compared the effectiveness of holistic and analytic rubrics based on the rater reliability and the MHA. We computed the rater reliability with Kendall's W, and the analytic category of evidence had an almost perfect agreement ($W = 0.93$). Moreover, the algorithmic model trained with the analytic rubric performed well on the accuracy and the weighted Cohen's kappa. Taking group A (the ratio of 9:1) as an example, the mean of accuracy is 0.88 for the analytic rubric on the testing dataset and is better than the holistic rubric (0.82). Similarly, the weighted Cohen's kappa of the analytic rubric ranges from 0.76 to 0.82 and shows a higher value of 0.07 than the holistic rubric. In summary, the results show that the accuracies and weighted

Table 6.3 The Accuracy and the Weighted Cohen's Kappa of Analytic Rubric

Dataset	Claim		Evidence		Reasoning	
	Accuracy[a]	k^b	Accuracy[a]	k^b	Accuracy[a]	k^b
Training						
Group A	0.88 (0.88–0.89)	0.79 (0.78–0.81)	0.91 (0.91–0.92)	0.81 (0.80–0.82)	0.85 (0.85–0.86)	0.77 (0.77–0.78)
Group B	0.88 (0.87–0.89)	0.79 (0.78–0.80)	0.90 (0.90–0.91)	0.79 (0.78–0.80)	0.85 (0.85–0.86)	0.77 (0.77–0.78)
Group E	0.88 (0.87–0.89)	0.79 (0.78–0.81)	0.90 (0.89–0.92)	0.79 (0.76–0.82)	0.86 (0.84–0.87)	0.78 (0.76–0.80)
Group H	0.88 (0.84–0.91)	0.79 (0.73–0.84)	0.87 (0.85–0.90)	0.72 (0.67–0.76)	0.83 (0.80–0.86)	0.73 (0.68–0.77)
Testing						
Group A	0.90 (0.87–0.93)	0.82 (0.78–0.87)	0.89 (0.85–0.93)	0.76 (0.65–0.87)	0.86 (0.84–0.88)	0.79 (0.77–0.82)
Group B	0.89 (0.87–0.91)	0.80 (0.77–0.83)	0.89 (0.88–0.91)	0.76 (0.72–0.81)	0.85 (0.84–0.87)	0.78 (0.76–0.80)
Group E	0.89 (0.88–0.89)	0.79 (0.78–0.81)	0.90 (0.88–0.92)	0.78 (0.75–0.82)	0.85 (0.84–0.87)	0.77 (0.74–0.79)
Group H	0.89 (0.88–0.89)	0.80 (0.79–0.81)	0.89 (0.88–0.90)	0.76 (0.74–0.79)	0.85 (0.82–0.88)	0.76 (0.71–0.82)

[a] Accuracy (95% CI).
[b] Weighted Cohen's kappa (95% CI).

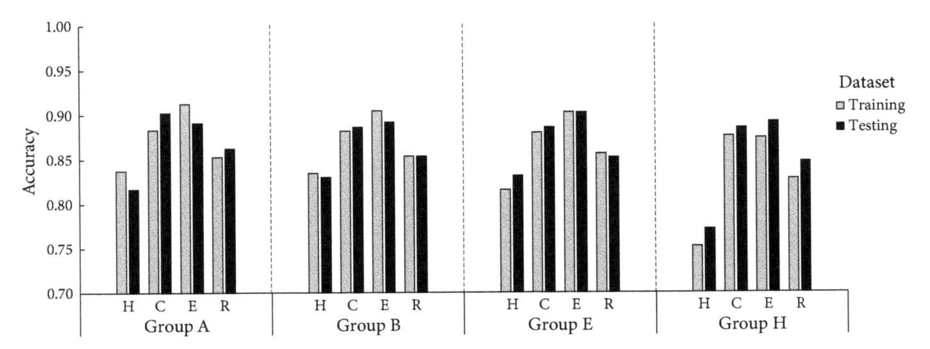

Figure 6.6 The accuracy of holistic and analytic rubrics among the groups.

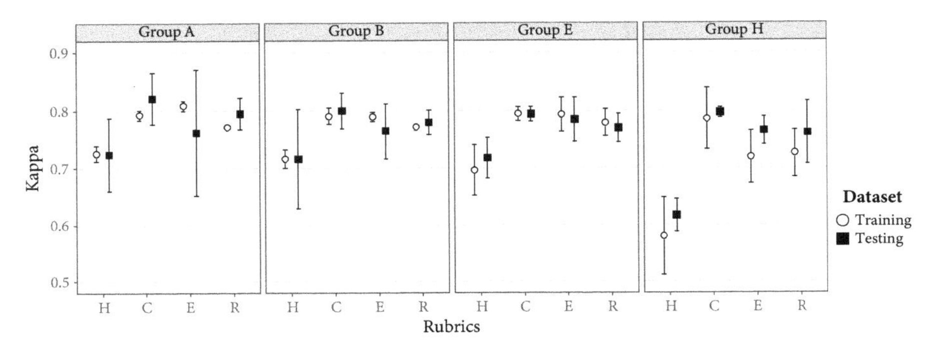

Figure 6.7 The weight Cohen's kappa of holistic and analytic rubrics among the groups.

Cohen's kappa of the analytic rubrics (claim, evidence, and reasoning) perform better than the holistic rubric (see Figure 6.6).

Conclusions

Educational research has put a lot of effort into understanding the learning characteristics and processes to support an optimal environment for learning. Several functions of ML could support school instruction to achieve educational purposes and match individual needs via automated scoring of students' performance. For instance, it can obtain an accurate understanding of the learner's unique individual needs through diagnosis and provide the necessary individualized scaffolding instruction to enhance his/her learning outcomes (Luan and Tsai 2021); it could also be employed in students' examination performance prediction and provide specific assistance (Tomasevic, Gvozdenovic, and Vranes 2020). More importantly, as expected, science learning that deals with complex and abstract contents in science, such as physics and chemistry, will lower MHA (Zhai, Shi, and Nehm 2021). ML has shown potential in the analysis of various tasks of assessment, such as complex, diverse, and structural constructs in authentic tasks, and of course, in reducing time-consuming human-grading efforts (Zhai et al. 2020a), alleviating teachers' grading burden and encouraging school teachers to employ ML in formative assessments in school practices.

From the Chinese language perspective, the research showed two major challenges for Chinese word segmentation (Ma and Chen 2004). One is clarifying the ambiguous segmentation such as 化學反應 (see the example in Figure 6.3). The other is identifying unknown words which do not exist in the corpus. To perform well in Chinese word segmentation, the researchers not only developed the specific rules and the matching algorithm (Sproat and Emerson 2003) but also built the corpus of the Chinese language (Xue et al. 2005). Therefore, we used the CKIP Tagger, which was developed based on the traditional Chinese corpora, to enhance word segmentation accuracy.

In our study, we found that the accuracies and weighted kappa values of the analytic rubrics (i.e., claim, evidence, and reasoning) outperformed those of the holistic rubrics. The automated scoring is suitable for science assessment in the Chinese language and can be used as a reference value for the development of relevant assessments. Although we are concerned that the lengths of students' responses were not long enough for such analyses, it was revealed that it was not a big issue in obtaining high accuracy and relatively satisfactory kappa values. This finding was consistent with Wang et al. (2021), who also found that the automated scoring accuracy did not differ substantially by student response lengths and did not significantly moderate MHA (Nehm and Haertig 2012). However, one must note that the length of student responses has weak relations with MHA (Liu et al. 2016). With the promising results from our study, as well as others, however, we still see many challenges in adapting ML in analyzing students' responses in the Chinese language due to the manner of their expressions and the implicit nature of the language. Moreover, students' alternative or incomplete expressions, confusing labels, and redundant information (Zhai, He, and Krajcik 2022) might over- or underestimate students' performance on the task. Finally, the most important challenges are to support teachers' formative assessment via the use of such automated scoring in school teaching and to adopt it for students with different background knowledge and needs. Further research is needed to overcome these challenges.

Acknowledgments

This study is supported by Ministry of Science and Technology, Taiwan, under Grant MOST108-2511-H-003-011-MY3. The authors would like to thank Joe Krajcik, Xiaoming Zhai, and Peng He for their assistance in the early stages of this study and are also grateful to all the students and teachers who participated in this study.

References

Corder, G. W., and Foreman, D. I. 2009. Nonparametric Statistics for Non-statisticians: *A Step-by-Step Approach*. Chichester, UK: Wiley.

Cunningham, C. M., and Kelly, G. J. 2017. "Epistemic Practices of Engineering for Education." *Science Education* 101, no. 3: 486–505. https://doi.org/10.1002/sce.21271

Duschl, R. 2008. "Science Education in Three-Part Harmony: Balancing Conceptual, Epistemic, and Social Learning Goals." *Review of Research in Education* 32, no. 1: 268–91. https://doi.org/10.3102/0091732x07309371

Gobert, J. D., Sao Pedro, M., Raziuddin, J., and Baker, R. S. 2013. "From Log Files to Assessment Metrics: Measuring Students' Science Inquiry Skills Using Educational Data Mining." *Journal of the Learning Sciences* 22, no. 4: 521–63. https://doi.org/10.1080/10508406.2013.837391

Huang, C.-J., Wang, Y.-W., Huang, T.-H., Chen, Y.-C., Chen, H.-M., and Chang, S.-C. 2011. "Performance Evaluation of an Online Argumentation Learning Assistance Agent." *Computers & Education* 57, no. 1: 1270–80.

Jescovitch, L. N., Scott, E. E., Cerchiara, J. A., Merrill, J., Urban-Lurain, M., Doherty, J. H., and Haudek, K. C. 2021. "Comparison of Machine Learning Performance Using Analytic and Holistic Coding Approaches across Constructed Response Assessments Aligned to a Science Learning Progression." *Journal of Science Education and Technology* 30, no. 2: 150–67. https://doi.org/10.1007/s10956-020-09858-0

Jiménez-Aleixandre, M. P., and Crujeiras, B. 2017. "Epistemic Practices and Scientific Practices in Science Education." In *Science Education: An International Course Companion*, edited by K. S. Taber and B. Akpan, 69–80. Rotterdam: Sense Publishers. https://doi.org/10.1007/978-94-6300-749-8_5

Jordan, M. I., and Mitchell, T. M. 2015. "Machine Learning: Trends, Perspectives, and Prospects." *Science* 349, no. 6245: 255–60. https://doi.org/10.1126/science.aaa8415

Krajcik, J. S. 2021. "Commentary-Applying Machine Learning in Science Assessment: Opportunity and Challenges." *Journal of Science Education and Technology* 30, no. 2: 313–18. https://doi.org/10.1007/s10956-021-09902-7

Kuo, B. C., Li, C. H., and Huang, C. Y. 2021. "Applying Google BERT to Enhance the Correct Rate of Automatic Scoring in Chinese Writing." *Psychological Testing* 68, no. 1: 53–74.

Lamb, R., Hand, B., and Kavner, A. 2021. "Computational Modeling of the Effects of the Science Writing Heuristic on Student Critical Thinking in Science Using Machine Learning." *Journal of Science Education and Technology* 30, no. 2: 283–97. https://doi.org/10.1007/s10956-020-09871-3

Lee, H.-S., Gweon, G.-H., Lord, T., Paessel, N., Pallant, A., and Pryputniewicz, S. 2021. "Machine Learning-Enabled Automated Feedback: Supporting Students' Revision of Scientific Arguments Based on Data Drawn from Simulation." *Journal of Science Education and Technology* 30, no. 2: 168–92. https://doi.org/10.1007/s10956-020-09889-7

Linn, M. C., Gerard, L., Ryoo, K., McElhaney, K., Liu, O. L., and Rafferty, A. N. 2014. "Computer-Guided Inquiry to Improve Science Learning." *Science* 344, no. 6180: 155–56. https://doi.org/10.1126/science.1245980

Liu, O. L., Rios, J. A., Heilman, M., Gerard, L., and Linn, M. C. 2016. "Validation of Automated Scoring of Science Assessments." *Journal of Research in Science Teaching* 53, no. 2: 215–33. https://doi.org/10.1002/tea.21299

Lottridge, S., Wood, S., and Shaw, D. 2018. "The Effectiveness of Machine Score-Ability Ratings in Predicting Automated Scoring Performance." *Applied Measurement in Education* 31, no. 3: 215–32. https://doi.org/10.1080/08957347.2018.1464452

Luan, H., and Tsai, C.-C. 2021. "A Review of Using Machine Learning Approaches for Precision Education." *Educational Technology & Society* 24, no. 1: 250–66. https://www.jstor.org/stable/26977871

Ma, W. Y., and Chen, K. J. 2004. "Design of CKIP Chinese Word Segmentation System." *Chinese and Oriental Languages Information Processing Society* 14, no. 3: 235–49.

Maestrales, S., Zhai, X., Touitou, I., Baker, Q., Schneider, B., and Krajcik, J. 2021. "Using Machine Learning to Score Multi-dimensional Assessments of Chemistry and Physics." *Journal of Science Education and Technology* 30, no. 2: 239–54. https://doi.org/10.1007/s10956-020-09895-9

Mao, L., Liu, O. L., Roohr, K., Belur, V., Mulholland, M., Lee, H.-S., and Pallant, A. 2018. "Validation of Automated Scoring for a Formative Assessment That Employs Scientific Argumentation." *Educational Assessment* 23, no. 2: 121–38.

Mayfield, E., Adamson, D., and Rosé, C. 2014. *LightSide Researcher's Workbench User Manual.* Retrieved November 12, 2015.

McNeill, K. L., and Krajcik, J. 2008. "Scientific Explanations: Characterizing and Evaluating the Effects of Teachers' Instructional Practices on Student Learning." *Journal of Research in Science Teaching* 45, no. 1: 53–78. https://doi.org/10.1002/tea.20201

McNeill, K. L., Lizotte, D. J., Krajcik, J., and Marx, R. W. 2006. "Supporting Students' Construction of Scientific Explanations by Fading Scaffolds in Instructional Materials." *Journal of the Learning Sciences* 15, no. 2: 153–91. https://doi.org/10.1207/s15327809jls1502_1

McNeill, K. L., and Martin, D. M. 2011. "Claims, Evidence, and Reasoning." *Science and Children* 48, no. 8: 52–56. http://www.jstor.org/stable/43176206

Ministry of Education in Taiwan. 2018. Curriculum Guidelines of 12-year Basic Education for Elementary, Junior High Schools and General Senior High Schools—Natural Sciences. https://www.naer.edu.tw/eng/PageSyllabus?fid=148

National Research Council (NRC). 2014. *Developing Assessments for the Next Generation Science Standards.* Washington, DC: The National Academies Press. https://doi.org/10.17226/18409.

Nehm, R. H., Ha, M., and Mayfield, E. 2012. "Transforming Biology Assessment with Machine Learning: Automated Scoring of Written Evolutionary Explanations." *Journal of Science Education and Technology* 21, no. 1: 183–96. https://doi.org/10.1007/s10956-011-9300-9

Nehm, R. H., and Haertig, H. 2012. "Human vs. Computer Diagnosis of Students' Natural Selection Knowledge: Testing the Efficacy of Text Analytic Software." *Journal of Science Education and Technology* 21, no. 1: 56–73. https://doi.org/10.1007/s10956-011-9282-7

NGSS Lead States. 2013. *Next Generation Science Standards: For States, By States.* Washington, DC: National Academies Press. https://doi.org/doi:10.17226/18290

OECD. 2017. *PISA for Development Assessment and Analytical Framework: Reading, Mathematics and Science, Preliminary Version.* Paris: OECD Publishing.

Pellegrino, J. W. 2014. "A Learning Sciences Perspective on the Design and Use of Assessment in Education." In *The Cambridge Handbook of the Learning Sciences*, 2nd ed., edited by R. K. Sawyer, 233–52. Cambridge: Cambridge University Press. https://doi.org/10.1017/CBO9781139519526.015.

Rosenberg, J. M., and Krist, C. 2021. "Combining Machine Learning and Qualitative Methods to Elaborate Students' Ideas about the Generality of Their Model-Based Explanations." *Journal of Science Education and Technology* 30, no. 2: 255–67. https://doi.org/10.1007/s10956-020-09862-4

Schwarz, C. V., Passmore, C., and Reiser, B. J. 2017. *Helping Students Make Sense of the World Using Next Generation Science and Engineering Practices.* Richmond, VA: NSTA Press.

Sproat, R., and Emerson, T. 2003. "The First International Chinese Word Segmentation Bakeoff." In *Proceedings of the Second SIGHAN Workshop on Chinese Language Processing, Sapporo, Japan*, 133–43. Association for Computational Linguistics.

Tomasevic, N., Gvozdenovic, N., and Vranes, S. 2020. "An Overview and Comparison of Supervised Data Mining Techniques for Student Exam Performance Prediction." *Computers & Education* 143: 103676. https://doi.org/10.1016/jcompedu.2019.103676

Wang, C., Liu, X., Wang, L., Sun, Y., and Zhang, H. 2021. "Automated Scoring of Chinese Grades 7–9 Students' Competence in Interpreting and Arguing from Evidence." *Journal of Science Education and Technology* 30, no. 2: 269–82. https://doi.org/10.1007/s10956-020-09859-z

Xue, N., Xia, F., Chiou, F. D., and Palmer, M. 2005. "The Penn Chinese Treebank: Phrase Structure Annotation of a Large Corpus." *Natural Language Engineering* 11, no. 2: 207–38. https://doi.org/10.1017/S135132490400364X

Zhai, X. 2021. "Practices and Theories: How Can Machine Learning Assist in Innovative Assessment Practices in Science Education." *Journal of Science Education and Technology* 30, no. 2: 139–49. https://doi.org/10.1007/s10956-021-09901-8

Zhai, X., Haudek, K., and Ma, W. 2022. "Assessing Argumentation Using Machine Learning and Cognitive Diagnostic Modeling." *Research in Science Education* 53: 405–24. https://doi.org/10.1007/s11165-022-10062-w

Zhai, X., Haudek, K., Shi, L., Nehm, R., and Urban-Lurain, M. 2020a. "From Substitution to Redefinition: A Framework of Machine Learning-Based Science Assessment." *Journal of Research in Science Teaching* 57, no. 9: 1430–59. https://doi.org/10.1002/tea.21658

Zhai, X., He, P., and Krajcik, J. 2022. "Applying Machine Learning to Automatically Assess Scientific Models." *Journal of Research in Science Teaching* 59: 1765–94. https://doi.org/10.1002/tea.21773
Zhai, X., Krajcik, J., and Pellegrino, J. W. 2021. "On the Validity of Machine Learning-Based Next Generation Science Assessments: A Validity Inferential Network." *Journal of Science Education and Technology* 30, no. 2: 298–312. https://doi.org/10.1007/s10956-020-09879-9
Zhai, X., Shi, L., and Nehm, R. H. 2021. "A Meta-analysis of Machine Learning-Based Science Assessments: Factors Impacting Machine-Human Score Agreements." *Journal of Science Education and Technology* 30, no. 3: 361–79. https://doi.org/10.1007/s10956-020-09875-z
Zhai, X., Yin, Y., Pellegrino, J. W., Haudek, K. C., and Shi, L. 2020b. "Applying Machine Learning in Science Assessment: A Systematic Review." *Studies in Science Education* 56, no. 1: 111–51. https://doi.org/10.1080/03057267.2020.1735757.

7

Exploring Attributes of Successful Machine Learning Assessments for Scoring of Undergraduate Constructed Response Assessment Items

Megan Shiroda, Jennifer Doherty and Kevin C. Haudek

Introduction

Calls from national organizations including the American Association for the Advancement of Science and the National Research Council have advocated for refocusing science education to core concepts and scientific skills (AAAS 2011; NRC 2012). With this call, there has been a push for more authentic assessment practices that measure knowledge-in-use, such as constructed response assessments, as they provide better insight into student thinking (Krajick 2021). Indeed, constructed response assessments have been found to increase teacher insight about student learning, allowing them to adjust teaching strategies to achieve learning outcomes (Gerard and Linn 2016). Unfortunately, this method of assessment has a heavier time burden for evaluation than multiple-choice assessments, making it difficult to implement in the large classes commonly found in introductory college STEM courses. Machine learning (ML) has increased the use of authentic formative assessments in STEM by automating the process of evaluation and feedback using text classification computer scoring models (CSMs). Such CSMs use natural language processing and ML to classify responses into categories and have been used in a variety of classrooms for short text, concept-based assessments, including biology (Ha et al. 2011; Jescovitch et al. 2020; Sieke et al. 2019), chemistry (Dood et al. 2020; Noyes et al. 2020), physics (Çınar et al. 2020; Maestrales et al. 2021), and statistics (Kaplan et al. 2014). Text classification CSMs have also been used in education research studies to assess student learning at large scales, which would be difficult using only human scoring approaches (Pelletreau et al. 2016; Uhl et al. 2021). While the creation of text classification CSMs for a variety of topics and disciplines has been successful (reviewed in Zhai et al. 2020b; Zhai, Shi, and Nehm 2021), the development process is still time and effort intensive, as both the assessment items and CSMs typically require multiple rounds of development and revision (Kaplan et al. 2014; Urban-Lurain et al. 2015). The human involvement during the development of CSMs, especially in supervised

Megan Shiroda et al., *Exploring Attributes of Successful Machine Learning Assessments for Scoring of Undergraduate Constructed Response Assessment Items*. In: *Uses of Artificial Intelligence in STEM Education*. Edited by: Xiaoming Zhai and Joseph Krajcik, Oxford University Press. © Oxford University Press (2024). DOI: 10.1093/oso/9780198882077.003.0007

ML applications, is still a significant barrier and impedes the expansion of this use of ML in science education (Zhai et al. 2020b). Further, a given CSM is unique to the concept or topic being assessed, meaning they usually have limited generalizability for new item contexts (Brew and Leacock 2013; McGraw-Hill Education 2014). These barriers limit the concepts and contexts that can be assessed using constructed responses and thereby restrict teachers and researchers in their use of constructed response assessments. The challenge of producing additional assessment items and CSMs may be addressed by artificial intelligence (AI) methods. AI may be useful in determining features of assessment items and/or technical features of CSMs that lead to successful CSM development or may be able to identify problematic steps in a design process. By reducing the number of iterations and/or time spent in development of CSMs, AI may enhance the creation or accuracy of CSMs.

The difficulty in CSM development could in part be due to the number of variables that can affect computer scoring success, including examinee, machine, technical, and assessment features (Lottridge, Wood, and Shaw 2018; Zhai, Shi, and Nehm 2021). For the features associated with examinees, there is considerable but inconsistent research indicating that the performance of CSMs can be affected by student language proficiency (Ha and Nehm 2016a, 2016b; Liu et al. 2016; Wilson et al. 2023), country of origin (Bridgeman, Trapani, and Attali 2012), achievement level (Bridgeman, Trapani, and Attali 2012), gender (Shermis 2015), socioeconomic status (Shermis et al. 2017), and institution (Ha et al. 2011; Shiroda et al. 2021). Success of CSMs can also be affected by the rubric used to classify the responses (Nehm and Haertig 2012; McGraw-Hill Education 2014), the set of responses used to train the CSM (Nehm, Ha, and Mayfield 2012), model validation methods (Nehm, Ha, and Mayfield 2012; Zhai et al. 2020b), ML approach (Zhai et al. 2020b), and the reliability of human coders when assigning scores to responses (Bridgeman, Trapani, and Attali 2012; Lottridge, Wood, and Shaw 2018; Nehm and Haertig 2012). Finally, features of the assessment item and the responses themselves can be important. This can include response length (Nehm and Haertig 2012; Liu et al. 2014; Mao et al. 2018), the scenario or context of the assessment item (Zhai et al. 2020c), and item difficulty (McGraw-Hill Education 2014; Zhai et al. 2020a). Other work has also found that the structure of the assessment item itself can affect the outcome of CSM development (Brew and Leacock 2013; Liu, Lee, and Linn 2011). Specifically, constructed response items that have a forced choice component lead to higher human–CSM agreement than items that do not (Brew and Leacock 2013; Liu, Lee, and Linn 2011). In addition to these features of the assessment and model, there is the added difficulty of the considerable language diversity in responses, in that students can explain complex STEM concepts in a variety of ways. While some work has suggested that the variety of ways students can express an idea can be problematic for CSMs for short constructed responses in science (Jescovitch et al. 2020; Lottridge, Wood, and Shaw 2018; Maestrales et al. 2021; Shiroda et al. 2021), no work has quantitatively examined the relationship between the diversity of student language and model performance.

Students use different formal and informal language, as evidenced by their words, phrases, and sentences to communicate their thinking. For example, students can supply explanations that include scientific jargon or provide informal explanations of phenomenon. Previous work developing CSMs for STEM assessments has observed that this variety affects the success of the CSMs (Jescovitch et al. 2020; Lottridge, Wood, and Shaw 2018; Maestrales et al. 2021; Shiroda et al. 2021). While observed during CSM development, the diversity of student language is difficult to quantify in part due to the short length of many constructed responses. Traditionally, lexical diversity can be thought of as the range of words a student uses in a sample of text. This approach focuses on the repetition of words in a writing sample and cannot be applied to short texts under a hundred words (Choi and Jeong 2016; Tweedie and Baayen 1998; Zenker and Kyle 2021). As most constructed responses to short answer assessment are under a hundred words, no traditional lexical diversity metric can be applied to examine responses individually. In addition to the length requirement, current lexical diversity metrics offer an incomplete picture of the diversity of text within a *corpus* of constructed responses as it does not compare the words used in one response to the other responses (Jarvis 2013; Shiroda, Fleming, and Haudek 2023). To better understand the diversity of language that students use in constructed responses, we recently examined a corpus using diversity measures commonly used in ecology to better assess the text diversity in the corpus overall and to compare among categorical groups of responses to determine if different response features statistically affect language (Shiroda, Fleming, and Haudek 2023). These metrics, including Whittaker's beta (β), species turnover, and Bray–Curtis dissimilarity distance, compare the words used in a given response to every other response in the data set, allowing for better quantification of differences in language. Other measures, including richness (S), Shannon's diversity index (H'), and Simpson's diversity index (D) examine repetition of words in individual responses similar to traditional measures of lexical diversity. Within that work, we also described a visualization technique called ordination that is used in diverse fields to examine complex data (Shiroda, Fleming, and Haudek 2023). Ordination uses dimension reduction to project multifaceted data into two or three dimensions, which can then be graphed into a biplot. When applied to a constructed response corpus, each response is represented by a point with similar responses plotted more closely together based on word similarity. Afterwards, categorical data, such as assessment features, human-assigned scoring, and respondent characteristics, can be overlaid on the biplot to look for patterns. We have previously used this technique to gain a better understanding of differences in language used by students in constructed responses between institutional types, ways of scientific thinking, and timing of response collection (Shiroda, Fleming, and Haudek 2023). In order to apply these metrics to text usage, we apply natural language processing methods for content analysis to collections of student responses. Briefly, these text extraction methods identify words and phrases in student responses and present these features as *n-grams* in order to generate a document term matrix (Jurka et al. 2013). Some of the text pre-processing steps can be changed, such as stemming and stop word removal, in order to focus the matrix on the most pertinent text features for a given assessment or corpus. The resulting matrix is then used to calculate diversity measures or as input for ordination. We imagine these ordination techniques could also be useful to improve the process of CSM development.

Study Context

Over the past several years, our group developed over seventy CSMs that predict the classification of student reasoning aligned to learning progressions using constructed response items. These assessment items target college-level science content and span five scientific processes in the field of physiology: bulk flow, diffusion, ion flow, mass balance, and water movement (Michael et al. 2017). Each assessment item has an associated coding rubric based on a learning progression framework. Learning progression frameworks are empirically based, ordinal frameworks that describe increasingly more scientific reasoning that students use as they gain proficiency in a topic (Corcoran, Mosher, and Rogat 2009). Learning progression frameworks can support research to understand how undergraduates learn to reason using key disciplinary principles. However, learning progression frameworks also represent a challenge to developing ML-based CSMs (Zhai et al. 2020b). This challenge is thought to be multifaceted. As the rubrics are holistic, the rubric bins or levels are commonly less defined than analytical rubrics. This is in part because student thinking is not distinct within a learning progression but instead requires overlapping or additive ideas. For example, in this work, the highest level within the mass balance items requires students to explain how inputs and outputs interact in a system, while students at lower levels only include either the input or the output (Scott et al. 2023). This leads to an overlap in language across the levels which likely contributes to difficulty in creating accurate CSMs for this topic. In addition, within a level of the learning progression, it is likely that responses will contain infrequent or incorrect ideas that must still be recognized by the CSM as a potential way to fall into a given learning progression level. For example, Jescovitch et al. (2019) reported difficulty with a specific rubric bin in an ion movement assessment item (also used as part of this study) as the bin contained student responses with numerous types of mistakes. Mistakes that were less common were rarely classified correctly, leading to low CSM performance for that particular rubric bin (Jescovitch et al. 2019). Similarly, Shiroda et al. (2021) found that unique ways of discussing human weight loss resulted in reduced model performance.

Given the difficulty of applying natural language processing and supervised ML constructed responses aligned to learning progressions, we sought to better understand the variable success we have had developing CSMs for this set of items. We first sought to explore attributes of the items, rubrics, and training sets that have been previously examined for their role in CSM success, including item context, the inclusion of forced choice, the number of rubric bins or CSM bins, and the length of responses in our first research question. To address qualitative observations by other groups that diversity of language impacts CSM success, we applied new methods for quantifying and visualizing the diversity of language students use to construct short responses to determine whether language diversity of the constructed responses corpus contributes to overall CSM performance. To better understand what attributes impact CSM development and assist in the creation of CSMs, we address the following research questions:

1. Is item context, item structure, the number of rubric bins, training set size, the number of CSM bins, or response length correlated to overall scoring accuracy (Cohen's kappa) within this set of CSMs?
2. Do diversity metrics traditionally used in ecology correlate to model or bin scoring accuracy when applied to language within a constructed response corpus?
3. Does visualization of the similarity and differences in the language of responses via ordination methods provide insight into the performance and development of CSMs?

To examine which assessment and data set features are associated with CSM accuracy, we use outputs of natural language processing and ML model scoring. We use natural language processing methods, along with supervised ML, as part of the CSM generation and further use natural language processing to identify student word and phrase usage for quantification and comparison in language diversity metrics. Use of dimension reduction techniques in AI is common, especially in unsupervised ML (Murphy 2012). This is due to the multivariate nature of many of the large data sets, leading to a huge number of dimensions. This is also true for datasets associated with text-scoring models, since the resulting text matrix can become very large. Using specific ordination techniques, like detrended correspondence analysis, provide advantages to interpretability of the output, since the primary dimension centers on relatedness of sites, or as we have applied it, text in student constructed responses (Shiroda, Fleming, and Haudek 2023). Further, some ordination techniques can handle high-zero datasets, which are common in the application of natural language processing and ML to science assessments. In this work, we utilize a dimensionality reduction technique with natural language processing to explore how text in responses compare to one another and how item characteristics are associated with groupings of responses.

Methods

Response collection

Responses to these items were collected from undergraduates enrolled in biology or physiology courses from multiple classrooms by instructors at different institutions, including both two- and four-year colleges, as previously described (Jescovitch et al. 2020; Scott et al. 2023). To collect a range of student thinking, we targeted major, non-major, introductory biology, and advanced physiology students pre- and post-instruction of the relevant topics of the items. The number of institutions, instructors, and time points is dependent on the item. Each response was collected via a low-stakes online survey, quiz, or homework. The research data collection and study were approved by IRBs at the research institutions (University of Washington IRB ID STUDY00001316 and Michigan State University IRB x17-196e).

Dataset

These items and accompanying CSMs were developed through the Learning Progressions on the Development of Principle-based Reasoning in Undergraduate Physiology (LeaP UP) collaboration. Items and rubrics from this project align with learning progression frameworks for undergraduate understanding, including mass balance (Scott et al. 2023) and flux (Scott, Wenderoth, and Doherty 2020; Doherty et al. 2023). The associated coding rubrics for the assessment items are aligned to these learning progression levels, making each rubric ordinal in nature. As each learning progression is created to reflect student thinking, rubrics are variable in their number of scoring levels or bins. Some of these bins or levels were combined during CSM development, resulting in fewer predictive bins in the CSM, but the rubrics maintain the ordinal nature of the coding rubric and learning progression (see Table 7.1 for rubric bins and Table 7.2 for CSM bins). Model development is an iterative process that involves a question development cycle and training of a supervised machine learning model to build a CSM (Urban-Lurain et al. 2015). The training model is evaluated using a tenfold cross-validation method (Zhai et al. 2020b). Herein, we included all CSMs that have established rubrics and response datasets. These models are in different stages of training and testing and include CSMs that are publicly usable via https://beyondmultiplechoice.org. For each item, the information for the CSM that achieved the highest performance for accuracy in predicting human scores as measured by Cohen's kappa (κ) is provided and used for analysis. We report κ as a single measure of overall model performance for comparison purposes, as this is the most common metric reported for CSMs in science education, and the measure accounts for chance agreements between raters (Zhai, Shi, and Nehm 2021; McHugh 2012). The assessment items span five key scientific principles within physiology: bulk flow (BF; $n = 9$), diffusion (DF; $n = 13$), ion movement (IM; $n = 14$), mass balance (MB; $n = 22$), and water movement (WA; $n = 14$). The items are set in eight discipline relevant contexts (i.e., physiological systems) including cardiovascular ($n = 11$), digestive ($n = 2$), generic ($n = 2$), neurophysiology ($n = 13$), plant physiology ($n = 21$), renal ($n = 7$), respiratory ($n = 11$), and skeletal-muscular ($n = 4$). Each assessment item asks students to explain a phenomenon in a context and include at least one explain question, which prompts students to write their response in a text box; however, the overall structure of the assessment items does vary. Only four items contain a single explain component, while the others include multiple questions or parts to which students respond using separate text boxes. Explain/explain items have two separate but related explain questions ($n = 13$). For some items, forced choice questions were also combined with an explain component for forced choice/explain item structure ($n = 22$) or forced choice/explain/forced choice/explain ($n = 4$) item structure. The forced choice selections alone are not

Table 7.1 Assessment Item Descriptions

Process	Item Name	Subtitle	Context	Item Structure	Rubric Bins	Notes
Bulk Flow						
	Asthma tidal volume	-	Respiratory	Ex/Ex	10	Single item and rubric
	Blood pressure gradients	-	Cardiovascular	FC/Ex	8	These are separate items that differ based on Context and Complexity but are all scored with the same rubric
	Blood pressure gradients across species	-				
	Phloem pressure gradients	-	Plant Physiology			
	Phloem pressure gradients across species	-				
	Pressure gradients in Tubes	-	Generic			
	Changes in tidal volume	-	Respiratory	Ex	7	Single item and rubric
	Contrasting blood pressure gradients	Part 1	Cardiovascular	FC/Ex	8	Two-part item designed to be given together. Scored with two separate rubrics
		Part 2	Cardiovascular	FC/Ex	8	
	Decreased blood flow through coronary	Gradient	Cardiovascular	ID/Ex	6	Single item that has separate rubrics for resistance and gradient ideas
		Resistance				
	Decreased blood flow to brain	Gradient	Cardiovascular	ID/Ex	6	Single item that has separate rubrics for resistance and gradient ideas
		Resistance				
	Decreased phloem sap flow	Gradient	Plant Physiology	ID/Ex	5	Single item that has separate rubrics for resistance and gradient ideas
		Resistance	Plant Physiology	ID/Ex	5	

Continued

Table 7.1 *Continued*

Process	Item Name	Subtitle	Context	Item Structure	Rubric Bins	Notes
Diffusion						
	Alveolar oxygen diffusion	-	Respiratory	FC/Ex/FC/Ex	8	Single item and rubric but similar to those marked.*
	Decreased auxin diffusion out of cells	Gradient	Plant Physiology	FC/Ex	6	Single item that has separate rubrics for resistance and gradient ideas
		Resistance			5	
	Decreased oxygen diffusion into blood	Gradient	Respiratory	ID/Ex	6	Single item that has separate rubrics for resistance and gradient ideas
		Resistance			5	
	Diffusion gradient	Part 1	Plant Physiology	FC/Ex	6	Two-part item designed to be given together. Scored with two separate rubrics
		Part 2			8	
	Mesophyll carbon dioxide diffusion	-	Plant Physiology	FC/Ex/FC/Ex	8	Single item and rubric but similar to those marked.*
	Oxygen diffusion in water	-	Generic	FC/Ex/FC/Ex	8	Single item and rubric but similar to those marked.*
	Increased oxygen diffusion into muscles	Gradient	Respiratory	ID/Ex	6	Single item that has separate rubrics for resistance and gradient ideas
		Resistance			4	
	Serine Diffusion	Gradient	Digestive	FC/Ex	5	Single item that has separate rubrics for resistance and gradient ideas
		Resistance			3	

Ion Movement					
Action potential peak change	-	Neurophysiology	FC/Ex/FC/Ex	11	Single item and rubric
Sinoatrial action potential Ca^{++}	-	Cardiovascular	FC/Ex	10	Single item and rubric
Decreased Na^{+} flow into neuron	Gradient	Neurophysiology	ID/Ex	6	Single item that has separate rubrics for resistance and gradient ideas
	Resistance			6	
Equilibrium potential (Cl^{-})	-	Neurophysiology	ID/Ex	10	Single item and rubric
Equilibrium potential (K^{+}, animal cell)	-	Neurophysiology	ID/Ex	11	These are separate items that differ based on Context and Complexity but are all scored with the same rubric
Equilibrium potential (K^{+}, generic)	-	Generic	ID/Ex	9	
Equilibrium potential (K^{+}, neuron)	-	Neurophysiology	ID/Ex	11	
Equilibrium potential (K^{+}, plant/guard cell)	-	Plant Physiology	ID/Ex	10	
Equilibrium potential (K^{+})	-	Neurophysiology	ID/Ex	11	
Glutamate EPSP	-	Neurophysiology	FC/Ex	12	Single item and rubric
Resting membrane potential	-	Neurophysiology	Ex	12	Single item and rubric
Resting membrane potential [K^{+}] changed	-	Neurophysiology	FC/Ex	10	Single item and rubric
Mass Balance					
Explain alveolar pO_2	CVR Identify Flux	Respiratory	Ex/Ex	9 5	Six individual items with different contexts that share the same rubrics. Each item can be scored for CVR and Identifying Flux
Explain aorta blood flow	CVR Identify Flux	Cardiovascular	Ex/Ex	9 5	
Explain leaf glucose levels	CVR Identify Flux	Plant Physiology	Ex/Ex	9 5	
Explain root cell auxin levels	CVR Identify Flux	Plant Physiology	Ex/Ex	9 5	
Explain skeletal sarcoplasm Ca^{++} level	CVR Identify Flux	Skeletal muscle	Ex/Ex	9 5	

Continued

Table 7.1 *Continued*

Process	Item Name	Subtitle	Context	Item Structure	Rubric Bins	Notes
	Explain synapse serotonin levels	CVR	Neurophysiology	Ex/Ex	9	
		Identify Flux			5	
	Predict alveolar pO_2	CVR	Respiratory	FC/Ex	9	Six individual items with different contexts that share the same rubrics. Each item can be scored for CVR and Identifying Flux
		Identify Flux			5	
	Predict aorta blood flow	CVR	Cardiovascular	FC/Ex	9	
		Identify Flux			5	
	Predict leaf glucose levels	CVR	Plant Physiology	FC/Ex	9	
		Identify Flux			5	
	Predict root cell auxin levels	CVR	Plant Physiology	FC/Ex	9	
		Identify Flux			5	
	Predict skeletal sarcoplasm Ca^{++} level	CVR	Skeletal muscle	FC/Ex	10	
		Identify Flux			5	
Water Movement						
	Increased reabsorption at collecting duct	Gradient	Renal	ID/Ex	6	Single item that has separate rubrics for resistance and gradient ideas
		Resistance			5	
	Increased reabsorption at proximal tubule	Gradient	Renal	ID/Ex	6	Single item that has separate rubrics for resistance and gradient ideas
		Resistance			5	

Increased glomerular filtration	Pressure	Renal	ID/Ex	6	Single item that has separate rubrics for resistance, pressure, and gradient ideas
	Gradient			6	
	Resistance			5	
Stop glomerular function		Renal	ID/Ex	11	Single item and rubric
Water into and out of capillaries	Part A	Cardiovascular	Ex	9	Two-part item designed to be given together. Scored with two separate rubrics
	Part BC		ID/Ex	10	
Water into and out of guard cells	Part A	Plant Physiology	Ex	9	
	Part BC		ID/Ex	11	Two-part item designed to be given together. Scored with two separate rubrics
Increased water into growing plant cell	Pressure	Plant Physiology	ID/Ex	6	Single item that has separate rubrics for resistance, pressure, and solute ideas
	Resistance			5	
	Solute			6	

Item names can be used to view the full text items on https://beyondmultiplechoice.org or can be linked to Table 7.2 for model information. The number of rubric bins reflects the coding rubric. Notes are provided to clarify the setup of the assessment items as some were scored with multiple rubrics, while other groups of items share rubrics. Item structure refers to the item as whole or the subpart of the question if there is a subtitle provided. CVR: covariational reasoning; Ex: explain; FC: forced choice; ID: identify.

Table 7.2 Model Descriptions

Item Name	Item Shorthand	Training Set Size	κ	CSM Bins	Model Notes
Asthma tidal volume	BF_ASTHMANS	951	0.732	6	-
Blood pressure gradients Blood pressure gradients across species Phloem pressure gradients Phloem pressure gradients across species Pressure gradients in tubes	BF_ALLTUBES	2907	0.851	3	Single model used to score items of different contexts and complexity.
Changes in tidal volume	BF_CANDLE2	1035	0.795	5	-
Contrasting blood pressure gradients	BF_TUBES_DEEPDIVE	1053	0.855	3	-
	BF_TUBES_DEEPDIVE	999	0.860	3	-
Decreased blood flow through coronary Decreased blood flow to brain	BF_COR & PASSOUT_R	1256	0.851	3	Single model used to score two items of different contexts.
Decreased blood flow through coronary Decreased blood flow to brain	BF_COR & PASSOUT_G	1256	0.793	3	Single model used to score two items of different contexts.

Shorthand names are used throughout the paper. Item names can be used to view items on https://beyondmultiplechoice.org. CSM bins is the number of bins used in the CSM; κ is unweighted Cohen's kappa. Notes are provided to clarify the setup of the CSM items as some were used to score multiple items since the items shared a topic.

sufficient for the student to answer the entirety of the question. For example, the student may be asked to pick whether they expect concentration to go up, down, or stay the same, then are prompted to explain why. Finally, items could include an identify component, in which students have an open response but are more likely to list features relevant to the item prompt than construct full-sentence explanations ($n = 29$). For example, the assessment may ask the student to *identify* ways that the concentration of an ion could be affected and then ask to *explain* why the things that were identified would affect ion concentration. Similar item structures have been used by other authors who develop CSMs (Liu, Lee, and Linn 2011; Mao et al. 2018; Zhu et al. 2017).

Developing CSMs using Constructed Response Classifier

To develop the CSMs, we used the Constructed Response Classifier tool, which uses natural language processing and supervised ML processes and has been used previously to score short text constructed responses in science assessments (Jescovitch et al. 2020; Noyes et al. 2020). The R code and documentation for a set of web applications using the Constructed Response Classifier tool are available at https://github.com/BeyondMultipleChoice/AACRAutoReport. Student constructed responses that have been human-coded using rubrics are used as inputs to the Constructed Response Classifier tool. The Constructed Response Classifier extracts text features using natural language processing techniques, then performs an ensemble of eight individual ML algorithms during model training (Jurka et al. 2013). The output of each algorithm is a classification prediction for each response for a given rubric. These individual outputs from each algorithm were combined to make a final categorization prediction using a simple voting scheme. The computer model was generated using a tenfold cross-validation approach. CSMs were developed uniquely for each assessment item and rubric. We started with a default set of model parameters and then iteratively adjusted and tested ML model parameters for each item. For example, the Constructed Response Classifier tool allows for the inclusion or exclusion of numbers in the text responses. Overall, scoring accuracy for each CSM was measured using accuracy and κ as a measure of agreement between human- and CSM-assigned scores during the cross-validation procedure (Zhai, Shi, and Nehm 2021). During model training, other measures of CSM performance at each rubric bin or level (e.g., accuracy, specificity, sensitivity) are used to evaluate and refine the CSM. These metrics provide diagnostic information about which bin or level is most problematic and help target changes to model parameters. However, these bin or level metrics do not provide much information about the overall model performance across all levels. Here, we report only the overall (unweighted) κ measure of the developed CSM (Fleiss and Cohen 1973). Cohen's kappa allows us to use a single overall measure of the CSM that works for ordinal data, multiclass predictions, and variable numbers of bins or levels in each CSM. Further, we were interested in exploring possible associations of the item attributes with overall CSM performance, as opposed to item attributes that correlate with CSM performance of specific rubric bins or levels. We acknowledge that using only κ as a measurement of CSM performance can be problematic (Ferri, Hernández-Orallo, and Modroiu 2009; Chicco and Jurman 2020). For example, larger sample sizes are more likely to achieve higher κ since more responses are used to train the ML model. However, we decided to use κ as a measure as it remains commonly used and could be easily compared to other literature that has compared CSMs using κ (Zhai, Shi, and Nehm 2021). We used the highest κ resulting from cross-validation during model development as we do not have separate testing datasets available for all CSMs. When individual rubric bins are examined for a subset of assessment items, the percent accuracy for each bin or level is used instead of κ. Bin accuracy is calculated by dividing the number of correctly coded responses in a given bin by the total number of responses that were coded in that bin by human coders.

Creation of the Data Matrices

The data matrices used in lexical work have responses as rows and individual words as columns, with each cell containing the frequency of a given word in a given constructed responses. For each of the matrices described, responses coded as zeroes by humans in the rubric (i.e., off-task or non-relevant answer) were removed from the dataset, as this code was not consistently used across the models and can greatly skew the diversity techniques. A raw data matrix containing word frequencies for each response was created using natural language processing in WordStat (v.8.0.23, 2004–18, Provalis Research) after the use of snowball (English) stemming and without correcting spelling errors. This matrix was used to calculate the text diversity measures. A second matrix was created that reflects the word processing settings used in the creation of the corresponding CSM. Unless otherwise stated, these settings were the exclusion of the words "and," "a," "the," and "in" and the removal of numbers and symbols. We also excluded any words not appearing in at least three responses, as patterns cannot be detected with a lower frequency. Certain models had additional settings in the text processing steps. For IM_ANEION, "it," "at," and "as" were also removed from the text, and the numbers −90, −91, −76, −77, −81, −80, and −79 were replaced with the phrase "Equilibrium potential." For IM_RESTING, the words "greater," "higher," and "stronger" were replaced with the word "differ." Finally, for both MB_PRECALCIGPH and MB_RHIZOGPH, numbers were kept as features in the data matrix. Finally, a third matrix containing the human scores and CSM-predicted scores was also created. The latter two matrices were used for ordination, while the first was used to calculate diversity metrics.

Analysis and Calculations

Cohen's kappa (κ) was used as a measure of inter-rater agreement (Fleiss and Cohen 1973), in this case to compare human consensus scores and CSM-predicted scores for each model. This results in a number between 0 and 1, with 1 representing perfect agreement. We calculated the percent accuracy of CSMs for individual rubric bins (or levels) by dividing the number of correctly coded responses by the CSM by the total number of responses with that human-assigned scores.

For diversity metrics, words were stemmed using snowball (English) without misspellings being corrected. All ecological diversity metrics were performed in PC-ORD using the first, raw matrix described earlier (version 7.08; McCune and Mefford 2018). Richness (S) is the number of non-zero elements in a row, or the number of unique words within a single response. Shannon's diversity index (H') is calculated using the formula $\sum Pi \times ln\,(Pi)$, where Pi is the proportion of the ith word in the entire dataset (Shannon 1948). Simpson's diversity index (D) is $1 - \Sigma\ (Pi \times Pi)$, where Pi is the proportion of the ith word in the entire dataset (Simpson 1949). Simpson and Shannon are calculated for each individual constructed responses and then averaged to determine the measure for the corpus as a whole (Jurasinski, Retzer, and Beierkuhnlein 2009). Whittaker beta diversity is calculated using the formula $\frac{\alpha}{\gamma}$, where γ is the total number of words in the pair of responses and α is the shared number of words (Whittaker 1967; 1969). Species turnover is calculated by the formula $(s_1 - c) + (s_2 - c)$, where s_1 is the number of words in the first response, s_2 is the number of words in the second response, and c is the number of words in both responses (McCune and Mefford 2018). Bray–Curtis (Sorensen) dissimilarity distance measures the percent dissimilarity between two responses and is calculated using the formula $1 - \frac{2W}{A+B}$, in which W is the sum of shared abundances and A and B are the sums of abundances in individual responses (McCune and Mefford 2018). Whittaker's beta, species turnover, and Bray–Curtis dissimilarity are calculated using every possible pairing in the dataset. These numbers are then averaged to derive a single number for the dataset. The balance, a given training set, was calculated using Shannon's entropy (H). With a dataset of n, with k classes of size c_i, $H = \sum_{i=1}^{k} \frac{c_i}{n} log \frac{c_i}{n}$ (Shannon 1948).

Ordination Techniques

We applied detrended correspondence analysis as previously described (Shiroda, Fleming, and Haudek 2023). Briefly, detrended correspondence analysis is one of the most widely used ordination methods in ecology, accepts data that are not normally distributed, and uniquely allows for quantification of species turnover in the biplot (Palmer 2019). Ordination techniques require a primary matrix that contains the information that needs to be reduced, in this case the frequencies of each word in each response in a given corpus. Data matrices were produced as described earlier.

The detrended correspondence analysis was performed and visualized in PC-ORD (version 7.08; McCune and Mefford 2018). For program settings, rare words were down-weighted, and 999 was selected as the seed number. Scores were calculated for words using weighted averaging. We examined the significance of each axis using 999 randomizations. All biplots are depicted with raw scores as the axis. A hundred units on the x-axis is equivalent to one half change in species turnover.

Statistical Analysis

Associations between item or model feature and model κ, bin percent accuracy, or percent error were examined using the Pearson correlation coefficient (Pearson's r). The statistical power was determined via the associated Pearson's r using the R values and the number of samples (n; https://www.socscistatistics.com/tests/pearson/default2.aspx). Associations are considered weak if r is below 0.4, moderate if between 0.4 and 0.6, and strong if greater than 0.6 (Dancey and Reidy 2007; https://www.socscistatistics.com/pvalues/pearsondistribution.aspx). These results are reported in the format of "r(degrees of freedom) = the r statistic, p = p-value" where the degrees of freedom is the number of tested pairs minus 2. Categorical data were examined using a one-way ANOVA with post hoc Tukey HSD to examine pairwise comparisons. Within the test, pairwise p-values are provided unless the F-statistic from the ANOVA found there was no significance between the overall means, in which case the f-ratio and p-value are provided.

Results

We created a dataset of forty-nine items (Table 7.1) and seventy-two accompanying CSMs (Table 7.2) which were developed through the Learning Progressions on the Development of Principle-based Reasoning in Undergraduate Physiology (LeaP UP) collaboration. All the assessment items can be found on https://beyondmultiplechoice.org by the item name (Table 7.1). Each of the items asks students to explain a phenomenon and includes at least one explain prompt. In addition, some items also include an identify question, which prompts students to list ideas, or a forced choice, which allows students to select a prewritten short answer such as "inside the cell" or "it will increase." This set of items examines post-secondary student proficiency in applying the physiological principles of mass balance and flux identified by Modell (2000). The principle of mass balance examines changes in the amount of a given substance in a compartment based on the inputs and outputs of the system (Michael and Modell 2021; Scott et al. 2023). Students must identify the different inputs and outputs and apply covariational reasoning to explain how total mass can be affected. The principle of flux examines the passive movement of matter down gradients and requires students to reason about the effects of all the gradients and resistances in each system (Michael and McFarland 2011). The items span five topics or scientific processes pertinent to physiology. Bulk flow (BF), diffusion (DF), ion movement (IM), and water movement (WA) are all types of flux, while mass balance (MB) is its own grouping. The items also cover eight physiological system contexts including cardiovascular, digestive, generic, neurophysiology, plant physiology, renal, respiratory, and skeletal muscular. The items are scored using holistic rubrics that place responses along a learning progression, which describe levels of reasoning from developing (lower levels) to more expert-like (higher levels; Corcoran, Mosher, and Rogat 2009; Scott et al. 2023). There are frequently multiple ways that responses can be placed into a single holistic level within a learning progression. That is, many holistic learning progression levels have sublevels in a coding rubric for a given item. Therefore, there are typically more coding bins associated with a rubric (Table 7.1) than just the number of levels in the learning progression. During subsequent CSM development, these rubric bins may be collapsed back into a single-level bin for CSM scoring or can be coded separately by the CSM, frequently resulting in a different number of rubric bins than CSM bins (Table 7.2). The training set sizes used to build the CSMs range from 344 to 2907 with an average of 791.1 responses per item. CSM performance is reported using κ and ranges from 0.49 to 0.92, with an average of 0.70.

Scoring Accuracy Varies by Item Structure, Scientific Process, and the Number of Bins

Training Set Features: As the same ML application was used for all these items, we cannot examine some features that have been previously found to contribute to model success, including ML supervision, model validation method, and ML algorithm(s). We did, however, examine the effect of the size of the training set (Table 7.2) on scoring accuracy. We found a weak positive correlation between the training sample size and the accuracy of the model, as measured by κ; however, this result was not significant (r (70) = 0.014, p = 0.9). We have observed during model creation that the success of a model overall can be influenced by the balance of the codes in the dataset, meaning that each coding bin is equally (or near equally) represented in the training set, as opposed to the total number of responses in the set. We found a weak, negative correlation between the balance of codes in the training set and CSM accuracy, but this result was not significant (Table 7.3; r (70) = −0.34; p = 0.33).

Assessment Features: The set of assessment items was developed for post-secondary physiology education; therefore, some possible assessment features do not apply (e.g., student level), as they are all constructed response questions intended for college students. The holistic rubrics used in this study are different from an analytic rubric, in which individual concepts are coded, as there is often more than one way to be classified within a given holistic level. While our group has previously examined deconstructing holistic rubrics into a series of analytic rubrics and demonstrated that well-designed analytic rubrics could be used to achieve similar CSM success (Jescovitch et al. 2020), all the CSMs in this dataset are trained using cores from holistic rubrics.

Table 7.3 Summary of Tested Model Features and Results

Measure	Feature	*n*	Min.	Max.	Avg	Relationship	Statistic	Significance
	Training sample size	72	344	2907	791.1	Weak positive	Pearson	*ns*
	Model bins	72	2	12	4.4	Weak negative	Pearson	0.005
	Rubric bins	72	3	12	7.4	Weak negative	Pearson	0.033
	Item structure	72			Categorical		ANOVA	<0.001
	Scientific process	72			Categorical		ANOVA	<0.05
	Context	68			Categorical		ANOVA	*ns*
	Shannon entropy (balance)	10	0.8640	0.9955	0.9460	Weak negative	Pearson	*ns*
Overall model accuracy (κ)	Bray–Curtis distance	10	69.75	81.97	75.24	Weak negative	Pearson	*ns*
	Species turnover	10	1.7	2.5	2	Weak negative	Pearson	*ns*
	Richness (S)	10	16.6	30.7	26.2	Weak negative	Pearson	*ns*
	Shannon's diversity index (H')	10	2.60	3.22	3.03	Weak negative	Pearson	*ns*
	Simpson's diversity index (D)	10	0.9020	0.9516	0.9378	Weak negative	Pearson	*ns*
	Whittaker's beta (β)	10	29.7	42.8	36.2	Moderate positive	Pearson	*ns*
	Word count	10	8029	72,148	35,617.2	Weak negative	Pearson	*ns*
	Centroid minimum distance	10	1.28	9.37	4.84	Weak negative	Pearson	*ns*
	Centroid maximum distance	10	12.50	114.88	72.32	Weak positive	Pearson	*ns*
	Centroid average distance	10	6.73	66.03	39.79	Weak positive	Pearson	*ns*
	Bray–Curtis distance	43	61.58	86.76	73.06	Weak negative	Pearson	*ns*
	Species turnover	43	1.4	2.9	1.9	Weak negative	Pearson	*ns*
	Richness (S)	43	11.8	40.7	25.9	Weak positive	Pearson	*ns*
	Shannon's diversity index (H')	43	2.21	3.49	3.02	Weak negative	Pearson	*ns*
Bin percent accuracy	Simpson's diversity index (D)	43	0.8412	0.9623	0.9374	Weak negative	Pearson	*ns*
	Whittaker's beta (β)	43	5.3	44.1	20.2	Weak positive	Pearson	0.004
	Centroid minimum distance	43	1.28	60.20	14.98	Weak positive	Pearson	*ns*
	Centroid maximum distance	43	7.18	114.88	65.26	Weak positive	Pearson	*ns*
	Centroid average distance	43	5.13	95.39	40.35	Weak positive	Pearson	0.052
Percent error	Distance between centroids	168	1.3	114.9	42.4	Weak negative	Pearson	<0.001

n: number of models or bins used to calculate statistic; Min: minimum; Max: maximum; Avg: average.

While all the items are developed for physiology, they span different scientific processes and contexts. We found scoring accuracy varied based on the five scientific processes: bulk flow, diffusion, ion movement, mass balance, and water movement. We had the greatest success overall with CSMs for items in bulk flow and diffusion, followed closely by water movement, with an average κ of 0.821, 0.821, and 0.739, respectively (Table 7.3). There is no statistical difference between CSMs accuracy among these three processes (One-way ANOVA, Tukey HSD; $p > 0.05$). We did observe a difference in CSM accuracy between items targeting ion movement ($\kappa = 0.726$) and bulk flow ($p = 0.019$) and diffusion ($p = 0.019$). There is no statistical difference between the performance of the CSMs for ion movement and water movement. Finally, the CSMs associated with mass balance items have the lowest average κ of 0.544, which is significantly lower than all the other concepts (One-way ANOVA, Tukey HSD; $p < 0.001$). In contrast, we did not observe a difference in CSM accuracy based on item context. While a few items were set in the context of the digestive system or skeletal muscular systems, or in a generic context, most items used a cardiovascular, neurophysiology, plant physiology, renal, or respiratory context. We did not find any significant difference in CSM performance among these contexts, with the range of κ averages between 0.679 and 0.781 (One-way ANOVA, f-ratio = 0.6731; $p = 0.61$).

The assessment items also have different structures. While each item contains at least one explain component, some items also include an identify or forced choice components as part of the item. CSMs for items which contained only Ex (either one or two parts) prompts were the least successful (average $\kappa = 0.582$; Table 7.3). This difference was significant in comparison to both the inclusion of a forced choice (One-way ANOVA, Tukey HSD; $p < 0.001$) or an identify question ($p < 0.001$) coupled with an Ex prompt in forming the entire item. CSMs for the identify and explain format were the most successful ($\kappa = 0.765$), followed by the inclusion of a forced choice ($\kappa = 0.712$). The difference in CSMs accuracy between identify & explain and forced choice & explain was not significant (One-way ANOVA, Tukey HSD; $p = 0.27$). In support of this, we also observed that inclusion of the student responses from identify or forced choice questions when developing CSMs for the explanations improves the overall model performance (*data not shown*). Of the fifty-five models that include these components, only one model performed better when the response from the forced choice or identify component was excluded during model training.

We also examined whether there was any effect on the CSM performance based on the number of human-coded rubric bins. We found a weak but significant negative correlation between the number of rubric coding bins (or levels) and scoring accuracy ($r(41) = -0.252$, $p = 0.033$). In addition, we commonly collapse bins into holistic levels; therefore, we also examined whether there was an association between the number of bins in the final CSM and κ. Similar to the previous results, we found a weak but significant negative correlation between the number of bins in the model and model success ($r(41) = -0.324$, $p = 0.005$; Table 7.3). Together, this indicates that models with fewer coding rubric and model bins are more successful overall.

Measures of Language Diversity Do Not Strongly Correlate to Model Success

Previously we used ecological diversity measures to assess the student text contained within a constructed response corpus (Shiroda, Fleming, and Haudek 2023). We applied these measures to investigate possible associations between human–machine κ and six diversity metrics for student responses using a subset of ten items. We selected one high and one low κ model from each category to evenly represent the different processes in the data set (Table 7.4).

Richness (S) is the number of nonzero elements in a matrix row or the number of unique words in a response. This is somewhat similar to response length, which has been found to have variable effect on model success (Liu et al. 2014; Mao et al. 2018; Nehm and Haertig 2012). Within individual items, responses ranged from an average of 16.6 unique words to 30.7, with an overall average of 26.2 unique words in responses to all ten items. This measure has a weak, nonsignificant correlation to the success of the model ($r(8) = -0.177, p = 0.63$). There is a larger range of richness (from 11.8 to 40.7) within individual bins of each item rubric in the dataset. We did not find a correlation between richness of the individual bins κ ($r(41) = 0.0006, p = 0.99$). This may be because richness is more heavily linked to the learning progression level of the response in previous work (Shiroda, Fleming, and Haudek 2023). In general, we found the same pattern in this dataset as responses assigned to the highest learning progression level had the fewest average unique words (20.6), while responses aligned to the lowest level had the most unique words (30.2). Responses aligned to the middle levels had an average of 27.2 unique words.

Simpson's index of diversity (D) and Shannon's diversity (H') examine the diversity of language within a given constructed response in slightly different ways. Each measure had a weak negative correlation with overall scoring accuracy but was not significant ($r(8) = -0.137$ and -0.182, respectively; $p > 0.5$) We found the same pattern of a weak, negative correlation with percent bin accuracy ($r(41) = -0.100$ and -0.046, respectively; $p > 0.5$). These results suggest that the diversity of student language within a response does not affect scoring accuracy. Ecological metrics can also measure the similarity or dissimilarity between pairs of responses. This would reveal whether a dataset's or group's responses (i.e., responses within a given bin) are more or less similar to each other. Whittaker's beta (β) diversity, Bray–Curtis dissimilarity, and species turnover are all slightly different ways of calculating this type of diversity. Bray–Curtis dissimilarity and species turnover had similar results of weak negative correlations with the overall scoring accuracy but were not significant ($r(8) = -0.246$ and -0.168, respectively; $p > 0.5$). We found the same pattern of a weak, negative correlation with percent bin accuracy ($r(41) = -0.063$ and 0.002; $p > 0.5$). In contrast, for β, we found a moderate but not significant association with κ ($r(8) = 0.5703; p = 0.085$) and a weak, but significant association with percent bin accuracy ($r(41) = 0.4267$; $p = 0.004$). β is the total number of words in two responses divided by the shared words between two responses. Low values represent many shared words between responses, while high values indicate few words are shared. For both κ and percent accuracy, a more successful model (i.e., higher κ and higher percent accuracy)

Table 7.4 Language Diversity Metrics

Item shorthand	κ	Avg length	Total words	H	BC	β	Species turnover	S	H'	D	Centroid distance		
											Min	Max	Avg
BF_ASTHMANS	0.742	43.0	39,444	0.968	76.01	35.0	2.1	29.8	3.22	0.952	7.03	92.83	52.17
BF_TUBES_DEEPDIVE	0.855	22.7	23,867	0.946	69.75	42.8	1.7	17.6	2.71	0.922	6.42	56.62	37.75
DF_ANIMOLE	0.816	45.9	30,378	0.894	73.31	35.2	1.9	28.1	3.10	0.942	3.47	114.88	66.03
DF_OXYG	0.719	53.5	24,984	0.874	81.97	38.8	2.5	30.7	3.17	0.945	9.15	47.05	31.37
IM_ANEION	0.721	64.6	68,182	0.986	74.53	38.0	2.0	30.1	3.15	0.943	3.40	80.93	44.38
IM_RESTING	0.621	48.3	72,148	0.995	76.92	37.2	2.1	30.1	3.17	0.947	2.82	67.13	41.45
MB_PRECALCIGPH—CV	0.603	37.2	26,310	0.978	75.96	33.0	2.1	27.1	3.12	0.948	3.02	83.67	35.06
MB_RHIZOGPH—IDF	0.465	45.5	31,510	0.969	73.72	32.7	1.9	27.5	3.09	0.943	9.37	71.89	42.26
WA_STARLING	0.649	21.1	8029	0.986	76.60	29.7	2.1	16.6	2.60	0.902	2.44	12.50	6.73
WA_GCELL3	0.665	43.5	31,320	0.864	73.62	39.6	1.9	23.9	2.95	0.935	1.28	95.69	40.67

κ: Cohen's kappa; CR: constructed response; H: Shannon's entropy (balance); BC: Bray–Curtis distance; β: Whittaker's beta diversity; S: richness; H': Shannon's diversity index; D: Simpson's diversity index; Min: minimum; Max: maximum; Avg: average.

was associated with a higher β value in the set of responses. A larger β value can be achieved in two ways: increase the total words (nominator) in the compared set of responses or decrease the shared words (denominator) in the compared set of responses. To better understand the relationship between β and CSM κ, we calculated the number of total words for each model and tested its association with model success. We found a weak negative association that was not significant (-0.061; $p = 0.87$). This indicates that the association of β diversity of the responses with model success is most likely due to the lower number of shared words between responses. This could be interpreted as these CSMs target or identify a small set of very important words that are shared by responses in a given bin.

Dimension Reduction Techniques Can Reveal Potential Coding Problems and Solutions

Previously, we found that ordination techniques, a type of dimension reduction, can be used to visualize the lexical diversity in a corpus of constructed responses (Shiroda, Fleming, and Haudek 2023). Briefly, ordination techniques use a matrix of the words in each response to create a biplot in which responses that are more similar based on the presence and absence of words are closer together on the plot. While the axis of most reduction and ordination techniques cannot be labeled, detrended correspondence analysis has a defined first axis of species turnover or as we have applied it, the shared words between responses. While the high and low ends of the axis do not mean there are more or fewer words in a response, the spread between two points can be interpreted as the difference between the two based on shared words. Categorical data, such as the classification of responses into a rubric bin or level, can then be overlayed on the biplot. As text classification CSMs also rely on lexical differences between responses, we expected successful CSMs to have better separation of responses based on the overlayed categorical data. Indeed, we observed that items such as BF_ANIMOLE ($\kappa = 0.816$; Figure 7.1A) showed more distinct clustering of responses by rubric bins than a relatively inaccurate model, MB_RHIZOGPH_IDF ($\kappa = 0.465$; Figure 7.1B). For MB_RHIZOGPH_IDF, the most distinct grouping is Level 1, which is also the most successfully coded bin with 89% accuracy, while Levels 2, 3, and 4 are problematic in contributing to the low performance of the overall model and display 21, 50, and 72% accuracy, respectively. Based on these observations, we thought we might be able to use distances between the group centroids to better understand the accuracy of a given level within a model. We found that if responses in a particular level are commonly miscoded to another level (high percent error) by the CSM, the distance between those two group centroids tended to be lower ($r(166) = -0.334$; $p < 0.001$).

As this correlation is suggestive but not consistent for all models, we further investigated whether a given miscoded response tended to be closer to the group centroid to which it was miscoded. Using DF_OXYG as an example (Figure 7.2), responses coded as Level 2 were heavily miscoded to both Levels 1 and 3 by the CSM. In the biplot (Figure 7.2A), the centroid of Level 2 responses is [111.3, 286.9] while the centroids

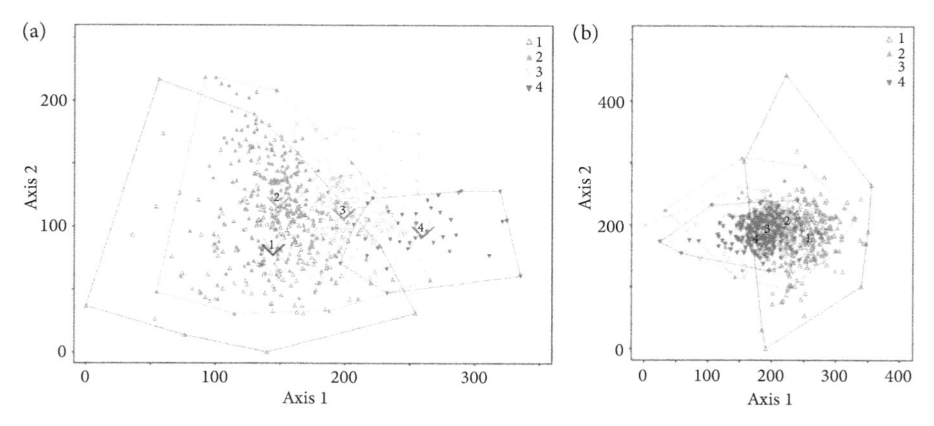

Figure 7.1 Ordination biplots depict the lexical diversity of human-scored student responses. Detrended correspondence analysis plots are overlaid with categorical data (human coding; shape). An example of a training set with an associated model with high predictive accuracy shows greater separation (a) than a training set associated with a model with lower predictive accuracy (b). Centroids of each category are marked by V with the associated bin name (1–4). Hulls are drawn around the outermost data points for each category.

for Levels 1 and 3 are [158.3, 251.1] and [120.4, 253.9], respectively. By removing Level 1 and 3 responses from the biplot and overlaying the CSM score (Figure 7.2B), we observed that the centroid of responses miscoded to Level 1 [113.5, 239.1] or Level 3 [121.4, 267.5] was closer to the Level 1 and 3 centroids from Figure 7.2A while the correct response centroid is located at [102.5, 311.1], closer to the centroid of Level 2 responses. However, this was not true of all individual responses, as there are responses (labeled 9, 30, 53, 61, and 248) that were miscoded by the machine that are more closely positioned to the Level 2 centroid of Figure 7.2A.

Since detrended correspondence analysis provided some insight into CSM errors, we also examined whether the resulting biplots would be useful in decisions on binning response categories separately or together, often referred to as "splitting" or "lumping" in qualitative analysis (Saldaña 2021). For example, during model development for PRECALCIGPH_CV, we found that models which separated the learning progression Level 3 responses into two bins (i.e., into 3.1 and 3.2) were more successful than grouping all Level 3 responses together and predicting the single Level 3 bin. We observe in the detrended correspondence analysis plots that there are distinct groupings of responses according to bins 3.1 and 3.2, supporting that the language is different enough to separate the responses and justify splitting Level 3 into subcodes (Figure 7.3A). In contrast, during development for the IM_RESTING CSM, Level 1 and 2 responses were heavily mis-coded to each other. In the detrended correspondence analysis, we found considerable overlap between the groups of responses, which resulted in an increase in model κ from 0.62 to 0.76 when the codes were "lumped," and responses binned together during modeling (Figure 7.3B). These findings are in line with previous literature that reported that more precisely defined bins

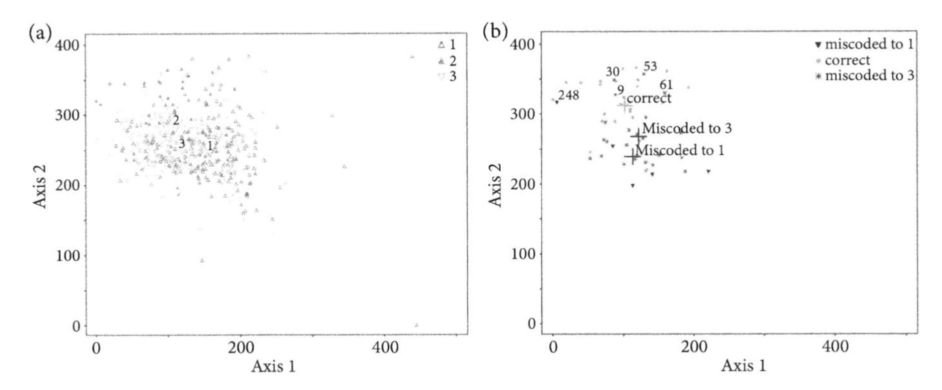

Figure 7.2 Ordination biplots provide insight into miscoded responses. (a) The detrended correspondence analysis plot of model DF_OXYG shows the relationship among the human-scored bins. Centroids are marked by V with the associated bin name (1–3). (b) All responses not human-scored to 2 are removed from the biplot for clarity. Shapes represent whether the CSM correctly scored the response (correct) or incorrectly (miscoded to 1/miscoded to 3). Centroids are indicated by plus signs.

are more successful for CSM predictions (Jescovitch et al. 2019; Leacock, Messineo, and Zhang 2013; Lottridge, Wood, and Shaw 2018).

Discussion

In this work, we sought to understand the features of the responses, training sets, and assessment items that contribute to the accuracy of a short answer text classification CSM. We hoped that by exploring these questions, we would be able to reduce the development time of new CSMs and thereby expand the use of AI-based assessments to new topics in science. We addressed these questions using outputs of natural language processing and supervised ML as part of text classification models for student, concept-based constructed responses. Further, we applied natural language processing and dimension reduction techniques to examine the diversity of student language in student scientific constructed responses. We propose that by better understanding the relationship of text in student responses, researchers can make better decisions during rubric development, human coding for supervised ML, and adjust ML feature parameters as part of CSMs development.

Our work examining assessment characteristics and performance of CSMs found two results that seem counterintuitive. First, we found a very low effect of training set size on CSM scoring accuracy (κ). Previous work has found that increasing the training set size typically increases individual scoring accuracy for short answer scoring in science assessment (Wang et al. 2021; Heilman and Madnani 2015), but there are also some reported exceptions (Ha, Urban-Lurain, and Merrill 2011). Others have postulated that other attributes of the items, such as the complexity of the topic being scored, likely contributed to the CSM accuracy despite the training set size

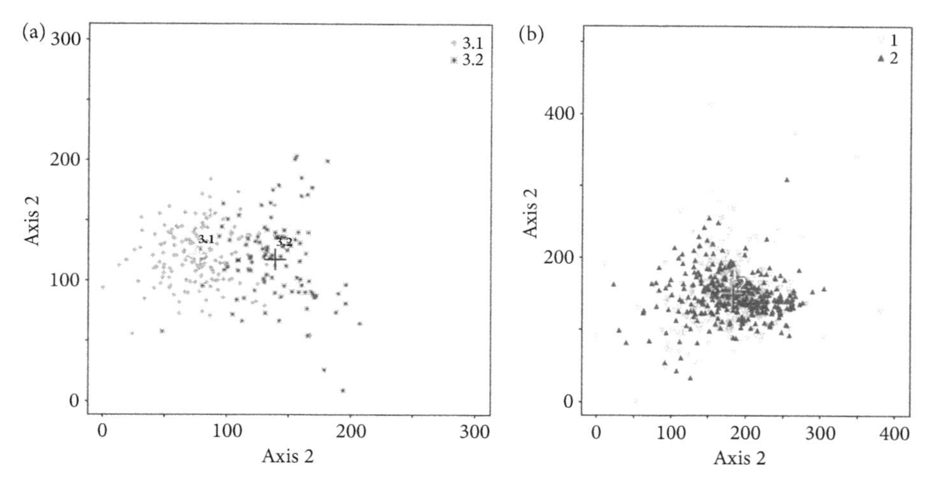

Figure 7.3 Ordination biplots can provide insight during CSM development. The detrended correspondence analysis biplots show the relationship between two human-coded bins that were more accurate when (a) separated or (b) combined for model development. Centroids of each category are marked by plus signs and the associated bin names.

(Ha, Urban-Lurain, and Merrill 2011; Haudek and Zhai 2021). Given other findings herein, it is likely that other features of the item and/or model, such as the scientific process targeted by the item, are more important than only training set size for some pairs of items and CSMs. The second surprising result is that unbalanced datasets had higher measures of CSM accuracy, as measured by κ. Previous work in CSM has found the opposite (Yang et al. 2002), and it is common practice in ML to balance data in the training set. As we usually see improvement in overall CSM performance with a more balanced training set, we suspect this result could be more indicative of how Cohen's kappa is calculated (Chicco and Jurman 2020). Specifically, if a low-occurring bin is not well scored, it has less of an effect on κ for the overall CSM than if a frequently occurring bin is consistently miscoded. This essentially means that for a balanced model, all bins must perform equally well, which is not necessarily true for an unbalanced dataset. This result, therefore, requires further scrutiny by examination of other measures of dataset imbalance and/or CSM performance at specific levels or bins.

Both the assessment scenario and subject domain in STEM have been proposed as features that could affect scoring accuracy (Zhai, Shi, and Nehm 2021). As all of our models in this study focus on physiology, we could not compare the subject domain (i.e., chemistry vs. biology), but we postulated that the scientific process targeted by the item and context used within the item could similarly affect CSM scoring accuracy. To our knowledge, this has not been directly tested previously with a large set of items and CSMs. We found CSMs for certain scientific processes were more accurate than others. Specifically, mass balance items had significantly lower κ than all the other concept categories; however, other shared attributes of the mass balance set of items and CSM could also be affecting success. For example, all the mass balance items share a common coding rubric and the same two tasks (covariational reasoning and identifying flux). Thus, we cannot untangle the contributions of processes, rubrics, and tasks for this set of items. Further, these items are also relatively new to the CSM development process, meaning we have not yet determined model settings that could greatly improve performance. These CSMs then represent models "in development" with the goal of achieving performance thresholds, in comparison to other items and CSMs (e.g., diffusion) that have achieved the target CSM thresholds and are considered complete. In contrast to mass balance, the ion flow CSMs have been through multiple rounds of development but remain problematic. We have attributed this to the large number of synonyms students use to respond to these questions. For example, the ions themselves and major ideas can be written out or given various notations and symbols by students. For example, *sodium* can be denoted as sodium, sodium ions, Na, and Na^+, and *equilibrium potential* can be written out or abbreviated E, Ena, Ena+, or communicated with the actual numeric value. The broad range of text to convey important scientific meaning is an identified problem in short-answer, concept-based CSMs, especially in science assessment (Brew and Leacock 2013; Jescovitch et al. 2020). To alleviate both these observations, most of the ion movement models include synonym replacement as part of the natural language processing process in the CRC tool, which greatly increases scoring accuracy.

Another significant item attribute that contributed to CSM success identified in this work was item structure. We observed during item development that students tended to provide clearer responses if given items with multiple questions with separate boxes to enter text into. For this reason, only four of the seventy-two items in the study contain only one explanation box. This finding seems to extend work on assessment items that use a multiple-choice followed by explanation format. In previous studies, researchers have found that prompting students for written explanations influences their multiple-choice selections within the same item (Koretsky, Brooks, and Higgins 2016) and reveals they have difficulty linking multiple ideas using explanation only prompts (Liu, Lee, and Linn 2011). We also found that the inclusion of a student's forced choice selection or written identify response along with their written explain component significantly increased CSM performance for categorization of their explanation response. To our knowledge, no work has directly tested the effect of a forced choice and identify question setup on scoring accuracy. We suspect increased performance could be for several reasons. First, the forced choice and identify questions provide stronger, consistent language patterns for the model to learn and may help narrow the lexical range of student responses. With forced choice, students are directly including the same set of words which are often heavily associated with the level of scientific thinking and therefore the coding bins. While students can use their own words in identify components, this part of the question tends to be less verbose than the explanation as students list their ideas, and there is usually a smaller set of variables or features students identify. For example, instead of explaining the complexity of an electrochemical gradient or how to change a gradient, within identify boxes, students will simply state "Change the gradient." In addition, providing students with forced choice distractors or asking them to identify relevant features in a question first may provide students a starting point from which to begin their explanations, resulting in less heterogeneous responses. Finally, including a forced choice or identify component limits the true open-endedness of the assessment task, which may be beneficial for CSM development (Brew and Leacock 2013). Despite including forced choice and identify components to our assessment items and associated CSMs, the models still rely mostly on the explain component as the correct forced choice will not result in a high level within the coding rubric or the CSM scoring. The inclusion of forced choice to constructed response items for STEM assessment has been used by other assessment groups (Liu, Lee, and Linn 2011; Zhu et al. 2017; Mao et al. 2018).

We found weak but statistically significant correlations between human–CSM κ and the number of bins in the coding rubric and model, indicating CSMs are more successful with fewer rubric bins and coding bins. This finding is supported in the literature by Leacock, Messineo, and Zhang (2013), who found that smaller, well-defined rubric concepts lead to higher scoring accuracy. We have noted while working with these models that though a satisfactory κ is obtained, many of the items with a high number of rubric-coding bins require more iterative development rounds for the CSM than those items and associated rubrics with a lower number of ideas. For example, within the ion flow concept, we had more difficulty with the CSMs for items that had over nine identified ideas in the rubric, while the model development for items with rubrics containing five to six bins only took one round of model training. However, this is not an absolute rule, as the mass balance IDF models all have a relatively low number of bins (five) but are among the CSMs that have exhibited low performance during model development. Together, this suggests that the number of model bins is not fully explanatory for model success. Indeed, other attributes of scoring rubrics have been found to influence model success. McGraw-Hill Education (2014) found CSMs had lower agreement with human coding if the ideas expressed were holistic as opposed to defined ideas. Additionally, Jescovictch et al. (2020) found that an analytical rubric was more successful for some specific models when compared directly to a holistic rubric in model training. Lottridge, Wood, and Shaw (2018) have also postulated that in addition to the number of bins, the complexity and overlap of the ideas in the bins are also important.

As other work has postulated that the complexity of the ideas expressed in responses and text overlap between bins affect CSM accuracy (McGraw-Hill Education 2014; Lottridge, Wood, and Shaw 2018; Leacock, Messineo, and Zhang 2013), we sought to find a metric that could be used to quantify the complexity and overlap of the text that students express in their responses. Ecological diversity metrics, when used with natural language processing, can reflect the range of language in constructed responses and have been used in conjunction with ordination methods to distinguish between groupings of responses (Shiroda, Fleming, and Haudek 2023). Unfortunately, we did not find a strong correlation between the ecological diversity measures we used and the associated human–CSM κ, with the exception of Whittaker's β. β showed a moderate, but not significant correlation with κ and a weak but significant percent bin scoring accuracy. As explained earlier, this measure is highly influenced by the number of shared words between responses, as it is the denominator in the formula. Since we did not observe a correlation between the total number of words in the constructed response corpus and model or bin accuracy alone, we think these observed correlations with β are largely due to a lower number of shared words between responses, which would produce higher β values. We believe the associated improvement in CSM performance could be because the model has a more distinct set of words that it associates with a given bin. If too many words are shared within a bin, it is more difficult for the model to learn the pattern in the language relevant to the underlying science or physiology construct of the assessment item.

We were hopeful that these diversity measures could be used more diagnostically to help determine whether a CSM will be more or less accurate based on the set of collected responses; however, there could be several reasons why these measures do not more strongly correlate with CSM accuracy. First, the diversity measures weigh all words in a matrix equally, while the ML algorithms are able to weight specific text features which are associated with the rubric bins. Since the rubric bins prioritize science content through proper words and phrases, we would expect science-relevant words to be extremely important in the ML algorithms (Nehm, Ha, and Mayfield 2012). We encourage future work to examine the diversity of science versus non-science (i.e., informal) text in student responses and the relationship to CSMs performance. Second, a major difference between the ML algorithms and the diversity metrics is the use of text feature grain size. To use our diversity metrics, we created a matrix of single words. In general, most of the CSMs studied here use unigrams and bigrams (one word and sequences of two words) to create the features used by the model; however, some models also use tri- and quad-grams to create the feature matrix for ML input. Within this work, we elected to only use individual words as including bi-, tri, and quad-grams because including all these combinations would result in matrices with thousands of columns with mostly zeros in the rows. As these matrices are already high zero datasets, we did not want to further compound this issue.

In contrast to the output values of the diversity metrics, the application of dimension reduction in ordination biplots from detrended correspondence analysis appears to provide some useful information about CSM performance. First, the average distance between groupings of responses by assigned bin and the percent accuracy of the bin was very close to significant and should be further investigated with a larger dataset. This, in combination with the significant negative correlation between percent error and group centroid distance for miscoded responses, supports our hypothesis that CSMs are more accurate if the language in responses classified in each rubric bin is distinct. This can also be visually observed in the groupings within biplots (as shown in Figure 7.1). Examining miscoded responses in Figure 7.2B also support that the more similar individual responses are to other groupings based on the text contained in responses, the more likely responses are to be miscoded. While this result is not surprising since the model relies on language patterns, we think it can be useful in better understanding a dataset during the model development process. We demonstrate one potential use of the biplot visualizations in Figure 7.3. Depending on the approaches, number of codes predicted, and algorithms (among other variables) used, training a single model may take up to an hour or more for large data sets. By using the ordination plots to examine different binning based on human-assigned codes, researchers could make more informed decisions on binning combinations before beginning CSM training, thereby saving time during model development. Alternatively, researchers could use biplot visualizations to assist decision-making about code lumping and splitting as part of the iterative work of human coding and CSM training to establish well-performing CSMs.

We have summarized the findings of this study, as well as the literature cited herein in Table 7.5. These citations are the only ones used within this paper and do not represent an exhaustive literature review of all automatic text scoring in science assessment. For a more thorough review please refer to Zhai, Shi, and Nehm (2021). Despite these conclusions, we also recognize several limitations of this study. First, this is an observational study, not a controlled experiment. Each of these CSMs and the associated assessment items contain multiple features that affect model success. Other studies directly compare an individual feature of an item, rubric, or model development and therefore have fewer potentially confounding factors. However, such studies are not always generalizable and the results found for a given CSM may not apply to another. Therefore, we see value in our *post-hoc* analysis in that it compares seventy-two different CSMs. A second limitation is that these models are not all in the same stages of development. Specifically, the ion movement items were some of the first this group worked on while the mass balance items are the most recent. Finally, some models have a low number of responses in the training set. This is partly due to when the items were developed but also due to the popularity of the assessment item itself. Some items target ideas usually learned in specific upper-level undergraduate classes and are therefore likely to be used in fewer courses, while other items target foundational ideas and common systems and thus are used in large-enrollment, introductory life sciences classes, resulting in a higher number of collected responses.

Future Directions

There are many remaining challenges in CSM development that AI can help address. Although some AI approaches, such as natural language processing and ML, are used to construct CSMs, there are opportunities to engage other AI approaches to aid the development process of CSMs. First, other dimension reduction techniques in AI should continue to be explored, with the goal of explainable groupings of short texts. We encourage continued exploration of other unsupervised clustering or learning methods to find potentially useful patterns in text groupings. These identified patterns can then be examined to ensure relevance to the assessment construct or their effect on performance of predictive algorithms. Such patterns may lead to better identification and/or diagnosis of potential miscodes from CSMs or additional information to use as input in predictive algorithms. To this point, another remaining challenge is the size of the text-feature matrix for comparison of short text responses. For this work, we used a matrix limited to individual words, primarily due to the increased difficulty of extracting patterns from large, high zero matrices. Generating a feature matrix via natural language processing could allow us to focus the matrix by extracting the most important words or phrases associated with a corpus. This could help focus the ordination techniques in a similar way to the CSMs, resulting in more informative ordination plots. Finally, as pointed out by others (Lottridge, Wood, and Shaw 2018; Zhai, Shi, and Nehm 2021), there are many variables, including those

Table 7.5 Summary of Findings and Supporting Literature for Features Affecting CSM Performance

	Feature	This study	Related literature
Assessment features	Question structure	Inclusion of FC or ID feature increases accuracy	Brew and Leacock (2013); Liu, Lee, and Linn (2011)
	Item context	Scientific process contributes to model success, but item context does not.	Zhai et al. (2020c)
	Number of rubric bins	Fewer rubric bins increase kappa.	Leacock, Messineo, and Zhang (2013); Lottridge, Wood, and Shaw (2018)
	Overlap of ideas	Separation of ideas based on separated language improves CSM accuracy.	Jescovitch et al. (2020); Lottridge, Wood, and Shaw (2018); McGraw-Hill Education (2014)
	Rubric type	Not examined as all rubrics are based on ordinal learning progressions.	Jescovitch et al. (2020); McGraw-Hill Education (2014); Nehm and Haertig (2012)
Item difficulty	Not examined as all items are designed for similar courses.	McGraw-Hill Education (2014); Zhai et al. (2020a)	
CSM training	Model Validation	Not examined as all items were developed with the same model validation method.	Nehm et al. 2012; Zhai et al. 2020b
Training set responses	Training set size	No statistical effect.	Ha et al. (2011); Heilman and Madnani (2015); Wang et al. (2021)
	Balance of training set	No statistical effect.	Yang et al. (2002)
	Diversity of student language	No consistent statistical effect.	Jescovitch et al. (2019); Jescovitch et al. (2020); Lottridge, Wood, and Shaw (2018); Maestrales et al. (2021); Shiroda et al. (2021)
	Response length	No statistical effect.	Liu et al. (2014); Mao et al. (2018); Nehm and Haertig (2012); Nehm, Ha, and Mayfield (2012)
	Student demographics	Not examined as demographic information was not readily available for all training sets.	Bridgeman, Trapani, and Attali (2012); Ha and Nehm (2016a, 2016b); Ha et al. (2011); Liu et al. (2016); Shermis (2015); Shermis et al. (2017); Shiroda et al. (2021); Wilson et al. (2023)

Note: These citations are only ones used within this paper and do not represent an exhaustive literature review. For a more thorough review please refer to Zhai et al. (2021).

of the assessment items, respondents, and CSM, which likely affect CSM success. Although we have tried to examine a few of these features specifically, future applications of AI could utilize other learning methods to identify which of these variables associate individually or as groups of variables with CSM outcomes. The goal of such an application would be transfer learning to the creation of new items, rubrics, and CSMs with minimal human involvement. One challenge to applying AI to such a problem is that many reported studies in ML-based science assessments do not report technical features of the CSM (Zhai et al. 2020b) or report different metrics of performance (Zhai, Shi, and Nehm 2021), thus limiting the available model information for such a large-scale study.

Acknowledgments

We thank members of the Automated Analysis of Constructed Response research group and collaborative LeaP UP project for helpful discussions about this study. We also thank Lauren Jescovitch and Juli Uhl, who worked on the development of several of the CSMs used in this work. This material is based upon work supported by the National Science Foundation under Grants 1323162 and 1660643. Any opinions, findings, and conclusions or recommendations expressed in this material are those of the author(s) and do not necessarily reflect the views of the National Science Foundation.

References

American Association for the Advancement of Science. 2011. *Vision and Change in Undergraduate Biology Education: A Call to Action*. Washington, DC.

Brew, C., and Leacock, C. 2013. "Automated Short Answer Scoring: Principles and Prospects." In Handbook of Automated Essay Evaluation, edited by M. D. Shermis and J. Burstein. London: Routledge. https://doi.org/10.4324/9780203122761.ch9

Bridgeman, B., Trapani, C., and Attali, Y. 2012. "Comparison of Human and Machine Scoring of Essays: Differences by Gender, Ethnicity, and Country." *Applied Measurement in Education* 25, no. 1: 27–40.

Chicco, D., and Jurman, G. 2020. "The Advantages of the Matthews Correlation Coefficient (MCC) over F1 Score and Accuracy in Binary Classification Evaluation." *BMC Genomics* 21, no. 1: 6. https://doi.org/10.1186/s12864-019-6413-7

Choi, W., and Jeong, H. 2016. "Finding an Appropriate Lexical Diversity Measurement for a Small-Sized Corpus and Its Application to a Comparative Study of L2 Learners' Writings." *Multimedia Tools and Applications* 75, no. 21: 13015–22. https://doi.org/10.1007/s11042-015-2529-1

Çınar, A., Ince, E., Gezer, M., and Yilmaz, Ö. 2020. "Machine Learning Algorithm for Grading Open-Ended Physics Questions in Turkish." *Education and Information Technologies* 25: 3821–44. https://doi.org/10.1007/s10639-020-10128-0

Corcoran, T. B., Mosher, F. A., and Rogat, A. 2009. *Learning Progressions in Science: An Evidence-Based Approach to Reform*. New York: Center on Continuous Instructional Improvement.

Dancey, C. P., and Reidy, J. 2007. *Statistics without Maths for Psychology*. London: Pearson Education.

Dood, A. J., Dood, J. C., Cruz-Ramírez de Arellano, D., Fields, K. B., and Raker, J. R. 2020. "Analyzing Explanations of Substitution Reactions Using Lexical Analysis and Logistic Regression

Techniques." *Chemistry Education Research and Practice* 21: 267–86. https://doi.org/10.1039/C9RP00148D

Doherty, J. H., Scott, E. E., Cerchiara, J. A., Jescovitch, L. N., McFarland, J. L., Haudek, K. C., and Wenderoth, M. P. 2023. "What a Difference in Pressure Makes! A Framework Describing Undergraduate Students' Reasoning about Bulk Flow down Pressure Gradients." *CBE—Life Sciences Education 22*, no. 2. https://doi.org/10.1187/cbe.20-01-0003

Ferri, C., Hernández-Orallo, J., and Modroiu, R. 2009. "An Experimental Comparison of Performance Measures for Classification." *Pattern Recognition Letters* 30, no. 1: 27–38. https://doi.org/10.1016/j.patrec.2008.08.010

Fleiss, J. L., and Cohen, J. 1973. "The Equivalence of Weighted Kappa and the Intraclass Correlation Coefficient as Measures of Reliability." *Educational and Psychological Measurement* 33, no. 3: 613–19. https://doi.org/10.1177/001316447303300309

Gerard, L. F., and Linn, M. C. 2016. "Using Automated Scores of Student Essays to Support Teacher Guidance in Classroom Inquiry." *Journal of Science Teacher Education* 27, no. 1: 111–29.

Ha, M., and Nehm, R. H. 2016a. "The Impact of Misspelled Words on Automated Computer Scoring: A Case Study of Scientific Explanations." *Journal of Science Education and Technology* 25, no. 3: 358–74.

Ha, M., and Nehm, R. 2016b. " Predicting the Accuracy of Computer Scoring of Text: Probabilistic, Multi-model, and Semantic Similarity Approaches." Paper in proceedings of the National Association for Research in Science Teaching, Baltimore, MD, April 14–17.

Ha, M., Nehm, R. H., Urban-Lurain, M., and Merrill, J. E. 2011. "Applying Computerized-Scoring Models of Written Biological Explanations across Courses and Colleges: Prospects and Limitations." *CBE—Life Sciences Education* 10, no. 4: 379–93.

Haudek, K. C., and Zhai, X. 2021. " Exploring the Effect of Construct Complexity on Machine Learning Assessments of Argumentation." Paper presented at Annual International Meeting of the National Association for Research in Science Teaching (NARST), virtual.

Heilman, M., and Madnani, N. 2015. "The Impact of Training Data on Automated Short Answer Scoring Performance." In *Proceedings of the Tenth Workshop on Innovative Use of NLP for Building Educational Applications*, 81–85. https://doi.org/10.3115/v1/W15-0610

Jarvis, S. 2013. "Capturing the Diversity in Lexical Diversity." *Language Learning* 63: 83–106. https://doi.org/10.1111/j.1467-9922.2012.00739.x

Jescovitch, L. N., Doherty, J. H., Scott, E. E., Cerchiara, J. A., Wenderoth, M. P., Urban-Lurain, M., Merrill, J., and Haudek, K. C. 2019. "Challenges in Developing Computerized Scoring Models for Principle-Based Reasoning in a Physiology Context. Paper Set: Measuring Complex Constructs in Science Education: Applications of Automated Analysis." Paper presented at the Annual International Meeting of the National Association for Research in Science Teaching (NARST). Baltimore, MD, Mar 31–Apr 3.

Jescovitch, L. N., Scott, E. E., Cerchiara, J. A., Merrill, J. E., Urban-Luain, M., Doherty, J. H., and Haudek, K. C. 2020. "Comparison of Machine Learning Performance Using Analytic and Holistic Coding Approaches Across Constructed Response Assessments Aligned to a Science Learning Progression." *Journal of Science Education and Technology* 30: 150–67. https://doi.org/10.1007/s10956-020-09858-0

Jurka, T., Collingwood, L., Boydstun, A., Grossman, E., and Atteveldt, W. 2013. "RtextTools: A Supervised Learning Package for Text Classification." *The R Journal* 5: 6–12. https://doi.org/10.32614/RJ-2013-001.

Jurasinski, G., Retzer, V., and Beierkuhnlein, C. 2009. "Inventory, Differentiation, and Proportional Diversity: A Consistent Terminology for Quantifying Species Diversity." *Oecologia* 159: 15–26. https://doi.org/10.1007/s00442-008-1190-z

Kaplan, J. J., Haudek, K. C., Ha, M., Rogness, N., and Fisher, D. G. 2014. "Using Lexical Analysis Software to Assess Student Writing in Statistics." *Technology Innovations in Statistics Education* 8, no. 1. Retrieved from https://escholarship.org/uc/item/57r90703

Koretsky, M. D., Brooks, B. J., and Higgins, A. Z. 2016. "Written Justifications to Multiple-Choice Concept Questions during Active Learning in Class." *International Journal of Science Education* 38, no. 11: 1747–65. https://doi.org/10.1080/09500693.2016.1214303

Krajcik, J. S. 2021. "Commentary—Applying Machine Learning in Science Assessment: Opportunity and Challenges." *Journal of Science Education and Technology* 30, no. 2: 313–18. https://doi.org/10.1007/s10956-021-09902-7

Leacock, C., Messineo, D., and Zhang, X. 2013. "Issues in Prompt Selection for Automated Scoring of Short Answer Questions." In Annual Conference of the National Council on Measurement in Education, San Francisco, CA.

Liu, O. L., Brew, C., Blackmore, J., Gerard, L., Madhok, J., and Linn, M. C. 2014. "Automated Scoring of Constructed-Response Science Items: Prospects and Obstacles." *Educational Measurement: Issues and Practice* 33, no. 2: 19–28. https://doi.org/10.1111/emip.12028

Liu, O. L., Lee, H.-S., and Linn, M. C. 2011. "An Investigation of Explanation Multiple-Choice Items in Science Assessment." Educational Assessment 16, no. 3: 164–84. https://doi.org/10.1080/10627197.2011.611702

Liu, O. L., Rios, J. A., Heilman, M., Gerard, L., and Linn, M. C. 2016. "Validation of Automated Scoring of Science Assessments." *Journal of Research in Science Teaching* 53, no. 2: 215–33. https://doi.org/10.1002/tea.21299

Lottridge, S., Wood, S., and Shaw, D. 2018. "The Effectiveness of Machine Score-Ability Ratings in Predicting Automated Scoring Performance." *Applied Measurement in Education* 31, no. 3: 215–32.

Maestrales, S., Zhai, X., Touitou, I., Baker, Q., Schneider, B., and Krajcik, J. 2021. "Using Machine Learning to Score Multi-dimensional Assessments of Chemistry and Physics." *Journal of Science Education and Technology* 30, no. 2: 239–54. https://doi.org/10.1007/s10956-020-09895-9

Mao, L., Liu, O. L., Roohr, K., Belur, V., Mulholland, M., Lee, H.-S., and Pallant, A. 2018. "Validation of Automated Scoring for a Formative Assessment That Employs Scientific Argumentation." Educational Assessment 23, no. 2: 121–38.

McCune, B., and M. J. Mefford. 2018. PC-ORD. Multivariate Analysis of Ecological Data. Version 7.08

McGraw-Hill Education CTB. 2014. *Smarter Balanced Assessment Consortium Field Test: Automated Scoring Research Studies (in Accordance with Smarter Balanced RFP 17)*. Monterey, CA: McGraw-Hill.

McHugh, M. L. 2012. "Interrater Reliability: The Kappa Statistic." *Biochemia Medica (Zagreb)* 22, no. 3: 276–82. PMID: 23092060; PMCID: PMC3900052.

Michael, J., Cliff, W., McFarland, J., Modell, H., and Wright, A. 2017. *The Core Concepts of Physiology: A New Paradigm for Teaching Physiology*. New York: Springer. https://doi.org/10.1007/978-1-4939-6909-8

Michael, J. A., and McFarland, J. 2011. "The Core Principles ("Big Ideas") of Physiology: Results of Faculty Surveys." *Advances in Physiology Education* 35, no. 4: 336–41. https://doi.org/10.1152/advan.00004.2011

Michael, J., and Modell, H. 2021. "Validating the Core Concept of 'Mass Balance.'" *Advances in Physiology Education* 45, no. 2: 276–80. https://doi.org/10.1152/advan.00235.2020

Modell, H. I. 2000. "How to Help Students Understand Physiology? Emphasize General Models." *Advances in Physiology Education* 23, no. 1: S101–107.

Murphy, K. P. 2012. *Machine Learning: A Probabilistic Perspective*. Cambridge, MA: MIT Press.

National Research Council. 2012. *A Framework for K–12 Science Education: Practices, Crosscutting Concepts, and Core Ideas*. Washington, DC: National Academies Press.

Nehm, R. H., Ha, M., and Mayfield, E. 2012. "Transforming Biology Assessment with Machine Learning: Automated Scoring of Written Evolutionary Explanations." *Journal of Science Education and Technology* 21, no. 1: 183–96.

Nehm, R. H., and Haertig, H. 2012. "Human vs Computer Diagnosis of Students' Natural Selection Knowledge: Testing the Efficacy of Text Analytic Software." *Journal of Science Education and Technology* 21, no. 1: 56–73.

Noyes, K., McKay, R. L., Neumann, M., Haudek, K. C., and Cooper, M. M. 2020. "Developing Computer Resources to Automate Analysis of Students' Explanations of London Dispersion Forces." *Journal of Chemical Education* 97, no. 11: 3923–36. https://doi.org/10.1021/acs.jchemed.0c00445

Palmer, M. W. 2019. "Gradient Analysis of Ecological Communities (Ordination)." In Handbook of Environmental and Ecological Statistics, edited by A. Gelfand, M. Fuentes, P. Hoeting, and R. L. Smith, 241–74. Boca Raton, FL: CRC Press.
Pelletreau, K. N., Andrews, T., Armstrong, N., Bedell, M. A., Dastoor, F., Dean, N., Erster, S., et al. 2016. "A Clicker-Based Study That Untangles Student Thinking about the Processes in the Central Dogma." *CourseSource*. https://doi.org/10.24918/cs.2016.15
Saldaña, J. 2021. The Coding Manual for Qualitative Researchers. London: Sage.
Scott, E. E., Wenderoth, M. P., and Doherty, J. H. 2020. "Design-Based Research: A Methodology to Extend and Enrich Biology Education Research." *CBE—Life Sciences Education* 19, no. 3. https://doi.org/10.1187/cbe.19-11-0245
Scott, E. E., Cerchiara, J., McFarland, J. L., Wenderoth, M. P., and Doherty, J. H. 2023. "How Students Reason about Matter Flows and Accumulations in Complex Biological Phenomena: An Emerging Learning Progression for Mass Balance." *Journal of Research in Science Teaching* 60, no. 1: 63–99. https://doi.org/10.1002/tea.21791
Shannon, C. E. 1948. "A Mathematical Theory of Communication." *Bell System Technical Journal 27*, no. 3: 379–423.
Shermis, M. D. 2015. "Contrasting State-of-the-Art in the Machine Scoring of Short Form Constructed Responses." *Educational Assessment* 20, no. 1: 46–65.
Shermis, M. D., Mao L., Mulholland, M., and Kieftenbeld, V. 2017. "Use of Automated Scoring Features to Generate Hypotheses Regarding Language-Based DIF." *International Journal of Testing* 17, no. 4: 351–71.
Shiroda, M., Uhl, J. D., Urban-Lurain, M., and Haudek, K. C. 2021. "Comparison of Computer Scoring Model Performance for Short Text Responses across Undergraduate Institutional Types." *Journal of Science Education and Technology* 31: 117–28. https://doi.org/10.1007/s10956-021-09935-y.
Shiroda, M., Fleming, M. P., and Haudek, K. C. 2023. "Ecological Diversity Methods Improve Quantitative Examination of Student Language in Short Constructed Responses in STEM." *Frontiers in Education* 8. https://www.frontiersin.org/articles/10.3389/feduc.2023.989836
Sieke, S. A., McIntosh, B. B., Steele, M. M., and Knight, J. K. 2019. "Characterizing Students' Ideas about the Effects of a Mutation in a Noncoding Region of DNA." *CBE—Life Sciences Education* 18, no. 2. https://doi.org/10.1187/cbe.18-09-0173
Simpson, E. H. 1949. "Measurement of Diversity." *Nature* 163, no. 4148: 688. Bibcode:1949Natur. 163.688S. https://doi.org/10.1038/163688a0.
Tweedie, F. J., and Baayen, R. H. 1998. "How Variable May a Constant be? Measures of Lexical Richness in Perspective." *Computers and the Humanities* 32: 323–52. https://doi.org/10.1023/A:1001749303137
Uhl, J. D., Sripathi, K. N., Meir, E., Merrill, J., Urban-Lurain, M., and Haudek, K. C. 2021. "Automated Writing Assessments Measure Undergraduate Learning after Completion of a Computer-Based Cellular Respiration Tutorial." *CBE—Life Sciences Education* 20, no. 33. https://doi.org/10.1187/cbe.20-06-0122.
Urban-Lurain, M., Cooper, M. M., Haudek, K. C., Kaplan, J. J., Knight, J. K., Lemons, P. P., Lira, C. T., et al. 2015. "Expanding a National Network for Automated Analysis of Constructed Response Assessments to Reveal Student Thinking in STEM." *Computers in Education Journal* 6, no. 2: 65–81.
Wang, C., Liu, X., Wang, L., Sun, Y., and Zhang, H. 2021. "Automated Scoring of Chinese Grades 7–9 Students' Competence in Interpreting and Arguing from Evidence." *Journal of Science Education and Technology* 30: 269–82. https://doi.org/10.1007/s10956-020-09859-z
Wilson, C. D., Haudek, K. C., Osborne, J. F., Buck Bracey, Z. E., Cheuk, T., Donovan, B. M., Stuhlsatz, M. A. M., Santiago, M. M., and Zhai, X. 2023. "Using Automated Analysis to Assess Middle School Students' Competence with Scientific Argumentation." *Journal of Research in Science Teaching* 61, no. 1: 38–69. https://doi.org/10.1002/tea.21864
Whittaker, R. H. 1967. "Gradient Analysis of Vegetation." *Biological Reviews* 42: 207–64.
Whittaker, R. H. 1969. "Evolution of Diversity in Plant Communities." *Brookhaven Symposia in Biology* 22: 178–95.

Yang, Y., Buckendahl, C. W., Juszkiewicz, P. J., and Bhola, D. S. 2002. "A Review of Strategies for Validating Computer Automated Scoring." *Applied Measuremeant in Education* 15, no. 4: 391–412.

Zenker, F., and Kyle, K. 2021. "Investigating Minimum Text Lengths for Lexical Diversity Indices." *Assessing Writing* 47. https://doi.org/10.1016/j.asw.2020.100505

Zhai, X., Haudek, K., Shi, L., Nehm, R., and Urban-Lurain, M. 2020a. "From Substitution to Redefinition: A Framework of Machine Learning-Based Science Assessment." *Journal of Research in Science Teaching* 57, no. 9: 1430–59. https://doi.org/10.1002/tea.21658

Zhai, X., Yin, Y., Pellegrino, J., Haudek, K., and Shi, L. 2020b. "Applying Machine Learning in Science Assessment: A Systematic Review." Studies in Science Education 56, no. 1: 111–51.

Zhai, X., Haudek, K., Stuhlsatz, M., and Wilson, C. 2020c. "Evaluation of Construct-Irrelevant Variance Yielded by Machine and Human Scoring of a Science Teacher PCK Constructed Response Assessment." Studies in Educational Evaluation 67: 1–12. https://doi.org/10.1016/j.stueduc.2020.100916

Zhai, X., Shi, L., and Nehm, R. H. 2021. "A Meta Analysis of Machine Learning Based Science Assessments: Factors Impacting Machine Human Score Agreements." *Journal of Science Education and Technology* 30: 361–79. https://doi.org/10.1007/s10956-020-09875-z

Zhu, M., Lee, H., Wang, T., Liu, O.L., Belur, V., and Pallant, A. 2017. "Investigating the Impact of Automated Feedback on Students' Scientific Argumentation." *International Journal of Science Education* 39, no. 12: 1648–68. https://doi.org/10.1080/09500693.2017.1347303.

8

AI-Based Diagnosis of Student Reasoning Patterns in NGSS Assessments

Lei Liu, Dante Cisterna, Devon Kinsey, Yi Qi, and Kenneth Steimel

National science standards such as the Next Generation Science Standards (NGSS; NGSS Lead States 2013) emphasize the deployment of multiple dimensions of science learning to make sense of the world, including doing science and the application of both disciplinary and cross-disciplinary concepts. Effectively noticing, interpreting, and then responding to students' ways of reasoning can be challenging and time-consuming for teachers in a classroom setting, particularly with the complexity of the standards' performance expectations. Scientific reasoning engages students in developing and testing hypotheses about how to make sense of natural phenomena. In science education, engaging students in active reasoning about the natural world can improve their ability to relate their observations with scientific principles in making sense of the world and solving real-world problems (Zimmerman 2007). Leveraging existing NGSS-aligned assessment data, we utilized machine-learning techniques to create artificial intelligence (AI) tools to support the understanding of student reasoning based on their written explanations. With high-quality assessment data, it is possible to train the machine to learn from human-annotated constructed response (CR) data to classify various patterns and identify strengths and weaknesses in students' reasoning (Kaldaras, Akaeze, and Krajcik 2021). The validity of the AI-based classification of student reasoning patterns is critical (Zhai, Krajcik, and Pellegrino 2021) and is related to four relevant assumptions:

(1) there are sufficient student data from high-quality assessments, well aligned with the three-dimensional learning framework described in the NGSS standards;
(2) there is a well-described framework that unpacks specific characteristic features of each student reasoning pattern (SRP);
(3) there are reliable human-annotated student responses for the machine to learn from; and
(4) advanced machine learning techniques are applied and iteratively validated.

This chapter describes a project exploring how a machine-learning approach can be utilized to respond to the national need to support multidimensional science learning. In particular, machine-learning techniques were applied to tackle the challenge of identifying various SRPs in making sense of scientific phenomena. The chapter

Lei Liu et al., *AI-Based Diagnosis of Student Reasoning Patterns in NGSS Assessments.* In: *Uses of Artificial Intelligence in STEM Education.* Edited by: Xiaoming Zhai and Joseph Krajcik, Oxford University Press.
 DOI: 10.1093/oso/9780198882077.003.0008

includes six sections. The first section discusses the need to understand student reasoning. The second section describes the assessment items and student data used in the study. The third section elaborates on a theoretical framework of student reasoning patterns and features for each pattern. The fourth section of the chapter focuses on the development and validation of an AI tool to automate the classification of SRP. The fifth section reports on a cognitive interview study, as part of the validation process, that involved students' use of the AI tool and findings from that study. The last section extends to discuss the validity issues related to the AI-based classification of SRP, its potential uses, limitations, and future research.

Student Reasoning Patterns (SRP)

Reasoning involves logical actions such as analyzing, proving, evaluating, explaining, inferring, justifying, and generalizing (Australian Curriculum, Assessment, and Reporting Authority [ACARA] 2015). In the context of science education, scientific reasoning includes developing testable questions, testing hypotheses, and drawing appropriate conclusions by coordinating empirical evidence and theory, which each requires identifying patterns from data or information and drawing inferences for the purpose of explaining scientific phenomena or solving problems. Student reasoning patterns refer to various ways of thinking when making sense of a natural phenomenon or trying to solve a problem. Student reasoning in science learning contexts relates to information seeking (Kuhn 2010) through interacting with the learning environments. Starting at young ages, children begin their scientific reasoning to make sense of the world around them by asking questions such as the following: Why do things move? Why do leaves change color? Why is there day and night? Similar to scientists and philosophers, students start shaping their own reasoning patterns to satisfy human inherent curiosity in making sense of the world using the power of observations and logic skills even at a very young age (Jirout and Klahr 2012). Klahr, Zimmerman, and Jirout (2011) characterized scientific reasoning in terms of two principal features: scientific content and inquiry processes. Similarly, the NGSS implies that scientific reasoning integrates knowledge and skills (i.e., three-dimensional science learning), in other words, to engage students in science practices to develop conceptual understanding within and across scientific domains.

There has been abundant research on how scientists reason (e.g., Kind and Osborne 2017; Klahr and Carver 1995); however, there has been less research on how students reason, particularly reasoning involving various dimensions of science learning. Research has identified scientists' distinct "styles of reasoning" (Kind and Osborne 2017) that differ in their ontological focus, methodologies, and epistemology. It is also argued that the notion of styles of reasoning is "a cultural argument for the values of an education in the sciences" (Kind and Osborne 2017, 10). In addition, it was stated that these styles of reasoning involve the three dimensions of knowledge required by the NGSS, namely disciplinary core ideas (DCIs), science and engineering practices (SEPs), and crosscutting concepts (CCCs). However, there is less documentation of student reasoning patterns in science learning that involve these three dimensions of knowledge. With more NGSS-aligned assessments available, there are opportunities to conduct research on characteristic features in student reasoning.

Evidence from NGSS-Aligned Assessment to Classify SRP

Teachers often rely on data collected from assessments to evaluate and determine the strengths and weaknesses of their students at different stages of learning (Krajcik 2021). Assessments, if appropriately designed, can be useful tools for providing data and evidence to support teachers in understanding and evaluating student reasoning in science. NGSS-aligned assessments require students to apply both core scientific concepts and essential practices to conduct higher-order reasoning (National Research Council 2014). As states implement assessments aligned to the NGSS, new assessment approaches are being applied to measure multiple dimensions of science. These newly designed assessments can help evoke common student reasoning patterns while making sense of science (e.g., ecological phenomena). By identifying patterns in student reasoning, teachers can generate better opportunities to solicit and build on students' ways of reasoning as resources for instructional planning. Given the multiple dimensions deployed in NGSS-aligned assessment, teachers are facing tremendous challenges in making sense of student data and providing constructive feedback to support student reasoning (Kaldaras and Haudek 2022). There are needs of both theoretical and technology tools to support science teachers to interpret and make use of student assessment data to inform their instructional planning. It is a time-consuming effort to make sense of student reasoning, which is likely to be specific to scientific concepts and/or practices.

Here we describe a scenario-based ecosystem assessment task as an example that requires students to use their understanding of the CCC of systems and system models, and knowledge of trophic relationships among organisms in ecosystems to come up with an argument through engaging in the practice of model-based argumentation, measuring a bundle of adapted performance expectations (i.e., MS-LS2-4 and MS-LS2-5) from the NGSS. To complete the task, students must use a modeling tool and a simulation to figure out the best method to control a corn rootworm infestation that affects corn yield. The simulation provided data to evaluate how the two control methods (using predators vs. growing a trap crop) would help reduce the population of corn rootworms in a farm ecosystem. Students evaluated the effectiveness of each method through a simulated activity and evidence-based reasoning. Figure 8.1 presents data generated from the simulation of the first control method (using predators—harvestmen). The CR item asked students to construct an explanation of why adding harvestmen (a predator) into the farm ecosystem in Years 3 through 5 was not helpful to reduce the corn rootworm population and increase the corn yield. To answer this question, students were expected to construct an explanation based on both evidence or data generated from the simulation (SEP dimension) and relevant science principles that describe the system mechanisms in the ecosystem, including relationships between system components (DCI/CCC dimensions).

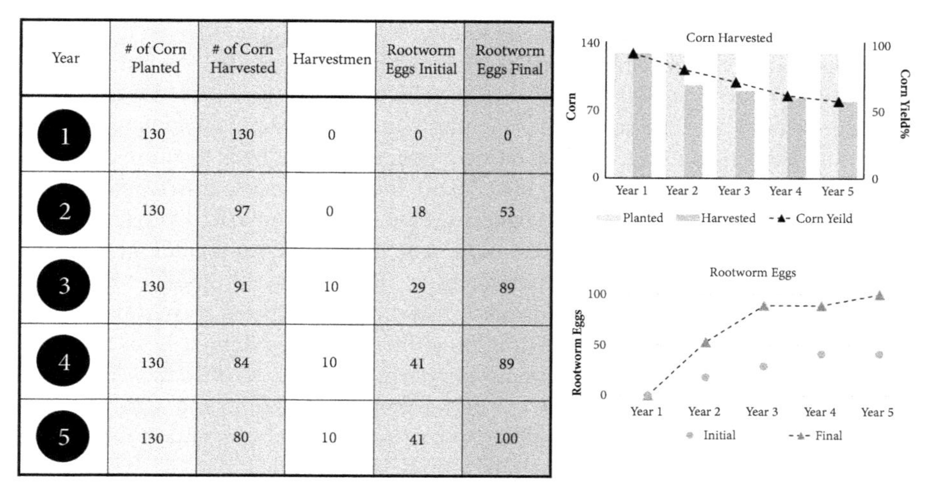

Year	# of Corn Planted	# of Corn Harvested	Harvestmen	Rootworm Eggs Initial	Rootworm Eggs Final
1	130	130	0	0	0
2	130	97	0	18	53
3	130	91	10	29	89
4	130	84	10	41	89
5	130	80	10	41	100

Figure 8.1 Data generated from a simulation of adding harvestmen (a predator organism) into the ecosystem to resolve the corn harvest problem.

A Theoretical Framework for SRP

Learning theories on how students reason help to make sense of machine learning, generate innovative applications of AI, and enhance the significance of its application value. In the domain of science education, research has explored how young children engaged in scientific reasoning and used evidence to support their reasoning (Chinn and Brewer 1998; Kuhn, Amsel, and O'Loughlin 1988; Masnick and Morris 2008). Some research showed that many students did not coordinate data or evidence with theory (e.g., Kuhn, Amsel, and O'Loughlin 1988). In other words, there is a clear separation between data and theory in students' explanation. Other research found that students tended to use data to retain their theories but ignored anomalous data that conflicted with their theories (Chinn and Brewer 1998). The NGSS calls for a new paradigm of science learning that requires integrating multiple dimensions of science to make sense of phenomena. Assessments aligned with the NGSS provide opportunities for students to explore natural phenomena and demonstrate both their scientific knowledge and science practices. It is desired that students actively participate in more meaningful activities (e.g., investigating simulated natural phenomena) while conducting evidence-based reasoning like a scientist or engineer. This type of reasoning requires integrating the science practice (e.g., analyzing and interpreting data) with scientific theories or principles (e.g., system mechanisms in ecosystems). This new paradigm requires an updated learning theory or framework of how students reason in relation to the dimensions in science learning.

In the ecosystem assessment item described in "Evidence from NGSS-Aligned Assessment to Classify SRP," students were asked to use data from a simulation of a farm ecosystem to explain why adding a predator into the system did not solve the rootworm infestation that impacts the corn field. We identified several typical student reasoning patterns by analyzing student responses. Some students focused on describing observations and data only, while others only provided scientific principles without referring to data or evidence. Finally, we found some students attempted to integrate both data and scientific principles into their reasoning. Diagnosing these reasoning patterns is useful for generating personalized feedback to address gaps in student reasoning (e.g., Nazaretzky et al. 2022). In science classrooms, teachers need help to identify student reasoning patterns. Figure 8.2 summarizes key features of SRPs elicited in this ecosystem assessment item. The examples include highlighted evidence associated with the features for each SRP. Pattern A responses include a description of data patterns or inclusion of data only, thus labeled as unidimensional and related to the SEP dimension (text underlined and highlighted in blue color). Pattern B responses include descriptions of system mechanisms only, thus labeled as unidimensional focusing on DCI/CCC dimension (text in italics and highlighted in orange). Pattern A + B responses include both data or data patterns and system mechanisms, thus labeled as multidimensional with both SEP and DCI/CCC dimensions. For responses that lack essential evidence associated with any dimension, they were labeled as unidentifiable pattern.

Development and Validation of an AI-Supported Classification Tool

With recent rapid improvements in AI research, machines are getting better at analyzing, understanding, and even responding to natural language. Recently there have been a few research efforts focusing on automated scoring related to NGSS learning (e.g., Haudek et al. 2012; Kaldaras, Akaeze, and Krajcik 2021; Kaldaras and Haudek 2022; Wilson et al. 2023; Zhai, He, and Krajcik 2022), including our SPIN-NGSS NSF grant (Liu, Cisterna, and Cahill 2020). Liu et al. (2016) identified eleven studies investigating automated text scoring of open-ended science items as post-hoc analysis of student responses, with only a few exploring the instructional potentials (e.g., Linn et al. 2014). Zhai, Krajcik, and Pellegrino (2021) investigated the validity challenges of machine-scoring. One potential risk identified is that student performance might be impacted by other variables, particularly in performance-based assessments with high demand for technology and novel forms of assessments. However, providing only a score is insufficient to support learning and teaching and teachers need support to understand student reasoning. In a systematic review of applying machine learning in science assessment, Zhai et al. (2020) stated that machine learning helps teachers evaluate and interpret students' performance immediately to adjust their teaching strategies although they pointed out that the majority of the studies included in the review focused on examining the accuracy of the machine learning, but not as much on the uses of machine learning to support classroom learning and teaching activities.

To help teachers better attend to students' ways of reasoning, our team has developed machine-learning models to automate the diagnosis of student reasoning patterns based on key features related to the NGSS dimensions. These models provide both a reasoning pattern label and evidence in student responses associated with the pattern. As part of this process, content experts first coded a set of

Student Reasoning Patterns	Description of Student Response Characteristics	Example Student Responses – Phase 2 (INCEpTION)
Pattern A: Unidimensional Reasoning (SEP)	Includes data patterns and/or data points only (e.g., description of system component population change, number of system components in certain year), but not scientific reasoning.	...adding harvestmen...didn't help to increase the percent corn yield because there became more rootworms every year and the same amount of harvestmen in years 3, 4, and 5...There were only 10 harvestmen with 89 and 100 rootworms.
Pattern B: Unidimensional Reasoning (DCI/CCC)	Includes system mechanisms only (e.g., function of system components, trophic relationship between system components), but not reference to data patterns.	Because the *rootworms where lying eggs* and they [harvestmen] couldn't stop it and when they tried it just made it worse.
Pattern A + B: Multidimensional Reasoning (SEP and DCI/CCC)	Includes both population data and/or data patterns and relevant scientific reasoning (naïve or scientific)	...there were not enough harvestmen per initial rootworm eggs. In the years Jonah did use harvestmen, the number of harvestmen remained the same. The initial rootworm eggs continued to increase. There were not enough *harevestmen to destroy all the eggs...*
Unidentifiable	Responses that are too vague or irrelevant.	I don't understand the graphs.

Figure 8.2 Student reasoning patterns in an ecosystem assessment item.

Note: The highlighted text indicates the segments of students' responses associated with each reasoning pattern.

student responses. Then, natural language processing (NLP) experts used the human-annotated codes to train computers to develop automated models. The automation includes evidence annotation (i.e., identifying parts of responses related to the NGSS dimensions), SRP classification (i.e., classifying entire responses with a reasoning pattern label), and real-time feedback (i.e., generating real-time automated feedback to students associated with specific reasoning patterns). Details on these steps follow.

Evidence Annotation and AI Model Building

Annotations were developed using the INCEpTION annotation tool (Klie, de Castilho, and Gurevych 2020). This tool allows annotation of document-level (i.e., individual student responses) and span-level (i.e., text segments within an individual student response) information with relative ease. The document-level annotation generates an SRP classification (i.e., what reasoning pattern the response illustrates). The span-level annotation provides evidence for the SRP classification, which is helpful for students and teachers to understand what a specific SRP classification is assigned. For evidence coding, we selected and highlighted texts in student responses related to specific NGSS dimensions. The evidence annotation looked for three types of evidence in student responses: SEP—corresponding to pattern A; DCI/CCC—corresponding to pattern B; and PROMPT—corresponding to when students copied the question prompt into their responses. The purpose of this human annotation was to gather human-generated codes based on a student learning model to train an automated model that can potentially provide useful information to teachers to help them interpret student responses according to the NGSS dimensions. The highlighted texts could be useful information when provided to teachers as evidence of student learning associated with the three dimensions of science learning.

Several rounds of annotation training and reliability coding were conducted to establish adequate agreement before conducting the AI model building. To evaluate span-level evidence code agreement, we evaluated span similarity. For span similarity, we used an intersection-over-union strategy and considered a span a match if the intersection-over-union ratio was greater than 0.8.

For evidence annotation AI model building, two different neural network architectures were used: multilabel sequence tagging and a conditional random field (CRF) approach. Both of these network architectures incorporated fine-tuning of BERT (Devlin et al. 2018), a large neural model trained by Google on massive amounts of English texts. The multilabel sequence tagging model predicts multiple tags for each word in the input, while the CRF model collapses overlapping DCI/CCC and SEP sequences into an OVERLAP tag. For the ecosystem assessment item, the CRF model achieved a macro-average F-score of 0.812 at the word level, while the multilabel sequence tagging model achieved an F-score of 0.813. The CRF model produced spans that more closely approximated human annotations (e.g., fewer discontinuities) but rarely matched annotated highlighted texts perfectly.

Label Annotation and AI Model Building

The first phase of model building for SRP labels focused on predicting a response-level reasoning pattern label. The prediction was tied with the evidence annotation. As shown in Figure 8.2, responses with blue highlights/underlined only (i.e., evidence for SEP dimension) got a prediction of pattern A label; responses with orange highlights/italicized only (i.e., evidence for DCI/CCC dimension) got a prediction of pattern B label; responses with both color highlights got a prediction of pattern A + B label; responses with no color codes got a prediction of the unidentifiable label. In addition, we explored using human codes of the SRP labels for AI model building. For the ecosystem assessment item, a traditional feature-based support vector classifier (SVC) and a neural approach using a large pre-trained transformer model were compared, showing significantly better performance using the pre-trained transformer model.

We measured agreement between four human coders in terms of pairwise Cohen's kappa. The first round of SRP coding showed poor agreement, with kappa only ranging between 0.34 and 0.48. However, after iterative training as well as revisions to the coding protocol, performance improved and remained satisfactory for the remainder of the effort, ranging from 0.67 to 0.83. To resolve discrepancies between annotators, the annotators adjusted the SRP annotations in cases where there were disagreements. Some learning out of this revision process was that the characteristics of student reasoning need to be better elaborated with examples of multiple ways that students intend to express their ideas. For example, some students tended to cite the raw data provided in the task, while others tended to describe data patterns based on their analysis results. Both cases were coded under the SEP dimension.

Real-Time Automated Feedback

Following the success of AI model building for the first CR item, we created an interface that embedded an AI-model that supported real-time automated diagnosis and feedback generation when students submit their responses. This immediate feedback would help students identify gaps in their reasoning for revisions and improvements.

We deployed the AI models in an online tool to automatically provide feedback on student responses to the ecosystem assessment item. When a student submitted a response, the online tool generated both diagnoses and feedback information to support students' reflection on their responses, including (1) classified reasoning patterns related to the NGSS dimensions, (2) color codes added to students' responses to help students identify the text in their answers associated with each SRP, and (3) feedback prompts to support students in revising their responses. For example, if the student response includes text only related to the reasoning pattern SEP, the feedback reminds students to consider bringing in other NGSS dimensions into their reasoning. If the student response shows a multidimensional pattern, the feedback prompts suggest students review their responses to make them more convincing or include alternative explanations. Figure 8.3 shows an example of the feedback generated when an answer included the multidimensional reasoning pattern.

Result of Automated Annotation

Dimension	Description	Color
SEP	Science and Engineering Practice (data patterns or data points)	blue
DCI/CCC	Crosscutting Concept and Disciplinary Core Ideas (systems mechanisms)	orange
Overlapped text	Overlapped texts in SEP and DCI/CCC dimensions	**brown**

Resoning Type:

Integrated reasoning: this response contains a mix of practice and system mechanisms.
Here are some additional things to consider:

- Are there other possible alternative explanations?
- Can you elaborate a bit more about how the concept relates to the data cited in your response?
- How can you make this argument more convincing?

Original Response

Adding the harvestmen to the crops was beneficial, but did not completely eliminate the problem of rootworms. This is because the rootworms continued to lay eggs at the same rate as before, and therefore continued to muliply. The percent of corn yield did not increase on effect of this.

Automatic Annotation

adding *the harvestmen to the crops was* beneficial, *but did not completely eliminate the problem of rootworms.* this is because the **rootworms continued to lay eggs** at the same rate as before, and therefore continued to multiply. the percent of corn yield did not increase on effect of this.

Figure 8.3 Example of automated feedback provided to a student response that includes a multidimensional reasoning pattern.

A Cognitive Interview Study

Similar to any other innovation development, validation is an important process for AI model building to ensure that such model is performing as it should, in terms of its design objectives and its utility for users. Questions related to the validation include the following: Does the AI model generate accurate diagnosis? Does the information generated by the AI model support students' next step learning? How do students react to the information generated by the AI tool? Cognitive interview studies may help answer some of these questions. In cognitive interview studies, interviewers can probe students when observing any cues of the uncertainty of respondents. In addition, the interviewers may also ask follow-up questions to collect information on how students perceive the functionalities of the AI tool and the information generated by the AI models. Student data collected from these studies can be used to identify gaps in AI models, particularly gaps in diagnosis accuracy and feedback effectiveness.

To validate the implementation of the AI models for the ecosystem assessment item, we conducted forty-five sessions of interviews with middle and high school students. Each session was approximately sixty minutes long. Among the forty-five students, there were five 6th graders, twelve 7th graders, nine 8th graders, ten 9th graders, and nine 10th graders. Twenty-four of the students identified as female, and twenty-one as male. In terms of ethnicity, students primarily identified as one or more ethnicity (fifteen students), followed by Asian/Asian-American (fourteen students), White/Caucasian (eight students), Black/African American (two students), Hispanic/Latino(a) (two students), and the rest preferred not to answer. We developed a protocol to guide students during the cognitive interview session, followed by interview questions. Each student read the assessment item and submitted an initial response. The AI tool generated real-time diagnosis information and real-time feedback about the reasoning pattern, indicating whether their answers were unidimensional or multidimensional with color-coded evidence associated with each dimension (see Figure 8.3). Based on the initial feedback generated by the tool, students had the opportunity to revise and submit new responses multiple times if they wanted. In each session, interviewers asked students for their interpretation of the feedback features presented in the dashboard and their thought process to make revisions: What does the tool tell you about your response? Why are some parts of your response highlighted in (blue/underlined, orange/italicized, brown/bolded)? What do you think the highlighted text tells you about your response? Is this feedback helpful to understand the aspects of your response that were good? Does the feedback help you understand where you can make improvements? etc.

Forty out of forty-five students revised their initial responses after receiving AI-generated feedback. Thirty students made one revision, and the other ten students made more than one revision. There were multiple response paths students took when revising their responses. Some were able to move from a unidimensional pattern to a multidimensional pattern with only one revision, while other students needed multiple revisions to achieve a multidimensional pattern.

When identifying gaps in the AI model, we identified two errors in AI diagnosis for SRP. One error related to student use of a different expression—"harvestmen removed rootworms," unlike most students who used "got rid of" or "kill" in their expressions. This expression described a system mechanism. However, the AI diagnosis failed to capture the DCI/CCC dimension in this specific response. The second error occurred when a student typed, "he did not add enough harvestman to kill enough root warms," in which the AI failed to recognize the DCI/CCC dimension. A possible interpretation was the typo in "warms" instead of "worms." We discussed these errors with an AI expert and updated the AI model to count in alternative ways of student expressions when describing predator–prey relationships and the impact of typos or misspellings in classifying student responses.

To explore the effect of real-time feedback on student performance, we analyzed how the AI-generated feedback impacted students' revisions of their initial responses. In each session, each student participant was prompted if they understood the automated diagnosis and feedback and if they would go back to revise and resubmit their response based on the feedback. We found forty out of forty-five students made at least one attempt to revise their responses, and 58% of the responses were diagnosed as pattern A + B after the first revision (see Figure 8.4). The results indicated that most students were able to use the feedback to revise their initial responses. For the five students who did not revise their responses, four of them had their initial responses diagnosed as pattern A + B and were not sure what additional information they should add to improve their responses. In total, after receiving the immediate feedback, 96%

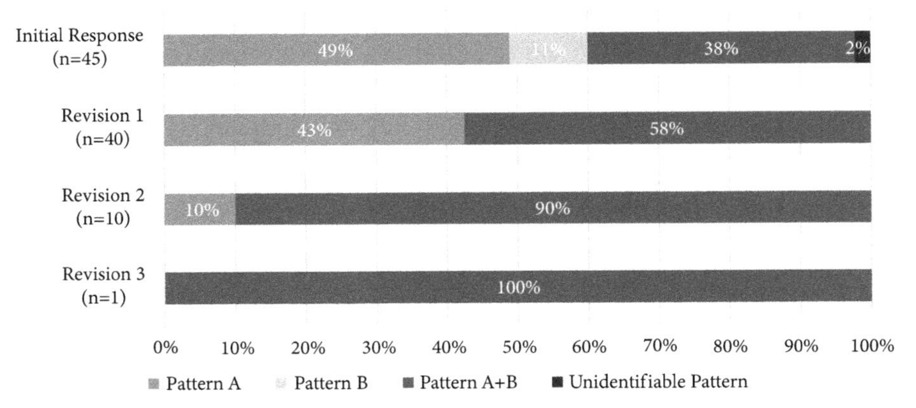

Figure 8.4 Student initial and revised responses.

of students who initially had unidimensional reasoning patterns (i.e., pattern A or pattern B) revised their responses, and about 70% of the revised responses were improved to be multidimensional reasoning pattern (i.e., pattern A + B). This indicated that the AI-generated diagnosis and feedback supported students to improve their multidimensional reasoning skills. For the remaining 30% of students who revised their initial responses, the revisions led to more elaborated descriptions of relevant dimension(s) in the initial responses, although the feedback did not lead to adding an additional dimension to their responses. For example, one student's initial response was:

> When adding the harvestmen, we did not see an increase in the corn yield due to that they didn't decrease the population of rootworms enough. From the chart and graphs, we see that as the number of corns harvested decreases, the amount of initial and final rootworm eggs increases. For example, in year 3, we can see that only around 70% of the corn is harvested and there is 89 rootworms. In year 5, we can see that there is around 62% corn harvested and there is 100 rootworms. With the population of rootworms increasing, more and more corn is being destroyed, therefore resulting in a decrease in the harvested corn. To conclude, the harvestmen where not able to control the rootworm population, which is causing a great decrease in harvested corn.

And the revised response was:

> When the population of harvestmen were added, there was not a decrease in rootworm eggs because it was not able to contain the rootworm population enough. From the chart and graphs, we see that as the number of corn harvested decreases, the amount of initial and final root worm eggs increases. For example, in year 3, we can see that only around 70% of the corn is harvested and there is 89 rootworms. In year 5, we can see that there is round 62% corn harvested and there is 100 rootworms. With the population of rootworms increasing, there was no potential for

> the harvestmen to be able to control the population. With the population of rootworms constantly on the rise, more and more corn was being destroyed and less corn was able to be harvested. To conclude, the harvestmen where not able to control the rootworm population, which is causing a great decrease in harvested corn.

This example showed that the student's revision focused on adding more data to elaborate why adding harvestmen did not control the rootworm population, which indicated that the feedback could be further improved to help students understand what dimension was included in their initial response and what dimensional information was missing.

In addition, we found that some students noted the feedback prompts helped them reflect on the NGSS dimensions included in their responses. For example, student 13 made three attempts to revise their responses (an initial response of pattern A + B), but in a very succinct way. In the following revision attempts, the student provided more detailed descriptions with more data from the graphs. In the last attempt, the student leveraged the feedback prompts to provide more detailed statements about the scientific principles and elaborated reasoning in the DCI/CCC dimension by adding more detailed system mechanisms. The student said that the feedback prompt "Can you elaborate a bit more about how the concept relates to the data cited in your response?" helped him to include a scientific principle about trophic relationships in the explanation to make sense of the data. Furthermore, we noted that although some student responses reflected the same SRP pattern after several revision attempts, they tended to include more descriptive statements based on the feedback. For example, student 7 made two revision attempts to review the initial response, but both revised responses were of pattern A. The student said the feedback prompt helped her improve her reasoning: "Yes . . . it's clear that most of what I wrote was just straight data points," but she was unsure of how to use the feedback to improve the response to be pattern A + B. Overall, the analysis suggests that the feedback tool helped students refine their ideas both *within* a reasoning pattern and to move their responses to another reasoning pattern. We identified three potential improvement aspects in the current feedback prompts. First, most students mentioned that they did not have direct instruction on the three NGSS dimensions (i.e., SEP, DCI, CCC), indicating the feedback should either avoid using those terms or provide more explanations on those terms. Second, some students mentioned specific examples of system mechanisms or scientific principles would be helpful, indicating the feedback should include specific examples. Third, some students with multidimensional reasoning patterns thought they should move to unidimensional reasoning when they received the feedback rather than further elaborating their responses, indicating the feedback should explicitly identify the desired reasoning pattern and acknowledge achievements students have made so far.

Overall, we found the cognitive interview study was indeed helpful in identifying gaps in both the AI model accuracy and potential improvements for AI-generated feedback. This type of validation process reminded us of weaving student language into AI model building and refinement and considering potential misinterpretations from students in revising feedback generation.

Discussion

This chapter described the conceptualization of the SRP framework related to the practice of interpreting and analyzing data and the ecosystem core concept, which was a starting point to define what AI can do to support students in using multiple dimensions to make sense of natural phenomena. AI applications in education are on the rise, given its potential to support individualized learning and teaching. Amidst the challenges of implementing the NGSS in classrooms, AI techniques have the potential to support teachers in diagnosing student reasoning patterns and inform their instruction. The product of AI diagnosis and feedback has the potential to enhance teachers' use of science assessments to facilitate student learning through individualized and immediate feedback (e.g., Lee et al. 2021). The automated diagnosis of student reasoning patterns can support teachers to interpret and use student data to make evidence-based instructional decisions. In these efforts, it is essential to validate the AI models (Zhai, Krajcik, and Pellegrino 2021). The validity of the AI models depends on the data used for the AI model building and refinement, how the unpacking of student cognition supports AI model building, the reliability of the data source that the machine is learning from (e.g., human codes), and the machine-learning techniques that are applied.

The process of validation needs to start at the beginning of conceptualizing the AI model and its purpose. To develop an AI model that can support NGSS learning and teaching, researchers have to define at a fine-grained level what machines can learn about student cognition related to various dimensions of science reasoning. As multiple efforts to further unpack other practices and core ideas of the NGSS to broaden AI use in the NGSS era are being considered, this unpacking is necessary to provide guidance and directions for what information can be generated by AI tools to provide useful information to support classroom learning and teaching.

The development and refinement of AI models require key steps of collecting or using data to train models and iteratively deploying the model to collect new data to refine and retrain the models. To develop AI models to support NGSS learning and teaching, we have to use NGSS-aligned assessment data. Rigorous alignment studies should precede the AI model building to make sure the assessment is well aligned with the NGSS standards. Once initial AI models are developed, it is also important to deploy the model with the target users to collect their perceptions on the AI-generated information and explore whether the AI models truly achieve their intended purposes. Cognitive interviews can be one of the many methods used in the validation process (Liu et al. 2016). It is always helpful to use the data generated from the validation studies to identify gaps, biases, or errors in the AI models, as well as refine the cognition model and retrain the AI models. The cognitive lab study from this project was one way to investigate students' interpretation of automated diagnosis and feedback. Additional efforts are needed to continue exploring how teachers and students use the AI-supported tools in classrooms to support their learning and teaching (Zhai et al. 2020).

Finally, it is important to note that there are tasks machines can do with the rapid development of AI, but AI cannot replace humans (Zhai and Nehm 2023), such as teachers' roles in classrooms. The hope is to leverage AI applications to empower teachers to focus on more complex tasks, particularly those that require accumulated knowledge about their students through daily interactions. Future research is needed to investigate how AI tools are implemented and used by teachers in classroom settings and what teacher roles are essential for fully taking advantage of AI tool use.

Acknowledgments

This material is based upon work supported by the National Science Foundation under Grant 2000492 and the Institute of Education Sciences under Grant R305A170456. Any opinions, findings, and conclusions or recommendations expressed in this material are those of the author(s) and do not necessarily reflect the views of the National Science Foundation and the Institute of Education Sciences—US Department of Education.

References

Australian Curriculum, Assessment and Reporting Authority (ACARA). 2015. Australian Curriculum: Mathematics. http://www.australiancurriculum.edu.au/Mathematics/

Chinn, C. A., and Brewer, W.F. 1998. "An Empirical Test of a Taxonomy of Responses to Anomalous Data in Science." *Journal of Research in Science Teaching* 35: 623–54. https://doi.org/10.1002/(SICI)1098-2736(199808)35:6%3C623::AID-TEA3%3E3.0.CO;2-O

Devlin, J., Chang, M. W., Lee, K., and Toutanova, K. 2018. "Bert: Pre-training of Deep Bidirectional Transformers for Language Understanding." *arXiv preprint arXiv*:1810.04805.

Haudek, K. C., Prevost, L. B., Moscarella, R. A., Merrill, J., and Urban-Lurain, M. 2012. "What Are They Thinking? Automated Analysis of Student Writing about Acid–Base Chemistry in Introductory Biology." *CBE—Life Sciences Education* 11, no. 3: 283–93.

Jirout, J., and Klahr, D. 2012. "Children's Scientific Curiosity: In Search of an Operational Definition of an Elusive Concept." *Developmental Review* 32, no. 2: 125–60. https://doi.org/10.1016/j.dr.2012.04.002

Kaldaras, L., Akaeze, H., and Krajcik, J. 2021. "Developing and Validating Next Generation Science Standards-Aligned Learning Progression to Track Three-Dimensional Learning of Electrical Interactions in High School Physical Science." *Journal of Research in Science Teaching* 58, no. 4: 589–618. https://doi.org/10.1002/tea.21672

Kaldaras, L., and Haudek, K. C. 2022. "Validation of Automated Scoring for Learning Progression-Aligned Next Generation Science Standards Performance Assessments." *Frontiers in Education* 7: 968289. https://doi.org/10.3389/feduc.2022.968289

Kind, P. E. R., and Osborne, J. 2017. "Styles of Scientific Reasoning: A Cultural Rationale for Science Education?" *Science Education* 101, no. 1: 8–31. https://doi.org/10.1002/sce.21251

Klahr, D., and Carver, S. M. 1995. "Scientific Thinking about Scientific Thinking." *Monographs of the Society for Research in Child Development* 60, no. 4: 137–51. http://www.jstor.org/stable/1166059?origin=JSTOR-pdf

Klahr, D., Zimmerman, C., and Jirout, J. 2011. "Educational Interventions to Advance Children's Scientific Thinking." *Science* 333, no. 6045: 971–75. https://doi.org/10.1126/science.1204528

Klie, J. C., de Castilho, R. E., and Gurevych, I. 2020, July. "From Zero to Hero: Human-in-the-Loop Entity Linking in Low Resource Domains." In Proceedings of the 58th Annual Meeting of the Association for Computational Linguistics, 6982–993. https://aclanthology.org/2020.acl-main.624/

Krajcik, J. S. 2021. "Commentary—Applying Machine Learning in Science Assessment: Opportunity and Challenges." *Journal of Science Education and Technology* 30, no. 2: 313–18. https://doi.org/10.1007/s10956-021-09902-7

Kuhn, D., Amsel, E., and O'Loughlin, M. 1988. *The Development of Scientific Thinking Skills.* San Diego, CA: Academic Press.

Kuhn, D. 2010. "Teaching and Learning Science as Argument." *Science Education* 94, no. 5: 810–24.

Lee, H. S., Gweon, G. H., Lord, T., Paessel, N., Pallant, A., and Pryputniewicz, S. 2021. "Machine Learning-Enabled Automated Feedback: Supporting Students' Revision of Scientific Arguments Based on Data Drawn from Simulation." *Journal of Science Education and Technology* 30, no. 2: 168–92. https://doi.org/10.1007/s10956-020-09889-7

Linn, M. C., Gerard, L., Ryoo, K., McElhaney, K., Liu, O. L., and Rafferty, A. N. 2014. "Computer-Guided Inquiry to Improve Science Learning." *Science* 344, no. 6180: 155–56. https://doi.org/10.1126/science.1245980

Liu, L., Cisterna, D., and Cahill, A. 2020. "Student Reasoning Patterns in NGSS Assessments." STEM for All Video Showcase 2020. https://multiplex.videohall.com/presentations/2043

Liu, O. L., Rios, J. A., Heilman, M., Gerard, L., and Linn, M. C. 2016. "Validation of Automated Scoring of Science Assessments." *Journal of Research in Science Teaching* 53, no. 2: 215–33. https://doi.org/10.1002/tea.21299

Masnick, A. M., and Morris, B. J. 2008. "Investigating the Development of Data Evaluation: The Role of Data Characteristics." *Child Development* 79, no. 4: 1032–48. https://doi.org/10.1111/j.1467-8624.2008.01174.x

National Research Council. 2014. *Developing Assessments for the Next Generation Science Standards.* Washington, DC: National Academies Press.

Nazaretsky, T., Bar, C., Walter, M., and Alexandron, G. 2022, March. "Empowering Teachers with AI: Co-designing a Learning Analytics Tool for Personalized Instruction in the Science Classroom." In *LAK22:* 12th International Learning Analytics and Knowledge Conference, 1–12. https://doi.org/10.1145/3506860.3506861

NGSS Lead States. 2013. *Next Generation Science Standards: For States, By States.* Washington, DC: National Academies Press.

Wilson, C., Haudek, K., Osborne, J., Stuhlsatz, M., Cheuk, T., Donovan, B., Bracey, Z., Mercado, M., and Zhai, X. 2023. "Using Automated Analysis to Assess Middle School Students' Competence with Scientific Argumentation." *Journal of Research in Science Teaching* 1–32. https://doi.org/10.1002/tea.21864

Zhai, X., and Nehm, R. 2023. "AI and Formative Assessment: The Train Has Left the Station." *Journal of Research in Science Teaching* 60, no. 6: 1390–98. https://doi.org/10.1002/tea.21885

Zhai, X., Yin, Y., Pellegrino, J. W., Haudek, K. C., and Shi, L. 2020. "Applying Machine Learning in Science Assessment: A Systematic Review." *Studies in Science Education* 56, no. 1: 111–51. https://doi.org/10.1080/03057267.2020.1735757

Zhai, X., Krajcik, J., and Pellegrino, J. 2021. "On the Validity of Machine Learning-Based Next Generation Science Assessments: A Validity Inferential Network." *Journal of Science Education and Technology* 30, no. 2: 298–312. https://doi.org/10.1007/s10956-020-09879-9

Zhai, X., He, P., and Krajcik, J. 2022. "Applying Machine Learning to Automatically Assess Scientific Models." *Journal of Research in Science Teaching* 59, no. 10: 1765–94.

Zimmerman, C. 2007. "The Development of Scientific Thinking Skills in Elementary and Middle School." *Developmental Review* 27, no. 2: 172–223. https://doi.org/10.1016/j.dr.2006.12.001.

PART II
AI TOOLS FOR TRANSFORMING STEM LEARNING

9
Artificial Intelligence-Based Scientific Inquiry

Anna Herdliska and Xiaoming Zhai

Introduction

The past decade has seen substantial changes in science and the way in which science is conducted. Scientists approach complex problems regarding health, energy, and environments, and the increasing complexity of these problems has facilitated new methods and innovative technologies that help tackle these challenging problems. Among these, artificial intelligence (AI), a subfield of computer science in which intelligence is exhibited by machines or software to make human-like decisions and analyses (Legg and Hutter 2007; McCarthy et al. 1956; Nilsson and Nilsson 1998; Norvig and Intelligence 2002; Poole, Mackworth, and Goebel 1998), is particularly resonating. The most substantial discoveries in science in recent years have benefited from AI (Gil et al. 2014). More importantly, research has seen that AI is changing how scientists conduct scientific inquiry to solve problems and how they approach the problems (Kitano 2021). These changes demand corresponding competence related to understanding and using AI for scientists to be able to succeed in conducting investigations. This competence, yet, is not likely to be automatically generated from scientists' regular work.

To solve this problem, our education system needs to prepare students to become future scientists. These future scientists and citizens should possess such competencies and be able to understand and conduct AI-based scientific inquiry. This competence is critical, not only for those who aim to become scientists but also for other students—as they are likely to live in an era when AI will be ubiquitously embedded in every aspect of their life (Zhai 2022). How could future citizens be able to survive and succeed in their careers if they are not able to use AI to investigate problems and figure out solutions? This problem can be solved only if we introduce AI-based scientific inquiry to K–12 students, in a way that science is manifested, so that they can develop such competence.

To tackle this problem, we developed AI-based inquiry activities for middle school students, aiming to improve their understanding and ability to conduct AI-involved scientific inquiry. Specifically, this study introduced Teachable Machine (Google 2023), an AI application, to science classrooms. Teachable Machine utilizes the core technology of AI–machine learning (ML), to develop algorithms that could solve complex, authentic problems. More than a hundred middle school students learned

Anna Herdliska and Xiaoming Zhai, *Artificial Intelligence-Based Scientific Inquiry*. In: *Uses of Artificial Intelligence in STEM Education*. Edited by: Xiaoming Zhai and Joseph Krajcik, Oxford University Press.
DOI: 10.1093/oso/9780198882077.003.0009

this method and used it to conduct AI-based scientific inquiry. We examined students' understanding of AI and their competence in conducting AI-based inquiry. This chapter answers two questions:

(1) How did students understand AI and use it to practice AI-based science inquiry after learning and experiencing Google Teachable Machine from this program?
(2) What performance patterns of AI-based inquiry did students demonstrate after learning and experiencing Google Teachable Machine from this program?

Artificial Intelligence

Historically, AI has been defined as a computer program's ability to think, reason, and solve problems with human-like competency (McCarthy et al. 1956). Good (1987) further proposed that AI is best defined as a system that is designed to explore human cognition in an efficient, unbiased, and error-free manner. AI can be broken down into subsets based on the particular traits or capabilities that a researcher would like to observe in their functioning system. These traits include reasoning and problem-solving, knowledge representation, planning, learning, natural language processing, motion and manipulation, social intelligence, and general intelligence (Norvig and Intelligence 2002). Each of these traits can provide a huge web of applications across disciplines. Recent development in AI has seen such innovations in using computers to mimic human intelligence and problem-solving abilities in solving complex problems (Benvenuti et al. 2023; Zhai, Nyaaba, and Ma 2023). The new development features a learning process, termed machine learning (ML), which goes beyond following a simple "if–then" command and is able to gain experience generating responses (Mitchell 1997). ML allows computers to complete actions and make decisions that are not based directly on code (Samuel 2000). The aforementioned characteristic has enhanced the intellectual capacity of AI, potentially emulating advanced cognitive functions.

With the fast-growing features of ML, AI is predicted to become the center of industries and science within the United States and globally in the next generation (Xivuri and Twinomurinzi 2021). This focus on AI will necessitate a shift in education to enhance student skills in the areas of problem-solving, creative thinking, and fundamental thinking skills (Shin 2021; Zhai 2022). Not doing so would result in an unprepared, technology-illiterate workforce, and a population incapable of making informed decisions regarding the use of technology in science work.

Artificial Intelligence in Science Teaching and Learning

Due to the significant potential of AI, researchers have positioned AI as a critical stride to enhance science teaching and learning. The earliest mention of AI or ML in science education was accomplished through the publication of Ron Good's article "Artificial Intelligence and Science Education," in 1987. Good related AI and ML to science education and provided the first insight into making connections between the ability of machines to process information and make decisions, and human cognition and rationalization of problems. The author relates the intelligence of machines to problem-solving ability rather than simply recalling information. He uses this idea throughout the article to suggest that this characteristic will cause AI to become a widespread trend in science education in the future. Therefore, it was said that AI would be able to model student thinking, teacher thinking, educational environments, and authentic scenarios. These proposed models relate well to what is now seen in science education and set the stage for AI-based science inquiry.

Currently, within the field of science education, AI can be used to support adaptive learning environments that are flexible, inclusive, engaging, and personalized. Many applications have been developed that can effectively track student behavior, assignment submission, and class attendance in order to support at-risk students and others (Zhai 2021). Among these, many categories of AI applications have most recently been developed for this support, including but not limited to automatic scoring, personal tutors, and collaborative learning. These applications have been shown to allow students access to adaptive, personalized learning supports, which are able to monitor student knowledge, feedback, and even affective states (Luckin et al. 2016).

ML, being used to automatically score assessments in many scientific content areas, aims to meet the nature of science learning, which requires performance assessments or constructed responses to elicit complex thinking. Applications in this area have been shown to have substantial accuracy for scoring student performance on assessment tasks (Nehm, Ha, and Mayfield 2012; Sung et al. 2021; Zhai, Shi, and Nehm 2021). In addition, ML has provided effective methods in which to use intelligent agents to facilitate customized learning and personalized tutoring (Wang and Shen 2021). Moreover, a few studies existing involve other areas of AI applications in science education. For example, one research group out of the University of Denver has been working to develop accessibility tools for visually or hearing-impaired students in science classrooms (Watters et al. 2020). Several groups are exploring the roles of facial recognition in evaluating the emotions and feelings of students in science classes (Ezquerra et al. 2022; Liaw et al. 2021). Additionally, researchers are working to use facial recognition and ML to identify epistemic beliefs and misconceptions about science content (Luan and Tsai 2021). Despite the uses of AI in science learning, a deeper integration of AI with scientific inquiry is yet to be recognized in science education. Allowing students access to larger sets of information will also increase the amount of authentic data or information that students can access during science inquiry.

AI-Based Scientific Inquiry

The role of science education must be to prepare students for their futures in today's world and supplement this in the future to allow success in job opportunities and personal decision-making for citizens. Current science learning is aimed at a three-dimensional approach, as set out by the National Research Council's (2012) *Framework for K-12 Science Education*. The three dimensions include science and engineering practices (SEP), crosscutting concepts (CCC), and disciplinary core ideas (DCI). SEPs include context-based classroom activities that allow students to engage in scientific practices, such as asking scientific questions, developing models, designing and carrying out investigations, using mathematical and computational thinking, constructing explanations, designing solutions, engaging in arguments from evidence, and obtaining, evaluating, and communicating information. CCCs include big ideas that connect different domains of science. They include patterns, proportion and scale, systems, and models, energy and matter, stability and change, and structure and function. DCIs are the required content knowledge in a given science discipline, including key ideas about the science area of interest. Additionally, there has been a more recent push to emphasize the importance of scientific phenomena to promote instruction aligned with the Next Generation Science Standards (Committee on Guidance on Implementing the Next Generation Science Standards et al. 2015; NGSS Lead States 2013). Science phenomena include natural, observable phenomena that can lead to the development of a solution or investigation by students (Achieve 2017). By using these approaches, students are often prompted to be authentically engaged with a problem. Students must create new ideas in science in order to effectively learn and develop these skills to solve problems. The more frequently that students are exposed to authentic, real situations in science, the more they will be able to refine these practices (Bybee 2006; Duschl and Grandy 2008).

AI is an innovative tool that can enrich the authentic experiences that students have when working with data. Due to its substantial promise and affordance, AI has been applied to transform the way science is conducted. For example, scientists spend much time examining scientific assumptions; when such options are numerous or challenging to differentiate due to the system's complexity, scientists could leverage AI to significantly reduce the time of testing assumptions. Such new ways of scientific inquiry are evident in a new paradigm in science research, shortening the time for significant scientific discoveries and being able to solve extraordinarily complex problems.

The new development of scientific inquiry using AI led by scientists must be reflected in science education. Historically, as seen with the incorporation of Watson and Crick's discovery of DNA's structure into biology curricula, educational systems have always strived to keep pace with groundbreaking scientific advancements. In our current era, characterized by rapid technological progress, fields such as biotechnology, quantum physics, and AI are evolving at an unprecedented rate. To ensure students are prepared for the future, it is crucial that their education mirrors these advancements. Furthermore, the very essence of science education extends beyond mere factual knowledge; it is about imbibing the process of scientific inquiry itself. By aligning education with the latest scientific methodologies, we cultivate critical thinking and a genuine understanding of science among students. This alignment not only equips students with relevant knowledge but also bolsters global competitiveness, as evidenced by the superior performance of countries that regularly update their science curricula in international competitions.

Likewise, as AI continues to develop, it is critical to allow students exposure to this new technology through three-dimensional learning. Scientists are applying AI to solve authentic science problems. If science education aims to prepare students with scientific literacy, AI has to be incorporated into science learning in a way that reflects how science is conducted so that students can understand AI-based science inquiry. On the other side, if AI will be used as learning technology, it must be used in a way that promotes true cognition of scientific thinking and practices. Learning technologies must be used to support three-dimensional science inquiry and place students in situations that allow them to actively construct connections between science content and practices (Krajcik and Mun 2014). Having students use and program AI systems is not effective on its own; instead, AI as a learning technology must be constructed in a way that promotes higher-order thinking in scientific practices in order to be beneficial to science learners. Moreover, feedback from higher education institutions consistently emphasizes the necessity of contemporary and robust foundational skills for incoming students. Thus, reflecting the latest development of AI for scientific inquiry in education is not just beneficial—it's essential for future readiness and global relevance.

AI-based inquiry positioned in three-dimensional science learning requires students to work with datasets and make reasonable decisions about programming so that they can better explain phenomena or design solutions. A strong connection exists between using AI as an inquiry strategy and three-dimensional learning in science. AI could also be used as a strategy to allow students to work with scientific phenomena in an innovative way (Zhou et al. 2020). By being involved in AI-enhanced inquiry, students could work with and explore new patterns of data within topics (NRC 2012). For example, in typical science learning, students observe the phases of mitosis under a microscope, identify the phases based on appearance, and record their findings. In an AI-enhanced inquiry example, students would work with large datasets to reason with and make decisions about cell processes in different parts of the cell cycle by leveraging the data analysis power of AI. A more authentic or situated approach could allow students to apply this machine to a realistic scenario mirroring scientists' work (i.e., cancer research or treatment). However, little to no reports exist of the benefits of involving AI in scientific inquiry. A huge area of growth is available to utilize the learning benefits of AI as a means to integrate science inquiry while enhancing a learner's experience to include decision-making, creativity, computational thinking, and logical reasoning (Shin 2021).

Teachable Machine

AI-based inquiry could be a relevant use of effective technology in science classrooms. Studies involving AI-based inquiry are not widely present in science education, and thus it is the role of science education to incorporate AI applications, such as Google's Teachable Machine (GTM), in learning activities. GTM is a web-based tool that allows users to train their own machine-learning models using self-collected data. GTM uses TenssorFlow.js, a Javascript-based ML library, to build models. Models are founded in a pre-trained neural network that utilizes transfer learning as the core technique. When a user creates classes and inputs data (e.g., images) the final layer of the neural network is formed to generate the model. Once the final layer is formed, users can test the effectiveness of their teachable machine by using an integrated web camera or by uploading a file.

GTM is designed to be easy to use, even for those without a background in ML and coding. It allows users to train models for image and audio classification tasks without writing ML code. With image classification, users can upload images and label them. Then, the machine will learn to recognize those objects and apply the learned knowledge (i.e., algorithmic models) to classify new images. With audio classification, users can upload audio samples and label them, and then the machine will learn to recognize those sounds. When inputting the data into GTM, users must group the data based on the labels into different classes (Figure 9.1a). After uploading the classified training samples, users can start the training process by selecting the pre-programmed option, "Train Model." A trained model can be used to predict or classify new data, but it is suggested that the users first validate the model by using new data. Users can compare GTM predictions with human labels to validate the accuracy of the algorithmic model developed. A validated algorithmic model can be used to conduct work (an example to classify cats and dogs refers to Figure 9.1b). GTM allows users to import data as classes without manual coding.

GTM was selected as a learning application due to its user-friendliness and compatibility with other Google applications. The program is highly accessible to students with varying backgrounds and programming knowledge due to the pre-trained neural network that exists within this program. Teachers can immediately implement this tool without the need to instruct students on programming or require prerequisite knowledge of ML programming language. There have been some studies and research on using GTM in education (e.g., Carney et al. 2020). These studies have found that the tool can be effective in helping students use ML and AI in an interactive and engaging way. Strategic use of GTM as a scientific inquiry tool can support literacy in technology, reinforcement of scientific content, and quality three-dimensional knowledge, resulting in high levels of authentic, situated learning within science classrooms.

Methods

Participants

This study collected data from 128 eighth-grade students, who enrolled in high school biology in a suburban Atlanta Title I school. The student sample includes 52% female and 48% male. The demographic makeup of the sample is 29% Black, 28% Asian, 28% White, 11% Latinx, and 4% other races. Among all the participants, 86% of the students were identified as gifted and talented, and all students had a minimum of one previous exposure to ML. To ensure the privacy of students, all identifying information was removed from project files, and randomized numbers were assigned to student project files for analysis purposes.

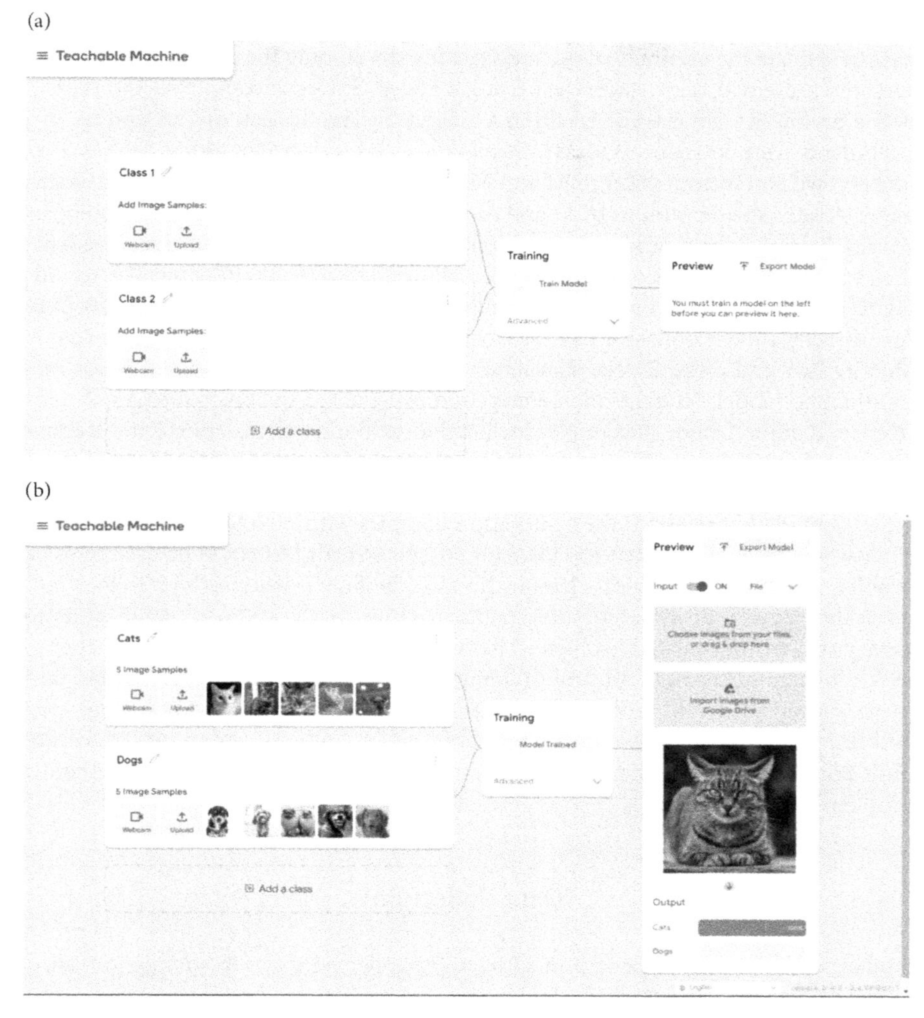

Figure 9.1 GTM interfaces of computer training (a) and classifications between dogs and cats (b).

Procedure: AI-Based Inquiry Using Teachable Machine

This study developed AI-based inquiry tasks by adopting GTM, given its lower requirements of coding or programming experience for users. Participating teachers and students in this study had access to GTM. Students worked to complete an AI-integrated biological classification unit. This unit involved an introduction to GTM. Students were asked to first identify a real-world problem that is investigable and then develop a solution using GTM. After having an investigable question, students worked in groups of three to four to collect images as data points. They then used GTM to train the machine to develop an algorithmic model and then used new data to validate the accuracy of the model. After developing the algorithmic models, students presented their studies via Google Slides. Students completed the project over a period of eight class days within a biological classification unit of study.

Students were introduced to ML through a series of introductory activities. Day one involved an introduction to AI and ML. Direct instruction was provided to students to learn the definitions of AI and ML. Examples of AI and ML as technologies within the daily lives of students were identified and shared in small groups. Students then engaged in a discussion applying their knowledge to ethical dilemmas surrounding AI and ML. Day two involved learning about how to use the GTM. Students were first directly shown how to create a teachable machine model that would correctly identify cats and dogs. Direct instruction involved teachers uploading photos and training the model. Students then engaged in using GTM to classify images of non-science examples. Student examples included identifying types of sport balls, student wearing glasses, types of popular cartoon characters, and types of cars. Day three involved students in the development of project ideas. Students engaged in a station-based activity that required the exploration of topics within biological classification. They were challenged to develop ideas about how ML and AI could be used to solve problems involving biological classification. In the final portion of the project, students developed a proposal for a teachable machine that would use classification to solve a real-world, situated problem. The proposals were evaluated by the teacher to check for the inclusion of all project components, testability using GTM, and ability to solve a real-world problem. Students had five project working days to develop and program their teachable machine. Additionally, students were required to produce a presentation, which required them to discuss the role of ML in their authentic problem-solving.

Data Collection

Student artifacts and presentation slides were collected via web submission using Google Suite applications. To guide their presentation, the teacher provided a guideline that student presentations must address: (1) What is AI? (2) What is Google Teachable Machine? (3) What is your research question? (4) How did you develop your teachable machine? (5) What is the real-world application of your teachable machine? Project files were completed and submitted using Google Slides. A total of thirty-eight student projects were collected for analysis.

Data Analysis

Student artifacts and slides were analyzed and initially coded using a deductive methodology. Deductive reasoning can be thought of as top-down reasoning, which follows a premise or rule that will always apply to a specific case. This strategy provides sound reasoning to support a claim with direct, clear evidence. In order to generate this evidence, a coding framework was developed.

Coding Framework

A coding framework was developed based on the foundational ideas underlying this study, including aspects of AI-based scientific inquiry, the SEPs and content knowledge, and the authors' goal of applying authentic solutions to problems within science. Authors first reviewed student project presentation files to identify the initial coding categories (see Figure 9.2) and the corresponding descriptions of the codes. An iterative process was employed by the authors to finalize the coding categories and the descriptions, which includes students' understanding of AI, problem development, quality of the dataset, algorithm validation, algorithm development, problem development, sample size, and limits of AI (see Table 9.1).

The coding criteria were determined to act as critical components of understanding the role of AI and ML in developing solutions to scientific problems. The primary expectation and outcome for student learning centers around developing an understanding of AI and problem-solving. The first two criteria, "AI understanding" and "problem development," focus on students' ability to define "AI" itself and to suggest authentic science problems that are potentially solvable by using AI. If students do not meet these two criteria, it is unlikely that they will be able to develop a project in

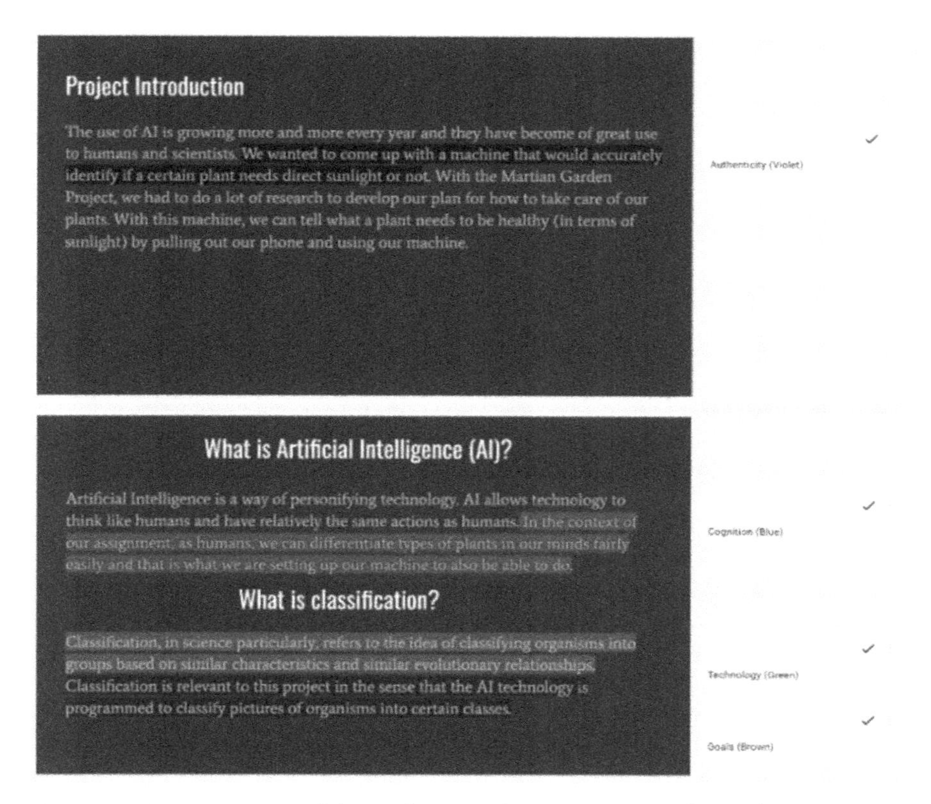

Figure 9.2 Demonstration of the application of categories using the Deductive Buckets method (above), as described by Galman (2016), and one student's artifact (below).

Table 9.1 Coding Rubric for Student Presentation Files

Code Aspect	Level 1	Level 2	Level 3
AI understanding	Student does not provide an accurate definition nor understanding of AI.	Student somewhat defines AI.	Student correctly defines AI and suggests that it mimics human behavior.
Problem development	Student does not suggest a realistic and AI-investigable problem to be solved.	Student suggests an AI-investable problem that is somewhat associated to society.	Student suggests an AI-investigable problem that is associated to society.
Quality of dataset	Student does not consider the quality of the data chosen to train the algorithm.	Student considers the quality of the data somewhat.	Student considers that the type of data selected for the algorithm is critical to the success of their project.
Algorithm development	Student does not show any evidence of understanding that algorithms must be trained to develop models for a dataset.	Student somewhat shows understanding that algorithms must be trained to develop models for a dataset.	Student recognizes that algorithm must be trained to develop models for a dataset.
Algorithm validation	Student provides no evidence that ML algorithmic models can accurately solve problems.	Student provides some evidence that ML algorithmic models can accurately solve problems.	Student provides evidence that ML algorithmic models can accurately solve problems.
Sample size	Student has a small dataset (less than 10 pictures per sample) and does not demonstrate an understanding of sample size.	Student has a larger dataset (20–30 pictures per category) but does not demonstrate an explanation or reasoning for choosing a larger number of data.	Student has a large dataset (30 or more pictures in each category) or demonstrates an understanding of the importance of a large sample size.
Limits of AI	Student does not show any understanding or consideration of limits in using algorithms for classification.	Student recognizes at a basic level that AI is not perfect.	Student shows an understanding of the imperfections that exist in AI systems.

this area. Additionally, students must be able to generate a research question that is testable through ML. Again, this is to ensure that students truly understand the ability of AI and ML to solve scientific problems.

Also involving the consideration of AI as a technology, students must consider the quality of their dataset when using algorithms. Students must be able to evaluate the quality of their data and understand the patterns, which the preset algorithms in GTM will follow to validate their dataset. Thus, the coding criteria of quality of the dataset, algorithm development, and algorithm validation were determined to make connections to student ability to generate a functional model to test their research question. The final coding criteria involves considering sample size and the limitations of AI in solving problems. Both of these criteria are of critical importance for students to understand AI-based scientific inquiry, as these must be considered when designing scientific protocols to investigate questions.

Coding Process

Using the coding rubrics, the authors coded students' presentation files and artifacts. The holistic style rubric evaluates students' ability to demonstrate an understanding and use of AI within their presentation. These qualities were determined to effectively summarize student understanding of how AI can be utilized to investigate science phenomena and solve scientific problems.

Two science education experts with expertise in K–12 science education, AI-based instruction, and science education research coded the students' project files and artifacts. The process began by utilizing a set of five example project files and artifacts. An initial meeting was held to introduce coding methodology using the predesigned rubric. After this initial meeting, raters independently coded the five examples and took notes about their scoring methodology. Meetings were held to discuss the codes. The discrepancies were discussed until a consensus was met, and minor revisions were made to the rubric to meet and promote consistency within coding. The inter-rater reliability was checked to ensure a cutoff of Cohen's kappa of 0.75, which represents high reliability (Fleiss, Levin, and Paik 2013). The scoring process continued with each expert coding the entire data set independently, and inter-rater reliability was recalculated and found to be > 0.75.

Latent Class Analysis (LCA)

LCA, an analytic approach, was used to identify patterns within the dataset to address RQ2 (Oberski 2016). A total of six class solutions were tested, and the best solution was determined through considerations of multiple fit indices, including Akaike information criteria (AIC), Bayesian information criteria (BIC), and sample size-adjusted Bayesian information criteria (aBIC). For AIC, BIC, and aBIC, smaller values are associated with an improved model fit (Nylund-Gibson and Choi 2018). AIC is based on the likelihood function and penalizes the addition of parameters, which usually favor a complex model; BIC considers the likelihood of the model but imposes a heavier penalty for adding additional parameters compared to AIC. As a result, BIC often favors simpler models. aBIC is an adjusted version of the BIC that takes into account the sample size. The adjustment for sample size can be particularly useful in situations where the sample size is either very large or very small. All analysis was completed in Mplus v. 8.5.

Results

Overview of Students' Understanding and Performance on AI-Based Inquiry

Students' understanding and performance on AI-based inquiry is summarized in Table 9.2. Results indicate that a commendable strength lies in the students'

Table 9.2 Student Distributions (%) at Levels for Each of the Seven Aspects

Level	AI understanding	Problem development	Quality of dataset	Algorithm development	Algorithm validation	Sample size	Limits of AI
3	92.86	85.71	21.43	0.00	50.00	47.62	9.52
2	7.14	9.52	7.14	11.90	0.00	40.48	2.38
1	0.00	4.76	71.43	88.10	50.00	11.90	88.10

foundational grasp of AI. Results indicate that an overwhelming majority have not only mastered the definition of AI in the context of "AI understanding" (92.86% at level 3) but also its application in "problem development" (85.71% at level 3). Their ability to associate AI-investigable problems with societal issues is notably robust. This foundational strength, however, contrasts sharply with their understanding of the intricacies involved in the actual implementation of AI.

When delving into the practicalities of AI, particularly in algorithm development and algorithm validation, disparities become evident. The absence of any student achieving a comprehensive understanding of algorithm training is alarming. This gap is further accentuated when juxtaposed against the even split in "algorithm validation" (50% at level 3), revealing a bifurcation in the cohort's capabilities. While half can substantiate the accuracy of ML algorithmic models, the other half exhibits a palpable deficiency (50% at level 1).

The importance of data, in terms of both quality and quantity, presents another contrasting picture. The majority's lack of consideration for the "quality of dataset" (71.43% at level 1) is a stark divergence from their relatively better understanding of "sample size" (47.62% at level 3). While many recognize the significance of large sample sizes in AI model training, their inability to discern the quality of data underscores a fragmented comprehension of data's role in AI.

Lastly, the "limits of AI" emerges as a poignant area of concern. The vast majority's (88.10% at level 1) limited understanding of the imperfections and potential biases in AI systems starkly contrasts with their foundational grasp of AI. This suggests that while students might understand what AI is and its potential applications, they might not fully appreciate its limitations or the ethical considerations that accompany its use.

In summation, while the cohort exhibits a strong foundational understanding of AI and its societal relevance, there are discernible gaps in their grasp of the practical and ethical nuances of AI implementation. This interplay of strengths and weaknesses offers valuable insights for future pedagogical strategies.

Student Understanding and Performance Patterns in AI-Based Inquiry

To examine the potential patterns of students in AI-based inquiry, we conducted LCA. In Table 9.3, the AIC, BIC, and aBIC values are delineated. For the sake of model

Table 9.3 LCA Fit Indices

K	LL	BIC	aBIC	AIC
2	−154.389	394.745	322.720	354.779
3	−143.393	417.605	308.001	356.787
4	−138.714	453.099	305.917	371.429
5	−134.186	488.895	304.134	386.372

Note: K = number of classes; LL = log-likelihood; BIC = Bayesian information criterion; aBIC = sample-size-adjusted BIC; AIC = Akaike information criterion.

stability, the log-likelihood is also incorporated as a referential metric. The optimal model, as indicated by the minimal values of AIC and BIC, was when K = 2. However, considering the limited sample size of this investigation, the aBIC was further scrutinized. It was observed that when K = 3, the aBIC value was significantly reduced to 308.001, in contrast to the aBIC value of 322.720 for K = 2. Elevating K to 4 or 5 exerted only marginal effects on the aBIC value. Consequently, it was ascertained that a value of K = 3 offers the most fitting model representation.

Upon evaluating the estimated posterior probabilities, the distribution of students across the three classes was discerned to be 71, 7, and 22%, respectively. Furthermore, to gauge the precision of classification, the entropy statistic was employed. This metric, which oscillates between 0 and 1, serves as an aggregate measure of classification assurance across all entities and classes. An entropy value approaching 1 signifies a more definitive classification. Elevated entropy values imply that entities can be distinctly categorized into latent classes, whereas diminished entropy values hint at potential vagueness in class affiliation. In the present analysis, an entropy value of 0.987 was recorded, signifying an exceptionally rigorous classification.

The three latent classes developed provided insight into a pattern that exists within student learning throughout the AI-based inquiry project. The latent classes described categories in which the components of the rubric could be placed in order to describe the level of mastery a student group demonstrated when completing the project (see Figure 9.3).

Pragmatic innovators. Class 1 students predominantly demonstrate an intermediate grasp in their understanding of AI concepts. In AI understanding (U1), with a score of 2.00, they somewhat define AI. This is exemplified by a level 2 response given by student group 2, which states, "AI is a way of personifying technology," showing a limited ability to define and explain AI. This proficiency level is shared with Class 3 but surpasses the foundational understanding of Class 2. Their high proficiency in problem development (U2), as evidenced by a score of 3.00, is particularly noteworthy. For instance, student group 4 shared a problem about wild berries, stating, "Some berries found in the wild can cause death and sickness . . . This device, if put into an app or microcontroller, could make sure you are choosing the right dining option." However, their foundational grasp in quality of dataset (U3), with a score of 1.00, indicates potential areas for improvement, a challenge they share with both Class 2 and Class 3.

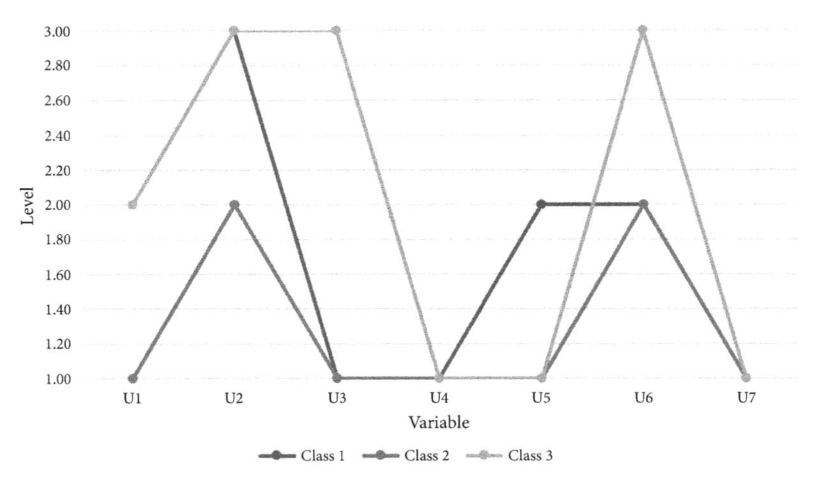

Figure 9.3 Plot of three classes from LCA.

Foundational explorers. Class 2 students, in contrast, predominantly exhibit a foundational understanding across most aspects. Their basic grasp in AI understanding (U1), with a score of 1.00, places them a step behind both Class 1 and Class 3. Their intermediate proficiency in problem development (U2) and sample size (U6), with scores of 2.00, offers a glimmer of their potential. However, their foundational understanding in quality of dataset (U3), algorithm development (U4), and limits of AI (U7), all with scores of 1.00, aligns them with the other classes in some areas. For instance, student group 10 describes their project, "This project will help you understand and be able to use AI programming, and it will show you how to classify different types of organisms." In this example, the students do not propose a problem that is solvable, but rather a benefit of using their project.

Holistic visionaries. Class 3 students present a more varied performance profile. Their intermediate understanding in AI understanding (U1), with a score of 2.00, aligns them with Class 1. Their high proficiency in problem development (U2) and sample size (U6), both with scores of 3.00, showcases their deep grasp in these areas. For instance, student group 3, which addressed overfishing, stated, "Overfishing . . . Well, simply put, we need to protect different species of fish . . . They need to be protected." However, their foundational understanding in quality of dataset (U3), algorithm development (U4), and limits of AI (U7), all with scores of 1.00, reveals areas of potential improvement. For instance, student group 12 displayed misconceptions, stating that "GTM creates a perfect solution to categorizing the types of infections that a human could have. This AI can immediately stop pandemics in our world." However, a few, like student group 20, recognized the imperfections, noting, "This AI program can only distinguish certain organisms by comparing and contrasting pictures, so sometimes, its predictions may be wrong. But keep in mind that even humans can have a hard time distinguishing different kingdoms just by looking at the pictures."

In essence, the student responses further illuminate the strengths and areas of improvement for each class, painting a vivid picture of their understanding and application of AI concepts. The pragmatic innovators of Class 1 exhibit a balanced approach to AI, demonstrating both a theoretical understanding and a practical application. Their intermediate grasp of AI's definition combined with a strong ability to associate AI problems with societal issues showcases their pragmatic approach to innovation. The foundational explorers of Class 2, while primarily exhibiting a foundational understanding across most aspects, hint at a budding potential, especially in their ability to somewhat associate AI with real-world problems. Their journey appears to be in its early stages, with ample room for growth and exploration. Lastly, the holistic visionaries of Class 3 present a comprehensive view of AI. Their deep understanding of AI's societal relevance and the importance of sample size is commendable. However, their challenges in recognizing the nuances of data quality and algorithm development suggest a vision that, while broad, still requires refinement in certain areas. Together, these classes represent a spectrum of understanding and application in the realm of AI, from foundational knowledge to visionary thinking.

Discussion

The integration of AI into science education, as illuminated by this study, is emblematic of the broader shifts occurring in the educational landscape. As we navigate deeper into the twenty-first century, the intricate dance between science and AI becomes increasingly central to our understanding of both domains and to produce AI literate citizens (Yang 2022). This study, positioned at this critical juncture, offers a rich tapestry of insights that are pivotal for educators, students, and policymakers alike. The transformative potential of AI in reshaping modern scientific methodologies is both profound and far-reaching. Its unparalleled capacity to analyze vast datasets, discern intricate patterns, and emulate human-like decision-making processes has expanded the horizons of what's possible within scientific inquiry. This seismic shift in the scientific paradigm underscores the pressing need for the next generation to not only have a foundational understanding of AI but also to be adept at harnessing its potential within scientific contexts. Such a skill set is no longer a mere enhancement but an essential component of modern scientific literacy, ensuring that students are primed to thrive in an era where AI's influence permeates every facet of our existence.

Our study's deep dive into student engagement with AI-based scientific inquiry, as encapsulated by the three distinct latent classes, provides a nuanced understanding of the myriad ways learners interact with and internalize AI concepts. The pragmatic innovators, with their balanced approach; the foundational explorers, who are at the cusp of their AI journey; and the holistic visionaries, who exhibit a broader yet nuanced understanding, each represent unique facets of the learning spectrum. This rich diversity underscores the imperative for an educational approach that is both adaptive and responsive, ensuring that the multifaceted learning needs of each student archetype are met with precision and empathy.

The role of AI in science education, as delineated by our findings, is both multifaceted and transformative. While AI's potential as a game-changer in education has been acknowledged in prior literature (Lameras and Arnab 2021), our study ventures into uncharted territories by examining its tangible and transformative impact on scientific inquiry. The three-dimensional approach to science learning, emphasizing scientific practices, crosscutting concepts, and core ideas, emerges as an ideal scaffold for the integration of AI. However, the journey is not devoid of challenges. The observed gaps in students' pragmatic and ethical application of AI underscore critical areas that warrant focused pedagogical attention.

In terms of its seminal contribution to the academic discourse, this study carves a niche for itself. The intersection of AI and science education has been a burgeoning area of interest, but our research delves deeper, offering a granular exploration of AI's role in science education. By proposing AI-based scientific inquiry, this study not only underscores the transformative potential of AI in reshaping science education but also charts a visionary path forward. The identification of distinct student archetypes and their nuanced engagement with AI provides a fresh, multidimensional perspective, enriching the discourse and offering actionable insights for educators. Moreover, by embedding AI within the three-dimensional science learning framework, the study beckons further exploration, research, and dialogue, setting the stage for a new era in science education.

Conclusion and Limitations

Even with its abundance of current uses, a frightening majority of people, according to a survey conducted by the Mozilla Foundation (2017), claim to not know much about AI or its uses. The survey revealed that the majority of Mozilla Firefox users felt that the words "concerned" and "curious" best described their feelings about AI in our world today. Research also revealed that many people have misunderstandings of AI bias (Bewersdorff et al. 2023), which generates unnecessary AI technophobia (Zhai and Krajcik 2022). The confluence of AI and science education, as elucidated by this study, heralds a transformative era in pedagogical practices. As AI continues to evolve and redefine boundaries across sectors, its seamless integration into science education emerges as both a timely and strategic imperative. This study, with its intricate weave of insights and findings, serves as a beacon, guiding educators and stakeholders through this transformative journey.

The findings of this study underscore the pressing need for a recalibration of science curricula, ensuring they resonate with the demands and opportunities of an AI-centric world. The diverse learning patterns observed among students emphasize the need for educators to adopt a more individualized, responsive, and forward-thinking approach to teaching. Recognizing and celebrating the heterogeneity of student experiences and perspectives is paramount.

By proposing AI-based scientific inquiry, this study makes a groundbreaking contribution to the field. It not only underscores the transformative potential of AI in enriching science education but also offers a visionary blueprint for its integration.

As the boundaries between science and AI become increasingly fluid, it is incumbent upon educators, policymakers, and stakeholders to ensure that students are equipped with the requisite skills, knowledge, and mindset. This study, with its depth and breadth of insights, serves as a foundational pillar in this endeavor, offering a roadmap for future research, exploration, and pedagogical innovation.

Acknowledgments

This material is based upon work supported by the National Science Foundation (NSF) under Grant 2101104, 2138854. Any opinions, findings, conclusions, or recommendations expressed in this material are those of the author and do not necessarily reflect the views of the NSF.

References

Achieve, Next Gen Science Storylines, and STEM Teaching Tools. 2017. "Using Phenomena in NGSS-Designed Lessons and Units."

Bauer, J. 2022. "A Primer to Latent Profile and Latent Class Analysis." In *Methods for Researching Professional Learning and Development: Challenges, Applications and Empirical Illustrations*, edited by M. Goller, E. Kyndt, S. Paloniemi, and C. Damşa, 243–68. New York: Springer International Publishing.

Benvenuti, M., Cangelosi, A., Weinberger, A., Mazzoni, E., Benassi, M., Barbaresi, M., and Orsoni, M. 2023. "Artificial Intelligence and Human Behavioral Development: A Perspective on New Skills and Competences Acquisition for the Educational Context." *Computers in Human Behavior*, 107903.

Bewersdorff, A., Zhai, X., Roberts, J., and Nerdel, C. 2023. "Myths, Mis-and Preconceptions of Artificial Intelligence: A Review of the Literature." *Computers and Education: Artificial Intelligence*, 100143.

Bybee, R. W., Taylor, J. A., Gardner, A., Van Scotter, P., Powell, J. C., Westbrook, A., and Landes, N. 2006. *The BSCS 5E Instructional Model: Origins and Effectiveness*, vol. 5, 88–98. Colorado Springs, CO: BSCS.

Carney, M., Webster, B., Alvarado, I., Phillips, K., Howell, N., Griffith, J., Jongejan, J., Pitaru, A., and Chen, A. 2020. "Teachable Machine: Approachable Web-Based Tool for Exploring Machine Learning Classification." In *CHI: EA '20: Extended Abstracts of the 2020 CHI Conference on Human Factors in Computing Systems*, 1–8. New York: Association for Computing Machinery.

Committee on Guidance on Implementing the Next Generation Science Standards, Board on Science Education, Division of Behavioral and Social Sciences and Education, and National Research Council. 2015. *Guide to Implementing the Next Generation Science Standards.* Washington, DC: National Academies Press.

Duschl, R. A., and Grandy, R. E. 2008. "Reconsidering the Character and Role of Inquiry in School Science: Framing the Debates." In *Teaching Scientific Inquiry*, edited by R. A. Duschl and R. E. Grandy, 1–37. Leiden: Brill.

Ezquerra, A., Agen, F., Rodríguez-Arteche, I., and Ezquerra-Romano, I. 2022. "Integrating Artificial Intelligence into Research on Emotions and Behaviors in Science Education." *Eurasia Journal of Mathematics Science and Technology Education* 18, no. 4: em2099.

Fleiss, J. L., Levin, B., and Paik, M. C. 2013. *Statistical Methods for Rates and Proportions.* London: Wiley.

Galman, S. C. 2016. *The Good, the Bad, and the Data: Shane the Lone Ethnographer's Basic Guide to Qualitative Data Analysis.* London: Routledge.

Gil, Y., Greaves, M., Hendler, J., and Hirsh, H. 2014. "Amplify Scientific Discovery with Artificial Intelligence." Science 346, no. 6206: 171–72.
Good, R. 1987. "Artificial Intelligence and Science Education." *Journal of Research in Science Teaching* 24, no. 4: 325–42.
Google. 2023. "Teachable Machine." Retrieved on April 2023. https://teachablemachine.withgoogle.com.
Kitano, H. 2016. "Artificial Intelligence to Win the Nobel Prize and Beyond: Creating the Engine for Scientific Discovery." *AI Magazine* 37, no. 1: 39–49.
Krajcik, J. S., and Mun, K. 2014. "Promises and Challenges of Using Learning Technologies to Promote Student Learning of Science." In *Handbook of Research on Science Education*, Volume II, edited by S. K. Abell and N. G. Lederman. 351–74. London: Routledge.
Lameras, P., and Arnab, S. 2021. "Power to the Teachers: An Exploratory Review on Artificial Intelligence in Education." *Information* 13, no. 1: 14.
Legg, S., and Hutter, M. 2007. "A Collection of Definitions of Intelligence." *Frontiers in Artificial Intelligence and Applications* 157, 17–24.
Liaw, H., Yu, Y.-R., Chou, C.-C., and Chiu, M.-H. 2021. "Relationships between Facial Expressions, Prior Knowledge, and Multiple Representations: a Case of Conceptual Change for Kinematics Instruction." *Journal of Science Education and Technology* 30, no. 2: 227–38.
Luan, H., and Tsai, C.-C. 2021. "A Review of Using Machine Learning Approaches for Precision Education." *Educational Technology and Society* 24, no. 1: 250–66.
Luckin, R., Holmes, W., Griffiths, M., and Forcier, L. B. 2016. *Intelligence Unleashed: An Argument for AI in Education*. London: Pearson.
McCarthy, J., Minsky, M., Rochester, N., and Shannon, C. 1956. The Dartmouth Summer Research Project on Artificial Intelligence. Artificial Intelligence: Past, Present, and Future.
Mitchell, T. 1997. *Machine Learning*. New York: McGraw-Hill.
National Research Council, Division of Behavioral and Social Sciences and Education, Board on Science Education, and Committee on a Conceptual Framework for New K-12 Science Education Standards. 2012. *A Framework for K-12 Science Education: Practices, Crosscutting Concepts, and Core Ideas*. Washington, DC: National Academies Press.
Nehm, R. H., Ha, M., and Mayfield, E. 2012. "Transforming Biology Assessment with Machine Learning: Automated Scoring of Written Evolutionary Explanations." *Journal of Science Education and Technology* 21, no. 1: 183–96.
NGSS Lead States. 2013. *Next Generation Science Standards: For States, By States*. Washington, DC: National Academies Press. https://doi.org/doi:10.17226/18290
Nilsson, N. J., and Nilsson, N. J. 1998. *Artificial Intelligence: A New Synthesis*. Burlington, MA: Morgan Kaufmann.
Norvig, P. R., and Intelligence, S. A. 2002. *A Modern Approach*. Upper Saddle River, NJ: Prentice Hall.
Nylund-Gibson, K., and Choi, A. Y. 2018. "Ten Frequently Asked Questions about Latent Class Analysis." *Translational Issues in Psychological Science* 4, no. 4: 440–61.
Oberski, D. 2016. "Mixture Models: Latent Profile and Latent Class Analysis." In *Modern Statistical Methods for HCI*, edited by J. Robertson and M. Kaptein, 275–87. New York: Springer International Publishing.
Poole, D., Mackworth, A., and Goebel, R. 1998. Computational Intelligence: A Logical Approach. Google Scholar Digital Library.
Samuel, A. L. 2000. "Some Studies in Machine Learning Using the Game of Checkers." *IBM Journal of Research and Development* 44, no. 1.2: 206–26.
Shin, S. 2021. "A Study on the Framework Design of Artificial Intelligence Thinking for Artificial Intelligence Education." *International Journal of Information and Education Technology*, 11, 9: 392–97. http://www.ijiet.org/vol11/1540-IJIET-1892.pdf
Sung, S. H., Li, C., Chen, G., Huang, X., Xie, C., Massicotte, J., and Shen, J. 2021. "How Does Augmented Observation Facilitate Multimodal Representational Thinking? Applying Deep Learning to Decode Complex Student Construct." *Journal of Science Education and Technology* 30, no. 2: 210–26.

Wang, C., and Shen, J. 2023. "Technology-enhanced collaborative learning in STEM." In *International Encyclopedia of Education*, 4th ed., edited by R. J. Tierney, F. Rizvi, and K. Ercikan, 207–14. Oxford: Elsevier.

Watters, J. D., Hill, A., Weinrich, M., Supalo, C., and Jiang, F. 2020. "An Artificial Intelligence Tool for Accessible Science Education." *Journal of Science Education for Students with Disabilities* 24, no. 1: 10.

Xivuri, K., and Twinomurinzi, H. 2021. "A Systematic Review of Fairness in Artificial Intelligence Algorithms." *Responsible AI and Analytics for an Ethical and Inclusive Digitized Society*, 271–84.

Yang, W. 2022. "Artificial Intelligence Education for Young Children: Why, What, and How in Curriculum Design and Implementation." *Computers and Education: Artificial Intelligence* 3: 100061.

Zhai, X. 2021. "Advancing Automatic Guidance in Virtual Science Inquiry: From Ease of Use to Personalization." *Educational Technology Research and Development* 69, no. 1: 255–58. https://doi.org/10.1007/s11423-020-09917-8

Zhai, X. 2022. "ChatGPT User Experience: Implications for Education." Available at SSRN: https://ssrn.com/abstract=4312418 or http://dx.doi.org/10.2139/ssrn.4312418

Zhai, X., and Krajcik, J. 2022. "Pseudo AI Bias." https://doi.org/10.48550/arXiv.2210.08141

Zhai, X., Nyaaba, M., and Ma, W. 2023. "Can AI Outperform Humans on Cognitive-demanding Tasks in Science?" Available at SSRN: https://ssrn.com/abstract=4451722 or http://dx.doi.org/10.2139/ssrn.4451722

Zhai, X., Shi, L., and Nehm, R. 2021. "A Meta-analysis of Machine Learning-Based Science Assessments: Factors Impacting Machine-Human Score Agreements." *Journal of Science Education and Technology* 30, no. 3: 361–79. https://doi.org/10.1007/s10956-020-09875-z

Zhou, X., Tang, J., Mushtaq, S., Wan, X., and Bai, Z. 2020. "Empowering Teachers to Integrate Machine Learning into K-12 Scientific Discovery." EduAI 2020 Workshop Paper. http://zhouxf.com/papers/EduAI_2020_paper_25.pdf

10
Supporting Simulation-Mediated Scientific Inquiry through Automated Feedback

Hee-Sun Lee, Gey-Hong Gweon and Amy Pallant

Introduction

The current vision for science learning calls for engaging students in the practices of science to learn disciplinary core ideas (National Research Council [NRC] 2012). While rewarding to students, learning disciplinary content through practices can pose enormous challenges for teachers in the classroom (Windschitl et al. 2012). Since students are likely to make progress at their own pace based on prior knowledge, experience, and interest (Stroupe 2014), formative assessment is needed to guide them (Bennett 2011; Goldin et al. 2017). The process of formative assessment includes (a) making diagnostic decisions on the quality of student work produced in the learning process and (b) providing feedback to facilitate student progress based on that diagnosis (Sadler 1989). When student inquiry happens within digitally constructed learning environments, this formative assessment function can be carried out through artificial intelligence (AI) (Gerard et al. 2015; Zhai et al. 2020). That is, we can design a computer-controlled automated feedback system to process students' performance data and make decisions on how to scaffold them until the intended learning goals are achieved (Deeva et al. 2021).

The development and classroom testing of an automated feedback system is complex, requiring multiple iterations to make the automated scoring more accurate and reliable and the automated feedback more relevant and meaningful for the intended purpose. Most published work has focused on a (final) version of the automated feedback system and examined its utility and impact. Often overlooked is the significant effort devoted to the design research process involved in developing the system, including securing large amounts of data needed to develop automated scoring, determining evidence-based learning trajectories, examining the types of discourse students engage in, and modifying the automated feedback features to create a more functional system. The goal of this chapter is to delineate these design aspects to inform the development of next-generation AI-enabled automated feedback systems for science practices.

First, we review automated feedback used in science education. Second, we use a conjecture map (Figure 10.1) to illustrate the design and research processes involved in the development of an automated feedback system called HASbot (Lee et al. 2019, 2021). Our initial conjecture prior to the HASbot development was that

Hee-Sun Lee, Gey-Hong Gweon and Amy Pallant, *Supporting Simulation-Mediated Scientific Inquiry through Automated Feedback*. In: *Uses of Artificial Intelligence in STEM Education*. Edited by: Xiaoming Zhai and Joseph Krajcik, Oxford University Press. © Oxford University Press (2024). DOI: 10.1093/oso/9780198882077.003.0010

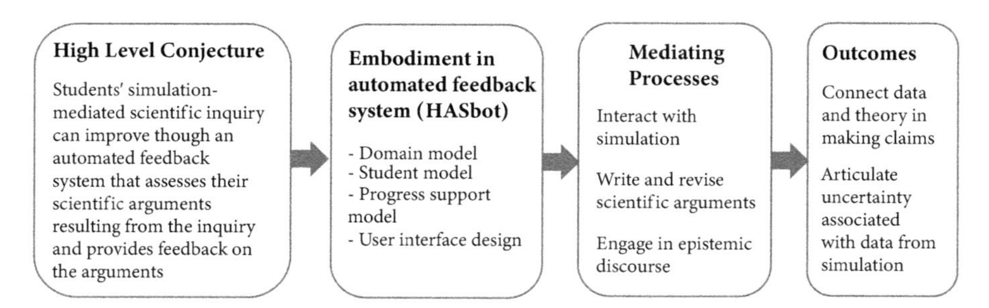

Figure 10.1 Conjecture map for design research with HASbot.

students' simulation-mediated scientific inquiry can be improved through the use of an automated feedback system if the system is able to both assess students' scientific arguments resulting from their inquiry and provide feedback to improve their arguments. Design ideas embodied in HASbot are described in terms of domain model, student model, progress support model, and user interface. We illustrate mediating processes and student outcomes based on various data sources we collected, such as student videos, log data, and artifacts. Lastly, we discuss design challenges encountered during HASbot research and future design considerations for developing more functional and sophisticated AI-enabled automated feedback systems in real-world classroom settings.

Automated Feedback in Science Education

When properly and practically designed, automated feedback can facilitate teacher use of formative assessment to support individual students as well as the entire class (Tansomboon et al. 2017). Formative assessment occurs during instruction often without students' recognition that they are being assessed (Black and William 1998). To be effective, formative assessment should be placed at the critical juncture where students put the most effort at achieving learning goals stated in the activities or tasks (Harlen and James 1997). The most important functions of formative assessment are diagnosis of the learner status as it connects to the intended learning outcomes and provision of feedback to learners for further improvement (Sadler 1989). While feedback can be provided by human agents such as teachers, tutors, or peers in any learning situation, automated feedback is provided in digitally constructed learning environments where automation between diagnosis and feedback based on student information is possible (Lee et al. 2019). For formative purposes, automated feedback concerns "information communicated to the learner that is intended to modify his or her thinking or behavior to improve learning" (Shute 2008, 153) or information communicated to teachers to modify their teaching strategies to improve student learning (Bennett 2011).

One of the early applications of automated feedback systems in education can be traced to intelligent tutoring systems (ITS) developed to teach mathematics and computer programing in the 1990s (Ahuja and Sille 2013; Narciss and Huth 2004).

In ITS applications, students advance based on their success or failure on a problem selected from a set of problems with various levels of difficulty. In the math and computer programing domains, problem difficulties can be defined based on prerequisite information or the number of operations needed to solve the problem. For example, adding three numbers is more difficult than adding two numbers. However, identifying the order of difficulties is much more complicated as science practices cannot be properly characterized in terms of the number of concepts or operations alone. Furthermore, binary decisions on students' performances do not provide much information on different ways in which students carry out science practices that often involve the creation, refinement, and use of representations (e.g., images, models, and data visualizations) or artifacts (e.g., explanations and arguments). Thus, current automated feedback designs in science education have sought to improve the depth and sophistication of scientific reasoning and performances in open-ended, under-defined inquiry tasks, rather than being successful in solving a larger number of problems through transfer of a well-defined thinking process (Duschl 2008).

Providing automated feedback based on student-generated textual responses to open-ended tasks has become prominent in the past decade (Zhai et al. 2020). In the most recent review of automated feedback systems published from 2008 to 2018, Deeva et al. (2021) identified 109 systems, 9 of which addressed science disciplines such as physics, biology, and Earth science. Applications of automated feedback benefitting student learning in real-world classrooms coincided with the purposeful use of natural language processing and machine-learning algorithms (Zhai et al. 2020) that enabled automated scoring of student-generated artifacts such as texts (Gerard, Kidron, and Linn 2019; Liu et al. 2016; Nehm, Ha, and Mayfield 2012), models (Zhai, He, and Krajcik 2022), and images (Pei, Xing, and Lee 2019), as well as behaviors captured in log data (Baker et al. 2013; Gobert et al. 2013; Sao Pedro et al. 2013). Studies have shown improvement in student artifacts and performances targeted by the automated feedback (Gerard, Kidron, and Linn 2019; Lee et al. 2019; Zhu et al. 2017), including for English language learners (Ryoo and Bedell 2019; Ryoo, Bedell, and Swearingen 2018), as well as the improvement in teachers' instruction based on automatically scored information shown to the teachers (Linn et al. 2014). While the development of automated feedback systems is complex, there is a dearth of literature delineating the design process, which we will address in this chapter using the case of HASbot.

Research Context

The purpose of HASbot was to provide real-time feedback to support students' written scientific argumentation and was integrated into student activities featured in an online curriculum module called "Will There Be Enough Fresh Water?" referred to as the water module hereafter. The water module consists of six activities and takes approximately six class periods for secondary school students to complete. Throughout the module, students engage in scientific inquiry using simulations, scientists' published data in tables and graphs, and journalists' photographs. There are eight argumentation tasks situated in a variety of scientific inquiry contexts, four of which involve simulations. The water module addresses scarcity and sustainability of fresh water on the surface of Earth; distribution and uses of fresh water; the flow of underground fresh water through rock layers with different porosities and permeabilities; and the impact of human use and development on fresh water availability. Students are encouraged to work in small groups to complete tasks in the water module. Teachers are expected to support students in carrying out inquiry investigations collaboratively (Sandoval 2005) and similarly to scientists' investigations (Lee and Songer 2003).

HASbot was developed in two stages. Stage 1 involved the collection of scientific arguments students wrote during the eight inquiry tasks in the water module. Fifteen middle and high school teachers across eleven states implemented the water module, and their 935 students provided the automated scoring sample data over a two-year period. We then developed automated scoring models based on the data. In Stage 2, we developed HASbot, which combined the automated scoring models with feedback statements. We then inserted HASbot into each inquiry task in the water module. We tested HASbot in several design cycles. This chapter addresses one design cycle where nine middle and high school teachers from seven US states and their 343 students used the water module with HASbot (HASbot testing sample). Among the students, 49% were female; 40% were non-White minority students; and 15% spoke English as a second language.

HASbot Automated Feedback System Design

We describe HASbot in four elements:

(1) *Domain model* represents the expert knowledge or performance students are expected to achieve. In science, the domain model needs to specify the age-appropriate representations of target scientific knowledge or practice that is contextualized in the task.
(2) *Student model* provides different types or ways in which students express or perform in the domain or the task. Information sources to build the student model can be artifacts students generate, processes in which they engage, behaviors captured during the learning process, verbal and nonverbal exchanges among students, and so on.
(3) *Progress support model* describes how students should be scaffolded to make progress on the task and relies on diagnostic information from the student model to provide customized and adjusted feedback.
(4) *User interface design* presents the arrangement, display, and function of the task, defines the type of interaction students will have, and delivers the feedback.

Figure 10.2 shows a schematic diagram for the HASbot design. The domain model provides a theoretical basis for the progress support model, influences the student model, and determines how to gather input from students through the user interface. The student model determines the machine learning (ML)-based diagnosis and

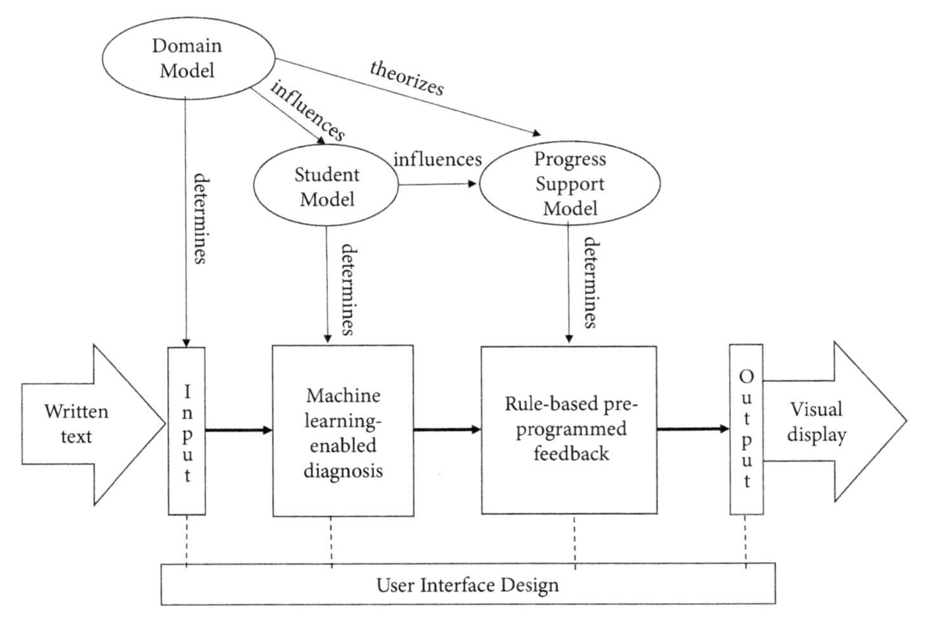

Figure 10.2 Schematic diagram for HASbot design.

influences the support students need in order to make progress. The progress support model determines the rule-based pre-programmed feedback mapped onto the ML-based diagnosis.

In HASbot, the domain model represents scientific argumentation associated with simulation-mediated scientific inquiry; the student model addresses how different levels of students' scientific argumentation are characterized in scoring rubrics and how students' written scientific arguments are automatically analyzed and diagnosed through automated scoring; the progress support model explains what feedback is needed to enable student progress toward writing increasingly sophisticated scientific arguments; and the user interface design illustrates how HASbot is integrated into the water module for classroom use. To illustrate the domain, student, and progress support models, we describe one of the simulation-mediated inquiry tasks in the water module, called the trap task.

Domain Model

How Should Scientific Argumentation in Simulation-Mediated Scientific Inquiry Be Represented?

Simulation-Mediated Scientific Inquiry

Carrying out scientific inquiry involves a range of practices such as posing questions; examining what is already known; planning and carrying out investigations; using tools to gather, analyze, and interpret data; constructing and using models; proposing answers, explanations, and predictions; and communicating results (NRC 1996). Scientific inquiry is situated in a particular science domain and follows the established epistemic norms in the respective scientific community (Sandoval and Reiser 2004). In order to carry out scientific inquiry, scientists need to create a version of reality using models that can be physical, mathematical, or computational and make observations or obtain data (Weisberg 2013). In this study, we focus on simulation-mediated scientific inquiry that is carried out to investigate complex systems (Wilensky and Rand 2015). Due to the unique affordances and limitations of simulations, we list three important types of epistemic understanding students must have in order to successfully engage in scientific inquiry. We use *epistemic* to mean relating to the domain-specific, knowledge-seeking process established in the science community (Elgin 2013).

First, students must know *representational abstraction* (Bar-Yam 2002). That is, a scientific simulation is a computational model of a real-world system that is defined by system properties and abstracted mathematical relationships (Morrison 2015). Students should compare a computational model with a real-world system so that they can interpret results from the simulation as a basis for understanding real-world phenomena.

Second, students must engage in *adequate interactions* with a simulation to obtain evidence from it. Computational models are based on algorithms, i.e., "sets of procedures that take a starting state as an input and specify how this state changes, ultimately yielding an output" (Weisberg 2013, 30). For example, to see how a computational model works, one must choose an input by setting initial conditions for an algorithmically described scientific phenomenon and then run the simulation to create an outcome. This simulation often needs to run multiple times before a scientist or a student can gain insights, write descriptions, or develop explanations about how the phenomenon works.

Third, students must recognize the limitations of a simulation due to *representational idealization*. A simulation has a limited purpose and design since it does not need to, and generally cannot, include all of the entities' properties and all factors associated with a complex system (Sterman 2002). Scientific inquiry with a simulation thus involves an idealized system configured to amplify aspects of the phenomenon the investigator intends to study. Moreover, abstracted mathematical relations among the properties of the entities comprising the complex system are approximations (Rowe 1994).

We expect these three types of epistemic understanding related to representational abstraction, representational idealization, and adequate interactions to be mentioned by students while carrying out simulation-mediated scientific inquiry.

Scientific Argumentation with Uncertainty

We used and interpreted Toulmin (1958)'s rhetorical structure of scientific arguments to fit the simulation-mediated inquiry tasks in the water module. According to Toulmin (1958), an argument has a claim that needs to be supported with data. Warrants are specific rationale that link data and claim in the context of simulation-based inquiry. Backing provides theories and premises that support the context-specific warrants. Qualifiers indicate the strength of the claim, and conditions of rebuttal specify situations that limit the applicability of the claim. Research on students' written scientific argument artifacts has studied students' responses to claim-data-warrants-backing (Clark et al. 2007; Erduran, Simon, and Osborne

2004; McNeill et al. 2006). Research also addressed conditions of rebuttals and qualifiers as part of investigating the coherence and validity of claim-evidence-reasoning over multiple candidate arguments (Kuhn 2010; Sampson 2010; Zohar and Nemet 2002).

In our conceptualization of arguments related to complex environmental systems, we consider a qualifier as the degree of uncertainty students express related to the evidence-based claim in light of theory (Lee et al. 2014). Environmental science topics have been frequently used for classroom scientific argumentation (Nussbaum, Sinatra, and Owens 2012) based on scientific data, journalistic reports, and simulations (Pallant and Lee 2015; Spiegelhalter, Pearson, and Short 2011). As environmental systems are complex, two types of scientific uncertainty exist: epistemic and ontic. Epistemic uncertainty occurs because investigators' theoretical and methodological assumptions and manifestations continue to evolve based on new evidence or understanding. Ontic uncertainty occurs because "the physical world has an element of irreducible elusiveness. The result of an experiment is not determined by the conditions under the control of the experimenter. The lack of control is not the experimenter's deficiency, but rather nature's indeterminism" (Ben-Haim 2014, 165). Epistemic uncertainty can thus be reduced as investigators gain knowledge and experience to make corrections and adjustments in the investigation. However, ontic uncertainty can never be reduced despite the investigators' best efforts because uncertainty "results from myriad factors both scientific and social, and consequently is difficult to accurately define and quantify" (Kandlikar, Risbey, and Dessai 2005, 444). As such, we expected students to express three epistemic understandings related to simulation-mediated inquiry with respect to representational abstractions, adequate interactions, and representational limitations to explain their level of uncertainty in their scientific argument.

To elicit students' scientific arguments, we use the uncertainty-infused scientific argumentation construct to account for system complexity and uncertainty when simulations are used as sources of evidence (Lee et al. 2014). The uncertainty-infused scientific argumentation construct includes two types of reasoning: one on how students use evidence to justify a claim based on scientific knowledge and the other on how students assign the level of uncertainty and attribute the sources of uncertainty. To elicit these two types of reasoning in scientific arguments, we use the following prompts: (1) multiple-choice claim, (2) constructed-response explanation, (3) uncertainty level from very uncertain to very certain on a five-point Likert scale, and (4) constructed-response uncertainty attribution. We placed these prompts at the end of each simulation-mediated scientific inquiry task.

Task Example

The trap task is the first simulation-mediated scientific inquiry investigation in the water module. It introduces the importance of fresh water availability and asks students to use the simulation to observe how rainwater moves through different rock and sediment layers with different degrees of permeability. See Figure 10.3. There is an introductory text before students run the groundwater simulation. After observing

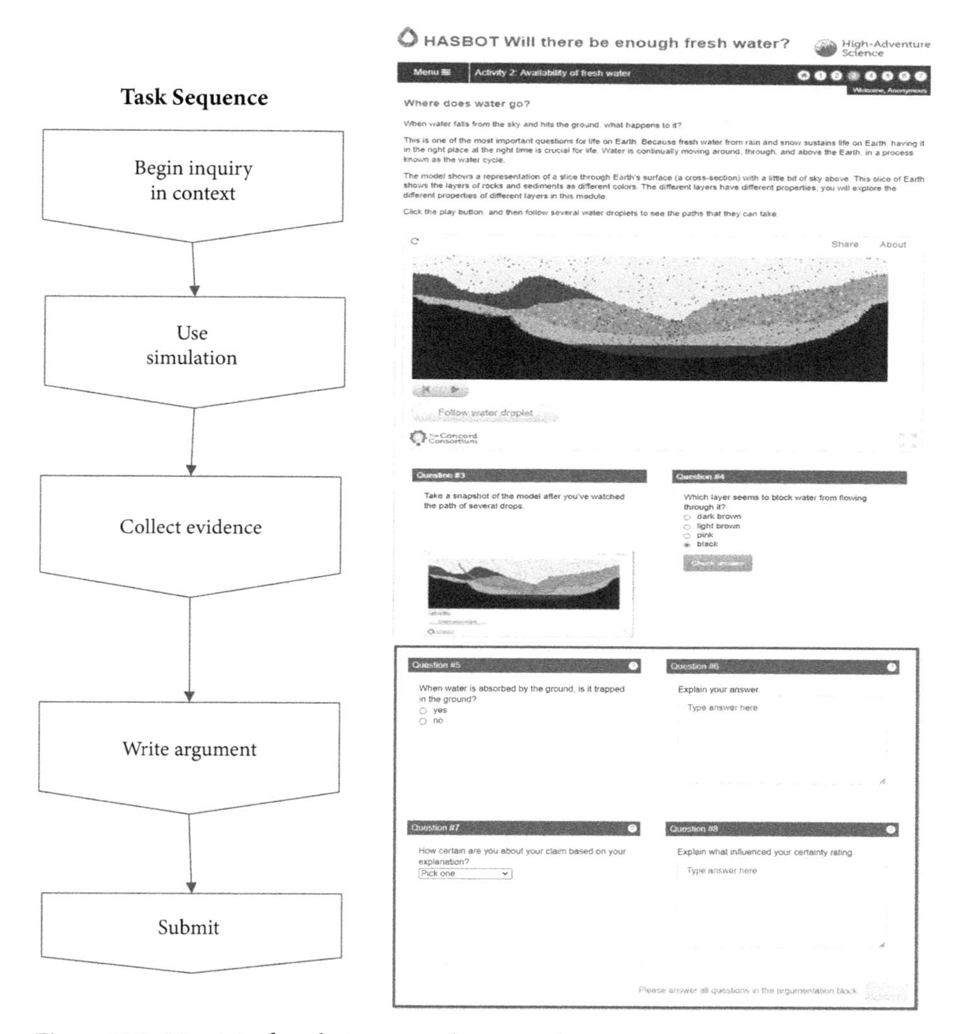

Figure 10.3 User interface design example: trap task.

the simulation and following water droplets, students take a snapshot of the simulation and are asked to draw the longest path a water droplet can take. To check whether students interpret the evidence as expected, students are asked to identify which layer in the simulation the water droplet cannot pass through. The uncertainty-infused scientific argumentation prompts follow for the question: "When water is absorbed by the ground, is it trapped in the ground?" To answer this claim prompt, students choose between yes and no. To explain the claim students chose, they respond to "Explain your answer." Students are then asked to choose from (1) very uncertain to (5) very certain related to the uncertainty rating prompt: "How certain are you about your claim based on your explanation?" Students respond to the uncertainty attribution prompt: "Explain what influenced your certainty rating."

Students have access to hints for each prompt. For selecting a claim, prompts include "Evidence may come from graphs and charts" and "A good claim is based on the evidence." For writing an explanation, "A good explanation combines evidence with scientific knowledge" and "When there is a model, you can describe what happened in the model." For selecting an uncertainty rating, "Your certainty rating can be based on how well the scientific knowledge fits the evidence from models, charts, or graphs" and "Your certainty rating can also reflect on the quality of the evidence or the investigation that produced the evidence." For writing an explanation for the uncertainty rating (uncertainty attribution), "Some topics are more certain than others. Consider the completeness of the evidence, biases in the evidence, and changes that could affect the trends over time."

Student Model

How Should Student Performances Be Recognized and Diagnosed?

Scoring Rubrics Reflecting Varied Epistemic Levels of Uncertainty-Infused Scientific Argumentation

In order to model students' performances in the simulation-mediated inquiry tasks, we focused on students' responses to the four-part uncertainty-infused scientific argumentation prompts. We developed a construct map that matches the underlying uncertainty-infused scientific argumentation construct and rubrics used to score students' responses to claim, explanation, and uncertainty attribution responses (see Figure 10.4). The construct consisted of five epistemic levels: no information, nascent, dogmatic, contextualized, and reflective. As students move from lower to higher epistemic levels, students' written scientific arguments become more and more sophisticated. We scored students' claims as 0 for incorrect/invalid claims and 1 for correct/valid claims from the science perspective. We scored explanations from 0 to 6 and uncertainty attributions from 0 to 4.

To score the explanation of the claim, we used the claim-evidence-reasoning approach (McNeill et al. 2006). That is, the most important elements in explaining a claim are data and reasoning. For the trap task, data students should collect were the following:

- Water droplets fall and absorb (infiltrate) into the ground.
- Water droplets move underground through the layers.
- Water droplets accumulate above the black (impermeable) layer.
- Some water droplets at the surface move back to the atmosphere.
- If water makes it to the surface from the underground, it can move back to the atmosphere.

Scientifically valid reasoning to use in the trap task included the following:

- Water cycles through the Earth system through precipitation, evaporation, and condensation.

Direction for increasingly sophisticated scientific argument (↑)

Scientific argument	Claim	Explanation of claim	Uncertainty attribution
Reflective Incorporates data and reasoning specific to the investigation context and reflects on simulation-based data as evidence		**(Score 6)** Fully elaborates scientifically valid data and reasoning	**(Score 4)** Mentions simulation limitations as evidence, e.g., representational abstraction, idealization, and adequacy
Contextualized Incorporates data or reasoning specific to the investigation context		**(Score 5)** Fully elaborates scientifically valid reasoning **(Score 4)** Fully elaborates scientifically valid data	**(Score 3)** Includes investigation-specific data patterns or causal mechanisms
Dogmatic Recognized the need for data/reasoning but does not have specific data/reasoning	**(Score 1)** Scientifically-valid claim	**(Score 3)** Partially elaborates scientifically valid data or reasoning **(Score 2)** Restates the claim	**(Score 2)** Mentions data, knowledge, and simulation that are not clearly or appropriately defined for the investigation
Nascent Uses common-sense argument not aligned with science	**(Score 0)** Scientifically-invalid claim	**(Score 1)** Includes incorrect or everyday data or reasoning	**(Score 1)** Uses personal knowledge or experience
No Information Does not provide information		**(Score 0)** blank or off-task, non-sensical responses	**(Score 0)** blank or off-task, non-sensical responses

Figure 10.4 Construct map for uncertainty-infused scientific argumentation.

- As the water table rises, water can move up to the surface.
- Underground water movement depends on both the porosity and permeability of the layers.

Using these two sets of data and reasoning, we identified scores 4 through 6: Score 4 explanations included data from the simulation without reasoning; score 5 explanations elaborated reasoning without data from the simulation; and score 6 explanations had both data and reasoning. Score 3 explanations included partially elaborated data or reasoning. Score 2 was given when students restated or made slight variations of the claim made in the multiple-choice claim prompt. Score 1 responses included only incorrect data and/or reasoning or used words such as "data" or "knowledge" without details from the task. Score 0 was assigned to blank, off-task, or "I don't know" responses. See Table 10.1 for the explanation scoring rubric with example responses for the Trap task.

For the uncertainty attribution, if students mentioned epistemic uncertainty associated with simulation-based data, such as representational idealization and abstraction, we assigned the highest score of 4. For example, a student mentioned

> although some is being evaporated there might be some water droplets that are trapped, because more go up when they are exposed to air. There could also be other factors such as amount of sunlight and other weather changes that are not shown in the diagram that could affect the amount of water being evaporated. In the diagram it seems there is constant precipitation so we would have to see the results in other weather conditions to evaluate this properly.

While recognizing that evaporation is a primary mechanism for not trapping the water droplets under the surface of the Earth, the student also noted that not all water droplets would be able to evaporate. As such, the claim that the groundwater is not trapped underground cannot be certain all the time. The student listed other factors not addressed in the simulation, such as weather conditions and sunlight availability.

In developing criteria for scores 0 to 3 below the highest score of 4 for the uncertainty attribution, we applied Kahneman and Tversky (1982)'s psychological analysis on uncertainty that distinguishes between internal and external attributions of uncertainty. We first assigned score 0 for no information, e.g., blank, off-task, or nonsensical responses. Internal attribution relies on personal theories or confidence without considering scientific norms, data, or evidence. We assigned score 1 for personal statements such as "I read about this" or "I am familiar with the water cycle." When students mentioned external attribution related to science, scores increased to 2 or higher. Score 2 responses attributed their uncertainty rating to data from the simulation without specifics. Score 3 was used for specific pieces of data and knowledge belonging to the context of a simulation-mediated scientific investigation. We also identified students who referred vaguely to data or knowledge without inquiry. See Table 10.2 for the uncertainty attribution scoring rubric with example responses for the trap task.

Validating Scoring Rubrics Representing Epistemic Progression

To validate our theorization of the progress in scientific arguments as shown in Figure 10.4, we applied the construct modeling approach proposed by Wilson (2005). We considered the uncertainty-infused scientific argumentation as a construct, i.e., an underlying ability that makes a claim based on data interpreted under scientific knowledge and critically evaluates the degree of uncertainty associated with the claim based on strengths and limitations of data and knowledge. Even though integers were used to distinguish different scoring levels in students' responses, they represented the order of progression. Therefore, the scores were initially given on an ordinal scale. Rasch analysis was used to psychometrically create an interval scale so that student scores and item difficulties could be compared and interpreted on that same

Table 10.1 Trap Task: Explanation Scoring Rubric, Example Responses, and Feedback (Adapted with permission from Lee et al. (2019))

Score	Student response examples	Feedback
Score 0 No information	• I made an educated guess.	You haven't explained your claim about whether or not water is trapped. Run the model and observe what happens to water as it moves underground. Explain why you think water is, or is not, trapped.
Score 1 Incorrect data or reasoning; nominal uses of "data" or "knowledge"	• Because that is what the model shows. • Yes, when the water is absorbed into the ground it becomes stuck there	Are you sure? Run the model again for a longer period of time. Use the "Follow a water droplet" button to watch where the water moves. Rewrite your explanation to include why you think water is (or is not) trapped underground.
Score 2 Restatement of the claim without data or reasoning	• Water moves on after a while, it is not trapped there forever. • The animation says it is trapped. • Because water can move	You made a claim without an explanation. Can you explain why water is (or is not) trapped underground? Provide specific evidence about how water moves through the model.
Score 3 Partially elaborated, scientifically valid data or reasoning	• Water can be evaporated. • Evaporation takes place so it is not trapped.	Your explanation needs more details. Can you provide specific evidence about how water moves in the model to support your claim? What makes it possible for water to move underground?
Score 4 Fully elaborated, scientifically valid data	• It is because all the water is just traveling down in the simulation, it just stays there. • They all go into the ground, but eventually all turn into water vapor.	You used evidence about how water moves through different layers in the model. What makes it possible for water to move underground?
Score 5 Fully elaborated, scientifically valid reasoning	• It is subject to evaporation depending on how far down it goes, and it can travel through ground flow into rivers, lakes, and streams.	You explained what makes it possible for water to move underground. Can you also add specific evidence about how water moves in the model?
Score 6 Fully elaborated and scientifically valid data with reasoning	• The water can be absorbed into the ground, but it can be released back into the atmosphere, as shown by the green dots by transpiration. Transpiration occurs from plants and trees releasing the water back into the atmosphere	You included evidence from the model and reasoning to support your claim. Great job!

Table 10.2 Trap Task: Uncertainty Attribution Scoring Rubric, Example Responses, and Feedback (Adapted with permission from Lee et al. (2019))

Score description	Student response examples	Feedback
Score 0 No information	• I'm not certain. • I am pretty sure I am right.	You haven't explained your certainty rating. What did you see in the groundwater model that influenced your certainty rating?
Score 1 Personal knowledge or experience	• I read about this yesterday. • I am familiar with the water cycle, but don't feel certain enough to mark "very certain." • We read it in the book.	You did not use scientific evidence. Your argument will be stronger if you evaluate the strengths and weaknesses of the evidence from the model. What are you certain about from the groundwater model?
Score 2 Nominal uses of data sources or vague mentions of investigation	• The graph clearly, obviously, and very blankly shows this idea. • There's a model.	You mentioned that the groundwater model influenced your certainty rating. Now, explain why you are certain or uncertain about your response.
Score 3 Investigation-specific data patterns or causal mechanisms	• Well after it rains there's always water on the ground, but after a while everything gets dry again. So, it is either still in the ground where we can't see or it has turned into vapor. • Well since in the picture it has the water looking like it's stuck in the ground. • Water can be evaporated from the ground.	You used scientific evidence or knowledge. Now, think about the potential weaknesses of your argument. Are there limitations to the groundwater model? What are they?
Score 4 Mentions of simulation limitations based on representational abstraction, representational idealization, and adequacy of simulation as data sources	• Because although some is being evaporated there might be some water droplets that are trapped because more go up when they are exposed to air. There could also be other factors such as amount of sunlight and other weather changes that are not shown in the diagram that could affect the amount of water being evaporated. In the diagram it seems there is constant precipitation so we would have to see the results in other weather conditions to evaluate this properly.	You used evidence from the model. You also recognized that the model is not a perfect representation of groundwater movement. That's a great start towards thinking like a scientist!

scale (Rasch 1966). As a result, Rasch analysis provided evidence that higher scores required greater amounts of an underlying ability on the construct (Bond and Fox 2007). Since our scoring levels across claim, explanation, and uncertainty attribution varied, we applied the Partial Credit Model (PCM) version of the Rasch analysis (Masters 1982) to the student argument data from the automated scoring sample from Stage 1.

Exploratory factor analysis (EFA) using principal axis factoring revealed that students' claims, explanation, and uncertainty attributions collectively contributed to a primary factor (Lee et al. 2019). We then carried out the Rasch–PCM analysis (Lee et al. 2019). Figure 10.5 shows item threshold locations on the logit for all eight scientific argumentation tasks in the water module. According to Figure 10.5, the item threshold locations associated with all of the explanation and uncertainty attribution scores increase as the scores increase across the eight tasks. This indicates that the progression of students' argument responses was captured adequately in the scores we assigned.

Automated Scoring Models

We developed automated scoring models using human-scored responses from Stage 1, which were also used for the Rasch–PCM analysis. Students' responses were scored by two human coders who worked together to develop the module, the scoring rubrics, and the feedback statements. The entire dataset was scored by one coder, and a randomly selected third of the data was scored by the other. The human–human agreement shows the reliability of scoring rubrics ranging from 0.86 to 0.96 in quadratic weighted kappa (QWK) for the explanations and from 0.87 to 0.96 for the uncertainty attributions across all eight scientific argumentation tasks in the water

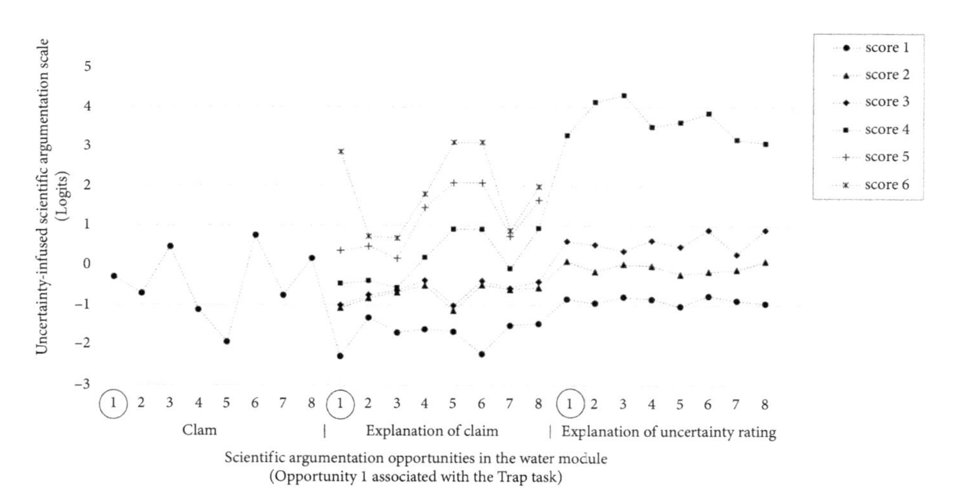

Figure 10.5 Item threshold locations across eight scientific argumentation tasks in the water module.

module. For the trap task, QWK between the two coders was 0.90 for the explanation and 0.90 for the uncertainty attribution.

Using c-raterML, a machine learning-based natural language processing engine developed by the Educational Testing Service (Heilman and Madnani 2013), we developed automated scoring models for each explanation prompt and each uncertainty attribution prompt (Mao et al. 2018). A total of sixteen scoring models, i.e., eight of them for explanations and the other eight for uncertainty attributions in the eight argumentation tasks, was developed for the water module. QWK between machine and human scores ranged from 0.70 to 0.92 for the explanations and from 0.85 to 0.91 for the uncertainty attributions across the eight argumentation tasks. QWK between machine and human scores was 0.78 for the explanation and 0.86 for the uncertainty attribution associated with the trap task.

Progress Support Model

What Feedback Is Needed and How Should It Be Delivered?

Feedback is an important part of learning in the classroom (Black et al. 2003; Hattie 2009). Students benefit more from immediate and task-specific feedback (Kulik and Fletcher 2016; Shute 2008) than delayed and task-general feedback (Dihoff, Brosvic, and Epstein 2003). Feedback can be provided in the forms of: (1) diagnostic feedback showing students whether their responses are correct or incorrect, or their level of performance; (2) suggestive feedback addressing hints, prompts, or ideas to take actions; (3) informative feedback providing additional information; and (4) motivational feedback through complementing and reassuring (Deeva et al. 2021).

Rasch–PCM analysisresults confirmed that the direction of progress on students' uncertainty-infused scientific argumentation follows the direction of score increases. Each score represents what epistemic level the response showed as well as the missing epistemic elements. We designed automated feedback to carry out diagnostic and suggestive functions so that students could recognize their progress based on score increases. In the diagnostic feedback part, the score students received was explained based on what it did or did not include. The suggestive feedback indicated what further information should be included and how that information could be obtained. For example, an explanation score of 3 in the trap task indicated that students needed to articulate their data and reasoning more clearly. As a result, students received feedback as follows:

> Your explanation needs more details. *[Diagnosis]*
>
> Can you provide specific evidence about how water moves in the model to support your claim? What makes it possible for water to move underground? *[Suggestion]*

The first sentence lets students know that their explanation was not clearly articulated. The second and third sentences suggest the next actions the students might take to improve data and reasoning in their explanation. Similarly, all feedback statements were configured to include diagnosis and suggestion statements. Table 10.1 lists feedback statements related to each explanation score, and Table 10.2 lists those related to each uncertainty attribution score.

User Interface Design

Figure 10.3 (right) shows the user interface design for the trap task presented to students as an interactive Web page on the computer screen. Students begin inquiry in the context of a specific question, use a simulation, collect evidence, and write a scientific argument. After students submit structured responses to the four-part uncertainty-infused scientific argumentation prompts, their responses are automatically scored in real time and feedback statements are delivered shortly thereafter. Figure 10.6 shows the interface design for displaying the automated score and feedback. We used a rainbow bar for students to quickly grasp their performance based on the numerical score and recognize room for further improvement. We placed automated feedback statements underneath the rainbow bar. Students can read, discuss, make revision decisions, and revise and resubmit if they want. The submit-feedback-revision process repeats until students decide to stop revising. The whole process of submitting, autoscoring, finding feedback matching the score, and displaying the score and feedback to students took two to five seconds.

Student Outcomes and Mediating Processes

We developed HASbot to help students revise their arguments so that they could better incorporate theory and evidence in their explanations and explicitly address affordances and limitations of the data drawn from the use of simulations. Since HASbot asked students to scrutinize data, it was possible that students also improved simulation-related aspects of inquiry. In this section, we describe student outcomes and mediating processes using the implementation data collected from the HASbot testing sample in Stage 2.

Overall Outcome: Improvement between Initial and Final Scientific Arguments

The percentage of students who made revisions after receiving automated feedback ranged from 51 to 67% across eight argumentation tasks in the water module (Lee et al. 2019). When students made revisions, their explanation and uncertainty attribution scores significantly improved, $p < 0.001$, based on paired samples t-tests. The effect size of the improvement in Cohen's d ranged from 0.20 SD to 0.65 SD for explanations. The effect size ranged from 0.51 SD to 0.99 SD for uncertainty attributions. In the trap task, 339 students submitted their responses to the uncertainty-infused scientific argumentation prompts; 67% of the students made revisions; students increased their explanation scores as a whole by 0.47 SD, $p < 0.001$, and their uncertainty attribution scores by 0.99 SD, $p < 0.001$.

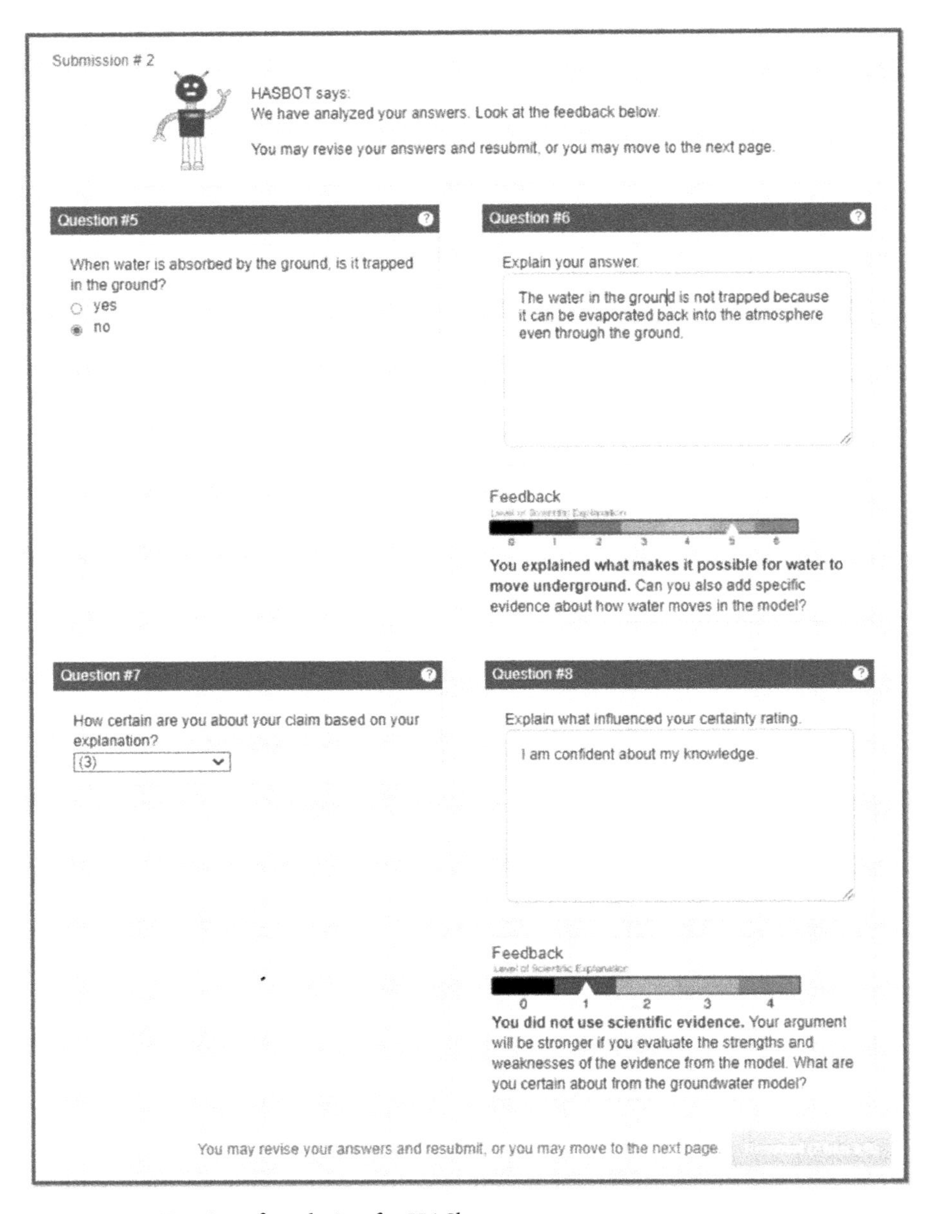

Figure 10.6 User interface design for HASbot.

Mediating Process 1: Engage in Epistemic Discourse

During Stage 2, we collected videos of nine student groups working in one teacher's environmental science class. The videos included student voices and computer screens as they worked through the trap task. Each group consisted of two or three students. During the trap task, the students encountered automated feedback for the first time in the water module. In total, 147 minutes of the videos were transcribed verbatim. On average, students in small groups took 16.3 minutes to finish the trap task.

We identified all episodes associated with the three types of epistemic discourse related to simulation-mediated inquiry before and after automated feedback. The first type of epistemic discourse concerns *phenomenon discourse* (P) about representational abstraction, i.e., mapping between simulated entities and real-world phenomena. Entities in the simulation are dots and different colored layers. Blue dots represent water droplets during the rain event while green dots represent evaporated water droplets. Blue-colored areas represent aquifers if present underground and lakes or rivers if present above ground. Layers with different colors represent different rock and sediment compositions. The phenomena in the simulation is the water flow above and below Earth's surface, including precipitating water droplets landing and infiltrating Earth's surface, moving through layers at different speeds, stopping at the black impermeable layer, rising as aquifers fill up, and evaporating from the surface. The second addresses *limitation discourse* (L) about representational idealization when students use a simulation as a tool to collect evidence. Limitations might include missing or simplified factors, sampling of data from the simulation, and lack of theory, analysis, or interpretation. The third type relates to *evidence discourse* (E) about the adequacy of simulation evidence during their collection, interpretation, and explanation of evidence in formulating scientific arguments about whether the groundwater is trapped.

Table 10.3 summarizes the distribution of these three types of discourse (P, L, and E) across the nine student groups in the simulation-mediated inquiry investigation steps. Before feedback, students used the simulation, collected evidence, and wrote arguments. After feedback, students evaluated automated scores and feedback, interacted with the simulation, or revised argument responses. Table 10.3 also includes automated scores students received on their first arguments and final arguments, if revised.

The duration of the whole discourse during the simulation-mediated inquiry ranged from nine minutes (G6) to twenty-four minutes (G8). Phenomenon discourse occurred in eight groups; evidence discourse occurred in all nine groups; and limitation discourse occurred in six groups. Over time, students' discourse tended to move from phenomenon to evidence to limitation. When students first engaged with the simulation, their discourse appeared to focus on representing the water movement phenomenon above and below the surface. The evidence discourse for most groups began to occur when students collected data with a snapshot of the simulation and further enriched when they wrote arguments. These results were in line with Sandoval (2005)'s assertion that epistemic discourse is more likely to occur when students create artifacts from inquiry-based instruction. However, limitation discourse was more difficult. It began to occur in two groups when students were asked to rate their uncertainty. These two groups were able to talk about uncertainty because they wondered about two different outcomes water droplets could take in the simulation: trapped or evaporated. Since precipitation fell periodically and groundwater continued to be recharged, the groundwater forming in the simulation

Table 10.3 Student Actions before and after Automated Feedback

	Before feedback actions			Argument scores	After feedback actions			Argument scores	Whole task
	Use simulation	Collect evidence	Write argument	Initial	Discourse	Simulation action	Argument revision	Revised	Duration (min)
G1	P	PE	E	1-4-4-1	EL	revisit	R	1-4-4-4	22
G2	–	PE	E	1-5-5-2	–	–	X	1-6-5-2	21
G3	–	–	PE	1-6-3-2	L	–	R	1-6-3-3	11
G4	PE	PE	–	1-5-4-2	PEL	Revisit & rerun	XUR	1-6-5-4	19
G5	–	–	E	1-4-3-3	–	–	–	–	13
G6	P	P	E	1-4-2-2	–	–	–	–	9
G7	P	P	E	0-5-5-3	EL	Revisit	XR	0-6-5-4	13
G8	–	P	EL	1-3-3-3	PEL	Revisit & rerun	XR	1-6-3-4	24
G9	–	PE	EL	1-4-5-4	–	–	–	–	15

Argument element: X: explanation; U: uncertainty rating; R: uncertainty attribution.
Epistemic discourse patterns: P: phenomenon discourse; E: evidence discourse; L: limitation discourse.

would not be dried out completely through evaporation. In such a case, there was uncertainty in making a claim that water is trapped or not. According to Kahneman and Tversky (1982)'s classification of uncertainty, people gain confidence in their claim based on the theory that explains the claim or the frequency of observations related to the claim. When lacking a theory, students can gain more confidence in their claim when they make frequent observations of the same outcome in the simulation.

When automated feedback was provided, five of the six groups that chose to revise began to engage in evidence discourse when revising the explanation or the limitation discourse when revising the uncertainty attribution. Among the five groups that engaged in evidence discourse, four groups revisited the simulation to clarify the meaning of the evidence and two groups reran the simulation to confirm their interpretation. That is, automated feedback prompted students to take a range of actions: engage more deeply with epistemic discourse related to simulation evidence and limitations, rerun the simulation, and revise argument responses. In particular, most groups' serious discourse around simulation limitations began in earnest after automated feedback on their uncertainty attribution was provided.

Mediating Process 2: Write and Revise Scientific Arguments

In the initial arguments submitted, all but one group claimed that groundwater was not trapped; explanations ranged from 3 (partially elaborated data or reasoning), 4 (fully elaborated data), to 5 (fully elaborated reasoning). Uncertainty attributions ranged from 1 (personal), 2 (nominal or unelaborated use of data), 3 (elaborated data within investigation), to 4 (evidence limitation). See Table 10.3. No groups' initial explanations and uncertainty attributions received the highest available scores, i.e., 6 and 4, respectively. After automated feedback was provided, three groups did not make any revisions; six groups made revisions (one group made one revision; three made two revisions; one made three revisions; and one made ten revisions). Among the six groups that revised, three groups revised both explanations and uncertainty attributions; two revised uncertainty attributions; and one revised explanations. Overall, uncertainty attributions were revised by five groups while explanations were revised by four groups. All revisions resulted in increases in automated scores students received after resubmission. Uncertainty ratings were mostly stable before and after revisions. Only one group changed their uncertainty rating from somewhat certain to very certain after carrying out two revisions on both explanation (from 5 to 6) and uncertainty attribution (from 2 to 3 to 4). Taken together, students' revisions and argument score changes indicate that the main function of automated feedback was achieved.

From the video analysis, we identified several ways students interacted with automated feedback beyond revising scientific arguments. First, automated feedback provided students with ideas for argument revisions. Student group G4 first claimed that the water is trapped because "the water moved slowest through the black layer, so slow that you might think it blocks the water movement." With that explanation, the group chose an uncertainty rating of 4. The following sequence of uncertainty attribution revision occurred:

Initial uncertainty attribution: "In the picture the rain drops kept on flowing and never trapped."
[Uncertainty attribution was based on observation of the model without mentioning evaporation or the blocking of groundwater (Score 2).]
HASbot: "You mentioned that the groundwater model influenced your certainty rating. Now, explain why you are certain or uncertain about your response."
First revision: "In the picture the rain drops kept on flowing and were never trapped. We are certain the water droplets are not trapped, because if they were they would stop flowing."
[The revision included more clearly articulated evidence from the simulation (Score 3).]
HASbot: "You used scientific evidence or knowledge. Now, think about the potential weaknesses of your argument. Are there limitations to the groundwater model? What are they?"
Second revision: "In the picture the rain drops kept on flowing and were never trapped. We are certain the water droplets are not trapped, because if they were they would stop flowing. However, layers further down may be able to stop it from flowing."
[Students used a factor that was not represented in the model that limited the claim based on evidence from the simulation (Score 4).]
HASbot: "You used evidence from the model. You also recognized that the model is not a perfect representation of groundwater movement. That's a great start towards thinking like a scientist!"

Second, low automated scores drove students to engage in the trap task further. High automated scores elicited a sense of achievement and satisfaction, e.g., "Yeah! It's a five, Yay! !" When students received high scores on their initial argument submissions, they did not discuss much about the content, the evidence, or the argument. However, unanticipated low scores surprised students. They were more likely to try to figure out what they had not done right and come up with a plan to get a higher score, such as revisiting the simulation and reinterpreting the evidence. For example, students in Group 4 received the following feedback: "Can you also add specific evidence about how water moves in the model?" The group went back to the simulation to add the water trap route and the water evaporation route:

G4S1: The water can pass every sediment layer but the black layer, the water moves through the layers easily on its way down to . . .
G4S2: The black layer stops.
G4S1: Ya. I don't . . . until it hits the black layer
G4S2: which will stop the water from sinking.
G4S1: from proceeding . . . Okay, so . . .
[going back to the model]

G4S1: Holy crap! *[after seeing in the model the entire landscape almost submerged]*
G4S1: There has got to be evaporation.
G4S2: I think so.

Third, explaining the claim was relatively easier for students than explaining the uncertainty rating. According to the teacher, students were rarely asked to assess the uncertainty of the evidence derived from the use of a simulation prior to using the water module. Only one group (G9) received the highest uncertainty attribution score of 4 after their first submission. Understandably, students needed to make sense of what it means to rate and explain uncertainty. For example, students in Group 1 wrote, "We are fairly certain of our answer because we were also able to think about our answers reasonably." They received a score of 1 on their uncertainty attribution, which meant their response was characterized as personal. The episode below illustrates the process of understanding what uncertainty meant in scientific argumentation (Lee et al. 2019, 615–16):

G1S1: A one? A one?
G1S2: Huh? How'd we get a one for that?
G1S1: We were fairly certain . . . *[after reading the feedback]* What are you certain about from the groundwater model?
G1S2: We were certain that the other one runs slower. We did well on the first one. *[Explanation Score 4]*
G1S1: I don't understand why we got through that *[explanation prompt]* really well.
G1S2: Then, we said, we said something else. We said that we . . .
G1S1: Hey, we're answering a completely different question than what it asked. That's why. [*Went back to the model to reexamine their evidence.]* It is asking us why we are certain about how the groundwater can get back up and be evaporated if it's not trapped!
G1S2: Yes!
G1S1: Are you certain of your answer?
G1S2: Oh, okay we figured it out.
G1S1: We are fairly certain, uh, wait, hold on . . . maybe it is trapped.
G1S2: No, it's not. We got a good score on explanation.
G1S1: Yeah, I know but it's not trapped . . . This is what it is asking. It's asking, we answered, why we thought it was not trapped.
G1S2: Then, how do you explain it?
G1S1: Okay, we are certain or we are fairly certain because . . . um, 30% of the water we get is groundwater. And in the model it showed that water was being evaporated afterwards. Also, in the model, it showed the water evaporating from sediments. *[Resubmitted uncertainty attribution and received a score of 3.]*

We also note that some wording of the feedback can be misunderstood. In particular, to reach a Score 4 in attributing uncertainty, students had to think about possible "limitations" to the evidence from the simulation. Two groups thought that limitations meant limiting the groundwater flow, instead of considering limitations in the evidence from the simulation. As such they were not able to engage in Epistemic discourse around simulation evidence.

Fourth, students became more deeply engaged with interpreting data in light of their knowledge after receiving feedback. For example, Group 1 went back to the simulation to reexamine their claim; they also elicited a piece of knowledge that could be useful in interpreting data. The information that "30% of the water we get is groundwater" was learned earlier in the water module. Students voluntarily elicited this piece of knowledge to justify that water could not be trapped forever in the ground if they were to use groundwater in their life. Thus, automated feedback helped this group of students not only engage in the simulation-mediated argumentation task at hand but also elicit knowledge and experience they felt relevant to make sense of data as part of writing argument responses.

Mediating Process 3: Interact with Simulation

In Stage 2, the curriculum server collected log data on the digital interactions and artifacts of the students who used the HASbot-integrated water module. Based on the log data, we discovered that 21.8% of the students reran the simulation after they read the automated feedback. In order to determine the adequacy of students' simulation interactions, we applied decision tree algorithms. Decision trees can be used to probabilistically predict the outcome variable from the predictor variables measured on a categorical or continuous scale (Baker et al. 2013). We first extracted several simulation interaction variables in the trap task such as the following:

- Number of times the student switched between simulation and answering questions (cui1)
- Number of times the simulation was run (m_n1)
- Average duration the simulation was run (m_at1)
- Number of water droplets followed (f_n1)
- Average time a water droplet was followed (f_at1)

We then used these variables to predict uncertainty attribution scores that addressed critical reasoning on the importance of data in making claims. We used decision tree algorithms for an exploratory purpose due to the small sample size and lack of strong theories to evaluate predictor variables on the outcome variable (Mingers 1989). We took 70% of the log data for training and 30% for cross-validation. The root node error reduction with decision tree splitting indicated that 41% of the students received an uncertainty attribution score of 3. This means that the root node error without decision tree splitting was 59% if Score 3 was used as prediction. Classification errors were reduced by 6% with decision tree splitting on the training dataset and 3% on the validation dataset for the trap task.

Figure 10.7 shows the decision tree output for the trap task. Each node in the tree has a single Boolean expression related to "true" or "false." For example, the first node in Figure 10.7 asks whether f_at1 (average amount of time a water droplet was followed) is smaller than 5.5 seconds. If yes, the Boolean expression in the next node asks

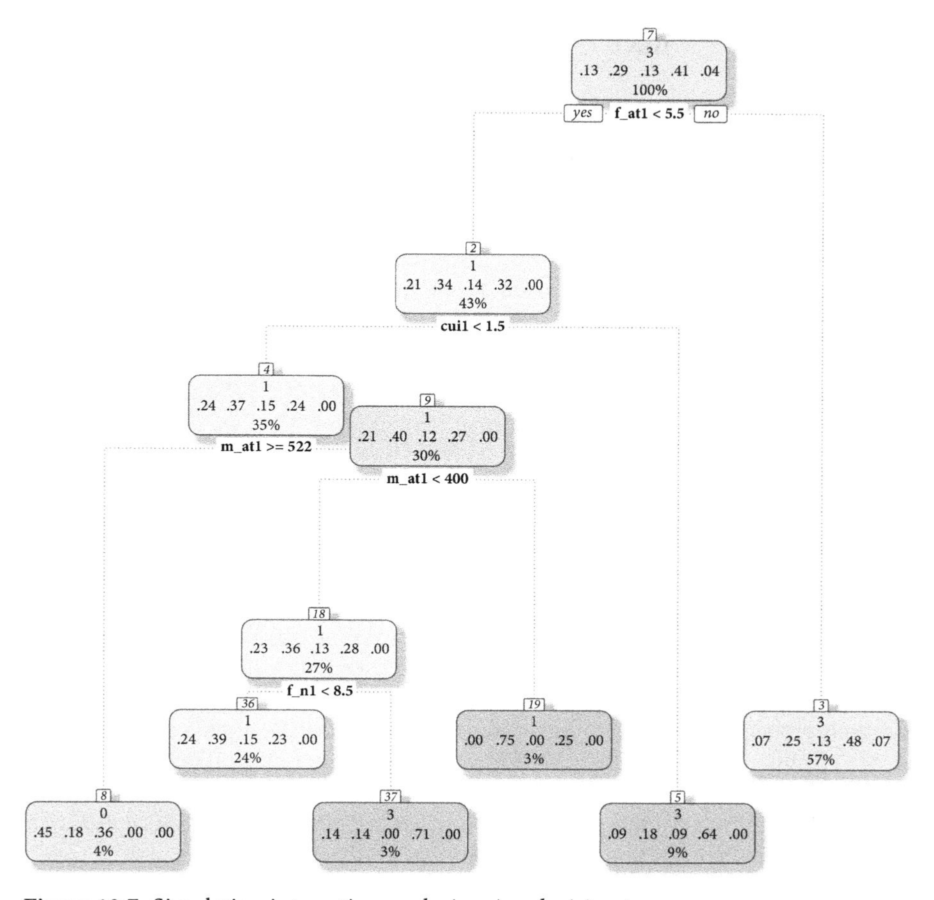

Figure 10.7 Simulation interaction analysis using decision tree.

whether cuil (number of times the student switched between simulation and answering questions) is smaller than 1.5. On the other hand, "No" at the first node leads to a terminal node showing percentage distribution across five uncertainty attribution scores. The top line in this terminal node is 3, showing the score with the largest percentage (48%). The middle line (0.07 0.25 0.13 0.48 0.07) shows the percentage distribution of 7, 25, 13, 48, and 7%, corresponding to Scores 0, 1, 2, 3, and 4. The third line (57%) shows the percentage of data that can be described by the Boolean decision sequence that ends at this terminal node. Other terminal nodes can be interpreted in a similar fashion. While the quantitative interpretation of the decision tree output is not straightforward, the strength of this analysis is that it provides human-readable criteria pointing out important factors. From this analysis, we identified the most important simulation interactions: (1) students followed water droplets for a long enough time, (2) the amount of time the trap simulation was run, and (3) the number of water droplets that were followed. These factors were incorporated to produce the simulation feedback in post-Stage 2 work (Lee et al. 2021).

AI Design Challenges: Automated Feedback for Science Practices

By harnessing AI's abilities to autoscore students' written responses through natural language processing, we developed the automated feedback system called HASbot. This design research described earlier showed how automated feedback can be used as scaffolds to engage students in deep epistemic discourse needed in scientific inquiry. However, we recognized that the design of HASbot could be further improved. We frame the discussion of HASbot findings and further improvement directions as AI design challenges for developing more accurate, responsive, and tailored automated feedback that can improve students' participation in science practices.

Challenge 1: Improving AI-Based Diagnostic Models

We tested the automated feedback system as part of the simulation-mediated inquiry that concluded with written scientific argumentation. Designed primarily for argument revisions, the automated feedback system we tested in this study provided diagnostic information about explanations and uncertainty attributions students submitted, along with suggestions for improvement. All nine groups we studied through video analysis read and reacted to automated scores and feedback in one way or another, though not all of them revised their arguments. However, the argument scores improved in six of the nine groups that revised their argument responses. That is, not all students who needed revisions revised, and not all students who revised improved.

One way to improve automated scoring is to use learning theories. Since automated scores are the main information used to provide feedback, it is important to develop a scoring rubric that matches the development of the targeted knowledge, practice, or reasoning. In order to devise the learning trajectory, manifesting appropriate learning theories is essential. In this study, we used multiple theories to characterize scientific argumentation with a simulation. To characterize what constitutes scientific arguments, we applied Toulmin (1958)'s rhetorical structure of argument and applied recent studies on supporting students' development of scientific arguments. Since evidence-based knowledge claims cannot be absolutely certain, we identified two types of scientific uncertainty: ontic uncertainty associated with the natural phenomenon under investigation and epistemic uncertainty associated with methods applied to discover how the phenomenon works. Since we cannot expect students to articulate these two types of scientific uncertainty, we sought other theories on how people without scientific training reason about uncertainty in everyday life. Kahneman and Tversky (1982)'s work identified personal and external sources of uncertainty. In science, externalization of uncertainty means students begin to realize limitations related to the investigation context or the scientific theories they are using.

Another way to improve the accuracy of automated scoring models is to increase the training sample (Zhai, Shi, and Nehm 2021). During Stage 1, we developed automated scoring models twice while student argument data were collected over a two-year period. In developing initial automated scoring models, we used 695 explanations and 671 uncertainty attributions for the trap task. The human–human agreement in QWK was 0.92 for the explanation and 0.90 for the uncertainty attribution. The human–machine agreement was 0.72 and 0.79, respectively. One school year later, we collected more scientific argument data and added them to the previous year's data. When we developed new automated scoring models with the 935 explanations and 909 uncertainty attributions, both data sizes increased from 695 and 671, respectively. The human–human agreement remained steady from the previous year's automated scoring models, 0.90 for the explanation and 0.90 for the uncertainty attribution. The human–machine agreement, however, improved from 0.72 to 0.78 for the explanation and from 0.79 to 0.86 for the uncertainty attribution.

Challenge 2: Improving Automated Feedback Design and Strategies for Science Practice

The current emphasis on learning through science "practice" stems from the expectation that "although it may be out of reach to think and act scientifically exactly as scientists do, students can be taught, in some basic form, scientifically powerful ways of reasoning and acting that capture what is particular about science—ways of reasoning and acting that develop reliable knowledge claims and are underpinnings of science's epistemic privilege" (Ford 2015, 1041). Science practice can be defined as "the learnable and valued dimensions of disciplinary work, both tacit and explicit, that people develop over time in a specific place, such as a laboratory, field station, or classroom" (Stroupe 2015, 1034). Science practice is cultivated by the communities of various science disciplines in conceptual, social, epistemic, and material dimensions (Lehrer and Schauble 2006). The conceptual dimension concerns various forms of subject matter knowledge established in the discipline, including theories, concepts, and ideas. The social dimension addresses interactions among participants that build and incorporate communal norms of formulating, using, advancing, and critiquing ideas for the purpose of progress (Ford 2015). The epistemic dimension provides a philosophical basis for what counts as scientific knowledge and how it ought to be obtained (Sandoval 2005). The material dimension addresses the importance of adaptation of science practice amenable to a variety of physical, inscriptional, technological, or computational resources used in carrying out science practices (Manz, Lehrer, and Schauble 2020; Pickering 1995).

As we expand the meaning of science practices in all four dimensions, automated feedback can aim to address any one or a combination of different dimensions. In the case of HASbot, we developed automated feedback by translating scientists' simulation-mediated inquiry for students in terms of content, epistemic, and material dimensions. HASbot did not address providing feedback to explicitly scaffold social interactions among students or between students and teachers. Difficulties are anticipated in devising feedback to address these four practice dimensions because developing adequate models for domain, student, and progress support is not straightforward.

When theories on student learning are well established, such as in the case of scientific argumentation (Erduran, Simon, and Osborne 2004; Lee et al. 2014; Manz 2015) or scientific experimentation (Duschl and Bybee 2014; Manz, Lehrer, and Schauble 2020), diagnosing student performances and scaffolding based on the diagnosis can be pre-programed similarly to HASbot. For instance, we already knew that good scientific arguments must have data and reasoning. As such, we created feedback statements to point out missing argument elements and how to examine and obtain those elements. We then prepared one set of feedback statements for each explanation and uncertainty attribution score. While that feedback design worked to improve students' argument revision scores, we realized that students received the same automated feedback over and over when their revisions did not meet the criteria for the next score. We observed frustrations with students who wanted to improve. This indicates that there should be a diverse range of feedback statements for the same diagnosis, especially when there is a high likelihood that a score increase is difficult.

When the connection between diagnosis and feedback is difficult due to lack of theories or precedents, AI can be used to develop pedagogical intelligence from data alone in a particular learning context. For example, we applied decision tree algorithms to find patterns between simulation interaction variables and students' critical thinking on data captured in the uncertainty rating explanations. We were able to find that the amount of time and the number of water droplets followed were important. In fact, in the next version of HASbot, students were provided with simulation feedback based on real-time analysis of their simulation interactions in addition to argument feedback (Lee et al. 2021).

Moreover, we can think about incorporating the epistemic affect dimension to provide automated feedback when scaffolding science practices. Epistemic affect is referred to as "feelings and emotions experienced within science, such as the excitement of having a new idea or irritation at an inconsistency" (Jaber and Hammer 2016, 189). Epistemic affect not only engages students in the practice but also monitors, controls, and stabilizes the practice over multiple trials. AI can look into how to identify and measure epistemic affect while students engage in digitally mediated learning environments, so that automated feedback can effectively address the affect dimension of doing science through practice.

Challenge 3: Soliciting Larger Impacts through Teacher Buy-in

We examined how students made use of automated feedback to engage in epistemic discourse to carry out simulation-mediated scientific inquiry. However, the impact of automated feedback may also depend upon how teachers orient students to take advantage of scientific argument revision opportunities. In addition, teachers can provide additional scaffolding to individual students or the classroom as a whole. Teachers' demand for automated scoring and feedback has been increasing. For instance, when we recruited teachers for subsequent curriculum implementation studies (post-Stage 2), we asked whether they would be interested in modules that offer automated scoring of open-ended questions in the module. Seventy-eight percent of the 132 middle and high school Earth science teachers said yes. The most important reason cited by teachers was related to saving time so they could give frequent formative and summative assessment, check student progress, and use time for other important matters such as preparing materials, monitoring progress, and assisting struggling students. As the HASbot-integrated water module became available to the general public, more teachers have implemented the module. During the 2020–21 school year, the curriculum server recorded 952 teachers and 46,684 students using the module in their classrooms. During the 2021–22 school year, the module was used by 965 teachers and 41,174 students. We expect that these numbers will grow as long as the module is available online. Therefore, teacher training and professional development is important if we are to transform science classrooms using AI-enabled automated feedback.

Challenge 4: Addressing Equity Concerns in AI

ML has emerged as a main AI tool for developing automated scoring models because its performance is known to be more accurate and less resource intensive than the programming based on lexical analyses, is comparable to human scores, and is closer to students' ideas represented in interviews than multiple-choice items (Mao et al. 2018). ML refers to a characteristic of a computer program whose performance improves by continuously "learning" from the data fed to the program. As a result, the quality of the automated scoring models depends upon the data fed to the algorithm. That is, if automated scoring models are developed with texts written predominantly by fluent English speakers and scored without regard to different sociocultural considerations, then the scientifically normative linguistic features are likely to be privileged (Cheuk 2021). For this reason, there is an urgent call for addressing equity issues in developing automated scoring algorithms. Systematic bias can lead to construct-irrelevant variance, which compromises the validity of formative assessment. Furthermore, innovations in AI algorithms must occur as insights from data follow the law of large numbers where frequently occurring patterns are reinforced by larger numbers included in the sample while less-frequent patterns can become ignored.

Conclusion

In this chapter, we described HASbot, an AI-based automated feedback system, in terms of domain, student, and progress support models, as well as the user interface design that incorporated these three models. Research on mediating processes and outcomes showed how the intended students' learning via simulation-mediated inquiry was facilitated with the help of automated feedback on scientific arguments. Based on our reflections on the HASbot design and research, we challenge the AI community to think about how science practices can be supported in conceptual, social, epistemic, and material dimensions for linguistically and socioculturally diverse students.

Acknowledgments

This material is based on work supported by the National Science Foundation under Grant DRL-1220756, DRL-1418019, and DRL-1812362. Any opinions, findings, conclusions, or recommendations expressed in this material are those of the authors and do not necessarily reflect the views of the National Science Foundation.

References

Ahuja, N. J., and Sille, R. 2013. "A Critical Review of Development of Intelligent Tutoring Systems: Retrospect, Present and Prospect." *IJCSI International Journal of Computer Science Issues* 10, no. 4: 39–48.

Baker, R., Hershkovitz, A., Rossi, L. M., Goldstein, A. B., and Gowda, S. M. 2013. "Predicting Robust Learning with the Visual Form of the Moment-by-Moment Learning Curve." *Journal of the Learning Sciences* 22: 639–66.

Bar-Yam, Y. 2002. "General Features of Complex Systems." In *Encyclopedia of Life Support Systems (EOLSS)*, Vol. I, 1–10. Paris: UNESCO.

Ben-Haim, Y. 2014. "Order and Indeterminism: An Info-Gap Perspective." In *Error and Uncertainty in Scientific Practice: History and Philosophy of Technoscience*, edited by M. Boumans, G. Hon, and A. C. Petersen, 157–76. London: Routledge.

Bennett, R. E. 2011. "Formative Assessment: A Critical Review." *Assessment in Education: Principles, Policy and Practice* 18, no. 1: 5–25.

Black, P., Harrison, C., Lee, C., Marshall, B., and William, D. 2003. *Assessment for Learning: Putting It into Practice*. New York: McGraw-Hill Education.

Black, P., and Wiliam, D. 1998. "Assessment and Classroom Learning." *Assessment in Education* 5, no. 1: 7–72.

Bond, T. G., and Fox, C. M. 2007. *Applying the Rasch Model*. Mahwah, NJ: Lawrence Erlbaum Associates.

Cheuk, T. 2021. "Can AI Be Racist? Color-Evasiveness in the Application of Machine Learning to Science Assessments." *Science Education* 105, no. 5: 825–36.

Clark, D., Sampson, V., Weinberger, A., and Erkens, G. 2007. "Analytic Frameworks for Assessing Dialogic Argumentation in Online Learning Environments." *Educational Psychology Review* 19: 343–74.

Deeva, G., Bogdanova, D., Serral, E., and Snoeck, M. 2021. "A Review of Automated Feedback Systems for Learners: Classification Framework, Challenges and Opportunities." *Computers & Education* 162: 104094.

Dihoff, R. E., Brosvic, G. M., and Epstein, M. L. 2003. "The Role of Feedback during Academic Testing: The Delay Retention Effect Revisited." *The Psychological Record* 53: 533–48.

Duschl, R. 2008. "Science Education in Three-Part Harmony: Balancing Conceptual, Epistemic, and Social Learning Goals." *Review of Research in Science Education* 32: 268–91.

Duschl, R. A., and Bybee, R. W. 2014. "Planning and Carrying Out Investigations: An Entry to Learning and to Teacher Professional Development around NGSS Science and Engineering Practices." *International Journal of STEM Education* 1, no. 1: 12.

Elgin, C. Z. 2013. "Epistemic Agency." *Theory and Research in Education* 11, no. 2: 135–52.

Erduran, S., Simon, S., and Osborne, J. 2004. "TAPping into Argumentation: Developments in the Application of Toulmin's Argument Pattern for Studying Science Discourse." *Science Education* 88: 915–33.

Ford, M. J. 2015. "Educational Implications of Choosing 'Practice' to Describe Science in the Next Generation Science Standards." *Science Education* 99, no. 6: 1041–48.

Gerard, L., Kidron, A., and Linn, M. C. 2019. "Guiding Collaborative Revision of Science Explanations." *International Journal of Computer-Supported Collaborative Learning* 14: 1–34.

Gerard, L., Matuk, C., McElhaney, K., and Linn, M. C. 2015. "Automated, Adaptive Guidance for K-12 Education." *Educational Research Review* 15: 41–58.

Gobert, J., Sao Pedro, M., Raziuddin, J., and Baker, R. 2013. "From Log Files to Assessment Metrics for Science Inquiry Using Educational Data Mining." *Journal of the Learning Sciences* 22, no. 4: 521–63.

Goldin, I., Narciss, S., Foltz, P., and Bauer, M. 2017. "New Directions in Formative Feedback in Interactive Learning Environments." *International Journal of Artificial Intelligence in Education* 27, no. 3: 385–92.

Harlen, W., and James, M. 1997. "Assessment and Learning: Differences and Relationships between Formative and Summative Assessment." *Assessment in Education: Principles, Policy & Practice* 4, no. 3: 365–79.

Hattie, J. 2009. *Visible Learning: A Synthesis of over 800 Meta-analyses Relating to Achievement.* London: Routledge.

Heilman, M., and Madnani, N. 2013. "HENRY-CORE: Domain Adaptation and Stacking for Text Similarity." In *Second Joint Conference on Lexical and Computational Semantics (*SEM)*, vol. 1, 96–102.

Jaber, L. Z., and Hammer, D. 2016. "Learning to Feel Like a Scientist." *Science Education* 100, no. 2: 189–220.

Kahneman, D., and Tversky, A. 1982. "Variants of Uncertainty." *Cognition* 11, no. 2: 143–57.

Kandlikar, M., Risbey, J., and Dessai, S. 2005. "Representing and Communicating Deep Uncertainty in Climate-Change Assessments." *Comptes Rendus—Geoscience* 337, no. 4: 443–55.

Kuhn, D. 2010. "Teaching and Learning Science as Argument." *Science Education* 94, no. 5: 810–24.

Kulik, J. A., and Fletcher, J. D. 2016. "Effectiveness of Intelligent Tutoring Systems: A Meta-analytic Review." *Review of Educational Research* 86, no. 1: 42–78.

Lee, H.-S., Liu, O. L., Pallant, A., Roohr, K. C., Pryputniewicz, S., and Buck, Z. E. 2014. "Assessment of Uncertainty-Infused Scientific Argumentation." *Journal of Research in Science Teaching* 51, no. 5: 581–605.

Lee, H.-S., Gweon, G-H., Lord, T., Paessel, N., Pallant, A., and Pryputniewicz, S. 2021. "Machine Learning-Enabled Automated Feedback: Supporting Students' Revision of Scientific Arguments Based on Data Drawn from Simulation." *Journal of Science Education and Technology* 30, no. 2: 168–92.

Lee, H.-S., Pallant, A., Pryputniewicz, S., Lord, T., Mulholland, M., and Liu, O. L. 2019. "Automated Text Scoring and Real-Time Adjustable Feedback: Supporting Revision of Scientific Arguments Involving Uncertainty." *Science Education* 103, no. 3: 590–622.

Lee, H.-S., and Songer, N. B. 2003. "Making Authentic Science Accessible to Students." *International Journal of Science Education* 25, no. 8: 923–48.

Lehrer, R., and Schauble, L. 2006. "Scientific Thinking and Science Literacy." In *Handbook of Child Psychology: Child Psychology in Practice*, edited by W. Damon, R. Lerner, K. R. A, and I. E. Sigel, 153–96. Chichester: Wiley.

Linn, M. C., Gerard, L., Ryoo, K., McElhaney, K., Liu, O. L., and Rafferty, A. N. 2014. "Computer-Guided Inquiry to Improve Science Learning." *Science* 344, no. 6180: 155–56.

Liu, O. L., Rios, J. A., Heilman, M., Gerard, L., and Linn, M. C. 2016. "Validation of Automated Scoring of Science Assessments." *Journal of Research in Science Teaching* 53, no. 2: 215–33.

Manz, E. 2015. "Representing Student Argumentation as Functionally Emergent from Scientific Activity." *Review of Educational Research* 85, no. 4: 553–90.

Manz, E., Lehrer, R., and Schauble, L. 2020. "Rethinking the Classroom Science Investigation." *Journal of Research in Science Teaching* 57, no. 7: 1148–74.

Mao, L., Liu, O. L., Roohr, K., Belur, V., Mulholland, M., Lee, H.-S., and Pallant, A. 2018. "Validation of Automated Scoring for a Formative Assessment That Employs Scientific Argumentation." *Educational Assessment* 23, no. 2: 121–38.

Masters, G. N. 1982. "A Rasch Model for Partial Credit Scoring." *Psychometrika* 47: 149–73.

McNeill, K. L., Lizotte, D. J., Krajcik, J., and Marx, R. W. 2006. "Supporting Students' Construction of Scientific Explanations by Fading Scaffolds in Instructional Materials." *Journal of the Learning Sciences* 15, no. 2: 153–91.

Mingers, J. 1989. "An Empirical Comparison of Pruning Methods for Decision Tree Induction." *Machine Learning* 4: 227–43.

Morrison, M. 2015. *Reconstructing Reality: Models, Mathematics, and Simulations*. Oxford: Oxford University Press.
Narciss, S., and Huth, K. 2004. "How to Design Informative Tutoring Feedback for Multi-media Learning." In *Handbook of Research on Educational Communications and Technology*, edited by H. M. Niegemann, D. Leutner, and R. Brunken, 181–95. Mahwah, NJ: Lawrence Erlbaum.
National Research Council. 1996. *National Science Education Standards*. Washington, DC: National Academies Press.
National Research Council. 2012. *A Framework for K-12 Science Education: Practices, Crosscutting Concepts, and Core Ideas*. Washington, DC: National Academies Press.
Nehm, R. H., Ha, M., and Mayfield, E. 2012. "Transforming Biology Assessment with Machine Learning: Automated Scoring of Written Evolutionary Explanations." *Journal of Science Education and Technology* 21, no. 1: 183–96.
Nussbaum, E. M., Sinatra, G. M., and Owens, M. C. 2012. "The Two Faces of Scientific Argumentation: Applications to Global Climate Change." In *Perspectives on Scientific Argumentation: Theory, Practice, and Research*, edited by M. S. Khine, 17–38. Cham: Springer.
Pallant, A., and Lee, H.-S. 2015. "Constructing Scientific Arguments Using Evidence from Dynamic Computational Climate Models." *Journal of Science Education and Technology* 24, no. 2: 378–95.
Pei, B., Xing, W., and Lee, H.-S. 2019. "Using Automatic Image Processing to Analyze Visual Artifacts Created by Students in Scientific Argumentation." *British Journal of Educational Technology* 50, no. 6: 3391–404.
Pickering, A. 1995. *The Mangle of Practice: Time, Agency, and Science*. Chicago: University of Chicago Press.
Rasch, G. 1966. *Probabilistic Models for Some Intelligence and Attainment Tests*. Chicago: University of Chicago Press.
Rowe, W. D. 1994. "Understanding uncertainty." *Risk Analysis* 14, no. 5: 743–50.
Ryoo, K., and Bedell, K. 2019. "Supporting Linguistically Diverse Students' Science Learning with Dynamic Visualizations through Discourse-Rich Practices." *Journal of Research in Science Teaching* 56, no. 3: 270–301.
Ryoo, K., Bedell, K., and Swearingen, A. 2018. "Promoting Linguistically Diverse Students' Short-Term and Long-Term Understanding of Chemical Phenomena Using Visualizations." *Journal of Science Education and Technology* 27, no. 6: 508–22.
Sadler, R. 1989. "Formative Assessment and the Design of Instructional Systems." *Instructional Science* 18: 119–44.
Sampson, V. 2010. "Argument-Driven Inquiry as a Way to Help Students Learn How to Participate in Scientific Argumentation and Craft Written Arguments: An Exploratory Study." *Science Education* 95: 217–57.
Sandoval, W. A. 2005. "Understanding Students' Practical Epistemologies and Their Influence on Learning through Inquiry." *Science Education* 89, no. 4: 634–56.
Sandoval, W. A., and Reiser, B. J. 2004. "Explanation-Driven Inquiry: Integrating Conceptual and Epistemic Scaffolds for Scientific Inquiry." *Science Education* 88: 345–72.
Sao Pedro, M. S., Baker, R. S., Gobert, J. D., Montalvo, O., and Nakama, A. 2013. "Leveraging Machine-Learned Detectors of Systematic Inquiry Behavior to Estimate and Predict Transfer of Inquiry Skills." *User Modeling and User-Adapted Interaction* 23: 1–39.
Shute, V. J. 2008. "Focus on Formative Feedback." *Review of Educational Research* 78, no. 1: 153–89.
Spiegelhalter, D., Pearson, M., and Short, I. 2011. "Visualizing Uncertainty about the Future." *Science* 333, no. 6048: 1393–400.
Sterman, J. D. 2002. "All Models Are Wrong: Reflections on Becoming a Systems Scientist." *System Dynamics Review* 18, no. 4: 501–31.
Stroupe, D. 2014. "Examining Classroom Science Practice Communities: How Teachers and Students Negotiate Epistemic Agency and Learn Science-as-Practice." *Science Education* 98, no. 3: 487–516.
Stroupe, D. 2015. "Describing 'Science Practice' in Learning Settings." *Science Education* 99, no. 6: 1033–40.

Tansomboon, C., Gerard, L. F., Vitale, J. M., and Linn, M. C. 2017. "Designing Automated Guidance to Promote Productive Revision of Science Explanations." *International Journal of Artificial Intelligence and Education* 27: 729–757.
Toulmin, S. 1958. *The Uses of Argument*. Cambridge: Cambridge University Press.
Weisberg, M. 2013. *Simulation and Similarity: Using Models to Understand the World*. Oxford: Oxford University Press.
Wilensky, U., and Rand, W. 2015. *An Introduction to Agent-Based Modeling: Modeling Natural, Social, and Engineered Complex Systems with NetLogo*. Cambridge, MA: MIT Press.
Wilson, M. 2005. *Constructing Measures: An Item Response Modeling Approach*. Mahwah, NJ: Lawrence Erlbaum Associates.
Windschitl, M., Thompson, J., Braaten, M., and Stroupe, D. 2012. "Proposing a Core Set of Instructional Practices and Tools for Teachers of Science." *Science Education* 96, no. 5: 878–903.
Zhai, X., He, P., and Krajcik, J. 2022. "Applying Machine Learning to Automatically Assess Scientific Models." *Journal of Research in Science Teaching* 59, no. 10: 1765–94.
Zhai, X., Shi, L., and Nehm, R. 2021. "A Meta-analysis of Machine Learning-Based Science Assessments: Factors Impacting Machine–Human Score Agreements." *Journal of Science Education and Technology* 30, no. 3: 361–79.
Zhai, X., Yin, Y., Pellegrino, J. W., Haudek, K. C., and Shi, L. 2020. "Applying Machine Learning in Science Assessment: A Systematic Review." *Studies in Science Education* 56, no. 1: 111–51.
Zhu, M., Lee, H.-S., Wang, T., Liu, O. L., Belur, V., and Pallant, A. 2017. "Investigating the Impact of Automated Feedback on Students' Scientific Argumentation." *International Journal of Science Education* 39, no. 12: 1648–68.
Zohar, A., and Nemet, F. 2002. "Fostering Students' Knowledge and Argumentation Skills through Dilemmas in Human Genetics." *Journal of Research in Science Teaching* 39, no. 1: 35–62.

11

Using Evidence-Centered Design to Develop an Automated System for Tracking Students' Physics Learning in a Digital Learning Environment

Marcus Kubsch, Adrian Grimm, Knut Neumann, Hendrik Drachsler and Nikol Rummel

In recent years, machine learning has gained traction in research on assessments in science education (Zhai, Yin, et al. 2020). One focus of this work has been to increase the automaticity in science assessments (Zhai, Haudek, et al. 2020), i.e., automated scoring or coding of existing assessment instruments using supervised machine-learning techniques (e.g., Liu et al. 2016; Maestrales et al. 2021; Moharreri, Ha, and Nehm 2014). While there is still ongoing development, the basic methodology employed in this kind of work is a straightforward application of supervised machine learning based on existing datasets from valid and reliable instruments (e.g., Wilson et al. 2023). But how can one use machine learning to validly and reliably assess students' learning not in defined assessment situations but rather based on the artifacts they create when they engage in digital learning environments?

This question naturally comes up when we think about *why* automating science assessment is such a desirable goal—as evidenced by the productivity of this area of research (Zhai, Haudek, et al. 2020). Automaticity in science assessment is a key requirement for providing tailored support for students' learning, e.g., adaptive feedback or adaptive scaffolds. The effect of support such as feedback critically depends on the extent to which it meets students' individual needs (e.g., Narciss et al. 2014). Meeting individual students' needs then requires a continuous assessment of students' learning. As evidenced by work on intelligent tutoring systems (Corbett, Koedinger, and Anderson 1997), this is possible using data from students' performances on individual tasks. However, intelligent tutoring systems typically do not meet the vision of modern science instruction outlined, for example, in the *Framework for K–12 Science Education* (National Research Council 2012) or the German *Bildungsstandards* (Sekretariat der ständigen Konferenz der Kultusminister der Länder in der Bundesrepublik Deutschland 2020). Existing, high-quality instructional materials such as *OpenSciEd* (OpenSciEd 2019), in contrast, typically lack a tutoring function; that is, an automatic assessment of students' learning and provision of respective support. As De Jong et al. (2023) point out, incorporating tutoring functionality into

Marcus Kubsch et al., *Using Evidence-Centered Design to Develop an Automated System for Tracking Students' Physics Learning in a Digital Learning Environment.* In: *Uses of Artificial Intelligence in STEM Education.* Edited by: Xiaoming Zhai and Joseph Krajcik, Oxford University Press. © Oxford University Press (2024). DOI: 10.1093/oso/9780198882077.003.0011 high-quality instructional materials would enable teachers to provide more individual support to students in developing the competence in science envisioned in policy documents such as the *Framework* or the *Bildungsstandards.* This requires moving from automating the analysis of traditional assessment instruments to extending instructional units by an automated analysis of the artifacts that students produce as a function of instruction. However, frameworks or procedures for doing so are currently lacking (see also Kubsch, Czinczel, et al. 2022).

Thus, we set out to develop a framework and procedure for developing algorithmic models (so-called detectors) for the automated tracking of learning in existing curricular units that align with the vision of modern science instruction, i.e., units that emphasize knowledge-in-use and follow project-based pedagogy (Krajcik and Shin 2014). Assessments that capture knowledge-in-use, i.e., students' usage of their knowledge in science practices, have successfully been developed (Harris et al. 2016, 2019) by building off of evidence-centered design (ECD) (Mislevy, Almond, and Lukas 2003; Mislevy and Haertel 2007). Thus, we also started our development with ECD as a basis. In this chapter, we will describe the procedure and framework we developed, provide in-depth examples, and discuss issues of validity and reliability of the resulting detectors.

Evidence-Centered Design

The evidence-centered design approach to assessment is the product of conceptual and practical work pursued by Robert Mislevy and colleagues (see, e.g., Kim, Almond, and Shute 2016; Mislevy 2016; Mislevy, Almond, and Lukas 2003; Mislevy and Haertel 2007; Pellegrino, DiBello, and Goldman 2015; Rupp et al. 2012). The ECD approach understands assessment as a process of evidentiary reasoning—in principle similar to Kane's approach to validity (Kane 1992). This process involves the delineation of three spaces as shown in Figure 11.1: the claim, evidence, and task space. The process begins with the delineation of the claim space; that is, specification of the claims that one intends to make about a construct such as students' competence. This involves unpacking the complexes of knowledge and skills that constitute competence in a domain through analysis of the domain. Thorough unpacking and precise formulation of the knowledge students are expected to have and how they are expected to use it is most critical in this step. In the next step, evidence statements are formulated. These statements should describe as clearly as possible the features of student performances that will be accepted as evidence that a student has met what is specified in the claim space. Then the form of tasks that are expected to elicit the desired performances are specified. This involves defining fixed features that tasks must or must not have and variable features that may vary across tasks addressing the same claim. This part of the procedure leads to the design phase of the assessment argument. Precisely formulated claims and evidence statements that describe concrete performances will support the development of tasks better aligned with the construct (as specified by the claim space).

Once the tasks are developed, the next step is to define an evidentiary scheme for the tasks. Based on the performances expected from students, one needs to specify

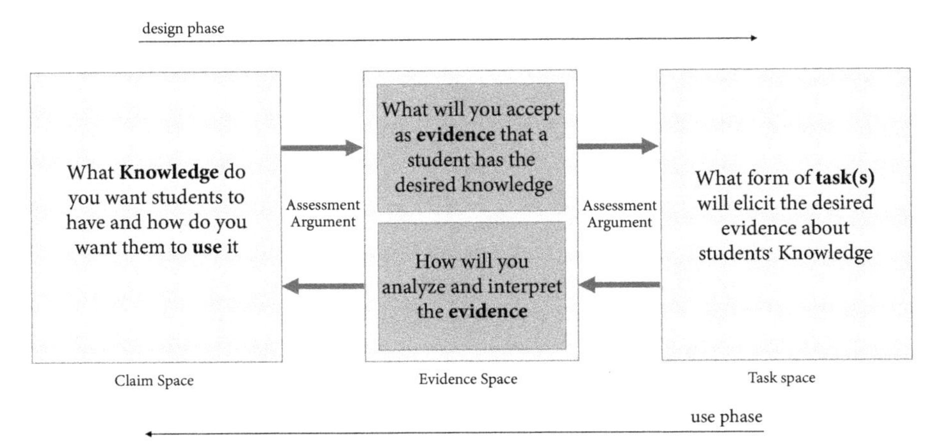

Figure 11.1 Simplified representation of evidence-centered design (adapted from Kubsch, Czinczel, et al. 2022).

how those performances will be evaluated in light of the evidence statements and how these evaluations will be combined into evidence supporting (or not supporting) the claims about the construct (e.g., students' knowledge). A scoring guide that includes a description of all possible performances, precise information on how each performance is scored, and how these scores "add up" into a total score ensures that total scores are indeed reflective of students' mastery of the construct. This part may be considered the use phase of the assessment argument. Together, both phases of the argument aim to ensure an optimal alignment of claims, evidence, and tasks.

Using Evidence-Centered Design for the Automated Analysis of Learning

In order to extend existing instructional units by the functionality of an automated analysis of students' learning, we need data about students' learning (e.g., artifacts that students are creating as a function of instruction) and algorithmic models that translate that data into information about student learning. For an on-the-fly assessment, the data need to be readily available in digital form; that is, they need to be obtained through students engaging in the use of digital technologies to produce the artifacts in question. The algorithmic models, in turn, need to be aligned with a domain-specific model of students learning that delineates how students progress in developing competence in the respective domain.

In the context of this chapter, competence is understood as the combined knowledge, skills, and abilities needed to solve problems in a domain across a wide range of contexts (Neumann 2013; Neumann, Schecker, and Theyßen 2019; Ufer and Neumann 2018). The nature of competence as a complex construct requires delineating the specific knowledge, skills, and abilities that make up competence in a domain. This process is also referred to as *competence modeling*, the result being the *model of competence* or *competence model.* Models describing how students progress in developing competence in a domain are also referred to as *models of competence development* (Schecker and Parchmann 2006; Ufer and Neumann 2018) or *learning progressions* (Duncan and Rivet 2018). In order to assess competence and, more importantly, the development of competence, levels of competence and competence development need to be further characterized by learning performances. That is, in addition to the knowledge, skills, and abilities that constitute competence, it is important to describe how the knowledge, skills, and abilities are combined and used to solve problems typical for the domain across contexts in which these problems typically occur.

The automated assessment of learning increasingly draws on (supervised) machine-learning approaches. Machine learning is a widely used technology where the machine "learns" from existing data. This learning is reflected in the (incremental) adjustment of parameters in a mathematical model. Once a model has been trained, that is, once the parameter values provide the best predictive accuracy based on the existing data, it can be utilized to automatically make predictions for new data (Hastie, Tibshirani, and Friedman 2009). In machine-learning terms, specific data used to make predictions are referred to as attributes or features. Features can refer to product data (e.g., an option chosen in a multiple-choice item, a response to an open-response item, or a drawing created in response to a prompt) but also process data (e.g., mouse movements, wait times) on different grain sizes (e.g., correct/incorrect answer or ideas used in an answer). The outcomes predicted are referred to as labels.

When features and labels are given and machine learning is used to find a function that maps the features onto the labels, this is generally called *supervised machine learning*. In a supervised machine-learning approach, algorithmic models are typically constructed by firstly scoring a dataset using human raters (also referred to as human labeling) and then, secondly, developing and training machine-learning models that link the human labels to specific feature sets using the training data. Hence, using supervised machine learning to automatically assess learning requires labels and scoring rubrics as a basis for scoring a dataset in terms of these labels, as well as a set of features and algorithmic models that can link the set of features to the labels. In our case, the labels are indicators of the learning performances or, on a finer grain size, knowledge, skills, and abilities, and the features are diverse data sources ranging from options selected in drop-down menus over text to mouse movements.[1]

In order to integrate such a supervised machine-learning procedure with an ECD approach, we extended the latter as described by Pellegrino, DiBello, and Goldman (2015) and as depicted in Figure 11.2: The *domain-specific model of learning* is an instance of what is called the claim space in Figure 11.1 and the *task model* reflects the task space in Figure 11.1. The *domain-specific model of learning* is defined by a competence model. This model defines the knowledge, skills, and abilities to be assessed and serves as a basis for specifying learning performances, i.e., specific usages of knowledge in scientific practices, in order to characterize the integration and use of the defined knowledge, skills, and abilities to meet specific learning performances.

[1] For clarity and to improve readability we will focus on these types of data throughout the remainder of the chapter.

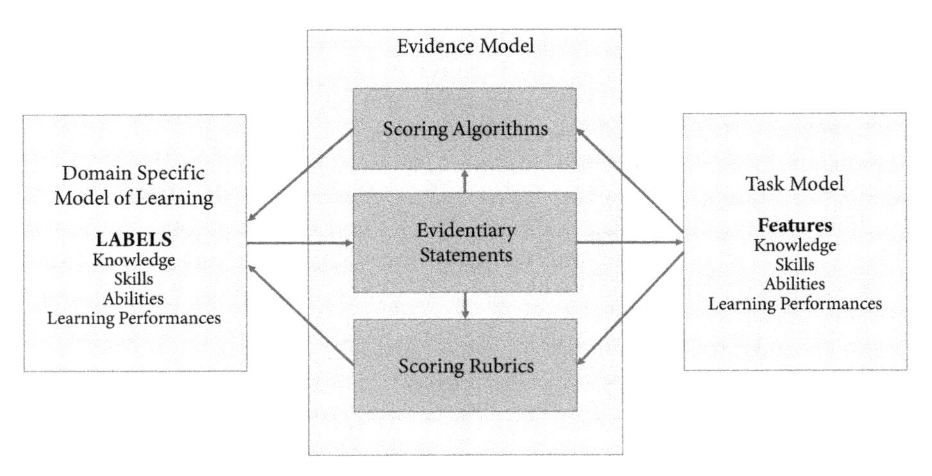

Figure 11.2 Evidence-centered design of algorithmic models for the automated assessment of learning.

Hence, the claim space specifies the labels. The task space is defined by a task model, i.e., the specification of tasks that can yield evidence about learning. Both spaces are linked by the *evidence model*. The evidence model is the representation of the competence model in the evidence space. For each knowledge, skill, and ability, as well as each learning performance, the evidence model holds one or more evidentiary statements that define what will be considered as evidence that students hold the respective knowledge, skills, or abilities or have met a specific learning performance. The evidentiary statements not only need to align with the task model such that the task model specifies what tasks exactly will yield such evidence, but also provide guidance for the specification of what aspects of student responses will (possibly) hold information with respect to the evidentiary statements. That is, the task model includes the features.

In terms of the supervised machine-learning process involved in the development of automated scoring, scoring rubrics are needed that allow for labeling performances on the respective tasks and algorithmic models are needed that link the labels to specific feature patterns. The development of both is guided by evidentiary statements. Hence, the evidentiary statements are at the core of the process of developing machine-learning detectors using our adapted ECD approach.

Developing Machine-Learning Detectors for an Automatized Analysis of Learning

In the section "Using Evidence-Centered Design for the Automated Analysis of Learning," we introduced and discussed a framework for the development of algorithmic models of the automated assessment of learning. We will now present a procedure for putting the framework to use. Figure 11.3 provides an overview of the steps in

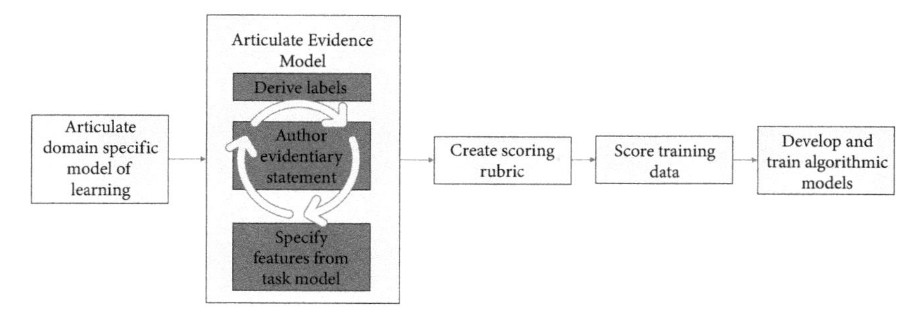

Figure 11.3 Overview of the steps in the procedure for the development of an automated assessment for existing curriculum materials.

the procedure of developing automated scoring models for the automated analysis of learning in existing curriculum materials: (1) articulating a domain-specific model of learning, (2) articulating an evidence model in an iterative process, (3) creating scoring rubrics, (4) scoring training data, and (5) developing and training machine-learning models. In the following, we will discuss each step and provide examples. To better situate these examples, we will begin this section with a short description of the context in which the curriculum materials were developed and the dataset used in the analyses presented here.

The Curriculum Materials

The units were developed as short, four- to six-class-period-long curriculum replacement units for the use in German middle school physics instruction and were implemented in the learning management system Moodle (Dougiamas and Taylor 2003). All units focused on the core concept of energy and followed project-based pedagogy (Krajcik and Shin 2014); that is, the units were driven by inquiry into phenomena, engaged students' need-to-know, and emphasized the integration of scientific practices and disciplinary knowledge or knowledge-in-use. More specifically, each unit started with setting up a driving question on energy and related phenomena that motivated the following lessons (e.g., "Why do laptops sometimes overheat?"). This driving question was then divided into three smaller sub-driving questions that students needed to answer by engaging in numerous scientific practices, such as conducting investigations or constructing explanations. The units concluded by synthesizing the answers to the sub-driving questions to answer and reflecting on the original driving question. In consequence, the tasks that students engaged in ranged from multiple-choice or cloze-type questions to constructed response, data analysis, and investigation tasks. Figure 11.4 shows a typical constructed response task.

The dataset used for the analyses presented in this chapter consists of 2835 responses from 305 students to 38 different constructed response items in German.

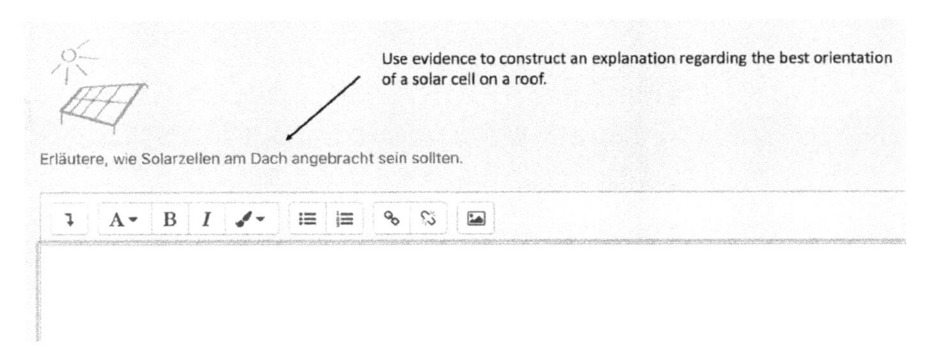

Figure 11.4 Constructed response example task.

On average, students answered 9.3 tasks, and the average word count per response was 25.48.

Articulate Domain-Specific Model of Learning

The first step in the development of automated machine-learning detectors for an automatized analysis of learning is the articulation of a domain-specific model of learning in terms of how students progress in developing competence in a domain. This domain-specific model of learning is informed by the literature on learning progressions (Duncan and Rivet 2018) and can take the form of a sequence of learning performances that map onto the instructional activities. In the context of our project, we drew on a learning progression of energy proposed by Neumann et al. (2013). The learning progression (Figure 11.5) defines four aspects of energy: manifestations of energy, energy transfer and transformations, energy dissipation, and energy conservation. For each of these aspects and across these aspects, different levels of integration exist. The different levels of integration, mirroring the central tenets of the knowledge-integration perspective (Clark and Linn 2013) and cognitive theories (Anderson and Schunn 2000; McClelland and Cleeremans 2009), correspond with the number of normative ideas related to the aspect and the number of connections between them. In consequence, increasing knowledge about energy is characterized by having more and stronger connections between these ideas (e.g., Kubsch et al. 2019). However, students may also have non-normative ideas about aspects of energy (Duit 2014), and connections between normative and non-normative ideas may inhibit the development of a well-structured knowledge base.

Articulate Evidence Model

The next step in the process of developing automated detectors of student learning is the articulation of an evidence model. This process typically starts with

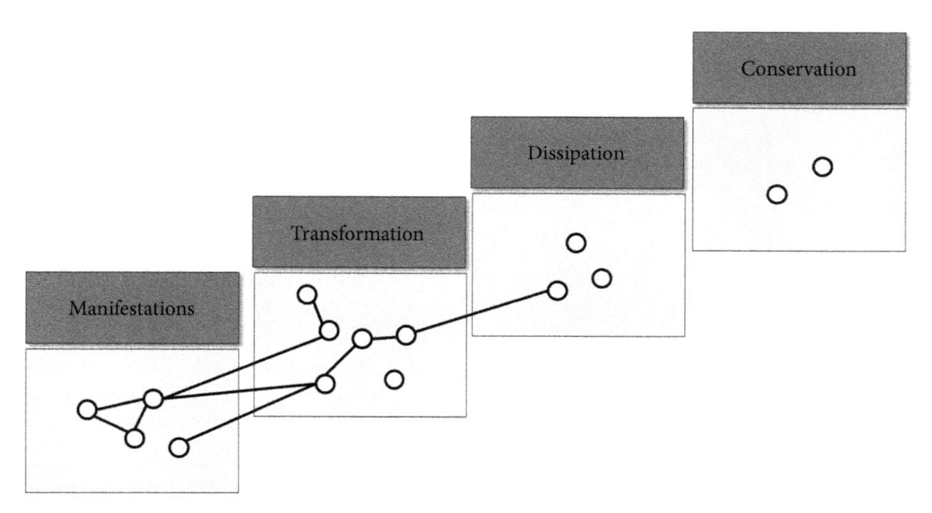

Figure 11.5 Learning progression of energy according to Neumann et al. (2013).

the authoring of evidentiary statements for each articulated learning performance (Harris et al. 2016), followed by the articulation of labels and the specification of features. In the case that instructional units and tasks already exist, the derivation of labels from the domain-specific model of learning, the specification of features from the task model, and the authoring of evidentiary statements need to happen simultaneously in an iterative process. Based on the available tasks, one needs to derive what learning performance the tasks reflect, what respective evidentiary statements are, and what features could be informative regarding the evidentiary statements. This needs to happen iteratively across the set of tasks in the learning environment, as the sensible grain size of learning performances and evidentiary statements will likely change as the tasks are analyzed one by one. We employed the following process:

Derive Labels from the Domain-Specific Model of Learning

To derive labels from the competence model for the knowledge, abilities, and skills (e.g., typical knowledge elements and scientific practices) and to formulate learning performances (e.g., how the knowledge is used in scientific practices), a good starting point is to write down the sample solution for a fully correct answer of a given task. Based on this sample solution, one can draw on the domain-specific model of learning to identify what knowledge, skills, and abilities are required to arrive at the sample solution and how they need to be integrated into a learning performance. The knowledge, skills, abilities, and learning performances now serve as labels.

In the context of our project, we found that the units emphasized ideas about manifestations of energy and energy transformation. Further, scientific practices focused on constructing explanations, conducting investigations, and analyzing data. Since the units were designed for use in early middle school, these practices were implemented in highly scaffolded ways; e.g., in the case of constructing explanations,

Table 11.1 Learning Performances Reflecting Increasing Integration of Knowledge about Manifestations and Transformations of Energy

Increasing integration ↑	Manifestations	Transformation
	M4. Students use multiple manifestations of energy with multiple variables in their answers.	T4. Students use multiple transformations between more than two forms of energy in their answers.
	M3. Students use multiple manifestations of energy with at least one of their variables in their answers.	T3. Students use one transformation between more than two forms of energy in their answers.
	M2. Students use one manifestation of energy with at least two of its variables in their answers.	T2. Students use multiple transformations between two forms of energy in their answers.
	M1. Students use one manifestation of energy with at least one of its variables in their answers.	T1. Students use one transformation between two forms of energy in their answers.

students are supposed to justify their answers, but the usage of structures such as claim, evidence, and reasoning is not required. As a result, the derived labels for learning performances in Table 11.1 emphasize knowledge components and their integration but de-emphasize scientific practices. Besides the labels for learning performances, labels for individual knowledge elements, e.g., different manifestations of energy, such as light energy or thermal energy, and different transformations of energy, such as the transformation of radiant energy into electric energy, were derived.

Author Evidentiary Statements

Evidentiary statements with respect to the actual tasks need to be formulated in alignment with the labels for the learning performances and—if of interest—also for the knowledge, skills, and abilities. Thus, this step is about defining what exactly is accepted as evidence for supporting the claim that learners have met the learning performances or have the specified knowledge, skills, and abilities; that is, what students will need to do in order to demonstrate proficiency. Evidentiary statements should be as precise as possible.

Table 11.2 provides examples of evidentiary statements for a selection of labels from a constructed response task about the optimal orientation of a solar cell.

Specify Features from Task Model

Depending on the task format (e.g., multiple-choice vs. open-ended responses), available modalities of the data (e.g., answers to a multiple-choice test, process data such as log-files of student interactions with a digital learning environment, or eye-tracking data of the students answering the questions), and the complexity of the labels (e.g.,

Table 11.2 Labels and Evidentiary Statements

Label category	Label	Evidentiary statement
Knowledge element	M.Radiant	Students' answer links light to energy.
Knowledge element	T.Radiant-Electric	Students' answer acknowledges that a solar cell converts radiant into electric energy.
Scientific practice	Constructing explanations	Students' answer includes a justification for the claim(s) made.
Learning performance	T1	Students' answer establishes a (normative) link between radiant energy and the electric energy output of a solar cell.

Note: M.Radiant is the label for the manifestation of energy in radiation; T.Radiant-Electric is the label for transformations of radiation into electric energy; constructing explanations is the label for aspects of the scientific practice of constructing explanations, T1 is the label for the learning performance T1 as specified in Table 11.1.

ranging from correct/incorrect to specific epistemic beliefs), the features can vary greatly. In the case of our data, we focused on open-ended text responses. For text data, examples of sample features are the length of text answers or the presence or absence of certain words; more complicated features could include hierarchical rules about word strings (e.g., Li, Gobert, and Dickler 2017). Among the most advanced methods for text data is using transformer language models such as BERT (Devlin et al. 2019) to create contextual embeddings of the relevant text data (students' answers in our case).

Create Scoring Rubrics

Once the evidence model is articulated, i.e., labels have been derived, evidentiary statements have been written, and features have been defined in an iterative process, scoring rubrics for human coding need to be developed. In essence, these documents capture the information in the evidentiary statements and features for each task but organize them in a way that supports an effortless and reliable coding process for the human coders. Typically, this includes providing detailed examples as well as a discussion of borderline cases to support the coding process.

Score Training Data

When rubrics have been developed, the next step is the actual coding. For reliable coding, it is important to instruct the coders, check for drift (i.e., coders deviating from the specifications of the rubric over time), and assess intercoder reliability.

In the context of our project, coding was performed by instructed student workers, and drift checks were implemented in the form of regular reviews of coded data. Finally, intercoder reliability was assessed on the basis of approximately 10% of the data, randomly selected and independently coded by two coders. Spearman's rho was chosen as a measure of inter-rater reliability to account for the ordinal character of our codes. An average Spearman's rho of 0.97 with a minimum of 0.68 indicated substantial intercoder reliability.[2]

Develop and Train Algorithmic Models

Once the data are scored, algorithmic models for automated scoring can be developed and trained. In case the features include specifications that do not allow for simple rule-based algorithmic models, such as searching for keywords or specific sequences of actions in log data, machine-learning methods can provide a solution. Given enough data and computing, even complex mappings between labels and features can be learned (Maestrales et al. 2021; Zhai, He, and Krajcik 2022; Zhai, Haudek et al. 2020).

In our project, we used supervised machine learning to analyze students' responses to the constructed response tasks.[3] Figure 11.6 depicts the basic steps in developing and training respective algorithmic models. First, students' texts are fed into a natural language processing system to obtain a representation of the texts suitable for the following steps. Next, using resampling techniques, the data are split into training and test data. The training data are then used for fitting algorithmic models of varying complexity and computational demands ranging from complex neural networks to keyword approaches to find an algorithmic model that presents the best balance in terms of model fit, model complexity, and computational demand. At last, model quality is determined based on the accuracy with which the model predicts the labels in the test data.

Table 11.3 shows the predictive accuracy of these models for labels reflecting different knowledge elements. Predictive accuracy is evaluated using the so-called F_1-score. The F_1-score is the harmonic mean of precision and recall. To explain these terms,

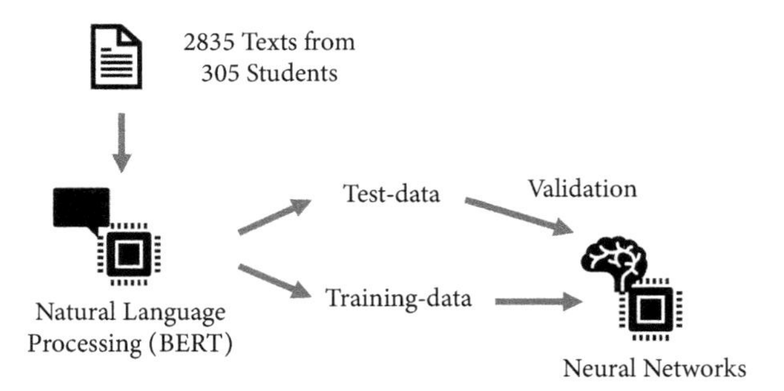

Figure 11.6 Procedure of using supervised machine learning for the training of algorithmic models.

[2] We used Spearman's rho because our codes had multiple levels and Spearman's rho is sensitive to nonexact but adjacent matches, whereas other measures like Cohen's kappa only capture exact matches, i.e., are most appropriate to use with nominal data.

[3] For a detailed description of the development of the algorithmic models and discussion of model performance, see Gombert et al. (2022).

Table 11.3 Predictive Accuracy of Different Models for Selected Labels

Model	Labels							Macro. F_1
	Electric energy	Electric indicator	Thermal energy	Thermal indicator	Transformation process	Radiant energy	Radiant indicator	
Multitask-GBERT-large	**93.29**	**89.29**	**90.53**	**90.36**	**91.89**	**91.07**	**90.46**	**90.98**
Explainable boosting machine	90.68	78.78	83.60	87.84	86.67	86.33	89.14	86.15
Logistic regression	87.44	78.91	83.58	85.92	81.14	84.30	88.60	84.27
Ridge regression	89.91	78.25	82.10	83.13	82.15	87.11	86.00	84.09
Decision tree	87.72	79.18	76.80	82.14	78.89	78.72	83.26	80.96
Keywords (odds ratio)	61.90	18.77	76.89	81.21	61.78	49.49	80.53	61.51
Number of answers where the label was coded as present.	222	308	123	424	235	194	616	
Number of answers where the label was coded as absent.	904	629	347	169	891	653	231	

Note. Bold numbers indicating highest scores.

consider the following examples where there are ten true instances of a label in the data. Now, suppose that an algorithm identifies eight instances of this label in the data, but only four of those are correctly identified by the algorithm. The resulting precision is 4/8 = 0.5, as precision is the fraction of correct classifications (4) among the total number of classifications (8). The resulting recall is 4/10 = 0.4, as recall is the fraction of correct classifications of a label (4) among the total number of occurrences of that label (10) in the data. In sum, high precision means that a model provides more correct than incorrect classifications, whereas high recall means that a model detects most of the instances of a label. In consequence, higher values of the F_1-score indicate better model accuracy. Note that the F_1-score is rescaled so that it ranges from 0 to 100 instead of 0 to 1. Thus, based on the F_1-score, the Multitask GBERT-large model (a model based on the transformer language model BERT (Devlin et al. 2019) trained for German) has the best predictive accuracy. It outperforms the keyword-based approach by a large margin and still performs substantially better than the other model types.

Beyond Automated Assessment—Next Steps

In the preceding sections, we have detailed the steps of a procedure for developing an automated assessment in existing curriculum materials with the example of some of our own work. The resulting machine-learning models can now be utilized to track (individual) students' learning as they progress through the curriculum. Drawing on ECD, the labels that the machine-learning models predict are firmly rooted in the relevant domain-specific models of learning and can resolve students' state of learning at a fine-grain size.

However, being able to track and examine students' learning is—although challenging in its own right—only a necessary condition for the ultimate goal of providing tailored support for students' learning. While a discussion of how to provide tailored support for students' learning based on automated assessment in (digital) curriculum units is beyond the scope of this chapter, we still want to provide a brief discussion of these next steps.

As Figure 11.7 indicates, the information about students' learning obtained from students' artifacts using automated assessments can be utilized for tailored supports via two paths. The student path focuses on directly supporting students, e.g., through adaptive feedback or scaffolds. The teacher path focuses on supporting students by helping teachers in tailoring their instructive practice closer to the needs of their students, e.g., by providing actionable insights such as specific learning difficulties students may have.

Discussion

In this chapter, we have provided a framework—and described a respective procedure including detailed examples—for the theory-guided development of an automated system for the assessment of students' learning in digital learning environments.

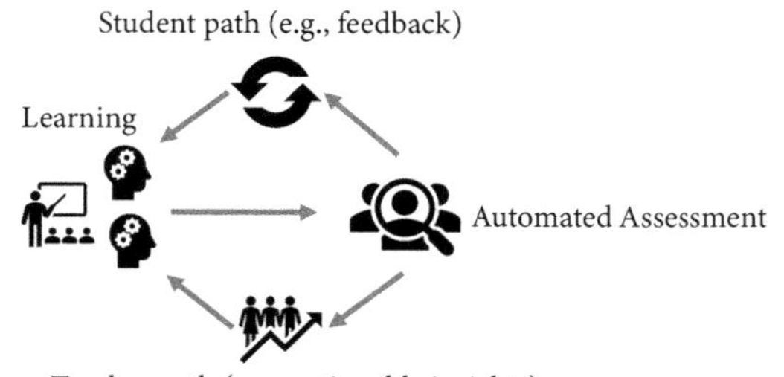

Figure 11.7 Possible paths of utilizing automated assessments for tailored instruction.

A key characteristic of our framework is that it is rooted in ECD (Mislevy, Almond, and Lukas 2003). Evidence-centered design helps to ensure the validity of the assessment as it aims at building a coherent line of argumentation for a validity argument (see Kane 1992; see also Zhai, Krajcik, and Pellegrino (2021) for a respective argument in the context of machine-learning-based assessments). While ECD is typically used to develop assessment tasks from scratch (e.g., see Harris et al. 2016), we developed a procedure with the aim of being able to automatically make valid and reliable inferences about students' learning from a set of given tasks in an existing curriculum.

While automaticity, as Figure 11.7 indicates, is key for scaling tailored instruction, it is also automaticity that demands the use of artificial intelligence (AI), more specifically, machine learning. Only with algorithmic scoring models developed with machine-learning techniques can we capture the complex constructs (see also Zhai, Haudek, et al. 2020) that modern science instruction demands (e.g., National Research Council 2012). Without the use of advanced machine-learning methods, we could only automatically assess simpler constructs, e.g., a traditional concept inventory (e.g., Hestenes, Wells, and Swackhamer 1992), potentially limiting assessment functionality (Zhai, Haudek, et al. 2020) as respective tasks can generally be considered to be less engaging than the carefully designed tasks in a learning environment that emphasizes complex constructs such as knowledge-in-use. Thus, AI plays a key role in negotiating the tension for automaticity, assessment functionality, and construct complexity.

In this chapter, we provided an example of how we used machine learning, more specifically supervised machine learning, to automatically score students' knowledge, skills, and learning performances based on how they engaged in knowledge-in-use tasks about energy. The best model we trained faithfully reproduces how humans score students' knowledge, skills, and learning performances. While this may sound impressive, a string of recent studies (e.g., Maestrales et al. 2021; see also Zhai, Yin, et al. 2020) has demonstrated that machines can indeed produce scores that mirror human scores for tasks targeting complex constructs. However, it is this very way in which the capabilities of automated scoring systems are assessed—the extent to which they reproduce human scores—that requires an in-depth discussion of issues of validity and bias.

Validity and Bias

When we discussed the performance of our machine-learning model, we relied on F_1-statistics that describe how well the trained model reproduces the scores of the humans who originally scored students' answers. This procedure (although calculated metrics and specific implementations of the process may vary) is the standard in research on automated assessment (see e.g., Lee et al. 2019; Liu et al. 2016; Maestrales et al. 2021). Sherin (2013) questions this approach as it considers human codes as the gold standard—an assumption that may not be warranted. Human codes can reflect bias, from small, unintentional deviations to outright racism (Cheuk 2021; Crawford 2021; Nelson 2020). As the quality of human codes is typically determined based on intercoder agreement, just as in our example, biases reflected in the codes and shared by the coders are hard to capture.

One way to capture potential biases is to investigate whether the model systematically performs differently for students with different demographic profiles. In fact, many studies on automated assessment investigate this aspect of their models. For example, Liu et al. (2016) investigated differential effects with respect to gender, native language, and whether students use a computer for homework and found no consistent effects for any of these variables. Another example is the work by Ha and Nehm (2016), in which they investigated the impact of misspelling on automated scoring. While students with English language learner status had significantly more spelling mistakes than native speakers of English, this did not lead to consistent differential effects. Thus, one may argue that warnings of bias in AI (Cheuk 2021; Crawford 2021; O'Neil 2016) and the potentially devastating effects such biases could have are unwarranted (see also Zhai and Krajcik 2022 and Zhai and Nehm 2023 for a discussion of how the warnings regarding the potentially detrimental effects of bias in machine learning may be attributed to misunderstandings, overexpectations, and inappropriate uses of machine learning).

However, we see at least three challenges for this positive conclusion regarding the role of bias in automated scoring. The first problem concerns the point that made it impossible for us to present an example of a bias analysis in this chapter: bias analyses require the collection of (highly) sensitive data, which may prohibit them. When laws (e.g., GDPR, European Commission (2018)) and regulations (for example Institutional Review Boards) demand data minimization, weighing the principle of data minimization against collecting sensitive data for bias analyses may not always favor collecting sensitive data for bias analyses (see also Grimm et al. (2023)). Such a result is even more probable when existing data are used, and there were no good reasons to collect sensitive demographic information during the original data collection. This is, in fact, the reason why we had no demographic data available to conduct bias analyses. The second problem is that even if respective data are available, bias may be hard to detect. Especially if we fear that an algorithm may discriminate against small minorities, available data may not allow us to meaningfully investigate for bias. Further, intersectional discrimination, i.e., discrimination because of more than one discrimination factor, such as gender or race combined, can lead to the same problem that the potentially targeted populations become too small to effectively investigate for bias. In consequence, a series of nonsystematic effects of demographic variables, e.g., as in Liu et al. (2016), may conceal intersectional bias. The third and final problem is that bias analyses are typically conducted without considering what the scores are actually used for; in other words, the system surrounding automated assessment (see Figure 11.7) is ignored. The accuracy of machine-learning models is typically assessed using F_1-scores. As described earlier, the F_1-score is an aggregate of precision and recall. High precision means that there are only a few false positives (instances incorrectly classified), and high recall means that there are only a few false negatives (instances of a label that were not classified). While using the F_1-score, which hides to what extent a model may be more susceptible to false positives or false negatives, may be sufficient for evaluating a machine-learning model for automated scoring on its own, it is not sufficient for evaluating an automated scoring model in the systemic context it is embedded in and for which we as science educators ultimately care about—such as a digital learning environment with adaptive feedback. Consider, for example, that an automated scoring model is used to determine whether someone who is working on a task gets a hint. Here, false positives, resulting in getting a hint although you do not need it, are probably less hurtful than false negatives, resulting in not getting a hint although it is needed. This example shows that evaluating an automated scoring model without considering the context in which it is used is hardly sensible. One could even go further and argue that the training of the model without considering the context it is to be used in is hardly sensible because during training, one could deliberately optimize for either maximizing precision or recall or balancing both. In sum, we argue that the role of bias in automated scoring remains a challenge.

We think that the framework presented in this chapter, which is building off of ECD, can—at least in part—help to address these challenges. A virtue of ECD is the transparency it brings to the process of developing automated assessments, as every decision requires justification, and the argumentative component leads to coherence between components. Further, when the domain-specific model of learning—the claim space in the terminology of Mislevy, Almond, and Lukas (2003)—and the evidence model are specified, we are typically considering the context in which the automated scoring model is later to be deployed. For example, the granularity on which we define labels, e.g., for students' knowledge, and write evidentiary statements will reflect what the aim of the assessment is. Zhai, Krajcik, and Pellegrino (2021) come to a similar conclusion when they discuss their approach of an inferential network for validity evidence which also builds foundationally on the core set of ideas in ECD.

Another avenue to addressing the challenges of bias in automated assessment may lie in utilizing AI in this process—but in different ways than before. As Kubsch, Krist, et al. (2022) argue, the science education community working on automated scoring has mostly explored the potential of supervised machine learning to build algorithmic scoring models that replicate human scores. In contrast, unsupervised machine-learning techniques, i.e., machine-learning methods that look for patterns in data, have rarely been used so far. As Sherin (2013) points out, these methods could help address the issue of bias in the scoring process. With *Computational Grounded Theory*, sociologist Nelson (2020) provides a method of how to integrate unsupervised machine learning in the human scoring process. Rosenberg and Krist (2020) have already successfully applied this method in the context of science education, leading to the discovery of a new code in a coding system.

Conclusion

In this chapter, we have introduced a framework for using ECD in the context of developing automated detectors for tracking students' learning in digital learning environments. Further, we have provided a procedure for applying this framework in a situation where tasks in a digital learning environment are already present, and the goal is to provide an automated assessment functionality for that learning environment. Finally, we have demonstrated the successful application of this procedure, drawing on a digital learning environment about energy. We hope that in these ways, our chapter provides a helpful contribution to the community in navigating the challenges and opportunities that AI holds for supporting students' science learning.

References

Anderson, J. R., and Schunn, C. 2000. "Implications of the ACT-R learning theory: No magic bullets." *Advances in Instructional Psychology, Educational Design and Cognitive Science* 1–33.

Cheuk, T. 2021. "Can AI Be Racist? Color-Evasiveness in the Application of Machine Learning to Science Assessments." *Science Education* sce.21671. https://doi.org/10.1002/sce.21671

Clark, D. B., and Linn, M. C. 2013. "The Knowledge Integration Perspective: Connections across Research and Education." In International Handbook of Research on Conceptual Change, edited by S. Vosniadou, 520–38. New York: Routledge.

Corbett, A. T., Koedinger, K. R., and Anderson, J. R. 1997. "Intelligent Tutoring Systems." In *Handbook of Human–Computer Interaction*, edited by M. G. Helander, T. K. Landauer, and P. V. Prabhu, 849–74. London: Elsevier.

Crawford, K. 2021. *Atlas of AI: Power, politics, and the planetary costs of artificial intelligence*. New Haven, CT: Yale University Press.

De Jong, T., Lazonder, A. W., Chinn, C. A., Fischer, F., Gobert, J., Hmelo-Silver, C. E., Koedinger, K. R., Krajcik, J. S., Kyza, E. A., Linn, M. C., Pedaste, M., Scheiter, K., and Zacharia, Z. C. 2023. "Let's Talk Evidence—The Case for Combining Inquiry-Based and Direct Instruction." *Educational Research Review* 39: 100536. https://doi.org/10.1016/j.edurev.2023.100536

Devlin, J., Chang, M.-W., Lee, K., and Toutanova, K. 2019. BERT: Pre-training of Deep Bidirectional Transformers for Language Understanding. *ArXiv:1810.04805 [Cs]*. http://arxiv.org/abs/1810.04805

Dougiamas, M., and Taylor, P. 2003. "Moodle: Using Learning Communities to Create an Open Source Course Management System." In Proceedings of EdMedia + Innovate Learning 2003, edited by D. Lassner and C. McNaught, 171–78. Waynesville, NC: Association for the Advancement of Computing in Education (AACE). https://www.learntechlib.org/p/13739

Duit, R. 2014. "Teaching and Learning the Physics Energy Concept." In Teaching and Learning of Energy in K-12 Education, edited by R. F. Chen, A. Eisenkraft, D. Fortus, J. Krajcik, K. Neumann, J. Nordine, and A. Scheff, 67–85. Springer, Cham. https://doi.org/10.1007/978-3-319-05017-1_5

Duncan, R. G., and Rivet, A. E. 2018. "Learning Progressions." In *International Handbook of the Learning Sciences*, edited by F. Fischer, C. Hmelo-Silver, S Goldman, and P. Reimann, 422–32. New York: Routledge.

European Commission. 2018. 2018 Reform of EU Data Protection Rules. https://eur-lex.europa.eu/eli/reg/2016/679/2016-05-04

Gombert, S., Di Mitri, D., Karademir, O., Kubsch, M., Kolbe, H., Tautz, S., Grimm, A., Bohm, I., Neumann, K., and Drachsler, H. 2022. "Coding Energy Knowledge in Constructed Responses with Explainable NLP Models." *Journal of Computer Assisted Learning* 39, no. 3: 767–86. https://doi.org/10.1111/jcal.12767

Grimm, A., Steegh, A., Kubsch, M., and Neumann, K. 2023. "Learning Analytics in Physics Education: Equity-Focused Decision-Making Lacks Guidance!" *Journal of Learning Analytics* 10, no. 1: 71–84. https://doi.org/10.18608/jla.2023.7793

Ha, M., and Nehm, R. H. 2016. "The Impact of Misspelled Words on Automated Computer Scoring: A Case Study of Scientific Explanations." *Journal of Science Education and Technology* 25, no. 3: 358–74. https://doi.org/10.1007/s10956-015-9598-9

Harris, C. J., Krajcik, J. S., Pellegrino, J. W., and DeBarger, A. H. 2019. "Designing Knowledge-in-Use Assessments to Promote Deeper Learning." *Educational Measurement: Issues and Practice* 38, no. 2: 53–67. https://doi.org/10.1111/emip.12253

Harris, C. J., Krajcik, J. S., Pellegrino, J. W., and McElhaney, K. W. 2016. Constructing *Assessment Tasks That Blend Disciplinary Core* Ideas, *Crosscutting Concepts*, and *Science Practices* for *Classroom Formative Applications*. Menlo Park, CA: SRI International.

Hastie, T., Tibshirani, R., and Friedman, J. H. 2009. *The Elements of Statistical Learning: Data Mining, Inference, and Prediction*, 2nd ed. London: Springer.

Hestenes, D., Wells, M., and Swackhamer, G. 1992. "Force Concept Inventory." *The Physics Teacher* 30, no. 3: 141–58.

Kane, M. T. 1992. "An Argument-Based Approach to Validity." *Psychological Bulletin* 112, no. 3: 527.

Kim, Y. J., Almond, R. G., and Shute, V. J. 2016. "Applying Evidence-Centered Design for the Development of Game-Based Assessments in Physics Playground." *International Journal of Testing* 16, no. 2: 142–63. https://doi.org/10.1080/15305058.2015.1108322

Krajcik, J. S., and Shin, N. 2014. "Project-Based Learning." In *The Cambridge Handbook of the Learning Sciences*, 2nd ed., edited by R. K. Sawyer, 275–97. Cambridge: Cambridge University Press. http://dx.doi.org/10.1017/CBO9781139519526.018

Kubsch, M., Czinczel, B., Lossjew, J., Wyrwich, T., Bednorz, D., Bernholt, S., Fiedler, D., Strauß, S., Cress, U., Drachsler, H., Neumann, K., and Rummel, N. 2022. "Toward Learning Progression Analytics—Developing Learning Environments for the Automated Analysis of Learning Using Evidence Centered Design." *Frontiers in Education 7*: 981910. https://doi.org/10.3389/feduc.2022.981910

Kubsch, M., Krist, C., and Rosenberg, J. M. 2022. "Distributing Epistemic Functions and Tasks—A Framework for Augmenting Human Analytic Power with Machine Learning in Science Education Research." *Journal of Research in Science Teaching* tea.21803. https://doi.org/10.1002/tea.21803

Kubsch, M., Nordine, J., Neumann, K., Fortus, D., and Krajcik, J. 2019. "Probing the Relation between Students' Integrated Knowledge and Knowledge-in-Use about Energy Using Network Analysis." *Eurasia Journal of Mathematics, Science and Technology Education* 15, no. 8: em1728. https://doi.org/10.29333/ejmste/104404

Lee, H., Pallant, A., Pryputniewicz, S., Lord, T., Mulholland, M., and Liu, O. L. 2019. "Automated Text Scoring and Real-Time Adjustable Feedback: Supporting Revision of Scientific Arguments Involving Uncertainty." *Science Education* 103, no. 3: 590–622. https://doi.org/10.1002/sce.21504

Li, H., Gobert, J., and Dickler, R. 2017. "Automated Assessment for Scientific Explanations in On-Line Science Inquiry." In Proceedings of the 10th International Conference on Educational Data Mining, 214–19. International Educational Data Mining Society.

Liu, O. L., Rios, J. A., Heilman, M., Gerard, L., and Linn, M. C. 2016. "Validation of Automated Scoring of Science Assessments." *Journal of Research in Science Teaching* 53, no. 2: 215–33. https://doi.org/10.1002/tea.21299

Maestrales, S., Zhai, X., Touitou, I., Baker, Q., Schneider, B., and Krajcik, J. 2021. "Using Machine Learning to Score Multi-Dimensional Assessments of Chemistry and Physics." *Journal of Science Education and Technology* 30, no. 2: 239–54. https://doi.org/10.1007/s10956-020-09895-9

McClelland, J. L., and Axel Cleeremans. 2009. "Connectionist Models." In *Oxford Companion to Consciousness*, edited by T. Byrne, Axel Cleeremans, and P. Wilken, Oxford: Oxford University Press.

Mislevy, R. J. 2016. "How Developments in Psychology and Technology Challenge Validity Argumentation: How Psychology and Technology Challenge Validity." *Journal of Educational Measurement* 53, no. 3: 265–92. https://doi.org/10.1111/jedm.12117
Mislevy, R. J., Almond, R. G., and Lukas, J. F. 2003. "A Brief Introduction to Evidence-Centered Design." ETS Research Report Series, CSE Report 632. Los Angeles, CA: National Center for Research on Evaluation, Standards, and Student Testing.
Mislevy, R. J., and Haertel, G. D. 2007. "Implications of Evidence-Centered Design for Educational Testing." *Educational Measurement: Issues and Practice* 25, no. 4: 6–20. https://doi.org/10.1111/j.1745-3992.2006.00075.x
Moharreri, K., Ha, M., and Nehm, R. H. 2014. "EvoGrader: An Online Formative Assessment Tool for Automatically Evaluating Written Evolutionary Explanations." *Evolution: Education and Outreach* 7, no. 1: 15. https://doi.org/10.1186/s12052-014-0015-2
Narciss, S., Sosnovsky, S., Schnaubert, L., Andrès, E., Eichelmann, A., Goguadze, G., and Melis, E. 2014. "Exploring Feedback and Student Characteristics Relevant for Personalizing Feedback Strategies." *Computers and Education* 71: 56–76. https://doi.org/10.1016/j.compedu.2013.09.011
National Research Council. 2012. *A Framework for K-12 Science Education*. Washington, DC: National Academies Press. http://www.worldcat.org/oclc/794415367
Nelson, L. K. 2020. "Computational Grounded Theory: A Methodological Framework." *Sociological Methods & Research* 49, no. 1: 3–42. https://doi.org/10.1177/0049124117729703
Neumann, K. 2013. "Mit welchem Auflösungsgrad können Kompetenzen modelliert werden? In welcher Beziehung stehen Modelle zueinander, die Kompetenz in einer Domäne mit unterschiedlichem Auflösungsgrad beschreiben?" *Zeitschrift für Erziehungswissenschaft* 16, no. S1: 35–39. https://doi.org/10.1007/s11618-013-0382-4
Neumann, K., Schecker, H., and Theyßen, H. 2019. "Assessing Complex Patterns of Student Resources and Behavior in the Large Scale." *Annals of the American Academy of Political and Social Science* 683, no. 1: 233–49. https://doi.org/10.1177/0002716219844963
Neumann, K., Viering, T., Boone, W. J., and Fischer, H. E. 2013. "Towards a Learning Progression of Energy." *Journal of Research in Science Teaching* 50, no. 2: 162–88. https://doi.org/10.1002/tea.21061
O'Neil, C. 2016. *Weapons of Math Destruction: How Big Data Increases Inequality and Threatens Democracy*, 1st ed. New York: Crown.
OpenSciEd. 2019. *OpenSciEd*. https://www.openscied.org
Pellegrino, J. W., DiBello, L. V., and Goldman, S. R. 2015. "A Framework for Conceptualizing and Evaluating the Validity of Instructionally Relevant Assessments." *Educational Psychologist* 51, no. 1: 59–81. https://doi.org/10.1080/00461520.2016.1145550
Rosenberg, J. M., and Krist, C. 2020. "Combining Machine Learning and Qualitative Methods to Elaborate Students' Ideas About the Generality of their Model-Based Explanations." *Journal of Science Education and Technology* 30: 255–67. https://doi.org/10.1007/s10956-020-09862-4
Rupp, A. A., Levy, R., Dicerbo, K. E., Sweet, S. J., Crawford, A. V., Calico, T., Benson, M., Fay, D., Kunze, K. L., Mislevy, R. J., and Behrens, J. T. 2012. "Putting ECD into Practice: The Interplay of Theory and Data in Evidence Models within a Digital Learning Environment." *Journal of Educational Data Mining* 4, no. 1: 49–110. https://doi.org/10.5281/ZENODO.3554643
Schecker, H., and Parchmann, I. 2006. "Modellierung naturwissenschaftlicher Kompetenz." *Zeitschrift Für Didaktik Der Naturwissenschaften* 12, no. 1: 45–66.
Sekretariat der ständigen Konferenz der Kultusminister der Länder in der Bundesrepublik Deutschland. 2020. *Bildungsstandards im Fach Physik für die Allgemeine Hochschulreife*.
Sherin, B. 2013. "A Computational Study of Commonsense Science: An Exploration in the Automated Analysis of Clinical Interview Data." *Journal of the Learning Sciences 22*, no. 4: 600–38. https://doi.org/10.1080/10508406.2013.836654
Ufer, S., and Neumann, K. 2018. "Measuring Competencies." In *International Handbook of the Learning Sciences*, edited by F. Fischer, C. Hmelo-Silver, S Goldman, and P. Reimann, 433–43. New York: Routledge.
Wilson, C. D., Haudek, K. C., Osborne, J. F., Buck Bracey, Z. E., Cheuk, T., Donovan, B. M., Stuhlsatz, M. A. M., Santiago, M. M., and Zhai, X. 2023. "Using Automated Analysis to Assess Middle School

Students' Competence with Scientific Argumentation." *Journal of Research in Science Teaching* 61, no. 1: 38–69. https://doi.org/10.1002/tea.21864

Zhai, X., Haudek, K., Shi, L., Nehm, R., and Urban-Lurain, M. 2020. "From Substitution to Redefinition: A Framework of Machine Learning-Based Science Assessment." *Journal of Research in Science Teaching* 57, no. 9: 1430–59. https://doi.org/10.1002/tea.21658

Zhai, X., He, P., and Krajcik, J. 2022. "Applying Machine Learning to Automatically Assess Scientific Models." *Journal of Research in Science Teaching* 59, no. 10: 1765–94. https://doi.org/10.1002/tea.21773

Zhai, X., and Krajcik, J. 2022. "Pseudo AI Bias." http://arxiv.org/abs/2210.08141

Zhai, X., Krajcik, J., and Pellegrino, J. W. 2021. "On the Validity of Machine Learning-Based Next Generation Science Assessments: A Validity Inferential Network." *Journal of Science Education and Technology* 30, no. 2: 298–312. https://doi.org/10.1007/s10956-020-09879-9

Zhai, X., and Nehm, R. H. 2023. "AI and Formative Assessment: The Train Has Left the Station." *Journal of Research in Science Teaching* 60, no. 6: 1390–98. https://doi.org/10.1002/tea.21885

Zhai, X., Yin, Y., Pellegrino, J. W., Haudek, K. C., and Shi, L. 2020. "Applying Machine Learning in Science Assessment: A Systematic Review." *Studies in Science Education* 56, no. 1: 111–51. https://doi.org/10.1080/03057267.2020.1735757.

12
Can AI-Based Scaffolding Promote Students' Robust Learning of Authentic Science Practices?

Janice D. Gobert, Haiying Li, Rachel Dickler and Christine Lott

Introduction

An intelligent tutoring system (ITS, henceforth) is currently defined as a computer system that delivers personalized instruction to students by using computational techniques to evaluate the learner in a variety of ways, including (but not limited to) their prior knowledge, competency/skill levels, motivation, and affective states. ITSs are programmed to provide instruction or remediation as needed (Gobert et al. 2023a) based on user/student data; providing instruction *aligned* to users' needs is why ITSs are referred to as "intelligent" (later in the document we unpack this). ITSs draw from three different disciplines, namely, computer science, science education, and cognitive psychology. Though drawing from three disciplines increases the potential for applications of ITSs to a wide variety of areas, this also presents some challenges because the pedagogical and theoretical underpinnings, research goals, and methodological/computational approaches of researchers/developers in each of the three academic fields may not always neatly align, which, in turn, influences the resulting ITS. In this chapter, we outline the components and key issues in ITSs relevant to our area of work, namely ITSs for science learning.

Components and Key Issues

ITSs formally came into existence when researchers began to seek ways that computers could *support* users' learning. To do so, they began to take a more comprehensive view of the student and what is needed in an ITS to support students, describing effective systems as needing to include an accurate representation of *what* is being taught, *who* is being taught, and importantly *how* best to teach it (Self 1974).

These descriptors, namely, the *what*, the *who*, *and* the *how*, translate into the core components required in ITSs. In ITSs, these are formally referred to as the architecture (Corbett, Koedinger, and Anderson 1997), and include (1) the *domain model*, which represents the knowledge, facts, rules, etc., that encompass the domain area being taught (e.g., a topic in science), (2) the *student model*, which represents the

Janice D. Gobert et al., *Can AI-Based Scaffolding Promote Students' Robust Learning of Authentic Science Practices?*.
In: *Uses of Artificial Intelligence in STEM Education*. Edited by: Xiaoming Zhai and Joseph Krajcik,
Oxford University Press. © Oxford University Press (2024). DOI: 10.1093/oso/9780198882077.003.0012

knowledge, misconceptions, and motivational and affective states of the user in some cases, and (3) the *tutoring model* (referred to as the scaffolding in our system, Inq-ITS (to be described later)), which includes how to provide personalized instruction and feedback based on information from the domain model (what needs to be learned) and student model (what the student knows/can do). Lastly, ITSs also include the *user interface model*, which is the interactive environment, including the graphics, text, widgets, etc., that students use to take actions in the system; these actions are used to generate or distill data about the students' learning processes (Mislevy et al. 2020).

Though all four components are needed to effectively enhance learning and instruction, it is the analysis of the student data that is needed for the ITS to react and support the student's specific needs; that is, the ITS needs to "know" what the student knows and/or can do, including their partial knowledge and developing competencies in order to provide targeted support and instruction.

There have been several different computational approaches used to develop the *student model* in ITS work (Chrysafiadi and Virvou 2013). Relevant to this chapter, the approach also varies with the domain of the ITS, e.g., math, etc. For example, in well-defined domains (Corbett and Anderson 1995), namely, those that have one correct answer, such as mathematics, the assessment of students' knowledge and skills is fairly straightforward. In these cases, to develop the student model, knowledge-engineering (Koedinger and MacLaren 2002) is used, then techniques, such as model tracing (Anderson et al. 1990), compare the student's knowledge and skills to those of an expert and intervenes when the system detects a difference between the student and expert.

The topic addressed in our work, science inquiry, however, is an ill-defined domain; that is, one for which there are many productive/correct and unproductive/incorrect ways to complete inquiry tasks (Kuhn 2005). These include (but are not limited to) the processes by which a learner forms a testable question, conducts an experiment to test their question, interprets and analyzes the resulting data, and then communicates their results. Because of the ill-defined nature of these tasks and the many, varied approaches that students can take in executing them, assessments of students' competencies upon which the student model is based on more complex than, for example, solving a mathematical problem. As such, this requires more nuanced computational techniques to assess students' competencies and, in turn, provide targeted tutoring, i.e., scaffolding (Gobert et al. 2023a).

Machine learning or data mining is a computational approach that is very well suited to the assessment and tutoring for ill-defined tasks, such as inquiry (Gobert et al. 2023b). In brief, machine learning allows a system to glean meaningful information about a student by distilling large amounts of user data (Baker and Yacef 2009), which informs the ITS about the knowledge of the learner; machine-learning techniques ultimately serve to automate the processes of analyzing users' actions. Because machine learning is based on large datasets, the result is a more nuanced understanding of the user, i.e., a better student model, which can identify a fuller range of student competencies and difficulties and be used to trigger more targeted, personalized supports. There are many benefits to applying machine learning to students' data, including logfiles that are generated as students work in an ITS (as in our system), making it uniquely suited to the assessment and tutoring of science inquiry practices/tasks. These benefits, referred to as the four V's (Laney 2001), are as follows. Machine learning can handle the *volume* of logfile data generated as students work on inquiry tasks, the *veracity* of log file data on students' competencies on a broad range of inquiry practices, the *velocity* at which log file data are generated as students conduct inquiry in real time, and the *variability* in students' process data on a broad range of inquiry practices. Machine learning has been used in ITSs in many ways, illustrating the benefits of all four V's. For example, it was used to create a library of learners' bugs to detect in real time when a student is off-task (Baker 2007) or is gaming the system (Baker et al. 2008), i.e., doing behaviors directly to receive hints instead of deeply engaging in learning. Similarly, machine learning, used in Inq-ITS for the assessment of students' competencies, has also been used on students' log files in real time to detect students' disengagement from learning (Gobert, Baker, and Wixon 2015).

Inquiry Learning: The Good, the Bad, and the Need for Scaffolding

The Next Generation Science Standards (NGSS Lead States 2013), a widely used framework for science education in the United States, was designed to improve students' science competencies. In brief, the NGSS describes authentic competencies for science that students K–12 are expected to learn; these also align with the goals of twenty-first-century skills frameworks (World Economic Forum 2015). In brief, the NGSS practices are as follows:

1. Asking questions (for science) and defining problems (for engineering);
2. Developing and using models;
3. Planning and carrying out investigations;
4. Analyzing and interpreting data;
5. Using mathematics and computational thinking;
6. Constructing explanations (for science) and designing solutions (for engineering);
7. Engaging in argument from evidence; and
8. Obtaining, evaluating, and communicating information.

At of the time of this writing, the NGSS Lead States (2013) has been adopted by forty-four states and Washington, DC, and despite this broad usage, the resources to assess and support the development of students' competencies on these are lagging behind (Pellegrino 2014), thereby specifying a need for an ITS that can both assess and support students' learning of these practices.

The NGSS Lead States (2013) as described above can be broadly thought of as the domain model(s) for our work, specifying what students should know and be able to demonstrate in science inquiry. There is a large body of research on inquiry learning across many science domains and levels of education (Kuhn 2005). A selection of practices (i.e., competencies) from the NGSS Lead States (2013) and the respective difficulties students exhibit on these are outlined below.

In brief, students have difficulties forming testable questions (NGSS practice 1), may not know what a hypothesis should look like (Njoo and de Jong 1993), and avoid posing questions that could be rejected (van Joolingen and de Jong 1993).

When designing and conducting investigations (NGSS practice 3), students do not plan which experiments to run (Glaser et al. 1992) and may not test their articulated questions (van Joolingen and de Jong 1993; Schauble et al. 1991). They gather insufficient evidence to test their questions (Shute and Glaser 1990; Schauble et al. 1991) by running only one trial or running the same trial repeatedly or by changing too many variables within the same trial (Shute and Glaser 1990).

Then, in analyzing and interpreting data (NGSS practice 4), students exhibit confirmation bias; i.e., they won't discard a hypothesis based on negative results (Klayman and Ha 1987) and draw conclusions based on confounded data (Klahr and Dunbar 1988). They don't relate the outcomes of experiments to theories being tested (Schunn and Anderson 1999) and have difficulty linking data back to hypotheses (Klahr and Dunbar 1988).

In constructing explanations (NGSS practice 6) and engaging in argument from evidence (NGSS practice 7), students have difficulty articulating and defending claims, use inappropriate and insufficient data in providing reasoning for their claims, and struggle to use evidence to support their claims (McNeill and Krajcik 2011).

Should inquiry practices be scaffolded/tutored? As regards the tutoring model, i.e., what support to provide to students, a key issue debated in science ITSs is the degree of learner control versus the amount of guidance built into the ITS. The debate focuses on what is more beneficial for students' learning, i.e., open-ended discovery learning or structured/scaffolded learning (de Jong et al. 2023; Hmelo-Silver, Duncan, and Chinn 2007; Kirschner, Sweller, and Clark 2006).

There are many reasons why we chose to scaffold, i.e., tutor, inquiry in Inq-ITS. First, as illustrated earlier, many students struggle with the full range of inquiry practices. Second, there are many key learner characteristics including students' goal orientation (Hershkovitz et al. 2011), engagement (Gobert, Baker, and Wixon 2015), and persistence (Al Mamun, Lawrie, and Wright 2022) that affect students' inquiry processes. Third, inquiry skills make a unique contribution to learning science outcomes over and above "big" variables, including intelligence (Shute and Glaser 1990), general reasoning ability (Schunn and Anderson 1999), and general metacognitive skills (Veenman and Elshout 1995). Fourth, since successful learners are more skilled at many inquiry tasks, including planning, data management, evidence generation and its interpretation, inferring irregularities in data, and providing explanations of findings (Schauble et al. 1991), scaffolding/tutoring inquiry processes may give students who are unskilled at inquiry a "leg up" at learning science (Gobert et al. 2023b). Lastly, open-ended inquiry has shown mixed results regarding efficacy (de Jong et al. 2023), leading to confusion and misconceptions (Brown and Campione 1994) and, in turn, failure to learn the science principles being targeted (Kirschner, Sweller, and Clark 2006).

Findings from Scaffolding Inquiry in Typical Contexts

There are several different types of scaffolds and formats for science inquiry. Types of scaffolds include adding explicit structures to inquiry task materials (White and Frederiksen 1998), such as example-based supports (van Gog and Rummel 2018). Scaffolds may be presented in pencil–paper format in which structural guidance supports particular steps of the practices (Reiser 2004), such as hypothesizing and collecting data (Martin et al. 2019), and constructing explanations (McNeill and Krajcik 2011). Scaffolding inquiry in these ways and typical contexts has had varying degrees of success on students' learning whereby students achieved success that they could not achieve on their own (Kirschner, Sweller, and Clark 2006). Further, scaffolding has led to transfer across settings; for example, designing controlled experiments, a lynchpin skill of inquiry, has been successfully scaffolded and demonstrated to transfer to other topics (Klahr and Nigam 2004), including experimenting with simulations (Sao Pedro 2013). Scaffolding data interpretation skills has been shown to be successful at helping students make connections between experimental data and real-world scenarios (Schauble et al. 1991), important to the NGSS and to scientific literacy more generally. Lastly, scaffolding students' explanations during inquiry, important to communicating findings (NGSS Lead States 2013), has also led to positive effects on learning (McNeill et al. 2006).

Scaffolding in Virtual Environments

Scaffolding can also be done within virtual environments (Quellmalz 2013; van Joolingen et al. 2005) at the end of an instructional unit or in some cases, in response to automated assessment of independent problems presented in the learning environment. Some learning environments support students through fixed scaffolding, which is when the same amount of scaffolding is provided to students, regardless of individual experience or performance. For instance, Tabak and Reiser's (2008) inquiry software provided fixed scaffolding to students and was found to benefit students' content and process understandings. Faded scaffolding (Martin et al. 2019) can also be useful to learning. For example, in Co-Lab, an online system that gradually reduces the presence of explicit goals to guide students' inquiry, students benefited from the scaffolds, compared to controls, for the inquiry task of planning their inquiry investigations (van Joolingen et al. 2005).

Another type of in-system scaffolding is personalized, adaptive guidance. This can be based on teachers' assessment of students' needs or can also be based on automated assessment of student competencies and difficulties and provided "just in time," when students need help (Anderson et al. 1995; Corbett and Anderson 1995). In some ITSs, adaptive scaffolding is based on students' level of mastery, namely, their performance on particular knowledge components (i.e., parts of skills) that are tracked in relation to an ideal model (i.e., model tracing discussed earlier; Anderson et al. 1995) and/or using Bayesian techniques (i.e., knowledge tracing; Corbett and Anderson 1995). These scaffolds have historically been provided in the form of personalized supports, i.e., pop-up messages, feedback from a pedagogical agent, or dialogue with a conversational agent (Graesser 2016). In general, scaffolding that is based on students' level of mastery and provided "just in time" by pedagogical agents can play an important role in the acquisition of skills by making learning more interactive and focusing students' attention where it is most needed (Li et al. 2018).

Personalized, adaptive scaffolding in real time is particularly important in complex settings such as science inquiry where each student may experience many difficulties that require support across a wide range of practices (Hmelo-Silver, Duncan, and Chinn 2007). While there are several online environments for science inquiry (e.g., PhET, Wieman et al. 2010; Co-Lab/Go-Lab, van Joolingen et al. 2005; BGuILE, Tabak and Reiser 2008), many of these tools lack automated scoring or personalized adaptive scaffolding of students' inquiry practices, despite its importance and potential for learning. Both SimScientist (Quellmalz 2013) and ChemVLab+ (Davenport, Rafferty, and Yaron 2018) use automated, personalized scaffolds in the form of increasingly specific pop-up messages when a student has been assessed as completing an element of the environment incorrectly (e.g., making an inaccurate prediction about a scientific phenomenon). However, their systems do not leverage machine learning on students' data, thereby limiting the generation of fine-grained student models. Next, we address the automated, personalized scaffolding in Inq-ITS, which is based on the assessment of students' inquiry competencies on a broad range of practices using patented AI algorithms (Gobert et al. 2023b) including machine learning, knowledge engineering, and natural language processing to analyze students' data in real time and provide targeted scaffolding to students, also in real time (Gobert et al. 2023a).

Inq-ITS

Inq-ITS (Inquiry-Intelligent Tutoring System, Gobert et al. 2023b) is a science platform with simulation-based labs in which middle and high school students conduct inquiry, including asking questions, developing and using models, planning and carrying out investigations, analyzing and interpreting data, and constructing explanations.

Inq-ITS elicits and collects evidence of students' proficiency at inquiry practices as they engage in rich, authentic inquiry tasks with simulations. From solely an assessment perspective, conducting assessment of students' inquiry competencies in real time within a simulation environment like Inq-ITS provides a desirable context to assess students' competencies in the context in which they are developing (Mislevy et al. 2020); hence, this is an authentic performance assessment of students' competencies at *doing* science. Furthermore, and importantly, tracking students' interactions within a simulation environment that is instrumented to collect, distill, and aggregate log data provides rigorous assessment data upon which scaffolding is based. Thus, we are assessing the competencies that science learning environments like Inq-ITS and others (Quellmalz 2013) were designed to foster (Gobert et al. 2023b).

Specifically, as students work in Inq-ITS, rich, high-fidelity log files are collected via the *user interface* (a core component of ITSs, Corbett, Koedinger, and Anderson 1997), which includes the collection of every mouse click, setting within a simulation, setting chosen on a widget, etc. (Gobert et al. 2023b). Then, based on these log files of click-steam data and students' writing, Inq-ITS automatically assesses students' inquiry competencies in real time based on knowledge-engineered and data-mined algorithms (Gobert, Baker, and Sao Pedro 2016; Gobert et al. 2019), and automatically scores students' writing based on natural language processing algorithms (Li, Gobert, and Dickler 2017). Our algorithms provide a very close match to human scorers, were *built on diverse student data* over multiple topics, and the generalizability of our algorithms was tested on new students *not* used to build models (Sao Pedro 2013; Sao Pedro, Baker, and Gobert 2013).

In brief, Inq-ITS' infrastructure rigorously captures all students' data and its algorithms generate real-time performance assessments of students' competencies in science inquiry practices. These algorithms are also used to generate real-time scaffolding/tutoring for students via a digital agent, Rex, described in detail later. The algorithms also drive alerts, which identify for educators the specific kinds of difficulties students have on a broad range of inquiry practices. These alerts are sent in real time to a teacher dashboard, Inq-Blotter, as students work. The dashboard also provides TIPS (*T*eacher *I*nquiry *P*ractice *S*upports), which guide teachers to do whole class instruction or differentiated instruction (for small groups), or provide 1:1 support (Gobert et al. 2023b).

Inq-ITS Scaffolds

We developed scaffolds that are triggered in real time by our underlying assessment algorithms. Our scaffolds were iteratively developed from actual teacher feedback, yielding predetermined responses that support students' specific struggles with a large range of inquiry practices (outlined earlier; Gobert and Sao Pedro 2017) as they conduct investigations within our system. Our system provides proactive scaffolds when our algorithms detect that the student needs help because on-demand help is subject to help abuse (Baker et al. 2008), and students may lack the metacognitive knowledge to realize that they are struggling (Aleven et al. 2016).

Our scaffolds are delivered directly following unproductive/incorrect inquiry performance on a specific practice, because this is more effective for students' learning compared to feedback provided at the end of the activity (Li et al. 2018). Scaffolds are delivered via our pedagogical agent, Rex, because pedagogical agents have been shown to be beneficial to learning (Mitrovic and Suraweera 2000). Our agent provides short textual descriptions, which have also been found to be an effective format for scaffolds (Rieber 2005).

Inq-ITS provides the following types of scaffolds.

1. Orienting scaffolds direct the student to the current task within the inquiry cycle since students have difficulties monitoring their progress (de Jong 2006).
2. Conceptual scaffolds provide a high-level hint to the student if they are unable to generate the appropriate strategy themselves.
3. Procedural scaffolds provide information about the procedure to use on the current task if a student is *not* able to generate the appropriate strategy themselves.

4. Instrumental scaffolds tell the student exactly what to do on the current task, i.e., a "bottom-out hint" (Aleven and Koedinger 2000), when a student is assessed as not able to generate the appropriate strategy themselves. These are useful for some students since explicit instruction can be effective for inquiry (Klahr and Nigam 2004) so that they do not become unmotivated and confused (Brown and Campione 1994).

Once we implemented our scaffolds into Inq-ITS, we evaluated their effectiveness in several studies in which students were randomly assigned to receive scaffolding for each practice (i.e., data collection, data analysis, warranting claims). The data from these studies, analyzed using Bayesian Knowledge Tracing (Corbett and Anderson 1995) and ANCOVAs, showed that students who received scaffolding were better able to both learn practices and transfer these competencies to new topics than students who did not receive scaffolding (Sao Pedro 2013; Gobert et al. 2018). One study (Li et al. 2018) demonstrated that students who received scaffolding across practices improved on these practices at a quicker rate relative to students who did not receive scaffolding. Studies on the real-time, adaptive scaffolding in Inq-ITS, however, have yet to examine the robustness of adaptive scaffolding on inquiry competencies over time and across topics, i.e., once scaffolding is removed. This is the topic of the study described next.

Testing the Transfer of Inq-ITS AI-Based Scaffolds across Topics and Time

In this study, we investigated whether adaptive scaffolding of inquiry practices on topic 1 is robust across topics at varying time intervals on future topics. One hundred and seven sixth-grade students from a middle school in the northeastern United States participated. Of the population of students at the middle school, 39.2% are White, 20.6% are Hispanic, 23.5% are Asian, 11% are Black, and the remaining students are two or more races.

Procedure and Materials

Students completed virtual labs in Inq-ITS (Gobert et al. 2023b) in the following order: animal cell (three simulation-based activities in which students investigated how changing the number of organelles in the animal cell affected the health of the cell), plant cell (three simulation-based activities in which students investigated how changing the number of organelles in the plant cell affected the health of the cell), genetics (three simulation-based activities in which students investigated how changing a mother monster's alleles impacted the traits of the monster's babies), and natural selection (four simulation-based activities in which students investigated how changing environmental factors impacted the presence of monsters with different traits).

Each of the four Inq-ITS simulation-based activities contains four stages in which students engage in practices aligned to the NGSS Lead States (2013): forming questions/hypothesizing, carrying out investigations/collecting data, analyzing and interpreting data, and communicating findings (see Figures 12.1a, b, c, d for screenshots of the animal cell lab). At the time of this study, adaptive, real-time scaffolding was available within the first three stages of the simulation-based activity. Students' performance on the science inquiry subpractices of asking questions/forming hypotheses, carrying out investigations/collecting data, and interpreting and analyzing data are scored using EDM and KE algorithms, which allows for real-time, adaptive scaffolds at a fine-grained level (Gobert et al. 2013).

In our system, if the algorithms determine that a student is having difficulty with a particular practice, Rex, our virtual pedagogical agent, appears on the screen with a text bubble to present different types of information, or scaffolds, depending on the difficulty the student is encountering (see Figure 12.1e for an example of one type of scaffold regarding the planning and carrying out investigations phase in the animal cell lab). As a student encounters difficulty on a science practice, they must address the hint from Rex accurately to move forward in the system. Students are first provided with an orienting hint, which reminds the students of the inquiry task they are working on. If the difficulty persists, the system adapts the scaffold presented by offering a conceptual hint, which is a high-level hint that further explains the subpractice at hand. This leaves the option for the student to generate the appropriate skill or strategy needed for the particular inquiry task. However, if these higher-level scaffolds are not enough and a student is still struggling, this can be followed with more explicit information in a procedural hint, which offers more assistance by providing details about the steps involved in the current inquiry task. Finally, if these prior levels of scaffolds are unable to yield a successful result, the student may receive an instrumental scaffold, which explains the exact steps to carry out in order to move forward on a particular inquiry task (see examples of each of these earlier in the chapter). Thus, as students demonstrate increased difficulty on a task, the system adapts with more explicit scaffolds to support the student on the inquiry practice with which they are engaged. It is possible that Rex might not pop up for a student at all during a scaffolded activity if the student demonstrates perfect performance on all inquiry practices on his/her first attempt. In the present study, students had real-time, adaptive Rex scaffolding available only in the first simulation-based topic (out of the four) that they completed (i.e., animal cell).

Measures

The dependent variables in the present study were the students' scores on the four inquiry practices automatically assessed by knowledge engineered rules and machine-learned algorithms in the first three stages of the Inq-ITS system, as described in the section "Procedure and Materials." The four practices and their corresponding subcomponents by which they were measured include: (1) generating

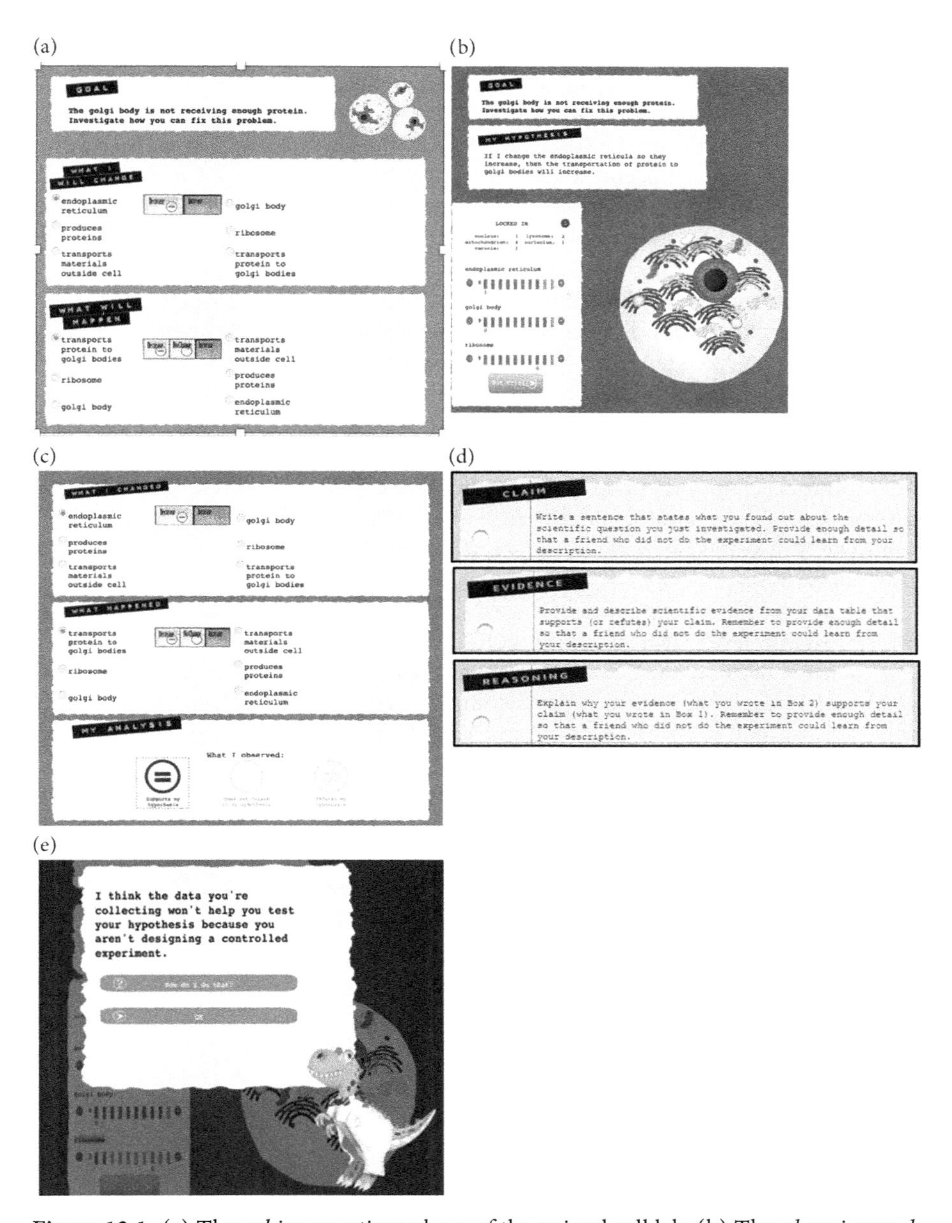

Figure 12.1 (a) The *asking questions* phase of the animal cell lab. (b) The *planning and carrying out investigations* phase of the animal cell lab. (c) The *analyzing and interpreting data* phase of the animal cell lab. (d) The *constructing explanations* phase of the animal cell lab. (e) Example of a Rex scaffold during the *planning and carrying out investigations* phase of the animal cell lab.

Adapted from Gobert, Sao Pedro, and Betts (2023b).

hypotheses, which was measured by identifying an IV (independent variable) and DV (dependent variable); (2) collecting data, which was measured by testing the hypothesis, running pairwise targeted and controlled trials, and conducting a controlled experiment; (3) interpreting data, which was measured by correctly selecting the IV and DV for a claim, correctly interpreting the relationship between the IV and DV, and correctly interpreting the hypothesis/claim relationship; and (4) warranting claims, which was measured by warranting the claim with more than one trial, warranting with controlled trials, correctly warranting the relationship between the IV and DV, and correctly warranting the hypothesis/claim relationship. Each inquiry practice subcomponent was automatically coded as 0 points if incorrect or 1 point if correct using the knowledge engineering and educational data-mining techniques in Inq-ITS that have been validated in prior studies (Gobert et al. 2013). For the first activity (where students had the opportunity to receive scaffolding from Rex and reattempt inquiry practices), the analyses used students' performance on their first attempts for each inquiry practice before they received any scaffolding from Rex. The average score on each of the four inquiry practices across all of the activities within a topic (i.e., the average hypothesizing score across all three animal cell activities) was used for analyses.

One of the independent variables used in the present study was inquiry practice, which had four levels: hypothesizing, collecting data, interpreting data, and warranting claims. This study also had a variable for time of completion with four levels: at Time 1 (December 2017), students completed the first Inq-ITS simulation-based topic (i.e., animal cell with Rex's support); at Time 2 (January 2018), students completed the second topic (i.e., plant cell); at Time 3 (March 2018), students completed the third topic (i.e., genetics); and at Time 4 (June 2018) students completed the fourth topic (i.e., natural selection). There was a forty-day gap between completion of the first to second and second to third topics, and about ninety days between the completion of the third to last topic. The four inquiry practices and time of topic completion (i.e., first, second, third, and fourth time) were the two within-subject factors. The purpose of the study was to investigate whether there was any significant growth in and transfer of inquiry performance over time after removing the adaptive scaffolding provided only in the first topic.

Analyses and Findings

Repeated measures analyses were carried out to investigate whether students' performance on each of the inquiry practices was robust after adaptive scaffolding was removed following completion of the first topic. Table 12.1 presents an overview of the means, standard deviations, minimum, and maximum scores.

Performance on Inquiry Practices: Main Effect of Practices

Results of the repeated measures multivariate test for overall inquiry score were significant: $F(3, 104) = 26.59$, $p < 0.001$, $\eta^2 = 0.434$. Results for tests of within-subjects effects for practice were also significant: $F(3, 318) = 43.85$, $p < 0.001$, $\eta^2 = 0.293$. The pairwise comparisons of overall inquiry score (see Figure 12.2) showed that students

Table 12.1 Statistics for Inquiry Practice × Time of Completion Across Four Virtual Labs (N = 107)

Time	Hypothesis		Data collection		Interpretation		Warranting	
	M (SD)	Min (Max)	M(SD)	Min (Max)	M (SD)	Min (Max)	M (SD)	Min (Max)
1 (*Day* = 1)	0.79 (0.21)	0.33 (1.00)	0.73 (0.26)	0.00 (1.00)	0.82 (0.18)	0.42 (1.00)	0.66 (0.27)	0.00 (1.00)
2 (*Day* = 40)	0.91 (0.15)	0.33 (1.00)	0.90 (0.19)	0.00 (1.00)	0.88 (0.21)	0.00 (1.00)	0.82 (0.28)	0.00 (1.00)
3 (*Day* = 80)	0.86 (0.24)	0.00 (1.00)	0.86 (0.24)	0.00 (1.00)	0.77 (0.25)	0.08 (1.00)	0.72 (0.28)	0.00 (1.00)
4 (*Day* = 170)	0.90 (0.20)	0.13 (1.00)	0.92 (0.14)	0.38 (1.00)	0.81 (0.21)	0.19 (1.00)	0.75 (0.24)	0.25 (1.00)

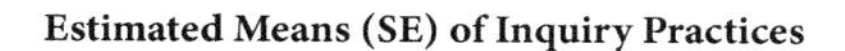

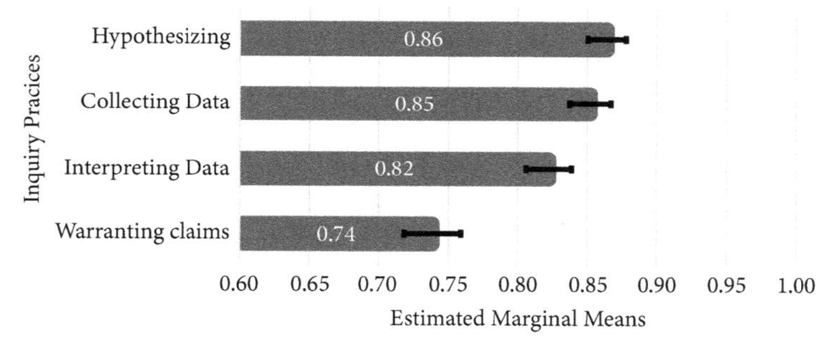

Figure 12.2 Estimated means (SE) of inquiry practices.

achieved higher scores on hypothesizing practice than on interpreting data practice ($p < 0.001$, Cohen's $d = 0.27$) and warranting claims practice ($p < 0.001$, $d = 0.70$). Students' collecting data scores were also significantly higher than interpreting data ($p = 0.028$, $d = 0.18$) and warranting claims ($p < 0.001$, $d = 0.61$). Moreover, the interpreting scores were significantly higher than warranting claims scores ($p < 0.001$, $d = 0.44$). These results revealed that students' inquiry proficiencies vary with different practices. They have the highest proficiency in hypothesizing and collecting data, followed by interpreting and warranting practices.

Growth over Time: Main Effect of Time

Results of the repeated measures analysis showed a significant multivariate effect for time, F (3, 104) = 20.93, $p < 0.001$, $\eta^2 = 0.376$. Results of the tests for within-subjects effects were also significant for time, F (3, 318) = 19.97, $p < 0.001$, $\eta^2 = 0.159$. The pairwise comparisons of overall inquiry performance over time showed that students achieved higher inquiry scores at Time 2 ($p < 0.001$, Cohen's $d = 0.68$), Time 3 ($p = 0.039$, Cohen's $d = 0.27$), and Time 4 ($p < 0.001$, Cohen's $d = 0.53$) relative to Time 1 (see Table 12.1). Results showed that inquiry scores were significantly lower at Time 3 than at Time 2 ($p < 0.001$, Cohen's $d = 0.36$) (see Figure 12.3a).

The topics completed at Time 1 and Time 2 were animal cell and plant cell, respectively, and therefore were similar in terms of the difficulty of content. Both topics are taught as part of the NGSS Lead States (2013) middle school "Life Science Strand 1 (From Molecules to Organisms: Structures and Processes)." The increase in inquiry practice scores from Time 1 to Time 2 indicated that students benefitted from the adaptive scaffolding at Time 1 and demonstrated growth in inquiry performance, i.e., had further honed this practice at Time 2. The topics at Time 3 and Time 4 were more complex than the topics completed at Time 1 and Time 2, but students still demonstrated growth in inquiry competencies at Time 3 and Time 4 relative to Time 1. However, at Time 3, students' inquiry performance decreased relative to Time 2. This drop in inquiry performance is likely explained by a change in the difficulty of topic (i.e., plant cell to genetics) since genetics is one of the more difficult life science topics for middle and high school students (Stewart 1982), requiring mathematical understandings of probability in addition to scientific content (Corbett et al. 2010). Even though there is a decrease in scores from Time 2 to Time 3 due to the increase in the complexity of the topic (i.e., genetics), the performance at Time 3 still significantly improved relative to Time 1. Overall, these findings indicate that our scaffolding of students' inquiry competencies is robust since scaffolding was removed after the first topic but its effects were maintained over 40, 80, and 170 days for the overall inquiry practice score.

Growth over Time: Interaction between Time and Inquiry Practices

Results of the repeated measures multivariate analyses also showed a significant two-way interaction between time and inquiry practice: $F(9, 98) = 11.00, p < 0.001, \eta^2 = 0.503$. Results for tests of within-subjects effects were also significant for this interaction: $F(9, 954) = 9.28, p < 0.001, \eta^2 = 0.080$. Pairwise comparisons (see Figure 12.3b) showed that for the practice of hypothesizing, students performed significantly higher at Time 2 ($p < 0.001$, Cohen's $d = 0.69$), Time 3 ($p = 0.020$, $d = 0.34$), and Time 4 ($p < 0.001$, $d = 0.54$), than at Time 1. A similar pattern was found for the practice of

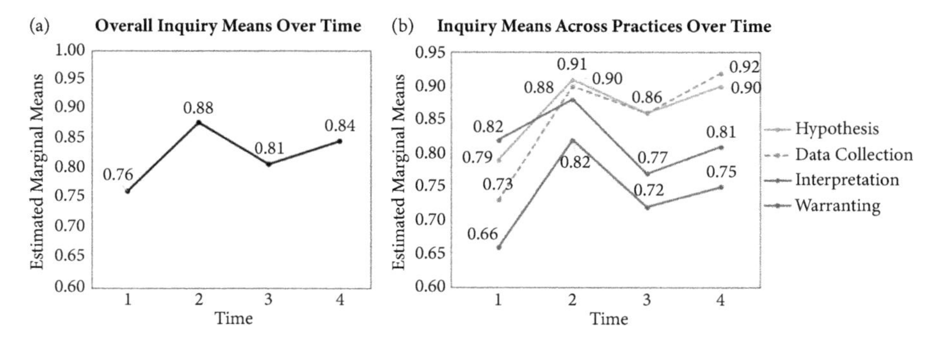

Figure 12.3 (a) Overall inquiry means over time. (b) Inquiry means across practices over time.

collecting data; i.e., students performed significantly higher at Time 2 ($p < 0.001$, $d = 0.73$), Time 3 ($p < 0.001$, $d = 0.54$), and Time 4 ($p < 0.001$, $d = 0.88$), than at Time 1. This pattern was not found for the practice of interpreting data or for the practices of warranting claims. A different pattern emerged for the practice of warranting claims. Specifically, students achieved higher scores at Time 2 ($p < 0.001$, $d = 0.56$) and Time 4 ($p = 0.004$, $d = 0.35$) than at Time 1 for the practice of warranting claims.

The findings for the specific practices of hypothesizing and data collection are similar to those found for the main effect of time. There was continuous growth in performance, i.e., a honing of practices, for hypothesizing and collecting data from Time 1 to Time 2, to Time 3, and to Time 4. These patterns demonstrate a growth in student performance for the practices of hypothesizing and collecting data regardless of the difficulty of the topic from Time 1 to Time 4. For the practice of warranting claims, however, a significant increase was found only when comparing Time 1 to Time 2 and when comparing Time 1 to Time 4. For the practice of warranting claims, the difficulty of content (i.e., genetics) perhaps influenced performance at Time 3, where there was not a significant improvement in scores.

We found that students achieved better interpreting data performance at Time 2 than at both Time 3 ($p < 0.001$, $d = 0.46$) and Time 4 ($p = 0.009$, $d = 0.32$). We also found that students achieved higher warranting claims scores at Time 2 than at Time 3 ($p =0.003$, $d = 0.34$). The decreasing performance on interpreting data practice from Time 2 to Time 3 and from Time 2 to Time 4 is likely due to the increasing complexity of topics from plant cell (Time 2) to genetics (Time 3) and natural selection (Time 4). This phenomenon also occurred in warranting claims performance, decreasing from Time 2 to Time 3, likely due to the increase in difficulty of the topic (genetics). Another possibility is that these practices, namely, interpreting data and warranting claims, interact with content knowledge to a greater degree (than hypothesizing and data collection). This is also commensurate with our transfer findings, i.e., that hypothesizing and data collection transfer across content areas and over time.

Discussion of Study's Findings

In this study, we investigated the efficacy of our scaffolding using students' performances on various inquiry practices at different time intervals and across different topics, thereby addressing far transfer in two different ways. Our results showed, in general, that our scaffolding was robust for hypothesizing and collecting data practices because students' competencies continued to improve when evaluated after 40, 80, and 170 days, regardless of topic difficulty. Specifically, we were interested in whether adaptive scaffolding of inquiry practices on one topic is enough to support student performance on different topics completed at various time intervals in the future. As such, these represent metrics of far transfer. Despite the difficulty of moving from less difficult topics (i.e., animal and plant cells) to more advanced topics (i.e., genetics and natural selection), we found that the effects of scaffolding were still highly robust in terms of student performance relative to the first inquiry topic. This pattern was consistent across the practices of hypothesizing and collecting data. For the practices of interpreting data and warranting claims, growth was influenced by the topic's difficulty, as identified in prior studies (Gobert et al. 2018).

In sum, these findings suggest that adaptive scaffolding in one topic in an ITS can benefit student inquiry learning even after scaffolding is removed and that the effect of adaptive scaffolding is maintained after long periods of time ranging from about 40 to about 170 days. Our interpretation of these findings is that the procedural support given by Rex, the pedagogical agent, for inquiry practices is greatly supporting the acquisition and refinement of competencies, which undergirds students' inquiry. The effects of adaptive scaffolding were also apparent across topics in life science, some of which were more difficult than others. We note that the success of the learning of inquiry practices, as evidenced by far transfer, may depend on both increasing difficulty of inquiry practices and increasing complexity of inquiry topics. Overall, the findings in the present study inform assessment designers and researchers that, if properly designed, scaffolding aimed at supporting students' competencies on various inquiry practices can greatly benefit students' deep learning of and performance on inquiry practices such that their learning is robust and can be transferred to other topics, even when these topics are presented long after the original scaffolding.

Concluding Comments

The chapter presented Inq-ITS (Gobert et al. 2023a, b), an ITS for science that is used in fifty states and multiple countries for real-time performance assessment and real-time scaffolding of science inquiry practices, as described by reform documents such as the NGSS Lead States (2013) and twenty-first-century skills frameworks (World Economic Forum 2015).

In brief, since science inquiry is an ill-defined domain, there were many considerations that needed to be accounted for in the design and development of an ITS for science practices. These were utilized in Inq-ITS, its tasks, and the computational and analytic techniques to collect students' data and assess students' competencies on inquiry practices and scaffold students on these practices in real time.

Regarding the key basic components or architecture of an ITS for science, Inq-ITS' *domain model* was designed to reflect the knowledge and competencies expected by the NGSS Lead States (2013). The *user interface model* elicits and collects students' interactions within the system, i.e., both the work products that students generate and processes that students engage in (i.e., particular "behaviors" exhibited during inquiry tasks; Mislevy et al. 2020). The *student model* represents students' knowledge and competencies, and the *tutoring model* integrates data from the student and domain models to provide targeted support to students in real time. These four ITS components are all critical so that an ITS can react on the basis of each student's knowledge and skills, including their partial knowledge and developing skills.

As demonstrated by the findings presented here, when these core components are properly operationalized and combined to assess and provide support to students on inquiry practices in real time, there are great benefits to students' learning of science competencies that can be transferred to other topics, long after scaffolding. Furthermore, utilizing machine learning in ITSs, as is done in our system, allows for all assessments and scaffolds (as well as alerts, and TIPS to teachers; Gobert et al. 2023b) to be generated in real time, and at scale, providing a much-needed resource for students and teachers in order to realize reform policies worldwide.

Acknowledgments

This work was supported by the National Science Foundation (NSF-DRL-1,252,477) and the US Department of Education (R305A210432). The opinions expressed are those of the authors and do not represent views of the National Science Foundation or the US Department of Education.

References

Al Mamun, M. A., Lawrie, G., and Wright, T. 2022. "Exploration of Learner-Content Interactions and Learning Approaches: The Role of Guided Inquiry in the Self-directed Online Environments." *Computers & Education* 178: 104398. https://doi.org/10.1016/j.compedu.2021.104398

Aleven, V., and Koedinger, K. 2000. "Limitations of Student Control: Do Students Know When They Need Help?" In Proceedings of the 5th International Conference on Intelligent Tutoring Systems, ITS 2000, edited by G. Gauthier, C. Frasson, and K. VanLehn, 292–303. Berlin: Springer-Verlag.

Aleven, V., Roll, I., McLaren, B. M., and Koedinger, K. R. 2016. "Help Helps, But Only So Much: Research on Help Seeking with Intelligent Tutoring Systems." *International Journal of Artificial Intelligence in Education* 26, no. 1: 205–23.

Anderson, J. R., Boyle, C. F., Corbett, A. T., and Lewis, M. W. 1990. "Cognitive Modeling and Intelligent Tutoring." *Artificial Intelligence* 42, no. 1: 7–49.

Anderson, J. R., Corbett, A. T., Koedinger, K. R., and Pelletier, R. 1995. "Cognitive Tutors: Lessons Learned." *Journal of the Learning Sciences* 4, no. 2: 167–207.

Baker, R. S. 2007. "Modeling and Understanding Students' Off-Task Behavior in Intelligent Tutoring Systems." In *Proceedings of the SIGCHI Conference on Human Factors in Computing Systems, ACM*, 1059–68. http://dx.doi.org/10.1145/1240624.1240785

Baker, R. S. J. d., Corbett, A. T., Roll, I., and Koedinger, K. R. 2008. "Developing a Generalizable Detector of When Students Game the System." *User Modeling and User-Adapted Interaction* 18, no. 3: 287–314.

Baker, R. S., and Yacef, K. 2009. "The State of Educational Data Mining in 2009: A Review and Future Visions." *Journal of Educational Data Mining* 1, no. 1: 3–17.

Brown, A. L., and Campione, J. C. 1994. "Guided Discovery in a Community of Learners." In Classroom Lessons: Integrating Cognitive Theory and Classroom Practice, edited by K. McGilly, 229–70. Cambridge, MA: MIT Press.

Chrysafiadi, K., and Virvou, M. 2013. "Student Modeling Approaches: A Literature Review for the Last Decade." *Expert Systems with Applications* 40, no. 11: 4715–29.

Corbett, A. T., and Anderson, J. R. 1995. "Knowledge Decomposition and Subgoal Reification in the ACT Programming Tutor." In Proceedings of AIED '95, 7th World Conference on Artificial Intelligence in Education, 1–7.

Corbett, A. T., Koedinger, K. R., and Anderson, J. R. 1997. "Intelligent Tutoring Systems." In *Handbook of Human–Computer Interaction*, edited by M. G. Helander, T. K. Landauer, and P. V. Prabhu, 849–74. Amsterdam: North-Holland.

Corbett, A., Kauffman, L., Maclaren, B., Wagner, A., and Jones, E. 2010. "A Cognitive Tutor for Genetics Problem Solving: Learning Gains and Student Modeling." *Journal of Educational Computing Research* 42: 219–39.

Davenport, J. L., Rafferty, A. N., and Yaron, D. J. 2018. "Whether and How Authentic Contexts Using a Virtual Chemistry Lab Support Learning." *Journal of Chemical Education* 95, no. 8: 1250–59.

de Jong, T. 2006. "Computer Simulations—Technological Advances in Inquiry Learning." *Science* 312: 532–33.

de Jong, T., Lazonder, A. W., Chinn, C. A., Fischer, F., Gobert, J., Hmelo-Silver, C. E., Koedinger, K. R., Krajcik, J. S., Kyza, E. A., Linn, M. C., Pedaste, M., Scheiter, K., and Zacharia, Z. C. 2023. "Let's Talk Evidence—The Case for Combining Inquiry-Based and Direct Instruction." *Educational Research Review* 39: 100536. https://doi.org/10.1016/j.edurev.2023.100536

Glaser, R., Schauble, L., Raghavan, K., and Zeitz, C. 1992. "Scientific Reasoning across Different Domains." In *Computer-Based Learning Environments and Problem-Solving*, edited by E. DeCorte, M. Linn, H. Mandl, and L. Verschaffel, 345–71. Heidelberg: Springer-Verlag.

Gobert, J. D., Baker, R. S., and Sao Pedro, M. A. 2016, June. "Inquiry Skills Tutoring System." US Patent no. 9,373,082 (issued).

Gobert, J. D., Baker, R.S., and Wixon, M. B. 2015. "Operationalizing and Detecting Disengagement within Online Science Microworlds." *Educational Psychologist* 50, no. 1: 43–57.

Gobert, J., Moussavi, R., Li, H., Sao Pedro, M., and Dickler, R. 2018. "Real-Time Scaffolding of Students' Online Data Interpretation during Inquiry with Inq-ITS Using Educational Data Mining." In Cyber-Physical Laboratories in Engineering and Science Education, edited by M. Auer, A. K. M. Azad, A. Edwards, and T. de Jong, 191–217. New York: Springer.

Gobert, J. D., and Sao Pedro, M. 2017. "Digital Assessment Environments for Scientific Enquiry Practices." In The Wiley *Handbook of Cognition and Assessment: Frameworks, Methodologies, and Applications*, edited by A. A. Rupp and J. P. Leighton, 508–34. Chichester: Wiley/Blackwell.

Gobert, J. D., Sao Pedro, M.A., Betts, C.G. 2023b. "An AI-Based Teacher Dashboard to Support Students' Inquiry: Design Principles, Features, and Technological Specifications." In *Handbook of Research on Science Education*, edited by N. Lederman, D. Zeidler, and J. Lederman, Vol. 3, 1011–44. London: Routledge. doi.org/10.4324/9780367855758

Gobert, J., Sao Pedro, M., Betts, C., and Baker, R. S. 2019, January. "Inquiry Skills Tutoring System (Child Patent for Additional Claims to Inq-ITS)." U.S. Patent no. 10,186,168 (issued).

Gobert, J. D., Sao Pedro, M. A., Li, H., and Lott, C. 2023a. "Intelligent Tutoring Systems: A History and an Example of an ITS for Science." In *International Encyclopaedia of Education*, edited by R.Tierney, F. Rizvi, K. Ercikan, and G. Smith, Vol. 4, 460–70. Amsterdam: Elsevier. doi.org/10.1016/B978-0-12-818630-5.10058-22

Gobert, J. D., Sao Pedro, M., Raziuddin, J., and Baker, R. S. 2013. "From Log Files to Assessment Metrics: Measuring Students' Science Inquiry Skills Using Educational Data Mining." *Journal of the Learning Sciences* 22, no. 4: 521–63.

Graesser, A. C. 2016. "Conversations with AutoTutor Help Students Learn." *International Journal of Artificial Intelligence in Education* 26: 124–32.

Hershkovitz, A., Wixon, M., Baker, R. S. J. d., Gobert, J., and Sao Pedro, M. 2011. "Carelessness and Goal Orientation in a Science Microworld." In *Artificial Intelligence in Education, AIED 2011*, LNAI 6738, edited by G. Biswas, S. Bull, J. Kay, and A. Mitrovic, 462–65. Heidelberg: Springer. doi:10.1007/978-3-642-21869-9_70

Hmelo-Silver, C.E., Duncan, R.G., and Chinn, C.A. 2007. "Scaffolding and Achievement in Problem-Based and Inquiry Learning: A Response to Kirschner, Sweller, and Clark (2006)." *Educational Psychologist* 42: 99–107.

Kirschner, P. A., Sweller, J., and Clark, R. E. 2006. "Why Minimal Guidance During Instruction Does Not Work: An Analysis of the Failure of Constructivist, Discovery, Problem-Based, Experiential, and Inquiry-Based Teaching." *Educational Psychologist* 41, no. 2: 75–86.

Klahr, D., and Dunbar, K. 1988. "Dual Space Search during Scientific Reasoning." *Cognitive Science* 12, no. 1: 1–48.

Klahr, D., and Nigam, M. 2004. "The Equivalence of Learning Paths in Early Science Instruction: Effects of Direct Instruction and Discovery Learning." *Psychological Science* 15: 661–67.

Klayman, J., and Ha, Y.-w. 1987. "Confirmation, Disconfirmation, and Information in Hypothesis Testing." *Psychological Review* 94, no. 2: 211–28. https://doi.org/10.1037/0033-295X.94.2.211

Koedinger, K., and MacLaren, B. 2002. "Developing a Pedagogical Domain Theory of Early Algebra Problem Solving." CMU-HCII Tech Report, 02–100. Pittsburgh, PA.

Kuhn, D. 2005. *Education for Thinking*. Cambridge, MA: Harvard University Press.

Laney, D. 2001. "3D Data Management: Controlling Data Volume, Velocity and Variety." *META Group Research Note* 6: 70–73.

Li, H., Gobert, J., and Dickler, R. 2017. "Automated Assessment for Scientific Explanations in Online Science Inquiry." In Proceedings of the 10th International Conference on Educational Data Mining, edited by X. Hu, T. Barnes, A. Hershkovitz, and L. Paquette, 214–19. Wuhan: EDM Society.

Li, H., Gobert, J., Dickler, R., and Moussavi, R. 2018. "The Impact of Multiple Real-Time Scaffolding Experiences on Science Inquiry Practices." In *Lecture Notes in Computer Science*, 99–109. New York: Springer.

Martin, N. D., Tissenbaum, C. D., Gnesdilow, D., and Puntambekar, S. 2019. "Fading Distributed Scaffolds: The Importance of Complementarity between Teacher and Material Scaffolds." *Instructional Science* 47, no. 1: 69–98. doi: 10.1007/s11251-018-9474-0

McNeill, K. L., and Krajcik, J. S. 2011. *Supporting Grade 5-8 Students in Constructing Explanations in Science: The Claim, Evidence, and Reasoning Framework for Talk and Writing*. London: Pearson.

McNeill, K. L., Lizotte, D. J., Krajcik, J., and Marx, R. W. 2006. "Supporting Students' Construction of Scientific Explanations by Fading Scaffolds in Instructional Materials." *Journal of the Learning Sciences* 15, no. 2: 153–91.

Mislevy, R., Yan, D., Gobert, J., and Sao Pedro, M. 2020. "Automated Scoring with Intelligent Tutoring Systems." In *Handbook of Automated Scoring: Theory into Practice*, edited by D. Yan, A. Rupp, and P. Foltz, 403–22. London: Chapman and Hall.

Mitrovic, A., and Suraweera, P. 2000. "Evaluating an Animated Pedagogical Agent." *Intelligent Tutoring Systems* 1839: 73–82.

Next Generation Science Standards Lead States. 2013. *Next Generation Science Standards: For States, by States*. Washington, DC: National Academies Press.

Njoo, M., and de Jong, T. 1993. "Exploratory Learning with a Computer Simulations for Control Theory: Learning Processes and Instructional Support." *Journal of Research in Science Teaching* 30: 821–44.

Pellegrino, J. W. 2014. "A Learning Sciences Perspective on the Design and Use of Assessment in Education." In *The Cambridge Handbook of the Learning Sciences*, 2nd ed., edited by K. Sawyer, 238–58. Cambridge: Cambridge University Press.

Quellmalz, E. 2013. *SimScientists Model Progressions*. Grant awarded by Institute of Education Sciences (IES R305A130160).

Reiser, B. J. 2004. "Scaffolding Complex Learning: The Mechanisms of Structuring and Problematizing Student Work." *Journal of the Learning Sciences* 13, no. 3: 273–304.

Rieber, L. P. 2005. "Multimedia Learning in Games, Simulations, and Microworlds." In *The Cambridge Handbook of Multimedia Learning*, edited by R. E. Mayer, 549–67. Cambridge: Cambridge University Press. https://doi.org/10.1017/CBO9780511816819.034

Sao Pedro, M. A. 2013. Real-Time Assessment, Prediction, and Scaffolding of Middle School Students' Data Collection Skills within Physical Science Simulations. Worcester, MA: Worcester Polytechnic Institute.

Sao Pedro, M. A., Baker, R. S., and Gobert, J. D. 2013. "What Different Kinds of Stratification Can Reveal about the Generalizability of Data-Mined Skill Assessment Models." In Proceedings of the Third International Conference on Learning Analytics and Knowledge, 190–94.

Schauble, L., Glaser, R., Raghavan, K., and Reiner, M. 1991. "Causal Models and Experimentation Strategies in Scientific Reasoning." *Journal of the Learning Sciences* 1, no. 2: 201–38.

Schunn, C. D., and Anderson, J. R. 1999. "The Generality/Specificity of Expertise in Scientific Reasoning." *Cognitive Science* 23, 3: 337–70.

Self, J. A. 1974. "Student Models in Computer-Aided Instruction." *International Journal of Man-Machine Studies* 6, no. 2: 261–76.

Shute, V., and Glaser, R. 1990. "A Large-Scale Evaluation of an Intelligent Discovery World: Smithtown." *Interactive Learning Environments* 1: 55–71.

Stewart, J. H. 1982. "Difficulties Experienced by High School Students When Learning Basic Mendelian Genetics." *The American Biology Teacher* 44: 80–89.

Tabak, I., and Reiser, B. J. 2008. "Software-Realized Inquiry Support for Cultivating a Disciplinary Stance." *Pragmatics & Cognition* 16: 307–55.

van Gog, T., and Rummel, N. 2018. "Example-Based Learning." In *International Handbook of the Learning Sciences*, edited by F. Fischer, C. E. Helmo-Silver, S. R. Goldman, and P. Reimann, 201–9. London: Routledge.

van Joolingen, W. R., de Jong, T., Lazonder, A. W., Savelsbergh, E. R., and Manlove, S. 2005. "Co-Lab: Research and Development of an Online Learning Environment for Collaborative Scientific Discovery Learning." *Computers in Human Behavior* 21: 671–88.

van Joolingen, W. R., and de Jong, T. 1993. "Exploring a Domain through a Computer Simulation: Traversing Variable and Relation Space with the Help of a Hypothesis Scratchpad." In *Simulation-Based Experiential Learning*, edited by D. Towne, T. de Jong, H. Spada, 191–206. Berlin: Springer-Verlag.
Veenman, M. V. J., and Elshout, J. J. 1995. "Differential Effects of Instructional Support on Learning in Simulation Environments." *Instructional Science* 22: 363–83.
White, B. Y., and Frederiksen, J. R. 1998. "Inquiry, Modeling, and Metacognition: Making Science Accessible to All Students." *Cognition and Instruction* 16: 3–118.
Wieman, C. E., Adams, W. K., Loeblein, P., and Perkins, K. K. 2010. "Teaching Physics Using PhET Simulations." *The Physics Teacher* 48, no. 4: 225–27.
World Economic Forum. 2015. New Vision for Education: Unlocking the Potential of Technology. http://www3.weforum.org/docs/WEFUSA_NewVisionforEducation_Report2015.pdf.

13
AI-Scorer
An Artificial Intelligence-Augmented Scoring and Instruction System

Ehsan Latif, Xiaoming Zhai, Holly Amerman, and Xinyu He

Introduction

Research indicates that effective instructional decision-making relies on teachers' knowledge of students' thinking and their awareness of what students know, which can be gauged using complex, performance-based learning tasks (Pellegrino et al. 2001). However, classroom teachers can rarely elicit student thinking using these tasks due to the time and cost intensiveness of scoring students' responses (Zhai, Hadeuk, et al. 2020). The heavy scoring burden can reduce teachers' interest and thus prevents them from using complex assessment tasks; even if teachers are willing to use complex tasks and grade student-constructed responses, the scores received can delay ongoing instruction.

Recent work on automatic scoring that employs artificial intelligence (AI) has significantly advanced assessment practices. Using machine learning, a subset of AI that builds algorithmic models by "learning" from data, has shown the enormous potential of filling this gap to provide teachers with timely scores for instructional decision-making (Zhai, Yin, et al. 2020). The endeavor of automatic scoring presents complexities, in terms of both model development and the efficacious operation of such systems. More than a decade ago, Nehm, Ha, and Mayfield (2012) employed a commercial program, LightSide, to build an automatic scoring tool (EvoGrader) for biology classes. Later efforts by Liu et al. (2016) employed machine learning to automatically score scientific inquiry items that require students to write explanations for phenomena. More recently Wilson et al. (2024) employed an algorithmic ensemble approach to accurately score students' written arguments immediately. Liu et al. (2023) further developed a large language model SciEdBERT to score students' written arguments and explanations. These examples evident the potential of AI-based assessment tools that can help teachers better understand students' thinking in a timely fashion and thus support ongoing instructional decision-making and adjustments. However, as these studies showcase the potential of automatic scoring from the perspective of algorithm development and validation, studies on how to construct a system to implement these algorithmic models in practice haven't been conducted thoroughly. None of the principles or guidelines have yet been identified and published to support the development of AI-based assessment and instruction system.

Ehsan Latif, Xiaoming Zhai, Holly Amerman, and Xinyu He, *AI-Scorer*. In: *Uses of Artificial Intelligence in STEM Education*.
Edited by: Xiaoming Zhai and Joseph Krajcik, Oxford University Press.
DOI: 10.1093/oso/9780198882077.003.0013

To fill the gaps, this chapter presents an AI-augmented assessment and instruction system, AI-Scorer, including our design considerations, the architecture structure, and empirical evidence of user experience and perceptions. In doing so, we intend to deliberate on how an AI-augmented assessment and instructional system can optimally serve teachers and students through structured and systematic support. The following sections first review the existing literature on automatic scoring and instructional systems in science, technology, engineering, and mathematics (STEM) education. We then describe the design and architecture of AI-Scorer. Findings from an empirical study in terms of teachers' perceptions of AI-Scorer are also presented. Finally, we discuss future research directions.

Automatic Scoring and Instruction Systems

Automatic scoring systems are a critical milestone in learning technologies, which were built up on automatic scoring technologies (e.g., machine learning) and learning analytics (e.g., data mining, dashboard designs). These systems originally aimed to solve instructional problems for teachers, mentors, and academic professions (Teasley 2017). As the technologies evolved, student-centered learning theories began to be included in the design and students became the target users, as they may benefit from receiving automatic feedback and learning guides to self-regulate their learning (Gerard and Linn 2016; Matcha, Gašević, and Pardo 2019). Based on the variations of the users, automatic scoring systems can be categorized into three distinct types: teacher-as-user, student-as-user, and multiusers (Table 13.1).

Teachers-as-User Automatic Scoring System

Teachers' assessment practices in STEM have long suffered from the inefficiency of timely feedbacks. Teachers who use assessment tasks appreciate timely scores that can help them understand students' thinking to make immediate instructional decisions and meet students' learning needs. However, automatic scoring was not accessible

Table 13.1 Types of Automatic Scoring Systems

Type of system	Features
Teacher-as-user	The system is designed to support teachers' instructional decision-making. Teachers can receive timely scores, data analysis, visualization, and student performance reports.
Student-as-user	The system is designed to support students' customized learning. Students can receive timely scores, feedback, or learning scaffolds.
Multiusers	The system is designed to support interactive learning and teaching activities. Teachers, students, and other stakeholders (e.g., educational manager, parent) can receive timely diagnosis information to support sharing and interactions.

to teachers until the development of Clicker assessment systems in the late previous century (Mazur 1997). Clicker was an innovation in developing interactive learning environments as it enabled timely feedback in large-enrolled classes, particularly meeting the needs of college instruction. This method was spotlighted after Mazur (1997), and his Harvard Physics group successfully employed it in peer instruction and thus solved feedback problems in large-enrollment college physics classes. College students who used the Clicker rated it as an engaging and beneficial assessment system (Han and Finkelstein 2013).

A typical Clicker system is developed to support teachers' instructional decisions, which usually includes a keypad for students to send responses and a receiver at teachers' end connected to computers to receive responses. The software was developed to host and analyze the data and accommodate other classroom programs such as PowerPoint. The compatibility with other programs was critical as teachers would need the automatic scores to be embedded in their existing technologies (Trees and Jackson 2007). Clicker systems did yield some concerns in practice, such as the system's ability to communicate large-volume responses. Initially, Clicker systems were developed using infrared (IR) to communicate information. Because IR-based Clicker systems could not handle large-volume responses in large-scale classes, a type of Clicker using radio frequency (RF) was introduced and soon became popular (Barber and Njus 2007). RF-based Clickers not only could handle large-volume responses simultaneously but also were less expensive, which met the needs of large-scale classrooms. Despite the popularity of Clickers, they could only handle multiple-choice questions, which are difficult for capturing students' complex thinking when engaging in scientific practices.

Considering the automatic scoring of essays facilitated by large assessment companies (Williamson, Xi, and Breyer 2012), researchers started to use lexical features of students' written responses to assign scores. Early work in this area was conducted by the Automated Analysis of Constructed Responses (AACR) research group consisting of researchers with backgrounds in STEM disciplines, linguistics, and educational research from seven universities (Haudek et al. 2011). They used commercial programs such as IBM SPSS Text Analytics for Surveys (STAS) and the Summarization Integrated Development Environment from Carnegie Mellon University (SIDE; Mayfield and Rose 2010) to analyze students' written responses and thus examined students' understanding of biology concepts. The STAS approach needed users to build a word library to develop algorithmic models, which was time-consuming and inefficient. In comparison, SIDE—a commercial program—includes an existing word library and embedded algorithms. Using SIDE, the research group developed scoring models for assessing biology concepts in much less time and with much less effort. Nehm and his colleagues at Stony Brook University, a member institute of AACR, employed an advanced version of SIDE, LightSIDE, to develop an online automatic scoring tool: EvoGrader. LightSIDE embeds a set of supervised machine-learning algorithms and allows users to tune parameters when developing scoring algorithms. Moharreri, Ha, and Nehm (2014) used EvoGrader to develop algorithmic models for eighty-six assessment items generated from the Assessment of Contextual Reasoning about Natural Selection (ACORNS, Nehm and Haertig (2012)), a database of questions developed to assess students' reasoning about natural selection. They embedded

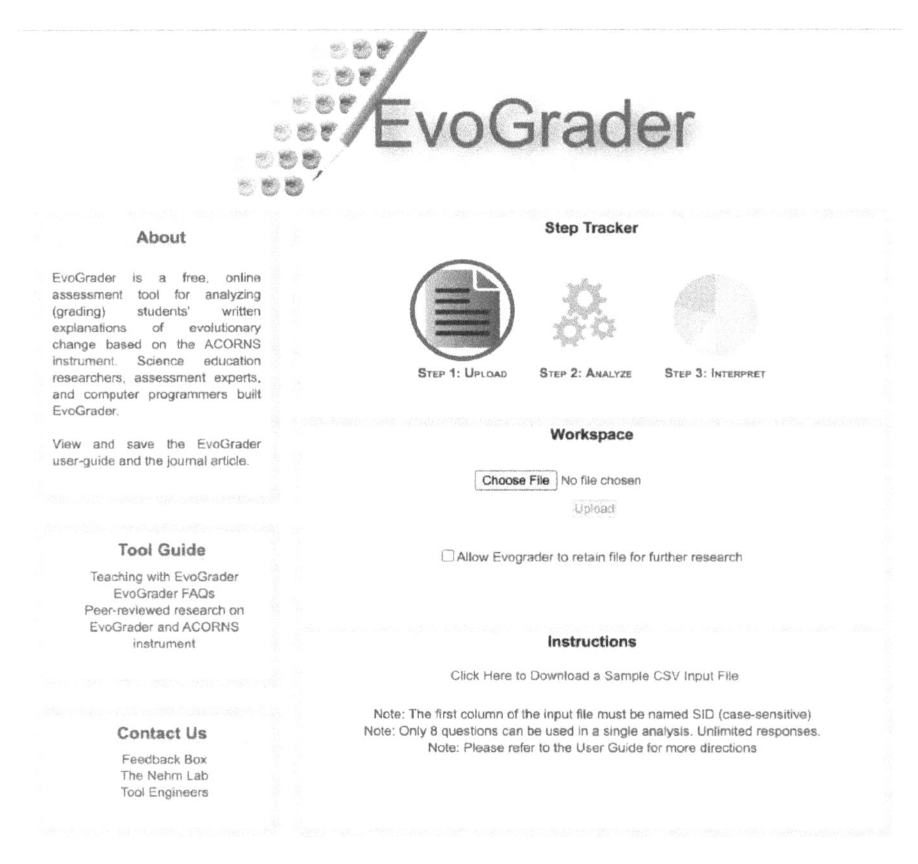

Figure 13.1 EvoGrader.

the algorithmic models in a web portal (http://www.evograder.org) so that teachers could send an online query and receive student scores immediately (see Figure 13.1).

One team member at Michigan State University adopted an ensemble machine algorithm approach to developing the online scoring tool AACR, which includes both exploratory and confirmatory analysis based on a design model (see Figure 13.2) (Urban-Lurian et al. 2013). Exploratory analysis combines automated qualitative and quantitative approaches to explore the datasets. For example, researchers could use text analysis software to extract key terms and disciplinary concepts from the responses and identify patterns and themes among ideas. These terms, concepts, and themes are used to aid in human rubric development. Using rubrics, both analytic and holistic, human experts can code student responses. During confirmatory analysis, lexical features are extracted and used as independent variables in statistical classification and/or supervised machine learning algorithms to predict expert human coding of responses. Finally, a predictive model is generated that can be used to completely automate the scoring of a new set of responses, predicting how experts would score the data.

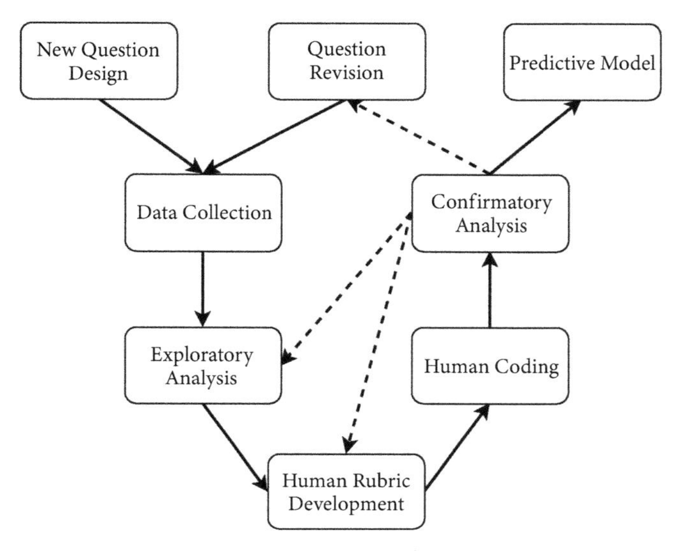

Figure 13.2 AACR design.

As for data visualization, most existing systems employ charts and figures with learning analytics to visualize the information. For example, the AACR scoring system provides visualized information to indicate the accuracy of machine scoring for each scoring category. The visualizations are found meaningful for teachers if they are designed to align with the learning goals (Rodriguez-Triana et al. 2015). Kasepalu et al. (2021) presented video recordings of students' collaborative activities in twenty-one in-service teachers' classrooms and supplied visualized analytics (e.g., social network analysis vignette) of these activities. They found that teachers perceived the analytical information as useful for them to better understand students' collaboration. Their results highlighted that purely added information, such as that delivered by the videos, cannot automatically inform teachers with meaningful instructional decisions.

The above-mentioned systems were designed to serve teachers primarily and directly and to help teachers make informed instructional decisions. They allow teachers to amass students' responses, observe a visualized analytical process, and read corresponding assessment reports. However, a gap remains between a system that furnishes information for teachers and one that teachers seek for their daily teaching endeavors. Holstein, McLauren, and Aleven (2019) investigated teachers' instructional needs and identified the knowledge that an automatic scoring system could offer: (1) students' thinking processes, (2) which students are stuck, (3) which students are "almost there" and just need a nudge to reach mastery, (4) what learning support is needed, (5) "eyes in the back of my head," (6) students' misconceptions, and (7) which students are making careless errors. It is evident that teachers require more than a complete and timely analysis report of student responses. They also necessitate that the system categorically addresses their concerns about students' learning and assist them in managing the teaching processes. In this context, a teachers-as-users automatic scoring system necessitates meticulous design considerations regarding how to visualize its data analysis, the content to be included in the reports, and the auxiliary functions beyond collecting and analyzing student responses.

As for the assessment report, teacher-as-users automatic scoring systems should stress the educational context, including the objectives, background information, and relevant parameters (Gašević, Dawson, and Siemens 2015; Nguyen, Gardner, and Sheridan 2020). Echeverria et al. (2018) developed a data storytelling approach to help teachers visualize the learning datasets. This approach includes teachers' learning design, learners' data, and data storytelling elements. Echeverria et al. (2018) contend that teachers' pedagogical intentions can be translated into rules and be read by a data processing system. These rules can be applied by computers to interpret students' behavioral indicators. The data storytelling elements help teachers focus on critical information so they can capture these elements immediately.

To assist teachers in instruction, the system should also have additional interaction functions, including human–computer interaction and teacher–student interaction (Holstein, McLauren, and Aleven 2019). The goal of these interactional functions is to link teachers' diagnosis and decision-making to students' actual learning practices, for example, to alert teachers when students need intervention, to share the reports with other stakeholders, and to respond to students' questions online (Tissenbaum and Slotta 2019; He, Chen, and Zhai 2023).

Student-as-User Automatic Scoring System

The Inquiry Intelligent Tutoring System (Inq-ITS) developed by Gobert et al. (2013, Gobert, Sao Pedro, and Betts 2023) uses educational data mining to do real-time performance assessment of students' science inquiry practices via activities including online simulations. The Inq-ITS can analyze students' log-file data and written responses to infer students' scientific inquiry competencies (see Figure 13.3). Likewise, the Web-based Inquiry Science Environment (WISE) also employs automatic scoring (see Figure 13.4). WISE incorporates the c-raterML that can automatically score student responses, which are used to provide learning guidance (Linn et al. 2014). These systems both target student users and provide students with appropriate feedback. Formative feedback can be classified into three types: knowledge of results, knowledge of correct response, and elaborated feedback (Shute 2008). Among the three, elaborated feedback is the most effective formative feedback in a computer-based learning environment (Van der Kleij, Feskens, and Eggen 2015). Besides item-based feedback, students' log data and personal information are potential data sources for generating feedback.

Student-as-user systems are designed to provide effective feedback. In the designing process, designers consider essential information needed to be provided to students, avoidance of cluttering information, and the type of feedback including predictions or alerts of students' performance, reflections on students' tasks, or recommendations about learning strategies and resources (Bodily and Verbert 2017).

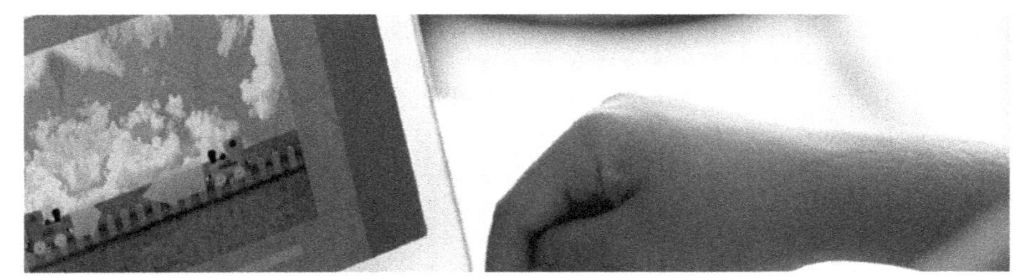

Figure 13.3 InqITS interaction page.

Although individual students are the first target, technology makes the sharing and interactions between students feasible. As collaborative learning is an essential part of formative learning, the privacy of automatic feedback needs to be considered such as sharing anonymous communications or feedback between groups (Roberts, Howell, and Seaman 2017).

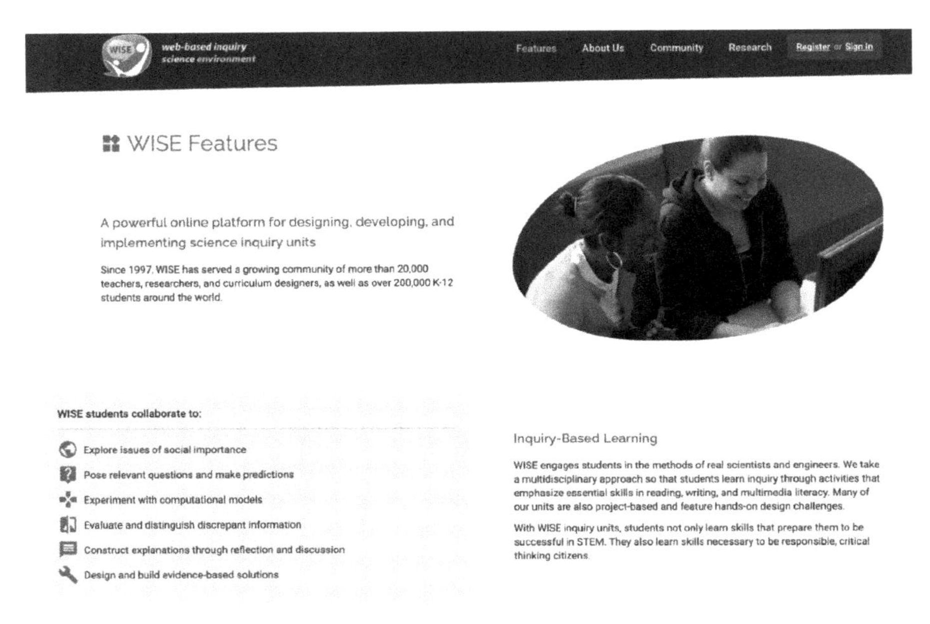

Figure 13.4 WISE Portal.

Multiuser Automatic Scoring System

Within the classroom milieu, the processes of teaching and learning are intrinsically intertwined, compelling instructional system designers to conceptualize systems that concurrently cater to both educators and learners. To serve both user groups optimally, such multiuser systems must inherently embody characteristics of both types of systems—providing teachers with quick-readable and accurate diagnosis information and students with appropriate feedback. The system also needs additional functions to support the interaction between and within groups of users (Verbert et al. 2013). This requires stakeholders to participate in the design and development of the system as early as possible and to determine the actual external and necessary internal limitations of the system (Greller and Drachsler 2012).

AI-Scorer

AI-Scorer is an assessment and instructional system designed for both teachers and students. It allows teachers to assess students' performance on tasks immediately. It automatically assesses learners' complex thinking in STEM learning using machine-learning models that can generate scores equally accurate to human experts (Amerman et al. 2022). With AI-Scorer, teachers will receive immediate scores of students' performance on learning tasks that can inform effective instructional decision-making. In addition, it allows storage of all learner-submitted materials for future reference. Teachers may utilize the system to track their student's progress, manage their classes, and provide timely feedback.

AI-Scorer is built upon a cloud service system that stores, transfers, and responds to relational information between algorithmic models and items. The user interfaces for teachers and students are built into a mobile app for both Android and iOS. Teachers and students will register and enter different interfaces based on their roles. Using this system, teachers can allocate items to their classes according to the learning topic. Students can submit their answers and immediately view their performance results. AI-Scorer also offers a researcher portal through which researchers can upload assessment items and algorithmic machine models that can automatically grade students' responses, view stored data, and analyze student performance. To serve teachers and students seamlessly, we designed the system with the following critical functions:

1. Scoring prediction via machine-learning algorithmic models;
2. Serving multiusers (e.g., students and teachers) through e-cloud storage;
3. Visualization of scores for feasible interpretations;
4. User's profile maintenance along with the details of items and scores; and
5. Class management and timely notifications of updated models to the subscribed users.

This section introduces the system design considerations, architecture, dataflow, and technical overview.

User-Centered Design Principles for the AI-Augmented Classroom Architecture

This study adopted a user-centered design approach frequently used in dashboard design, game design, wearable augmentations, etc. (Dollinger and Lodge 2018; Holstein et al. 2018). The user-centered design considers the diverse types of users, multiple aims, data interpretation needs, users' cognitions, learning sciences, sense-making of information, and the micropolitical and broader sociocultural settings in which sense-making happens (Jivet et al. 2018). To make sense of these user-related factors, designers must understand that the information generated and provided serves specific purposes within concrete environments, which limits the optimal design approaches. For example, teachers would have limited time during class to digest information-intensive dashboards; therefore, designers must bear teachers' cognitive load for interpreting dashboards in mind and only present the most critical information. If students in a classroom are from diverse backgrounds, the background information may also be critical for teachers to interpret the dashboard design. Designers need to present the critical information in such a way as to draw users' attention to the most instructionally relevant information.

Using Visualizations to Reduce User Cognitive Load

Visualization has always been a critical component in assessment and instructional systems. Ryan (2016) suggests that visualizations can be used to either explore or explain insights. However, most dashboards of AIs adopt the latter to explain the data insights. Our design uses visualizations to explain students' performance, promote efficient communication, and clarify ambiguity. Moreover, visualization is intentionally designed to engage users using different colors, lines, shapes, and sizes to highlight critical information. The visual information provided to users must be sufficient to understand students' learning process. The need to avoid extraneous data in digital teaching is highlighted at this point, focusing solely on the presentation of essential information.

Employing Goal-Oriented Design to Present Necessary Information

Given the diverse user goals of the system, the design can be significantly different. For a system such as AI-Scorer, designed to serve in-class learning and instructional decision-making, it is critical that the information provided must be able to draw users' attention and support immediate instructional decision-making. Therefore, the information presented must be selected—the most essential information instead of all information that is available. For example, we provided not only outcome information but also processing information, which is critical for teachers to understand their students' learning challenges by "at a glance" of the information provided; yet overly detailed information was avoided to simplify the interpretation processes. The dashboard provides information to promote users' sense-making and subsequent instructional decision-making.

In addition, AI-Scorer provides a filter function (according to performance expectations, grade bands, and topics) so that teachers and students can select the most appropriate information aligned with learning. We also stress that the information provided in the system is reliable. Users will receive the same result for the same action irrespective of the assessment questions or time of access. Also, our system adheres to the traditions of specific mobile kinds and operating systems, such as Android and iOS.

Identifying Information Grain Size and Synthesizing Levels to Facilitate Interpretations

It is critical to realize that raw assessment scores are difficult to interpret for most teachers. Using statistics, we may provide users (e.g., teachers) with fine grain-size information that is feasible to interpret (e.g., mean scores, deviations). Recent developments in learning analytics aim to provide synthesized information to teachers to support their instructional decision-making (Teasley 2017). AI-Scorer used cluster information to group students according to their task performance. Teachers may feasibly identify strategies to move the class forward with this grouping information. AI-Scorer also provides individual- and class-level performance information to meet teachers' instructional needs. The information provided is concise, accurate, and intended to tell stories of students at three levels to meet teachers' ongoing instructional needs.

Promoting Personalized Learning According to Students' Needs

A critical argument for adopting advanced technologies in the classroom is to provide personalized learning to fulfill individual students' needs (Zhai 2021). Given the diverse backgrounds and prior learning experiences, students need different learning supports and progress at varying paces. AI-Scorer as a multiuser system provides avenues for teachers to provide customized feedback to students as a complement to the automatic scores. Meanwhile, students can use the interactive feature to send questions, messages, or concerns to teachers. The dashboard emphasizes the use of a friendly and familiar mode of expression as well as an effective pedagogical agent to aid the learning process.

System Architecture

AI-Scorer is a cloud-based system that serves multiple users—teachers, students, and researchers. Complying with the design principles, the mobile interfaces for teachers and students provide the information needed to perform specific tasks with a personalized view for an individual student in each class. Cloud service for data backup and inferencing is set up and integrated to establish consistency in the system. Rapid response scoring functionality is implemented in the student portal so that one can receive feedback immediately after submitting responses. Students can use the feedback to reflect on and revise their responses. The system can handle procedural and administrative tasks such as creating a virtual class, filtering, assigning questions, and storing and downloading outcomes. Using these functions, teachers can manage their classes and provide customized support to their students. The system also supports evaluating overall class performance and individual student performance concerning the time spent on each task and the correctness of responses, as seen in Figure 13.5.

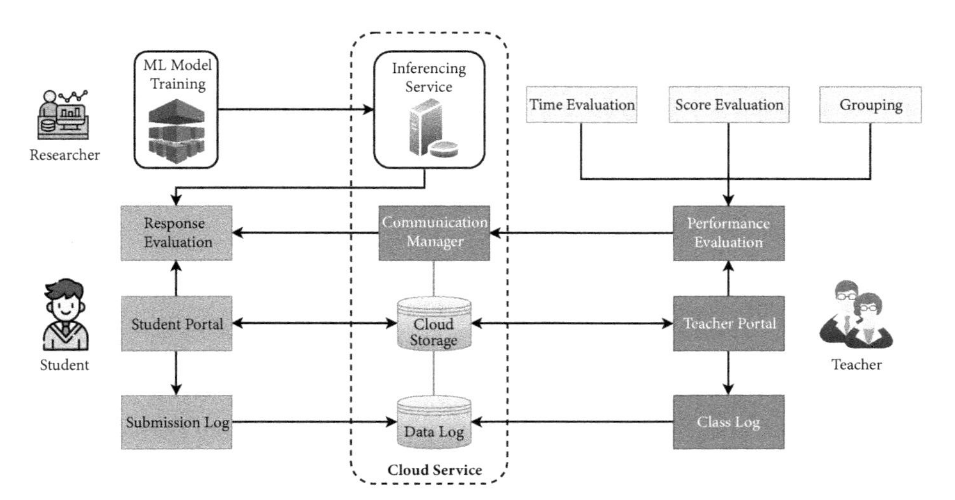

Figure 13.5 System architecture of AI-Scorer.

Dataflow Overview

Data flows between different components and users for communication and functioning of system can be seen in Figure 13.6. Mostly, data are in the form of a JSON request (Li et al. 2017), and only submission items will be sent as files to the system and stored in the cloud storage. According to Kunz et al. (2020), we designed two kinds of data in the system: residing and flowing. Residing data such as assessment items, submission files, and trained machine-learning scoring models resides in persistent cloud storage. However, data such as student responses, inferencing results, and user login credentials flow from the user to the cloud service for respective operations. In the case of model training, the researcher utilizes a model training service and provides assessment item data and the required machine-learning algorithm in the form of text and images as flowing data. Later, training services register the trained model for future inferencing to the inferencing service and store the model as residing data in cloud storage. In the case of automatic scoring, students submit responses as text or images to the inferencing services and receive scoring as flowing data. Student responses and scores are also retained in the cloud storage as residing data for persistence and record keeping. Teachers access the system through a communication manager and provide credentials as flowing data. Teachers can also view student responses as residing data and give remarks to each response which the student receives through the cloud as flowing data.

System Overview

We developed AI-Scorer for both Android and iOS users (teacher and student, see Figure 13.7). In addition, a Web portal has also been designed for researchers to create units, questions, and train models based on the provided response dataset. The functionality for each module is discussed in the following sections.

Teacher Portal

Teachers can register themselves to the system using a mobile application. Teachers can create virtual classes and register their students to the classes. They can develop virtual learning units and organize the existing assessment items in the unit. Teachers can also view the scores of students and give personalized comments for student responses.

Student Portal

Students can register to the system through a mobile application and register to any available class subject with the teacher's permission or be registered by their teachers to any class. If registered by their teacher, they will receive their user ID and passcode from the teacher. They can upload their responses to the server and get scores from the algorithmic models available for the class. Their scores and items will be stored in the server and visible to the teacher for manual grading and feedback. Students may also send comments to their teacher for any questions or concerns that may arise both before and after automatic scoring.

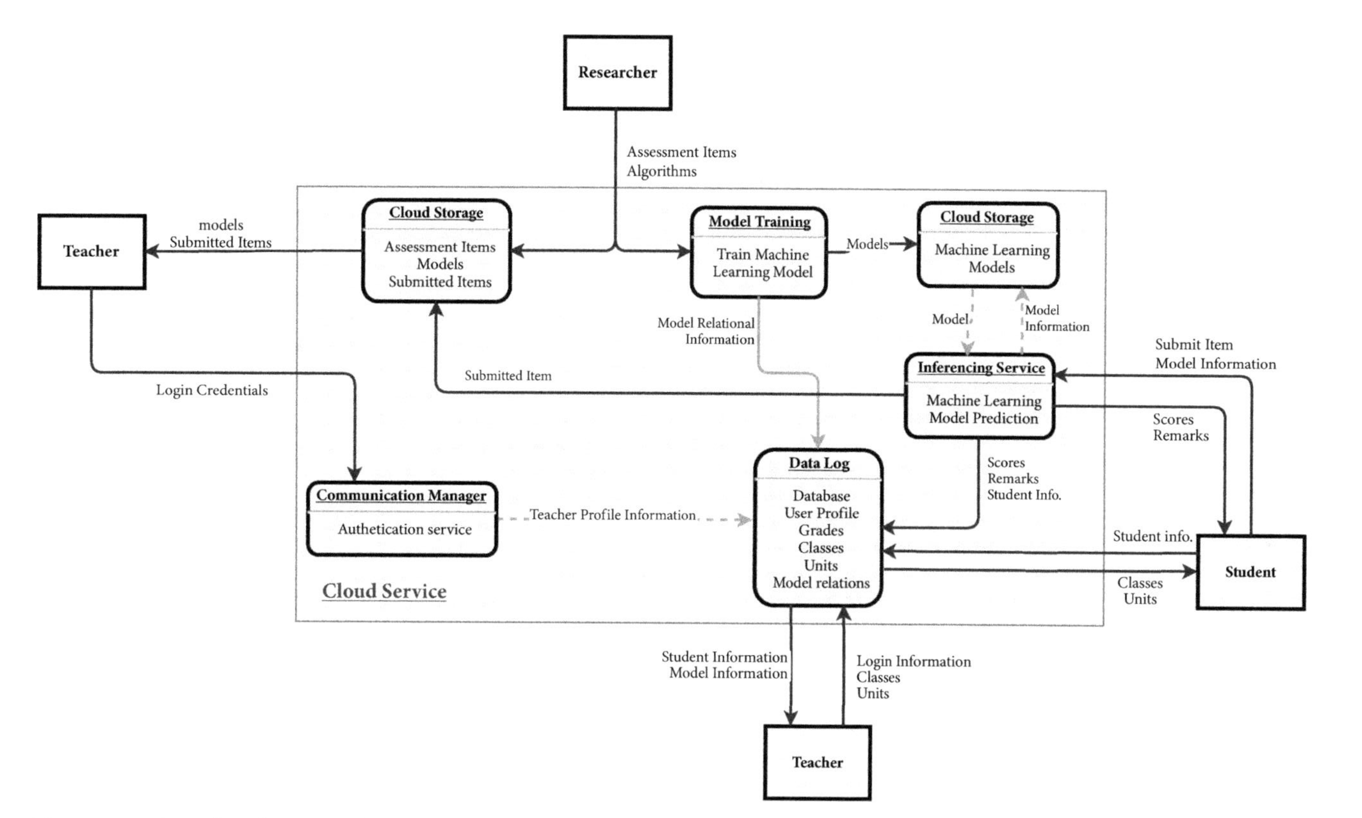

Figure 13.6 Dataflow diagram of AI-Scorer. Arrows indicate dataflow direction, and text above/below the arrow indicates the type of information in flow.

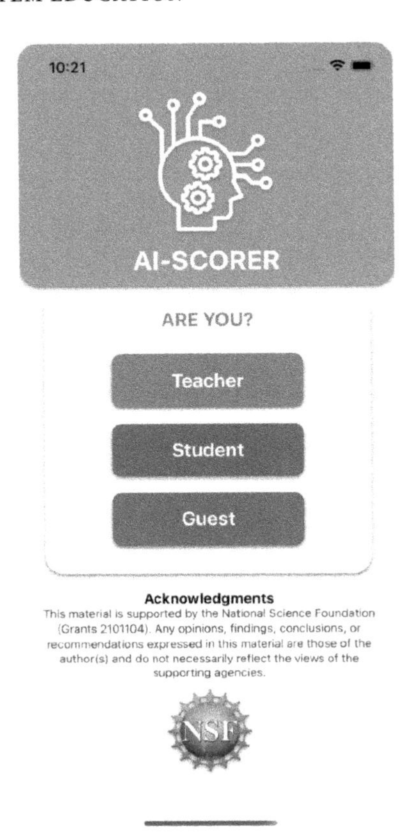

Figure 13.7 View of launch screen of AI-Scorer.

Researcher Portal

Researchers are responsible for developing tasks and machine-learning algorithmic models. They can also edit hyperparameters of the algorithmic models to achieve better accuracy if needed using our model customization feature. To achieve this, researchers must follow the steps outlined below:

1. Choose from available algorithmic models that are trained for the specific question.
2. If the accuracy/results provided by these models are not satisfactory, he can use the model customization feature to tweak the model's hyperparameters to improve it.
3. If the researcher wants to create the above workflow for more questions, they need to upload a corresponding dataset by going to the "add_question" portal.

Automated Scoring

Our Web portal has embedded algorithms for automatically scoring textual and visual responses. We have deployed well-researched image classifiers such as ResNet50

(Sharma, Jain, and Mishra 2018), CNN (Guo et al. 2022), and computationally inexpensive algorithms such as Mobi Net (Phan et al. 2020) for grading student-drawn visuals. Furthermore, we also have incorporated text-based classifiers such as Bidirectional Encoder Representations from Transformers (BERT) (González-Carvajal and Garrido-Merchán 2020), Naïve Bayes (Raschka 2014), and logistic regression (Shah et al. 2020) for scoring textual response. As discussed in the section "System Overview," researchers can select specific algorithms and use existing labeled data to train and develop scoring models using the Web portal and deploy the models on a cloud server. There are specific algorithm development, validation, and test procedures embedded in the system that can automatically be completed (Zhai, He, and Krajcik 2022). Once the algorithmic models are validated, teachers, students, and guest users can access the models. Students can submit their responses to the task and receive automatic scores in the form of performance expectations. In the following, we used one example task, "Gas Filled Balloons," to demonstrate how it works. There are five fine-grained performance expectations for this item (see Figure 13.8 for student interface design once a response is submitted):

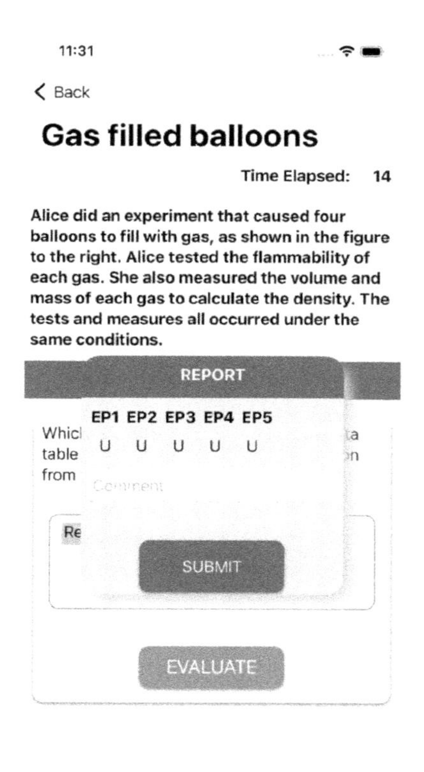

Figure 13.8 Student view of automated response screen.

Expectations 1, 4, and 5 (DCI): The student indicates that different substances have different molecules that must be made of different atoms, types, and numbers (or arrangements).

Expectations 2 and 3 (SEP/CCC): Students support a claim by referring to a pattern of data that the flammability of Gases A and as D is the same in the table (comparisons of data in different columns).

Performance Analyzer

Teachers can visualize the class performance and individual performance in terms of response time, individual student performance, whole class performance, and grouping information. Figure 13.9 shows four views of the teacher and student dashboards. The development of AI-Scorer is a collaborative and iterative process. Science education researchers, computer scientists, and experienced science teachers collaboratively work to design and revise the system. To better serve the major users, the team solicited comments from experienced teachers, piloted the systems, and revised the system in multiple rounds.

Empirical Study

The involvement of teachers in the preliminary stages of innovative technology development has proven critical to the overall success and implementation of the technology in the classroom (Mumtaz 2000). When initially examining teacher perceptions of this application, researchers determined that a focus on usability would be the most effective area of focus for designing and iterating changes to the application. Due to the lack of knowledge about AI-based educational applications, teachers

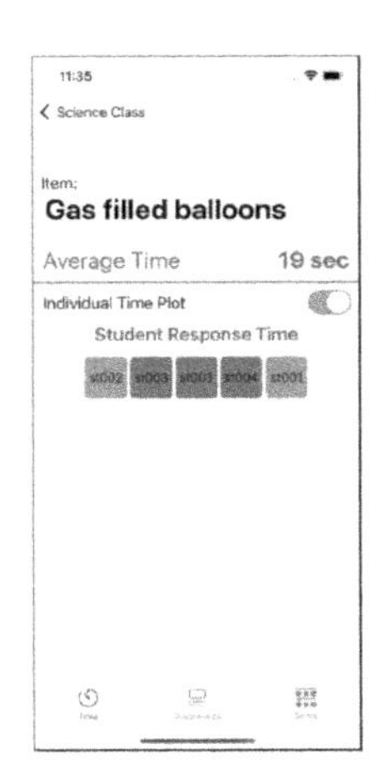

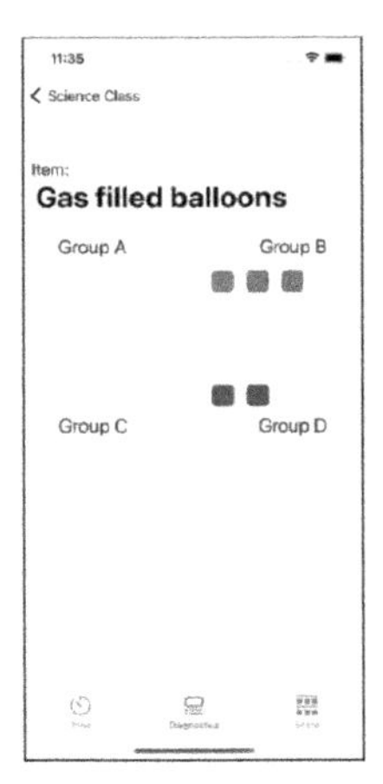

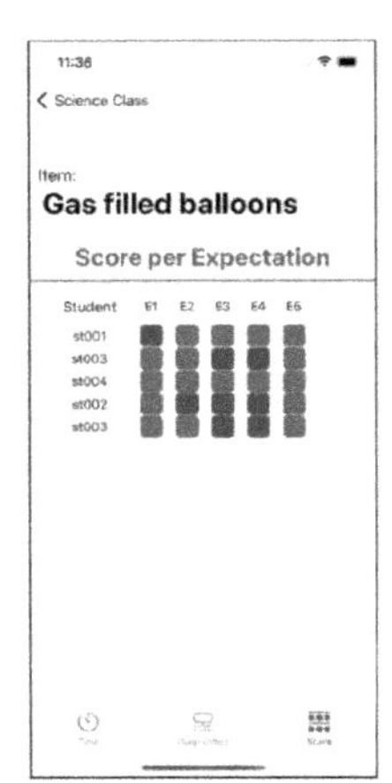

Figure 13.9 Teacher view of student performance analysis. From left to right: responding time; grouping information; individual performance on all five performance expectations; and individual student interface.

Deep Neural Network (Machine Learning)

In DNN ML, the computer looks for patterns in the data it is given, it determines the relationship between words, colors, picture, etc. It forms tight linkage between closely related items, and weak linkage between distantly-related items. Each of these linkage is called a "node" and this can be though of just as a neural network.

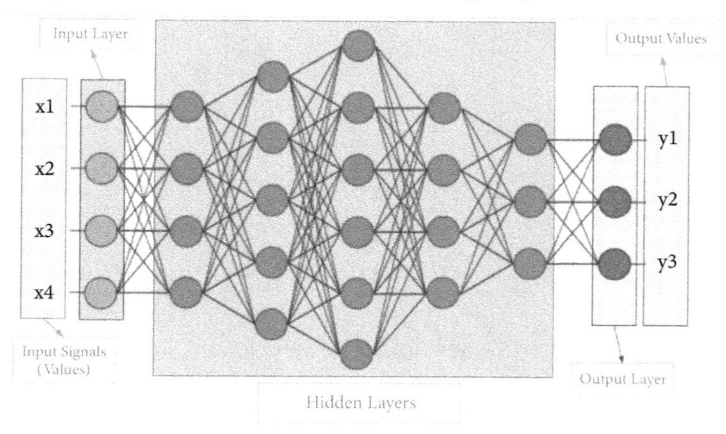

Figure 13.10 Screenshot of AI-overview video used with AI-Scorer teacher collaborators.

were given a brief introduction to AI via a prerecorded video (see Figure 13.10) and then interviewed in a semi-structured manner to elicit usable information to guide the development of the teacher and student-facing portions of AI-Scorer.

Methods

During the development of the AI-Scorer platform, three teachers were presented with an early version and asked to comment on the application based on their perceptions. In addition to the overview of AI-based technologies, as described previously, teachers were shown a brief video demonstrating the use of the AI-Scorer platform, including teacher and student interfaces, sample questions and responses, and an overview of how this would be used in the flow of teaching during a secondary science unit (see Figure 13.11). Teachers were given time and encouraged to ask as many clarifying questions as required to ensure they understood the application and its proposed use in the classroom. They were then provided several questions about their perceptions of the application. Questions to guide the semi-structured interview included the following:

1. How would you use this technology in your classroom?
2. Do you think that this technology would be easy to use? Why or why not?
3. What concerns or comments do you have about its usability?

Figure 13.11 Example of the initial grouping diagram shown to AI-Scorer teacher collaborators. (See Figure 13.9 for an updated version of the grouping screen, developed in response to the feedback from teachers.)

4. Do you have concerns about the design of this product, such as safety and security, and data management?
5. Do you have any suggestions about how we might improve the usefulness or usability of this platform?

Participants

Three secondary science teachers participated in the case study. T1 is a fifth-year science teacher in a large (2000+ students), diverse (76% Hispanic and Black), low-income (Title I), suburban high school in the southeastern United States. She teaches astronomy to mostly juniors and seniors but has also taught many other physical-science-oriented courses in the past. She self-describes her teaching as "student-driven," giving examples of "giving the power to the student" and students "taking responsibility for their own learning."

T2 is a mid-career (eleven years) teacher at the same school as T1 and is an experienced AP Physics and AP Computer Science instructor. He self-describes as a traditional teacher, saying, "The truth is, I'm not nearly as hands-on as I would like to be; I would love to do these long, very-low-structure, inquiry-based labs, but the tyranny of the AP exam keeps me from achieving that goal."

T3 is an experienced science teacher and is currently serving in a small (~200 students), private day and boarding high school in the southeastern United States. In the past, she has served at several public schools and only moved to the private school two years prior to the interview. She is currently teaching tenth-grade chemistry but has taught biology, physical science, and anatomy in the past. She self-describes her teaching as "traditional," stating that while technology is used in her classroom, it is mostly used by herself and her students to work through the "numerous chemistry problems they solve each day; there's a lot of direct instruction."

Thematic Coding

The goal of the teacher interviews was to solicit as many opinions, feelings, and perceptions as possible to inform the platform's design and usability for teachers. Due to this goal, interviews were then transcribed and coded using thematic coding (Braun and Clarke 2006). Codes were developed by the primary researcher for each participant independently and then were cross-referenced across the cases to discover themes present across the participants. A summary of the findings of the teacher interviews are shown in Table 13.2.

Usability

To analyze teachers' perceptions of the AI-Scorer's design usefulness, they were asked to share their thoughts on its usefulness in the classroom. The teachers' responses indicate a great excitement about AI-Scorer's potential use.

> **T2:** I'm actually, I'd like to say impressed, but I think blown away gets it better, if you achieve that that's kind of the golden ticket.

The teachers also expressed their desire to be able to view the student response scores in real-time, an important aspect of the AI-Scorer platform.

> **T1:** For me being able to check their progress monitor it would make better use of my time in the class, because I would only be checking on people whenever they're stuck, or whenever they need me to take kick the activity up to the next level for them.

Table 13.2 Summary of Findings from Teacher Interviews

Research goal	AI-Scorer	Other automatic scoring systems
Usability	Will help with using positive pedagogical approaches, such as progress monitoring	Do not have human–human agreements as high as AI-Scorer (ex. AP exam scoring)
Ease of use	Described as teacher friendly and valuable to learn to use	Other systems have required some level of learning curve

T2's description of the AI-Scorer platform as a "golden ticket" directly referred to its ability to automatically score student answers effectively. Specifically, teachers were told the algorithm had the ability to assign students' scores with a greater than 90% alignment with human scores. T2 further elaborated on this describing his experience as a table leader for AP exam scoring (a position that looks at readers' scores and ensures alignment), stating that he doubted he had ever seen 90% agreement in the AP reader's scoring. T1 further elaborated on the usability of having an automatically scored formative task for students, expressing her desire to differentiate instruction for students and the role that such a system could play in allowing for this.

Ease of Use

The goal of the AI-Scorer platform extends beyond the machine-learning automatic scoring capabilities to a system in which a teacher might be able to make instructional decisions from its results. Overall, the teachers believed that they could implement AI-Scorer easily and that the platform design was effective in its purpose. They also indicated they would be willing to spend the time dealing with any initial learning on the platform design and layout, given the overall functionality of having an auto-scored student response.

> **T1**: It certainly looks user-friendly.
> **T3**: I imagine that it would be like any other technology and that there would be a learning curve, and there would be some bumps. I think that the potential benefit would be worth that learning curve.

Of the responses on the ease of use of the AI-Scorer platform based on the design which teachers were presented, T3's response about being willing to have a "learning curve" to effectively utilize the system for its teaching and learning benefits was of particular interest to researchers. While technology developers often consider as many design structures to reduce the burden for users as they learn the new system, research shows, especially among teachers, there is often a disconnect between a desire to use and the willingness and actual implementation in classrooms (Chen 2011). For designers, the combination of an easy-enough to use design along with a usefulness that encourages the effort from users to learn the system is often the true goal of the design process. The teachers we spoke with indicated that the AI-Scorer platform held this combination of ease-of-use and usability.

Discussion

The AI-Scorer system introduced in this chapter represents a significant advancement in the field of educational technology, particularly in the realm of automated assessment in STEM education. One of its most distinguishing features is its multiuser functionality, which addresses a gap in existing literature and technology.

While previous systems like the Inquiry Intelligent Tutoring System by Gobert et al. (2013) and the Web-based Inquiry Science Environment by Linn et al. (2014) have made strides in automated assessment, they often focus on either the teacher or the student. AI-Scorer, however, is designed to serve both user groups optimally, aligning with calls for more inclusive and comprehensive systems in educational technology (Greller and Drachsler 2012; Verbert et al. 2013).

The integration of three-dimensional science learning into the AI-Scorer system represents a pivotal step forward in aligning educational technology with contemporary pedagogical frameworks. The system's design is deeply rooted in the principles of the *Framework for K–12 Science Education* (National Research Council 2012) and the *Next Generation Science Standards* (NGSS Lead States 2013), which advocate for a more integrated approach to science education that encompasses disciplinary core ideas (DCIs), science and engineering practices (SEPs), and crosscutting concepts (CCCs). This alignment is particularly evident in the fine-grained performance expectations embedded within the system, which are designed to assess students' understanding across these three dimensions.

Another notable contribution of AI-Scorer is its incorporation of a variety of machine-learning algorithms for scoring. Traditional systems often employ a single type of algorithm, thus limiting their versatility and adaptability to different types of assessment items (Shah et al. 2020; Sharma, Jain, and Mishra 2018). In contrast, AI-Scorer's use of multiple algorithms, ranging from image classifiers like ResNet50 to text-based classifiers like BERT, allows for a more nuanced and comprehensive assessment, making it a more versatile tool in educational settings. AI-Scorer's multidimensional approach allows for a more holistic assessment of student understanding, capturing not only what students know but also how they apply their knowledge in different contexts. This is in line with the NGSS's emphasis on the interconnectedness of scientific knowledge and practice (NGSS Lead States 2013).

Furthermore, the user-centered design approach of AI-Scorer sets it apart from many existing systems. While the importance of user-centered design in educational technology has been acknowledged (Dollinger and Lodge 2018; Holstein et al. 2018), it is less often put into practice in a meaningful way. By involving teachers in the preliminary stages of development, AI-Scorer ensures that the system is not only technologically advanced but also pedagogically sound. This approach aligns with recent calls for more user-centered designs that consider the diverse needs and contexts of educational settings (Jivet et al. 2018).

The real-time feedback mechanism in AI-Scorer also addresses a critical need in educational settings for immediate formative assessment. While the importance of timely feedback has been discussed in the literature (Shute 2008; Van der Kleij, Feskens, and Eggen 2015), fewer systems have successfully implemented this feature. AI-Scorer not only provides real-time feedback but also allows for personalized learning experiences, a feature often lacking but critically important in current educational technologies (Zhai 2021). The system's real-time feedback mechanism is particularly well-suited for the formative assessment of three-dimensional learning. The immediacy of the feedback allows teachers to make instructional decisions that are responsive to students' ongoing development across all three dimensions. This is a significant advancement over traditional systems, which often provide feedback that is either delayed or limited in scope, thus missing the opportunity for timely instructional adjustments (Pellegrino et al. 2001).

Lastly, the empirical validation of AI-Scorer through teacher interviews adds a layer of credibility and practicality to the system. This addresses a significant gap in the literature concerning the usability and practicality of such technologies in real-world educational settings (Mumtaz 2000). The feedback from teachers not only validates the system's design but also provides valuable insights into its potential for broader implementation and impact. Teachers' feedback indicated that the system would be particularly useful for progress monitoring, a key component of formative assessment that is often challenging to implement effectively in the context of three-dimensional science education (Kingston and Nash 2011).

In summary, AI-Scorer makes several significant contributions to the field, from its multiuser functionality and diverse algorithmic approaches to its user-centered design and real-time feedback mechanisms. These features, backed by empirical validation, position it as a leading tool in the evolving landscape of educational technology and automated assessment.

Conclusion

In conclusion, the AI-Scorer system represents a significant and transformative contribution to the field of educational technology, with particular emphasis on enhancing the quality and scope of three-dimensional science learning. This is in direct alignment with the *Framework for K–12 Science Education* and the *Next Generation Science Standards* (NGSS Lead States 2013). Unlike traditional automated scoring systems, which often focus narrowly on content knowledge (Shute 2008; Van der Kleij, Feskens, and Eggen 2015), AI-Scorer offers a multifaceted, real-time feedback mechanism that encompasses disciplinary core ideas, science and engineering practices, and crosscutting concepts. This holistic approach to assessment and feedback not only fills a critical gap in the existing literature but also provides an innovative, pedagogically sound, and practically applicable tool for modern science education (Greller and Drachsler 2012; Teasley 2017). The system's capability to adapt to the complexities of three-dimensional science learning makes it a groundbreaking asset for educators striving to meet the diverse and evolving needs of their students.

The empirical study involving teachers serves as a robust validation of the system's usability and its high potential for real-world classroom implementation (Chen 2011; Mumtaz 2000). The teachers' expressed willingness to navigate the initial learning curve is particularly noteworthy, as it indicates a recognition of the system's long-term pedagogical benefits. This is a testament to the system's user-centered design, a feature that has been consistently cited as crucial for the successful adoption and scalability of educational technologies (Dollinger and Lodge 2018; Holstein et al. 2018). In this context, AI-Scorer does not merely serve as another educational tool but stands as a pioneering model for future research and development in educational technology. It offers a scalable, effective, and empirically validated solution that has the potential to revolutionize both teaching and learning in the science classroom, thereby setting a new standard for what is achievable through the integration of artificial intelligence in educational settings (Jivet et al. 2018; Verbert et al. 2013).

Acknowledgments

The chapter was funded by National Science Foundation. Awards 2101104 (PI: Xiaoming Zhai), 2100964 (PI: Joseph Krajcik), 2101166 (PI: Yue Yin), and 2101112 (PI: Christopher Harris). The authors acknowledge the PASTA team members from University of Georgia, Michigan State University, University of Illinois Chicago, and WestEd.

References

Amerman, H., Zhai, X., Latif, E., He, P., and Krajcik, J. 2022. "Does Transformer Deep Learning Yield More Accurate Sores on Student Written Explanations than Traditional Machine Learning." Paper presented at American Educational Research Association, 2023 Annual Conference, Chicago, IL.

Barber, M., and Njus, D. 2007. "Clicker Evolution: Seeking Intelligent Design." *CBE—Life Sciences Education* 6, no. 1: 1–8.

Bodily, R., and Verbert, K. 2017. "Review of Research on Student-Facing Learning Analytics Dashboards and Educational Recommender Systems." *IEEE Transactions on Learning Technologies* 10, no. 4: 405–18.

Braun, V., and Clarke, V. 2006. "Using Thematic Analysis in Psychology." *Qualitative Research in Psychology* 3, no. 2: 77–101.

Chen, J. L. 2011. "The Effects of Education Compatibility and Technological Expectancy on e-Learning Acceptance." *Computers & Education* 57, no. 2: 1501–11.

Dollinger, M., and Lodge, J. M. 2018, March. "Co-creation Strategies for Learning Analytics." In Proceedings of the 8th International Conference on Learning Analytics and Knowledge, 97–101.

Echeverria, V., Martinez-Maldonado, R., Granda, R., Chiluiza, K., Conati, C., and Buckingham Shum, S. 2018, March. "Driving Data Storytelling from Learning Design." In Proceedings of the 8th International Conference on Learning Analytics and Knowledge, 131–40.

Gašević, D., Dawson, S., and Siemens, G. 2015. "Let's Not Forget: Learning Analytics Are about Learning." *TechTrends* 59, no. 1: 64–71.

Greller, W., and Drachsler, H. 2012. "Translating Learning into Numbers: A Generic Framework for Learning Analytics." *Journal of Educational Technology & Society* 15, no. 3: 42–57.

Gerard, L. F., and Linn, M. C. 2016. "Using Automated Scores of Student Essays to Support Teacher Guidance in Classroom Inquiry." *Journal of Science Teacher Education* 27, no. 1: 111–29.

Gobert, J. D., Sao Pedro, M.A., and Betts, C.G. 2023. "An AI-Based Teacher Dashboard to Support Students' Inquiry: Design Principles, Features, and Technological Specifications." In Handbook of Research on Science Education, Vol. III, edited by N. Lederman, D. Zeidler, and J. Lederman, 1011–44. Amsterdam: Elsevier.

Gobert, J. D., Sao Pedro, M., Raziuddin, J., and Baker, R. S. 2013. "From Log Files to Assessment Metrics: Measuring Students' Science Inquiry Skills Using Educational Data Mining." *Journal of the Learning Sciences* 22, no. 4: 521–63.

González-Carvajal, S., and Garrido-Merchán, E. C. 2020. "Comparing BERT against Traditional Machine Learning Text Classification." arXiv Preprint arXiv:2005.13012.

Guo, W., Xu, G., Liu, B., and Wang, Y. 2022. "Hyperspectral Image Classification Using CNN-Enhanced Multi-level Haar Wavelet Features Fusion Network." *IEEE Geoscience and Remote Sensing Letters* 19: 1–5.

Han, J. H., and Finkelstein, A. 2013. "Understanding the Effects of Professors' Pedagogical Development with Clicker Assessment and Feedback Technologies and the Impact on Students' Engagement and Learning in Higher Education." *Computers and Education* 65: 64–76.

Haudek, K. C., Kaplan, J. J., Knight, J., Long, T., Merrill, J., Munn, A., Nehm, R., Smith, M., and Urban-Lurain, M. 2011. "Harnessing Technology to Improve Formative Assessment of Student Conceptions in STEM: Forging a National Network." *CBE—Life Sciences Education* 10, no. 2: 149–55.

He, X., Chen, Y., and Zhai, X. 2023, April. "Automatically Generated Assessment Reports for Teachers' Formative Uses: A Review of AutoRs." Roundtable presented at the annual meeting of the American Educational Research Association (AERA), Chicago, IL.

Holstein, K., Hong, G., Tegene, M., McLaren, B. M., and Aleven, V. 2018, March. "The Classroom as a Dashboard: Co-designing Wearable Cognitive Augmentation for K-12 Teachers." In Proceedings of the 8th International Conference on Learning Analytics and Knowledge, 79–88.

Holstein, K., McLaren, B. M., and Aleven, V. 2019. "Co-designing a Real-Time Classroom Orchestration Tool to Support Teacher–AI Complementarity." *Journal of Learning Analytics* 6, no. 2: 27–52.

Jivet, I., Scheffel, M., Specht, M., and Drachsler, H. 2018, March. "License to Evaluate: Preparing Learning Analytics Dashboards for Educational Practice." In Proceedings of the 8th International Conference on Learning Analytics and Knowledge, 31–40.

Kasepalu, R., Chejara, P., Prieto, L. P., and Ley, T. 2021. "Do Teachers Find Dashboards Trustworthy, Actionable and Useful? A Vignette Study Using a Logs and Audio Dashboard." *Technology, Knowledge and Learning* 27, no. 3: 971–89.

Kingston, N., and Nash, B. 2011. "Formative Assessment: A Meta-analysis and a Call for Research." *Educational Measurement: Issues and Practice* 30, no. 4: 28–37.

Kunz, I., Casola, V., Schneider, A., Banse, C., and Schütte, J. 2020, October. "Towards Tracking Data Flows in Cloud Architectures." In 2020 IEEE 13th International Conference on Cloud Computing (CLOUD), 445–52.

Li, Y., Katsipoulakis, N. R., Chandramouli, B., Goldstein, J., and Kossmann, D. 2017. "Mison: A Fast JSON Parser for Data Analytics." *Proceedings of the VLDB Endowment 10*, no. 10: 1118–29.

Linn, M. C., Gerard, L., Ryoo, K., McElhaney, K., Liu, O. L., and Rafferty, A. N. 2014. "Computer-Guided Inquiry to Improve Science Learning." *Science* 344, no. 6180: 155–56.

Liu, Z., He, X., Liu, L., Liu, T., and Zhai, X. 2023. "Context Matters: A Strategy to Pre-train Language Model for Science Education." In *International Conference on Artificial Intelligence in Education*, 666–74. Cham, Switzerland: Springer Nature.

Liu, O. L., Rios, J. A., Heilman, M., Gerard, L., and Linn, M. C. 2016. "Validation of Automated Scoring of Science Assessments." *Journal of Research in Science Teaching* 53, no. 2: 215–33.

Matcha, W., Gašević, D., and Pardo, A. 2019. "A Systematic Review of Empirical Studies on Learning Analytics Dashboards: A Self-Regulated Learning Perspective." *IEEE Transactions on Learning Technologies* 13, no. 2: 226–45.

Mayfield, E., and Rosé, C. 2010, June. "An Interactive Tool for Supporting Error Analysis for Text Mining." In Proceedings of the NAACL HLT 2010 Demonstration Session, 25–28.

Mazur, E. 1997, March. "Peer Instruction: Getting Students to Think in Class." In American Institute of Physics Conference Proceedings, 981–88.

Moharreri, K., Ha, M., and Nehm, R. H. 2014. "EvoGrader: An Online Formative Assessment Tool for Automatically Evaluating Written Evolutionary Explanations." *Evolution: Education and Outreach* 7, no. 1: 15.

Mumtaz, S. 2000. "Factors Affecting Teachers' Use of Information and Communications Technology: A Review of the Literature." *Journal of Information Technology for Teacher Education* 9, no. 3: 319–42.

National Research Council, Division of Behavioral, Board on Science Education, & Committee on a Conceptual Framework for New K-12 Science Education Standards. 2012. *A framework for K-12 science education: Practices, crosscutting concepts, and core ideas.* National Academies Press.

Nehm, R. H., Ha, M., and Mayfield, E. 2012. "Transforming Biology Assessment with Machine Learning: Automated Scoring of Written Evolutionary Explanations." *Journal of Science Education and Technology* 21, no. 1: 183–96.

Nehm, R. H., and Haertig, H. 2012. "Human vs. Computer Diagnosis of Students' Natural Selection Knowledge: Testing the Efficacy of Text Analytic Software." *Journal of Science Education and Technology* 21, no. 1: 56–73.

Next Generation Science Standards (NGSS) Lead States. 2013. *Next Generation Science Standards: For States, by States.* Washington, DC: National Academies Press.

Nguyen, A., Gardner, L., and Sheridan, D. 2020. "A Design Methodology for Learning Analytics Information Systems: Informing Learning Analytics Development with Learning Design." In *Hawaii International Conference on System Sciences 2020* (HICSS-53).

Pellegrino, J. W., Glaser, R., Chudowsky, N., and National Resource Council. 2001. *Knowing What Students Know: The Science and Design of Educational Assessment.* Washington, DC: National Academies Press.

Phan, H., He, Y., Savvides, M., and Shen, Z. 2020. "Mobinet: A Mobile Binary Network for Image Classification." In Proceedings of the IEEE/CVF Winter Conference on Applications of Computer Vision, 3453–62.

Raschka, S. 2014. "Naive Bayes and Text Classification Introduction and Theory." *arXiv preprint arXiv:1410.5329.*

Roberts, L. D., Howell, J. A., and Seaman, K. 2017. "Give me a Customizable Dashboard: Personalized Learning Analytics Dashboards in Higher Education." *Technology, Knowledge and Learning* 22, no. 3: 317–33.

Rodríguez-Triana, M. J., Martínez-Monés, A., Asensio-Pérez, J. I., and Dimitriadis, Y. 2015. "Scripting and Monitoring Meet Each Other: Aligning Learning Analytics and Learning Design to Support Teachers in Orchestrating CSCL Situations." *British Journal of Educational Technology* 46, no. 2: 330–43.

Ryan, L. 2016. *The Visual Imperative: Creating a Visual Culture of Data Discovery.* Burlington, MA: Morgan Kaufmann.

Shah, K., Patel, H., Sanghvi, D., and Shah, M. 2020. "A Comparative Analysis of Logistic Regression, Random Forest and KNN Models for the Text Classification." *Augmented Human Research* 5, no. 1: 1–16.

Sharma, N., Jain, V., and Mishra, A. 2018. "An Analysis of Convolutional Neural Networks for Image Classification." *Procedia Computer Science* 132: 377–84.

Shute, V. J. 2008. "Focus on Formative Feedback." *Review of Educational Research 78*, no. 1: 153–89.

Teasley, S. D. 2017. "Student Facing Dashboards: One Size Fits All?" *Technology, Knowledge and Learning* 22, no. 3: 377–84.

Tissenbaum, M., and Slotta, J. 2019. "Supporting Classroom Orchestration with Real-Time Feedback: A Role for Teacher Dashboards and Real-Time Agents." *International Journal of Computer-Supported Collaborative Learning* 14, no. 3: 325–51.

Trees, A. R., and Jackson, M. H. 2007. "The Learning Environment in Clicker Classrooms: Student Processes of Learning and Involvement in Large University-Level Courses Using Student Response Systems." *Learning, Media and Technology* 32, no. 1: 21–40.

Urban-Lurain, M., Prevost, L., Haudek, K. C., Henry, E. N., Berry, M., and Merrill, J. E. 2013, October. "Using Computerized Lexical Analysis of Student Writing to Support Just-in-Time Teaching in Large Enrollment STEM Courses." In *2013 IEEE Frontiers in Education Conference (FIE)*, 1709–15.

Van der Kleij, F. M., Feskens, R. C., and Eggen, T. J. 2015. "Effects of Feedback in a Computer-Based Learning Environment on Students' Learning Outcomes: A Meta-analysis." *Review of Educational Research* 85, no. 4: 475–511.

Verbert, K., Duval, E., Klerkx, J., Govaerts, S., and Santos, J. L. 2013. "Learning Analytics Dashboard Applications." *American Behavioral Scientist* 57, no. 10: 1500–9.

Williamson, D. M., Xi, X., and Breyer, F. J. 2012. "A Framework for Evaluation and Use of Automated Scoring." *Educational Measurement: Issues and Practice* 31, no. 1: 2–13.

Wilson, C. D., Haudek, K. C., Osborne, J. F., Buck Bracey, Z. E., Cheuk, T., Donovan, B. M., Stuhlsatz, M. A. M., Santiago, M. M., and Zhai, X. 2024. "Using Automated Analysis to Assess Middle School Students' Competence with Scientific Argumentation." *Journal of Research in Science Teaching* 61, no. 1: 38–69.

Zhai, X. 2021. "Advancing Automatic Guidance in Virtual Science Inquiry: From Ease of Use to Personalization." *Educational Technology Research and Development: ETR & D* 69, no. 1: 255–58.
Zhai, X., Haudek, K., Shi, L., Nehm, R., and Urban-Lurain, M. 2020. "From Substitution to Redefinition: A Framework of Machine Learning-Based Science Assessment." *Journal of Research in Science Teaching* 57, no. 9: 1430–59.
Zhai, X., Yin, Y., Pellegrino, J. W., Haudek, K. C., and Shi, L. 2020. "Applying Machine Learning in Science Assessment: A Systematic Review." *Studies in Science Education* 56, no. 1: 111–51.
Zhai, X., He, P., and Krajcik, J. 2022. "Applying Machine Learning to Automatically Assess Scientific Models." *Journal of Research in Science Teaching* 59, no. 10: 1765–94. https://doi.org/10.1002/tea.21773.

14
Smart Learning Partner
Chinese Core Competency-Oriented Adaptive Learning System

Lei Wang, Cong Wang, Quan Wang, Jiutong Luo and Xijuan Li

Introduction

In today's fast-paced and rapidly evolving technological world, adaptive learning systems (ALSs) are gaining immense popularity in the field of science education. These systems offer a personalized and adaptive learning experience, catering to the individual needs and preferences of the learners. Moreover, assessing core competencies is a complex undertaking that requires a comprehensive consideration of various factors, including the nature of core competencies, assessment objectives, assessment methods, assessment indicators, and data analysis (Duong 2016; Holmes and Hooper 2000; Kawshala 2017). To tackle this, a systematic research and design approach is necessary.

The development of adaptive learning systems that can automatically collect student performance data (Crawford 2000), such as online learning management systems and automated assignment grading systems (Lee et al. 2021; Wang et al. 2021), is crucial to support the automation of the assessment process. Nonetheless, it's vital to study how to effectively apply the results of core competency assessment to teaching practice.

The Smart Learning Partner system is one such adaptive learning system that has been developed with a focus on the core competencies in science education, aiming to enhance the learning experience of students by integrating advanced technologies and methodologies that align with the core competencies. This chapter outlines the Smart Learning Partner system, including its features, competency integration, design, implementation, and use in science education.

Literature Review

Core Competency in Science Education

The proposal of core competency can be regarded as a sign of the shift from a knowledge-oriented to a competency-oriented approach in education around the world. In response to challenges such as globalization of the knowledge economy

Lei Wang et al., *Smart Learning Partner*. In: *Uses of Artificial Intelligence in STEM Education*.
Edited by: Xiaoming Zhai and Joseph Krajcik, Oxford University Press. © Oxford University Press (2024).
DOI: 10.1093/oso/9780198882077.003.0014

and rapid technological development, countries and regions have defined the connotations and developed frameworks of core competency based on their own social, economic, and educational development needs (Duong 2016; Holmes and Hooper 2000; Kawshala 2017).

In 2006, the European Union proposed the "European Reference Framework for Lifelong Core Competency," which defines competency as the combination of knowledge, skills, and attitudes that are appropriate to a particular context (European Commission 2007) and as the foundation for personal achievement and development, social integration, and successful employment (Williamson, Xi, and Breyer 2012; Zhai, Haudek, et al. 2020). It elaborates on the eight core competency contents, including native language communication, foreign language communication, mathematical competency, basic scientific and technological competency, digital competency, learning to learn, social and civic competency, and creativity and innovation.

In 2009, the Partnership for 21st Century Skills in the United States developed the "Framework for 21st Century Learning" (Trilling and Fadel 2009), which identifies three indispensable sets of skills for the twenty-first century: learning and innovation skills, digital competency skills, and career and life skills (Bernhardt 2015). These include critical thinking and problem-solving, communication and collaboration, creativity and innovation, information competency, media competency, information and communication technology competency, adaptability and flexibility, initiative and self-direction, social and cross-cultural skills, productivity and accountability, and leadership and responsibility.

In 2016, the general framework for students' development of core competency in China was officially released, defining students' development of core competency as "the essential qualities and key abilities that students should possess to meet the needs of lifelong and social development" (Xin et al. 2016). It involves three aspects: cultural foundation, autonomous development, and social participation, and is comprehensively manifested in six core literacies, including humanistic accomplishment, scientific spirit, learning to learn, healthy living, responsibility, and innovative practice.

Starting from the essential characteristics of each discipline, the General Senior High School Curriculum Standards issued in 2017 and the Compulsory Education Curriculum Standards issued in 2022 condensed the core competencies of each subject, realized the specific expression of core competencies in specific disciplines, and clarified the correct values, essential qualities, and key abilities that students should achieve after learning the course. For example, the core competencies that information technology curriculum should cultivate include information awareness, computational thinking, digital learning and innovation, and information social responsibility. These four core elements are not isolated from each other, but support and blend with each other in terms of content, depend on and penetrate each other logically, and jointly promote the improvement of students' digital competency and skills.

In various countries and regions, there are relatively well-formed frameworks for core competencies. After decades of development, cognitive diagnosis has also developed many mature and stable cognitive diagnosis models. However, research on measuring core competencies based on cognitive diagnosis is still in its early stages.

The cognitive model of a disciplinary field is constructed by disciplinary experts, including cognitive attributes such as core competency, disciplinary knowledge, and disciplinary skills, as well as the hierarchical structural relationships among them. Test items should cover each cognitive attribute, and multiple measurements should be taken for each attribute (Williamson, Xi, and Breyer 2012; Zhai, Haudek, and Ma 2023). By establishing a binary association matrix (Q matrix) between cognitive attributes and test items, cognitive diagnostic testing using student response data can provide cross-validated evidence and support for intervention program design (Zhang, Jang, and Chahine 2021). The cognitive diagnostic model serves as a bridge linking student test responses to their levels of mastery of underlying cognitive attributes and is crucial for effective cognitive diagnosis. When selecting a cognitive diagnostic model, it is essential to maintain consistency between its cognitive assumptions and the test takers' response mechanisms in the test items and to develop an appropriate diagnostic model based on specific measurement needs. Finally, the cognitive diagnostic results can be interpreted and analyzed from the perspectives of test item scores and the core competency embedded in the disciplinary field's cognitive model to attribute individual or group performance of different test takers.

Stages of the cognitive diagnostic process include constructing a domain cognitive model, developing cognitive diagnostic test items, defining test attribute matrices, selecting cognitive diagnostic models, and interpreting cognitive diagnostic results (Zhang, Jang, and Chahine 2021). The domain cognitive model is used to represent cognitive attributes and their hierarchical relationships, which can be obtained through subject experts or literature review. The cognitive diagnostic model is crucial for implementing cognitive diagnostic testing, and there are several typical models, such as linear logistic model, rule space model, attribute hierarchy model, DINA model, and multidimensional item response theory model. In terms of applications, previous research has mainly focused on academic ability testing, but in recent years, attention has shifted towards assessing core competencies (de la Torre 2009; Fischer 1973; Leighton, Gierl, and Hunka 2004; Tatsuoka 1983). For example, Gierl, Zheng, and Cui (2008) have used cognitive diagnostic analysis for personalized analysis of chemistry competency test items and for assessing mathematical core competencies based on the rule space model.

Adaptive Learning Systems (ALS) in STEM

Martin et al. (2020) conducted a systematic review of research on adaptive learning and found that adaptive feedback and adaptive navigation were the most investigated adaptive targets. There was significant diversity within studies emphasizing the adaptive target, within both the instructional model and the content model. This emphasizes the need for adaptive learning researchers to consider the broader scope of the adaptive learning model, including the source and target. Therefore, future studies should focus more on adaptive learning as a learning technology to improve its ability and availability in individual learning and personalized growth.

Martin et al. (2020) designed an adaptive learning framework that combines elements from two previous frameworks (Figure 14.1; Shute and Towle 2003; Vandewaetere, Desmet, and Clarebout 2011). It includes a learner model, an instructional model, and a content model. Additionally, it has an adaptive engine to make adjustments based on the learner's needs.

The learner model is a representation of the characteristics of a learner, including their attributes, preferences, knowledge, proficiency, motivational and emotional aspects, and individual differences (Vandewaetere, Desmet, and Clarebout 2011). This model is used to adapt learning to the needs and characteristics of the learner.

One of the biggest advantages of ALS is their ability to provide students with more personalized learning materials (Matt 2016). The content model, also known as the expert or domain model, refers to the content or knowledge base for the course (Vandewaetere, Desmet, and Clarebout 2011). This content model could involve concepts that build on each other and includes a learning map with relationships between different ideas and how the course content is delivered to the learner (Martin et al. 2020). The construction of domain-specific knowledge and cognitive models often requires the participation of domain-specific experts who, based on a review of existing research literature, determine the objectives and content of cognitive diagnosis aimed at that particular field.

The instructional model, which is a tool used to adapt instruction to meet the needs of learners based on their individual learning styles and the content being taught. Given that it provides a framework for determining what content is presented to learners (Vandewaetere, Desmet, and Clarebout 2011), adaptive learning systems can support teacher involvement by providing them with real-time data

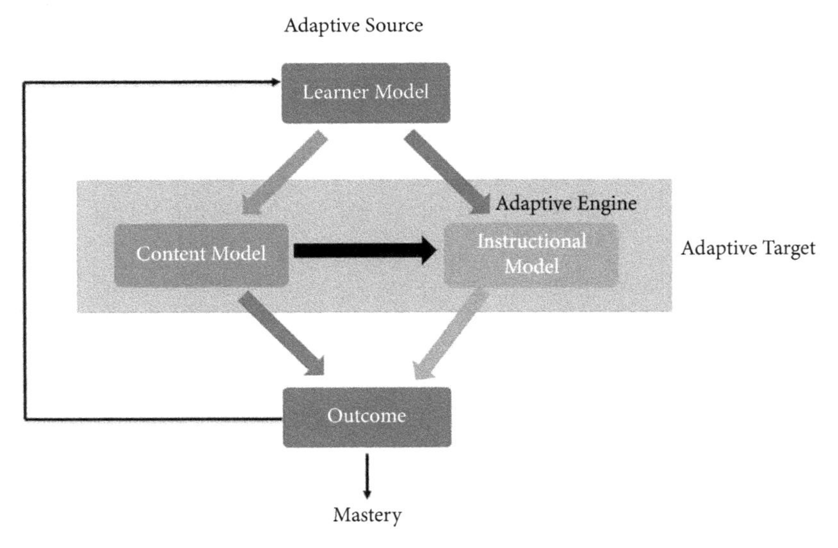

Figure 14.1 Adaptive learning models framework from. Shute and Towle (2003) and Vandewaetere, Desmet, and Clarebout (2011).

on student performance and allowing them to adapt their instruction accordingly (Keuning and van Geel 2021). This allows them to focus on the areas that are most in need of attention, and to use their time more effectively to support student learning. It also defines the techniques and tools used to adapt instruction, such as pacing, format, and sequencing (Martin et al. 2020). Keuning and van Geel (2021) discussed the use of adaptive learning systems with teacher dashboards in Dutch schools to improve differentiated instruction. The findings suggest that teacher dashboards can support teachers by providing up-to-date information about student progress but using them also requires new skills and knowledge such as interpreting information and understanding how the ALS calculates data.

The adaptive engine is an AI-based sequence generator that creates a learning map with instructional content, including knowledge and cognition, for learners in an instructional model. According to Shute and Towle (2003), the adaptive engine is responsible for selecting a topic, identifying objectives, sequencing them, and presenting them in a way that meets the learner's needs until mastery is achieved. ALS in science education involve the use of algorithms to collect and analyze data on student performance, providing valuable insights for educators and researchers (Lee et al. 2021; Zhai 2022). Supervised machine learning is where the algorithm is trained using labeled data. Supervised machine learning is also used in various ways such as automated assigning scores, classification, recognition, and predicting. For instance, it has been used to assign scores to students' scientific explanations (Liu et al. 2016), classify students' responses to physics questions (Nakamura et al. 2016), identify key learning goals (Okoye, Summer, and Bethard 2013), and predict group project performance by analyzing students' online discussion and work patterns (Yoo and Kim 2014). ALS also provide students with immediate feedback on their performance, allowing them to identify areas for improvement and receive guidance on how to overcome obstacles (Attali and Powers 2008; Lee et al. 2021; Mao et al. 2018; van der Kleij and Adie 2018; Zhu, Liu, and Le 2020). For example, an ALS named HASbot has been integrated with an online curriculum module called the "water module" which is designed for secondary school students and revolves around the crucial concept that fresh water is essential and scarce in sustaining life (Lee et al. 2019; Lee et al. 2021). This system is based on a simulation-based instructional approach, comprised of multiple sub-problems. Following a student's response to a certain constructed-response item, the computer provides scores and corresponding feedback. Through the employment of personalized feedback, students undertake adaptive learning by modifying their argumentative positions. Furthermore, ALS can track students' progress over time and provide teachers and administrators with valuable insights into student performance, enabling them to make data-driven decisions about instruction (Krajcik 2021; Zhai, Yin, et al. 2020). In Pan, Cayton-Hodge, and Feng's (2015) and Shute, Ke, and Wang's (2017) studies, their sophisticated game-based assessment systems gather a wide range of data on the user's performance, including response time and the use of hints, to provide personalized feedback. This type of assessment is called "stealth assessment," where the individual is unaware of the assessment process during their engagement with the game. These insights can be used to improve the effectiveness of science education and better understand how students learn (Martin et al. 2020).

Ling and Chiang (2022) developed an online learning platform and adaptive course content, as well as a corresponding assessment mechanism (checkpoints), based on the educational theory of adaptive instruction. This was achieved by progressively designing learning units to form a learning path. In addition, an online learning feedback platform and teaching assistants were available to help resolve difficulties encountered by students while learning program design with the instructor, providing solutions to problems in program design learning and instruction. The study found that adaptive instruction can better control students' learning situations, identify students' problems early, and provide timely and appropriate assistance to help improve students' different levels and qualities. Moreover, the study results also indicate that assistance provided by teaching assistants and online teaching platforms can provide more resources to fulfill the ideas of adaptive instruction.

Azevedo et al. (2022) provided an overview of self-regulated learning (SRL) research conducted over the past decade using MetaTutor, a hypermedia-based intelligent tutoring system (Figure 14.2). MetaTutor was designed to support college students in learning about the human circulatory system while developing their SRL skills. The system is based on SRL models, multimedia learning principles, AI, and prior research on SRL. Analytical techniques used in this research include educational data-mining techniques, such as cluster analysis and sequence mining, unsupervised machine-learning techniques to examine complex eye-tracking data and facial expressions of emotion, dynamical systems modeling, and machine-learning algorithms to predict performance at the end of the learning session.

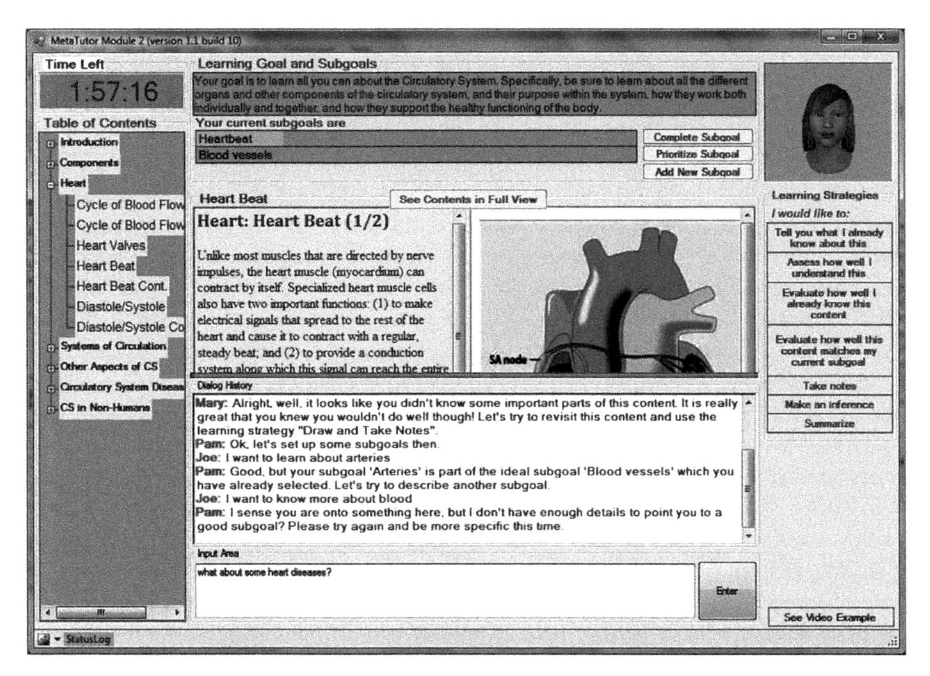

Figure 14.2 MetaTutor's main interface elements from Azevedo et al. (2022).

These techniques have been used to examine metacognitive and cognitive behaviors during learning with MetaTutor, and have been shown to provide more comprehensive insights than traditional inferential statistics. The research conducted with MetaTutor has contributed significantly to our understanding of SRL and has the potential to inform the design of effective learning technologies that promote SRL.

Zulfiani, Suwarna, and Miranto (2018) developed the ScEd-Adaptive Learning System (ScEd-ASL) by applying computer-based instruction to students' visual, aural, read/write, and kinesthetic learning styles (Figure 14.3). The uniqueness of this media is its integration of science materials, accommodating both fast and slow learners and matching their learning styles. ScEd-ASL was found to be highly effective for students with kinesthetic learning style, followed by aural, read/write, and visual learning styles.

Aguar et al. (2017) conducted a case study using the Web-based adaptive learning system Adaptive Learning for Interdisciplinary Collaborative Environments (ALICE) to promote interdisciplinary instruction. The study discussed instructional design factors, including structured materials, assessment development, and other instructional design considerations through the exploration of a case study implementing ALICE in a graduate level systems biology course. The influence of ALICE on instructional design aspects was detailed and discussed while providing the architecture and guidelines to incorporate ALICE in one's course. The study suggests that with the help of ALICE, the classroom environment should shift from a lecture-based approach to a discussion-based setting to encourage interdisciplinary collaborative thinking and problem-solving.

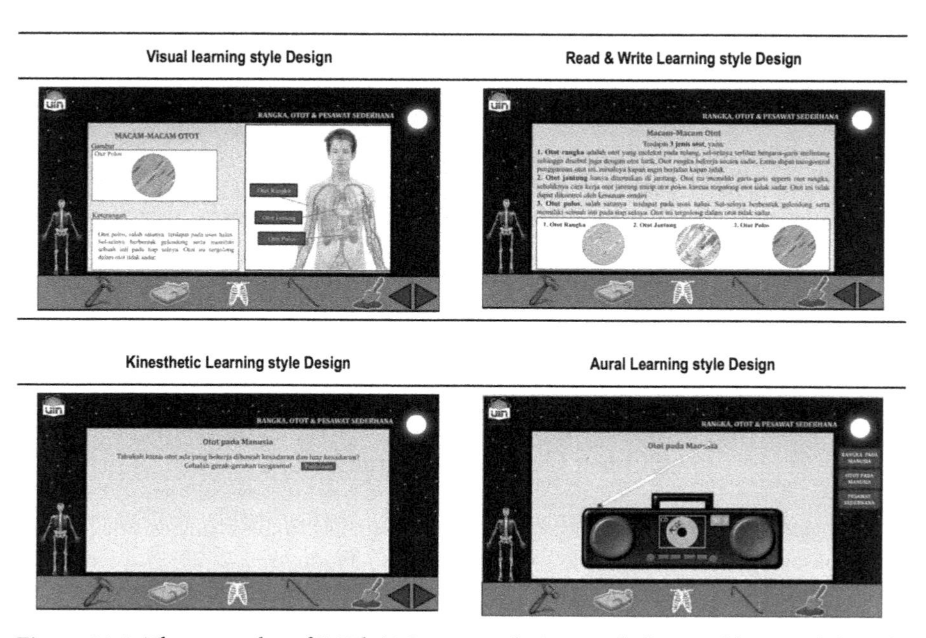

Figure 14.3 The examples of ScEd-ALS content design result from Zulfiani et al. (2018).

Studies have shown that ALS can improve student outcomes in science subjects. The effectiveness of ALS in science education has been demonstrated through various studies, with some reporting improved student performance and satisfaction compared to traditional teaching methods. Previous studies have implemented adaptive instruction in online computer programming courses and assessed the students' learning outcomes (Si, Kim, and Na 2014). The findings indicated that students in the adaptive instruction group performed better than those in the fixed instruction group. Moreover, recent research revealed that adaptive teaching competence has a substantial impact on students' academic achievement (Brühwiler and Vogt 2020). In conclusion, the implementation of ALS in science education offers numerous benefits and has the potential to revolutionize the way students learn and engage with subject matter.

However, these systems also present several challenges that must be addressed in order to fully realize their potential. By carefully considering the costs and benefits, and by working to overcome the challenges, schools and teachers can ensure that ALS are implemented in a way that is effective, efficient, and equitable for all students.

Solving the challenges faced by core competency developing-oriented teaching means making full use of the advantage of emerging information technology. Within the context of education, this means conceptualizing the whole learning process as a large data collection. It also requires modeling the structure of subject knowledge, ability, and competency toward realizing the performance of students' subject competency diagnosis and analysis to promote the development of students' subject ability and competency. To do so, the Smart Learning Partner (SLP) platform (http://slp.bnu.edu.cn) has been established by the Advanced Innovation Center for Future Education of Beijing Normal University. In this chapter, we talk about the development and potential uses of this platform toward meeting these goals.

Research Questions

(1) How does SLP support core competency-oriented accurate teaching and assessment?
(2) How should SLP be applied to promote the development of students' subject competency through adaptive learning?

The Theoretical Framework for the Construction of SLP

Subject Competency Framework

The subject competency framework (SCF) (Figure 14.4) in this study was developed based on our prior work (Wang 2016; Wang 2017; Wang et al. 2022). Subject competency refers to the stable psychological regulation mechanisms that students need to carry out cognitive and problem-solving activities when they face subject research objects and problem contexts (Feng 1986; Wang et al. 2022; Yang 2012). There are

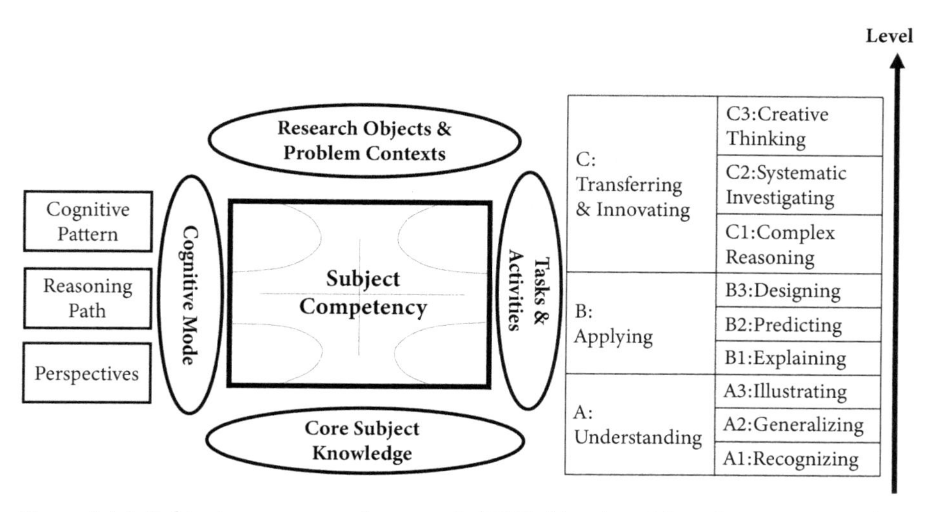

Figure 14.4 Subject competency framework (SCF) (developed based on Wang 2016).

four essential components contributing to students' subject competency. They are subject core knowledge (lower dimension), cognitive mode (left dimension), research objects and problem contexts (upper dimension), as well as tasks and activities (right dimension) (Wang 2016). These four dimensions are closely linked. When students encounter research objects and problem contexts (upper dimension), they need to use cognitive mode (left dimension) based on their subject core knowledge (lower dimension) to complete corresponding tasks and activities (right dimension).

Regarding different "research objects and problem contexts" (Figure 14.4, upper dimension), students' cognitive and problem-solving activities can be summarized into three categories:

(a) the input of knowledge and experience, i.e., learning and understanding, including mental processes such as observing and fetching information, remembering and recognizing information, generalizing, correlating and integrating, illustrating, demonstrating, and arguing;
(b) the initial output of knowledge and experience, i.e., applying practical activities, including mental processes such as analyzing, explaining, inferring, predicting, and designing; and
(c) the advanced output of knowledge and experience, i.e., transferring and innovative activity, including complex reasoning and problem-solving, systematic inquiry (hypothesis, design, implement, model building), and creative thinking (critical thinking, evaluate, reflect) (Anderson et al. 2001; Bloom et al. 1956; Kuhn 2010; Mullis and Martin 2013; National Academy of Sciences 2013; Novak 1961; Wang 2016; Wang and Zhi 2016; Wu and Wang 2007).

According to the ideas mentioned above, the upper dimension (research objects and problem contexts) and right dimension (tasks and activities) of SCF are developed. The right dimension includes three categories: (a) understanding, (b) applying, and (c) transferring and innovating. There are nine corresponding subcategories, respectively (see Figure 14.4). Students need higher-order cognitive and problem-solving activities/thinking skills when the research objects are complex and problem contexts are unfamiliar.

The stable psychological regulatory mechanism is the essence of subject competency, which includes directed and performance regulation (Wang 2016). According to Feng (1986), declarative knowledge provides directed regulation for successful completion of subject competency-related activities from a psychological perspective. Procedural knowledge and strategical knowledge offer performance regulation (Anderson et al. 2001; Bloom et al. 1956; Feng 1986). Therefore, on its own, subject core knowledge is a fundamental but insufficient foundation for subject competency (Harlen 2010). It is notable that subject competency can only be obtained when students' cognitive perspectives (e.g., analyze the substance from elemental and particle perspectives, explore the substance property from category and valence perspectives) and cognitive patterns (e.g., understand matter and its change from both macroscopic and microscopic levels) are sufficient (Zhang, Lei, and Treagust 2021). Zhang and her colleagues state that cognitive patterns contain four aspects that students should form in chemistry learning, namely, macro–micro, qualitative–quantitative, fragmented–systematic, and static–dynamic. Thus, we claim that cognitive perspectives play an important role in students' subject competency (Wang 2016; Zhang, Lei, and Treagust 2021). Accordingly, the left and lower dimensions of SCF are developed.

Based on the above, a four-dimensional subject competency framework is constructed (Figure 14.4; Wang 2016). The SCF reveals key variables of students' subject competency. It is suggested to integrate the above four dimensions (Figure 14.4) to form students' specific performance expectations (PE) as indicated by the SCF-based framework. Students' PE can be reflected by their subject competency regarding different "understanding (A)—applying (B)—transferring and innovating (C)" categories and subcategories (Figure 14.4, right dimension). For example, B2 examines students' predicting competency, e.g., predicting the chemical properties of simple unknown substances based on the principles of substance category, elemental valence, metathesis reaction, and redox reaction perspectives (Wang 2021; Wang et al. 2022).

In addition, the four-dimensional SCF can be further modified regarding various subjects and themes to generate a thematic-specific model for each discipline. This model is not only the evaluation and diagnosis framework of subject competency performance, but also the cultivation and development path of subject competency. The nine subject research teams (Chinese, mathematics, English, physics, chemistry, biology, geography, history, and politics) of Beijing Normal University foster the SCF-based teaching and assessment to promote students' competency development. Therefore, this study takes the SCF model as the theoretical framework to construct an assessment–learning–teaching system for subject competency development in SLP.

By using SCF as the theoretical framework of SLP, SLP has different characteristics from other AI-based assessment platforms in the field of science education. The core is the disciplinary knowledge graph and the subject competency performance expectation based on the SCF. The commonness of the disciplinary knowledge graph constructed by each platform is greater than the difference. The feature of the SLP platform is to build the subject knowledge graph based on the subject core knowledge dimension of SCF (Figure 14.4, lower dimension) and to focus on the big ideas of each subject. However, the subject competency performance expectation is the biggest reason that makes SLP different. The PE, which integrates the SCF's four dimensions, is the core of the specific content section in the SLP. PE itself is the key for teachers to design teaching and assessment objectives, and to clarify the level students should reach. In addition, every item in every assessment instrument in SLP and every teaching micro-resource (an instructional video specifically designed for a PE, usually 3–8 minutes long) is developed according to PE and can be coded with PE. What's more, instead of dividing the ability level of items according to the scoring rate in the past, we can accurately predict the level of items through SCF and PE, and explain whether students can achieve this PE and achieve this subject competency through the performance of students in answering specific items.

Construction of Ideas and Key Elements of the SLP

The assessment–learning–teaching system in SLP is based on the SCF. SLP selects core knowledge and activity experience (relevant experience that students gain from the experiments that the curriculum standards require students to do in their daily study) with the subject competency development value to construct disciplinary knowledge graphs, develops a subject competency PE system of core knowledge and activity experience, and develops a series of assessment instruments and micro-course resources. These assessment instruments and micro-course resources are developed according to the PEs. Besides, they are coded from several dimensions, such as core concept, cognitive mode, subject core competency, and problem contexts. As a result, a subject competency development-oriented assessment–learning–teaching system including a subject knowledge graph, subject competency PE system, assessment instruments, and micro-course resources has been built in SLP, as shown in Figure 14.5 (Wang et al. 2019).

Based on the above, SLP can comprehensively and accurately diagnose and analyze students' subject competency performance, push learning resources, and design and implement teaching in different stages of students' learning (Wang et al. 2019). In this way, the integration, precision, and individuation of the assessment–learning–teaching system for subject competency can be realized, and the development of students' subject competency can be promoted.

The AI Techniques Underlying the SLP

There are several AI techniques used in the SLP. First, machine learning, especially the knowledge-tracking model, is used to build student models and estimate students'

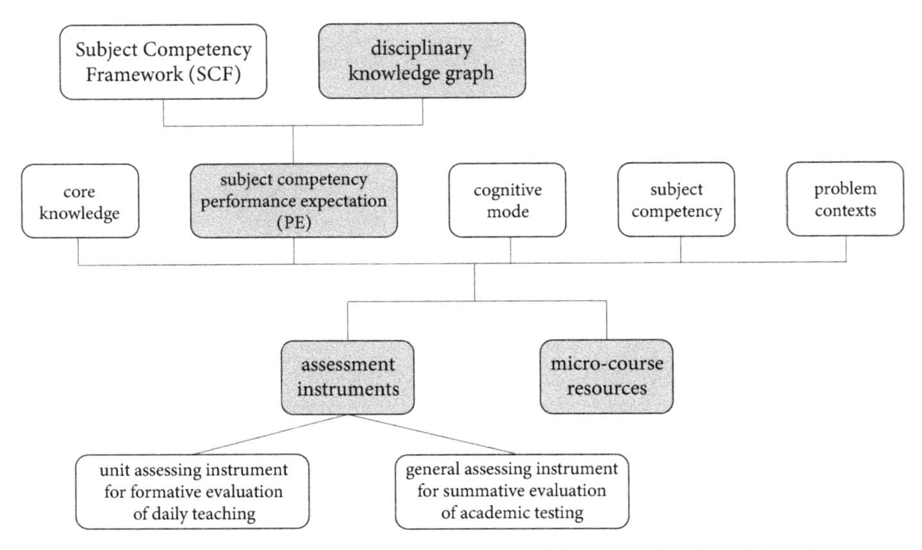

Figure 14.5 Construction ideas and key elements of the SLP (developed based on Wang et al. 2019).

proficiency at the concept level (Chen et al. 2018). In this platform, the designers specifically incorporated knowledge structure information and the relationships (e.g., prerequisite relations) between different concepts into well-known models (e.g., Bayesian knowledge tracing and deep knowledge tracing). Second, the SLP also provides a cognitive graph that shows an individual learner's cognitive status on the knowledge structure (Pian et al. 2019), which is called an adaptive learning cognitive map as well (Luo and Yu 2022; Wan and Yu 2020). The adaptive learning cognitive map has two versions, i.e., individual and collective. The individual map could not only support the teacher's understanding of a specific student's learning status (Luo and Yu 2022) but also support the student's self-awareness and reflective thinking during the learning process (Pian et al. 2019). Accordingly, the collective map could provide teachers with a whole picture of students' learning status and thus inform their pedagogical decision. Meanwhile, the knowledge-based recommendation approach, which aims to provide the best-fit learning materials for students based on their needs shown from the adaptive learning cognitive map (Luo and Yu 2022; Niu, Li, and Luo 2023), is used to generate personalized learning recommendations by the system. To better support and interpret the recommendations and suggestions from the system, the design team has also attempted to integrate explainable AI techniques into the SLP (Lu et al. 2020). Furthermore, the SLP could also be used as a platform for homework and examinations. In this case, the graph convolutional network models are used to grade students' both text and formula answers for some subjects, such as math, physics, and chemistry (Tan et al. 2023). Finally, the learning analytic approach and data visualization techniques are used in the SLP for both the learning process (e.g., materials clicked, videos watched, tests finished) and examinations (Luo, Wang, and Yu 2022; Luo and Yu 2022). Specifically, the learning reports of mid-term and final exams are visualized with different graphs and tables to make the data more understandable for teachers and useful for their instruction (Luo, Wang, and Yu 2022).

The Supporting Role of SLP in Assessment, Learning, and Teaching

The assessment–learning–teaching system in SLP lays a foundation for teaching and assessment to promote the development of students' subject competency. It can effectively support the accurate determination of subject competency development goals, online diagnosis and analysis of subject competency performance, and accurate and personalized recommendations for subject competency development resources.

Supporting the Accurate Determination of Subject Knowledge Graph and Subject Competency Development Goals

According to the content requirements of curriculum standards, experts in each subject analyze the curriculum content from the perspective of subject ontology and student learning, and establish the knowledge graph of level 1, 2, and 3 topics (core concept). In chemistry, for example, there are six level 1 topics (i.e., inorganic matter and its application), twenty-four level 2 topics (i.e., metals and their compounds), and eighty-six core concepts (i.e., iron and its compounds).

Under each core concept, a 3 × 3 (A, B, C, A1–A3, B1–B3, C1–C3) performance expectation is constructed based on the SCF and with the SCF's right dimension as the main progressive variable. Taking iron and its compounds as an example (see Figure 14.6), there are twenty-six PEs under this core concept, such as "A2 Generalizing: Establishing associations of properties, reaction phenomena, and applications of ferrite and ferrite"; "B1 Explaining: Explaining the simple and unfamiliar reactions of iron and its important compounds based on category and valence perspectives"; and "C2 Systematic Investigating: Systematically exploring the properties of unfamiliar iron-containing substances (e.g., ferrous oxalate)."

The subject competency PE system is helpful for teachers to accurately analyze the teaching content, set teaching objectives, and help students to clarify the learning content and development goals (Wang et al. 2019).

Supporting Online Diagnosis and Analysis of Students' Subject Competency Performance

Effective teaching should pay attention to the process of "teaching–learning–assessment" and "test-assisted learning" as the core mechanism of accurate teaching in the context of smart education (Peng and Zhu 2017). Aligned, a series of assessment instruments can be constructed based on the subject competency

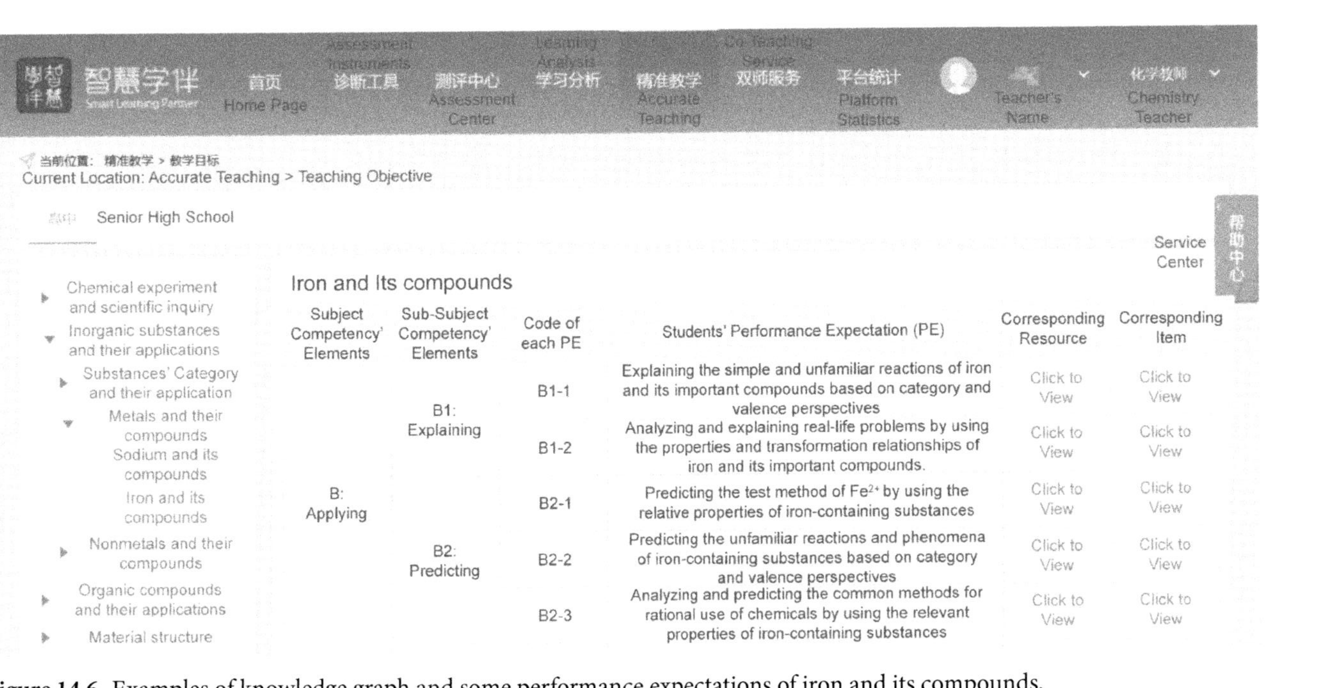

Figure 14.6 Examples of knowledge graph and some performance expectations of iron and its compounds.

knowledge graph and PE to timely diagnose and track students' subject competency performance at different stages of learning. These include (a) a unit assessing instrument for formative evaluation of daily teaching that assesses students' subject competency performance based on core concepts; and (b) a general assessing instrument for summative evaluation of academic testing that assesses students' academic performance based on the course content of the semester or academic year. Notably, at least one test question was developed for each performance expectation.

The development of disciplinary competency performance assessment instruments should: (a) follow the orientation of core competency, ask questions pointed to subject competency, and be closely related to core knowledge and experience, cognitive mode, and competency connotation; (b) create various and abundant problem situations with different complex degrees of strangeness and indirection; (c) use "choice, judgment, second-order diagnosis, open questions" and other diversified types of questions; (d) formulate the score standard according to the students' subject competency development level; and (e) code every score point from multiple dimensions, such as core knowledge, subject competency performance expectation, subject core competency, and problem contexts.

After students take the subject competency test with SLP and teachers mark non-multiple-choice questions, students' subject ability performance can be accurately diagnosed by the SLP. SLP can analyze students' performance from multiple dimensions that include knowledge and experience, the overall performance of subject competency, first-level subject competency performance, second-level subject competency performance, specific subject competency performance expectation, and specific test question answering performance. SLP can also find the advantages and problems of students' subject competency development from individual and class diagnosis reports and analyze the known points, obstacle points, and development points in depth. On this basis, students can better understand their subject advantages and problems toward developing their subject competency. In turn, teachers can better understand the problems and advantages of students' subject competency development, clarify teaching objectives, identify key and difficult points, and accurately design and implement teaching based on the evidence of students' performance.

Supporting Personalized Recommendations of Resources for Students' Subject Competency Development

A series of micro-course resources oriented by subject competency was constructed based on the SCF and PE. When we developed micro-course resources in SLP, we followed the orientation of promoting the development of students' subject competency. We set the subject competency development goal of each micro-course resource based on corresponding subject competency PE and subject competency development goals. We also paid attention to inspiration, making ideas and methods of problem-solving explicit, while taking into account the interestingness and diversity. Notably, at least one micro-resource was developed for each performance expectation.

By realizing the accurate diagnosis and personalized recommendation of micro-course resources based on students' subject competency performance on SLP, students can better master the core ideas and methods in problem-solving and develop subject competency. Likewise, teachers can recommend students to learn micro-course resources according to teaching needs.

Application Models Based on the SLP

The assessment–learning–teaching system in SLP can effectively support the teaching that promotes the subject competency development of students. Through teaching practice, this chapter proposes independent learning and classroom teaching application models based on SLP to promote the subject competency development of students.

Independent Learning Model

Based on the disciplinary knowledge graph and subject competency performance expectation system, students can define learning objectives (see Figure 14.6 for an example). Based on the assessment instruments and diagnosis reports, students can carry out self-diagnosis and reflection, and better identify their own advantages and problems in the development of subject competency. Based on the micro-course resources, students can accurately learn according to their own problems and advantages, establish cognitive perspectives, form reasoning paths, and improve subject competency (see Figure 14.7 for an example).

The independent learning model is shown in Figure 14.8. According to the requirements of independent learning, students can choose the core concepts, understand the core concepts, complete the online assessment of subject competency, and obtain the diagnostic report of subject competency performance. Based on the diagnostic report and subject competency PE system, students can identify problems and advantages of their own subject competency development, learn recommended micro-course resources, break through difficulties, develop advantages, and improve subject competency.

The core of effective independent learning is to uncover students' strengths and weaknesses based on the assessment of subject competency performance. If students are weak in the subject competency performance of a core concept, it is necessary to accurately diagnose which subject competency PE connects to students' weakness so as to push micro-course learning resources accurately. For example, the weak performance of students' understanding (A) competency through accurate diagnosis clearly relates to students' A2-1, A3-1, and A3-2 subject competency PE, leading to the weak performance of the second-level subject competency elements of generalizing (A2) and illustrating (A3), thus leading to the weak performance of understanding (A) competency. Therefore, students should be recommended

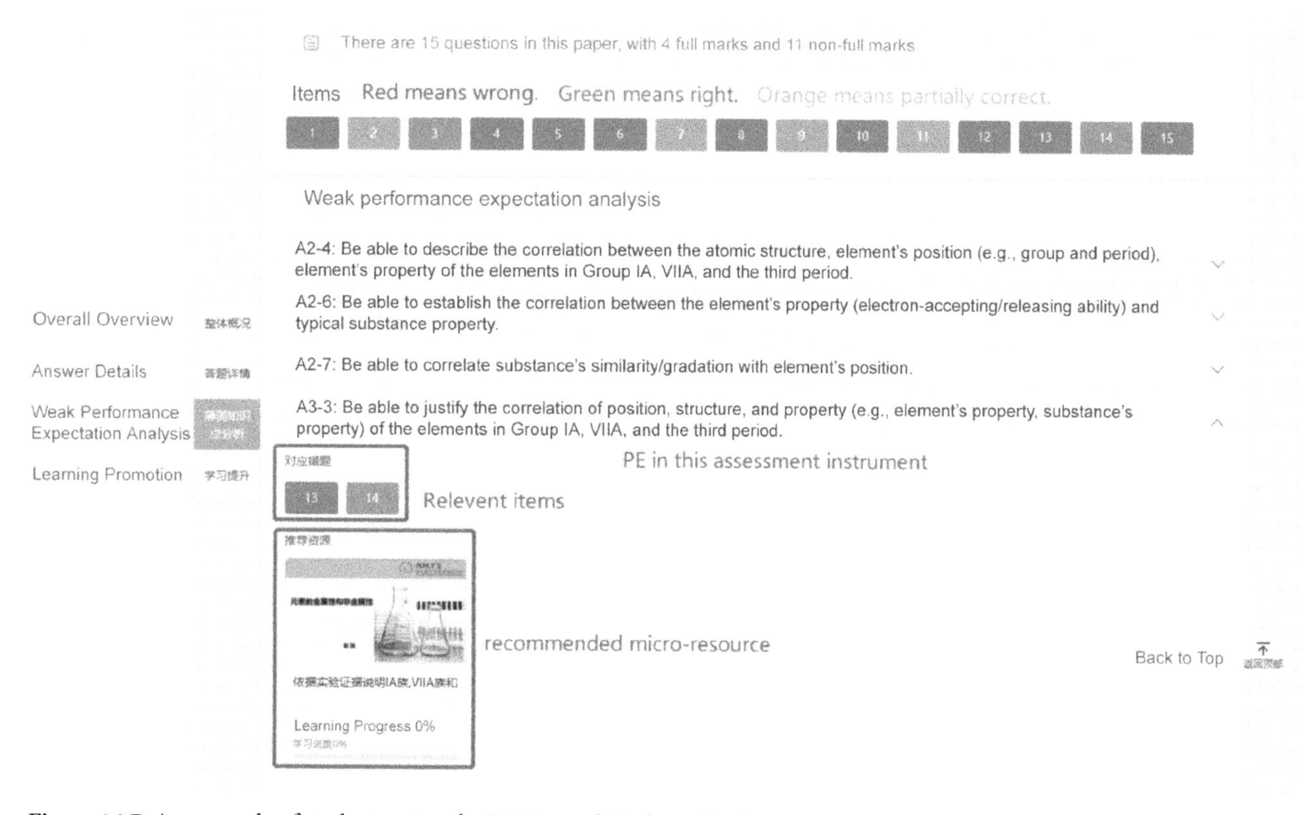

Figure 14.7 An example of students using the SLP to study independently.

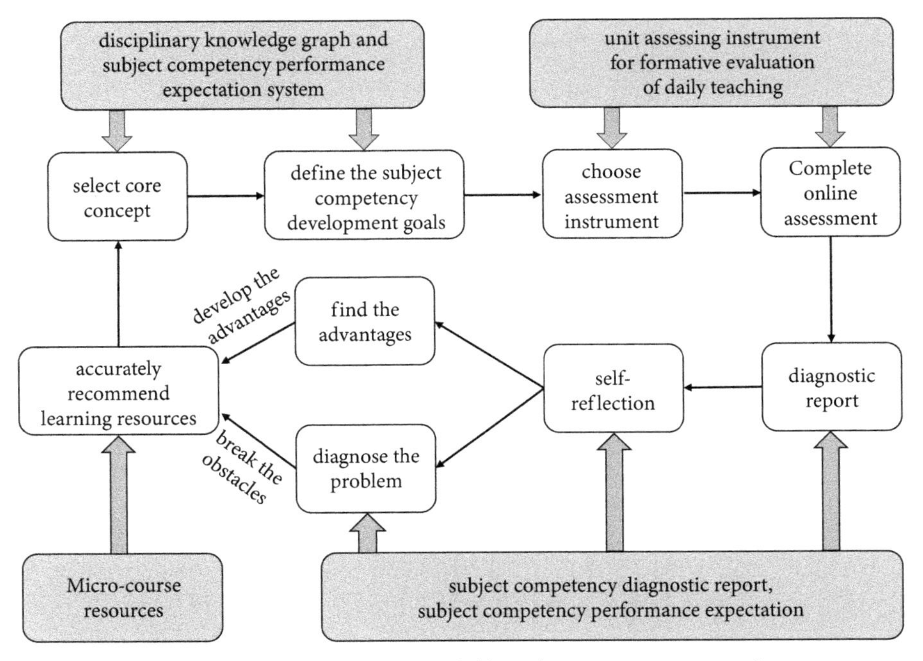

Figure 14.8 The independent learning model based on SLP to promote the development of students' subject competency.

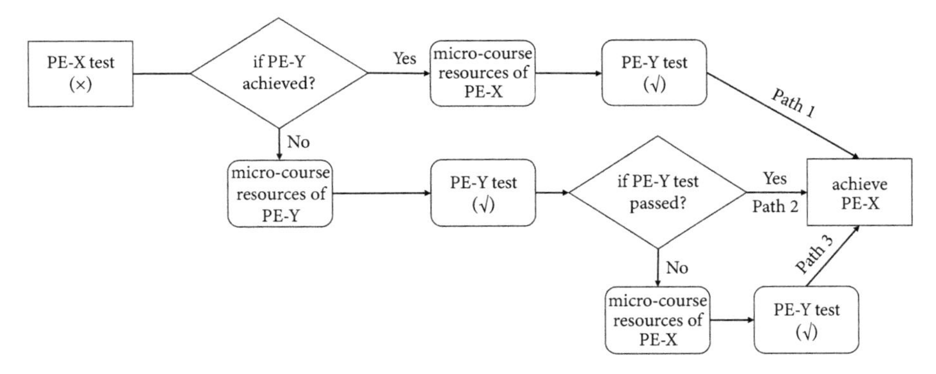

Figure 14.9 Tests and resources recommended for adaptive learning.

corresponding micro-course learning resources to support the development of the A2-1, A3-2, and A3-2 PE.

If students have weak performance in a PE, it is a way of thinking to directly recommend the learning resources of the corresponding PE. At the same time, there are also correlations between different core concepts and different PEs. For example, the weak performance of students' PE-X may be due to the weak performance of PE-X itself, the weak performance of its associated PE-Y, or the weak performance of both PE-X and -Y. Therefore, there are three recommended learning paths, as shown in Figure 14.9. Path 1 indicates that the weak performance of students' PE-X is not caused by PE-Y, but because PE-X itself has not been achieved. It is necessary to recommend the micro-course learning resource of PE-X for the student. Path 2 shows that the weak performance of students' PE-X is caused by PE-Y, and PE-X can be completed if PE-Y is reached first. Path 3 shows that the weak performance of students' PE-X is related to both PE-X and -Y. It is necessary to break through PE-Y first and then PE-X. For students with weak performance in PE-X, different students can achieve this PE through different paths according to their differences in subject competency performance. In SLP, students can adjust their learning content according to their subject competency performance, and continuously improve their learning path based on data-driven and learning analysis to achieve subject competency.

Classroom Teaching Model

Based on the disciplinary knowledge graph and subject competency PE system, teachers can more clearly define the structure of teaching knowledge content and the development goals of subject competency. This would help to accurately design and select teaching objectives, problem contexts, activities, and tasks, and at the same time, explicit cognitive perspectives and reasoning paths and optimize teaching behavior. Based on the assessment instruments and diagnostic reports, teachers can understand the strengths and weaknesses of students' subject competency development, identify the key and difficult points of teaching, and accurately design and implement teaching according to the evidence of students' performance. Based on micro-course resources, teachers can deeply understand the subject competency PE and problem-solving methods toward reflecting on and improving their teaching.

Therefore, SLP can guide teachers to change from "specific knowledge implementation-oriented" to "subject competency development-oriented" teaching, help to clarify the functional value of core teaching content to subject competency development, assist teachers in designing diverse and graded subject competency activities in different links of teaching, and promote teachers' teaching behavior more toward the cultivation of students' subject competency. In turn, teachers can help students to establish core cognitive perspectives, form reasoning paths, and realize the development of students' subject competency. Based on SLP, the development of students' subject competency can be promoted before class, during class, and after class. The details are as follows:

Before class: Teachers release subject competency-oriented unit assessment instruments to students, and students complete self-diagnosis of subject competency performance on the SLP platform. The SLP platform pushes the diagnosis report of subject competency performance to students, and students can carry out independent learning according to the individual diagnosis report.

In class: Based on the diagnostic results of students' subject competency performance, teachers can use specific activities and tasks to have in-depth conversations with students, and help students establish cognitive perspectives and reasoning paths. Teachers use micro-course resources to promote students' reflection and group discussion, deepen their cognitive perspectives and reasoning paths, and promote the development of students' subject competency. At the same time, teachers can use unit assessment instruments to timely diagnose and feedback the development of students' subject competency, to ensure the generation of classroom activities.

After class: Teachers release subject competency-oriented unit assessment instruments to students, and students complete self-diagnosis of subject competency performance on the SLP platform. The shortcomings of subject competency performance can be further studied by themselves using micro-course resources. At the same time, teachers can urge students to study according to the individual subject competency diagnosis report and reflect on teaching according to the class subject competency diagnosis report.

Discussion

The use of cognitive diagnosis technology to measure core competency is an important advance to respond to the current education evaluation reform and adapt to the requirements of the new curriculum standards. This study introduces a perspective of cognitive diagnosis, which uses SCF as an intermediary and relies on the team-developed Smart Learning Partner platform to design learning performance tasks with learning indicator attributes. The study establishes internal logical connections between learning performance tasks and the core competency and subject knowledge, achieving effective measurement and visual representation of subject knowledge and core competency based on data evidence. This study forms a complete closed-loop path that integrates the measurement of subject knowledge and core competency, the discovery of subject strengths and weaknesses, and precise teaching and learning. It provides a reference solution for implementing large-scale measurement of subject core competency.

The indicator system can categorize and systematize the subject knowledge, forming a knowledge map. This knowledge map is not just a simple classification but also shows the relationships and logical connections between concepts, helping learners establish a complete knowledge framework, thereby better understanding and mastering the inherent logical structure of the subject, which has significant advantages in the content model. Compared to Lee et al.'s (2019) system (HASbot), the knowledge map of SLP covers all the knowledge and skill requirements of compulsory education, rather than focusing on only scientific argumentation. This means that SLP can provide more comprehensive and systematic educational support, helping students to master the core knowledge and skill requirements of various subjects (National Research Council 2007). Based on the knowledge map, the indicator system can also design advanced learning paths, dividing knowledge points into different learning stages according to logical relationships and learning difficulties, and setting corresponding learning goals and evaluation standards for each stage. As a result, learners can follow a systematic and planned learning path, not only improving learning efficiency, but also better mastering knowledge.

The platform visualizes students' mastery of knowledge using learning cognitive maps based on core concepts in each subject area. Different textures are used to represent different levels of mastery, enabling students to understand their own proficiency in different core concepts and to adjust their learning pace accordingly. Teachers can also gain insight into the overall performance of their classes and identify which core concepts the class excels in and where they need improvement, in order to adjust their teaching plans accordingly and improve the quality of assessments.

In terms of core competency, the platform presents visualizations of students' personal core competency development trends and their individual and class-wide comprehensive performance levels on a radar chart. This allows students to see their core competency diagnostic results and trends over time and compare them longitudinally. At the same time, students can compare their personal core competency performance with the class's overall performance and identify their own subject strengths and weaknesses. The platform enables subject teachers and class teachers to pinpoint each student's individual needs; develop tailored teaching interventions, subject-specific teaching activities, and assessment tasks; and ultimately cultivate students' core competency.

The indicator system can intelligently recommend the most suitable resources and learning paths for learners based on multiple factors, such as their learning history, interests, and learning styles. These recommendations are not only based on algorithmic models but also on the knowledge map and advanced learning paths of the indicator system, ensuring that the resources obtained by learners meet their learning needs and also help them advance smoothly along the advanced learning path. Through cognitive diagnostic results, students and teachers can utilize the high-quality micro-lesson resources provided by the platform for self-reinforcement and teaching intervention. These resources cover all core concepts of the nine subjects in secondary schools and are annotated with learning indicators by subject experts, establishing a connection with the test questions used in the cognitive diagnostic process. When students receive their diagnostic reports, the platform will make precise recommendations for learning resources based on the weak knowledge points reflected in the report, providing direct access to learning materials. Teachers can also use the platform's micro-lesson resources to develop students' follow-up learning plans and reinforcement measures and push micro-lessons that match the students' subject ability levels based on the development rules of subject strengths. This helps students avoid incorrect answering patterns and design more targeted teaching intervention plans, ultimately improving classroom teaching effectiveness. Additionally, using the platform's micro-lesson resources can save teachers preparation time and allow them to have more time for instructional design and student Q&A.

References

Anderson, L. W., Krathwohl, D. R., Airasian, P. W., Cruikshank, K. A. and Wittrock, M. C. 2001. *A Taxonomy for Learning, Teaching, and Assessing: A Revision of Bloom's Taxonomy of Educational Objectives*. San Antonio: Pearson Education.

Attali, Y., and Powers, D. 2008. "Effect of Immediate Feedback and Revision on Psychometric Properties of Open-Ended Gre® Subject Test Items." *ETS Research Report Series* 2008, no. 1: i–23.

Aguar, K., Sanchez, C. C., Beltran, D. B., Safaei, S., Asefi, M., Arnold, J., Portes, P. R., Arabnia, H. R., and Gutierrez, J. B. 2017. "Considerations on Interdisciplinary Instruction and Design Influenced by Adaptive Learning: A Case Study Involving Biology, Computer Science, Mathematics, and Statistics." arXiv: Physics Education.

Azevedo, R., Bouchet, F., Duffy, M., Harley, J., Taub, M., Trevors, G., . . . and Cerezo, R. 2022. "Lessons Learned and Future Directions of Metatutor: Leveraging Multichannel Data to Scaffold Self-regulated Learning with an Intelligent Tutoring System." *Frontiers in Psychology* 13: 813632.

Bernhardt, P. 2015. "21st Century Learning: Professional Development in Practice." *The Qualitative Report.*

Bloom, B., Englehart, M. D., Furst, E. J., Hill, W. H., and Krathwohl, D. 1956. "Taxonomy of Educational Objectives Handbook I: The Cognitive Domain." *British Journal of Educational Studies* 14, no.3: 119.

Brühwiler, C., and Vogt, F. 2020. "Adaptive Teaching Competency: Effects on Quality of Instruction and Learning Outcomes." *Journal of Educational Research Online* 12, no. 1: 119–42.

Chen, P., Lu, Y., Zheng, V., and Bian, Y. 2018. "Prerequisite-Driven Deep Knowledge Tracing." In *IEEE Conference on Data Mining (ICDM'2018)*, 39–48. IEEE.

Crawford, B. A. 2000. "Embracing the Essence of Inquiry: New Roles for Science Teachers." *Journal of Research in Science Teaching* 37, no. 9: 916–37.

de la Torre, J. 2009. "DINA Model and Parameter Estimation: A Didactic." *Journal of Educational and Behavioral Statistics* 34, no. 1: 115–30.

Duong, O. T. K. 2016. "Developing Core Competencies of Students through Competence-Based Assessment at Ho Chi Minh City University of Technology and Education." *Online Journal for Technical and Vocational Education and Training in Asia* 7: 1–17.

European Commission. 2007. *Key Competences for Lifelong Learning: European Reference Framework*. Brussels: Publications Office of the European Union.

Feng, Z. 1986. "The Generalization Experience Theory of Ability." *Journal of Beijing Normal University (Social Science)* 1, no. 1: 27–34.

Fischer, G. H. 1973. "The Linear Logistic Test Model as an Instrument in Educational Research." *Acta Psychologica* 37, no. 6: 359–74.

Gierl, M. J., Zheng, Y., and Cui, Y. 2008. "Using the Attribute Hierarchy Method to Identify and Interpret Cognitive Skills That Produce Group Differences." *Journal of Educational Measurement* 45, no. 1: 65–89.

Harlen, W. 2010. *Principles and Big Ideas of Science Education.* Hatfield: Association for Science Education.

Holmes, G., and Hooper, N. 2000. "Core Competence and Education." *Higher Education* 40: 247–58.

Kawshala, B. A. H. 2017. "Theorizing the Concept of Core Competencies: An Integrative Model beyond Identification." *International Journal of Scientific and Research Publications* 7: 253–56.

Keuning, T., and van Geel, M. 2021. "Differentiated Teaching With Adaptive Learning Systems and Teacher Dashboards: The Teacher Still Matters Most." *IEEE Transactions on Learning Technologies* 14, no. 2: 201–10.

Krajcik, J. S. 2021. "Commentary—Applying Machine Learning in Science Assessment: Opportunity and Challenges." *Journal of Science Education and Technology* 2: 1–6.

Kuhn, D. 2010: "Teaching and Learning Science as Argument." *Science and Education* 94, no. 5: 810–24.

Lee, H., Pallant, A., Pryputniewicz, S., Lord, T., Mulholland, M., and Liu, O. L. 2019. "Automated Text Scoring and Real-Time Adjustable Feedback: Supporting Revision of Scientific Arguments Involving Uncertainty." *Science Education 103*, no. 3: 590–622.

Lee, H. S., Gweon, G. H., Lord, T., Paessel, N., Pallant, A., and Pryputniewicz, S. 2021. "Machine Learning-Enabled Automated Feedback: Supporting Students' Revision of Scientific Arguments Based on Data Drawn from Simulation." *Journal of Science Education and Technology 30*: 168–92.

Leighton, J. P., Gierl, M. J., and Hunka, S. M. 2004. "The Attribute Hierarchy Method for Cognitive Assessment: A Variation on Tatsuoka's Rule-Space Approach." *Journal of Educational Measurement 41*, no. 3: 205–37.

Ling, H. C., and Chiang, H. S. 2022. "Learning Performance in Adaptive Learning Systems: A Case Study of Web Programming Learning Recommendations." *Frontiers in Psychology* 13: 770637.

Liu, O. L., Rios, J. A., Heilman, M., Gerard, L., and Linn, M. C. 2016. "Validation of Automated Scoring of Science Assessments." *Journal of Research in Science Teaching 53*, no. 2: 215–33.

Lu, Y., Wang, D., Meng, Q., and Chen, P. 2020. "Towards Interpretable Deep Learning Models for Knowledge Tracing." In *International Conference on Artificial Intelligence in Education*, 185–90. Cham: Springer.

Luo, J., and Yu, S. 2022. "Implementing a Key-Competence-Based Subject Knowledge Learning Tool in Chinese Middle Schools: The Direct and Sustained Effects." *Interactive Learning Environments*, 1–20.

Luo, J., Wang, M., and Yu, S. 2022. "Exploring the Factors Influencing Teachers' Instructional Data Use with Electronic Data Systems." *Computers & Education* 191: 104631.

Mao, L., Liu, O. L., Roohr, K., Belur, V., Mulholland, M., Lee, H.-S., and Pallant, A. 2018. "Validation of Automated Scoring for a Formative Assessment that Employs Scientific Argumentation." *Educational Assessment 23*, no. 2: 121–38.

Martin, F., Chen, Y., Moore, R. L., and Westine, C. D. 2020. "Systematic Review of Adaptive Learning Research Designs, Context, Strategies, and Technologies from 2009 to 2018." *Educational Technology Research and Development 68*, no. 4: 1903–29.

Matt, B. 2016. "A Framework for Adaptive Learning Design in a Web-Conferencing Environment." *Journal of Interactive Media in Education 2016*, no. 1: 11.

Mullis, I. V. S., and M. O. Martin. 2013. *TIMSS 2015 Assessment Frameworks*. Chestnut Hill, MA: TIMSS and PIRLS International Study Center.

Nakamura, C. M., Murphy, S. K., Christel, M. G., Stevens, S. M., and Zollman, D. A. 2016. "Automated Analysis of Short Responses in an Interactive Synthetic Tutoring System for Introductory Physics." *Physical Review Physics Education Research 12*, no. 1: 010122.

National Academy of Sciences. 2013. *Next Generation Science Standards*. Washington, DC: National Academies Press.

National Research Council. 2007. *Taking Science to School: Learning and Teaching Science in Grades K-8*. Washington, DC: National Academies Press.

Niu, S. J., Li, X., and Luo, J. 2023. "Multiple Users' Experiences of an AI-Aided Educational Platform for Teaching and learning." In *AI in Learning: Designing the Future*, edited by H. Niemi, R. D. Pea, and Y. Lu, 215–31. Cham: Springer.

Novak, J. D. 1961. "An Approach to the Interpretation and Measurement of Problem Solving Ability." *Science and Education* 45, no. 2: 122–31.

Okoye, I., Sumner, T., and Bethard, S. 2013. "Automatic Extraction of Core Learning Goals and Generation of Pedagogical Sequences through a Collection of Digital Library Resources." In *Proceedings of the 13th ACM/IEEE-CS Joint Conference on Digital Libraries—JCDL '13*, 67.

Pan, X., Cayton-Hodges, G., and Feng, G. 2015. "Tablet-Based Math Assessment: What Can We Learn from Math Apps?" *Education Technology & Society 18*: 3–20.

Peng, H., and Zhu, Z. 2017. "Measurement-Assisted Learning: A Core Mechanism of Precision Instruction in Smart Education," *e-Education Research* 3: 94–103.

Pian, Y., Lu, Y., Chen, P., and Duan, Q. 2019. "Coglearn: A Cognitive Graph-Oriented Online Learning System." In *2019 IEEE 35th International Conference on Data Engineering (ICDE)*, 2020–23. IEEE.

Shute, V., and Towle, B. 2003. "Adaptive E-Learning." *Educational Psychologist 38*, no. 2: 105–14.

Shute, V., Ke, F., and Wang, L. 2017. "Assessment and Adaptation in Games." In *Techniques to Improve the Effectiveness of Serious Games*, Advances in Game Learning, edited by P. Wouters and H. van Oostendorp, 59–78. Cham: Springer.

Si, J., Kim, D., and Na, C. 2014. "Adaptive Instruction to Learner Expertise with Bimodal Process-oriented Worked-out Examples." *Journal of Educational Technology & Society 17*, no. 1: 259–71.

Tan, H., Wang, C., Duan, Q.L., Lu, Y., Zhang, H., and Li, R. 2023. "Automatic Short Answer Grading by Encoding Student Responses via a Graph Convolutional Network." *Interactive Learning Environments* 31, no. 3: 1636–50.

Tatsuoka, K. K. 1983. "Rule Space: An Approach for Dealing with Misconceptions Based on Item Response Theory." *Journal of Educational Measurement 20*: 345–54.

Trilling, B., and Fadel, C. 2009. *21st century skills: Learning for life in our times*. Chichester, UK: *John Wiley and Sons*.

van der Kleij, F., and Adie, L. 2018. "Formative Assessment and Feedback Using Information Technology." In *Second Handbook of Information Technology in Primary and Secondary Education*, edited by J. Voogt, G. Knezek, R. Christensen, and K.-W. Lai, 601–15. Cham: Springer.

Vandewaetere, M., Desmet, P., and Clarebout, G. 2011. "The Contribution of Learner Characteristics in the Development of Computer-Based Adaptive Learning Environments." *Computers in Human Behavior 27*, no. 1: 118–30.
Wan, H., and Yu, S. 2020. "A Recommendation System Based on an Adaptive Learning Cognitive Map Model and Its Effects." *Interactive Learning Environments* 31, no. 3: 1821–39.
Wang, C., Liu, X., Wang, L., Sun, Y., and Zhang, H. 2021. "Automated Scoring of Chinese Grades 7–9 Students' Competence in Interpreting and Arguing from Evidence." *Journal of Science Education and Technology 30*, no. 2: 269–82.
Wang, L. 2016. "Exploring Performance and Intrinsic Composition of Disciplinary Competency—Based on the Multi-integrative Model of 'Learning-Applying -Innovating." *Educational Research* 37, no. 9: 83–92.
Wang, L. 2017. *Research on the Competency of Chemistry Subject Based on Students' Core Competency.* Beijing: Beijing Normal University Press.
Wang, L., Wang, Q., Kong, S., Hu, J., and Chen, X. 2022. "Subject Competency Framework in Fostering High-End Lesson Study—A Case of Teaching 'Properties of Iron Salts' Unit in a Senior High School." *International Journal for Lesson and Learning Studies* 11, no. 2: 73–90.
Wang, L., and Zhi Y. 2016. "Research on Chemistry Subject Competency and Its Performance", *Journal of Educational Studies* 12, no.4: 46–56.
Wang, Lei, Zhou, D., Zhi, Y., Huang, Y., Hu, J., and Chen, Y. 2019. "The Construction and Application Model of an Integration System for the Improvement of Disciplinary Competence in Smart Learning Partner." *China Educational Technology* 1: 28–34.
Wang, Q. 2021. *Research on the Academic Quality Evaluation of Inorganic Matter Subject for High School Students Based on the New Curriculum Standards.* Beijing: Beijing Normal University.
Williamson, D. M., Xi, X., and Breyer, F. J. 2012. "A Framework for Evaluation and Use of Automated Scoring." *Educational Measurement: Issues and Practice 31*, no. 1: 2–13.
Wu, J., and Wang, Z. 2007. *Theory of Chemical Learning.* Nanning: Guangxi Education Publishing House. [in Chinese]
Xin, T., Jiang, Y., Chongde, L., Baoguo, S., and Xia, L. 2016. "On the Connotation, Characteristics and Framework Orientation of Students' Development Core Literacy." *Chinese Journal of Education* 6: 3–7.
Yang, Y. 2012. *Research on Measurement and Assessment of the Competence in Discipline of Chemistry.* Shanghai: East China Normal University.
Yoo, J., and Kim, J. 2014. "Can Online Discussion Participation Predict Group Project Performance? Investigating the Roles of Linguistic Features and Participation Patterns." *International Journal of Artificial Intelligence in Education* 24, no. 1: 8–32.
Zhai, X. 2022. "Assessing High-School Students' Modeling Performance on Newtonian Mechanics." *Journal of Research in Science Teaching* 59: 1313–53.
Zhai, X., Haudek, K., Shi, L., Nehm, R., and Urban-Lurain, M. 2020. "From Substitution to Redefinition: A Framework of Machine Learning-Based Science Assessment." *Journal of Research in Science Teaching* 57, no. 9: 1430–59.
Zhai, X., Haudek, K. C., and Ma, W. 2023. "Assessing Argumentation Using Machine Learning and Cognitive Diagnostic Modeling." *Research in Science Education* 53, no. 2: 405–24.
Zhai, X., Yin, Y., Pellegrino, J. W., Haudek, K. C., and Shi, L. 2020. "Applying Machine Learning in Science Assessment: A Systematic Review." *Studies in Science Education* 56, no. 1: 111–51.
Zhang, J., Jang, E., and Chahine, S. 2021. "A Systematic Review of Cognitive Diagnostic Assessment and Modeling through Concept Mapping." *Frontiers of Contemporary Education* 2: 41.
Zhang, L., Lei, W., and Treagust. D. F. 2021. "Discipline-Specific Cognitive Factors That Influence Grade 9 Students' Performance in Chemistry." *Chemistry Education Research and Practice* 22, no. 4: 813–41.
Zhu, M., Liu, O. L., and Lee, H.-S. 2020. "The Effect of Automated Feedback on Revision Behavior and Learning Gains in Formative Assessment of Scientific Argument Writing." *Computers & Education* 143: 103668.
Zulfiani, Z., Suwarna, I. P., and Miranto, S. 2018. "Science Education Adaptive Learning System as a Computer-Based Science Learning with Learning Style Variations." *Journal of Baltic Science Education* 17, no. 4: 711.

PART III
AI-BASED STEM INSTRUCTION AND TEACHER PROFESSIONAL DEVELOPMENT

15
A Systematic Review on Artificial Intelligence in Supporting Teaching Practice
Application Types, Pedagogical Roles, and Technological Characteristics

Lehong Shi and Ikseon Choi

Introduction

Artificial intelligence (AI) promises to perform human-like cognitive tasks like learning, problem-solving, handling complexity, and making rational decisions (Guilherme 2019; Russell 2010; Spector and Ma 2019). Within the educational context, embedded in intelligent applications such as intelligent tutoring systems (ITS) (Gerard, Kidron, and Linn 2019; Dickler 2019; Gobert et al. 2023b), teaching assistants (Goel and Polepeddi 2018), and machine-learning (ML)-based automatic scoring systems (Gobert et al. 2013; Gobert and Sao Pedro 2016; Zhai et al. 2020a) AI presents significant potential to support teachers' instructional decision-making and transform their pedagogical practices. Extensive research has illustrated the promising roles of AI in supporting teachers' lesson design activities and providing learners with personalized scaffolding through customized feedback and recommendations (Edwards and Cheok 2018; Yun, Kim, and Choi 2013). AI has also shown potential in alleviating teachers' concerns regarding the breadth of domain-specific knowledge they must possess (Roll and Wylie 2016; Wenger 1987) and in assessing students' written responses to provide timely and informative feedback (Gobert 2019; Zhai et al. 2020a; Zhai et al. 2020b; Zhai, Shi, and Nehm 2021). Moreover, recent studies have advocated combining machine and human intelligence to facilitate teachers' immediate instructional decision-making and actions within dynamic educational contexts (Chounta et al. 2022; Paiva and Bittencourt 2020). Recognizing the significant potential of AI in enhancing teachers' pedagogical practices, numerous researchers, organizations, and stakeholders have emphasized the importance of teachers swiftly adopting AI into their instructional practices. Some scholars are enthusiastic about the use of AI applications, such as social robots, to address the prevailing teacher shortage (Edwards and Cheok 2018; Morita et al. 2018; Mubin et al. 2013; Serholt et al. 2017) with the notion of robot teachers gaining favor (Sharkey 2016).

While acknowledging the potential of AI to support current teaching practices, the role of AI is a vital inquiry that necessitates careful reflection and thorough

Lehong Shi and Ikseon Choi, *A Systematic Review on Artificial Intelligence in Supporting Teaching Practice.*
In: *Uses of Artificial Intelligence in STEM Education.* Edited by: Xiaoming Zhai and Joseph Krajcik,
Oxford University Press. © Oxford University Press (2024). DOI: 10.1093/oso/9780198882077.003.0015

investigation. Haristiani (2019) posed a crucial question regarding the driving forces of the potential of AI in teaching: AI advancements, teachers' innovative integrations of AI, or other factors. Many have emphasized the significance of technological advances, suggesting that teachers' previous responsibilities and roles have been shaped and potentially diminished due to the advent of AI in education (Williamson 2016). Some review studies have endeavored to examine the potential of AI in educational contexts from various perspectives. For instance, AI functionalities in education have been categorized into several domains, such as profiling and prediction, assessment and evaluation, adaptive systems and personalization, and intelligent tutoring systems (Chen, Chen, and Lin 2020; Hwang et al. 2020; Zawacki-Richter et al. 2019). Baker and Smith (2019) classified AI tools into three categories based on who directs the use of AI: learner-directing, instructor-directing, and system-directing tools. Ouyang and Jiao (2021) also categorized three types of AI and learner relationships within the learner-directing AI tools. Furthermore, Xu and Ouyang (2021) identified three roles AI can play in teaching and learning, including serving as a new subject, a direct mediator, or a supplementary assistant. Notably, few review studies were found to explicitly investigate the impact of AI on teachers' pedagogical practices from the perspective of teachers themselves. However, such a pedagogical perspective is essential in designing and promoting AI technology within teachers' classroom practices.

It is of primary interest in this study to systematically review the literature on AI in education studies to investigate how AI can support and transform teachers' pedagogical practices in classrooms through analyzing the pedagogical roles and characteristics of AI. The findings of this study are expected to contribute to a deeper understanding of how teachers incorporate AI into classrooms to enhance their instruction. The following research questions guide the study:

(1) What are the grade levels, subject domains, and contexts in which AI has been integrated into teaching?
(2) What are the technological functionalities of AI that support and enhance teaching?
(3) What pedagogical roles of AI emerge when teachers incorporate AI into their instruction?
(4) What unique characteristics does AI exhibit in supporting teachers' instructional practices?

Analytical Framework

The existing body of literature emphasizes that the effectiveness of technology integration in education can be measured by the degree to which technology becomes an integral part of pedagogy practice (De Koster, Volman, and Kuiper 2017; Harris 2005; Howard et al. 2015; Zhai et al. 2019). Accordingly, the successful implementation of technology in instructional settings depends on its alignment with teachers' pedagogical objectives and purposes (e.g., Okojie, Olinzock, and Okojie-Boulder 2006). Studies have demonstrated that teachers perceive technology as valuable when it

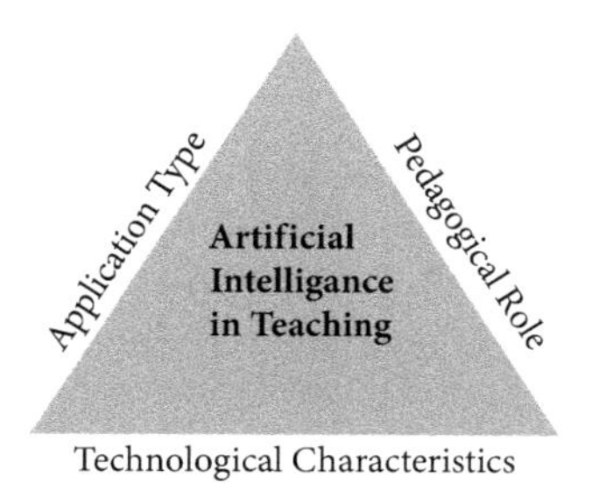

Figure 15.1 The proposed three-dimensional analytical framework.

offers significant pedagogical potential in supporting various aspects of their teaching practices, including classroom management, grading, and decision-making (Howard et al. 2015; McKnight et al. 2016). Moreover, it is essential to recognize that each technology possesses distinct characteristics that influence its impact on pedagogy. It is crucial to consider the unique attributes of specific technologies in relation to pedagogical practices (Zhai and Jackson 2023).

Our inquiry has elucidated three fundamental considerations for the effectiveness of AI integration into teaching practices: (1) the selection and implementation of AI technologies; (2) the pedagogical roles of AI and associated pedagogical benefits in teaching; and (3) the unique characteristics exhibited by AI in its capacity to support and reinforce pedagogy. In response to these concerns, we proposed a three-dimensional analytical framework, encompassing *application type*, *pedagogical role*, and *technological characteristics* (see Figure 15.1). The dimension of *application type* refers to the specific AI applications and the associated technologies employed in teaching. Since AI has the potential to facilitate and promote instructional decision-making and pedagogical innovation, it is crucial to categorize its *pedagogical roles* to comprehend its pedagogy affordance and benefits. The *technological characteristics* highlights the distinctive features of AI technology when incorporated into teaching practices.

Application Type

In the discourse of technology integration in education, it is crucial to understand the technological features inherent in the discussed technology (ChanLin et al. 2006; Inan and Lowther 2010). This principle also applies to AI technology. In the case of AI applications in teaching, we emphasize a foundational comprehension of the types of AI technology across three key aspects. Firstly, we categorize the AI systems and applications utilized in educational settings, given the diverse range of AI technologies available in supporting teaching practices. Secondly, a close examination of its design features becomes necessary within a given AI system or application. Remarkably, including a teacher dashboard within an AI system allows educators to effectively engage and interact with AI technology. Investigating such design features provides valuable insights into how AI can effectively integrate into the instructional process. Lastly, we examine the degree of teachers' involvement in designing AI-integrated instructions.

Pedagogical Role

A fundamental assumption underlying the integration of technology in education is the potential to yield pedagogical benefits for users, including teachers and students (Zhai et al. 2020a). Building upon this assumption, we highlight the importance of examining AI used from the perspective of teachers' pedagogical practices. To investigate the specific pedagogical potential of AI for teachers, we delve into its potential roles in teaching and explore how these roles can support and innovate teachers' pedagogical practices. Understanding the pedagogical roles of AI in teaching is crucial as it enables a clear differentiation between AI and traditional technologies in terms of their support for teachers.

Technological Characteristics

AI is often considered a revolutionary and disruptive innovation (Manyika et al. 2017) compared with conventional technologies. It is crucial to discern the distinctiveness of AI technology in order to delve deeper into its influence on teaching practices. AI includes multiple distinctive features that have diverse implications in the field of education. However, this study focuses on uncovering AI's uniqueness solely from the perspective of teachers' pedagogy. It is not our goal to provide a comprehensive overview of all characteristics of AI within the educational context.

The proposed framework presents a concise argument for comprehending the potential of AI in teaching, encompassing its technological functionalities, pedagogical roles, and unique characteristics. This framework serves as a roadmap for the process of literature selection, coding, analysis, and findings reported in this study. Guided by this framework, we conducted a systematic search and analysis of the literature pertaining to AI in educational studies, aiming to address the research questions at hand. The first question focuses on investigating the contextual factors surrounding AI integration in teaching, while the subsequent three questions correspond to the three dimensions of the framework, respectively.

Method

Eligibility Criteria

To address the research questions in accordance with the analytical framework, a set of inclusive and exclusive rules were established to guide the search for relevant studies (see Table 15.1), employing a comprehensive literature review methodology (Onwuegbuzie and Frels 2016).

Literature Selection

To facilitate a comprehensive literature selection process and ensure the inclusion of high-quality studies, an extensive search was conducted across multiple academic databases, including EBSCOhost, ERIC, ProQuest, Web of Science, ScienceDirect,

Table 15.1 The Inclusion and Exclusion Criteria for the Literature Search

	Criteria	Rational
Inclusion	Study focus	Studies that integrated AI technology to support or improve teaching mentioned how AI helps teachers in classrooms even though the study focuses on student learning.
	Study type	Studies that provide empirical evidence (e.g., qualitative, quantitative, or mixed-method studies) to explain the pedagogical benefits of AI in teaching.
	Study purpose	Studies explained the integration of AI in pedagogy and teacher performance, although student learning might be another essential purpose for many studies.
	Participants	The primary focus of research is integrating AI in K–12 classrooms or postsecondary contexts.
	Time range	Studies conducted in the past decade (i.e., 2010–22) since we focus mainly on recent studies of AI in education.
	Study quality	Written in the English language and peer-reviewed journal articles.
Exclusion	Study focus	Studies that only focus on student learning, without any information on how AI benefits teachers' pedagogy.
	Study type	However, studies that discussed AI technology in education focus on AI system description and evaluation rather than implementation in practice.
	Study purpose	Studies that were theoretical or conceptual papers without empirical data to report how teachers integrate AI in teaching.

and Google Scholar. We employed two sets of keywords to retrieve relevant articles: (1) AI-related keywords, such as artificial intelligence, machine learning, deep learning, virtual assistant, intelligent tutoring system, and social robots; and (2) teaching-related keywords, like teaching, instruction, scaffolding, facilitation, and feedback. The initial search generated 1327 studies.

To ensure the integrity and relevance of the study, we took a rigorous screening process. Initially, duplicate studies (n = 235) were removed. Subsequently, the titles and abstracts of the remaining studies were carefully reviewed to exclude articles that focused on the design and testing of AI systems rather than the implementation of AI in teaching (n = 451). Furthermore, studies (n = 339) lacking empirical evidence of AI utilization in teaching were excluded. To maintain a consistent level of quality, additional exclusions were made for conference papers, book chapters, dissertations (n = 262), and studies without accessible full-text versions. Additionally, we utilized the snowball search strategy to search for omitting studies, resulting in four additional articles. Ultimately, we identified 44 studies that met the eligibility criteria for further full-text analysis to answer the four research questions.

Coding of AI Features in Teaching

The analysis of the eligible studies followed a qualitative inductive content analysis approach, drawing on the work of Elo and Kyngäs (2008) and Mayring (2014). Prior to the coding process, a coding protocol was developed, aligning with the proposed

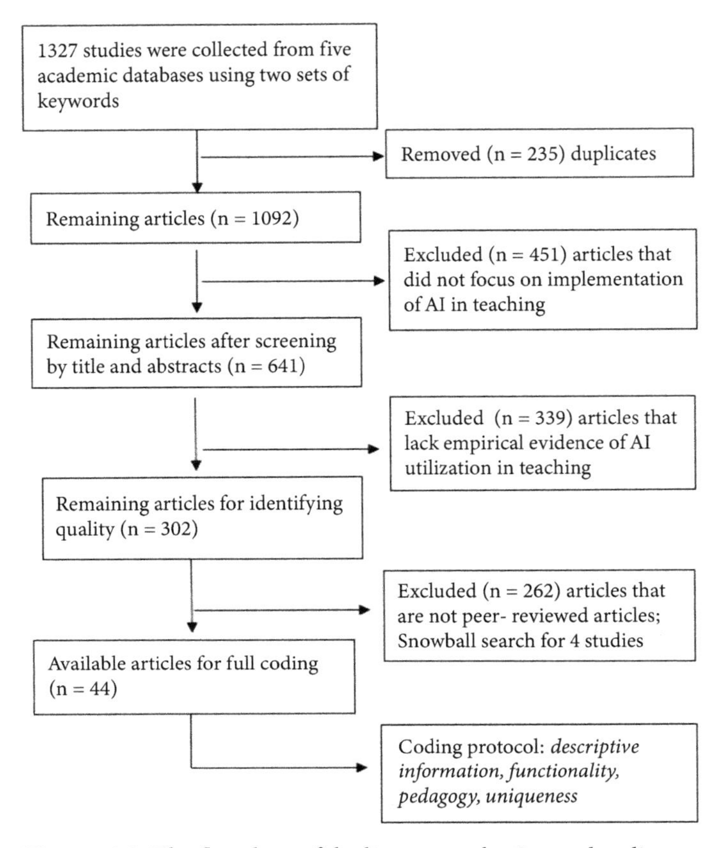

Figure 15.2 The flowchart of the literature selection and coding process.

analytical framework. The coding protocol encompassed four key sections: *descriptive information*, *application type*, *pedagogical role*, and *technological characteristics*. Descriptive information coding involves capturing details such as the author(s), years of publication, article title, grade level, subject domain, and integration settings of each study. The application type was coded by the AI systems or tools, the presence of a teacher dashboard, and the extent of teacher involvement in the design and development process. The pedagogical role was coded on the various way of AI in supporting and facilitating teaching. Finally, the technological characteristics of AI were extracted by identifying its unique attributes across different pedagogical roles of AI in supporting teaching.

Following the development of the coding protocol, two coders first coded one-fifth of the eligible studies to establish inter-rater reliability. Cohen's kappa coefficient was at 0.895, indicating substantial agreement (McHugh 2012) between the two coders. We discussed and resolved any discrepancies to iteratively revise the coding protocol for extracting relevant data. Subsequently, the first coder independently coded the remaining studies, adhering to the finalized coding protocol. Figure 15.2 presents the flowchart of the literature search and coding process.

Results

The Educational Context of Reviewed Studies

Educational Levels

Studies included in the analysis were across various grade levels. As indicated in Table 15.2, postsecondary and elementary schools emerged as the most extensively studied grade levels, constituting approximately one-third of the reviewed studies ($n = 17$ and 11, respectively). Middle schools accounted for the following considerable proportion of research attention.

Subject Matter Domains

Our investigation also focused on identifying the subject matter domains in which AI was employed to enhance teaching practices. As depicted in Table 15.2, the analysis revealed that science, in the general sense, received the highest frequency of research attention ($n = 17$). Mathematics was the second most explored subject domain ($n = 7$), followed by computer science ($n = 6$). A smaller proportion of studies examined the integration of AI into language teaching activities conducted by teachers. It is worth noting that a considerable body of research investigated how AI facilitates language learning for students without explicitly mentioning the involvement of teachers (Haristiani 2019; Woo and Choi 2021). Most researchers primarily focused on leveraging AI to support teachers' pedagogical practice in science ($n = 24$), with three articles specifically addressing biology and four articles discussing physics.

To gain a comprehensive understanding of the utilization of AI across various educational levels and subject domains, we analyzed the distribution of subject areas within four grade levels across the studies included in our review. The findings indicated that the distribution of subject domains in middle school studies exhibited similarities to those in high school studies, as illustrated in Figure 15.3. Notably, the implementation of AI to support teachers' language teaching activities was exclusively identified within the K–elementary school-level studies. Conversely, no studies were identified that explored the integration of AI into teachers' pedagogy for computer science across elementary to high school levels. Also, general science emerged as the most extensively studied subject domain at the K–elementary and middle school levels.

Educational Setting

As shown in Table 15.2, a substantial majority of the studies ($n = 32$) were conducted within the confines of a formal educational context, specifically within classroom settings. The remaining studies investigated the integration of AI in teaching within informal settings, including online learning platforms and after-school programs. The prevalence of studies conducted in formal educational settings is in line with the recognition of AI's potential to support diverse pedagogical practices in which teachers assume a crucial role.

Table 15.2 Educational Contexts and Technological Features of Reviewed Studies

Variables	Categories	Number of studies	Percentage (100%)
Educational level	K–elementary	11	25
	Middle school	9	20.45
	High school	7	15.9
	Postsecondary	17	38.64
Subject matter	General science	17	38.64
	Biology	3	6.81
	Physics	4	9.09
	Computer science	6	13.64
	Math	7	15.91
	Language	3	6.81
	No specified	4	9.09
Educational setting	Formal	32	72.72
	Informal	12	27.28

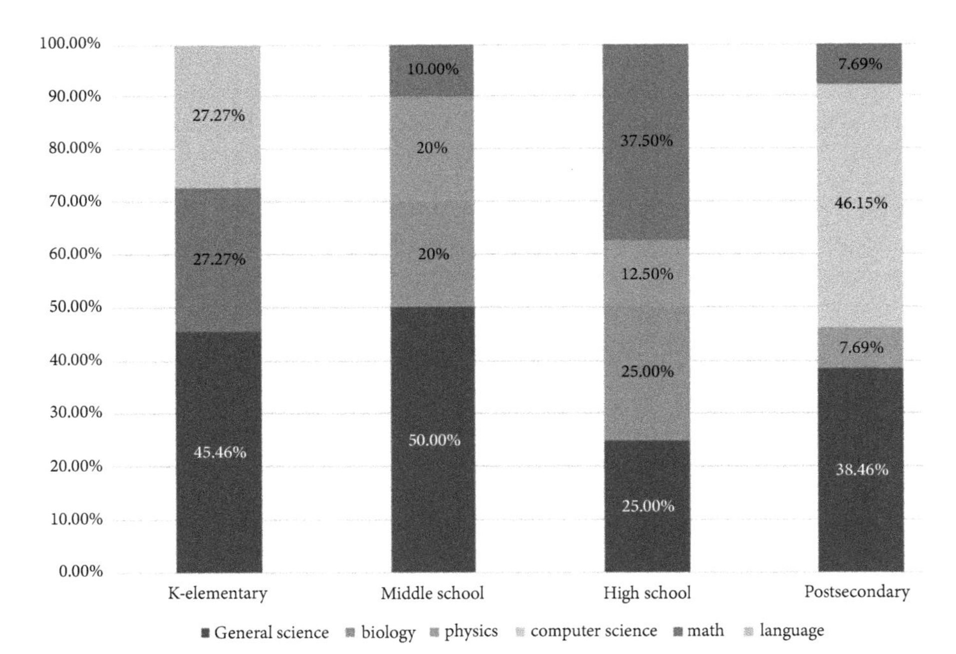

Figure 15.3 Relationship between educational levels and subject domains of the reviewed studies on AI applications in teaching.

AI Application Types in Teaching

To answer RQ2, we analyzed the data from three critical technological features outlined in the analytical framework: the types of AI applications employed, the degree of teachers' involvement in designing AI-integrated instructions, and the interface provided for teacher and AI interaction.

We categorized the integration of AI technologies into teachers' pedagogical practices across different subject domains and educational levels into five distinct types, as presented in Table 15.3. Firstly, social robots were employed in nine studies to assist teachers in facilitating students' learning in language, science, and safety activities (e.g., Fridin 2014; Hashimoto, Kato, and Kobayashi 2011; Morita et al. 2018). Secondly, intelligent tutoring systems, discussed in fourteen studies, can guide student learning, monitor their progress (e.g., Arroyo et al. 2014; Dickler 2019; Gobert et al. 2023b), and provide teachers with timely reports and feedback (e.g., Adair, Dickler, and Gobert 2020). Thirdly, pedagogical agents, such as chatbots and anthropomorphous virtual characters (Veletsianos and Russell 2014) were investigated in five studies, supporting teachers in various instructional activities within and outside the classroom (e.g., Chin, Dohmen, and Schwartz 2013; Goel and Polepeddi 2018; Huang and Shiu 2012) through its interactions with learners and teachers. For example, Jill Watson (Goel and Polepeddi 2018), an AI virtual teaching assistant, was developed to assist teachers in an online course by communicating with students, responding to inquiries, grading assignments, and providing prompt feedback, enabling teachers to focus more on core instructional activities. Fourthly, various teacher decision support tools were discussed in the literature, For instance, the teacher responding tool provides teachers with automated, students-specific recommendations for teachers to notice, interpret, and respond to students' ideas (Bywater et al. 2019). Van Leeuwen et al. (2015) examined the teacher-supporting tools that present summaries, visualization, and analysis of students' participation for teachers to guide collaborative learning. Other teacher decision support tools, such as tools to promote teacher and AI partnership (e.g., Paiva and Bittencourt 2020), expert decision-making process visualization tools (e.g., Cukurova, Kent, and Luckin 2019), and prediction systems/tools to support teachers' decision on individual students' intervention such as at-risk students (e.g., Hung et al. 2017; Moreno-Marcos et al. 2020) and monitor student engagement (e.g., Hussain et al. 2018) were explored. Lastly, automated assessment tools were employed to aid teachers in scoring students' written responses and providing timely feedback (e.g., Gerard and Linn 2016; Zhai, Shi, and Nehm 2021).

To investigate the interaction between teachers and AI, we conducted a specific analysis of teacher interfaces and teacher involvement in the design process. As depicted in Table 15.3, out of the forty-four reviewed studies, only approximately one-fifth (n = 10) discussed the mechanisms through which teachers collaborated with researchers in designing AI-integrated curriculum/activities or AI tools/systems (i.e., Gerard and Linn 2016; Morita et al. 2018). For instance, teachers collaborated with researchers to develop five robotic modes aligned with different learning goals based on their curriculum and teaching objectives (Chang et al. 2010). Furthermore, we examined whether the AI systems had a teacher interface to facilitate better

Table 15.3 Educational Contexts and Technological Features of Reviewed Studies

Variables	Categories	Number of studies	Percentage (%)
AI applications	Social robots	9	20.45
	Intelligent tutoring systems	14	31.82
	Pedagogical agents	5	11.36
	Teacher decision support tools	8	18.18
	Automated assessment tools	8	18.18
Teacher-involved design	Yes	10	22.72
	No	34	77.29
Teacher interface	Yes	15	34.09
	No	29	65.91

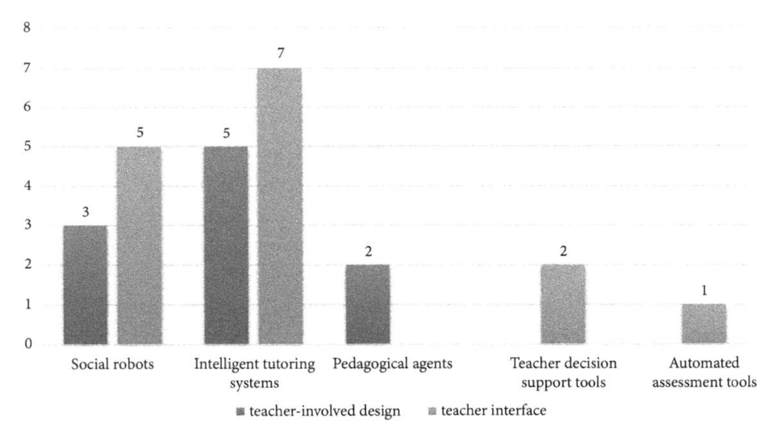

Figure 15.4 The distribution of teacher-involved design and teacher interface across the five types of AI technologies in reviewed studies.

communication among teachers, students, and AI, particularly in displaying student data to teachers. Only fifteen out of the forty-four studies emphasized the features of the teacher interface (e.g., teacher dashboard) and how it presented student data to teachers (i.e., Arroyo et al. 2014; Bywater et al. 2019; Dickler, Gobert, and Sao Pedro 2021; Hashimoto, Kato, and Kobayashi 2011; Hussain et al. 2018).

Figure 15.4 illustrates the distribution of two critical technological functionalities: teacher-involved systems or curriculum/activity design and teacher dashboards across the five AI technology types examined in the reviewed studies. Five of the ten studies that mentioned teacher-involved systems or curriculum/activity design were related to intelligent/adaptive learning systems. The teacher interface feature was observed in intelligent/adaptive learning systems (seven studies) and social robots (five studies).

The Pedagogical Roles of AI to Support Teachers' Instructional Practices

Following a thorough analysis of diverse AI systems and tools employed to support and enhance teaching within the studies reviewed, we identified three pedagogical roles that AI assumes in facilitating teaching, including (1) *AI as an instruction partner*, (2) *AI as an evaluation partner*, and (3) *AI as a pedagogical decision partner*. Table 15.4 provides an overview of each pedagogical role of AI along with its associated features, supported by reference examples.

AI as an Instructional Partner

The findings indicate that AI, when employed to assist teachers as an instructional partner, fulfills three distinct roles: (a) serving as an independent *tutor/instructor*, as evidenced in fourteen studies (e.g., Arroyo et al. 2014; Buttussi and Chittaro 2020); (b) functioning as a *teaching assistant*, as demonstrated in sixteen studies (e.g., Dickler 2019; Goel and Polepeddi 2018; Hashimoto, Kato, and Kobayashi 2011); and (c) acting as a *teaching aid tool*, mentioned in ten studies (e.g., Hung et al. 2017; Van Leeuwen et al. 2015).

Independent Tutor/Instructor

Numerous AI systems demonstrate their potential to function as knowledgeable tutors or instructors, facilitating students' knowledge and skill acquisition by offering immediate instruction, guidance, tutorials, supervision, and hints.

Intelligent tutoring systems aim to replicate the effective practices of one-on-one human tutoring to enhance student learning outcomes (Baker 2016). Several intelligent tutoring systems (e.g., Gobert et al. 2013; Graesser, Li, and Forsyth 2014) incorporate pedagogical strategies employed by human experts (Kara and Sevim 2013). Sometimes AI virtual tutor avatars, such as Rex in the Inquiry ITS (Gobert et al. 2018), have been introduced to substitute human teachers. These intelligent machine tutors/instructors can analyze individual students' progress and engagement, creating comprehensive learner profiles and alleviating the burden on teachers to possess extensive knowledge and pedagogical expertise while monitoring student advancement.

Advanced educational robots have also been implemented as robot tutors (Yun, Kim, and Choi 2013) to substitute teachers' roles partially or temporarily in classroom settings. These robot teachers adopt roles as authoritative figures or explicit sources of knowledge through storytelling, conversation-based interactions, and human-like behaviors (Buttussi and Chittaro 2020; Fridin 2014; Hashimoto, Kato, and Kobayashi 2011). For instance, Saya, a humanoid robot with a female appearance, has been deployed as a teacher in classrooms (Hashimoto, Kato, and Kobayashi 2011). In Saya's "lecture mode," she explains class content. In contrast, in the "interactive mode," she engages in interactive behaviors such as paying attention to students, looking around the classroom, and conversing with students using head and eye movements. Furthermore, to interact with humans, Saya can express human-like facial expressions,

Table 15.4 The Pedagogical Roles of AI and Reference Examples

AI pedagogical roles with teachers	Attributes	Sub-categories	Reference examples
AI as an instruction partner	AI facilitates and substitutes part of teaching role to instruct student learning activities	Independent tutor/instructor	Arroyo et al. (2014); Buttussi and Chittaro (2020); Paiva and Bittencourt (2020)
		Teaching assistant	Chang et al. (2010); Dickler (2019; Dickler, Gobert, and Sao Pedro 2021); Goel and Polepeddi (2018); Hashimoto, Kato, and Kobayashi (2011)
		Teaching aid tool	Bywater et al. (2019); Hung et al. (2017); Van Leeuwen et al. (2015)
AI as an evaluation partner	AI tracks and assesses students' learning progress and outcomes with timely feedback	Track students' progress in real-time	Van Leeuwen et al. (2015); Hussain et al. (2018); Yu (2017)
		Assess students' performance in various domains	Adair, Dickler, and Gobert (2020); Dickler (2019); Dickler, Gobert, and Sao Pedro (2021); Ghali, Ouellet, and Frasson (2016); Hung et al. (2017)
		Elicit complex performance	Adair, Dickler, and Gobert (2020); Huang et al. (2011); Käser et al. (2017); Ghali, Ouellet, and Frasson (2016); Smith et al. (2019)
		Provide timely scoring and feedback	Bywater et al. (2019); Gerard and Linn (2016); Gerard, Kidron, and Linn (2019); Huang et al. (2011)
AI as a pedagogical decision partner	AI can inform teachers of the appropriate content, pedagogy, and strategies to make instructional decisions.	Prescriptive recommendations	Arnold and Pistilli (2012)
		Descriptive recommendations	Adair, Dickler, and Gobert (2020); Hussain et al. (2018)
		AI insights drive teachers' decision-making	Gerard and Linn (2016); Gobert et al. (2018); Miller et al. (2015); Van Leeuwen et al. (2014)

including surprise, fear, anger, and happiness. Social robots functioning as tutors or mentors can adapt their actions based on students' learning styles, personalities, and emotional states, offering personalized student learning assistance (Westlund et al. 2016).

Teaching Assistant

The analysis reveals that AI can serve as a teaching assistant, providing timely support and aiding teachers in various instructional activities, including identifying students' needs, answering questions, and reminding students of deadlines (Gerard, Kidron, and Linn 2019; Goel and Polepeddi 2018; Morita et al. 2018). We identified two types of AI teaching assistants: virtual teaching assistants (VTA), such as chatbots (Goel and Polepeddi 2018), and physically embodied teaching assistants, like humanoid social robots (Chang et al. 2010). An example of the VTA is Jill Watson (Goel and Polepeddi 2018), which is a conversational chatbot assisting teachers in an online course to respond to student queries, grade assignments, and provide feedback timely.

Teaching Aid Tool

Through our review, we have identified AI technologies that can serve as valuable teaching aid, acting as platforms or tools to enhance teachers' instructional activities. Firstly, AI can be a teaching platform by providing teachers with materials and resources to facilitate dynamic instructional activities. For instance, Yu (2017) developed a feedback system that enables teachers to collect student responses and communicate with them through a dual-channel mechanism. Secondly, AI can be an intelligent tool to support teachers in various pedagogical activities (Van Leeuwen et al. 2014; Smith et al. 2019). These tools offer specific functionalities that assist teachers in their instructional tasks. For instance, Smith et al. (2019) developed a multimodal computational model capable of automatically analyzing student writing and drawings in elementary science learning, providing valuable insights to teachers. Another example is the teacher-responding tool (Bywater et al. 2019), which utilizes natural language processing techniques to offer feedback recommendations to teachers.

AI as an Evaluative Partner

Our analysis has unveiled that AI technology has the potential to evaluate students' performance processes and outcomes, playing the role of an evaluation partner with teachers. We classified this role into the following four aspects.

Track Students' Progress in Real-Time

AI monitors student performance by identifying their progress and challenges, producing informative reports that provide actionable insights to inform and facilitate teachers' decision-making and subsequent pedagogical actions. Shin et al. (2022) conducted a study on an AI-enabled prediction system for formative assessment practices in elementary school math classrooms. This system automatically monitors and detects students' progress in various learning states by analyzing their performance scores, providing valuable information for teachers to make informed decisions about future assessments, and providing appropriate scaffolding for specific students.

AI systems also can detect when a student is struggling or deviating from the expected trajectory (Gobert and Sao Pedro 2016). This ability gives teachers predictive analytics on student difficulties and early warnings to identify at-risk students (Arnold and Pistilli 2012; Jayaprakash et al. 2014). Teacher alerts (Dickler 2019; Gobert 2019; Gobert and Sao Pedro 2016; Gobert, Sao Pedro, and Betts 2023a) and time-series clustering approaches (Hung et al. 2017) have been utilized to notify teachers when students face challenges or to detect at-risk students in learning, enabling early intervention to support student success. Course Signals is an example of a system that predicts student success in real-time, determines the reasons behind students being at risk, and provides this information to instructors (Arnold and Pistilli 2012). Armed with valuable information from AI, teachers can approach students to gain a deeper understanding of their off-track performance and provide the necessary assistance.

Assess Students' Performance in Various Domains

The reviewed studies revealed that AI has the potential to assist teachers in monitoring and predicting students' cognitive and metacognitive performance, analyzing their learning engagement, and detecting their emotional states (Hung et al. 2017; Hussain et al. 2018; Käser et al. 2017; Moreno-Marcos et al. 2020). Various intelligent tutoring systems continuously monitor and analyze students' behaviors and cognition to evaluate their mastery of concepts, skills, and activities within the content domain (e.g., Arroyo et al. 2014; Dickler 2019; Gerard and Linn 2016; Gobert et al. 2013). For instance, Käser et al. (2017) employed dynamic Bayesian networks for student modeling performance, enabling instructors to adapt their instructional strategies to meet individual student needs. Hussain et al. (2018) developed an automated disengagement tracking tool that forecasts students' engagement in an online course, assisting instructors in modifying their instruction to enhance student engagement. Moreover, affect-sensitive ITS can identify and responsively address learners' affective states, including confusion, frustration, boredom, and engagement, enabling teachers to become aware of students' emotional states and adjust their instruction accordingly (e.g., Arroyo et al. 2014). By providing real-time insights into students' behavior interactions, cognitive performance, and emotional states, AI empowers teachers to accurately track student performance and make informed instructional adjustments.

Elicit Complex Performance

Various innovative assessment construct types were employed in ML-based assessment practices. From the analysis, we identified that written explanation and argumentation (e.g., Adair, Dickler, and Gobert 2020; Huang et al. 2011; Smith et al. 2019), essays (e.g., Gerard and Linn 2016; Gerard, Kidron, and Linn 2019), simulations (e.g., Käser et al. 2017), and games (e.g., Ghali, Ouellet, and Frasson 2016) were typically utilized when introducing ML into assessment practices.

Many intelligent tutoring systems employ students' behavioral activities and written artifacts to evaluate their performance. These systems collect data on students' behavior and interactions with the system, enabling teachers to track their progress throughout the learning process. An example of such a system is the Inquiry ITS, which employs educational machine algorithms to assess students' cognitive performance and their practice at each stage of scientific investigations (Adair, Dickler, and Gobert 2020; Dickler 2019; Gobert et al. 2018).

Provide Timely Scoring and Feedback

ML-based assessments automatically score students' various performance-based constructs using advanced ML algorithms. Many studies have reported the high accuracy of ML in scoring performance-based tasks. Some of the studies used traditional ML approach (e.g., Gerard and Linn 2016; Gerard, Kidron, and Linn 2019; Huang et al. 2011; Käser et al. 2017; Smith et al. 2019; Zhai et al. 2020b; Zhai, Haudek, and Ma 2022), but recent studies are leveraging deep learning (Zhai, He, and Krajcik 2022) and large language models (Liu et al. 2023; Wu et al. 2023).

Furthermore, many ML-based automatic scoring systems provide teachers with personalized feedback and report on students' performance (Adair, Dickler, and Gobert 2020; Dickler, Gobert, and Sao Pedro 2021; Shin et al. 2022), thus allowing teachers' prompt instructional adjustments and scaffolding (e.g., Gerard, Kidron, and Linn 2019; Huang and Shui 2012; Smith et al. 2019).

AI as a Pedagogical Decision Partner

The literature analysis revealed that some AI systems and applications offered pedagogical recommendations and suggestions to guide teachers' practices and instructional decision-making.

Some AI systems provide prescriptive recommendations to teachers, such as the Course Signals system (Arnold and Pistilli 2012), which provides instructors with specific actions to take based on AI's analysis of student behavior, such as sending an email to a student to discuss their course activities when they are inactive or falling behind peers. Also, the system offers suggested text for the email to help instructors talk with the student.

Several studies have reported using descriptive and dynamic AI recommendations for pedagogical strategies teachers can choose from and integrate into their teaching practices. An example is the teacher inquiry practice support (TIPS) (Adair, Dickler, and Gobert 2020), which offers teachers four categories of support: orienting, conceptual, procedural, and instrumental. By incorporating one or more AI recommendations with their pedagogical knowledge and strategies, teachers can provide personalized and timely scaffolding to students.

AI applications also offer teachers valuable insights into students' learning processes, allowing them to make data-driven instructional adjustments. For example, the Teacher's Partner, an AI-powered tool designed to collaborate with human intelligence (Paiva and Bittencourt 2020), automatically retrieves and processes students' online learning data to generate visualizations of their learning patterns and trends. This information about ongoing pedagogical situations and students' learning events during online learning empowers teachers to make informed decisions and offer personalized assistance. In the case of Reasoning Mind, teachers use real-time AI-provided reports to identify students struggling with specific concepts and engage in proactive remediation (Miller et al. 2015). Additionally, the Virtual Collaborative Research Institute system provides real-time information on student participation in collaborative chat, allowing teachers to take immediate action to improve the quality of collaborative discussions, mainly targeting individuals or groups facing difficulties (Van Leeuwen et al. 2014, 2015).

The Profile of AI's Unique Characteristics

To answer RQ4, we identified three distinctive characteristics of AI in supporting teaching: *AI–teacher interactivity*, *automaticity*, and *autonomy*, which collectively contribute to the profile of AI characteristics in teaching.

AI–Teacher Interactivity

Following the social behavior norms to interact with human teachers, a wide range of AI systems and applications in the eligible studies displayed the uniqueness of AI–teacher interactivity. AI and teachers interact and communicate in a natural and interpersonal manner (Chen, Park, and Breazeal 2020) using various approaches, including written messages, dialogue, and actions and behaviors in the cognition, social, and emotional domains (Buttussi and Chittaro 2020; Chen, Park, and Breazeal 2020; Fridin 2014). Natural language processing (NLP) models and systems were utilized to process and comprehend complex human written and spoken languages, enabling information exchange between teachers and AI. For example, teacher reports (Adair, Dickler, and Gobert 2020; Dickler 2019) present human-actionable text and graphs on student performance to facilitate teacher interaction. Social robots like KindSAR (Fridin 2014) engage in textual and verbal communication with teachers during their assistance in instructional activities. Intelligent tutoring systems like AutoTutor employ conversational interaction through simulated human tutorial dialogue designs (Graesser, Li, and Forsyth 2014).

Furthermore, some AI systems use nonverbal cues. They detect and interpret human body movements and behavior, including eye movements, hand gestures, and facial expressions, to communicate with and respond to users, including teachers. Humanoid robots like Nao (Ros et al. 2016), Saya (Hashimoto, Kato, and Kobayashi 2011), and Pepper (Morita et al. 2018) utilize various body cues, such as head movements, blinking eyes, and spatial orientation, to engage in communication and interaction with teachers and their students.

It is important to note that while some research has focused on investigating how AI can detect and monitor users' emotional states in educational settings, few studies explored and discussed the emotional dimension of teacher and AI interaction.

Nevertheless, some studies have examined the emotional impact of AI on teachers, including aspects like trust and perceived AI competence (Indira, Hermanto, and Pramono 2020; Serholt et al. 2017; Sharkey 2016). Additionally, the current AI–teacher interactivity primarily entails one-way interaction, with AI suggesting information, strategies, and guidance to teachers for enhanced pedagogy (e.g., Chen, Chen, and Lin 2020; Ros et al. 2016; Buttussi and Chittaro 2020).

AI Automaticity

In the reviewed studies, we identified that many AI systems and tools can automatically perform various tasks, such as tracking students' performance and challenges, analyzing their progress data, and providing timely feedback and guidance, which refers to AI automaticity. AI automaticity reflects the capability of AI to automatically process substantial amounts of data and information to detect and understand the occurrences within teaching and learning environments.

AI automaticity is observed in ML-enabled assessments (Zhai et al. 2020a), where AI can automatically score students' performance-based responses, such as written essays, drawings, and simulations, to provide teachers with automated scores (Gerard and Linn 2016; Gerard, Kidron, and Linn 2019; Käser et al. 2017; Zhai et al. 2020a; Zhai et al. 2020b) and feedback and guidance (Mehmood et al. 2017; Nehm, Ha, and Mayfield 2012).

AI automaticity is also found in automatically identifying student problems (Dickler 2019; Jayaprakash et al. 2014), alerts on students' challenges (Adair, Dickler, and Gobert 2020; Dickler 2019), and recommending teaching materials and resources (Adair, Dickler, and Gobert 2020; Gobert, Sao Pedro, and Betts 2023a; Gobert et al. 2023b; Heylen et al. 2004; Matthews et al. 2012) to promote instructional decision-making and action-taking. For instance, many intelligent tutoring systems (e.g., Arroyo et al. 2014; Dickler 2019; Gerard and Linn 2016; Gobert et al. 2023b) can automatically score students' interactions with the system and their progress to generate student performance reports, enabling teachers to better prepare their lessons and implement interventions and scaffolding strategies more effectively.

AI Autonomy

Arguably various AI systems could be distinguished from traditional educational technologies by the capacity to adaptively, if not autonomously, perform tasks within dynamic situations with less or no human intervention (Kara and Sevim 2013; Lundie 2016). This highlights a distinctive feature—AI autonomy, which refers to the level of agency an AI system possesses in selecting from different options and implementing its selections independently (Gunderson and Gunderson 2004). However, this area of AI technology continues to grow, raising psychological, ethical, and philosophical questions, such as AI consciousness and ethical responsibility (Meissner 2020).

According to the literature, AI autonomy manifests in various forms when AI fulfills the identified pedagogical roles. At the same time, we admit the overlap and blur of the boundaries between automaticity and autonomy. Most intelligent tutoring systems that independently adapt to individual students' learning needs and pace can provide teachers with performance reports, feedback, and recommendations. When AI takes on the role of a teaching assistant or pedagogical agent, such as Jill Watson (Goel and Polepeddi 2018), it can autonomously make decisions regarding answering questions, grading assignments, providing feedback, and interacting with students. AI demonstrates a certain level of agency to determine when and how to support students and teachers without further intervention by humans. Some AI-enabled assessment systems and tools can grade student work and provide actionable feedback and recommendations based on independent machine judgment without needing teacher consultation.

It is clear that, in our review, AI autonomy in teaching is still limited. Nonetheless, careful exploration of AI technology advancements and emerging dialog on AI autonomy among stakeholders would be necessary. AI autonomy arguably enables AI to enhance teaching by performing independent work in grading, analysis, and decision-making, thus reducing the workload for teachers in certain aspects of their pedagogical responsibilities.

Discussion

Over the past decade, there has been a growing interest in exploring the potential impact of AI technology on teaching and learning from varied aspects, such as teacher–AI complementarity and cooperation in classroom orchestration (Holstein, McLaren, and Aleven 2019; Kang et al. 2023) and the potential of AI in transforming teachers' pedagogy (Edwards and Cheok 2018). Nonetheless, we posit that a fundamental imperative resides in comprehending the scope of AI's capabilities and its potential contributions to teachers' pedagogical practices, approached through a pedagogically oriented lens. In this study, we systematically reviewed forty-four empirical studies based on the proposed framework to shed light on the current state of AI applications in teaching, the pedagogical roles of AI, and its distinctive characteristics in supporting and impacting various pedagogical activities of teachers.

Our findings reveal that advanced AI technology could significantly transform and shift teachers' traditional practices and roles. For example, AI can track students' progress, score written responses, and provide personalized scaffolding and feedback. Understanding the capabilities of AI in the context of teaching offers a complementary perspective for researchers, practitioners, and other stakeholders to explore further and discuss the evolving roles of teachers in the era of AI. In what follows, we discussed our study's significant findings and contributions to the existing literature, highlighting the knowledge gained from understanding the pedagogical contributions of AI.

AI Promotes Instruction to Meet the Customized Needs of Students

The intricacies associated with students' cognitive, metacognitive, and emotional states present a significant challenge for teachers in delivering personalized instruction and facilitating timely learning experiences (Gobert et al. 2018). Meeting the individualized needs of each student in an equal and inclusive manner can be exceptionally demanding for teachers.

Our study has revealed that AI technology has the potential to effectively assist teachers in addressing these challenges through various means. For instance, the teaching assistant can support teachers by providing students with adaptive and personalized learning resources, materials, and feedback (e.g., Gobert et al. 2013; Goel and Polepeddi 2018; Graesser, Li, and Forsyth 2014).

Importantly, AI systems can automatically track and diagnose students' progress and difficulties, manage their behavior, and predict their performance (Arroyo et al. 2014; Howard et al. 2017). These systems can also provide teachers real-time data on individual students' progress (e.g., Gobert et al. 2013) and offer teacher support (e.g., Adair, Dickler, and Gobert 2020). The data-driven insights provided by AI can facilitate teachers in delivering personalized instruction and scaffolding to students timely (Dickler, Gobert, and Sao Pedro 2021).

Furthermore, teachers in traditional settings often encounter difficulties in identifying and appropriately responding to students' emotional states and their cognitive and metacognitive performance. Our review findings indicate that affective AI systems, leveraging facial and speech recognition technologies, can detect students' emotional states (Heylen et al. 2004). This technology gives teachers automatic information on students' emotional states, enabling them to make informed decisions and adjust their instruction accordingly. Consequently, utilizing affective AI systems can enhance teachers' ability to support their students' emotional needs more effectively and efficiently.

Teachers Can Assess Student Performance Innovatively and Timely

Conventional technologies have significantly impacted classroom assessment by enabling computer-based assessment items and digital representation. However, most computer-based traditional evaluations rely on multiple-choice items, which may not fully capture students' complex cognitive abilities and higher-order thinking. Performance-based assessments and open-ended questions have been considered advantageous alternatives to address these assessment limitations. Yet, it was challenged by the limited time and resources for scoring and delayed feedback. Our review highlights the potential of AI to overcome such challenges.

Our review has identified a range of intelligent tutoring systems that can evaluate students' progress and interactions with the systems (Adair, Dickler, and Gobert 2020; Dickler 2019; Gobert et al. 2018). These intelligent tutoring systems are designed to provide and visualize in-process assessments, offering teachers detailed reports on students' progress at various stages of the learning process to support informed decisions.

AI-based assessments can afford performance-based assessments with timely and personalized feedback, promoting authentic learning activities (Zhai et al. 2020a; Zhai et al. 2020b) even in large classrooms (Zhai 2021). Various authentic assessment constructs, including written explanations and arguments (Adair, Dickler, and Gobert 2020; Zhai, Haudek, and Ma 2022), essays (Gerard and Linn 2016; Gerard, Kidron, and Linn 2019), simulations (Käser et al. 2017), and games (Ghali, Ouellet, and Frasson 2016), can be implemented, leveraging the potential of AI and ML. AI-based assessment can accurately score students' written responses with precision comparable to human scoring (Zhai, Shi, and Nehm 2021) while providing detailed and personalized feedback and reports on students' performance. By providing teachers with comprehensive information about students' performance, AI-based innovative assessment can assist them in making informed instructional decisions (Zhai and Nehm 2023).

The functions and roles of AI in tracking students' behavior and interactions with the system and scoring their written responses highlight the automaticity of AI. This prominent attribute denotes its ability to process vast amounts of data and information efficiently. The reviewed studies indicate that AI automaticity can support teachers in assessing students' progress and facilitate their lesson planning and instructional adaptations.

AI Participates in Classroom Communication and Interaction

The achievement of instructional objectives has traditionally relied on effective communication and interaction between teachers, students, and the available teaching resources in learning environments. While conventional technologies have been used as tools or platforms to facilitate classroom communication, our study suggests that AI is progressively emerging as a communicative agent (Reeves 2016) in classroom communication and interaction (Guzman and Lewis 2020), as it assumes various roles that demonstrate its characteristic of AI–human interactivity. In terms of the communication mode between teachers and AI, Edwards and Edwards (2017) argue that "the machine is increasingly being designed to teach and learn through interaction and to be responsive to natural teaching and learning methods employed by their human partners" (487). As a result, several contemporary communication variables, such as immediacy, interaction, and social and emotional attraction (Edwards and Cheok 2018), have garnered significant attention in research on human–intelligent machine communication.

Various AI technologies (e.g., virtual teaching agents, ITS, and social robots) can engage in automatic communication and interaction with teachers through oral or written discourse (Reeves 2016) in the domains of behavior, cognition, and social-emotional aspects (Buttussi and Chittaro 2020; Chen, Chen, and Lin 2020; Fridin 2014). We claim this interaction as the characteristic of AI–teacher interactivity, evident in several identified AI pedagogical roles. For instance, when AI functions as a teaching assistant to support instructional activities, it requires frequent communication with teachers to update its performance in tasks such as grading assignments and responding to questions (Goel and Polepeddi 2018). Similarly, when AI assists teachers in monitoring student progress, it must interact with them to convey information about students' advancements and challenges through various natural means, such as text and dialogue (Gerard and Linn 2016; Gobert et al. 2018). Our review indicates that AI is being developed to engage in a message exchange with teachers in classroom communication. This marks a departure from traditional technology primarily used for communication between teachers and students (Guzman and Lewis 2020).

AI Becomes an Emergent Partner in Teaching

Some researchers have raised the argument that the advancement of AI technology holds the potential for assuming significant social roles within educational contexts (e.g., Edwards and Cheok 2018; Morita et al. 2018; Mubin et al. 2013; Serholt et al. 2017; Sharkey 2016). These arguments have raised critical concerns, such as AI trust, AI replacement, and teacher apprehension (Lindner and Romeike 2019; Serholt et al. 2017; Sharkey 2016; van Ewijk, Smakman, and Konijn 2020). To ensure the successful integration of AI in teaching, Mubin et al. (2013) proposed the significance of clearly defining the roles of teachers and AI. While it is hard to describe such roles clearly in this complex arena, our review contributes to the literature by elucidating the potential pedagogical benefits of AI in teaching and how it can support, rather than replace, teachers.

Within this study, we have identified three pedagogical roles for AI to support and enhance teaching practices in three domains, including instruction, evaluation, and pedagogical decision-making. Our findings suggest that AI enables teachers to accomplish many previously unattainable tasks. Through continuous monitoring of student's progress and providing real-time reports and alerts regarding their academic and emotional well-being, AI can facilitate teachers' personalized and timely instructional support (Holstein, McLaren, and Aleven 2019; Qin, Li, and Yan 2020). Furthermore, AI-based assessment tools and their automaticity can empower teachers to employ authentic assessment tasks and deliver prompt scoring and personalized feedback. Our study underscores the emerging significance of AI in the classroom, where it serves as a platform or collaborator for teachers rather than a replacement.

Nevertheless, our review has revealed that studies describing fully autonomous AI instructors evoke apprehension. Instead, several studies have advocated for a hybrid approach that combines teachers' expertise and human qualities with the capabilities of AI to enhance student support (Kent 2022; Manyika et al. 2017). By augmenting teacher intelligence with machine intelligence, teachers can provide personalized guidance, support, and pedagogy that adapt to the ever-changing dynamics of educational environments.

While our review has shed light on the potential of AI in supporting teachers in education, significant gaps remain in the current literature. Although several studies have explored the possibility of AI in formal settings and subjects such as science, language arts, and computer science, further research is warranted to investigate the use of AI in informal settings, including remote teaching and field trips, as well as in other subject domains, such as social studies. While numerous studies have focused on the interactions between learners and AI, only a small percentage has examined how AI can support teachers. Moreover, to foster effective collaboration between teachers and AI, involving teachers in the design process and providing them with interfaces that enable seamless interaction with AI is imperative. However, the literature on these matters is limited, necessitating further research.

Conclusion and Limitations

Based on the proposed three-dimensional analytical framework, the current study analyzes the applications of AI in enhancing teachers' pedagogical practices. Based on the application types of AI, we categorized three distinct pedagogical roles of AI and identified its technological characteristics in supporting teaching practices. The findings highlight that teachers can effectively partner with AI to augment student learning by comprehending and harnessing the various roles and features of specific AI systems or tools. Through our systematic review, we present comprehensive evidence from the literature to initiate ongoing discussions and explorations concerning the benefits and transformations brought about by AI in the context of teaching.

Notwithstanding the identification of pedagogical roles and characteristics of AI in teaching, our study is subject to certain limitations. Firstly, although we conducted a comprehensive search of studies across educational levels and subject domains to understand the topic, we recognize that AI applications and systems may vary in their implementation across different subject domains, potentially presenting distinct roles in supporting teachers. Secondly, for this study, we excluded research that solely focused on how students utilize AI without considering the activities of teachers in AI-integrated educational environments. While such studies may provide relevant insights or evidence for classifying AI's pedagogical roles in teaching, they were not included in this study to ensure the quality of the synthesis.

References

Adair, A., Dickler, R., and Gobert, J. 2020. "Supporting Teachers Supporting Students: Iterative Development of TIPS in a Teacher Dashboard." In *The Interdisciplinarity of the Learning Sciences, 14th International Conference of the Learning Sciences (ICLS) 2020*, edited by M. Gresalfi and I. S. Horn, 1769–70. International Society of the Learning Sciences.

Arnold, K. E., and Pistilli, M. D. 2012. "Course Signals at Purdue: Using Learning Analytics to Increase Student Success." In *Proceedings of the 2nd International Conference on Learning Analytics and Knowledge*, 267–70. New York: ACM.

Arroyo, I., Woolf, B. P., Burelson, W., Muldner, K., Rai, D., and Tai, M. 2014. "A Multimedia Adaptive Tutoring System for Mathematics That Addresses Cognition, Metacognition and Affect." *International Journal of Artificial Intelligence in Education* 24, no. 4: 387–426.

Baker, R. S. 2016. "Stupid Tutoring Systems, Intelligent Humans." *International Journal of Artificial Intelligence in Education* 26, no. 2: 600–14. http://dx.doi.org/10.1007/s40593-016-0105-0

Baker, T., and Smith, L. 2019. *Educ-AI-tion Rebooted? Exploring the Future of Artificial Intelligence in Schools and Colleges.* Nesta Foundation.

Buttussi, F., and Chittaro, L. 2020. "Humor and Fear Appeals in Animated Pedagogical Agents: An Evaluation in Aviation Safety Education." *IEEE Transactions on Learning Technologies* 13, no. 1: 63–76. https://doi.org/10.1109/TLT.2019.2902401

Bywater, J. P., Chiu, J. L., Hong, J., and Sankaranarayanan, V. 2019. "The Teacher Responding Tool: Scaffolding the Teacher Practice of Responding to Student Ideas in Mathematics Classrooms." *Computers & Education* 139: 16–30.

Chang, C. W., Lee, J. H., Wang, C. Y., and Chen, G. D. 2010. "Improving the Authentic Learning Experience by Integrating Robots into the Mixed-Reality Environment." *Computers and Education* 55, no. 4: 1572–78.

ChanLin, L. J., Hong, J. C., Horng, J. S., Chang, S. H., and Chu, H. C. 2006. "Factors Influencing Technology Integration in Teaching: A Taiwanese Perspective." *Innovations in Education and Teaching International* 43, no. 1: 57–68.

Chen, H., Park, H. W., and Breazeal, C. 2020b. "Teaching and Learning with Children: Impact of Reciprocal Peer Learning with a Social Robot on Children's Learning and Emotive Engagement." *Computers and Education* 150.

Chen, L., Chen, P., and Lin, Z. 2020a. "Artificial Intelligence in Education: A Review." *IEEE Access* 8: 75264–78. https://doi.org/10.1109/ACCESS.2020.2988510

Chin, D. B., Dohmen, I. M., and Schwartz, D. L. 2013. "Young Children Can Learn Scientific Reasoning with Teachable Agents." *IEEE Transactions on Learning Technologies* 6, no. 3: 248–57. https://doi.org/10.1109/TLT.2013.24

Chounta, I. A., Bardone, E., Raudsep, A., and Pedaste, M. 2022. "Exploring Teachers' Perceptions of Artificial Intelligence as a Tool to Support Their Practice in Estonian K-12 Education." *International Journal of Artificial Intelligence in Education* 32, no. 3: 725–55.

Cukurova, M., Kent, C., and Luckin, R. 2019. "Artificial Intelligence and Multimodal Data in the Service of Human Decision-Making: A Case Study in Debate Tutoring." *British Journal of Educational Technology* 50, no. 6: 3032–46.

De Koster, S., Volman, M., and Kuiper, E. 2017. "Concept-Guided Development of Technology in Traditional and Innovative Schools: Quantitative and Qualitative Differences in Technology Integration." *Educational Technology Research and Development* 65: 1325–44.

Dickler, R. 2019. An Intelligent Tutoring System and Teacher Dashboard to Support Students on Mathematics in Science Inquiry. Doctoral dissertation, Rutgers University, School of Graduate Studies.

Dickler, R., Gobert, J., and Sao Pedro, M. 2021. "Using Innovative Methods to Explore the Potential of an Alerting Dashboard for Science Inquiry." *Journal of Learning Analytics* 8, no. 2: 105–22.

Edwards, B. I., and Cheok, A. D. 2018. "Why Not Robot Teachers: Artificial Intelligence for Addressing Teacher Shortage." *Applied Artificial Intelligence* 32, no. 4: 345–60.

Edwards, A., and Edwards, C. 2017. "The Machines Are Coming: Future Directions in Instructional Communication Research." *Communication Education* 66, no. 4: 487–88.

Elo, S., and Kyngäs, H. 2008. "The Qualitative Content Analysis Process." *Journal of Advanced Nursing* 62, no. 1: 107–15. https://doi.org/10.1111/j.1365-2648.2007.04569.x

Fridin, M. 2014. "Storytelling by a Kindergarten Social Assistive Robot: A Tool for Constructive Learning in Preschool Education." *Computers and Education* 70: 53–64. https://doi.org/10.1016/j.compedu.2013.07.043

Gerard, L. F., and Linn, M. C. 2016. "Using Automated Scores of Student Essays to Support Teacher Guidance in Classroom Inquiry." *Journal of Science Teacher Education* 27, no. 1: 111–29.

Gerard, L., Kidron, A., and Linn, M. C. 2019. "Guiding Collaborative Revision of Science Explanations." *International Journal of Computer-Supported Collaborative Learning* 14: 1–34.

Ghali, R., Ouellet, S., and Frasson, C. 2016. "LewiSpace: An Exploratory Study with a Machine Learning Model in an Educational Game." *Journal of Education and Training Studies* 4, no. 1: 192–201.

Gobert, J. 2019. Inq-Blotter: Designing Supports for Teachers' Real Time Instruction (NSF-IIS-1902647). Awarded by the. National Science Foundation.

Gobert, J. D., Moussavi, R., Li, H., Sao Pedro, M., and Dickler, R. 2018. "Scaffolding Students' On-line Data Interpretation during Inquiry with Inq-ITS." In *Cyber-physical Laboratories in Engineering and Science Education*, edited by M. E. Auer, A. K. M. Azad, A. Edwards, and T. de Jong, 191–218. Cham: Springer

Gobert, J., and Sao Pedro, M. 2016. Inq-Blotter: A Real-Time Alerting Tool to Transform Teachers' Assessment of Science Inquiry Practices (NSF-IIS-1629045). Awarded from the National Science Foundation.

Gobert, J. D., Sao Pedro, M., Raziuddin, J., and Baker, R. S. 2013. "From Log Files to Assessment Metrics: Measuring Students' Science Inquiry Skills Using Educational Data Mining." *Journal of the Learning Sciences* 22, no. 4: 521–63.

Gobert, J. D., Sao Pedro, M.A., and Betts, C.G. 2023a. "An AI-Based Teacher Dashboard to Support Students' Inquiry: Design Principles, Features, and Technological Specifications." In *Handbook of Research on Science Education*, edited by N. Lederman, D. Zeidler, and J. Lederman, Vol. 3, 1011–44. London: Routledge. https://doi.org/10.4324/9780367855758

Gobert, J. D., Sao Pedro, M. A., Li, H., and Lott, C. 2023b. "Intelligent Tutoring Systems: A History and an Example of an ITS for Science." In *International Encyclopaedia of Education*, edited by R.Tierney, F. Rizvi, K. Ercikan, and G. Smith, Vol. 4, 460–70. Amsterdam: Elsevier.

Goel, A. K., and Polepeddi, L. 2018. "Jill Watson: A Virtual Teaching Assistant for Online Education." In *Learning Engineering for Online Education*, 120–43. London: Routledge.

Graesser, A. C., Li, H., and Forsyth, C. 2014. "Learning by Communicating in Natural Language with Conversational Agents." *Current Directions in Psychological Science* 23: 374–80.

Guilherme, A. 2019. "AI and Education: The Importance of Teacher and Student Relations." *AI and Society* 34, no. 1: 47–54. https://doi.org/10.1007/s00146-017-0693-8

Gunderson, J. P., and Gunderson, L. F. 2004. "Intelligence ≠ Autonomy ≠ Capability." *Performance Metrics for Intelligent Systems, PERMIS.*

Guzman, A. L., and Lewis, S. C. 2020. "Artificial Intelligence and Communication: A Human–Machine Communication Research Agenda." *New Media and Society* 22, no. 1: 70–86.

Haristiani, N. 2019. "Artificial Intelligence (AI) Chatbot as Language Learning Medium: An Inquiry." *Journal of Physics: Conference Series* 1387, no. 1: 012020. Bristol: IOP Publishing.

Harris, J. 2005. "Our Agenda for Technology Integration: It's Time to Choose." *Contemporary Issues in Technology and Teacher Education* 5, no. 2: 116–22.

Hashimoto, T., Kato, N., and Kobayashi, H. 2011. "Development of Educational System with the Android Robot SAYA and Evaluation." *International Journal of Advanced Robotic Systems* 8, no. 3: 28.

Heylen, D., Vissers, M., op den Akker, R., and Nijholt, A. 2004. "Affective Feedback in a Tutoring System for Procedural Tasks." In Affective Dialogue Systems, ADS 2004, edited by E. André, L. Dybkjær, W. Minker, and P. Heisterkamp, Lecture Notes in Computer Science, Vol. 3068, 244–53. Berlin: Springer.

Holstein, K., McLaren, B. M., and Aleven, V. 2019. "Co-designing a Real-Time Classroom Orchestration Tool to Support Teacher–AI Complementarity." *Journal of Learning Analytics* 6, no. 2: 27–52.

Howard, S. K., Chan, A., Mozejko, A., and Caputi, P. 2015. "Technology Practices: Confirmatory Factor Analysis and Exploration of Teachers' Technology Integration in Subject Areas." *Computers & Education* 90: 24–35.

Howard, C., Jordan, P., di Eugenio, B., and Katz, S. 2017. "Shifting the Load: A Peer Dialogue Agent That Encourages its Human Collaborator to Contribute More to Problem Solving." *International Journal of Artificial Intelligence in Education* 27, no. 1: 101–29.

Huang, C. J., Wang, Y. W., Huang, T. H., Chen, Y. C., Chen, H. M., and Chang, S. C. 2011. "Performance Evaluation of an Online Argumentation Learning Assistance Agent." *Computers and Education* 57, no. 1: 1270–80.

Huang, S.-L., and Shiu, J.-H. 2012. "A User-Centric Adaptive Learning System for e-Learning 2.0." *Journal of Educational Technology & Society* 15, no. 3: 214–25.

Hung, J. L., Wang, M. C., Wang, S., Abdelrasoul, M., Li, Y., and He, W. 2017. "Identifying at-Risk Students for Early Interventions—A Time-Series Clustering Approach." *IEEE Transactions on Emerging Topics in Computing* 5, no. 1: 45–55.

Hussain, M., Zhu, W., Zhang, W., and Abidi, S. M. R. 2018. "Student Engagement Predictions in an e-Learning System and Their Impact on Student Course Assessment Scores." *Computational Intelligence and Neuroscience* 6, no. 347: 186.

Hwang, G.-J., Xie, H., Wah, B. W., and Gašević, D. 2020. "Vision, Challenges, Roles and Research Issues of Artificial Intelligence in Education." *Computers and Education: Artificial Intelligence* 1: 100001. https://doi.org/10.1016/j.caeai.2020.100001

Inan, F. A., and Lowther, D. L. 2010. "Factors Affecting Technology Integration in K-12 Classrooms: A Path Model." *Edu Technology Research and Development 58*: 137–54.

Indira, E. W. M., Hermanto, A., and Pramono, S. E. 2020. "Improvement of Teacher Competence in the Industrial Revolution Era 4.0." In *International Conference on Science and Education and Technology (ISET 2019)*, 350–52. Dordrecht: Atlantis Press.

Jayaprakash, S. M., Moody, E. W., Lauria, E. J. M., Regan, J. R., and Baron, J. D. 2014. "Early Alert of Academically At-Risk Students: An Open-Source Analytics Initiative." *Journal of Learning Analytics* 1, no. 1: 6–47.

Kang, J., Kang, C., Yoon, J., Ji, H., Li, T., Moon, H., and Han, J. 2023. "Dancing on the Inside: A Qualitative Study on Online Dance Learning with Teacher-AI Cooperation." *Education and Information Technologies* 28: 1211–41.

Kara, N., and Sevim, N. 2013. "Adaptive Learning Systems: Beyond Teaching Machines." *Contemporary Educational Technology* 4, no. 2: 108–20.

Käser, T., Klingler, S., Schwing, A. G., and Gross, M. 2017. "Dynamic Bayesian Networks for Student Modeling." *IEEE Transactions on Learning Technologies* 10, no. 4: 450–62.

Kent, D. 2022. Artificial Intelligence in Education: Fundamentals for Educators. KOTESOL DCC.

Lindner, A., and Romeike, R. 2019. "Teachers' Perspectives on Artificial Intelligence." In ISSEP 2019: 12th International Conference on Informatics in Schools: Situation, Evaluation and Perspectives. At Larnaca, Cyprus.

Liu, Z., He, X., Liu, L., Liu, T., and Zhai, X. 2023. "Context Matters: A Strategy to Pre-train Language Model for Science Education." In *AI in Education 2023*, edited by N. Wang, G. Rebolledo-Mendez, V. Dimitrova, N. Matsuda, and O. C. Santos, Vol. CCIS 1831, pp. 1–9. Cham: Springer. https://doi.org/10.1007/978-3-031-36336-8_103

Lundie, D. 2016. "Authority, Autonomy and Automation: The Irreducibility of Pedagogy to Information Transactions." *Studies in Philosophy and Education* 35, no. 3: 279–91.

Manyika, J., Chui, M., Miremadi, M., Bughin, J., George, K., Willmott, P., and Dewhurst, M. 2017. "A Future That Works: AI, Automation, Employment, and Productivity." *McKinsey Global Institute Research, Tech. Rep 60*: 1–135.

Matthews, K., Janicki, T., He, L., and Patterson, L. 2012. "Implementation of an Automated Grading System with an Adaptive Learning Component to Affect Student Feedback and Response Time." *Journal of Information Systems* 23, no. 1: 71–84.

Mayring, P. 2014. "Qualitative Content Analysis Theoretical Foundation, Basic Procedures and Software Solution." In *Approaches to Qualitative Research in Mathematics Education. Advances in Mathematics Education*, edited by A. Bikner-Ahsbahs, C. Knipping, and N. Presmeg, 365–80. Dordrecht: Springer. http://www.beltz.de

McHugh, M. L. 2012. "Interrater Reliability: The Kappa Statistic." *Biochemia medica* 22, no. 3: 276–82.

McKnight, K., O'Malley, K., Ruzic, R., Horsley, M. K., Franey, J. J., and Bassett, K. 2016. "Teaching in a Digital Age: How Educators Use Technology to Improve Student Learning." *Journal of Research on Technology in Education* 48, no. 3: 194–211.

Mehmood, A., On, B. W., Lee, I., and Choi, G. S. 2017. "Prognosis Essay Scoring and Article Relevancy Using Multi-text Features and Machine Learning." *Symmetry* 9, no. 1: 11.

Meissner, G. 2020. "Artificial Intelligence: Consciousness and Conscience." *AI and Society* 35, no. 1: 225–35. https://doi.org/10.1007/s00146-019-00880-4

Miller, W. L., Baker, R., Labrum, M., Petsche, K., Liu, Y-H., and Wagner, A. 2015. "Automated Detection of Proactive Remediation by Teachers in Reasoning Mind Classrooms." In *Proceedings of the 5th International Learning Analytics and Knowledge Conference*, 290–94.

Moreno-Marcos, P. M., Muñoz-Merino, P. J., Maldonado- Mahauad, J., Pérez-Sanagustín, M., Alario-Hoyos, C., and Delgado Kloos, C. 2020. "Temporal Analysis for Dropout Prediction Using Self-Regulated Learning Strategies in Self-paced MOOCs." *Computers and Education* 145, no. 103: 728.

Morita, T., Akashiba, S., Nishimoto, C., Takahashi, N., Kukihara, R., Kuwayama, M., and Yamaguchi, T. 2018. "A Practical Teacher–Robot Collaboration Lesson Application Based on PRINTEPS." *Review of Socionetwork Strategies* 12, no. 1: 97–126.

Mubin, O., Stevens, C. J., Shahid, S., Mahmud, A. A., and Dong, J. J. 2013. "A Review of the Applicability of Robots in Education." *Technology for Education and Learning* 1, no. 1: 1–7.

Nehm, R. H., Ha, M., and Mayfield, E. 2012. "Transforming Biology Assessment with Machine Learning: Automated Scoring of Written Evolutionary Explanations." *Journal of Science Education and Technology* 21, no. 1: 183–96. https://doi.org/10.1007/s10956-011-9300-9

Okojie, M. C., Olinzock, A. A., and Okojie-Boulder, T. C. 2006. "The Pedagogy of Technology Integration." *Journal of Technology Studies* 32, no. 2: 66–71.

Onwuegbuzie, A. J., and Frels, R. 2016. *Seven Steps to a Comprehensive Literature Review: A Multimodal and Cultural Approach*. Thousand Oaks, CA: Sage.

Ouyang, F., and Jiao, P. 2021. "Artificial Intelligence in Education: The Three Paradigms." *Computers and Education: Artificial Intelligence 2*: 100020.

Paiva, R., and Bittencourt, I. I. 2020. "Helping Teachers Help Their Students: A Human–AI Hybrid Approach." In *International Conference on Artificial Intelligence in Education*, 448–59. Cham: Springer.

Qin, F., Li, K., and Yan, J. 2020. "Understanding User Trust in Artificial Intelligence-Based Educational Systems: Evidence from China." *British Journal of Education Technology* 51, no. 5: 1693–710.

Reeves, J. 2016. "Automatic for the People: The Automation of Communicative Labor." *Communication and Critical/ Cultural Studies* 13, no. 2: 150–65.

Roll, I., and Wylie, R. 2016. "Evolution and Revolution in artificial intelligence in education. *International Journal of Artificial Intelligence in Education* 26, no. 2: 582–99. https://doi.org/10.1007/s40593-016-0110-3.

Ros, R., Oleari, E., Pozzi, C., Sacchitelli, F., Baranzini, D., Bagherzadhalimi, A., Sanna, A., and Demiris, Y. 2016. "A Motivational Approach to Support Healthy Habits in Long-term Child–Robot Interaction." *International Journal of Social Robotics* 8, no. 5: 599–617.

Russell, S. J. 2010. *Artificial Intelligence: A Modern Approach*. San Antonio, TX: Pearson Education.

Serholt, S., Barendregt, W., Vasalou, A., Alves-Oliveira, P., Jones, A., Petisca, S., and Paiva, A. 2017. "The Case of Classroom Robots: Teachers' Deliberations on the Ethical Tensions." *AI and Society* 32, no. 4: 613–31. https://doi.org/10.1007/s00146-016-0667-2

Sharkey, A. J. C. 2016. "Should We Welcome Robot Teachers?" *Ethics and Information Technology* 18, no. 4: 283–97. https://doi.org/10.1007/s10676-016-9387-z.

Shin, J., Chen, F., Lu, C., and Bulut, O. 2022. "Analyzing Students' Performance in Computerized Formative Assessments to Optimize Teachers' Test Administration Decisions Using Deep Learning Frameworks." *Journal of Computers in Education* 9, no. 1: 71–91.

Smith, A., Leeman-Munk, S., Shelton, A., Mott, B., Wiebe, E., and Lester, J. 2019. "A Multimodal Assessment Framework for Integrating Student Writing and Drawing in Elementary Science Learning." *IEEE Transactions on Learning Technologies* 12, no. 1: 3–15.

Spector, J. M., and Ma, S. 2019. "Inquiry and Critical Thinking Skills for the Next Generation: From Artificial Intelligence Back to Human Intelligence." *Smart Learning Environments* 6, no. 1: 1–11.

van Ewijk, G., Smakman, M., and Konijn, E. A. 2020. "Teachers' Perspectives on Social Robots in Education: An Exploratory Case Study." In *Proceedings of the Interaction Design and Children Conference, IDC 2020*, 273–80. https://doi.org/10.1145/3392063.3394397

Van Leeuwen, A., Janssen, J., Erkens, G., and Brekelmans, M. 2014. "Supporting Teachers in Guiding Collaborating Students: Effects of Learning Analytics in CSCL." *Computers & Education*, 79, 28–39.

Van Leeuwen, A., Janssen, J., Erkens, G., and Brekelmans, M. 2015. "Teacher Regulation of Cognitive Activities during Student Collaboration: Effects of Learning Analytics." *Computers & Education* 90: 80–94.

Veletsianos, G., and Russell, G. S. 2014. "Pedagogical Agents." In *Handbook of Research on Educational Communications and Technology*, 4th edition, edited by J. M. Spector, M. D. Merrill, J. Elen, and M. J. Bishop, 759–69. New York: Springer.

Wenger, E. 1987. *Artificial Intelligence and Tutoring Systems*. Los Altos, CA: Morgan Kauffman.

Westlund, J. K., Lee, J. J., Plummer, L., Faridi, F., Gray, J., Berlin, M., Quintus-Bosz, H., et al. 2016. "Tega: A Social Robot." In *The Eleventh ACE/IEEE International Conference on Human Robot Interaction*, 2016, 561.

Williamson, B. 2016. "Boundary Brokers: Mobile Policy Networks, Database Pedagogies, and Algorithmic Governance in Education." In *Research, Boundaries, and Policy in Networked Learning*, edited by T. Ryberg, C. Sinclair, S. Bayne, and M. de Laat, 41–57. New York: Springer.

Woo, J. H., and Choi, H. 2021. "Systematic Review for AI-Based Language Learning Tools." *arXiv preprint arXiv:2111.04455.*

Wu, X., He, X., Li, T., Liu, N., and Zhai, X. 2023. "Matching Exemplar as Next Sentence Prediction (MeNSP): Zero-shot Prompt Learning for Automatic Scoring in Science Education." In *AI in Education 2023*, edited by N. Wang, G. Rebolledo-Mendez, N. Matsuda, O. C. Santos, and V. Dimitrova, Vol. LNAI 13916, 401–13. New York: Springer. https://doi.org/https://doi.org/10.1007/978-3-031-36272-9_33

Xu, W., and Ouyang, F. 2021. "A Systematic Review of AI Role in the Educational System Based on a Proposed Conceptual Framework." *Education and Information Technologies* 27: 4195–223.

Yu, Y. C. 2017. "Teaching with a Dual-Channel Classroom Feedback System in the Digital Classroom Environment." *IEEE Transactions on Learning Technologies* 10, no. 3: 391–402.

Yun, S.-S., Kim, M., and Choi, M.-T. 2013. "Easy Interface and Control of Tele-education Robots." *International Journal of Social Robotics* 5, no. 3: 335–43.

Zawacki-Richter, O., Marín, V. I., Bond, M., and Gouverneur, F. 2019. "Systematic Review of Research on Artificial Intelligence Applications in Higher Education—Where Are the Educators?" *International Journal of Educational Technology in Higher Education* 16, no. 1: 39. https://doi.org/10.1186/s41239-019-0171-0

Zhai, X. 2021. "Practices and Theories: How Can Machine Learning Assist in Innovative Assessment Practices in Science Education." *Journal of Science Education and Technology* 30, no. 2: 139–49.

Zhai, X., Haudek, K., and Ma, W. 2022. "Assessing Argumentation Using Machine Learning and Cognitive Diagnostic Modeling." *Research in Science Education* 53, 405–24. https://doi.org/https://doi.org/10.1007/s11165-022-10062-w

Zhai, X., Haudek, K. C., Shi, L., Nehm, R., and Urban-Lurain, M. 2020a. "From Substitution to Redefinition: A Framework of Machine Learning-Based Science Assessment." *Journal of Research in Science Teaching* 57, no. 9: 1430–59. https://doi.org/10.1002/tea.21658

Zhai, X., He, P., and Krajcik, J. 2022. "Applying Machine Learning to Automatically Assess Scientific Models." *Journal of Research in Science Teaching* 59, no. 10: 1765–94.

Zhai, X., and Jackson, D. F. 2023. "A Pedagogical Framework for Mobile Learning in Science Education." In *International Encyclopedia of Education*, 4th edition, edited by R. J. Tierney, F. Rizvi, and K. Ercikan, 215–23. Amsterdam: Elsevier.

Zhai, X., and Nehm, R. H. 2023. "AI and Formative Assessment: The Train Has Left The Station." *Journal of Research in Science Teaching* 60, no. 6: 1390–98.

Zhai, X., Shi, L., and Nehm, R. H. 2021. "A Meta-analysis of Machine Learning-Based Science Assessments: Factors Impacting Machine-Human Score Agreements." *Journal of Science Education and Technology* 30: 361–79.

Zhai, X., Yin, Y., Pellegrino, J. W., Haudek, K. C., and Shi, L. 2020b. "Applying Machine Learning in Science Assessment: A Systematic Review." *Studies in Science Education* 56, no. 1: 111–51.

Zhai, X., Zhang, M., Li, M., and Zhang, X. 2019. "Understanding the Relationship between Levels of Mobile Technology Use in High School Physics Classrooms and the Learning Outcome." *British Journal of Educational Technology* 50, no. 2: 750–66.

16

A Design Framework for Integrating Artificial Intelligence to Support Teachers' Timely Use of Knowledge-in-Use Assessments

Peng He, Namsoo Shin, Xiaoming Zhai and Joseph Krajcik

Introduction

In a world marked by incessant changes, individuals need usable knowledge (referred to as "knowledge-in-use") that will enable them to navigate life's demands and flourish in an ever-evolving future (National Research Council [NRC] 2011; 2012a). In the context of science education, knowledge-in-use underscores the application of scientific knowledge to make sense of meaningful phenomena or solve challenging problems (He et al. 2023a; Krajcik et al. 2023; Li et al. 2024; NRC 2012b). The *Framework for K–12 Science Standards* in the US (hereafter referred to as the *Framework*; NRC 2012b) addresses this concept by establishing three-dimensional (3D) performance expectations (NGSS Lead States 2013) that integrate the three dimensions of scientific knowledge—disciplinary core ideas (DCIs), crosscutting concepts (CCCs), and scientific and engineering practices (SEPs) across K–12 STEM education. However, these ambitious goals pose a challenge to traditional assessment methods, such as multiple-choice questions, particularly in classroom settings (NRC 2014). Newly devised 3D assessments (e.g., Harris et al. 2019; He et al. 2023b) typically utilize performance-based constructed responses. The timely analyses of these assessments present a significant hurdle for teachers, but even when these analyses are available, interpreting these scores for immediate instructional adjustments presents an even greater challenge for teachers.

Emerging digital technologies, including artificial intelligence (AI), could potentially assist teachers in addressing these challenges. Up to this point, STEM education researchers have harnessed AI techniques (e.g., machine learning [ML], learning analytics) to explore numerous critical domains. For instance, these technologies have been leveraged to address the challenges of classroom assessments (e.g., Zhai et al. 2020), including automatic scoring (Liu et al. 2014), student feedback (e.g., Lee et al. 2021), learning guidance (e.g., Ryoo and Linn 2016), and the automated generation of student reports (e.g., Matuk et al. 2016). Researchers have also employed ML to automate the scoring of students' responses on knowledge-in-use assessments (e.g., Zhai, He, and Krajcik 2022) and developed user-friendly Web portals or apps to furnish teachers with automatically generated student reports (e.g., Moharreri,

Peng He et al., *A Design Framework for Integrating Artificial Intelligence to Support Teachers' Timely Use of Knowledge-in-Use Assessments*. In: *Uses of Artificial Intelligence in STEM Education*. Edited by: Xiaoming Zhai and Joseph Krajcik, Oxford University Press. © Oxford University Press (2024). DOI: 10.1093/oso/9780198882077.003.0016

Ha, and Nehm 2014). Nevertheless, even with timely student reports, teachers may encounter difficulties interpreting students' performances and making effective instructional decisions (Bennett 2018). Prior research suggests that a comprehensive understanding of knowledge-in-use assessments and actionable knowledge, such as content-specific instructional strategies, is essential for teachers to determine their subsequent instructional moves (Bennett 2018; Furtak 2017). In the intricate social environment of a classroom, the process of instructional decision-making places significant cognitive demands on teachers (Blackley, Redmond, and Peel 2021; Sweller 1988).

This chapter delves into the utilization of knowledge-in-use assessments as a means to alleviate the cognitive load on teachers and facilitate timely and effective instructional decisions. It further proposes a design framework to guide the integration of AI for teachers' use of knowledge-in-use assessments to support their timely instructional decision-making in science classrooms. Two key questions guide our exploration: (1) What information do teachers require to make timely instructional decisions that foster student knowledge-in-use? (2) How can AI assist teachers in making timely instructional decisions to enhance student knowledge-in-use?

Theoretical Perspectives and Design Framework

Extensive literature underscores the importance of teacher instructional decisions as a pivotal element in improving teaching (Blackley, Redmond, and Peel 2021; Clough, Berg, and Olson 2009; Schoenfeld 2010; Shavelson 1986). Shavelson and Stern's (1981) teacher cognition theory forms the cornerstone of this perspective, positing that teachers' thoughts, judgments, and decisions form a synergistic cognitive process integral to teaching. According to this theory, teachers base instructional decisions on an amalgamation of information about students, subject matter, and the educational environment. They make these "real-time" or "in-flight" decisions during classroom interactions, often without ample time for extensive reflection or information gathering. This section explores previous research, providing a synopsis of the theoretical perspectives on instructional decisions, knowledge-in-use assessments, and the application of AI in assessment practices to aid teacher decision-making.

Conceptualizing Instructional Decision-Making

Research spanning over the past four decades has sought to shed light on the cognitive processes that underpin teachers' instructional decisions by developing several conceptual models. These models typically employ critical components or multiple-step processes to elucidate teachers' decision-making activities.

Prominent conceptual models for understanding teachers' instructional decisions often draw upon schema theory as it applies to teacher cognition (Leinhardt and Greeno 1986; Shavelson and Stern 1981; Westerman 1991). Schema theory, as proposed by Piaget (1952), suggests that humans organize knowledge into units, or schemas, to store and retrieve information. This construct has been pivotal to cognitive psychologists seeking to understand the interplay of factors critical to the instructional decision-making process (Adams and Collins 1979; Rumelhart 1980). Teacher instructional decision-making, considered a complex cognitive skill, requires a constellation of interrelated schemata to utilize information for instructional actions (Leinhardt and Greeno 1986). For example, Shavelson and Stern (1981) proposed a decision-making framework that includes: (a) antecedent conditions, (b) teacher characteristics, (c) cognitive processes of information selection and integration, (d) consequences for teachers and students, and (e) teacher evaluations of judgments, decisions, and teaching routines. Expanding on this, Shavelson (1986) identified three schemata integral to teacher cognition: scripts, scenes, and propositional structures.

Alternatively, some models illustrate the teacher decision-making process sequentially, such as Schoenfeld's (2010) goal-oriented decision-making framework. In his prior work, Schoenfeld (1998) described a theory of teaching-in-context that includes teachers' beliefs, goals, and knowledge to make instructional decisions. Building upon his prior work, Schoenfeld (2010) proposed the goal-oriented decision-making framework that illustrates "one's decisions about what goals to pursue, and how to pursue them, are made based on one's current resources, goals, and orientations" (Schoenfeld 2010, 8). Based on his fundamental argument, teacher interactional decision takes place as follows: (a) enters a classroom situation with a specific body of resources, goals, and orientations; (b) takes in and orients to the classroom situation with knowledge; (c) establishes goals; (d) makes goal-oriented decisions, consciously or unconsciously; and (e) takes and monitors the actions iteratively. He suggested that teachers' decisions are driven by their anticipated goals and the resources they have at their disposal, including knowledge in its various forms—facts, procedural and conceptual knowledge, and problem-solving strategies. Schoenfeld (2010) emphasized that teachers' dispositions, beliefs, values, and metacognitive abilities, like monitoring and self-regulation, also shape their instructional decisions and actions.

Despite the insights offered by these models, making instructional decisions promptly remains a formidable challenge for teachers, particularly for those at the beginning of their careers. Such decisions necessitate real-time processing of vast amounts of classroom information (Blackley, Redmond, and Peel 2021). Given the limitations in data collection and speedy processing, teachers often struggle to make immediate, appropriate instructional decisions without support.

Utilizing Classroom Assessments for Instructional Decision-Making

Classroom assessment serves as a crucial tool for collecting student learning information, which subsequently informs teachers' decision-making processes in classrooms (Anderson 2003). This process results in an instructional interplay among teachers, students, and disciplinary knowledge. Teachers utilize classroom assessment data to gauge students' comprehension levels, inform lesson planning, and differentiate instruction (Borko, Roberts, and Shavelson 2008; Hamilton et al. 2009; Kerr et al. 2006).

In the realm of science education, assessments predicated on knowledge-in-use are extensively employed to facilitate student 3D learning. Anchored in the concept of situated learning (Greeno, Collins, and Resnick 1996), these assessments are intricate constructs due to the demand they place on students to apply 3D knowledge—DCIs, SEPs, and CCCs—to comprehend phenomena and solve problems. Consequently, traditional assessment formats like multiple-choice and matching items typically will not suffice (NRC 2014) to measure such knowledge. Existing literature posits that performance-based tasks generate tangible products or performances, serving as evidence of learning. These tasks can manifest as student-written text responses, plans for conducting investigations, or drawn models (NRC 2014).

Nevertheless, the complex nature of these knowledge-in-use tasks presents a formidable challenge for both developers and practitioners of such assessments. Scoring and interpreting the results of students' performance on these assessment tasks also pose significant difficulties. In our previous research, we adopted an evidence-centered design approach (Mislevy and Haertel 2006) to develop knowledge-in-use tasks suitable for classroom use (Harris et al. 2019). To assess students' constructed responses, we designed holistic (Harris et al. 2019; Li et al. 2021) and analytic rubrics (He et al. 2023b), providing valuable assessment information for both teachers and students. Nonetheless, difficulties persist in the presentation and interpretation of assessment information to effectively support teachers' instructional decisions and stimulate students' science learning in everyday classrooms.

Leveraging AI in Assessment Practices for Instructional Decision-Making

Machine learning (ML), a subset of AI technology, applies algorithms to autonomously score student responses on intricate performance-based assessments, thereby providing immediate results for students and teachers. Automated scoring through ML has been utilized by researchers to cultivate personalized student feedback (Lee et al. 2021) and adaptive learning systems (Gerard and Linn 2016), and to support teachers in timely adjustments to their instruction (Ghali, Ouellet, and Frasson 2016). Researchers have categorized ML into three basic and commonly used approaches: supervised, unsupervised, and semi-supervised (Murphy 2012; Zhu and Goldberg 2022). Of these, supervised ML has been established as a mature and commonly used approach in science education. However, unlike unsupervised and semi-supervised ML, supervised ML requires human intervention, as the machine learns from human-scored student response data to construct an algorithmic model, which it then uses to score new cases automatically. Numerous researchers have leveraged the supervised ML approach to construct algorithms for automatically scoring student responses using analytic and/or holistic scoring rubrics (Jescovitch et al. 2021; Li, Liu, and Krajcik 2023a).

Researchers have employed natural language processing to score student-constructed written responses on assessment tasks, especially for assessing student scientific explanations (Ha and Nelm 2016) and argumentation (Mao et al. 2018). Furthermore, convolutional neural networks have been used to score more challenging tasks, such as student-drawn models online (Zhai, He, and Krajcik 2022) and in paper–pencil formats (Li, Liu, and Krajcik 2023a). These studies have provided robust evidence of ML scoring's high accuracy and agreement with trained human experts in scoring student-written and -drawn constructed responses. By utilizing these immediate ML scores, some researchers have created automated guidance or student feedback systems to support personalized and adaptive learning (Zacharia et al. 2015), especially in scientific argumentation (Lee et al. 2021), explanation (Gerard et al. 2016; Tansomboon et al. 2017), and student-generated concept diagrams (Ryoo and Linn 2016). ML can significantly alleviate teacher workload by scoring student-constructed responses and providing timely feedback.

However, the generation of comprehensive, immediate reports on students' performance for both individuals and the entire class, which can enable teachers to adjust their instruction in a timely manner, remains a challenge. To our knowledge, only a few dashboards have been developed for science teachers. Some of these dashboards provide student information about understanding scientific inquiry, such as the WISE dashboard (Matuk et al. 2016), the CK Biology curriculum dashboard (Acosta and Slotta 2018), and the SAIL Smart Space tablet tool (Tissenbaum and Slotta 2019). Regrettably, these dashboards either do not provide alerts (Acosta and Slotta 2018; Matuk et al. 2016) or solely provide alerts (Tissenbaum and Slotta 2019) for teachers when students complete an activity. In response to these shortcomings, Dickler and colleagues (2021) developed Inq-ITS, a science-intelligent tutoring system, providing teachers with data on students' inquiry practices, such as forming questions/hypothesizing, collecting data, analyzing and interpreting data, and constructing explanations. However, these dashboards are either content-focused or practice-specific. None of them present information about student knowledge-in-use performance. The field still has a limited understanding of how AI-based information can support teachers' timely instructional decisions, especially with respect to knowledge in use.

Design Framework

Building from the aforementioned literature and theoretical perspectives, we present a comprehensive design framework (see Figure 16.1) that utilizes AI to guide teachers in employing knowledge-in-use assessments to enhance their timely instructional decision-making. This framework, grounded in schema theory (Piaget 1952) and goal-oriented theory (Schoenfeld 2010), facilitates the organization and interpretation of multifaceted information for teacher decision-making (Shavelson 1986). Furthermore, cognitive load theory (Sweller 1988) forms the basis for utilizing AI to process information and recommend appropriate instructional strategies.

As shown in Figure 16.1, the design framework comprises three main components: an automated report dashboard for displaying assessment information, instructional strategies to aid teacher decision-making, and professional development to train teachers on the use of this AI-empowered decision-making system.

To leverage AI for making timely instructional decisions, teachers need to engage with the AI system through professional learning support. Subsequently, they review

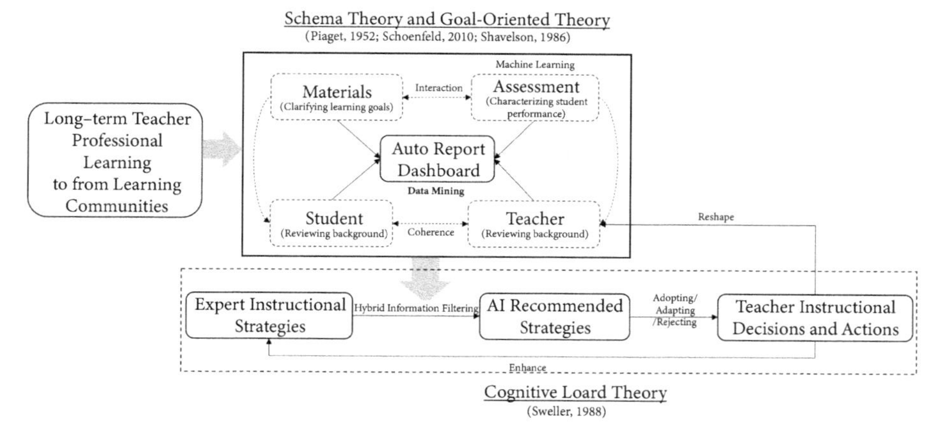

Figure 16.1 A design framework for guiding teacher use of AI-based classroom assessments to support instructional decisions.

the automated report dashboard. The AI system filters this dashboard's information and proposes suitable instructional strategies. Ultimately, teachers maintain their authority to adopt, modify, or reject the AI-recommended strategies and make instructional decisions accordingly.

Implementing the Design Framework: An Early Stage

In this section, we delve into the design framework, discussing each phase with examples from our research. The section begins by introducing the case of Ms. Emily, a middle school science teacher facing challenges in making instructional decisions within her classroom. Subsequently, considering Ms. Emily's predicament, we elucidate the process we adopted for our project, which employs AI to assist teachers in utilizing knowledge-in-use assessments to enhance instructional decision-making.

Illustrative Case

Ms. Emily, a middle school science teacher, is guiding her class through an exploration of chemical reactions using a unit, "Chemical Reaction," that aligns with the NGSS. Over the initial lessons, her students have undertaken several experiments to investigate properties such as density, boiling point, and flammability of various substances, in addition to understanding why mass and volume are not properties of substances. Currently, they are on Lesson 5. Ms. Emily has just administered an online knowledge-in-use assessment task to gauge their grasp of the ideas (see Figure 16.2). In due course, all of her students ($N = 20$) complete the task, providing short text responses which they submit via the student portal.

Gas filled balloons (ID#: 034.02-c01)

Tap text to listen

Alice did an experiment that caused four balloons to fill with gas, as shown in the figure to the right. Alice tested the flammability of each gas. She also measured the volume and mass of each gas to calculate the density. The tests and measures all occurred under the same conditions. The data is in Table 1.

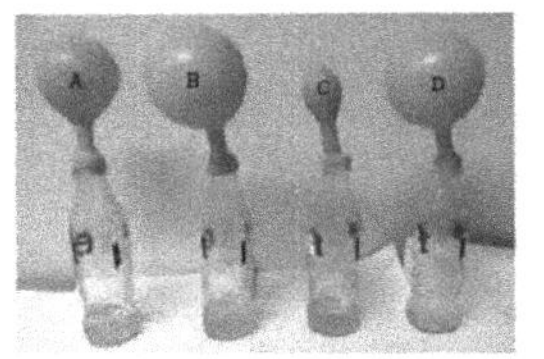

Table 1. Data of four gases in the balloons.

Sample	Flammability	Density	Volume
Gas A	Yes	0.089 g/L	180 cm^3
Gas B	No	1.422 g/L	270 cm^3
Gas C	No	1.981 g/L	35 cm^3
Gas D	Yes	0.089 g/L	269 cm^3

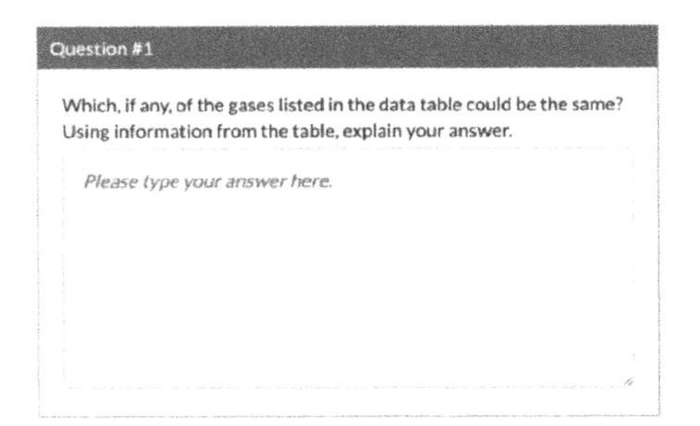
Question #1

Which, if any, of the gases listed in the data table could be the same? Using information from the table, explain your answer.

Please type your answer here.

Figure 16.2 An example of assessment tasks from the NGSA website. The assessment task was designed and stored online by the NGSA project. See the tasks via the official website: http://nextgenscienceassessment.org. All assessments are free to the public and are licensed under a Creative Commons Attribution-NonCommercial 3.0 license.

On the teacher portal, Ms. Emily reviews all the responses. She now faces the task of providing feedback on these responses and, more importantly, deciding the subsequent course of instruction based on her students' performance. This decision-making process presents a substantial challenge, as it necessitates the gathering, analysis, integration, and diagnosis of a wide array of information to ensure her instructional choices align with her class's current state of learning. Although she has access to an online platform (portal) that facilitates the collection of students' responses, the variability in each student's task performance complicates her analysis. She strives to accommodate the diverse responses from her students yet acknowledges, "This is too much and time-consuming. I wish I had a way to consolidate all responses and discern patterns." Faced with time constraints, Ms. Emily reluctantly selects only a portion of her students' responses and attempts to summarize the entire class's performance based on these chosen responses. The awareness that this summary may not fully represent all students' performance frustrates her, yet she must proceed to meet the day's lesson objectives.

The challenge experienced by Ms. Emily is a commonplace occurrence in science classrooms. Many science teachers encounter difficulties supporting student knowledge-in-use due to a lack of knowledge to interpret students' performance and provide instructional support tailored to student needs. As illustrated in Ms. Emily's case, considerable time and effort are expended in scoring students' responses and providing individualized feedback. While Ms. Emily can offer personalized feedback, given her familiarity with her students' learning experiences, and cultural and linguistic backgrounds, the extended time frame may negatively impact students' engagement and interest in their prior work, as they must wait for the teacher to finish providing feedback. Moreover, teachers, especially those new to the profession, may struggle to take the next instructional steps as they may be unfamiliar with the NGSS-aligned instructional knowledge. Even experienced educators can encounter difficulties as they may need to review extensive information, such as students' previous learning experiences and class performance. Furthermore, teachers' beliefs and past teaching experiences can also influence their instructional decisions. Therefore, making timely instructional decisions represents a complex and situational process without a linear mechanism, necessitating the need for innovative technologies, such as AI, to assist teachers. We now proceed to elaborate on our design framework for using AI to enhance teachers' instructional decisions, ultimately supporting students' development of knowledge-in-use.

Automatic Report Dashboard

The current literature has guided us to recognize three potential components of an automated report dashboard system: materials that assist teachers in clarifying learning goals (e.g., Schoenfeld 2010; Siuty, Leko, and Knackstedt 2018), assessment for diagnosing student performance (e.g., Anderson 2003; Datnow and Hubbard 2016), and the collation of student and teacher background information (e.g., Borko, Roberts, and Shavelson 2008).

Materials: Clarifying Learning Goals

The learning materials featured in an automatic report dashboard should aid teachers help to see whether students obtain the learning goals. The types of materials used in classrooms, including curriculum, assessment, and instructional guides, establish a learning context aimed at advancing student development towards a specific learning goal. It is crucial that high-quality materials, such as curriculum and assessment, align with standard-based learning goals (NRC 2006). Research suggests that novice teachers particularly benefit from high-quality materials to augment their disciplinary knowledge (Grossman and Thompson 2008) and enhance their instructional strategies (Valencia et al. 2006). Therefore, it is vital to gather information on the materials teachers employ in their classrooms.

In our current work, the assessment materials, such as the 3D assessment tasks, were designed using a modified evidence-centered design approach (Harris et al. 2019) to align with NGSS performance expectations (PEs) (NGSA 2023). Given the broad scope of an NGSS PE, we defined a set of learning performances (Harris et al. 2019) to elaborate on the requirements to achieve PEs. Each learning performance represents a smaller segment of a PE, integrating aspects of a DCI, a SEP, and a CCC. For instance, Table 16.1 illustrates a learning performance

Table 16.1 The Learning Performance for the "Gas-Filled Balloons" Task

<table>
<tr><td colspan="3">NGSS performance expectation: MS-PS1-2 Analyze and interpret data on the properties of substances before and after the substances interact to determine whether a chemical reaction has occurred.
Learning performance goal: Students analyze and interpret data to determine whether substances are the same based on characteristic properties.</td></tr>
<tr><td>Disciplinary core ideas</td><td>Scientific and engineering practices</td><td>Crosscutting concepts</td></tr>
<tr><td>PS1.A: Structure and properties of matter
Each pure substance has characteristic physical and chemical properties (for any bulk quantity under given conditions) that can be used to identify.
Elaboration of PS1.A:
- "Properties of substances" are substances' characteristics (quality or condition) that can be observed or measured, i.e., density, mp, bp, solubility, flammability, odor, mass, volume, and color.
- "Characteristic properties" are properties that are independent of the amount of the sample and that can be used to identify substances.
- Weight, mass, volume, shape, length/width, texture, and temperature are not characteristic properties of substances and may change.
- No two substances can have the same characteristic properties under the same conditions; if two materials have even one different characteristic property, they are different substances.</td><td>Analyzing and Interpreting data
- Summarize data using descriptive statistics.
- Identify relationships (e.g., linear and nonlinear, statistical).</td><td>Patterns
- Identify similarities across two or more quantities or properties (relative to a measurement error range) from models, verbal descriptions, or graphical representations.
- Categorize objects or entities based on similarities and differences from models, verbal descriptions, graphical representations, or data.
- Describe why quantities or properties are similar/different/differ by a specific amount or degree.</td></tr>
</table>

featuring a specific DCI, SEP, and CCC for the "gas-filled balloons" task (Figure 16.2). This learning performance shares the same practice (i.e., analyzing and interpreting data) and crosscutting concepts (i.e., patterns) with the NGSS PE (i.e., MS-PS1-2). However, the learning performance incorporates a portion of DCI which includes the characteristic properties of substances but omits the concept of chemical reactions. With respect to instructional decisions, teachers need to comprehend the learning performance goal, clarify the specifics of its dimensions for the assessment tasks in use, and understand its relationship with the corresponding NGSS PEs.

Assessment: Characterizing Student Performance

The automatic report dashboard's second element encapsulates a summary of students' performance on classroom assessment tasks. Research has indicated that the formative use of well-structured performance assessment tasks provides invaluable insights into student performance, enabling teachers to modify instruction (e.g., Alonzo 2019; Anderson 2003; Datnow and Hubbard 2016). Automated scoring of students' written and illustrated responses to these assessment tasks is now feasible (Zhai, He, Krajcik, and 2022). This technology allows teachers to rapidly access information about student performance in three domains: individual, group, and entire class performance.

In our research, we created analytic rubrics to gauge students' 3D learning performance (He et al. 2023b). Table 16.2 illustrates the scoring rubric and a student response for the "gas-filled balloons" task. The rubric consists of five criteria representing different dimensions. A student receives a point for each criterion met; otherwise, a zero is scored. For example, the response in Table 16.2 scores as "11,100"—the student has provided a correct "statement (C1)" and identified the "data patterns (C2 and C3)" but failed to justify why "flammability (C4)" and "density (C5)" serve to identify substances.

We enlisted individuals with subject-matter knowledge, notably undergraduates majoring in science-related fields, to score middle students' responses. The developers of the rubric conducted an orientation session to familiarize these scores with the scoring criteria. In the interest of inter-rater reliability (IRR), we assigned at least two scorers to evaluate a segment of student responses for each task. To verify IRR, we employed either Fleiss's kappa (Fleiss and Cohen 1973) or Cohen's kappa (Cohen 1960) calculations. Discrepancies between raters were addressed through discussion until a consensus was reached. This process was repeated until the IRR

Table 16.2 Scoring Rubric and Example for the "Gas-Filled Balloons" Task

Student response: Gases A and D could be the same gas because they have the same density and flammability.

Dimensions	Criteria	Score	
DCI	C1. Student states that gas A and gas D could be the same substance.	1	0
SEP+CCC	C2. Student describes the pattern (comparing data in different columns) in flammability data of gas A and gas D as the same in the table.	1	0
SEP+CCC	C3. Student describes the pattern (comparing data in different columns) in density data of gas A and gas D as the same in the table.	1	0
DCI	C4. Student indicates that flammability is one of the characteristic properties of identifying substances.	0	1
DCI	C5. Student indicates that density is one of the characteristic properties of identifying substances.	0	1

value exceeded 0.70, which signaled the commencement of scoring of various cases. In the official workbooks, we deliberately ensured a 15% overlap of cases, serving as a means of monitoring the stability of the IRR throughout the scoring process. All scores generated by the undergraduate scorers were subsequently used to train ML algorithms to automatically score new student responses. The synergistic application of rubrics and automatic scoring offers teachers prompt and precise data on students' 3D learning performance. This not only alleviates teachers' workload but also equips them to make effective and timely pedagogical decisions.

To aid teachers in interpreting student performance, we classified students' responses into four distinct groups based on their performance patterns on the three dimensions. Table 16.3 represents the four groups, distinguishing students who achieved understanding from those who require additional support. For instance, students with a "00011" pattern fall into Group C. These students have mastered the practice of "analyzing and interpreting data" and the crosscutting concept of "pattern" but require further instruction in understanding that "characteristic properties can be used to identify substances." The rubrics and grouping strategy enable the dashboard to present teachers with detailed student performance data at the individual, group, and class levels. Figure 16.3 displays class-wide progress and the number of students

Table 16.3 The Characteristics of Student Performance Groups

Group	Achieved	Student need support
Group A: *Support of DCI, SEP, and CCC*	Students have achieved: *N/A*	Students need support in: *DCI: understanding the characteristics properties vs. non-characteristic properties of substances* *SEP: analyzing and interpreting data* *CCC: looking for patterns in data*
Group B: *Support of SEP and CCC*	Students have achieved: *DCI: understanding the characteristics properties vs. non-characteristic properties of substances*	Students need support in: *SEP: analyzing and interpreting data* *CCC: looking for patterns in data*
Group C: *Support of DCI*	Students have achieved: *SEP: analyzing and interpreting data* *CCC: looking for patterns in data*	Students need support in: *DCI: understanding the characteristics properties vs. non-characteristic properties of substances.*
Group D: *Support of moving forward*	Students have achieved: *DCI: understanding the characteristics properties vs. non-characteristic properties of substances* *SEP: analyzing and interpreting data* *CCC: looking for patterns in data*	Students have achieved the task, and they need support to move forward.

in the four groups, as presented in the Web-based teacher dashboard (Latif and Zhai 2023). This AI-based teacher dashboard assists teachers in managing assessment data and interpreting student performance across different levels, facilitating instructional decision-making.

Student and Teacher Components: Reviewing Backgrounds

Teachers routinely utilize students' background information, encompassing prior knowledge, learning experiences, and non-academic characteristics (e.g., motivation, classroom behavior, and social-emotional skills) (Borko and Shavelson 1990; Perfecto 2012) to inform their instructional decisions. Studies have shown that experienced teachers possess more sophisticated knowledge in characterizing students than their novice counterparts (Borko and Shavelson 1990). Furthermore, teachers draw significantly from their teaching experiences, beliefs, orientations, and knowledge when shaping instructional decisions. Schoenfeld (1998) posited that teacher beliefs serve as the underlying framework for the goals they set out to achieve. These beliefs, in turn, sift their knowledge and information usage to make informed judgments or decisions (Borko, Roberts, and Shavelson 2008; Datnow and Hubbard 2016). It's also worth noting that teachers' beliefs and orientations are markedly influential in making instructional decisions (Schoenfeld 2010). Teachers' pedagogical beliefs shape their teaching orientations, which can range from teacher-centered, traditional to student-centered constructivist instruction (Ertmer and Ottenbreit-Leftwich 2010). Numerous studies have underscored the impact of teachers' professional experiences on their instructional decisions (e.g., Clough, Berg, and Olson 2009; Kippers et al. 2018; Schoenfeld 2010; Shavelson 1986; Trevisan, Phillips, and De Rossi 2021). Consequently, an automatic report system should account for teacher information, including their prior knowledge, teaching experience (professional learning, teaching beliefs and values, and teaching tenure), and educational background (degree, major, and subject matter).

Our design model outlines the interrelationships among these three components that warrant consideration in an automatic report dashboard. For instance, when teachers choose learning materials and establish learning objectives, their teaching experience and prior knowledge guide their decisions (e.g., Anderson 2003). Simultaneously, students' prior knowledge and learning experiences inform their performance on assessment tasks (e.g., Binder et al. 2019). The alignment between learning materials and assessment tasks (Fortus and Krajcik 2012; NRC 2006) determines whether students can meet the targeted learning goals. Furthermore, classroom interactions, such as teacher–student and student–student dialogues (Alonzo 2019), should influence the design of an automatic report system (see Phase 2 in Figure 16.2). Figure 16.3 showcases a teacher dashboard using the "gas-filled balloons" task as an example. The dashboard provides information on individual students and group performance, alongside instructional strategies aligned with the "gas-filled balloons" task. However, the dashboard has not yet incorporated information related to teacher and student backgrounds.

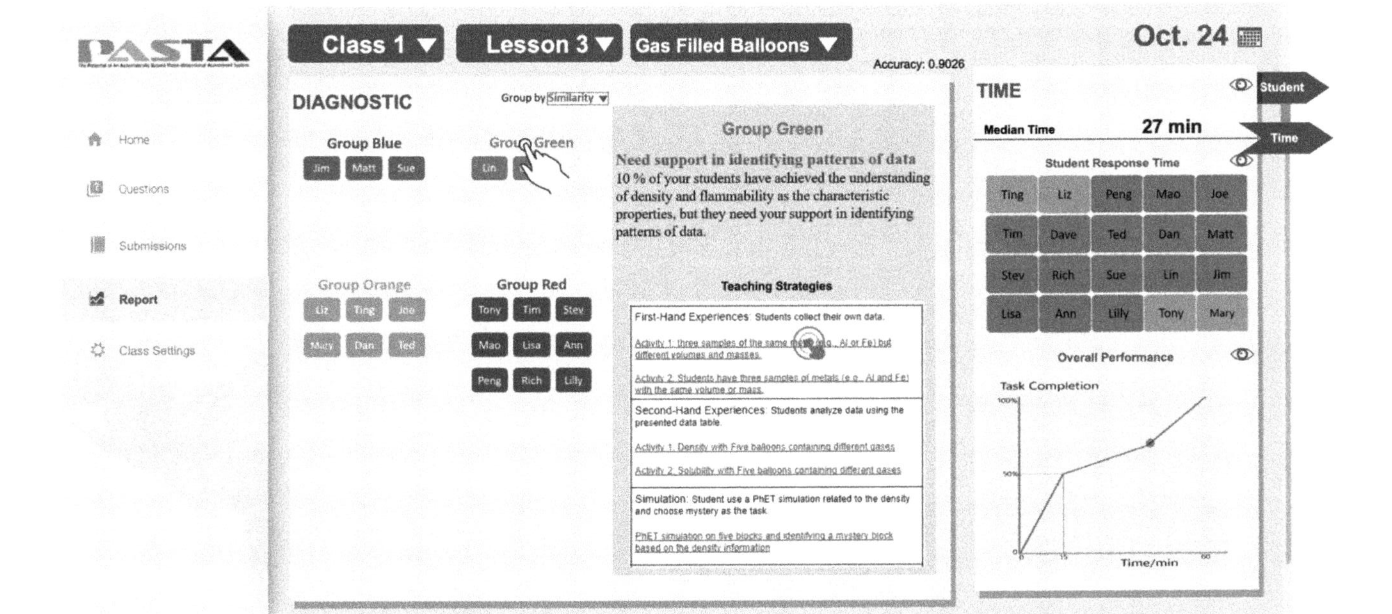

Figure 16.3 The teacher dashboard (adopted from Latif and Zhai 2023). The teacher dashboard presents the four groups (A, B, C, and D; see Table 16.3) as color groups (blue, green, orange, and red), respectively.

Instructional Strategies

Drawing upon the schema theory of teacher cognition, Shavelson (1986) posited that seasoned teachers possess superior "schemata" for instructional thinking compared to their less experienced counterparts. Furthermore, a teacher's factual knowledge regarding instruction can significantly drive forward educational progression (Berliner 1986). With AI's automatic scoring, teachers acquire critical information on individual students, collective group performance, and requisite student support. Consequently, instructional strategies, designed based on the research literature, can assist teachers with limited knowledge and teaching experience in making instructional decisions. We structured these strategies into three distinct categories: content-general, content-specific, and inclusive strategies (Clough and Corbett 2000; Mackenzie 2022; Magnusson, Krajcik, and Borko 1999). The general strategies originate from constructive and interactive perspectives of learning activities (Chi 2009). We underscore the need for our instructional strategies to engage students in independently and collaboratively constructing ideas based on the information presented. Our content-specific strategies concentrate on each 3D dimension to assist individual students or groups, such as those requiring DCI, SEP, or CCC support. Based on the literature, we designed the instructional strategies as practical and equitable. We integrated inclusive and culturally relevant strategies with content-specific strategies. Inclusive strategies capitalize on students' interests and backgrounds to engage them more profoundly and sustain their learning (NRC 2012b). Some exemplary inclusive strategies for science classrooms encompass fostering active listening, encouraging open-mindedness, developing social identities, respecting others' ideas, and suspending judgment (Mackenzie 2022). Accordingly, we delineated four types of 3D instructional strategies predicated on the learning materials: firsthand, secondhand, simulation, and multimodal experiences. Although a strategy might target one or two dimensions, the strategies engage learners using the 3-dimension.

Table 16.4 displays the features of instructional strategy examples from the "gas-filled balloons" task. We conducted one-hour interviews with six experienced teachers to explore their reflections and suggestions on instructional strategies. Thematic analysis guided our evaluation of the teacher interview data. We gleaned that our instructional strategies should be based on four key principles:

(a) goal orientation—teachers viewed the goal of 3D learning as the compass to guide the selection of instructional strategies;
(b) feasibility—teachers considered hands-on experiences such as manipulation, data collection, and observation as vital for students;
(c) cultural relevance—teachers deemed contextualization necessary, tying it to relevant phenomena and familiar objects;
(d) inclusion and fairness—teachers believed it essential to cater to language, learning modalities, and accessibility to foster fairness and equity.

We leveraged these critical principles to design instructional strategies that bolster teacher instructional decisions.

Table 16.4 Four Types of Instructional Strategies

Types	Essential features	Examples (for "gas-filled balloons task")
1. First-hand experience	Students collect data independently and have tangible experiences such as touching, feeling, manipulating objects, or conducting lab experiments/investigations.	1.1. Students work in small groups to collect and analyze mass, density, and volume data to identify the three samples. 1.2. Students work in small groups to find the data patterns. 1.3. Based on the data patterns, students elaborate on the characteristic properties (i.e., color and density) for identifying substances.
2. Second-hand experience	Students work on given data through teacher demonstrations, the Internet, or textbooks.	2.1. Teacher provides students with data about three gases (He, N_2, and CO_2)—density, volume, mass, and solubility. 2.2. Students work in small groups to find the data patterns. 2.3. Based on the patterns, students elaborate on the properties (i.e., density, solubility) for identifying substances.
3. Simulation experience	Students manipulate online simulations to conduct lab experiments/investigations.	3.1. Teacher guides students to use an online simulation (e.g., PhET) to identify the mystery block by collecting color, mass, volume, and density data. 3.2. Students work in small groups to find the data patterns. 3.3. Students use the data patterns to claim density as the characteristic properties to identify substances.
4. Multimodal experience	Students receive at least two reading sources: paper-version textbooks/articles, videos, simulation demonstrations, or online hypertexts.	4.1. Teacher uses PowerPoints to present students' information on the data patterns for characteristic and non-characteristic properties of substances with texts, images, and videos. 4.2. Students work in small groups to discuss how the data patterns can be used as evidence to support the claim that characteristic properties can be used to identify substances.

In our design model, the heterogeneous information in an automatic report dashboard serves as a sieve for the AI to recommend instructional strategies to enhance student learning. The AI evolves from its interactions with teachers, science education experts, and newly acquired data on student performance about which instructional strategies foster student 3D learning. Teachers familiarize themselves with the AI-recommended instructional strategies and take action. According to Schoenfeld (2010), subjective valuations heavily influence teacher instructional decisions.

He noted that teachers imbue their instructional decisions with personal values, which can make their decisions appear reasonable and justifiable, despite dissent from others. As a result, teachers with personal subjective valuations may vary in their decisions when provided with the AI-recommended strategies. For instance, teachers might directly adopt, revise based on their experiences, or integrate these AI-recommended strategies into existing ones. Teachers also reserve the right to reject the AI-recommended strategies and act based on their "schemata." Concurrently, teachers will recalibrate their orientations, beliefs, and knowledge by learning from expert instructional strategies. Ultimately, teachers' final instructional strategies will contribute to improving expert instructional strategies in the system.

Professional Learning Support

Even with automatic report dashboards and well-designed instructional strategies, teachers still require professional learning programs to effectively utilize AI-based assessments in making instructional decisions. Previous studies (e.g., Anderson 2003; Kippers et al. 2018) suggest that teacher participation in professional learning should foster teaching communities that bolster understanding of how to use, score, and interpret assessment data and enhance their comprehension of 3D learning and teaching. Professional learning should also cultivate teachers' capabilities to use AI systems. Hence, teachers need ample opportunities to navigate the automatic report dashboard and explore examples of expert instructional strategies that they may encounter in their classrooms. Professional learning should foster transparency, thereby establishing teachers' trust in using AI systems. Importantly, it is crucial to discuss how the AI system operates in professional learning, especially regarding the accuracy of automatic scoring and the recommendation of strategies. Teachers should also be involved in the process of rubric development to address the potential bias of scoring responses from students who are historically marginalized. In our work, we included teachers from minoritized and marginalized racial and ethnic groups to work with us on scoring students' responses to develop algorithms. We trained them to use our scoring rubrics. In turn, they provided feedback on the revision of the rubrics and discussed any discrepancies during the scoring process, which potentially reduced the bias in our machine training process.

Ultimately, professional learning should provide teachers with opportunities to learn from actual use cases on how other teachers make instructional decisions in diverse situations based on the information on the automatic report dashboard and AI-recommended strategies.

Discussions and Conclusions

Drawing from the relevant literature and theoretical foundations, we proposed a comprehensive design framework (Figure 16.1) that utilizes AI to enhance teachers' application of knowledge-in-use assessments for informed and timely instructional decisions. This framework guided the development of an automatic report dashboard and instructional strategies within an AI-based teacher decision-making system. This section discusses the framework's primary contributions, preliminary products, and future work.

Our study constructed a design framework based on the schema theory (Piaget 1952), goal-oriented theory (Schoenfeld 2010), and cognitive load theory (Sweller 1988). This facilitates the creation of AI-based teacher instructional decision systems for knowledge-in-use assessments in classrooms. Unlike existing studies (e.g., Blackley, Redmond, and Peel 2021; Clough, Berg, and Olson 2009; Schoenfeld 2010), this framework elucidates the critical components when teachers utilize AI for just-in-time decisions. This guide serves as a roadmap for researchers and designers in developing fundamental products, such as automatic report dashboards and instructional strategies. Furthermore, the design framework delineates how AI aids teachers in their decision-making processes. Building upon previous studies (e.g., Acosta and Slotta 2018; Matuk et al. 2016; Tissenbaum and Slotta 2019), AI can promptly generate individual and collective student information and consolidate diverse data to automatically propose research-based instructional strategies. Our preliminary exploration of this design framework has value for researchers and practitioners. Our automatic report dashboard with AI support offers automatic scoring and feedback for teachers and students, group information, and instructional strategies, thereby assisting teachers' instructional decisions. We posit that teachers can leverage these design products, particularly teacher collective feedback, and instructional strategies, when they use knowledge-in-use assessments to facilitate student learning. The proposed framework and products should be empirically tested and improved. For instance, cognitive interviews regarding teacher decision-making processes, classroom observations, and implementation field studies should be undertaken.

AI serves as a tool for the automated scoring of student artifacts and promises personalized, equitable, and inclusive learning. Incorporating automatic scoring, researchers can construct a robust automatic feedback system that considers student backgrounds and prior learning experiences. By synchronizing all information regarding teachers, students, and classrooms, researchers can establish a recommender system that supports teachers' prompt instructional decisions through well-designed instructional strategies. The complexity and high cognitive demands of teacher decision-making (Schoenfeld 2010; Shavelson and Stern 1981; Sweller 1988) can be eased by AI through just-in-time reporting of critical information. An AI recommender system could autonomously suggest the most suitable instructional strategy for teacher consideration with the aid of well-designed instructional strategies and timely data reports. Teachers maintain the discretion to use, modify, or replace the recommended strategies with their own. Moreover, AI plays a pivotal role in classrooms, transforming the conventional learning environment into a digital, AI-powered system. However, educational researchers must consider creating curriculum, instruction, assessment, and professional learning environments that accommodate teacher and student AI competencies (e.g., information and data literacy, safety, and digital content creation; see Pedró et al. 2019). Researchers need to use the most up-to-date knowledge of teaching and learning when designing these systems.

While significant strides have been made in developing automatic report dashboards and instructional strategies, the potential role of AI as a facilitator in enhancing teachers' instructional decisions remains largely unexplored. One key aspect to consider is that the construction of automatic report dashboards necessitates the integration of diverse and dynamic information. Current dashboards primarily incorporate reports of student performances on learning or assessment tasks, often overlooking other critical data sources. These include teacher and student background information, teacher–student interactions, and classroom discourses. The complexity of this dynamic and multifaceted information poses a significant challenge to innovative data collection techniques, such as face and non-visual sensors (Samadiani et al. 2019), and AI analysis approaches like text mining. For instance, researchers can collect data on student emotions and engagement from self-response surveys, from the experience sampling method (Schneider et al. 2016), or through facial recognition sensors that promptly detect student facial expressions (Samadiani et al. 2019). Furthermore, these dashboards will inevitably generate extensive log file data requiring organization and analysis, which necessitates the use of advanced technologies such as social network analysis (Freeman 2004) and text mining (Jiang et al. 2022). Moreover, the design of dashboards capable of displaying this hybrid information in an accessible, user-friendly manner presents its own unique set of challenges. This highlights the need for future research to focus on the efficient and effective integration of various types of data, as well as the creation of user-centric dashboard designs to best aid teachers in their instructional decision-making processes.

For AI-based instructional decision recommender systems to benefit teachers and students, they should exhibit accuracy, transparency, and impartiality. The incorporation of AI recommender systems in the realm of education is an emerging field that presents a significant challenge to researchers, largely due to the absence of comprehensive datasets for training AI algorithms (Luan et al. 2020; Pedró et al. 2019). While AI has the potential to mitigate subjective interpretation of data—given that ML algorithms realize on using datasets with variables that enhance their predictive accuracy—insufficient data often hampers the development of these algorithms for AI-based instructional strategy recommender systems. The dearth of data can result in inaccuracies in predicting teachers' decisions and inefficiencies in proposing relevant suggestions. Consequently, a fundamental question that arises is the guiding principles and approaches that can enable AI to learn from expert teachers' decisions and the limited datasets from teachers using the recommender systems. Additionally, transparency in the development and utilization of AI recommender systems is paramount to prevent the potential misuse of innovative technologies. AI-based instructional decision recommender systems hold the potential for bias and lack fairness unless developers take meticulous considerations during the design and application process (Ntoutsi et al. 2020). AI bias in instructional decisions can dishearten teachers and be detrimental to students. The bias in AI-based systems can originate from the programming and data sources (Li, Xing and Leite 2022), such as unbalanced sampling used in training AI algorithms, which could lead to biased scoring and injustices towards specific demographic groups. The manner in which data are collected or selected for use can also introduce bias, creating unfair circumstances for various cohorts (Li et al. 2023b). Future work should include humans from diverse backgrounds (e.g., teachers from minoritized and marginalized racial and ethnic groups) in the design and implementation process. Innovative approaches such as data argumentation and large language AI models (e.g., GPT) need to be further explored to minimize the bias in the algorithm development process. Fundamental research is also crucial for exploring ways to enhance transparency and impartiality in AI-based instructional decision-making processes, making AI work more effectively and equitably for all stakeholders.

In conclusion, this chapter delineates a design framework that guides teachers in leveraging AI for assessment-based instructional decisions. The framework encompasses three critical components that elucidate AI-based teacher instructional decisions. An early-stage application of this framework, including the creation of automatic report dashboards and instructional strategies, is also discussed. We posit that the proposed design framework has the potential to assist in the development of AI systems that enhance teacher instruction and student learning across diverse fields.

Acknowledgments

This study is supported by the National Science Foundation (Grants 2101104, 2100964). Any opinions, findings, conclusions, or recommendations expressed in this material are those of the authors and do not necessarily reflect the views of the National Science Foundation.

References

Acosta, A., and Slotta, J. D. 2018. "CKBiology: An Active Learning Curriculum Design for Secondary Biology." *Frontiers in Education* 3: 1–19.

Adams, M. J., and Collins, A. 1979. "A Schema-theoretic View of Reading." In *New Directions in Discourse Processing*, edited by R. O. Freedle, 1–22. Norwood, NJ: Ablex Publishing.

Alonzo, A. C. 2019. "Defining Trustworthiness for Teachers' Multiple Uses of Classroom Assessment Results." In *Classroom Assessment and Educational Measurement*, edited by S. M. Brookhart and J. H. McMillan, 120–45. London: Routledge.

Anderson, L. W. 2003. *Classroom Assessment: Enhancing the Quality of Teacher Decision Making*. London: Routledge.

Bennett, R. E. 2018. "Educational Assessment: What to Watch in a Rapidly Changing World." *Educational Measurement: Issues and Practice* 37, no. 4: 7–15.

Berliner, D. C. 1986. "In Pursuit of the Expert Pedagogue." *Educational Researcher* 15, no. 7: 5–13.

Binder, T., Sandmann, A., Sures, B., Friege, G., Theyssen, H., and Schmiemann, P. 2019. "Assessing Prior Knowledge Types as Predictors of Academic Achievement in the Introductory Phase of Biology and Physics Study Programmes Using Logistic Regression." *International Journal of STEM Education* 6: 1–14.

Blackley, C., Redmond, P., and Peel, K. 2021. "Teacher Decision-Making in the Classroom: The Influence of Cognitive Load and Teacher Affect." *Journal of Education for Teaching* 47, no. 4: 548–61.

Borko, H., Roberts, S. A., and Shavelson, R. 2008. "Teachers' Decision Making: From Alan J. Bishop to Today." In *Critical Issues in Mathematics Education*, edited by P. Clarkson and N. Presmeg, 37–67. Boston, MA: Springer.

Borko, H., and Shavelson, R. J. 1990. "Teacher Decision Making." In *Dimensions of Thinking and Cognitive Instruction*, edited by B.F. Jones and L. Idol, 311–46. London: Routledge.

Chi, M. T. H. 2009. "Active-Constructive-Interactive: A Conceptual Framework for Differentiating Learning Activities." *Topics in Cognitive Science* 1, no. 1: 73–105.

Clough, M. P., Berg, C. A., and Olson, J. K. 2009. "Promoting Effective Science Teacher Education and Science Teaching: A Framework for Teacher Decision-Making." *International Journal of Science and Mathematics Education* 7, no. 4: 821–47.

Clough, P., and Corbett, J. 2000. Theories of Inclusive Education: A Student′ s Guide. London: Sage.

Cohen, J. E. 1960. "A Coefficient of Agreement for Nominal Scales." Educational and Psychological Measurement 20, no. 1: 37–46.

Datnow, A., and Hubbard, L. 2016. "Teacher Capacity for and Beliefs about Data-Driven Decision Making: A Literature Review of International Research." *Journal of Educational Change* 17, no. 1: 7–28.

Dickler, R., Gobert, J., and Sao Pedro, M. 2021. "Using Innovative Methods to Explore the Potential of an Alerting Dashboard for Science Inquiry." *Journal of Learning Analytics* 8, no. 2: 105–22.

Ertmer, P. A., and Ottenbreit-Leftwich, A. T. 2010. "Teacher Technology Change: How Knowledge, Confidence, Beliefs, and Culture Intersect." *Journal of Research on Technology in Education* 42, no. 3: 255–84.

Fleiss, J. L., and Cohen, J. 1973. "The Equivalence of Weighted Kappa and the Intraclass Correlation Coefficient as Measures of Reliability." *Educational and Psychological Measurement* 33: 613–19.

Fortus, D., and Krajcik, J. 2012. "Curriculum Coherence and Learning Progressions." In *Second International Handbook of Science Education*, edited by B. Fraser, K. Tobin., and C. McRobbie, 783–98. Springer International Handbooks of Education, vol 24. Dordrecht: Springer.

Freeman, L. 2004. *The Development of Social Network Analysis. A Study in the Sociology of Science.* Vancouver: Empirical Press.

Furtak, E. M. 2017. "Confronting Dilemmas Posed by Three-Dimensional Classroom Assessment: Introduction to a Virtual Issue of Science Education." *Science Education* 101, no. 5: 854–67.

Gerard, L. F., and Linn, M. C. 2016. "Using Automated Scores of Student Essays to Support Teacher Guidance in Classroom Inquiry." *Journal of Science Teacher Education* 27, no. 1: 111–29.

Gerard, L., Ryoo, K., McElhaney, K., Liu, O. L., Rafferty, A., and Linn, M. 2016. "Automated Guidance for Student Inquiry." *Journal of Educational Psychology* 108, no. 1: 60–81.

Ghali, R., Ouellet, S., and Frasson, C. 2016. "LewiSpace: An Exploratory Study with a Machine Learning Model in an Educational Game." *Journal of Education and Training Studies* 4, no. 1: 192–201.

Greeno, J. G., Collins, A. M., and Resnick, L. B. 1996. "Cognition and Learning." In *Handbook of Educational Psychology*, edited by D. Berliner and R. Calfee, 15–46. London: Macmillan.

Grossman, P., and Thompson, C. 2008. "Learning from Curriculum Materials: Scaffolds for New Teachers?" *Teaching and Teacher Education* 24, no. 8: 2014–26.

Ha, M., and Nehm, R. 2016. "The impact of Misspelled Words on Automated Computer Scoring: A Case Study of Scientific Explanations." *Journal of Science Education and Technology* 25, no. 3: 358–74.

Hamilton, L., Halverson, R., Jackson, S. S., Mandinach, E., Supovitz, J., and Wayman, J. 2009. *IES Practice Guide: Using Student Achievement Data to Support Instructional Decision Making* (NCEE 2009-4067). Washington, DC: National Center for Education Evaluation and Regional Assistance.

Harris, C. J., Krajcik, J. S., Pellegrino, J. W., and DeBarger, A. H. 2019. "Designing Knowledge-in-Use Assessments to Promote Deeper Learning." *Educational Measurement: Issues and Practice* 38, no. 2: 53–67.

He, P., Chen, I.-C., Touitou, I., Bartz, K., Schneider, B., and Krajcik, J. 2023a. "Predicting Student Science Achievement Using Post-unit Assessment Performances in a Coherent High School Chemistry Project-Based Learning System." *Journal of Research in Science Teaching* 60, no. 4: 724–60.

He, P., Zhai, X., Shin, N., and Krajcik, J. 2023b. "Applying Rasch Measurement to Assess Knowledge-in-Use in Science Education." In *Advances in Applications of Rasch Measurement in Science Education*, edited by X. Liu and W. Boone, 315–47. New York: Springer.

Jescovitch, L. N., Scott, E. E., Cerchiara, J. A., Merrill, J., Urban-Lurain, M., Doherty, J. H., and Haudek, K. C. 2021. "Comparison of Machine Learning Performance Using Analytic and Holistic Coding Approaches across Constructed Response Assessments Aligned to a Science Learning Progression." *Journal of Science Education and Technology* 30, no. 2: 150–67.

Jiang, S., Nocera, A., Tatar, C., Yoder, M. M., Chao, J., Wiedemann, K., Finzer, W., and Rosé, C. P. 2022. "An Empirical Analysis of High School Students' Practices of Modelling with Unstructured Data." *British Journal of Educational Technology* 53, no. 5: 1114–33.

Kerr, K. A., Marsh, J. A., Ikemoto, G. S., Darilek, H., and Barney, H. 2006. "Strategies to Promote Data Use for Instructional Improvement: Actions, Outcomes, and Lessons from Three Urban Districts." *American Journal of Education* 112, no. 3: 496–520.

Kippers, W. B., Wolterinck, C. H., Schildkamp, K., Poortman, C. L., and Visscher, A. J. 2018. "Teachers' Views on the Use of Assessment for Learning and Data-Based Decision Making in Classroom Practice." *Teaching and Teacher Education* 75: 199–213.

Krajcik, J., Schneider, B., Miller, E., Chen, I.-C., Bradford, L., Baker, Q., Bartz, K., Miller, C., Li, T., Codere, S., and Peek-Brown, D. 2023. "Assessing the Effect of Project-Based Learning on Science Learning in Elementary Schools." *American Education Research Journal* 60, no. 1: 70–102.

Latif, E., and Zhai, X. 2023, April 13–16. "AI-SCORER: Principles for designing artificial intelligence-augmented instructional systems." Paper presented to the Annual Meeting of the American Educational Research Association, Chicago.

Lee, H. S., Gweon, G. H., Lord, T., Paessel, N., Pallant, A., and Pryputniewicz, S. 2021. "Machine Learning-Enabled Automated Feedback: Supporting Students' Revision of Scientific Arguments Based on Data Drawn from Simulation." *Journal of Science Education and Technology* 30, no. 2: 168–92.

Leinhardt, G., and Greeno, J. G. 1986. "The Cognitive Skill of Teaching." *Journal of Educational Psychology* 78, no. 2: 75.

Li, C., Xing, W., and Leite, W. L. 2022. "Toward Building a Fair Peer Recommender to Support Help-Seeking in Online Learning." *Distance Education* 43, no. 1: 30–55.

Li, T., Liu, F., and Krajcik, J. 2023a. "Automatically Assess Elementary Students' Hand-drawn Scientific Models Using Deep Learning of Artificial Intelligence." In *Proceedings of the Annual Meeting of the International Society of the Learning Sciences* (ISLS).

Li, T., Miller, E., Chen, I.C., Bartz, K., Codere, S., and Krajcik, J. 2021. "The Relationship between Teacher's Support of Literacy Development and Elementary Students' Modelling Proficiency in Project-Based Learning Science Classrooms." *Education 3-13: International Journal of Primary, Elementary and Early Years Education* 49, no. 3: 302–16.

Li, T., Chen, I., Miller, E., Miller, C., Schneider, B., and Krajcik, J. 2024. "The Relationships between Elementary Students' Knowledge-in-Use Performance and Their Science Achievement." *Journal of Research in Science Teaching* 61, no. 2: 358–418. https://doi.org/10.1002/tea.21900

Li, T., Reigh, E., He, P., and Adah Miller, E. 2023b. "Can We and Should We Use Artificial Intelligence for Formative Assessment in Science?" *Journal of Research in Science Teaching* 60, no. 6: 1385–89.

Liu, O. L., Brew, C., Blackmore, J., Gerard, L., Madhok, J., and Linn, M. C. 2014. "Automated Scoring of Constructed-Response Science Items: Prospects and Obstacles." *Educational Measurement: Issues and Practice* 33, no. 2: 19–28.

Luan, H., Geczy, P., Lai, H., Gobert, J., Yang, S. J., Ogata, H., Baltes, J., Guerra, R., Li, P., and Tsai, C. C. 2020. "Challenges and Future Directions of Big Data and Artificial Intelligence in Education." *Frontiers in Psychology* 11: 580820.

Mackenzie, A. H. 2022. "Inclusive Strategies for the Science Classroom." *The Science Teacher* 89, no. 5: 1–2.

Magnusson, S., Krajcik, J., and Borko, H. 1999. "Nature, Sources, and Development of Pedagogical Content Knowledge for Science Teaching." In *Examining Pedagogical Content Knowledge: The Construct and Its Implications for Science Education*, 95–132. Dordrecht: Springer Netherlands.

Mao, L., Liu, O. L., Roohr, K., Belur, V., Mulholland, M., Lee, H.-S., and Pallant, A. 2018. "Validation of Automated Scoring for a Formative Assessment That Employs Scientific Argumentation." *Educational Assessment* 23, no. 2: 121–38.

Matuk, C., Gerard, L., Lim-Breitbart, J., and Linn, M. 2016. "Gathering Requirements for Teacher Tools: Strategies for Empowering Teachers through Co-design." *Journal of Science Teacher Education* 27, no. 1: 79–110.

Mislevy, R., and Haertel, G. 2006. "Implications of Evidence-Centered Design for Educational Testing." *Educational Measurement: Issues and Practice* 25, no. 4: 6–20.

Moharreri, K., Ha, M., and Nehm, R. H. 2014. "EvoGrader: An Online Formative Assessment Tool for Automatically Evaluating Written Evolutionary Explanations." *Evolution: Education and Outreach* 7, no. 1: 15.

Murphy, K. P. 2012. *Machine Learning: A Probabilistic Perspective.* Cambridge, MA: MIT Press.

National Research Council. 2006. *Systems for State Science Assessment.* Washington, DC: National Academies Press.

National Research Council. 2011. *Assessing 21st Century Skills: Summary of a Workshop.* Washington, DC: National Academies Press.

National Research Council. 2012a. *Education for Life and Work: Developing Transferable Knowledge and Skills in the 21st Century.* Washington, DC: National Academies Press.

National Research Council. 2012b. *A Framework for K-12 Science Education: Practices, Crosscutting Concepts, and Core Ideas.* Washington, DC: National Academies Press.

National Research Council. 2014. *Developing Assessments for the Next Generation Science Standards.* Washington, DC: National Academies Press.

NGSS Lead States. 2013. *Next Generation Science Standards: For States, by States.* Washington, DC: National Academies Press.

NGSA. 2023. *Next Generation Science Assessment.* https://ngss-assessment.portal.concord.org

Ntoutsi, E., Fafalios, P., Gadiraju, U., Iosifidis, V., Nejdl, W., Vidal, M. E., Ruggieri, S., et al. 2020. "Bias in Data-Driven Artificial Intelligence Systems—An Introductory Survey." *Wiley Interdisciplinary Reviews: Data Mining and Knowledge Discovery* 10, no. 3: e1356.

Pedró, F., Subosa, M., Rivas, A., and Valverde, P. 2019. *Artificial Intelligence in Education: Challenges and Opportunities for Sustainable Development.* Paris: UNESCO.

Perfecto, M. R. G. 2012. "Contextual Factors in Teacher Decision Making: Extending the Woods Model." Asia-Pacific Education Researcher 21, no. 3: 474–83.

Piaget, J. 1952. *The Origins of Intelligence in Children.* Madison, CT: International Universities Press.

Rumelhart, D. E. 1980. "Schemata: The Building Blocks of Cognition." In *Theoretical Issues in Reading Comprehension*, edited by R. J. Spiro, B. C. Bruce, and W. E. Brewer, 33–58. Hillsdale, NJ: Lawrence Erlbaum Associates.

Ryoo, K., and Linn, M. C. 2016. "Designing Automated Guidance for Concept Diagrams in Inquiry Instruction." *Journal of Research in Science Teaching* 53, no. 7: 1003–35.

Samadiani, N., Huang, G., Cai, B., Luo, W., Chi, C. H., Xiang, Y., and He, J. 2019. "A Review on Automatic Facial Expression Recognition Systems Assisted by Multimodal Sensor Data." *Sensors* 19, no. 8: 1863.

Schneider, B., Krajcik, J., Lavonen, J., Salmela-Aro, K., Broda, M., Spicer, J., Bruner, J., et al. 2016. "Investigating Optimal Learning Moments in US and Finnish Science Classes." *Journal of Research in Science Teaching* 53, no.3: 400–21.

Schoenfeld, A. H. 1998. "Toward a Theory of Teaching-in-Context." *Issues in Education* 4, no. 1: 1–94.

Schoenfeld, A. H. 2010. *How We Think: A Theory of Goal-Oriented Decision Making and Its Educational Applications.* London: Routledge.

Shavelson, R. J. 1986, June. Interactive Decision-Making: Some Thoughts on Teacher Cognition. Invited address, I Congreso Internacional, "Pensamientos de los Profesores y Toma de Decisiones," Seville, Spain.

Shavelson, R. J., and Stern, P. 1981. "Research on Teachers' Pedagogical Thoughts, Judgments, Decisions, and Behavior." *Review of Educational Research* 51, no. 4: 455–98.

Siuty, M. B., Leko, M. M., and Knackstedt, K. M. 2018. "Unraveling the Role of Curriculum in Teacher Decision Making." *Teacher Education and Special Education* 41, no. 1: 39–57.

Sweller, J. 1988. "Cognitive Load during Problem Solving: Effects on Learning." *Cognitive Science* 12, no. 2: 257–85.

Tansomboon, C., Gerard, L. F., Vitale, J. M., and Linn, M. C. 2017. "Designing Automated Guidance to Promote Productive Revision of Science Explanations." *International Journal of Artificial Intelligence in Education* 27, no. 4: 729–57.

Tissenbaum, M., and Slotta, J. 2019. "Supporting Classroom Orchestration with Real-Time Feedback: A Role for Teacher Dashboards and Real-Time Agents." *International Journal of Computer-Supported Collaborative Learning* 14, no. 3: 325–51.

Trevisan, O., Phillips, M., and De Rossi, M. 2021. "Unpacking Teacher Decision-Making: Connecting Complex Elements." *Italian Journal of Educational Research* 27: 13–26.

Valencia, S. W., Place, N. A., Martin, S. D., and Grossman, P. L. 2006. "Curriculum Materials for Elementary Reading: Shackles and Scaffolds for Four Beginning Teachers." *The Elementary School Journal* 107, no. 1: 93–120.

Westerman, D. A. 1991. "Expert and Novice Teacher Decision Making." *Journal of Teacher Education* 42, no. 4: 292–305.

Zacharia, Z. C., Manoli, C., Xenofontos, N., De Jong, T., Pedaste, M., van Riesen, S. A., et al. 2015. "Identifying Potential Types of Guidance for Supporting Student Inquiry When Using Virtual and Remote Labs in Science: A Literature Review." *Educational Technology Research and Development* 63, no. 2: 257–302.

Zhai, X., Haudek, K. C., Shi, L., Nehm, R. H., and Urban-Lurain, M. 2020. "From Substitution to Redefinition: A Framework of Machine Learning-Based Science Assessment." *Journal of Research in Science Teaching* 57, no. 9: 1430–59.

Zhai, X., He, P., and Krajcik, J. 2022. "Applying Machine Learning to Automatically Assess Scientific Models." *Journal of Research in Science Teaching* 59, no. 10: 1765–94.

Zhu, X., and Goldberg, A. B. 2022. *Introduction to Semi-supervised Learning.* Berlin: Springer Nature.

17
Using AI Tools to Provide Teachers with Fully Automated, Personalized Feedback on Their Classroom Discourse Patterns

Abhijit Suresh, William R. Penuel, Jennifer K. Jacobs, Ali Raza, James H. Martin, and Tamara Sumner

Introduction

Academically productive discourse derives from theoretical and empirical research showing the effectiveness of highly interactive, socially constructed learning environments (Saxe et al. 2002; Vygotsky 1978; Webb et al. 2008). Over the past decade, a robust literature on accountable talk, and in particular the talk moves that promote rich discussions, has emerged (O'Connor, Michaels, and Chapin 2015; Resnick, Asterhan, and Clarke 2018). Research has consistently documented how implementing talk moves based on accountable talk promotes students' learning of challenging content (Resnick, Michaels, and O'Connor 2010; Walshaw and Anthony 2008; Webb et al. 2019) and contributes to educational equity (O'Connor and Michaels 2019; Patterson-Williams 2019). Our research team developed the TalkMoves application, which provides teachers with automated, personalized feedback on the talk moves captured by their videorecorded mathematics lessons. The central innovation in the TalkMoves application is the deep learning models that classify both teachers' and students' discourse moves. These models are embedded within an analytic engine that processes the recordings and generates analytics that are displayed on a user interface co-designed by teachers. The resultant tool provides teachers with a rich and meaningful representation of their classroom discourse for specific teaching episodes and over time, enabling reflective noticing and instructional shifts. Pilot data suggest that teachers who consistently used the application over a two-year period had significant increases in both their own talk moves and their students' use of talk moves. This study demonstrates the promise of artificial intelligence (AI) tools in professional development efforts intended to enhance teachers' pedagogical skills, particularly in the area of theory-based discourse improvements.

Abhijit Suresh et al., *Using AI Tools to Provide Teachers with Fully Automated, Personalized Feedback on Their Classroom Discourse Patterns*. In: *Uses of Artificial Intelligence in STEM Education*. Edited by: Xiaoming Zhai and Joseph Krajcik, Oxford University Press. © Oxford University Press (2024). DOI: 10.1093/oso/9780198882077.003.0017

Moves to Support Accountable Talk in Disciplinary Learning

In well-structured classroom discussions, student talk is important for supporting the growth of their disciplinary understandings in science, technology, engineering, and mathematics (STEM). In science and engineering, for example, although students may undertake work on their own to make sense of phenomena or solve problems, meaningful engagement in science and engineering practices necessarily involves taking one's ideas public and working with the ideas that other students have surfaced, in order to jointly construct knowledge (Berland et al. 2016; Michaels and O'Connor 2017; Wendell, Andrews, and Paugh 2019). In mathematics, sharing one's thinking through talk supports the development of a deep understanding of key concepts and engagement with practices such as constructing arguments and critiquing the reasoning of others (Cobb et al. 2001; O'Connor, Michaels, and Chapin 2015; Webb et al. 2015). When interacting with and designing technology, productive classroom talk serves important purposes of helping coordinate activity among groups of learners, considering tradeoffs in design choices, and building shared understandings (Mercer and Wegerif 2002; Rowell 2004). Across the disciplines, facilitating rich conversations is key to helping students learn to generate and apply knowledge, not just passively receive or memorize information (Resnick, Michaels, and O'Connor 2010).

Accountable talk is a framework for supporting the kind of talk that takes place during rich classroom discussions and can lead to student learning. Accountable talk grows out of an understanding of learning as fundamentally a social process derived from the writings of Vygotsky (Wertsch 1985), as well as conceptualization of academic disciplines as dialogic enterprises (Ford and Forman 2015; Resnick, Michaels, and O'Connor 2010). Teachers who embrace "dialogic teaching" encourage multivocal interactions in their classrooms that purposefully position students as active communicators and agentic sense-makers (Alexander 2020). Although accountable talk theory originated within the mathematics education literature, it has since been understood to be broadly applicable across academic disciplines (Michaels, O'Connor, and Resnick 2008), and has been extensively studied in both STEM (particularly math and science) and non-STEM content areas (e.g., language arts) (see Resnick, Asterhan, and Clarke 2015).

In a classroom culture where accountable talk is pervasive, students are both active speakers and listeners who generate and build on the ideas of others and ask one another questions aimed at deepening and clarifying their thinking (Michaels, O'Connor, and Resnick 2008). In addition, they adhere to standards of reasoning established within the class that demand all participants explain their ideas, search for and interrogate premises, and revise their views based on new knowledge and feedback (Resnick, Michaels, and O'Connor 2010). Third, the talk is accountable to knowledge grounded in shared investigations, theories, texts, or other publicly accessible information; speakers are expected to make explicit evidence they are using and challenge others when evidence is lacking (Michaels, O'Connor, and Resnick 2008). Importantly, accountable talk does not require use of formal registers of the disciplines or "proper" ways of speaking: it is accessible to everyone in the classroom.

These forms of talk are not common in contemporary US classrooms (Gallimore, Hiebert, and Ermeling 2014). Instead, much talk in classrooms involves the teacher telling students information or giving directives to students, using what has been called monologic or authoritarian discourse (Ford and Forman 2015; Michaels and O'Connor 2015; Nystrand 1997). In addition, the most common form of questioning of students involves not asking them to expand or clarify their thinking or give reasons for claims but instead serves the purpose of evaluating whether students have the correct understanding of a concept or answer to a problem (Kawanaka and Stigler 1999; Mehan and Cazden 2015). Such talk patterns in classrooms yield limited opportunities for students to express and elaborate on their thinking and offer little opportunity for collaborative knowledge building (Wells and Mejia-Arauz 2006). While there have been several successful efforts to promote accountable talk in classrooms (e.g., Billings and Fitzgerald 2002; Chapin and O'Connor 2012), long-held and dominant patterns of classroom instruction tend to be highly resilient despite concerted efforts to change them (Morris and Hiebert 2011). In addition, even in classrooms where accountable talk is prominent, equity issues remain apparent such as students' perceptions of their "right to speak" (Clarke 2015).

One strategy that has proven successful in supporting changes to classroom talk has been the introduction of *talk moves* to teachers as part of a sustained professional development effort (Chapin and O'Connor 2012). Talk moves are tools intended to help teachers achieve goals for facilitating discussions aligned with accountable talk (Michaels and O'Connor 2015). They form families of utterances derived from ethnographic studies of teachers who were successful in promoting rich, student-driven talk in their classrooms (e.g., O'Connor and Michaels 1993, 1996). Those families of utterance serve three broad instructional goals of ensuring (1) accountability to the learning community, (2) accountability to content knowledge, and (3) accountability to rigorous thinking (Resnick, Asterhan, and Clarke 2018). Using talk moves within each of these categories ensures that all students are engaged as active participants, encouraged to make mathematical claims, and asked to provide well-reasoned arguments (Michaels, O'Connor, and Resnick 2008).

Talk moves as discursive tools offer two key advantages for teachers seeking to create equitable cultures of accountable talk. First, a well-crafted talk move can provide a focused way to highlight important academic ideas while also socializing students to orient to one another's thinking (Chapin, O'Connor, and Anderson 2009). For example, the simple question, "Jamy, what evidence from our investigation do you think might support Hector's claim that the tree gets its mass from the air?" invites students to think with each other and encourages reasoning about a specific science idea. Second, many talk moves are relatively straightforward to learn and simple to implement even during "rapid-fire" classroom discussions, such as restating a student's contribution or providing adequate wait time, particularly once teachers are attuned to them (Edwards-Groves and Davidson 2020; Rawding and Wills 2012). As Michaels and O'Connor (2015) argue, "an utterance-level tool, a talk move, can be easy to remember and easy to pull out with a bit of practice" (350).

Providing Teachers with Feedback on Their Use of Talk Moves

There is compelling evidence that identifying and attending to teacher and student discourse patterns is extremely useful for educators' professional learning and improvement efforts (Lefstein et al. 2020). Receiving detailed feedback on one's teaching practice can be an essential mechanism for professional learning and growth but is often costly to implement (e.g., through coaching or video analysis). In particular, personalized feedback on the nuances of their classroom talk is challenging to provide reliably to teachers in a timely and useable manner.

In one effort to address this challenge, Correnti and colleagues (2015) developed a guide for improving instruction that enables the documentation and analysis of patterns of discourse across content areas. Users of the Analyzing Teaching Moves (ATM) Guide can identify opportunities that position students as learners from classroom discussions, mainly through teaching moves that invite their contributions and are responsive to their ideas. The research team developed visual displays of classroom discourse based on the ATM Guide, showing talk patterns and spotlighting what could be improved. In addition, the ATM Guide served as a vocabulary of well-defined discursive constructs for leaders and educators to draw on to communicate better and guide improvement. A professional development program that trained teachers to use the ATM Guide proved successful in providing a common vocabulary and shifting what they noticed during classroom discussions; however, it did not impact teachers' capacity to identify connections between discursive interactions and student learning opportunities (Scherrer and Stein 2013).

Chen and colleagues (Chen 2020; Chen et al. 2020; Chen, Clarke, and Resnick 2015) have documented even more success using their Classroom Discourse Analyzer (CDA), a Web-based tool that offers teachers visual feedback about their use of talk moves. The research team embedded the CDA within a professional development effort that was considerably longer than Scherrer and Stein's (2013) program and focused on analyses of teachers' own video-recorded lessons rather than precollected lesson transcripts. In a randomized controlled trial, teachers who received personalized feedback from the CDA significantly increased their use of dialogic talk and experienced changes in their beliefs and self-efficacy related to classroom talk (Chen 2020). Moreover, treatment teachers' students experienced significant growth in their mathematics achievement relative to the control group (Chen et al. 2020). However, similar to the ATM Guide, the CDA analyzer requires trained human coders to provide the detailed discursive information that is then presented to teachers.

Using Deep Learning Models for Natural Language Processing to Accelerate and Scale Discourse-Related Feedback

Machine learning and deep learning models have been used extensively in a variety of natural language processing (NLP) tasks, including in the domain of classroom discourse (Donnelly et al. 2016; 2017; Jensen, Pugh, and D'Mello 2021;

Klebanov et al. 2017; Odden, Marin, and Randolph 2021; Perrotta and Selwyn 2020; Wiley et al. 2017; Wilson et al. 2022). AI-based tools that utilize deep learning models for NLP have the potential to accelerate analyses of very large datasets, making feasible real-time (or near real-time) analyses of classroom talk that could ultimately lead to "a shift in distribution of features of discussion" in alignment with the goals of accountable talk (Rosé and Tovares 2015, 290). Research has shown that it is possible to fully automate the generation of information regarding teachers' discourse patterns by building on advances in NLP, automatic speech recognition, and deep learning (e.g., Song et al. 2021). A small number of research teams have recently trained computer models to automate discourse analyses from instructional episodes, detecting discursive features such as instructional talk, authentic teacher questions, elaborated evaluation, and uptake (Demszky et al. 2021; Jensen et al. 2020; Kelly et al. 2018).

Incorporating these models into professional learning tools that enable teachers to receive personalized information about their instructional practices is an important next step (Sionti et al. 2012). Wang and colleagues (2013; 2014) highlight the promise of providing teachers with AI-driven analyses of their discourse practices. They found that teachers who received automated feedback regarding the amount of teacher talk relative to student talk in their mathematics lessons significantly increased the quantity of student talk, suggesting that even basic information about teachers' discursive patterns, presented in a readily accessible format, can produce changes in the desired directions. A more recent example is TeachFX, a commercially available application that uses natural language processing to provide teachers with data analytics highlighting the discourse patterns in their recorded lessons, focused largely on the degree to which students are talking relative to their teacher. Ford and Welling-Riley (2021) report that some of the teachers who piloted TeachFX saw a 45% increase in student talk.

Numerous empirical questions remain about the potential of a fully automated system to provide teachers with detailed and actionable feedback related to their classroom discourse. In this chapter, we address two of these questions:

(1) To what degree can talk moves be accurately classified by deep learning models for natural language processing?
(2) What are teachers' perceptions of the usability and accuracy of an application that automatically classifies talk moves, and how does use of the application promote changes in their talk moves over time?

The TalkMoves Application

Application Overview

The TalkMoves application is a deployed system that uses automatic speech recognition and deep learning models to detect the presence of the teacher and student talk moves in recorded mathematics lessons, drawing on accountable talk theory (Jacobs et al. 2022; Suresh et al. 2021a,b). The well-defined nature of talk moves and the fact that they are firmly grounded in a large body of empirical research make them well-suited for NLP and machine-learning applications.

The deep learning models in the TalkMoves application were trained and evaluated using the TalkMoves dataset, which includes 567 transcripts from K–12 mathematics lessons. In total, these lesson transcripts comprise 174,186 annotated teacher utterances, 59,874 student utterances, and 1.8 million words (15,830 unique). The transcripts were curated from various sources, including research projects and websites, and were all derived from video recordings of actual classrooms. A detailed description of the TalkMoves dataset and how to access the public portion of these lessons are provided in Suresh et al. (2022a).

All of the transcripts in the TalkMoves dataset were human-annotated for ten teacher and student talk moves by one of two experienced annotators who were extensively trained on accountable talk and adhered to a detailed coding manual (the coding manual is also publicly accessible; see Suresh et al. 2022a). The talk moves included in the application, along with brief descriptions and examples, are shown in Table 17.1. These talk moves were selected for the following reasons: (1) they were suggested as especially important moves by experts in accountable talk, (2) they occurred frequently enough in our training dataset to reliably define and annotate, and (3) in combination they represent each accountable talk category for both teacher and students. These ten moves are not an exhaustive list of all possible talk moves; in future iterations of the application other candidate talk moves should be considered, particularly if they meet the criteria listed above.

The annotators established initial reliability with one another before applying the codes and again when they were approximately halfway through coding to ensure that their coding remained accurate and consistent. Inter-rater agreement, calculated using Cohen's kappa (McHugh 2012), was at least 0.88 for each student and teacher talk move at both time periods. Of the teacher sentences, 32.85% contained a talk move, and 58.29% of the student sentences contained a talk move. All sentences annotated by human experts, including those coded as not containing a talk move, served as the "ground-truth" training dataset for our models (Suresh et al. 2021b, 2022a).

The TalkMoves application consists of three interrelated components: (1) a cloud-based big data infrastructure to manage and process recordings of mathematics lessons, (2) automated speech recognition and deep learning models to classify talk moves, and (3) a personalized dashboard to visually display each teacher's feedback analytics for their individual lessons and their lessons over time. The application infrastructure is designed to process classroom recordings asynchronously and generate personalized feedback using Amazon Web Services (AWS). This infrastructure includes a processing pipeline, data management and storage, and feedback generation (see Figure 17.1).

First, teachers generate and upload classroom recordings, consisting of entire lessons or portions of lessons. The system collects the files, processing one video at a time through the pipeline. The audio is converted into a written transcript, which is then broken into sentences. Each sentence is designated as originating from the teacher or a student. Deep learning models then determine whether there is a talk move corresponding to each teacher or student sentence. Additional analytics are

Table 17.1 Teacher and Student Talk Moves Included in the TalkMoves Application

Category	Talk move	Description	Example
Teacher talk moves			
Learning community	Keeping everyone together	Prompting students to be active listeners and orienting students to each other	"What did Eliza just say her equation was?"
Learning community	Getting students to relate to another's ideas	Prompting students to react to what a classmate said	"Do you agree with Juan that the answer is 7/10?"
Learning community	Restating	Repeating all or part of what a student said word for word	"Add two here."
Content knowledge	Pressing for accuracy	Prompting students to make a mathematical contribution or use mathematical language	"Can you give an example of an ordered pair?"
Rigorous thinking	Revoicing	Repeating what a student said but adding on or changing the wording	"Julia told us she would add two here."
Rigorous thinking	Pressing for reasoning	Prompting students to explain, provide evidence, share their thinking behind a decision, or connect ideas or representations	"Why could I argue that the slope should be increasing?"
Student talk moves			
Learning community	Relating to another student	Using, commenting on, or asking questions about a classmate's ideas	"I didn't get the same answer as her."
Learning community	Asking for more info	Student requests more info, says they are confused or need help	"I don't understand number four."
Content knowledge	Making a claim	Student makes a math claim, or factual statement, or lists a step in their answer	"X is the number of cars."
Rigorous thinking	Providing evidence or reasoning	Student explains their thinking, provides evidence, or talks about their reasoning	"You can't subtract 7 because then you would only get 28 and you need 29."

applied to calculate other discursive features, such as how much talk came from the teacher versus the students. Finally, the system generates feedback based on the output from the model, which is visually displayed on a personalized dashboard using a Web interface. The entire system is fully automated and requires no human processing beyond the initial uploading of classroom recordings. Processing speed depends on the number of videos uploaded at one time and their file size; however, feedback is typically available within a few minutes of uploading.

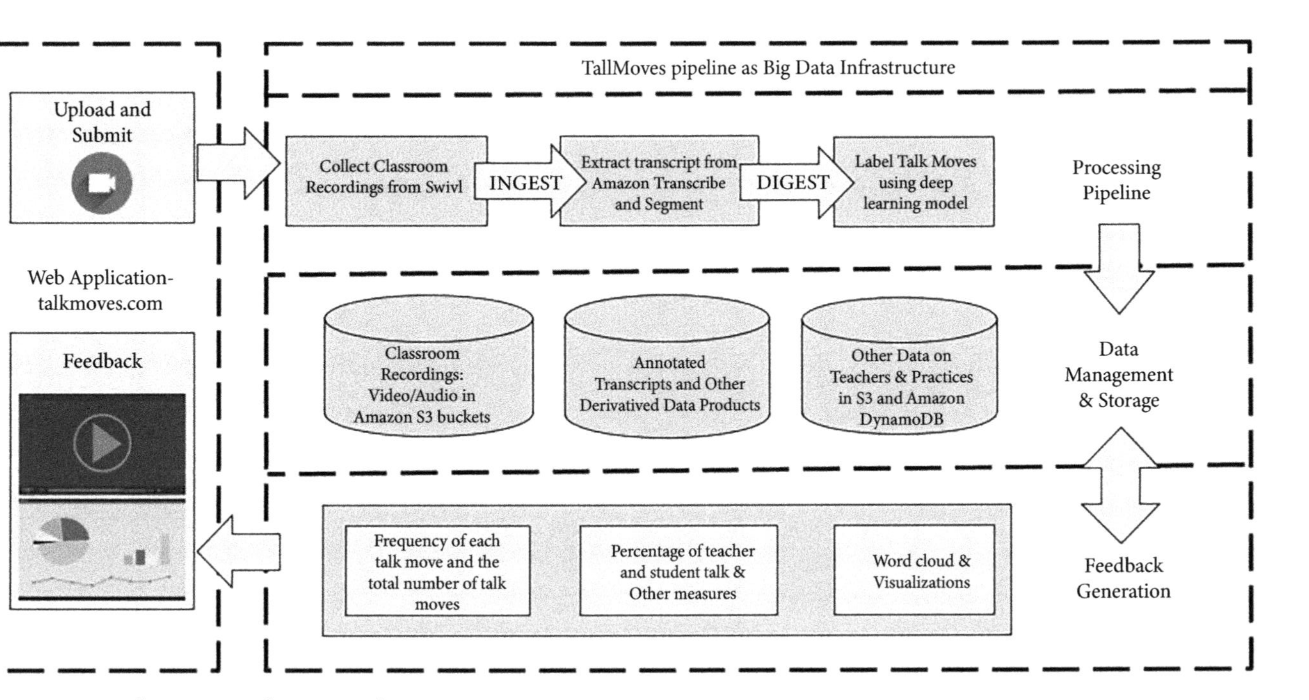

Figure 17.1 Talk Moves application architecture.

Model Development and Accuracy

The deep learning models included in the application take classroom transcripts as input and output the talk moves associated with each corresponding sentence. This can be formulated as a supervised multi-label sequence classification problem in machine learning. We trained two independent models to identify teacher and student talk moves automatically. We began with a bidirectional long short-term (bi-LSTM) network that can process sequences (both forward and backward) to understand and identify features that separate the different talk moves as well as sentences that do not contain a talk move. Of note is the uneven distribution pattern of the talk moves included in the TalkMoves dataset, with certain talk moves being much more frequently used during classroom lessons than others. This distribution pattern reflects natural variation in how teachers and students use talk moves in mathematics lessons, with some moves being more common than others. Furthermore, talk moves are "special" linguistic acts, meaning that they have a particular meaning for both the speaker and the listeners when they occur. Therefore it is not surprising that among all teacher and student sentences, the most common talk move label is "none," indicating that those sentences do not contain a talk move.

We explored different model architectures for performing sentence-level classification, including transformer models such as BERT (Devlin et al. 2019) and Roberta (Liu et al. 2019) (see Suresh et al. 2019, 2021a, 2022a for details). We tested the performance of BASE models (rather than standard large models), as these smaller models are better suited for deployment in user-facing applications. Among the BASE models, we found that the Roberta base performed the best for both teacher ($F_1 = 76.32\%$) and student sentence classification ($F_1 = 73.12\%$). Through further experimentation, we found that using additional contextual cues boosted the performance of the teacher model to an F_1-score of 78.92% (Suresh et al. 2022b).

Model performance was based on macro-F_1-scores, rather than simply calculating their degree of accuracy, due to the skewed distribution of talk moves. F_1 is the harmonic mean of precision and recall and calculated as $F_1 = 2 * (precision * recall)/(precision + recall)$. Precision is the fraction of retrieved talk moves that are relevant to the sentence and recall is the fraction of the talk moves that are successfully retrieved, where success is defined relative to a human rater's identification of talk moves. An F_1 score of 80% is roughly on par with well-trained human annotator performance. For the teacher models, the experiments were repeated with ten random seeds and the average score is reported. In contrast, the performance on the student models has high variance since only a limited number of student utterances were available to be used as the training data. The best performing models were deployed into the production pipeline of the TalkMoves application.

User Interface

The initial feedback interface for the TalkMoves application was generated using a collaborative design (co-design) process (Penuel, Roschelle, and Shechtman 2007) that included teachers, mathematics educators, and computer scientists. Research suggests that by actively including teachers in the development of new instructional materials and innovations, co-design helps to ensure the resulting products will be directly meaningful to their everyday teaching practice (Raza et al. 2021; Voogt, Pieters, and Handelzalts 2016). The co-design process yielded several guiding principles for the application, including the following: filming and uploading the classroom recordings should be simple, fast, and nondisruptive for teachers; the feedback should be presented in a professional, informative, and nonevaluative manner; and the interface should be intuitive, with easily interpretable graphics and minimal text (Jacobs et al. 2022).

When they use the TalkMoves application, teachers receive feedback on a personalized dashboard for each uploaded classroom recording. The dashboard displays the corresponding video and a variety of data analytics, primarily using graphics and visual representations (see Figure 17.2). Information is presented for the target lesson, the target lesson compared to all of the teachers' lessons, and the target lesson compared to the lessons from all other users of the application. The following analytics are generated for all teacher and student talk moves: (1) how many times each talk move was used, (2) the number of talk moves in this lesson compared to the teacher's average and the group's (all participating teachers) average, (3) the relative frequency of each accountable talk category, and (4) the number of talk moves during each quartile of the lesson. Additional information includes the relative percentage of teacher and student talk, a word cloud showing the most frequently used words, the percentage of one-word student utterances, teacher utterances followed by at least three seconds of wait time, and the number of (and most common) "mathematical terms" used by teachers and students.

Understanding how productive talk supports learning requires a longitudinal lens (Ford and Forman 2015; Mortimer and Scott 2003). To this end, the interface also provides teachers with visual displays of their lesson feedback over time (for all of their lessons or a selected subset). The "trends" section of the application offers information about teacher and student talk moves and a variety of other discourse features across a teacher's recorded lessons. Figure 17.3 shows an example of the feedback provided to one teacher about their students' talk moves in twelve uploaded lessons, illustrating changes in individual student talk moves over time as well as showing patterns in the relative frequency of each talk move category across lessons.

User Study

We conducted a user study to understand how a small set of teachers used the TalkMoves application in practice and to document their perceptions of the application's usability and accuracy, along with changes in their talk moves over time. The participating teachers were provided with an iPad and a Swivl, a hardware device designed to provide automated video capture for K–12 classrooms (Franklin et al. 2018), to self-record their lessons beginning in fall 2019. The user study was designed to be longitudinal, with teachers engaging with and providing feedback on iterative versions of the application as it was updated over two academic years.

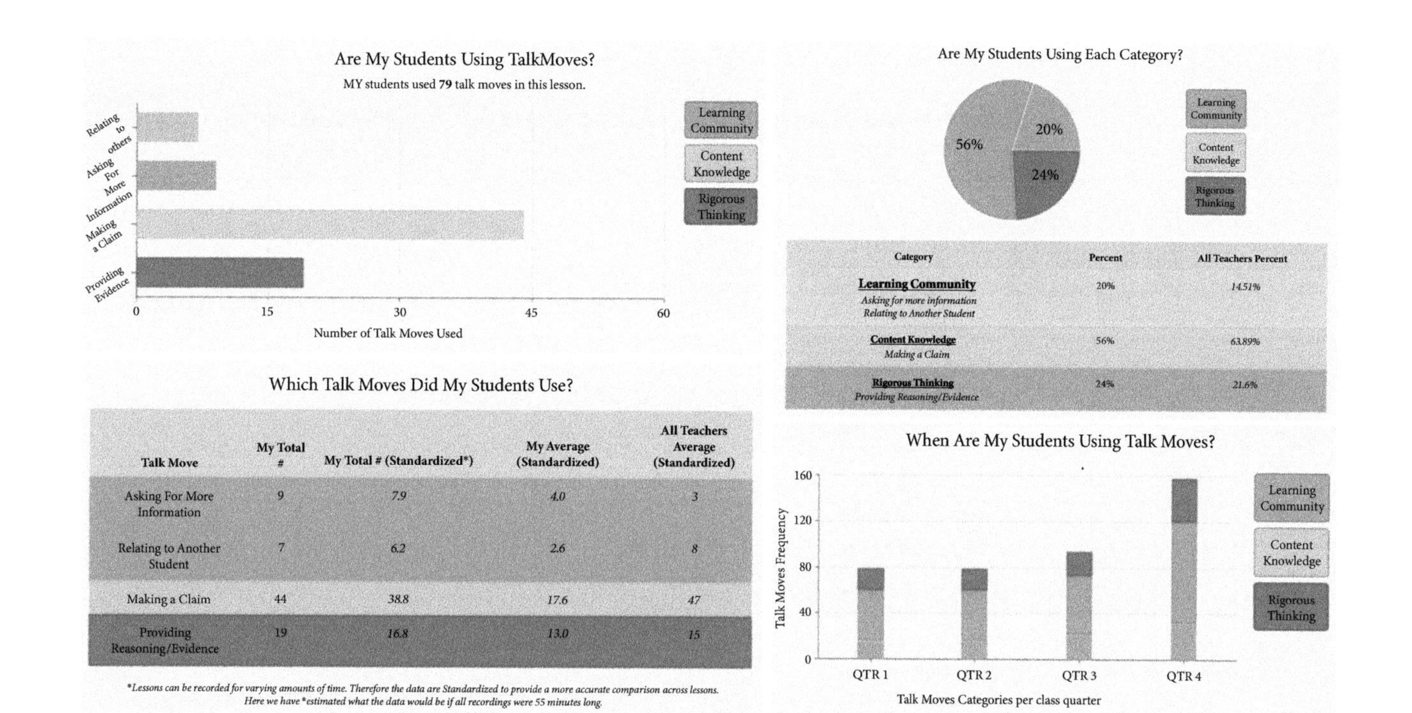

Figure 17.2 User interface displaying information about the teacher talk moves used during a selected lesson.

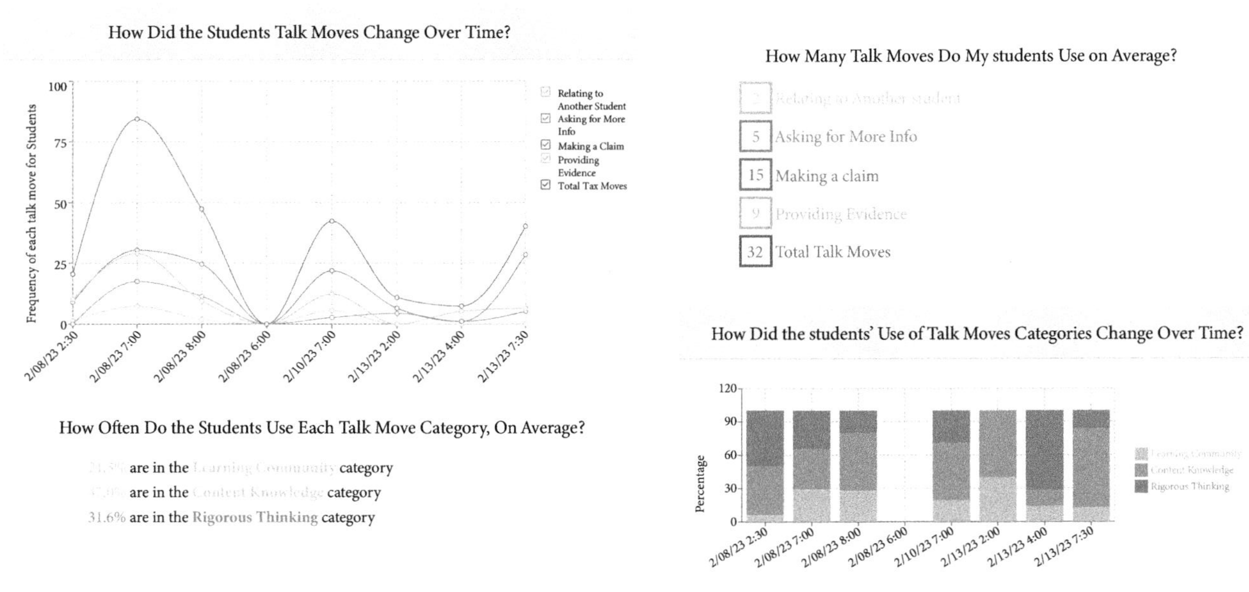

Figure 17.3 User interface displaying information about the student talk moves used across lessons.

An essential backdrop to this study was the COVID-19 pandemic, with face-to-face classroom instruction ceasing in the participating school districts from spring 2020 through at least fall 2020. During this time, the teachers engaged in various instructional models that included in-person, online, and hybrid classes. In the first school year of the study, the teachers recorded only in-person lessons. However, during the second school year, most of the teachers recorded both online and in-person (or hybrid) lessons. Our preliminary analyses suggest that there is no notable difference between these online and in-person lessons in terms of the frequency of talk moves, perhaps because the teachers who elected to continue with the study were increasingly attentive to using talk moves during their instruction.

Participants

Twenty-one teachers from two school districts in the western United States voluntarily consented to participate in the TalkMoves application pilot study beginning in the 2019–20 school year. The teachers spanned grades 4–12, with most teaching upper elementary school (71%). The participants were a relatively experienced group of teachers with four to thirty-two years of classroom teaching experience ($M = 15$). Twelve teachers continued their participation for a second school year (2020–21). Like the whole group, most of these continuing teachers taught elementary school ($n = 8$), and their average teaching experience was sixteen years.

Data Sources and Analyses

We used a mixed-methods, interpretive approach to studying teachers' experiences using the application (Creswell 2013) and collected a variety of qualitative and quantitative data. Qualitative data included responses from five surveys administered throughout the two-year period as well as two interviews. The surveys and interviews primarily focused on teachers' use and understanding of the application and its perceived utility value. Quantitative data come from the automated feedback on teachers' recorded mathematics lessons. Examples of this quantitative data include the frequency of each talk move in a given lesson, the total number of talk moves, and the percentage of talk by students.

Teachers' Use of the Tool

Because teachers were provided with the equipment to self-record their classrooms, they had complete autonomy over whether and how often to record. Although they were encouraged to record lessons on a regular basis (e.g., weekly or biweekly), teachers made their own decisions about when to record and generally did so intermittently. Furthermore, in this study, teachers' engagement with the application was designed as an independent, cyclical process. Ideally, teachers would review, reflect on, and make instructional changes based on the automated feedback generated for each lesson. However, the extent to which teachers elected to engage in such a process was an empirical question that we were able to examine in several ways.

Table 17.2 shows how often teachers recorded and the number of teachers who reported consistently reviewing the application's feedback during each year of the study. In Year 1, the twenty-one participating teachers each recorded ten lessons on average, with a wide range across teachers (recording between three and twenty-one lessons). Data from Year 2 are quite similar, with the twelve continuing teachers each recording fourteen lessons on average (ranging from one to thirty-one recordings).

Of the teachers who participated in the first year of the study, thirteen (62%) reported that they logged into the application and looked over the automated feedback for most or all of the lessons that they recorded. Five of the eight teachers who were infrequent viewers of their data in Year 1 elected to not continue in the second year, and three decided to continue participating. In other words, the teachers who chose to remain in the study for a second year were mostly (but not all) consistent reviewers of the application's feedback on their lessons. During Year 2, ten of the twelve participating teachers (83%) reported that they consistently reviewed the application's feedback.

Perceived Usability

The TalkMoves application was designed for teachers to learn to navigate independently, with no training related to either talk moves or the feedback displays. Encouragingly, teachers generally found the application straightforward and easy to use, though some initially had questions about the recording equipment and accessing the feedback on their lessons. Most of these early questions were related to challenges using the Swivl device or bugs in the application that were troubleshooted and fixed. Once teachers had recorded multiple lessons during the first year of the study, the majority reported that the recording equipment was easy or relatively easy to use (84%) and that it was easy or fairly easy to find the information they wanted on

Table 17.2 Teachers' Use of the TalkMoves Application during Years 1 and 2

	Year 1 (2019–2020)	**Year 2 (2020–21)**
Number of participating teachers	21	12
Total lessons recorded	210	163
Average # lessons recorded by each teacher	10	14
Range in # lessons recorded by each teacher	3–21	1–31
Number of teachers who consistently reviewed the application's feedback	13	10

the application (68%). When asked about the graphs and charts in the application, almost all of the teachers (89%) said they were easy or relatively easy to interpret, despite the application's minimal surrounding text.

One teacher enthusiastically described the application's functionality by saying, "It's very user-friendly, very intuitive. I mean, it's a plug and play, which is great for me." Another noted with a bit more hesitancy, "I wouldn't say that it's something that I feel 100% confident using or navigating, but I feel like I've been able to play around with it to figure some things out." Perhaps not surprisingly, by the second year of the study, the teachers who elected to continue using the application did not raise any concerns about its usability. However, as we will discuss next, there were some ongoing concerns around the accuracy of the automated feedback.

Perceived Accuracy

Teachers were asked about the degree to which they perceived the application's feedback as accurate and trustworthy throughout the user study. During the first year, in winter 2020, after the teachers had recorded at least a few lessons, most teachers (79%) rated the application as at least moderately accurate (i.e., 3 or higher on a 5-point scale) and 21% felt that it was somewhat inaccurate or not accurate. Most teachers correctly noted that the system was limited in detecting and automatically transcribing student speech, likely resulting in lower performance in feedback related to student speech. The research team provided suggestions about where teachers should place their microphones in the classroom to best pick up student voices, advice that may have supported teachers' efforts to ensure higher quality audio but raised flags about the accuracy of the fully automated process. At the beginning of the study, many teachers were particularly interested in the data on the percentage of student talk in their classrooms. They reported being disappointed that the application tended to under-report student utterances.

Between Years 1 and 2 of the study, the user interface was substantially redesigned to foreground talk moves and minimize attention on the amount of talk produced by teachers and students. Instead of prominently featuring visualizations depicting the *quantity* of talk produced by the students, the revised interface highlights the talk *quality*. Perhaps as a result of this redesign, teachers who continued participating for a second year reported paying closer attention to the feedback provided on talk moves and raised fewer concerns about the overall accuracy of the data. During interviews in fall 2020, most teachers (83%) shared that they found the application's feedback trustworthy and generally accurate. However, they pointed out that their frequency on some of the talk moves (particularly restating) were lower than expected. There were still concerns about the microphones not sufficiently capturing student talk during "turn and talks" or small group work (when many individuals were talking at once). One teacher explained, "I'm sure there are some small mistakes, but I don't think there are any major mistakes."

Classroom Impacts

We examined the effect of using the application for two school years on talk move frequency during mathematics lessons. Based on the video recordings uploaded by the twelve teachers who participated in both years of the user study, Figures 17.4 and 17.5 provide information on observable changes in their classroom instruction. Specifically, the figures show the average frequency of each teacher and student talk moves by semester (fall, spring) across the two school years (2019–20, 2020–21). With a few exceptions, talk moves were not notably different *within* a school year; however, significant changes occurred *across* years for this subset of teachers. We used the Wilcoxon signed ranks test for nonparametric data to compare the average frequency of talk moves in fall 2019 to spring 2021 (Table 17.3). These analyses showed that three of the six teacher talk moves and all four of the student talk moves increased significantly ($p < 0.05$) or nearly significantly ($p < 0.06$) over these two time periods (see Figure 17.4).

As in the model training dataset, the teacher talk moves "keeping everyone together" and "pressing for accuracy" were by far the most prevalent at each time point. The most common student talk move was "making a claim," which likely corresponds to occasions when their teachers "press for accuracy." Of note is the sharp increase in the frequency of students "providing evidence," despite the lack of a corresponding increase in teachers "pressing for reasoning." It is possible that revoicing students' contributions more often, or simply being invited more frequently to contribute to the classroom conversation, encourages students to explain or provide evidence related to their mathematical thinking.

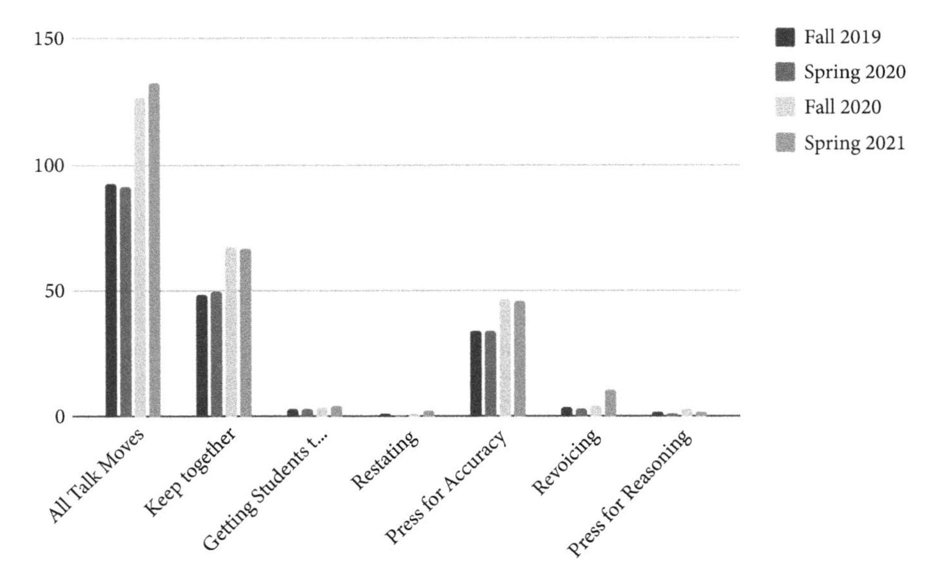

Figure 17.4 Average frequency of teacher talk moves per lesson during the 2019–20 and 2020–21 school years.

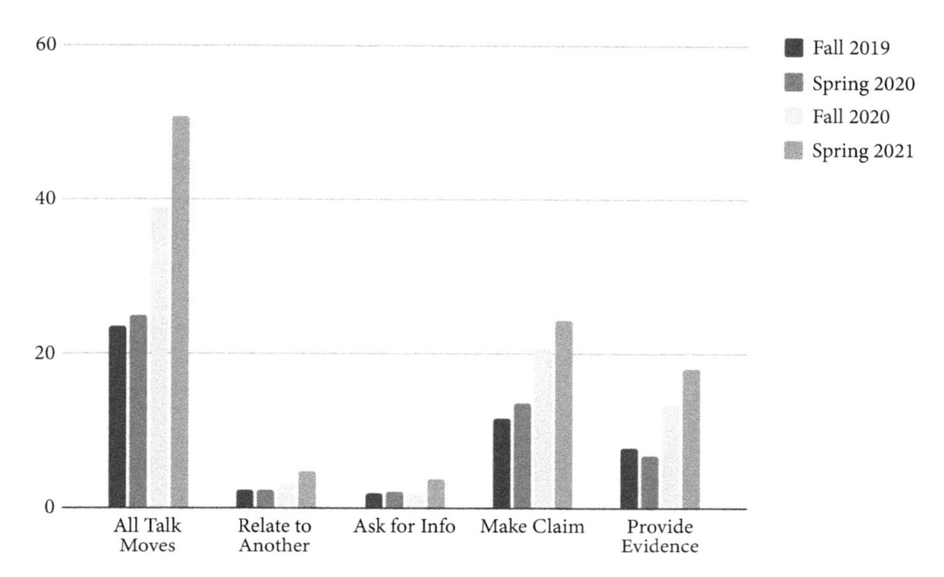

Figure 17.5 Average frequency of student talk moves per lesson during the 2019–20 and 2020–21 school years.

Table 17.3 Change in the Average Frequency of Teacher and Student Talk Moves per Lesson from Fall 2019 to Spring 2021

Talk move label	Fall 2019 Mean frequency	Spring 2021 Mean frequency	p-value
Teacher talk moves			
All teacher talk moves	100	129	$p < 0.003$
Keep students together	53	64	$p < 0.06$
Get students to relate	2	4	ns
Restating	2	3	ns
Press for accuracy	37	44	$p < 0.06$
Revoicing	4	11	$p < 0.001$
Press for reasoning	2	2	ns
Student talk moves			
All student talk moves	27	51	$p < 0.03$
Relate to another student	2	5	$p < 0.06$
Ask for info	2	4	$p < 0.04$
Make a claim	14	25	$p < 0.05$
Provide evidence	8	17	$p < 0.02$

Overall, these twelve users appeared especially motivated to receive feedback that could improve their discourse strategies. When asked to describe their use of the application at the end of the project, most teachers explicitly connected their use of the TalkMoves application to reflecting on their classroom discourse patterns (92%) and acting on those reflections in an intentional effort to change their instruction (75%), as shown in Table 17.4. Several teachers expressed that they would have liked to use the application more often, but felt constrained by the educational disruptions and stress caused by the COVID-19 pandemic. Over half of the teachers (58%) said that they would like to continue using the application, with some noting that it could support collaborative professional development efforts at their schools, such as in professional learning communities and with coaches.

Discussion

TalkMoves offers an example of an NLP application that leverages a well-theorized approach to academic discourse (accountable talk) and addresses a recognized challenge in education (providing personalized feedback at scale). This effort demonstrates how a new form of big data—classroom recordings—can be combined with advances in automated speech recognition and deep learning models and embedded within a user-friendly application to provide teachers with unique insights into their instruction and discourse routines. The deep learning models used in the TalkMoves application automatically recognize and classify critical features of classroom

Table 17.4 Number of Teachers Who Reported the Application Supported Reflection and/or Change

Teacher comments	Number of teachers	Illustrative quotes
Reflecting on discourse patterns	11	"I am always curious to see how much my students were talking during class. I usually look at the student talk data first. Then, I look at the teacher talk to see what kinds of talk moves I was using throughout the lesson." "While TalkMoves is far from perfect, it is by far the best reflective data I have ever used."
Changing discourse strategies	9	"The feedback inspires me to do some research and look into activities that get kids talking in different ways based on the feedback." "I saw categories that I wasn't using, or my wait time average, and made a conscious effort to improve upon those in upcoming lessons." "When I am not recording or thinking about talk moves specifically, I sometimes go on autopilot and just do what is comfortable. When I am using the talk moves app and thinking more about talk moves, I feel that I can more intentionally talk and elicit student responses!"

talk, generating information about teacher and student talk moves that is on par with domain-based instructional experts in terms of reliability. Evidence from an initial user study suggests that teachers perceive the application to be usable, and the feedback to be generally accurate, although there are some notable difficulties in capturing student audio and subsequent analyses derived from student speech data. Particularly promising is that engagement with the application over a two-year period appears to promote teachers' and students' overall use of talk moves. Due to the small sample size and the lack of a comparison group, these analyses should be considered exploratory only. Yet, they offer a glimpse of the potential for how AI-driven tools might impact teacher learning and change instruction to incorporate dialogic features more often.

The TalkMoves application, in its present form, does not advise teachers on whether or how to make instructional changes. Currently designed as a platform that primarily supports individual reflection, teachers must make sense of their own data, consider whether changes are warranted, and if so, adopt new instructional strategies aligned with their personal goals. The data-driven feedback provided to teachers in the form of visual analytics based on their classroom discourse is intended to serve as a mirror, rather than as an evaluation or call to action. The application does not offer pedagogical suggestions or set guideposts regarding which talk moves to use and how often. In part, this intentional neutrality is a design decision based on the participating teachers' expressed concerns that an automated tool should not offer judgments regarding their instruction or set unrealistic expectations without any knowledge of their instructional contexts, which would feel both uncomfortable and untrustworthy.

Notably, the accountable talk framework does not define an ideal number of talk moves for lessons on any disciplinary content. Such rigid guidelines would be fundamentally counter to the agentic positioning of both teachers and students in a dialogic classroom, where conversations take place organically, meaning is socially derived, and learning is co-constructed. Instead of setting benchmarks, the application provides information about a teacher's average number of talk moves (during a lesson and over time) and how that teacher's averages compare to their peers (in this case, the other pilot teachers). Users must then overlay their own interpretations of the data, drawing from their understanding of the instructional setting and critical self-reflection.

As developers, our intention was for the TalkMoves application to encourage pedagogical reflection, inquiry, and goal setting, particularly around classroom discourse practices. The monitoring of talk moves, derived from data on teachers' own lesson recordings, enables meaningful "informating" feedback (Zuboff 1988) by making previously hidden or tacit instructional activities visible in an effort to support noticing, learning, and intentional change. As such, the TalkMoves application offers teachers the opportunity to participate in a human–technology partnership that centers the reflective noticing (Sherin and Dyer 2017) of instructional patterns that may become targets for study and improvement.

Becoming adept in new teaching routines using the application will likely require a good deal of time, effort, and professional learning for most practitioners. The TalkMoves application can serve as an important tool by providing reliable, detailed, and longitudinal feedback; however, it would likely be best suited for collaborative use by teachers working in professional learning communities and/or with instructional coaches to ensure a clear understanding of the data, to become more knowledgeable about accountable talk theory and discourse-rich instruction, and to set realistic goals for incremental improvements in practice. In the future, it will be important to design educative and collaborative professional experiences that make intentional use of the application's automated feedback to promote dialogic classrooms where students' ideas, reasoning, and multiple points of view play a central role and become conversational norms (Hofmann and Ruthven 2018).

Limitations

In the following, we elaborate on three limitations in the study: challenges with automated speech recognition, limitations of the training dataset, and ideas for improving model performance.

Speech Recognition Challenges

A critical limitation of this work is the challenge of automated speech recognition (ASR) systems to recognize young children's speech accurately. In addition to errors detecting teacher talk and autogenerated speaker diarization, we have found that student talk is severely underestimated by Amazon Transcribe, which the application uses to automate speech-to-text transcript generation. This challenge has been noted by many in the field and can likely be attributed primarily to low confidence levels and errors brought on by acoustic variability, unpredictable articulation, and other behaviors common in children's language production (Booth et al. 2020; Gerosa, Giuliani, and Brugnara 2007).

To ascertain the extent to which speech recognition challenges impact the output of the deep learning models used in the application, we selected a few lesson transcripts at random and tested model performance on ASR output compared to gold-standard, human-created transcripts. Because the number of sentences in the ASR transcripts did not align with the gold standard, we compared the proportional distribution of teacher talk moves from both outputs, as seen in Figure 17.6. The distribution from the ASR output closely resembles that from the gold standard, suggesting that despite the differences in the transcripts the labeling of talk moves is quite similar. Further analyses are needed to validate the robustness of the model to word errors and to ensure similar accuracy with respect to the student talk moves.

Limited Training Dataset

The TalkMoves dataset was curated as a training set to develop the deep learning models used in the TalkMoves application. This dataset incorporates classroom transcripts that are human transcribed and annotated from real-world mathematics

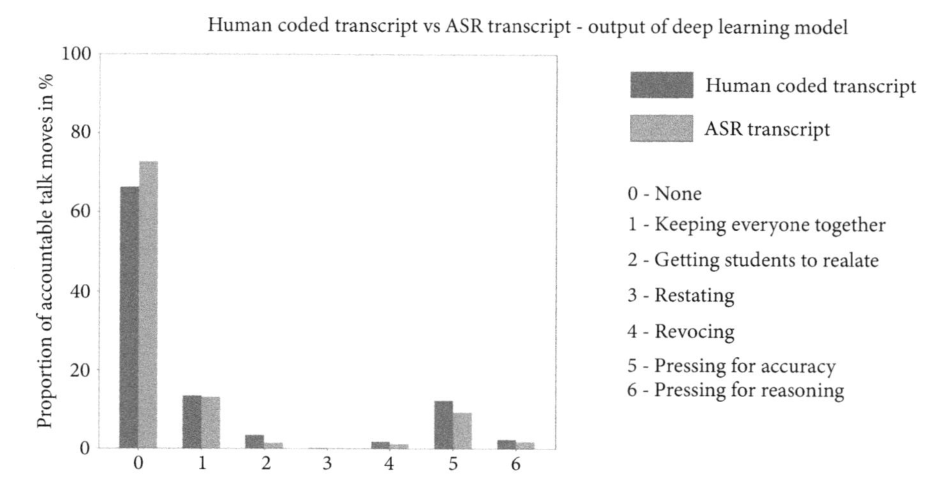

Figure 17.6 Proportional distribution of talk moves predicted using human-coded and ASR transcripts.

lessons. It is limited in scope, as recording and transcribing authentic mathematics classroom lessons involves significant human effort, along with the collection of numerous permissions from the participants, making the curation of such a dataset challenging and expensive. The transcripts included in the TalkMoves dataset are skewed towards female-taught, English-speaking, US middle school lessons (grades 6–8), although in many cases descriptive information about the lessons is unknown.

Improving Model Performance

Although performance reported on the teacher models is relatively stable and has been validated with ten different runs and random seeds, it could likely still be improved. For example, future improvement efforts might better account for the nonuniform distribution of talk moves. The nonuniform (i.e., imbalanced) nature of the data is a major concern when working with real word applications. The imbalance problem is commonly known to impede the performance of the predictive models (Singh and Anuradha 2015). Recent developments to overcome the imbalance problem have proven to provide significant improvement in predictive analysis, especially for classification (Hasib et al. 2020). A simple approach is to use a modified loss function that penalizes prediction of dominating classes (i.e., weighted loss) (Suresh et al. 2019). Similarly, SMOTE or synthetic minority oversampling data (Chawla et al. 2002) is a popular sampling technique to generate artificial samples to balance the distribution of data. The output of SMOTE is not a real representation of the text inside its feature space (i.e., mathematics classrooms) since much of the pertinent semantic, syntactic, and contextual information is not captured across the generated samples. An initial attempt to address the imbalanced problem using weighted loss or SMOTE did not yield any substantial performance improvements. Moreover, compared to the teacher models, the variance in performance on the student models is much more prominent since the number of student utterances available for fine-tuning was substantially fewer. The current performance of the student models (73% F_1) is the best of four different runs (i.e., not the average). The performance of the student models could likely be improved by using improvised ASR systems tailored to reliably recognize child speech and incorporating additional student utterances into the training dataset that capture rich conversations involving students.

Conclusion

Feedback on accountable talk is ripe for a machine-learning application due to the fact that such talk is well specified by the research literature, leading to automated classification with high levels of accuracy. In addition to the accountable talk, there is emerging literature on other discourse-based moves likely to support students' academic motivation and ensure equitable learning opportunities, such as relationship-building moves. For example, displaying empathy during teacher and student interactions has been demonstrated to promote caring relationships between teachers and students (Hackenberg 2010; Jaber, Southerland, and Dake 2018), which in turn have positive impacts on student achievement (O'Connor and McCartney 2007). Importantly, empathy can be operationalized as a discursive construct (Macagno et al. 2022) and modeled using NLP approaches (Alam, Danieli, and Riccardi 2018). Other high-frequency instructional phenomena similarly well articulated and relatively easy to identify, such as appropriate instructional tasks or scaffolds based on detected student errors, also lend themselves to AI-based classification systems that might offer useful guidance for teachers.

Teachers and educational leaders across content areas and grade levels appear enthusiastic about the potential of applications that provide automated, personalized information on essential instructional practices and seem eager to incorporate these tools into their ongoing professional learning (Chen et al. 2020; Scornavacco, Jacobs, and Harty 2022). Existing and novel professional development efforts that target improvements in classroom discourse driven by increased attention to facilitating productive talk (e.g., Aguilar and Telese 2019; Moser et al. 2022; O'Connor and Michaels 2019) would likely benefit from applications that automate individualized feedback at scale. The AI models used in the TalkMoves application appear to be reliably transferable to a range of related use cases, such as online mathematics tutoring, as another research team has already demonstrated (Balyan et al. 2022). Important next steps include expanding the technology to target a larger set of research-based best practices, embedding it within a well-articulated professional learning paradigm, and conducting rigorous studies of uptake, efficacy, and impacts on teaching and learning.

References

Aguilar, J., and Telese, J. 2019. "Learning Productive Mathematical Talk Moves through Mix-Reality Simulation: The Case of Pre-service Elementary Teachers in a Hispanic Serving Institution." In *Proceedings of Society for Information Technology and Teacher Education International Conference*, edited by K. Graziono, 2129–33. Las Vegas, NV: Association for the Advancement of Computing in Education. https://www.learntechlib.org/primary/p/207941/

Alam, F., Danieli, M., and Riccardi, G. 2018. "Annotating and Modeling Empathy in Spoken Conversations." *Computer Speech & Language* 50: 40–61. https://doi.org/10.1016/j.csl.2017.12.003

Alexander, R. 2020. *A Dialogic Teaching Companion*. New York: Routledge.

Balyan, R., Arner, T., Taylor, K., Shin, J., Banawan, M., Leite, W. L., and McNamara, D. S. 2022. "Modeling One-on-One Online Tutoring Discourse Using an Accountable Talk Framework." In *Proceedings of the 15th International Conference on Educational Data Mining*, edited by A. Mitrovic and N. Bosch, 477–83. Durham: International Educational Data Mining Society.

Berland, L. K., Schwarz, C. V., Krist, C., Kenyon, L., Lo, A. S., and Reiser, B. J. 2016. "Epistemologies in Practice: Making Scientific Practices Meaningful for Students." *Journal of Research in Science Teaching* 53, no. 7: 1082–12. https://doi.org/10.1002/tea.21257

Billings, L., and Fitzgerald, J. 2002. "Dialogic Discussion and the Paideia Seminar." *American Educational Research Journal* 39, no. 4: 907–41. https://doi.org/10.3102/00028312039004905

Booth, E., Carns, J., Kennington, C., and Rafla, N. 2020. "Evaluating and Improving Child-Directed Automatic Speech Recognition." In *Proceedings of the 12th Conference on Language Resources and Evaluation*, 6340–45. Marseille: European Languages Resources Association.

Chapin, S. H., and O'Connor, C. 2012. "Project Challenge: Using Challenging Curriculum and Mathematical Discourse to Help All Students Learn." In *High-Expectation Curricula: Helping All Students Succeed with Powerful Learning*, edited by C. Dudley-Marling and S. Michaels, 113–27. New York: Teachers College Press.

Chapin, S. H., O'Connor, M. C., and Anderson, N. C. 2009. *Classroom Discussions: Using Math Talk to Help Students Learn, Grades K-6*. Sausalito, CA: Math Solutions Publications.

Chawla, N. V., Bowyer, K. W., Hall, L. O., and Kegelmeyer, W. P. 2002. "SMOTE: Synthetic Minority over-Sampling Technique." *Journal of Artificial Intelligence Research* 16: 321–57.

Chen, G. 2020. "A Visual Learning Analytics (VLA) Approach to Video-Based Teacher Professional Development: Impact on Teachers' Beliefs, Self-efficacy, and Classroom Talk Practice." *Computers & Education* 144: 1–15. http://dx.doi.org/10.1016/j.compedu.2019.103670

Chen, G., Chan, C. K., Chan, K. K., Clarke, S. N., and Resnick, L. B. 2020. "Efficacy of Video-Based Teacher Professional Development for Increasing Classroom Discourse and Student Learning." *Journal of the Learning Sciences* 29, nos. 4–5: 642–80. http://dx.doi.org/10.1080/10508406.2020.1783269

Chen, G., Clarke, S. N., and Resnick, L. B. 2015. "Classroom Discourse Analyzer (CDA): A Discourse Analytic Tool for Teachers." *Technology, Instruction, Cognition and Learning* 10, no. 2: 85–105.

Clarke, S. N. 2015. "The Right to Speak." In *Socializing Intelligence through Academic Talk and Dialogue*, edited by L. B. Resnick, C. S. C. Asterhan, and S. N. Clarke, 167–80. Washington, DC: American Educational Research Association.

Cobb, P. A., Stephan, M., McClain, K., and Gravemeijer, K. 2001. "Participating in Classroom Mathematical Practices." *Journal of the Learning Sciences* 10, nos. 1 and 2: 113–63. https://doi.org/10.1207/S15327809JLS10-1-2_6

Correnti, R., Stein, M. K., Smith, M. S., Scherrer, J., McKeown, M. G., Greeno, J. G., and Ashley, K. 2015. "Improving Teaching at Scale: Design for the Scientific Measurement and Learning of Discourse Practice." In *Socializing Intelligence through Academic Talk and Dialogue*, edited by L. B. Resnick, C. S. C. Asterhan, and S. N. Clarke, 315–34. Washington, DC: American Educational Research Association.

Creswell, J. 2013. *Qualitative Inquiry and Research Design: Choosing among Five Approaches*, 3rd ed. Thousand Oaks, CA: Sage.

Demszky, D., Liu, J., Mancenido, Z., Cohen, J., Hill, H., Jurafsky, D., and Hashimoto, T. 2021. "Measuring Conversational Uptake: A Case Study on Student–Teacher Interactions." *arXiv preprint arXiv:2106.03873*

Devlin, J., Chang, M., Lee, K. and Toutanova, K. 2019. "BERT: Pre-training of Deep Bidirectional Transformers for Language Understanding." In Proceedings of the 2019 Conference of the North American Chapter of the Association for Computational Linguistics: Human Language Technologies, 4171–86. Minneapolis, MN: Association for Computational Linguistics. https://arxiv.org/pdf/1810.04805.pdf&usg=ALkJrhhzxlCL6yTht2BRmH9atgvKFxHsxQ

Donnelly, P. J., Blanchard, N., Samei, B., Olney, A. M., Sun, X., Ward, B., Kelly, S., Nystran, M., and D'Mello, S. K. 2016. "Automatic Teacher Modeling from Live Classroom Audio." In *Proceedings of the 2016 Conference on User Modeling Adaptation and Personalization*, 45–53. Halifax, Canada: Association for Computing Machinery. http://dx.doi.org/10.1145/2930238.2930250

Donnelly, P. J., Blanchard, N., Olney, A. M., Kelly, S., Nystrand, M., and D'Mello, S. K. 2017. "Words Matter: Automatic Detection of Teacher Questions in Live Classroom Discourse Using Linguistics, Acoustics, and Context." In Proceedings of the Seventh International Learning Analytics and Knowledge Conference, 218–27. Vancouver, Canada: Association for Computing Machinery. http://dx.doi.org/10.1145/3027385.3027417

Edwards-Groves, C., and Davidson, C. 2020. "Noticing the Multidimensionality of Active Listening in a Dialogic Classroom." *Australian Journal of Language and Literacy* 43, no. 1: 83–94.

Ford, M. J., and Forman, E. A. 2015. "Uncertainty and Scientific Progress in Classroom Dialogue." In *Socializing Intelligence through Academic Talk and Dialogue*, edited by L. B. Resnick, C. S. C. Asterhan, and S. N. Clarke, 143–56. Washington, DC: American Educational Research Association.

Ford, K., and Welling-Riley, K. 2021. "Student Talk in Science Class." *The Learning Professional* 42, no. 3: 58–61.

Franklin, R. K., O'Neill Mitchell, J., Walters, K. S., Livingston, B., Lineberger, M. B., Putman, C., Yarborough, R., and Karges-Bone, L. 2018. "Using *Swivl* Robotic Technology in Teacher Education Preparation: A Pilot Study." *TechTrends* 62, no. 2: 184–89. https://doi.org/10.1007/s11528-017-0246-5

Gallimore, R., Hiebert, J., and Ermeling, B. 2014. "Rich Classroom Discussion: One Way to Get Rich Learning." Teachers College Record, http://www.tcrecord.org ID Number: 17714.

Gerosa, M., Giuliani, D., and Brugnara, F. 2007. "Acoustic Variability and Automatic Recognition of Children's Speech." *Speech Communication* 49, nos. 10–11: 847–60. http://dx.doi.org/10.1016/j.specom.2007.01.002

Hackenberg, A. J. 2010. "Mathematical Caring Relations in Action." *Journal for Research in Mathematics Education* 41, no. 3: 236–73. https://doi.org/10.5951/jresematheduc.41.3.0236

Hasib, K. M., Iqbal, M., Shah, F. M., Mahmud, J. A., Popel, M. H., Showrov, M., Ahmed, S., and Rahman, O. 2020. "A Survey of Methods for Managing the Classification and Solution of Data Imbalance Problem." *Journal of Computer Science* 16, no. 11: 1546–57. arXiv:2012.11870

Hofmann, R., and Ruthven, K. 2018. "Operational, Interpersonal, Discussional and Ideational Dimensions of Classroom Norms for Dialogic Practice in School Mathematics." *British Educational Research Journal* 44, no. 3: 496–514. https://doi.org/10.1002/berj.3444

Jaber, L. Z., Southerland, S., and Dake, F. 2018. "Cultivating Epistemic Empathy in Preservice Teacher Education." *Teaching and Teacher Education* 72: 13–23. https://doi.org/10.1016/j.tate.2018.02.009

Jacobs, J., Scornavacco, K., Harty, C., Suresh, A., Lai, V. and Sumner, T. 2022. "Promoting Rich Discussions in Mathematics Classrooms: Using Personalized, Automated Feedback to Support Reflection and Instructional Change." *Teaching and Teacher Education* 122, 103631. https://doi.org/10.1016/j.tate.2022.103631

Jensen, E., Pugh, S. L., and D'Mello, S.K. 2021. "A Deep Transfer Learning Approach to Modeling Teacher Discourse in the Classroom." In *Proceedings of the 11th International Learning Analytics and Knowledge Conference*, 302–12. New York: Association for Computing Machinery. https://doi.org/10.1145/3448139.3448168

Jensen, E., Dale, M., Donnelly, P. J., Stone, C., Kelly, S., Godley, A., and D'Mello, S. K. 2020. "Toward Automated Feedback on Teacher Discourse to Enhance Teacher Learning." In *Proceedings of the*

2020 CHI Conference on Human Factors in Computing Systems, 1–13. https://doi.org/10.1145/3313831.3376418

Kawanaka, T., and Stigler, J. W. 1999. "Teachers' Use of Questions in Eighth-Grade Mathematics Classrooms in Germany, Japan, and the United States." *Mathematical Thinking and Learning* 1, no. 4: 255–78.

Kelly, S., Olney, A. M., Donnelly, P., Nystrand, M., and D'Mello, S. K. 2018. "Automatically Measuring Question Authenticity in Real-World Classrooms." *Educational Researcher* 47, no. 7: 451–64. http://dx.doi.org/10.3102/0013189X18785613

Klebanov, B., Burstein, J., Harackiewicz, J. M., Priniski, S. J., and Mulholland, M. 2017. "Reflective Writing about the Utility Value of Science as a Tool for Increasing Stem Motivation and Retention—Can AI Help Scale Up?" *International Journal of Artificial Intelligence in Education* 27, no. 4: 791–818. https://doi.org/10.1007/s40593-017-0141-4.

Lefstein, A., Louie, N., Segal, A., and Becher, A. 2020. "Taking Stock of Research on Teacher Collaborative Discourse: Theory and Method in a Nascent Field." *Teaching and Teacher Education* 88: 102954. https://doi.org/10.1016/j.tate.2019.102954

Liu, Y., Ott, M., Goyal, N., Du, J., Joshi, M., Chen, D., Levy, O., Lewis, M., Zettlemoyer, L., and Stoyanov, V. 2019. "Roberta: A Robustly Optimized BERT Pretraining Approach." *arXiv preprint arXiv:1907.11692.*

Macagno, F., Rapanta, C., Mayweg-Paus, E., and Garcia-Milà, M. 2022. "Coding Empathy in Dialogue." *Journal of Pragmatics* 192: 116–32. https://doi.org/10.1016/j.pragma.2022.02.011

McHugh, M. L. 2012. "Interrater Reliability: The Kappa Statistic." *Biochemia Medica* 22, no. 3: 276–82.

Mehan, H., and Cazden, C. 2015. "The Study of Classroom Discourse: Early History and Current Developments." In *Socializing Intelligence through Academic Talk and Dialogue*, edited by L. B. Resnick, C. S. C. Asterhan, and S. N. Clarke, 13–36. Washington, DC: American Educational Research Association.

Mercer, N., and Wegerif, N. 2002. "Is 'Exploratory Talk' Productive Talk?" In *Learning with Computers: Analysing Productive Interactions*, edited by P. Light and K. Littleton, 79–101. London: Routledge.

Michaels, S., O'Connor, C., and Resnick, L. B. 2008. "Deliberative Discourse Idealized and Realized: Accountable Talk in the Classroom and in Civic Life." *Studies in the Philosophy of Education* 27: 283–97. https://doi.org/10.1007/s11217-007-9071-1

Michaels, S., and O'Connor, C. 2015. "Conceptualizing Talk Moves as Tools: Professional Development Approaches for Academically Productive Discussions." In *Socializing Intelligence through Academic Talk and Dialogue*, edited by L. B. Resnick, C. S. C. Asterhan, and S. N. Clarke, 333–47. Washington, DC: American Educational Research Association.

Michaels, S., and O'Connor, C. 2017. "From Recitation to Reasoning: Supporting Scientific and Engineering Practices through Talk." In *Helping Students Make Sense of the World Using Next Generation* Science and Engineering Practices, edited by C. V. Schwarz, C. Passmore, and B. J. Reiser, 311–36. Richmond, VA: NSTA Press.

Morris, A. K., and Hiebert, J. 2011. "Creating Shared Instructional Products: An Alternative Approach to Improving Teaching." *Educational Researcher* 40, no. 1: 5–14. http://dx.doi.org/10.3102/0013189X10393501

Mortimer, E., and Scott, P. 2003. *Meaning Making in secondary science classrooms*. Philadelphia, PA: Open University Press.

Moser, M., Zimmermann, M., Pauli, C., Reusser, K., and Wischgoll, A. 2022. "Student's Vocal Participation Trajectories in Whole-Class Discussions during Teacher Professional Development." *Learning, Culture and Social Interaction* 34: 100633. https://doi.org/10.1016/j.lcsi.2022.100633

Nystrand, M. 1997. *Opening Dialogue: Understanding the Dynamics of Language and Learning in the English Classroom*. New York: Teachers College Press.

O'Connor, E., and McCartney, K. 2007. "Examining Teacher–Child Relationships and Achievement as Part of an Ecological Model of Development." *American Educational Research Journal* 44, no. 2: 340–69. https://doi.org/10.3102/0002831207302172

O'Connor, M. C., and Michaels, S. 1993. "Aligning Academic Talk and Participation Status through Revoicing: Analysis of a Classroom Discourse Strategy." *Anthropology and Education Quarterly* 24, no. 4: 318–55. http://dx.doi.org/10.1525/aeq.1993.24.4.04x0063k

O'Connor, M. C., and Michaels, S. 1996. "Shifting Participant Frameworks: Orchestrating Thinking Practices in Group Discussions." In *Discourse, Learning, and Schooling*, edited by D. Hicks, 63–103. New York: Cambridge University Press.

O'Connor, C., and Michaels, S. 2019. "Supporting Teachers in Taking up Productive Talk Moves: The Long Road to Professional Learning at Scale." *International Journal of Educational Research* 97: 166–75. https://doi.org/10.1016/j.ijer.2017.11.003.

O'Connor, C., Michaels, S., and Chapin, S. H. 2015. "'Scaling Down' to Explore the Role of Talk in Learning: From District Intervention to Controlled Classroom Study." In *Socializing Intelligence through Academic Talk and Dialogue*, edited by L. B. Resnick, C. S. C. Asterhan, and S. N. Clarke, 111–26. Washington, DC: American Educational Research Association.

Odden, O. B., Marin, A., and Rudolph, J. L. 2021. "How has *Science Education* Changed over the Last 100 Years? An Analysis Using Natural Language Processing." *Science Education* 105, no. 4: 653–80. https://doi.org/10.1002/sce.21623

Patterson, A. D. 2019. "Equity in Groupwork: The Social Process of Creating Justice in a Science Classroom." Cultural Studies of Science Education 14: 361–81. https://doi.org/10.1007/s11422-019-09918-x

Penuel, W. R., Roschelle, J., and Shechtman, N. 2007. "Designing Formative Assessment Software with Teachers: An Analysis of the Co-design Process." *Research and Practice in Technology Enhanced Learning* 2, no. 1: 51–74. https://doi.org/10.1142/S1793206807000300

Perrotta, C., and Selwyn, N. 2020. "Deep Learning Goes to School: Toward a Relational Understanding of AI in Education." *Learning, Media and Technology* 45, no. 3: 251–69. DOI: 10.1080/17439884.2020.1686017

Rawding, M. R., and Wills, T. 2012. "Discourse: Simple Moves That Work." *Mathematics Teaching in the Middle School* 18, no. 1: 46–51. https://doi.org/10.5951/mathteacmiddscho.18.1.0046

Raza, A., Penuel, W. R., Allen, A. R., Sumner, T., and Jacobs, J. K. 2021. "'Making It Culturally Relevant': A Visual Learning Analytics System Supporting Teachers to Reflect on Classroom Equity." In Proceedings of the 15th International Conference of the Learning Sciences, 442–49. International Society of the Learning Sciences. https://repository.isls.org/bitstream/1/7501/1/442-449.pdf

Resnick, L. B., Michaels, S., and O'Connor, M. C. 2010. "How (Well Structured) Talk Builds the Mind." In *Innovations in Educational Psychology: Perspectives on Learning, Teaching, and Human Development*, edited by D. Preiss and R. J. Sternberg, 163–94. New York: Springer.

Resnick, L., Asterhan, C. S. C., and Clarke, S. N., eds. 2015. *Socializing Intelligence through Academic Talk and Dialogue*. Washington, DC: American Educational Research Association.

Resnick, L. B., Asterhan, C. S. C., and Clarke, S. N. 2018. *Accountable Talk: Instructional Dialogue That Builds the Mind.* Geneva, Switzerland: International Academy of Education (IAE) and International Bureau of Education (IBE) of the United Nations Educational, Scientific and Cultural Organization (UNESCO).

Rosé, C. P., and Tovares, A. 2015. "What Sociolinguistics and Machine Learning Have to Say to Each Other about Interaction Analysis." In *Socializing Intelligence through Academic Talk and Dialogue*, edited by L. B. Resnick, C. S. C. Asterhan, and S. N. Clarke, 289–300. Washington, DC: American Educational Research Association.

Rowell, P. M. 2004. "Developing Technological Stance: Children's Learning in Technology Education." *International Journal of Technology and Design Education* 14: 45–59. https://doi.org/10.1023/B:ITDE.0000007362.21793.88

Saxe, G. B., Gearhart, M., Note, M. and Paduano, P. 2002. "Peer Interaction and the Development of Mathematical Understandings: A New Framework for Research and Educational Practice." In *Charting the Agenda: Educational Activity after Vygotsky*, edited by H. Daniels, 107–44. London: Routledge.

Scherrer, J., and Stein, M. K. 2013. "Effects of a Coding Intervention on What Teachers Learn to Notice during Whole-Group Discussion." *Journal of Mathematics Teacher Education* 16: 105–24. https://doi.org/10.1007/s10857-012-9207-2

Scornavacco, K., Jacobs, J. and Harty, C. 2022. "Automated Feedback on Discourse Moves: Teachers' Perceived Utility of a Big Data Tool." Paper presented to the annual conference of the American Educational Research Association, San Diego, CA.

Sherin, M. G., and Dyer, E. B. 2017. "Mathematics Teachers' Self-captured Video and Opportunities for Learning." *Journal of Mathematics Teacher Education* 20, no. 5: 477–95. http://dx.doi.org/10.1007/s10857-017-9383-1

Singh, A., and Anuradha, P. 2015. "A Survey on Methods for Solving Data Imbalance Problem for Classification." *International Journal of Computer Applications* 127, no. 15: 37–41. http://dx.doi.org/10.5120/ijca2015906677

Sionti, M., Ai, H., Rosé, C. P., and Resnick, L. 2012. "A Framework for Analyzing Development of Argumentation through Classroom Discussions." In *Educational Technologies for Teaching Argumentation Skills*, edited by N. Pinkwart and B. M. McLaren, 28–55. Oak Park: Bentham Science.

Song, Y., Lei, S., Hao, T., Lan, Z., and Ding, Y. 2021. "Automatic Classification of Semantic Content of Classroom Dialogue." *Journal of Educational Computing Research* 59, no. 3: 496–521. http://dx.doi.org/10.1177/0735633120968554

Suresh, A., Jacobs, J., Clevenger, C., Lai, V., Tan, C., Ward, W., Martin, J. and Sumner, T. 2021b. "Using AI to Promote Equitable Classroom Discussions: The TalkMoves Application." In Proceedings of the 2021 International Conference on Artificial Intelligence in Education, 344–48. Utrecht, The Netherlands. https://doi.org/10.1007/978-3-030-78270-2_61

Suresh, A., Jacobs, J., Harty, C., Perkoff, M., Martin, J. and Sumner, T. 2022a. "The TalkMoves Dataset: K-12 Mathematics Lesson Transcripts Annotated for Teacher and Student Discursive Moves." Presentation at the 13th International Conference Language Resources and Evaluation Conference. https://arxiv.org/abs/2204.09652

Suresh, A., Jacobs, J., Lai, V., Tan, C., Ward, W., Martin, J. and Sumner, T. 2021a. "Using Transformers to Provide Teachers with Personalized Feedback on Their Classroom Discourse: The TalkMoves Application." Paper presented at the Association for Advancement of Artificial Intelligence Symposium on Artificial Intelligence for K-12 Education. https://arxiv.org/pdf/2105.07949.pdf

Suresh, A., Jacobs, J., Perkoff, M., Martin, J. and Sumner, T. 2022b. "Fine-Tuning Transformers with Additional Context to Classify Discursive Moves in Mathematics Classrooms." In *Proceedings of the 17th Workshop on Innovative Use of NLP for Building Educational Applications*, 71–81. Seattle, WA: Association for Computational Linguistics. https://aclanthology.org/2022.bea-1.11.pdf

Suresh, A., Sumner, T., Jacobs, J., Foland, B., and Ward, W. 2019. "Automating Analysis and Feedback to Improve Mathematics Teachers' Classroom Discourse." *Proceedings of the Association for Advancement of Artificial Intelligence Conference on Artificial Intelligence* 33, no. 1: 9721–28. https://doi.org/10.1609/aaai.v33i01.33019721

Voogt, J. M., Pieters, J. M. and Handelzalts, A. 2016. "Teacher Collaboration in Curriculum Design Teams: Effects, Mechanisms, and Conditions." *Educational Research and Evaluation* 22, no. 3–4: 121–140. https://doi.org/10.1080/13803611.2016.1247725

Vygotsky, L. 1978. "Interaction between Learning and Development." *Readings on the Development of Children* 23, no. 3: 34–41.

Walshaw, M., and Anthony, G. 2008. "The Teacher's Role in Classroom Discourse: A Review of Recent Research into Mathematics Classrooms." *Review of Educational Research* 78, no. 3: 516–51. https://doi.org/10.3102/0034654308320

Wang, Z., Miller, K., and Cortina, K. 2013. "Using the LENA in Teacher Training: Promoting Student Involvement through Automated Feedback." *Unterrichtswissenschaft* 41, no. 4: 290–302.

Wang, Z., Pan, X., Miller, K. F., and Cortina, K. S. 2014. "Automatic Classification of Activities in Classroom Discourse." *Computers & Education 78*: 115–23. https://doi.org/10.1016/j.compedu.2014.05.010

Webb, N. M., Franke, M. L., Ing, M., Chan, A., De, T., Freund, D., and Battey, D. 2008. "The Role of Teacher Instructional Practices in Student Collaboration." *Contemporary Educational Psychology* 33, no. 3: 360–81. https://doi.org/10.1016/j.cedpsych.2008.05.003

Webb, N. M., Franke, M. L., Turrou, A. C., and Ing, M. 2015. "An Exploration of Teacher Practices in Relation to Profiles of Small-Group Dialogue." In *Socializing Intelligence through Academic Talk and Dialogue*, edited by L. B. Resnick, C. S. C. Asterhan, and S. N. Clarke, 87–98. Washington, DC: American Educational Research Association.

Webb, N. M., Franke, M. L., Ing, M., Turrou, A. C., Johnson, N. C., and Zimmerman, J. 2019. "Teacher Practices That Promote Productive Dialogue and Learning in Mathematics Classrooms." *International Journal of Educational Research* 97: 176–86. https://doi.org/10.1016/j.ijer.2017.07.009

Wells, G., and Mejia-Arauz, R. 2006. "Dialogue in the Classroom." *Journal of the Learning Sciences* 15, no. 3: 379–428. https://doi.org/10.1207/s15327809jls1503_3

Wendell, K. B., Andrews, C. J., and Paugh, P. B. 2019. "Supporting Knowledge Construction in Elementary Engineering Design." *Science Education* 103, no. 4: 952–78. https://doi.org/10.1002/sce.21518

Wertsch, J. V. 1985. *Vygotsky and the Social Formation of Mind*. Cambridge, MA: Harvard University Press.

Wiley, J., Hastings, P., Blaum, D., Jaeger, A. J., Hughes, S., Wallace, P., Griffin, T. D., and Britt, M. A. 2017. "Different Approaches to Assessing the Quality of Explanations Following a Multiple-Document Inquiry Activity in Science." *International Journal of Artificial Intelligence in Education* 27, no. 4: 758–90. https://doi.org/10.1007/s40593-017-0138-z.

Wilson, J., Pollard, B., Aiken, J. M., Caballero, M. D., and Lewandowski, H. J. 2022. "Classification of Open-Ended Responses to a Research-Based Assessment Using Natural Language Processing." *Physical Review Physics Education Research* 18: 010141. https://doi.org/10.1103/PhysRevPhysEducRes.18.010141

Zuboff, S. 1988. *In the Age of the Smart Machine: The Future of Work and Power*. New York: Basic Books.

18
Use of Machine Learning to Score Teacher Observations

Lydia Bradford

Introduction

Teacher observations are key in schools and districts providing professional learning opportunities and evaluation mandates. They also are used in education research to measure the fidelity of implementation in classroom-based interventions and their mediating effects for estimating the intervention's pathways that may drive the outcome effects. In both cases, observations can be expensive due to the high human capital costs. The observers must be trained on complex protocols, including new technologies, schedule times and travel to the classrooms, score teachers' and students' behavior-based protocol directions, and provide additional field-based evidence for their scores. Each hour spent inside a classroom can correspond to over an hour outside of the classroom for scoring, which is quite burdensome. Machine learning (ML) can be an asset for reducing time to score with reliable measures obtained from human observation training sets. With this goal of reducing the human capital burden and costs with ML, the first question is whether this is possible. Current work by Zhai, Haudek et al. (2020) has tested using ML to score observation open-ended responses in a very controlled environment where many experienced teachers give open-ended responses to questions from videos of teachers and then different raters score these responses with binary scores (0 and 1) and then the machine is trained and compared to these external raters. That work gives insight into how ML can be used to score text-based scores from teacher observations. However, many studies do not have such a controlled environment nor the funds to hire multiple independent raters for training the machine. In such a situation, the following questions arise: Can available data be used researchers to train the machine for scoring teacher observations? How can the researcher accomplish this? What additional concerns and cautions should the researcher consider.

Science educators have applied ML for various purposes, as described in a recent book (see Zhai, Yin et al. 2020). One example is how ML was used in two project-based learning science curriculum evaluations. This chapter takes on yet another potential use by demonstrating how to train and use ML to score observation field notes. Using observations from two science education interventions (Multiple Literacies in Project-Based Learning [ML-PBL]; Krajcik et al. 2023) and Crafting Engaging Science Environments ([CESE]; Schneider et al. 2022), this chapter describes how to

Lydia Bradford, *Use of Machine Learning to Score Teacher Observations*. In: *Uses of Artificial Intelligence in STEM Education*. Edited by: Xiaoming Zhai and Joseph Krajcik, Oxford University Press. © Oxford University Press (2024).
DOI: 10.1093/oso/9780198882077.003.0018

score teaching observations using text analysis and illustrates a framework for other researchers to use when training machines on their own observation protocols.

The Interventions and Observation Protocols

CESE was a high school chemistry and physics curriculum intervention, and ML-PBL was a third-grade science curriculum intervention. The high school intervention was implemented in both Michigan and California, while the third-grade intervention was implemented only in Michigan. The high school study included sixty-one schools with 4238 students and 129 teachers. The third-grade study included forty-six schools with 2371 students and 91 teachers. Both interventions showed positive treatment effects on students' science achievement scores.

Once the interventions were shown to be effective, the researchers turned to investigating the mediating effects driving the treatment. In anticipation of this question, the research design included observations of the treatment teachers and control teachers using a protocol aimed at understanding the different aspects of the intervention and scoring each teacher's fidelity to the intervention. This protocol included observer field notes and questions that scored each teacher on several criteria, which proved to be quite time-consuming for the observers. This led to the question of whether these could be more efficiently scored using ML, which is explored in this chapter.

Briefly, the observation protocol for both studies focused on what both teachers and students are doing in the classroom. Questions included teachers' and students' use of various aspects of project-based learning, the teachers' integration of different portions of the NGSS standards in the lesson, observed social and emotional constructs from the teachers and students (agency, persistence, and collaboration), and the teachers' adherence to both the lesson plan and the overall principles of project-based learning. These observations were designed to give insights into both the treatment and control classrooms, which allows the researcher to understand how well the treatment teachers implement the intervention and whether any of the control teachers use similar practices. It also provided data to understand which parts of the intervention may be more influential in the treatment effect. Finally, using the different social and emotional observed behaviors, the researcher could learn how the context may moderate the treatment effect.

These types of in-classroom observations are key for many research questions that look to understand treatment effects in science education research. However, training observers and funding their travel and time for taking and analyzing field notes is often a major human capital expense. There are, however, a couple of ways to try and reduce the cost of these in-class observations with technology.

One increasingly common procedure is to have teachers or researchers record videos of the classroom and have observers watch the videos and assign scores. This saves travel time and costs for the observers but increases the initial investment in high-quality cameras or recording devices. Devices such as "swivls" have become more common in education research, with some concerns about the quality of observations and distinguishing speakers (Johnson et al. 2019; McCoy, Lynam, and Kelly 2018). Using video to evaluate teachers was further developed by Measures of Effective Teacher Longitudinal Database (MET-LDB), a project funded by the Bill and Melinda Gates Foundation in 2009, where thousands of videos were recorded by teachers in their classrooms and added to a substantial database (White et al. 2014). From these videos, the project employed many observers to score the teachers on various evaluation protocols. However, simply using videos as opposed to in-person observations may lead to a loss in truly understanding what is going on in the classroom, but the reduction in cost or the increase in efficiency can be helpful when the budget is limited. A second alternative, which this chapter proposes, is to automate the scoring from the field notes to save the observer time after having observed the classrooms, taken notes, scored the information, and uploaded it all to a comprehensive, reliable, and valid database.

Training a Machine for Teacher Observation Scores

To evaluate the increased efficiency and accuracy of using ML, there are multiple steps. First, establishing a baseline comparison is key for determining whether the machine is performing well. In some ML instances, researchers will choose a metric cut-off to determine how well the machine is performing. For example, some may choose to set an accuracy cut-off of 0.8 as being a sufficiently accurate score for the machine. However, using a preset cut-off can ignore other benefits of using a machine, even with lower accuracy scores. In the teacher observation scoring, one benefit could be in increasing the number of observations by increasing the efficiency of conducting an observation. For this study, the baseline assumes no human involvement in the scoring of the field notes. Essentially, the baseline is the case where there is neither a human rater nor ML algorithms to predict scores, and these baseline scores are the best guess in their absence. The baseline is established by random assignment of scores by probabilities. This is done computationally; however, no ML is used. However, another baseline could be to train different humans to score the observation field notes and compare these scorers to the machine (similar to the work done in Zhai, Haudek et al. 2020).[1]

Once a baseline has been chosen, the next step in training a machine is choosing which ML algorithms to compare. There are more possible algorithms than any one research group could attempt to train and compare, and researchers continue to study which new algorithms produce the most reliable predictions. When choosing which models to compare, the end prediction goal and the data structure are major factors. For example, this study chose machine models that can predict multiple categories and have performed relatively well in the past with text analysis. The choice of metrics to compare the algorithms is also determined by the predictions such as accuracy, precision, and recall, all of which are used for categorical predictions, depending on what part of the prediction is important (Hossin and Sulaiman 2015) or mean-squared error for continuous predictions (Pelvris et al. 2022).

[1] This procedure is quite costly and was unable to be conducted at this time on these two large datasets.

Additionally, a large concern in ML is the overfitting of a prediction model from the algorithm. Overfitting happens when a model is trained precisely to one dataset but is unable to generalize to new settings. Hyperparameter tuning using cross-validation aims to address this issue. For training the model, the dataset is first split into training and testing sets, where the model is trained on a training set, and then the testing set is used to see how the model performs on different data. For the sub-samples for the cross-validation, the training set needs to be made into smaller training and testing sets, which are employed repeatedly to find the best hyperparameters that reduce overfitting of the training set and increase generalizability to new data. Hyperparameters come in many different forms. Some of the hyperparameters deal with overfitting by adding constraints to the model (see the specific constraints to each model in the section "Machine Learning Methods" and how they work), others deal with additional issues of generalizability of the model, and other hyperparameters deal with the direct structure of the model, such as the number of nodes in a neural network. Ultimately, the goal of tuning these hyperparameters is to find the prediction model that performs the best on the metrics on new data (Yang and Shami 2020).

This study reports all aspects of ML training and comparisons of different algorithmic methods (i.e., the multinomial logistic regression, Bernoulli naïve Bayes, random forest, decision trees, and recurrent neural networks [RNN]) to evaluate the plausibility of its use to score teacher observations. These processes and results are reported in this chapter.

Research Questions

The research questions for this chapter are:

1. Does using machine learning improve upon the baseline metric for scoring teacher observations?
2. Which machine-learning methods perform the best on accuracy, precision, recall, F_1-scores, and time to train when scoring these teacher observations?
3. Does including the identifier of the observer or question type increase the accuracy of the scores as compared to the models that do not include observer ID or question type?

Data

To prepare the data for the ML, the teacher observations from both interventions (ML-PBL and CESE) were combined with four variables: score, text evidence for the score, observer ID, and question number on the protocol. Each question within the observation protocol was separated into its own data points. Overall, there were 4925 data points from 25 different observers on 44 different questions for machine training and testing. In these 4925 data points, each data point had a score, text, observer ID, and question number; therefore, there were no missing data points in this specified dataset.

These data were then transformed so that the following methods could be employed for prediction. For the first four methods (logistic regression, naïve Bayes, decision tree, and random forest), which do not use the sequence of the text, the text data had all punctuation removed and transformed into a matrix of tokens for words. This was done using Scikit-Learn's CountVectorizer package. For the recurrent neural network, the text data maintains its sequential nature. So, for example, if the text contained the previous sentence, instead of creating a matrix of the words, the text would remain: "For the recurrent neural network, the text data maintains its sequential nature."

Once the data were prepared, the data were split into the training set (80%) and the testing set (20%). The training set is used for the hyperparameter tuning and training of the algorithms. The testing set takes the trained algorithm and evaluates it on accuracy, precision, recall, and F_1-scores. For the first iteration of training and testing of the models, the observer identification and question number were removed from the data. After the hyperparameter tuning for each method (multinomial logistic regression, naïve Bayes, decision tree, random forest, and the RNN) and each model was compared across the "optimized models" determined by their accuracy, precision, and recall metrics (see the sections "Hyperparameter Tuning" and "Metrics"), these variables were once again included in the data. For both variables (observer ID and question number), all categorical options of the observer ID and question number were dummy-coded for the training of the models. They were dummy-coded because the observer identification is a nominal data type; therefore, it cannot be input into the ML model as if it were continuous. Once dummy-coded, these variables were added to the top two algorithms, which were then trained and tested again.

Baseline

A baseline comparison for the ML algorithms was done by randomly assigning scores based on the distribution of scores in the dataset. This distribution of scores comes from the scores given by the observer on the forty-four different questions from the observation protocol in both the elementary and high school interventions. The distribution of the scores for the dataset is reported in Figure 18.1. This figure shows that the observers gave a score of 1 7% of the time, a score of 2 20% of the time, a score of 3 34% of the time, and a score of 4 39% of the time. It is important to note the low percentage of scores given a 1 (and to some extent a 2). This could possibly lead to issues in training the algorithm, in particular, issues in hyperparameter tuning due to not enough datapoints occurring at the lower end of the distribution during the cross-validations. Although this chapter does not explore this, stratification during splitting the training and testing sets and for the hyperparameter tuning may help to alleviate some of these imbalance issues.

The baseline is randomly permuted based upon the above distribution whereby a score is randomly assigned to a data point based upon the probability distribution. Based upon the above distribution, for the baseline scores, a score of 1 was assigned with a 0.07 probability, a score of 2 with a 0.20 probability, a score of 3 with a 0.34 probability, and a score of 4 with a 0.39 probability. Then the precision, recall, F_1-scores, and accuracy were calculated as the baseline comparison of precision,

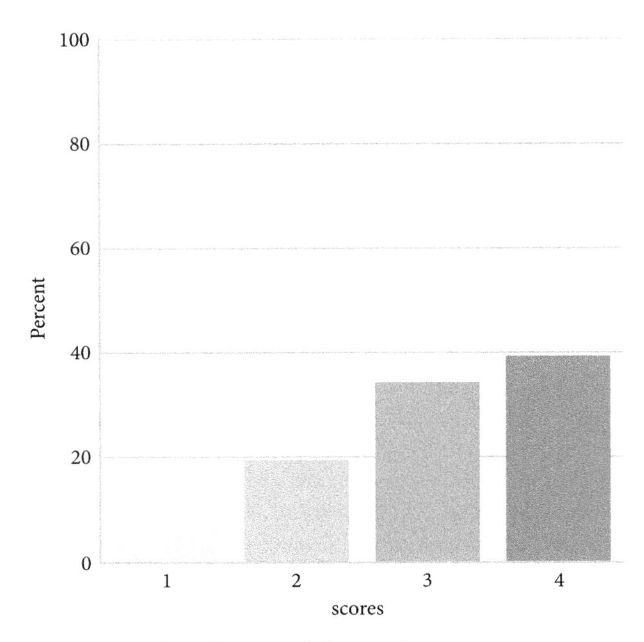

Figure 18.1 Distribution of observation scores.

recall, F_1-scores, and accuracy to which the ML methods are compared. (For further description of how these metrics are calculated, see "Metrics"). The baseline accuracy, precision, recall, and F_1-scores can be found in Table 18.4.

Machine-Learning Methods

All six chosen algorithms are classifier algorithms such that the outcome measure is not a continuous measure to be predicted but instead a "class" or category. Here in this example, the outcome is the score, which falls into four categories: either a score of 1, 2, 3, or 4. Although all are classifier algorithms, they differ in their methods of classification. There are other additional classifier algorithms (such as support vector machines and nearest-neighbor methods); however, these were chosen for this example for their clarity, ease of use, and appropriateness for text data. These algorithms were multinomial logistic regression, Bernoulli naïve Bayes, decision tree, random forest (Pedregosa et al. 2011), recurrent neural network (RNN; Abadi et al. 2015) and the Bidirectional Encoder Representations from Transformers (BERT; Devlin et al. 2018).

A multinomial logistic regression uses a one versus rest scheme so that the probability for each class is calculated using the multinomial logistic regression and compared to the other classes; for example, the probability of receiving a score of 1 versus receiving a score of 2, 3, and 4 together. This is calculated for each class, and the class with the highest probability is the predicted class. The probability of each class is calculated as follows:

$$\frac{exp\,(X_i W_k)}{\sum_{l=0}^{K-1} X_i W_l}$$

where X is in the input data, in this case the text data from the observations; W_k is the weights of the specified class; and W_l is the weights of the rest of the classes (Pedregosa et al. 2011). In the equation, W_k is the weights for a score of 1 and W_l is the weights for 2, 3, and 4. The weights are found using various computational solvers that are compared in the hyperparameter tuning. Once the probability from each class is calculated above, then the class with the highest probability is chosen for the predicted class. In the case of these data, that would be the score (1, 2, 3, 4) where the highest probability would be assigned the predicted score for that data point.

For the Bernoulli naïve Bayes, classification is done by estimating the posterior distribution of each class using Bayes rule, such that

$$P\left(c|d,\hat{\theta}\right) = \frac{P\left(c|\hat{\theta}\right)P\left(d|c,\hat{\theta}\right)}{P\left(d|\hat{\theta}\right)}$$

where c is the class, d is the text, and $\hat{\theta}$ is the parameter estimates, which are estimated using the word counts within each text (McCallum and Nigram 1998). Note that the Bernoulli naïve Bayes specifically assumes that the presence of each word in the text classifier is independent of the other words, simplifying the finding of the parameters for each word's probability in the text. Similar to the multinomial logistic regression, once the probabilities for each class are found based upon the text and parameters, the class (a score of 1, 2, 3, or 4) with the highest probability is assigned as the predicted score to the data point.

The classifications by decision tree and random forest come from similar frameworks, where a random forest is a series of decision tree classifiers done on different subsamples combined. Decision trees classify through nodes, leaves, and ultimately the proportion of the training set used to calculate probabilities. The nodes are areas where the data are split into different paths, and the leaves are the points where the data point is ultimately classified. In this study, the nodes and leaves are determined by the counts of words within the text. For example, it may be that the use of the word "Driving" more than a certain number of times could split the data between two nodes or even between a node and a leaf. Given how many word counts are in this study, visualization of the decision tree itself is not plausible.

Finally, recurrent neural networks build upon neural networks and have found wide usage in language processing. This study explored RNNs with bidirectional layers. The text data maintain their sequences so that the data are entered in with the words in order. The bidirectional layers process the text data forward and backwards simultaneously. For this study, the sequenced data are processed, and then passed through the bidirectional layers made up of long short-term memory networks and then passed through a dense layer and classified with a score of 1, 2, 3, or 4.

Hyperparameter Tuning

Before training and testing the different algorithms, hyperparameter tuning is an important step to increase accuracy while minimizing overfitting. The various hyperparameters of the different algorithms aim to regularize the parameters or algorithms in ways so that the parameter not only fits the specific dataset it is being trained on, but also uses different methods to increase accuracy depending on the type of dataset used. To find the optimal hyperparameters for the multinomial logistic regression, Bernoulli naïve Bayes, decision tree, and random forest, two methods of hyperparameter tuning through cross-validation were used sequentially. First, randomized search cross-validation was used across a larger spectrum of hyperparameter options (using Scikit-Learn's RandomizedSearchCV package), followed by a cross-validation search using every option pairing for a smaller spectrum around the optimal results found in the randomized search (using Scikit-Learn's GridSearchCV package). Each machine learning method has different hyperparameters to tune.

For the multinomial logistic regression, the hyperparameters included a penalty, the regularization strength, and the solver. Including a penalty aims to decrease overfitting of the model. There are three different penalty options for the multinomial logistic regression: ridge, lasso, and elastic net. The ridge option adjusts the weights downward, while the lasso option shrinks nonimportant weights to zero (Zhu and Hastie 2004), and the elastic net combines the two penalties (Cannarile et al. 2019). The regularization strength parameter determines the strength of the regularizer, and the solver is the different computation methods used to estimate the multinomial logistic regression (Minka 2003).

For the Bernoulli naïve Bayes Classifier, there is only one hyperparameter to tune, which is the smoothing parameter. The smoothing parameter is added to help deal with the categorical nature of the data used in the naïve Bayes classifier (Juan and Ney 2002). Essentially, within the naïve Bayes classifier, the classifier cannot handle cases that are completely new with none of the same data, more specifically, a data point that would have a zero probability. The smoothing parameter essentially adds a small amount of probability to each probability to ensure that no probability is equal to zero.

For the decision tree and random forest, the hyperparameters tuned include criterion, splitter, minimum split sample, and minimum sample per leaf (Breiman et al. 2017). There are two different criteria for the classification, and these are Gini and entropy, which use different probabilities of misclassification to determine the nodes of the tree. The Gini directly calculates the probability of misclassification of the nodes, whereas entropy takes the log of the probability. The splitter determines how the data are split at the node, whether it is the best split or the best random split. The minimum split sample indicates how many observations need to be included to split, and the minimum sample per leaf node is how many observations are needed in the final nodes. The random forest also included the option for whether the samples are bootstrapped or the entire sample is used.

A fivefold cross-validation method was used to find the best hyperparameters, using accuracy scores. The fivefold cross-validation was chosen for its ease of use and its benefits for reducing overfitting to the training set to increase generalizability, which was the goal of using machine learning here to predict scores for new sets of observations. For the fivefold cross-validation, the data are split into five groups of 20% of the data. In each fold, one of those 20% portions is used for testing, while the other 80% is used for training. Then the average accuracy scores of all five validations are compared across the hyperparameters. Hyperparameters with the highest average accuracy score across the five cross-validations were considered the best hyperparameters both in the cross-validation processes and in the tuning. For the RNN, cross validations were not used; instead, four different combinations of layers, dropout, and epochs were compared.

The hyperparameters and their options for all methods are reported in Table 18.1.

Metrics

Once each method was tuned, the methods were compared using accuracy, precision, recall, and F_1-scores. These metrics are ways to measure how the predicted values from the ML compare to the actual values given by the observer. For every text in the testing set, there will be a score from the machine and a score from the

Table 18.1 Hyperparameters and Their Options

Algorithm	Hyperparameter	Options
Multinomial logistic regression	Penalty	None, lasso, ridge, elastic-net
	Regularization strength (C)	Numbers between 0 and 4
	Solver	Newton-CG, SAG, SAGA, L-BFGS
Bernoulli naïve Bayes classifier	Smoothing parameter (alpha)	Numbers between 0 and 4
Decision tree	Criterion	Gini, entropy
	Splitter	Best, random
	Minimum split sample	Integers between 1 and 40
	Minimum sample per leaf	Integers between 1 and 20
Random forest	Bootstrap	True, false
	Maximum depth	Integers between 10 and 100
	Maximum features	Auto, square root
	Minimum leaf sample	1, 2, 4
	Minimum split sample	Integer between 1 and 10
	Number of estimators	Integers of 10 between 200 and 2000
Recurrent neural network	Number of bidirectional layers	1, 2
	Dropout	True, false
	Eepochs	10, 20

Table 18.2 Definitions of Metrics

Accuracy	$\frac{\textit{Total Predicted Correct (for all scores: } 1, 2, 3, 4)}{\textit{Total Predicted}}$
Precision	$\frac{\textit{Correctly predicted the score(for specific score: } 1, 2, 3, \textit{ or } 4)}{\textit{Total number of that specific scores(corresponding to the numberator)}}$
Recall	$\frac{\textit{Correctly predicted score(for specific score: } 1, 2, 3, \textit{ or } 4)}{\textit{Total number of the true score (corresponding to the numerator)}}$
F_1-Score	$2 \times \frac{precision \times recall}{precision + recall}$

Note: Accuracy uses the entire prediction and true scores, whereas precision and recall are calculated separately for each score.

original observer. The prediction is considered correct when the machine-predicted score equals the human observer score. Accuracy is the percent of all the scores that the machine correctly predicted. For example, if the machine correctly predicts 45 of the texts out of 100, the accuracy score would be 0.45. Accuracy gives a good overall view of how the machine compares to the observer; however, it fails to give more in-depth insights into how the machine performs in each category, which precision, recall, and F_1-scores do.

Precision takes all the times the machine gives a specific score (one, two, three, four) and gives the percentage of the time it is correct. For example, if the machine gives out 100 scores of three and of these 100 given threes, 60 are correct, then the precision score would be 0.6. On the other hand, recall takes all the times the observer gives a specific score (one, two, three, four) and gives the percentage of the observer scores that the machine correctly predicted. For example, if the observer scored a one 50 times, and the machine correctly scored those ones 25 times, then the recall would be 0.5. F_1-scores combine both recall and precision into one score. Table 18.2 shows how each of these metrics were calculated.

The top four methods were then compared by their efficiency, which is defined by their time to train, such that the method with the shortest time to train was determined to be the most efficient method. Time to train was calculated by subtracting the time after the parameters were estimated using the training set to the time right before the algorithm began training. After determining the method with the highest accuracy, precision, recall, F_1-scores scores, and efficiency, these methods were retrained using the addition variables of observer ID and then question number. These new predictions were compared to the original scores to understand the gain in predictions by including this additional non-text data.

Results

All methods—the multinomial logistic regression, Bernoulli naïve Bayes classifier, decision tree, random forest, and RNN—were able to have their hyperparameters fine-tuned and were then trained using the training set. The optimal hyperparameters were found, and the methods were compared on their accuracy, precision, recall, F_1-scores, and time to train using the testing set.

Optimal Hyperparameters

The optimal parameters for the ML methods were determined using fivefold cross-validation along with a random search across hyperparameters and then a grid search where their accuracy scores were compared for every combination of hyperparameters to find the most accurate hyperparameter. The most accurate ones were chosen as being the optimal and are reported in Table 18.3.

For the multinomial logistic regression, the optimal parameters were ridge for the penalty, a regularization strength of 0.303, and the L-BFGS solver. As ridge was chosen over lasso and elastic-net, this indicates that maintaining all features (all coefficients on the text counts) is important for the prediction of the scores. However, having ridge over no penalty and a regularization strength of 0.3030 (which indicates a strong regularizer) indicates that regularization is quite necessary for limiting overfitting. Finally, the optimal solver for this multinomial logistic regression is the LBFGS over the Newton-cg, sag, and saga computation methods for estimation, which may be due to the small size of the dataset.

For the Bernoulli naïve Bayes, the optimal smoothing parameter was found to be 0.433, which is smaller than one of the standard smoothing parameters, indicating that when the data are generalizing to new data, there is no need for a large adjustment to the probabilities.

For the decision tree, the optimal criterion was found to be entropy with a random splitter, a minimum split sample of 33, and a minimum sample per leaf of 1. The minimum sample splits indicate that there had to be at least 33 observations to split the tree, but there only had to be one observation to create a leaf or an end of the tree. The minimum split sample was on the higher end of the distribution, indicating that more data points were necessary for the split to avoid overfitting; however, the

Table 18.3 Optimal Hyperparameters

Multinomial logistic regression	**Naïve Bayes**	**Decision tree**	**Random forest**	**RNN**
Penalty: ridge	Smoothing parameter: 0.433	Criterion: entropy	Bootstrap: false	Number of bidirectional layers: 1
Regularization strength: 0.303		Splitter: random	Maximum depth: 65	Dropout: false
Solver: L-BFGS		Minimum split sample: 33	Maximum features: auto	Epochs: 20
		Minimum sample per leaf: 1	Minimum leaf sample: 1	
			Minimum split sample: 2	
			Number of estimators: 1800	

minimum sample per leaf allows the tree to create a final prediction based upon one observation, which may be due to the nature of specific words indicating a specific prediction. The random splitter over the best splitter was found to be optimal, which adjusts more for overfitting at the split. Entropy was chosen over Gini, which deals with the log loss as opposed to the pure prediction probabilities. Entropy improving over Gini makes theoretical sense given the distribution of scores with a lower number of scores in the lower ends of the distribution, where the Gini may exacerbate these issues of imbalance.

For the random forest, the optimal hyperparameters were not bootstrapping, with a maximum depth of 65, a minimum leaf sample of 1, a minimum split sample of 2, and 1800 estimators. Because the optimal choice included no bootstrapping, the entire dataset was used for finding each tree, and in this case, the number of trees is 1800. The max depth of each tree is 65, indicating that the trees can only split up to 65 times. This helps address issues of overfitting. Similar to the decision tree, the minimum leaf sample was 1, but for these trees, the minimum split sample was only two so that the tree could split with only two observations in the sample, creating. many more splits than would have been found in the decision tree.

Across all four of these hyperparameter choices, those chosen indicate that much adjustment was needed to limit the overfitting of the algorithms to the training set. For the RNN, the optimal hyperparameter indicated that one bidirectional layer was better than two, and twenty epochs improved upon ten. Finally, setting the dropout to false was found to increase accuracy over setting it to true. These optimal hyperparameters were used, and then each method was trained and timed for how long the training took. Once the models were trained, the testing data were passed through the model, and the predicted values were compared to the actual values of the testing data.

Model Comparison

Using the predicted values from the testing data compared to the actual values of the testing data, the multinomial logistic regression, Bernoulli naïve Bayes, decision tree, random forest, and RNN were compared to each other and to the baseline. The comparison of the models across precision, recall, F_1-scores, and accuracy is reported in Table 18.4.

None of the fine-tuned algorithms reached very high testing accuracy; however, they all increased accuracy by more than 100% compared to the baseline method. All accuracies fell between 0.49 and 0.57. The average precisions fell between 0.44 and 0.59, with the decision tree having the lowest precision and the random forest having the highest precision. The precision scores increased by more than 200% compared to the baseline method. The average recall scores fell between 0.44 and 0.53, with the decision tree having the lowest recall and the multinomial logistic regression having the highest recall. The average F_1-scores fell between 0.44 and 0.53, with the decision tree having the lowest F_1-score and the multinomial logistic regression and RNN

Table 18.4 Comparison of the Different Machine-Learning Methods

	Baseline	**Multinomial logistic regression**	**Bernoulli naïve Bayes**	**Decision tree**	**Random forest**	**Recurrent neural network**
Accuracy	0.32	0.57	0.56	0.49	0.56	0.57
Precision 1	0.02	0.58	0.39	0.37	0.66	0.56
2	0.18	0.50	0.51	0.33	0.53	0.47
3	0.34	0.51	0.50	0.47	0.51	0.52
4	0.43	0.65	0.69	0.59	0.64	0.66
Mean	0.24	0.56	0.52	0.44	0.59	0.55
Recall 1	0.01	0.39	0.41	0.39	0.32	0.43
2	0.19	0.41	0.43	0.25	0.20	0.34
3	0.36	0.52	0.57	0.49	0.61	0.58
4	0.40	0.73	0.65	0.62	0.79	0.71
Mean	0.24	0.53	0.52	0.44	0.48	0.52
F_1-score 1	0.01	0.47	0.40	0.38	0.43	0.49
2	0.18	0.45	0.47	0.29	0.29	0.40
3	0.35	0.51	0.53	0.48	0.56	0.55
4	0.42	0.69	0.66	0.60	0.70	0.68
Mean	0.24	0.53	0.52	0.44	0.50	0.53

having the highest F_1-scores. These also increase by more than 200% compared to the baseline method. The precision, recall, and F_1-scores vary greatly by score, with scores of 4 generally having the highest precision, recall, and F_1-scores and scores of 1 generally having the lowest precision, recall, and F_1-scores. This is true of the baseline method as well, which is intuitive since there are not as much data on the lower scores as not many teachers received these scores from the observers (see Figure 18.1).

All these methods have comparable accuracy and precision, recall, and F_1-scores and improve upon the baseline, so they were also compared on their efficiency or time to train. As the decision tree performed poorly compared to the other methods, it was not included in the final comparison on efficiency. The decision tree most likely performed worse compared to the other methods due to issues of overfitting that are common to decision trees (Kotsiantis 2013). The graph for their time to train is reported in Figure 18.2.

The RNN took the longest to train, with training time being 2391 seconds, while the Bernoulli naïve Bayes was the most efficient, taking only 0.006 seconds to train. The multinomial logistic regression took 1.34 seconds, and the random forest took 66.42 seconds. The Bernoulli naïve Bayes and multinomial logistic regression were by far the most efficient and thus the recommended methods for this observation scoring system, with tradeoffs between them. The multinomial logistic regression had slightly higher scores across precision, recall, and F_1-scores, and the Bernoulli naïve Bayes training was much faster than the multinomial logistic regression.

Additional Variables

Using the additional variables of observer ID, question number, and then both combined, the multinomial logistic regression and Bernoulli naïve Bayes were trained (using the 80% training set) and tested (using the 20% testing set) and had their accuracy scores calculated. The multinomial logistic regression and naïve Bayes were chosen because they were the most efficient (see Figure 18.2). These accuracy scores for including the observer, the question, and both are reported in Table 18.5.

Adding observer identification, question number, and both increased the accuracy slightly for the multinomial logistic regression but not for the Bernoulli naïve Bayes, so if using the multinomial logistic regression for scoring the observations, including these variables may be useful, but if using the Bernoulli naïve Bayes, using the text analysis only is sufficient.

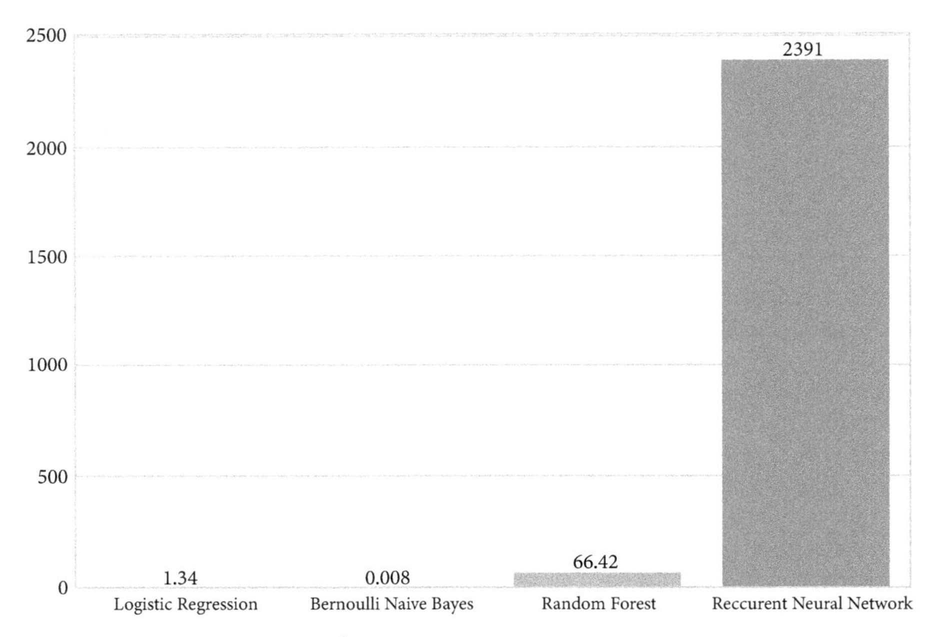

Figure 18.2 Time to train graph.

Table 18.5 Accuracy with Observer Identification and Question Number

Algorithm	Accuracy with observer	Accuracy with question	Accuracy with both
Multinomial logistic regression	0.58	0.60	0.61
Bernoulli naïve Bayes	0.57	0.56	0.58

Final Comparison: Multinomial Logistic Regression vs Baseline

The results so far have shown that the machine outperforms the baseline greatly on all metrics, but the machine is still not scoring very high compared to the human raters. This does not, however, give insight into the misclassification of the machine. Is the machine giving scores of 2 when the human rater scored it a 4, or is it giving 3's when the human rater is scoring a 4? This is an important question as it gives insights as to how well the machine is performing overall and how feasible it would be to use the machine over human raters. One way to evaluate this is to look at the confusion matrix of the predicted scores from the machine versus the actual scores. In the confusion matrix, the actual score is on the vertical axis, and the predicted scores are on the horizontal axis. Figures 18.3a and 18.3b, respectively, give the confusion matrix for the baseline predictions and the predictions from the trained multinomial logistic regression using both the question and observer identification. Note that the shades of green indicate greater numbers, so the darker the green, the more observations in that specific combination.

In both the baseline and the multinomial logistic regression, the highest number of observations is when a 4 is correctly predicted. In the baseline example, there is no pattern to when the baseline predicts incorrectly. The number of observations in a cell simply increases as the score increases since the probabilities of each score increase from 1 to 4. On the other hand, for the multinomial logistic regression, the machine confuses only those scores that are right above or right below the correct score. For example, if the human rater gave a score of 3, the machine may incorrectly score it either 2 or 4 but would not give it a score of 1. Similarly, if the human rater gave a score of 4, the machine may incorrectly score it a 3, but would not give it a score of 2 or 1.

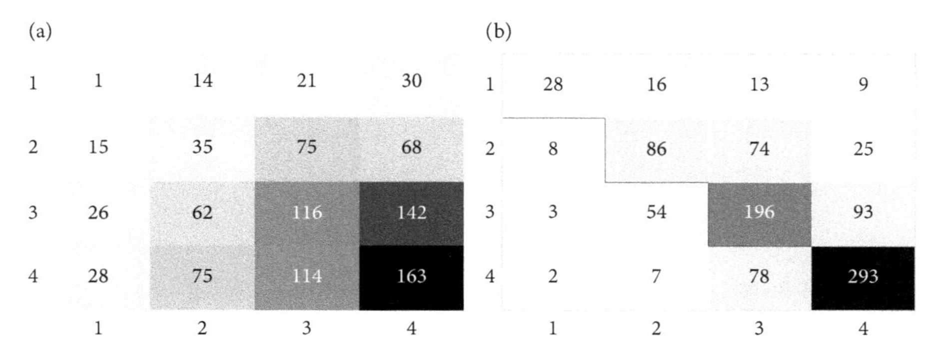

Figure 18.3 (a) Baseline confusion matrix vs (b) multinomial logistic regression confusion matrix.

Discussion

The accuracy scores discussed in "Results" lead to additional questions of how to improve the accuracy. One way to do so may be to stratify the data before splitting the data into the training and testing sets, as well as to use stratified cross-validation when tuning the hyperparameters (Zeng and Martinez 2000). Additional different types of algorithms may also be explored to try and increase accuracy, as well as more fine-tuning of the RNN. Finally, combining large language models with the classification may help to increase the accuracy of these methods (Kant et al. 2018). Exploring the confusion matrix also gives more insight into how the machine may be misclassifying the text, which may help to address areas that can be improved.

The confusion matrix presented earlier has three important implications. First, it is possible that the machine is misclassifying texts that are just around the cut-offs between 2's and 3's and between 3's and 4's. For example, the machine may be giving scores of 2's to teachers who barely received a score of 3 as opposed to a 2. However, the only way to evaluate this would be to try and ask the observers their original intention regarding the scoring. Second, this could also be considered a part of measurement error. Ultimately, many of the observation questions are trying to understand underlying constructs and trying to measure these constructs, which often leads to some sort of measurement error that may have occurred at the human rater level but can also be considered as occurring at the machine level as well. This leads to the final implication.

Given the assumption of measurement error that often underlies many important estimation techniques, using the scores of the machine may still lead to consistent estimation. This should be investigated further when considering using machine learning to score constructs that would have originally been scored by humans. In addition to investigating the confusion matrix, it may also be useful to evaluate the machine using inter-rater reliabilities (for this case, Kendall's W; Field 2005) between the machine and the observer, which gives a metric that considers the distance of the scores.

Overall, when trying to save time and resources, using a ML model to score teacher observations is a feasible and cost-efficient option, given that training data have already been collected. Note, that when developing an instrument, field testing an instrument is key to ensuring that it is reliable and valid; therefore, during these processes, the field test data would be an appropriate set of data upon which to train a ML model.

Conclusion

As machine learning becomes more of an option for the use of scoring, this chapter is designed to provide a general understanding of the kinds of methods that one can use with a finite dataset previously scored by humans. These methods have been chosen as they are appropriate for this type of data, popular, and easy to use. The current outcomes are not perfect but instead give the reader a sense of what kinds of data they are likely to receive, how to preprocess the data, and which methods may offer the best prediction given the dataset one has. So much of this is fluid and in the learning process; however, trying these different methods for one's own research interest is possible for researchers. See the hyperlink to git for the example code.[2] Note that the example code walks through how the ML process discussed here was completed;

[2] https://github.com/lydia-joy-bradford/ml4Tobservations

however, it does not include the "real" data from the confidential dataset. Additional analysis may also consider model comparison of inference models with ML scores versus human scores.

This example centers on using machine learning to score teacher observation protocols using text. This is an important aspect in many areas of science education research where scoring teacher observations is key for understanding the teacher mechanisms of an intervention or study. There may be other types of text data that may be scored in similar ways where these methods may give insight to researchers, such as open-ended survey responses from teachers.

Finally, some caution must be taken regarding the use of these ML methods, particularly when the accuracy, precision, recall, and F_1-scores are not at super high levels. These scores should not be used for high-stake considerations, nor for strong inferential studies, as the bias/inefficiency has not yet been explored as to how these scores may affect the model estimation and inference. However, in research with limited funds and time, these scores can give useful insights into general trends and statistics.

References

Abadi, M., Agarwal, A., Barham, P., Brevdo, E., Chen, Z., Citro, C., Corrado, G. S., et al. 2015. TensorFlow: Large-scale Machine Learning on Heterogeneous Systems. Software available from tensorflow.org.

Breiman, L., Friedman, J. H., Olshen, R. A., and Stone, C. J. 2017. *Classification and Regression Trees.* London: Routledge.

Cannarile, F., Compare, M., Baraldi, P., Diodati, G., Quaranta, V., and Zio, E. 2019. "Elastic Net Multinomial Logistic Regression for Fault Diagnostics of Onboard Aeronautical Systems." *Aerospace Science and Technology* 94: 105392.

Devlin, J., Chang, M.-W., Lee, K., and Toutanova, K. 2018. "Bert: Pre-training of Deep Bidirectional Transformers for Language Understanding." *arXiv preprint arXiv:1810.04805.*

Field, A. P. 2005. "Kendall's Coefficient of Concordance." *Encyclopedia of Statistics in Behavioral Science 2*: 1010–11.

Hossin, M., and Sulaiman, M. N. 2015. "A Review on Evaluation Metrics for Data Classification Evaluations." *International Journal of Data Mining and Knowledge Management Process* 5, no. 2: 1.

Johnson, E. S., Zheng, Y., Crawford, A. R., and Moylan, L. A. 2019. "Developing an Explicit Instruction Special Education Teacher Observation Rubric." *Journal of Special Education* 53, no. 1: 28–40.

Juan, A., and Ney, H. 2002. "Reversing and Smoothing the Multinomial Naive Bayes Text Classifier." In *Proceedings of the 2nd International Workshop on Pattern Recognition in Information Systems (PRIS 2002)*, Alacant (Spain), 200–12.

Kant, N., Puri, R., Yakovenko, N., and Catanzaro, B. 2018. "Practical Text Classification with Large Pre-trained Language Models." *arXiv preprint arXiv:1812.01207.*

Kotsiantis, S. B. 2013. "Decision Trees: A Recent Overview." *Artificial Intelligence Review* 39: 261–83.

Krajcik, J., Schneider, B., Millyer, E., Chen, I.-C., Bradford, L., Bartz, K., Baker, Q., et al. 2023. "Assessing the Effect of Project-Based Learning on Science Learning in Elementary Schools." *American Educational Research Journal* 60, no. 1: 70–102.

McCallum, A., and Nigam, K. 1998. "A Comparison of Event Models for Naive Bayes Text Classification." In *AAAI-98 Workshop on Learning for Text Categorization*, volume 752, 41–48. Madison, WI.

McCoy, S., Lynam, A., and Kelly, M. 2018. "A Case for Using Swivl for Digital Observation in an Online or Blended Learning Environment." *International Journal on Innovations in Online Education* 2, no. 2: .1–10.
Minka, T. P. 2003. "A Comparison of Numerical Optimizers for Logistic Regression." CMU Technical Report.
Pedregosa, F., Varoquaux, G., Gramfort, A., Michel, V., Thirion, B., Grisel, O., Blondel, M., et al. 2011. "Scikit-learn: Machine Learning in Python." *Journal of Machine Learning Research* 12: 2825–30.
Plevris, V., Solorzano, G., Bakas, N. P., and Ben Seghier, M. E. A. 2022, November. "Investigation of Performance Metrics in Regression Analysis and Machine Learning-Based Prediction Models." In *8th European Congress on Computational Methods in Applied Sciences and Engineering (ECCOMAS Congress 2022)*. European Community on Computational Methods in Applied Sciences.
Schneider, B., Krajcik, J., Lavonen, J., Salmela-Aro, K., Klager, C., Bradford, L., Chen, I.-C., et al. 2022. "Improving Science Achievement—Is It Possible? Evaluating the Efficacy of a High School Chemistry and Physics Project-Based Learning Intervention." *Educational Researcher* 51, no. 2: 109–21.
White, M., Rowan, B., Alter, G., and Greene, C. 2014. *User Guide to the Measures of Effective Teaching Longitudinal Database (MET LDB)*. Ann Arbor, MI: Inter-University Consortium for Political and Social Research, The University of Michigan.
Yang, L., and Shami, A. 2020. "On Hyperparameter Optimization of Machine Learning Algorithms: Theory and Practice." *Neurocomputing* 415: 295–316.
Zeng, X., and Martinez, T. R. 2000. "Distribution-Balanced Stratified Cross-Validation for Accuracy Estimation." *Journal of Experimental and Theoretical Artificial Intelligence* 12, no. 1: 1–12.
Zhai, X., Haudek, K. C., Stuhlsatz, M. A., and Wilson, C. 2020. "Evaluation of Construct-Irrelevant Variance Yielded by Machine and Human Scoring of a Science Teacher PCK Constructed Response Assessment." *Studies in Educational Evaluation* 67: 100916.
Zhai, X., Yin, Y., Pellegrino, J. W., Haudek, K. C., and Shi, L. 2020. "Applying Machine Learning in Science Assessment: A Systematic Review." *Studies in Science Education* 56, no. 1: 111–51.
Zhu, J. and Hastie, T. 2004. "Classification of Gene Microarrays by Penalized Logistic Regression." *Biostatistics* 5, no. 3: 427–43.

19

Widening the Focus of Science Assessment via Structural Topic Modeling

An Example of Nature of Science Assessment

David Buschhüter, Marisa Pfläging and Andreas Borowski

Introduction

Traditional assessment faces criticism assigned to the areas of focus, method, use/validity, and consequences (Lucas 2021). Meanwhile, machine learning (ML) has already increased authenticity, complexity, and automaticity in assessment (Zhai 2021; Zhai, Haudek, et al. 2020; Zhai, Yin, et al. 2020). However, it is less clear how ML techniques can support avoiding unintended consequences like negative impact on student motivation in the case of low test scores. In this example, we used unsupervised ML to uncover hypothetical learning gains inductively. We want to show that these techniques can help widen the assessment focus contributing to more strength-based assessments. By identifying learning gains, we do not intend to identify the learning process as a fine-grained learning trajectory. Instead, we search for evidence for learning using pre-post data. In particular, we investigate to what extent so-called structural topic models (STMs) can extract systematic differences in text responses before and after a teacher development program on supervision of students in scientific work and writing (Pfläging, Richter, and Borowski 2020). STMs can theoretically perform this task by including metadata, here the time point (pre or post). However, it needs to be analyzed to what extent human coders can reproduce the relationships between covariates and topic proportions. Such analysis is rarely conducted. We show that we can reproduce such effects by human coding even if the sample size is relatively small (N = 84 documents), which renders this method valuable for typically available datasets.

From a higher perspective, we demonstrate the feasibility of STMs as an epistemic tool for identifying relationships in science education in general inductively (e.g., by linking teacher texts on authentic performance assessments, such as explaining, planning, or reflecting [Kulgemeyer and Riese 2018; Miller 1990] to standardized test scores on dispositions, such as content, knowledge, or attitudes). Having more researchers use these models could help us notice research insights in our data that we would otherwise miss.

David Buschhüter, Marisa Pfläging, and Andreas Borowski, *Widening the Focus of Science Assessment via Structural Topic Modeling.* In: *Uses of Artificial Intelligence in STEM Education.* Edited by: Xiaoming Zhai and Joseph Krajcik, Oxford University Press. © Oxford University Press (2024). DOI: 10.1093/oso/9780198882077.003.0019

The Role of Unsupervised Methods of Machine Learning for STEM Assessment

Machine-Learning Techniques and Artificial Intelligence in STEM Assessment

Traditional assessments are often criticized for having significant limitations. Two prominent ones are a narrow focus (e.g., recall of knowledge instead of complex competencies) and limited methods of data collection (e.g., traditional multiple-choice tests instead of real-life performance situations) (Lucas 2021). AI and ML have the potential to revolutionize science, technology, enginnering, and mathematics (STEM) assessment by addressing these issues. Zhai, Haudek et al. (2020) analyzed how ML methods have impacted science assessment on dimensions of functionality, construct, and automaticity. In line with other analyses and reviews, their results include that ML allows assessment practices to target complex constructs, which addresses the issue of narrow focus (Zhai 2021; Zhai, Haudek et al. 2020; Zhai, Yin et al. 2020). ML has successfully been used to measure scientific argumentation and provide automatic feedback (Lee et al. 2021). Maestrales et al. (2021) were also able to score performance in scientific investigation using a large sample set of responses based on the framework for K–12 education (National Research Council 2012). Other complex constructs include explanation (Jescovitch et al. 2021) or teacher reflection (Wulff et al. 2021). The results of Zhai, Haudek et al. (2020) show that many ML studies also tend to provide authentic tasks (e.g., teacher reflection performance assessed through essays rather than multiple-choice tests). This addresses the issue of limited or "blunt" methods (Lucas 2021, 13). The combination of ML with technologies such as virtual or augmented reality (Sung et al. 2021) further contributes to the transformation toward more authentic assessment situations.

However, it is less clear how ML techniques can help address issues such as unintended consequences or ineffectiveness of test scores. Lucas (2021) highlights problems such as low student scores, causing students to feel like they have failed and have "not lived up to the expectations of their teachers, and indeed of society as a whole" (ASCL 2019, 28). Lucas (2021, 16) also explains that employers often use alternative approaches to focus on strengths, creating a more "balanced scorecard" than exam grades.

We believe unsupervised ML methods can be valuable in this regard. A consistent finding in literature reviews is that unsupervised ML is not very prevalent, while supervised ML is often employed because of its higher performance (Zhai, Haudek et al. 2020; Zhai, Yin et al. 2020). A meta-analysis of human–machine agreement shows that research employing supervised ML (κ = 0.70, 95% CI = 0.56, 0.83) achieved higher Cohen's κ values than unsupervised ML (κ = 0.50, 95% CI = 0.25, 0.75) (Zhai, Shi, and Nehm 2021). However, while supervised ML can provide accurate scoring, it is very labor intensive, because it needs human experts to annotate data manually (Zhai, Yin et al. 2020). In an assessment setting, this process also requires determining which performance is valuable and should be scored. This leads to unexpected findings going unnoticed. Unsupervised learning, on the other hand, does not have this issue. We argue that unsupervised ML offers a more student-centered approach to assessment. For example, Zehner, Sälzer, and

Goldhammer (2016) successfully employed clustering methods to group PISA item responses. Muldner et al. (2011) employed data-mining techniques to identify factors of gaming behavior with the Andes Intelligent Tutoring System (ITS), and Gao et al. (2022) showed that unsupervised ML can be used to identify problem-solving styles.

Two studies in science education leverage the power of unsupervised ML by finding relevant categories in student responses, which humans can confirm. Sherin (2013) used latent semantic analysis (LSA) to extract categories from student text, leading to a more nuanced category system for student conceptions. Rosenberg and Krist (2021) used unsupervised and supervised learning to revise a category system for student ideas, allowing for a more nuanced evaluation. In the following, we will present how structural topic models could be used to identify evidence for learning gains inductively (Fesler et al. 2019; Roberts, Stewart, and Airoldi 2016).

Structural Topic Models

For a preliminary understanding of structural topic models, it is helpful to understand a typical topic modeling approach such as latent Dirichlet allocation (LDA). In a nutshell, LDA (Blei, Ng, and Jordan 2003) is a method that helps extract topics given a corpus (collection) of texts and number *k*, specifying the number of topics that the algorithm should find in the collection. Here a topic is a probability distribution over the vocabulary of the corpus, and a document consists of a mix of words. The output provides the researcher with a distribution of words per topic being most representative and the distribution of topic proportions for every document.

STMs (Roberts, Stewart, and Tingley 2019) add to this by providing additional features such as correlated topics or—essential for identifying changes over time—the possibility of specifying covariates. The latter would enable us to extract not only categories but those categories with a statistical relationship with a variable of interest, given that such document properties are available to the researcher. For theory formation, this would help us to find not only categories (or variables) but also (e.g., causal) relations between such categories or variables. Functionally, it is reminiscent of methods such as structural equation modeling or path analysis (Green 2016; Karakaya-Ozyer and Aksu-Dunya 2018; Neuhaus and Borowski 2018). However, structural topic modeling can help us find categories simultaneously (Fesler et al. 2019; Roberts, Stewart, and Airoldi 2016).

From the perspective of educational assessment, STMs could identify changes in wording which could serve as evidence for learning, capturing learning gains in an exploratory manner. Figure 19.1 illustrates this aspect of structural topic modeling (similar to Blei 2012) in a science education example. We refer to the original paper for an in-depth presentation of STMs (Roberts, Stewart, and Tingley 2019).

If we can find a substantial statistical association between *time point* and prevalence, we can consider the topic as a candidate indicating a learning gain. However, it is important to reproduce the regression effect via human-coded topic proportion, as a general challenge in topic modeling is that topic models are often not well interpretable (Doogan and Buntine 2021). In the article “Reading Tea Leaves”

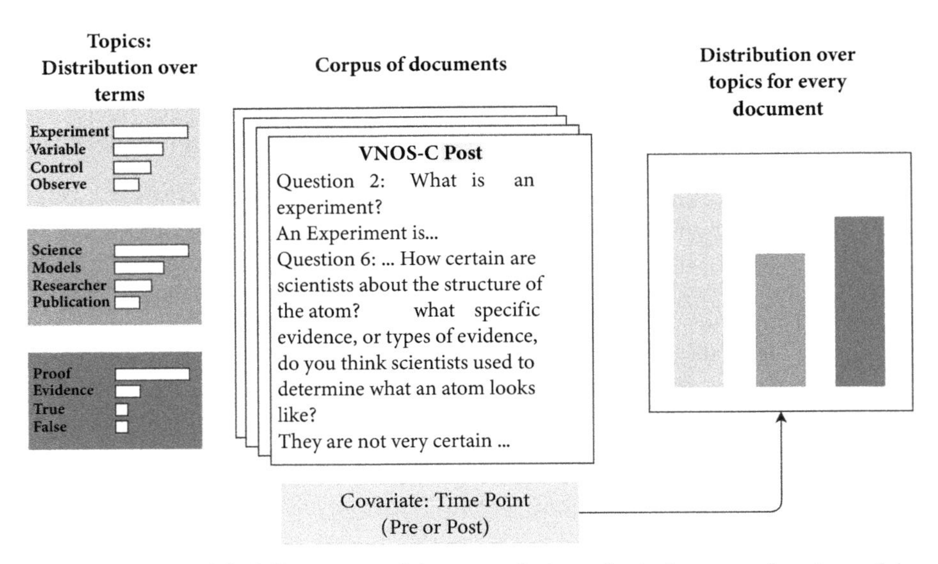

Figure 19.1 Simplified illustration of elements of a hypothetical structural topic model. If the purple topic proportion (purple bar) could be related to the covariate (here time point), this signifies that participants could write more on this topic in the post-test.

Chang et al. (2009, 288) write, "Practitioners typically assume that the latent space is semantically meaningful. . . . However, whether the latent space is interpretable is in need of quantitative evaluation."

Previous Use Cases of Structural Topic Models

STMs have been used successfully outside of STEM education. They are very prevalent in the political sciences (Roberts et al. 2014). Here we find research on the analysis of literature (Grajzl and Murrell 2019) or—more related to education—on how different topics in educational politics vary between international organizations (Windzio and Heiberger 2022). Roberts et al. (2014) also report that it should be possible to reach a substantial intercoder agreement between humans and machines.

STMs have also been proposed in the field of education for the extraction of topics that are related to other variables (Fesler et al. 2019). However, here, use cases are rarer. One typical example of the application in education is the analysis of trends in research or publications over time. Seitzer, Martens, and Martens (2021) analyze PISA publications' topics over time. Similar studies exist to analyze science education research trends (Mi, Lu, and Bi 2020). In such studies, the publication date are used as metadata.

Another use case is the application of massive open online courses (MOOCs). Reich et al. (2015) use STMs by identifying topics of more positive or negative feedback using the students' level of satisfaction as a covariate. They also identified more or less popular topics in a forum based on the covariate of being voted "up" or "down."

In STEM education research, we rarely find examples that use this method for assessment or evaluation. One exception is a comparison of traditional labs versus labs, which include inquiry-related tasks (Jeon et al. 2021). This research shows that STMs can help to systematically identify topics associated with inquiry-based writing. The authors provide summaries on a higher level and include an example set of documents representative of the topic (Jeon et al. 2021). Here STMs are used as an additional method. Therefore, it is sufficient that the authors only traced back the effect to some individual documents. Even if there is evidence that topic proportions are known to correlate with human-coded topic proportions (Roberts et al. 2014), it is worth noting the lack of studies trying to hand-code the texts based on their interpretation of the STM systematically to confirm their hypothesis, so that the anticipated effect occurs in the whole corpus. Furthermore, in order to draw inferences regarding assessment and research, we believe that it is often necessary to perform a secondary coding of the process to confirm that the first coder was not "reading tea leaves" (Chang et al. 2009, 288).

The Perspective of This Study

Context of This Use Case

This study aims to apply STMs to a science education example to investigate the usability of this method for widening the focus of an assessment. To reach this goal, we chose a longitudinal study so that we could employ *time point* as a covariate to identify evidence for potential learning gains. The content area of this study is nature of science (NOS) (Heering 2014; Lederman et al. 2002), embedded in the broader field of professional knowledge research and pedagogical content knowledge (PCK) (Hume, Cooper, and Borowski 2019; Shulman 1986).

We used a set of $N = 84$ booklets ("Views of Nature of Science Questionnaire C"; Lederman et al. 2002) in the analysis to estimate the final topic models. In this way, we hoped to illustrate that it is possible to use STMs successfully on typical-sized qualitative data, lowering the bar for other researchers to apply this method.

To enable a discussion of the findings, we will briefly summarize the literature on NOS and how it links to neighboring constructs and the nature of whole science. This shows that the measurement of NOS is a good candidate for widening the focus of our assessment.

Theoretical Background for This Use Case

There are several different approaches to conceptualizing the NOS (Arndt et al. 2020). The most prominent is the so-called minimum consensus approach (Lederman et al. 2002; Lederman 2006, 2007; McComas and Olson 1998; Osborne et al. 2003). The approach of Lederman (2006) conceptualizes NOS along with a consensus of the following seven aspects that are learnable and understandable by K–12 students as well as relevant for citizens in general (Lederman 2006, 304).

1. "Scientific knowledge is tentative (subject to change)."
2. "[Scientific knowledge] is empirically based (based on and/or derived at least partially from observations of the natural world)."
3. "[Scientific knowledge is] subjective (theory-laden, involves individual or group interpretation)."
4. "[Scientific knowledge] necessarily involves human inference, imagination, and creativity (involves the invention of explanations)."
5. "[Scientific knowledge] is socially and culturally embedded (influenced by the society/culture in which science is practiced)."
6. "Observations and inferences" should be distinct.
7. "Scientific theories and laws" have different functions and there are relationships between them.

These aspects of NOS are the theoretical basis for many studies (Neumann and Kremer 2013).

An established open-ended questionnaire to measure views about aspects of the NOS is the "Views of Nature of Science (VNOS) Questionnaire" (Lederman et al. 2002). Various versions of the VNOS Questionnaire exist, which have been used and further developed since the beginning of the 1990s in different studies to measure the views of K–12 students, college students, and pre- and in-service elementary and secondary science teachers. The VNOS-C enables researchers to study all seven aspects of the NOS as detailed by Lederman et al. (2002), and comprises ten open-ended questions (Lederman et al. 2002, 509), e.g.,

- "What, in your view, is science? What makes science (or a scientific discipline such as physics, biology, etc.) different from other disciplines of inquiry (e.g., religion, philosophy)?" (Question 1)
- "What is an experiment?" (Question 2)
- "Is there a difference between a scientific theory and a scientific law? Illustrate your answer with an example." (Question 5)
- "Science textbooks often represent the atom as a central nucleus composed of protons (positively charged particles) and neutrons (neutral particles) with electrons (negatively charged particles) orbiting that nucleus. How certain are scientists about the structure of the atom? What specific evidence **do you think** scientists used to determine what an atom looks like?" (Question 6)
- "Science textbooks often define a species as a group of organisms that share similar characteristics and can interbreed with one another to produce fertile offspring. How certain are scientists about their characterization of what a species is? What specific evidence **do you think** scientists used to determine what a species is?" (Question 7)

Whereas in some conceptualizations of NOS, aspects of the process of scientific inquiry are integrated (e.g., McComas and Olson 1998; Osborne et al. 2003) Lederman (2006; 2007) differentiates between the nature of the product of scientific inquiry—the nature of scientific knowledge (which corresponds to NOS)—and the nature of scientific inquiry (NOSI) which characterizes the process of scientific inquiry. Despite the distinction between NOS and NOSI, these are connected constructs, and they partly overlap (Lederman 2006, 2007; Schwartz, Lederman, and Lederman 2008). Schwartz, Lederman, and Lederman (2008) describe a theoretical framework for NOSI. Therefore, in accordance with Schwab (1962), NOSI includes seven aspects that are relevant for science education (Schwartz, Lederman, and Lederman 2008, 4–6):

1. Scientific questions to guide investigations;
2. Multiple methods of scientific investigations;
3. Multiple purposes of scientific investigations;
4. Justification of scientific knowledge;
5. Recognition and handling of anomalous data;
6. Distinction between data and evidence; and
7. Community of practice.

Comparing the aspect lists of NOS and NOSI, interconnections become clear. For example, empirically based scientific knowledge, which is "based on and/or derived from observations of the natural world (i.e., empirical)" (Lederman 2007, 834), emerges from studies with appropriate designs (which allow supporting scientific claims). Therefore, empirically based scientific knowledge (NOS aspect 2) is interrelated with the (multiple) methods of scientific investigations (NOSI aspect 2) and the justification of scientific knowledge (NOSI aspect 4).

Allchin (2011) opened a discussion on the minimum consensus approach of NOS not being broad enough to cover authentic competencies connected to the NOS approach, like being able to evaluate critically whether a particular source is scientific. He, therefore, introduced the idea of the nature of whole science, including concepts of SI and NOSI, which led to a functional NOS understanding and enabled scientific literacy. However, Schwartz, Lederman, and Abd-El-Khalick (2012) emphasize that NOS and NOSI are interlinked and part of different concepts.

Generally speaking, scholars have differing views on the conception or definition of NOS (Deng et al. 2011). Because of this theoretical discussion, a more inductive perspective on NOS and learning how students learn about a meta-perspective on science should not be underestimated, especially in situations where researchers disagree on the conceptualization of NOS. In simplified terms, we could ask more generally, "What do students learn when we teach them in classes relevant to NOS (including NOSI), SI, and scientific literacy?"

Such an approach would not need to start with a new data collection instrument. Learners could still be prompted to externalize their views on NOS. Using the VNOS-C could be a starting point because it prompts survey takers to write rich answers to the ten open-ended questions. The instrument is designed to score Lederman's seven aspects of NOS (2006, 2007). However, because of the interconnections between NOS and NOSI, there could also be hints of views about NOSI or other related constructs in some answers. For instance, the question "What is an experiment?" (Lederman et al. 2002, 509) should prompt responses on NOSI as well. It is even very similar to a question in the "Views of Scientific Inquiry (VOSI) Questionnaire": "What do you think a scientific experiment is? Give an example to support your answer" (Schwartz, Lederman, and Lederman 2008, 13). Therefore, it is evident that views about NOSI also become visible in answering the related question of the VNOS-C. This could also be the case for answers to further open-ended questions due to the interconnections between NOS and NOSI. Therefore, using the VNOS-C to evaluate a more holistic learning opportunity about science beyond the seven aspects of NOS (Lederman et al. 2006, 2007) has the potential to uncover further changes of views. As shown in Figure 19.1, a structural topic modeling approach could help extract these changes when used on VNOS-C data before and after an intervention that is not limited to NOS but where the VNOS-C has been utilized as the primary tool of evaluation. In "Teacher Development Program and Data Collection," we will describe such an intervention.

Teacher Development Program and Data Collection

Among other objectives, the longitudinal study investigates the effectiveness of a teacher development program on the supervision of students in scientific work and writing (Pfläging, Richter, and Borowski 2020). In some states of Germany, a seminar course is mandatory at the upper secondary school level (Bosse 2014). As part of these courses, students usually conduct a scientific investigation and report their results in a seminar paper which should have a "pre-scientific form" of a scientific thesis. The overarching goal of the science teacher training was to enable teachers to coach students in working and writing scientifically and to improve the teachers' competencies to evaluate (pre-)scientific thesis (Pfläging, Richter, and Borowski 2020). Therefore, the development program addressed the following:

1. Basic knowledge of NOS, (NO)SI, and scientific reasoning;
2. Competences concerning the evaluation of seminar papers and the evaluation of the scientific work process of students;
3. Competencies in supporting students in scientific work and writing; and
4. Competencies related to planning science seminar courses.

The teacher training was offered in an online and an in-person format. The teachers are equally distributed over the different formats. The two in-person programs took place from November 2019 to March 2020, and the two online training series from October 2020 to May 2021. The in-person classes took place on four event days à seven hours. The online classes were offered as six webinars (à 2–3.5 h; total 16 hours, incl. breaks). This format also included four self-directed learning units with videos and learning exercises (à 3–7 h; total approx. 18 h). The programs consist of four training modules over eighteen weeks (presence) and seventeen weeks (online). A description of the content and the program structure can be found in Figure 19.2.

The first three modules started with a prototypical historical example to address particular aspects of NOS by the minimum consensus approach (e.g., the aspect of tentativeness of scientific knowledge) and of NOSI (e.g., control of variables in scientific investigations), explicit and partly implicit. The aspects of NOS are connected to

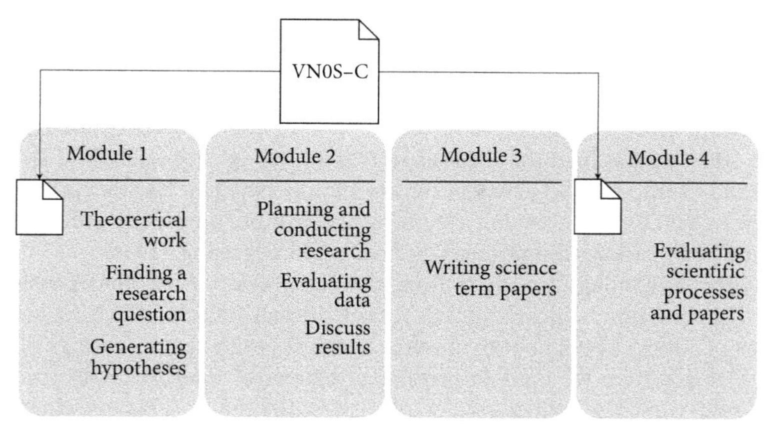

Figure 19.2 Structure of the teacher training (adapted from Pfläging, Richter, and Borowski 2020).

the criteria for preparing a written scientific paper. Following this, the teacher applied these prepared criteria in tasks to promote competencies in the learning goals (2) to (4) above. In terms of historical examples, the training contained the discovery of the vacuum, the discovery of X-rays, and the discovery of the structure model of DNA.

To evaluate the program concerning NOS, the teacher completed the VNOS-C questionnaire at the beginning of advanced training module 1 and the beginning of the last advanced training module 4. The testing time was restricted to sixty minutes. The answers to the VNOS-C were transcribed systematically. Restrictions regarding testing time hindered the researchers from employing instruments to measure NOSI or SI.

The training was intended for secondary school science teachers. A total of N = 42 teachers participated in the whole teacher professional development program and completed the VNOS-C questionnaire at both time points of the survey (Figure 19.2). The teachers' subjects can be found in Table 19.1. All participating teachers taught in the federal states of Berlin, Brandenburg, Hamburg, Saxony, and Bavaria.

Table 19.1 Distribution of Subjects over Teachers (N = 42 Teachers)

	Teachers with this subject **Number**	**Proportion***
Biology	23	55%
Chemistry	14	33%
Physics	10	24%
Other subjects	Less	Less

* The proportions do not add up to 100% because teachers in Germany teach generally more than one subject.

Research Question

Based on the theoretical background of NOS and the content of the teacher development program, VNOS-C responses could reveal evidence for additional learning gains in other aspects than the seven aspects of NOS (e.g., about NOSI). Therefore, we pose the question: To what extent can we identify potential learning gains outside the scope of VNOS-C concerning a learning opportunity on supervision of students in scientific work and writing using VNOS-C responses using STMs?

Primarily we conduct this study from the perspective of ML for assessment in STEM. This question is meaningful as it tests the feasibility of STMs for widening the focus of STEM assessment by finding categories outside the scoring rubric. To answer this question, we need to investigate aspects of interpretability and traceability (concerning the individual documents) of the topics. This question has the practical dimension of evaluating the teacher training described earlier. Furthermore, the investigation is meaningful from the perspective of the assessment of NOS and the neighboring constructs to meet the need for a more holistic assessment of an understanding of science, as many interventions do not focus solely on NOS itself.

Analysis

The data collection was performed as described in the section "Teacher Development Program and Data Collection." To answer the research question, we apply the approach of structural topic modeling to the VNOS-C questionnaire. The general idea is to add the variable *time point* as a covariate to measure and extract topics related to this variable (Figure 19.1). Suppose a topic has a positive relation to the variable *time point*. In that case, this signifies that the topic takes up a higher proportion in the post than in the pre-test and vice versa for a negative coefficient (e.g., mentioning less naïve views on NOS). To evaluate to what extent STMs are feasible for identifying new categories related to other variables, we focus on the following aspects:

(1) Interpretability: The topic can be interpreted and labeled as a candidate representing a learning gain on a basic level of interpretability.
(2) Curricular aspect of validity: The topic can be linked to the content of the teacher training program.
(3) Traceability: A human coder can reproduce the effect from pre to post suggested by the regression model.
(4) Objectivity: The effect from pre to post suggested by the regression model can be reproduced by another independent human coder with a sufficient intercoder agreement.

The analysis process in Figure 19.3 covers these aspects.

To be able to identify individual learning gains, we chose to include just teachers who took part in the pre- and post-test. Overall, $N = 84$ booklets, which translates to forty-two teachers, were analyzed. Including one-time participants would have

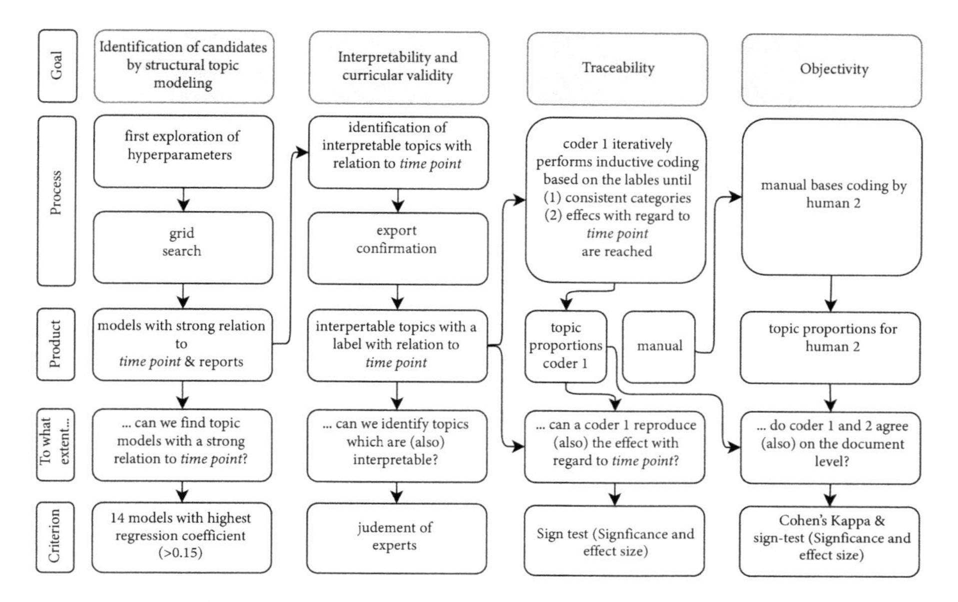

Figure 19.3 Analysis workflow.

led to a quasi-longitudinal interpretation, limiting our claims regarding hypothetical learning gains. The analysis was conducted using the r package stm (version 1.3.6). All texts were in German language and analyzed as such. Throughout the paper, we present English translations when, e.g., referring to terms or utterances from the texts.

As a first step, we explored hyperparameters to get the first impression of the impact that different hyperparameters would have, e.g., topic number, different stop-words, unit of analysis (analysis by question version or by booklet), and document unit (question, paragraph, or booklet). We decided to fit topic models question by question, as labeling the topics seemed easier than analyzing all questions simultaneously. Subsequently, we varied the topic number and the document unit systematically by performing a grid search over the following hyperparameters:

- Topic number = 2, 3, 4, 5, 6, 7, 8, 9, 10 (number of settings = 9)
- Document unit = response, paragraphs (number of settings = 2)

We estimated 180 models (9 × 2 = 18 for every one of the ten questions) and reported the regression coefficients concerning the covariate *time point* in this process. For all significant relationships, we constructed an R markdown-based report, which contained information to help interpret the topic and its role in the documents. The documents with the highest regression coefficients were then forwarded to the human analysis.

The aspects of interpretability, curricular validity, traceability, and objectivity are described in more detail below.

1. Interpretability: An expert human (expert 1, the first author of the paper, teaching a university seminar on the philosophy of science since 2014) used R markdown reports to judge whether the topic could be interpreted as a potential learning gain that might have occurred during the teacher training programs. The report contained the following elements:
   (a) Regression table concerning the effects of all topics on the variable *time point*;
   (b) Bar plots with the ten most frequent words for all topics;
   (c) Histogram of maximum topic proportions for each document;
   (d) Two box plots for the pre- and post-test of the topic proportion concerning the topics related to the variable *time point*;
   (e) Histogram of the difference in topic proportion related to the variable *time point* for every individual (proportion in the post minus pre proportion in the pre-test); and
   (f) Ten documents with the least and ten with the highest proportion regarding the topic related to the variable *time point* (original text and pre-processed versions). Based on the R markdown report, the expert identified candidate topics (e.g., "Role of Variables in Experiments") related to potential learning gains.
2. Curricular validity: The author of the teacher training program (expert 2) reviewed the candidates (see "Results") proposed by the first expert human. She had to discard any topics she could not link to the effects of the teacher training. In this step, additionally, we discarded one topic that was already part of the VNOS-Cs scoring rubric.
3. Traceability: Coder 1 (the same person as expert 1) marked the segments (defined as units of meaning) in several iterations based on the remaining topics, i.e., hypothetical learning gains until significant pre-post values and correlations were reached. During this iterative process, he also refined the definitions of the categories. Based on these definitions, coder 1 wrote a coding manual for coder 2 to reproduce this result in the following analysis step.
4. Objectivity: We used intercoder agreement to argue for objectivity. Coder 2 (the same person as expert 2) had the task of reproducing the same result as coder 1 based on the coding manual.

Results

Topic Modeling

As discussed, the analysis was conducted question by question. The formula *Prevalance ~ Timepoint* specified the association between topic prevalence and the time point in all models. For each model, we extracted the maximum of the absolute value of the regression coefficients (via stm package, r package stm). These values are displayed in Figure 19.4.

Of the estimated 180 models, we chose 14 models with the highest statistically significant regression coefficient (> 0.15) regarding the time point, meaning at least one

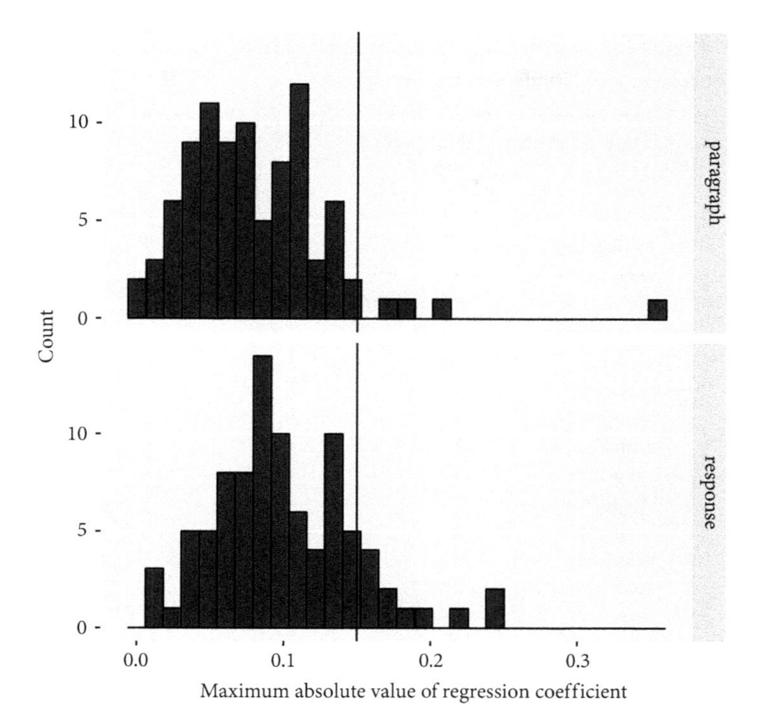

Figure 19.4 Histograms of maximum absolute values of regression coefficients for each model (paragraphs as documents = upper histogram, responses as documents = lower histogram).

of the topics had a regression coefficient higher than this threshold (Table 19.2). The number 14 (or threshold of 0.15) was an economic decision based on the time available for this step of the investigation and the distribution of the regression coefficients. In this way, we limited the interpretation to documents most likely to have reproducible effects when examined by a human. Figure 19.5 provides an overview of the VNOS-C models and questions.

Figure 19.5 shows an example of the distribution for the topic model on question 2, and Table 19.3 summarizes the regression equation for this example. Here topic 2 is the only topic to include terms such as "variables," "impact," or "method" in the ten most representative terms. As the regression table (see Table 19.3) shows, it is positively related to the time point, signifying an increase in the topic proportion throughout the teacher program.

Interpretability and Curricular Aspect of Validity

Based on the R Markdown reports, expert 1 identified five candidate topics that could be related to possible learning gains. The topic models related to these candidates or topic labels are marked in bold. These candidates were as follows:

Table 19.2 Topic Models with a Significant Relationship to Topic Prevalence and with at Least One Regression Coefficient Higher than 0.15

Question of VNOS-C	Document unit	Number of topics	Maximum regression coefficients	Number of effects
1	**paragraph**	**3**	**0.204**	**2**
2	**response**	**4**	**0.216**	**1**
3	paragraph	3	0.356	3
3	paragraph	9	0.165	4
3	response	6	0.180	1
4	response	7	0.158	1
5	paragraph	4	0.181	3
5	**response**	**2**	**0.243**	**2**
5	**response**	**3**	**0.247**	**2**
5	**response**	**7**	**0.196**	**2**
6	**response**	**4**	**0.159**	**1**
6	**response**	**6**	**0.161**	**1**
7	**response**	**2**	**0.172**	**2**
8	response	8	0.169	1

Potentially interpretable topic models with regard to the topic related to time point are marked in bold.

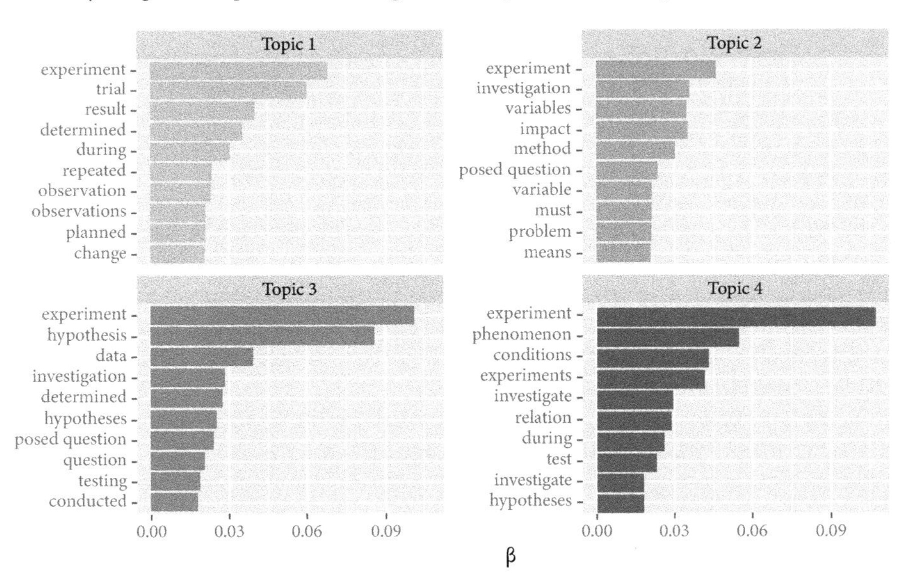

Figure 19.5 Distribution of probabilities (β) of the most representative terms for the three topics of a topic model related to the VNOS-C question "What is an experiment?" The original texts were in German, and the pre-processing included stemming. Because the stemming process differs in the two languages, we decided to provide English translations of German words related to German stems instead of a stemmed version.

Table 19.3 Prevalence Predicted by Time Point for Topic 2

	B	ΔB	t	p
Const.	0.351	0.049	7.224	<0.001
Time point	0.215	0.063	3.421	0.001

C1: Focus on specific subjects (biology, chemistry, physics) (increase) (question 1)
C2: Role of variables in experiments (increase) (question 2)
C3: Hierarchies law and theory (decrease) (question 5)
C4: Instrumental character of models as cognitive support (question 6)
C5: More general argumentations (increase) and fewer examples (decrease) (question 7)

We identified candidates 2, 4, and 5 as potential candidates for the traceability analysis. Out of the discussion with the expert, it emerged that there was no clear argumentation on why any specific subject (e.g., physics, biology) should have more prevalence after the teacher training candidate 1. Candidate 3 was discarded because it had already been part of the analysis based on the scoring rubric of VNOS-C.

The expert considered candidate 2 plausible because the aspect variable control was a specific part of the teacher development program (see Figure 19.2). Candidate 4 was considered as the teacher training had the general goal of teaching aspects of the philosophy of science. We hypothesized that this could have led teachers to think of models as less of a tool for teaching (help for understanding). Candidate 5 remained in the analysis because we believed that the philosophy focus helped the teachers make arguments more abstractly.

Traceability and Objectivity

From the traceability analysis, we could confirm two of the three candidates.

We noted an increase in segments that are "literally about control and variation of variables" (translated from the manual). Statements about variable control not using correct terminology were omitted (e.g., writing about "things" that must be held constant was not allowed in this category). The following example (translated from German) entirely belongs to the category:

> An experiment is the attempt of the proof (or contradiction) of a fact. For this purpose, a problem is simplified to such an extent that, ideally, only one variable remains that can be changed. By changing this variable, it can now be tested how the other considered variables change.

The other category (related to question 6: "Science textbooks often represent the atom as a central nucleus") summarized statements that either elicited models' function as visually illustrating (e.g., pictorial representation) or directly focused on models in teaching (e.g., writing about students): e.g., "That an atom looks like this is an older idea, but valuable, e.g., chemistry lessons to illustrate chemical bonds/reactions."

Table 19.4 summarizes the results for both candidates (topics) concerning the frequency of increasing and decreasing topic proportions.

We conducted a sign test to compare topic proportions because the distribution was inconsistent with the assumptions of the *t*-test or Mann-Whitney-U-test. For both topic proportions, a sign test shows to be significant:

- Candidate 2: $p = 0.039$, success rate = 10/12 ($Mdn_{pre} = Mdn_{post} = 0$).
- Candidate 4: $p < 0.001$, success rate = 12/12 ($Mdn_{pre} = Mdn_{post} = 0$)

Table 19.4 shows that for both candidates, the large majority does not change their topic proportion. However, in the following sense, the effect can be described as substantial: Figure 19.6 displays the human-coded topic proportions quantitatively for all teachers with more than 0% topic proportion in the pre- or post-test. Because there are no points on the diagonal, we can conclude that the teachers without a difference in topic proportions include no statements on the topics, neither in the pre- nor the post-test. We can also observe that most of the effect does not occur because teachers simply write more (C2) or less (C4) about the topic. Specifically, except for one time point in each analysis, all the points constituting the effect (blue points in C2; red points in C4) have a topic proportion of 0 (C2: in the pre-test, C4: in the post-test). The *p*-values reported here should be understood as pragmatic limits. They cannot be understood in terms of rigorous hypothesis testing, as the coding process went through several iterations. The same applies to the *p*-values related to the regression coefficients of the structural topic models.

In order to check for intercoder agreement, we calculated Cohen's kappa and performed the same significance test. Without further iterations, coder 2 reached almost perfect agreement $\kappa = 0.849$, 95% CI [0.682, 1.017], $p = 0 < 0.001$. And also reproduced a significant effect regarding the potential learning gains ($p = 0.039$, success rate = 8/9 ($Mdn_{pre} = Mdn_{post} = 0$) this analysis).

Regarding C4, in an initial round, the agreement was moderate at first ($\kappa = 0.364$, 95% CI [0.121, 0.606], $p = 0.005$, agreement = 76%). The reason, however, could be identified easily as coder 2 also selected statements including the visual aspect of the

Table 19.4 Number of Teachers with Positive and Negative Effects Based on the Topic Proportion

	Number of teachers	
Direction	**Candidate 2**	**Candidate 5**
Negative	2	12
Neutral	30	28
Positive	10	0
Total	42	40*

* Due to a lack of response two documents (two teachers) were excluded.

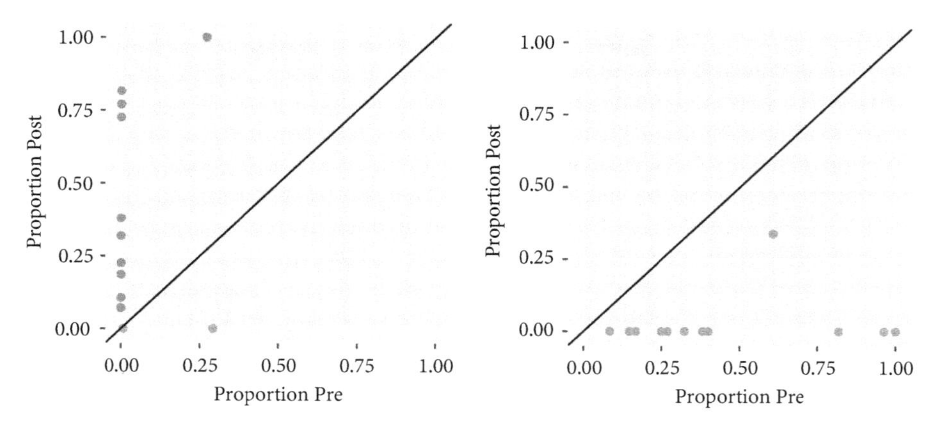

Figure 19.6 Human topic proportions for both topics and all teachers who write at least once about this topic.

atom, which do not include the function of the model as cognitive support. This was a mistake based on the coding manual and could easily be corrected. From the discussion, the reason for including this statement, however, was also influenced by the perspective of the second coder. As the main researcher, she had extensive coding experience using the VNOS-C. She also included these statements because statements on the look of an atom point to naïve realism and therefore indicate a naïve view of models and reveal a nontentative view of science. After adapting the coding instructions, an agreement of $\kappa = 0.914$ (95% CI [0.796, 1.032], $p < 0.001$, agreement = 98%) was reached. In her analysis, she could also reproduce a significant effect $p < 0.001$, success rate = 13/13 ($Mdn_{pre} = Mdn_{post} = 0$).

Discussion

The aim of this study was to investigate the suitability of STMs for identifying evidence of learning gains in STEM education assessment, with the perspective of broadening the focus of assessment. For this purpose, we analyzed the responses to the items of the VNOS-C before and after teacher training.

Results showed that it was indeed possible to identify evidence for additional learning gains through STMs outside of the scope of the seven aspects of NOS. Out of ten questions, two questions demonstrated evidence of teachers' improvements. One topic indicates that teachers have improved their language concerning experiments. This finding refers to the neighboring construct NOSI and is relevant in the context of whole science (Allchin 2011). As the teacher training also did cover NOSI aspects, related learning success could, in principle, be expected. However, the VASI (views about scientific inquiry; Lederman et al. 2014) would not necessarily uncover the nature of learning success at the technical language level. From this perspective, the employment of STMs remains beneficial.

The second finding refers to NOS and the function of models as an aid for visualization. While a quarter of the teachers write about this topic in the pre-test, they hardly mention it at the end of the teacher training. One implication for teacher training on NOS (Cullinane and Erduran 2023) might be that we should be aware that teachers arrive with a very classroom-centered view of science. This may interfere with their understanding of NOS and could be considered, particularly when teaching about the function of models. This result is also notable in the sense that it shows that decrease in topic proportion can be, in principle, interpreted as positive learning effects.

Although the study suggests that STMs can broaden the focus of assessment and provide additional information on students' learning gains, we have noted some limitations of the study. First, we cannot provide evidence on cognitive/substantial aspects of validity (Messick 1995; Zhai, Krajcik, and Pellegrino 2021), which would allow inferences on the cognitive processes and states. However, this is not an issue specific to STM. As Lederman et al. (2002) also suggested, VNOS answers can be validated in stimulated recall interviews.

A second limitation can be seen in the fact that the effects only impacted about 25% of the teachers. However, regarding C4, this proportion is the only one writing about models from this (problematic) perspective. After the training, almost no one retakes this view. From this angle, the effect is substantial.

A third limitation is that we did not evaluate the classification performance by using human–machine agreement, e.g., by using a test set. Sufficient performance would render the model feasible for automatic classification in a digital version of VNOS-C. Such research should generate value because there is no reliable and valid method for assessing NOS understanding in large groups to our information (McComas, Clough, and Nouri 2020). Future research could also investigate how feedback, including such additional learning gains, could be designed to have an impact as a more strength-based assessment (Lucas 2021). One option would be to present hypothetical learning gains to learners and decide together on the next steps of learning. We would also like to acknowledge that the process presented here is time-consuming. Future research could focus on methods that make this process more feasible, e.g., by having large language models support the identification of interpretable topics.

From a higher perspective, this research proposes a perspective on the role of unsupervised machine learning methods for assessment. Compared to supervised learning, these techniques have been used less (Zhai, Haudek, et al. 2020; Zhai, Yin, et al. 2020). We propose that unsupervised methods can be used to widen the focus of our assessments and focus on the learner and hope that this might further stimulate creative applications of unsupervised methods in STEM assessment and research. Identifying potential learning gains is just one example of applying STMs. We believe that STMs provide numerous opportunities, and we hope to see more useful applications in the future.

Acknowledgments

The data of this study data stems from a project supported by the Dr. Hans Riegel Foundation (project title: "Entwicklung, Durchführung und Evaluation einer Lehrkräftefortbildung zu Seminarkursen sowie zur Bewertung von naturwissenschaftlichen Seminararbeiten"). The opinions, findings, conclusions, or recommendations expressed by the authors do not necessarily reflect the views of the funders.

References

Allchin, D. 2011. "Evaluating Knowledge of the Nature of (Whole) Science." *Science Education* 95, 518–42. https://doi.org/10.1002/sce.20432

Arndt, L., Billion-Kramer, T., Wilhelm, M. and Rehm, M. 2020. "NOS-Modellierungen—Ein theoretischer Konflikt mit fehlender empirischer Basis. [NOS Modeling—A Theoretical Conflict with a Lack of Empirical Basis.]" *Progress in Science Education (PriSE)* 3(1), 35–45. https://doi.org/10.25321/prise.2020.994

ASCL [Association of School and College]. 2019. *The Forgotten Third: Final Report of the Commission of Inquiry*, Association of School and College Leaders, Leicester.

Blei, D. M., Ng, A. Y., and Jordan, M. I. 2003. "Latent Dirichlet Allocation." *Journal of Machine Learning Research* 3, nos. 4–5: 993–1022.

Blei, D. M. 2012. "Probabilistic Topic Models." *Communications of the ACM* 55, no. 4: 77–84. https://doi.org/10.1145/2133806.2133826

Bosse, D. 2014. "Lerngelegenheit Seminarkurs—wissenschaftspropädeutisches Arbeiten zwischen Hochschulvorbereitung und Berufsorientierung [Learning Opportunity Seminar Course—Scientific Propaedeutic Work between University Preparation and Career Orientation]." In *Abitur und Matura zwischen Hochschulvorbereitung und Berufsorientierung*, edited by F. Eberle, B. Schneider-Taylor and D. Bosse, 85–102. Wiesbaden: Springer VS.

Chang, J., Boyd-Graber, J., Gerrish, S., Wang, C., and Blei, D. M. 2009. "Reading Tea Leaves: How Humans Interpret Topic Models." In *Advances in Neural Information Processing Systems 22 - Proceedings of the 2009 Conference*, 288–96.

Cullinane, A., and Erduran, S. 2023. "Nature of Science in Preservice Science Teacher Education–Case Studies of Irish Pre-service Science Teachers." *Journal of Science Teacher Education* 34, no. 2: 201–23. https://doi.org/10.1080/1046560X.2022.2042978

Deng, F., Chen, D., Tsai, C. and Chai, C. S. 2011. "Students' Views of the Nature of Science: A Critical Review of Research." *Science Education* 95, no. 6: 961–99. https://doi.org/10.1002/sce.20460

Doogan, C., and Buntine, W. 2021. "Topic Model or Topic Twaddle? Re-evaluating Semantic Interpretability Measures." In *Proceedings of the 2021 Conference of the North American Chapter of the Association for Computational Linguistics*, 3824–48. Association for Computational Linguistics.

Fesler, L., Dee, T., Baker, R., and Evans, B. 2019. "Text as Data Methods for Education Research." *Journal of Research on Educational Effectiveness* 12, no. 4: 707–27. https://doi.org/10.1080/19345747.2019.1634168

Gao, Y., Zhai, X., Bulut, O., Cui, Y., and Sun, X. 2022. "Examining Humans' Problem-Solving Styles in Technology-Rich Environments Using Log File Data." *Journal of Intelligence* 10, no. 3: Article 3. https://doi.org/10.3390/jintelligence10030038

Grajzl, P., and Murrell, P. 2019. "Toward Understanding 17th Century English Culture: A Structural Topic Model of Francis Bacon's Ideas." *Journal of Comparative Economics* 47, no. 1: 111–35. https://doi.org/10.1016/j.jce.2018.10.004

Green, T. 2016. "A Methodological Review of Structural Equation Modelling in Higher Education Research." *Studies in Higher Education* 41, no. 12: 2125–55. https://doi.org/10.1080/03075079.2015.1021670

Heering, P. 2014. "Douglas Allchin: Teaching the Nature of Science: Perspectives and Resources." *Science and Education* 477–79. https://doi.org/10.1007/s11191-014-9706-x

Hume, A., Cooper, R., and Borowski, A., eds. 2019. *Repositioning Pedagogical Content Knowledge in Teachers' Knowledge for Teaching Science*. New York: Springer Nature. https://doi.org/10.1007/978-981-13-5898-2

Jeon, A., Kellogg, D., Khan, M. A., and Tucker-Kellogg, G. 2021. "Developing Critical Thinking in STEM Education through Inquiry-Based Writing in the Laboratory Classroom." *Biochemistry and Molecular Biology Education* 59: 140–50. https://doi.org/10.1002/bmb.21414

Jescovitch, L. N., Scott, E. E., Cerchiara, J. A., Merrill, J., Urban-Lurain, M., Doherty, J. H., and Haudek, K. C. 2021. "Comparison of Machine Learning Performance Using Analytic and Holistic Coding Approaches Across Constructed Response Assessments Aligned to a Science Learning Progression." *Journal of Science Education and Technology* 30, no. 2: 150–67. https://doi.org/10.1007/s10956-020-09858-0

Karakaya-Ozyer, K., and Aksu-Dunya, B. 2018. "A Review of Structural Equation Modeling Applications in Turkish Educational Science Literature." *International Journal of Research in Education and Science* 4, no. 1: 279–91.

Kulgemeyer, C., and Riese, J. 2018. "From Professional Knowledge to Professional Performance: The Impact of CK and PCK on Teaching Quality in Explaining Situations." *Journal of Research in Science Teaching* 55, no. 10: 1393–418. https://doi.org/10.1002/tea.21457

Lederman, J. S., Lederman, N. G., Bartos, S. A., Bartels, S. L., Meyer, A. A. and Schwartz, R. S. 2014. "Meaningful Assessment of Learners' Understandings about Scientific Inquiry—The Views about Scientific Inquiry (VASI) Questionnaire." *Journal of Research in Science Teaching* 51, no. 1: 65–83. https://doi.org/10.1002/tea.21125

Lederman, N. G. 2006. "Syntax Of Nature Of Science Within Inquiry And Science Instruction." In *Scientific Inquiry and Nature of Science. Implications for Teaching, Learning, and Teacher Education*, edited by L. B. Flick and N. G. Lederman, 301–17. Dordrecht: Springer. https://doi.org/10.1007/978-1-4020-5814-1_14

Lederman, N. G. 2007. "Nature of Science: Past, Present and Future." In *Handbook of Research on Science Education*, edited by S. K. Abell and N. G. Lederman, 831–79. Mahwah, NJ: Lawrence Erlbaum Associates.

Lederman, N. G., Abd-El-Khalick, F., Bell, R. L., and Schwartz, R. S. 2002. "Views of Nature of Science Questionnaire: Toward Valid and Meaningful Assessment of Learners' Conceptions of Nature of Science." *Journal of Research in Science Teaching* 39, no. 6: 497–521. https://doi.org/10.1002/tea.10034

Lee, H.-S., Gweon, G.-H., Lord, T., Paessel, N., Pallant, A., and Pryputniewicz, S. 2021. "Machine Learning-Enabled Automated Feedback: Supporting Students' Revision of Scientific Arguments Based on Data Drawn from Simulation." *Journal of Science Education and Technology* 30, no. 2: 168–92. https://doi.org/10.1007/s10956-020-09889-7

Lucas, B. 2021. *Rethinking Assessment in Education: The Case for Change.* East Melbourne, Australia: CSE Centre for Strategic Education.

Maestrales, S., Zhai, X., Touitou, I., Baker, Q., Schneider, B., and Krajcik, J. 2021. "Using Machine Learning to Score Multi-Dimensional Assessments of Chemistry and Physics." *Journal of Science Education and Technology* 30, no. 2: 239–54. https://doi.org/10.1007/s10956-020-09895-9

McComas, W. F., Clough, M. P. and Nouri, N. 2020. "Nature of Science and Classroom Practice: A Review of the Literature with Implications for Effective NOS Instruction." In *Nature of Science in Science Instruction. Rationales and Strategies*, edited by W. F. McComas, 67–111. Cham: Springer. https://doi.org/10.1007/978-3-030-57239-6_4

McComas, W. F. and Olson, J. K. 1998. "The Nature of Science in International Science Education Standards Documents." In *The Nature of Science in Science Education. Rationales and Strategies*, edited by W. F. McComas, 41–52. Dordrecht: Kluwer Academic. https://doi.org/10.1007/0-306-47215-5_2

Messick, S. 1995. "Validity of Psychological Assessment: Validation of Inferences from Persons' Responses and Performances as Scientific Inquiry into Score Meaning." *American Psychologist* 50, no. 9: 741–49. https://doi.org/10.1037/0003-066X.50.9.741

Mi, S., Lu, S., and Bi, H. 2020. "Trends and Foundations in Research on Students' Conceptual Understanding in Science Education: A Method Based on the Structural Topic Model." *Journal of Baltic Science Education* 19, no. 4: 551–68. https://doi.org/10.33225/jbse/20.19.551

Miller, G. 1990. "The Assessment of Clinical Skills/Competence/Performance." *Journal of the Association of American Medical Colleges* 65, no. 9: 63–67.

Muldner, K., Burleson, W., Van de Sande, B., and VanLehn, K. 2011. "An Analysis of Students' Gaming Behaviors in an Intelligent Tutoring System: Predictors and Impacts." *User Modeling and User-Adapted Interaction* 21, no. 1: 99–135. https://doi.org/10.1007/s11257-010-9086-0

National Research Council. 2012. *A Framework for K-12 Science Education: Practices, Crosscutting Concepts, and Core Ideas* (S. 13165). Washington, DC: National Academies Press. https://doi.org/10.17226/13165

Neuhaus, J., and Borowski, A. 2018. "Self-to-Prototype Similarity as a Mediator between Gender and Students' Interest in Learning to Code." *International Journal of Gender, Science and Technology* 10, no. 2: 233–52. https://genderandset.open.ac.uk/index.php/genderandset/article/view/497

Neumann, I. and Kremer, K. 2013. "Nature of Science und epistemologische Überzeugungen—Ähnlichkeiten und Unterschiede" ["Nature of Science and Epistemological Beliefs—Similarities and Differences"]. *Zeitschrift für Didaktik der Naturwissenschaften* 19: 209–32.

Osborne, J., Collins, S., Ratcliffe, M., Millar, R. and Duschl, R. 2003. "What 'Ideas-about-Science' Should Be Taught in School Science? A Delphi Study of the Expert Community." *Journal of Research in Science Teaching* 40, no. 7: 692–720. https://doi.org/10.1002/tea.10105

Pfläging, M., Richter, D. and Borowski, A. 2020. "Entwicklung einer Fortbildung zur Veränderung des Wissenschaftsverständnisses [Development of an advanced teacher training to change the understanding of science]." In *Naturwissenschaftliche Kompetenz in der Gesellschaft von morgen. Gesellschaft für Didaktik der Chemie und Physik. Jahrestagung in Wien 2019*, edited by S. Habig, 1059–62. University of Duisburg-Essen.

Reich, J., Tingley, D., Leder-Luis, J., Roberts, M. E., and Stewart, B. 2015. "Computer-Assisted Reading and Discovery for Student Generated Text in Massive Open Online Courses." *Journal of Learning Analytics* 2, no. 1: 156–84. https://doi.org/10.18608/jla.2015.21.8

Roberts, M. E., Stewart, B. M., and Airoldi, E. M. 2016. "A Model of Text for Experimentation in the Social Sciences." *Journal of the American Statistical Association* 111, no. 515: 988–1003. https://doi.org/10.1080/01621459.2016.1141684

Roberts, M. E., Stewart, B. M., and Tingley, D. 2019. "STM: An R Package for Structural Topic Models." *Journal of Statistical Software* 91, no. 2. https://doi.org/10.18637/jss.v091.i02

Roberts, M. E., Stewart, B. M., Tingley, D., Lucas, C., Leder-Luis, J., Gadarian, S. K., Albertson, B., and Rand, D. G. 2014. "Structural Topic Models for Open-Ended Survey Responses." *American Journal of Political Science* 58, no. 4: 1064–82. https://doi.org/10.1111/ajps.12103

Rosenberg, J. M., and Krist, C. 2021. "Combining Machine Learning and Qualitative Methods to Elaborate Students' Ideas About the Generality of Their Model-Based Explanations." *Journal of Science Education and Technology* 30, no. 2: 255–67. https://doi.org/10.1007/s10956-020-09862-4

Schwab, J. 1962. "The Teaching of Science as Enquiry." In *The Teaching of Science*, edited by J. J. Schwab and P. F. Brandwein, 1–103. Cambridge, MA: Harvard University.

Schwartz, R. S., Lederman, N. G. and Abd-El-Khalick, F. 2012. "A Series of Misrepresentations: A Response to Allchin's Whole Approach to Assessing Nature of Science Understandings." *Science Education* 96, no. 4: 685–92. https://doi.org/10.1002/sce.21013

Schwartz, R. S., Lederman, N. G. and Lederman, J. S. 2008. "An Instrument to Assess Views of Scientific Inquiry: The VOSI Questionaire." Paper presented at the international meeting of the National Association for Research in Science Teaching, Baltimore.

Seitzer, H., Martens, K., and Martens, K. 2021. "Placing PISA in Perspective: The OECD's Multicentric View on Education." *Globalisation, Societies and Education* 19, no. 2: 198–212. https://doi.org/10.1080/14767724.2021.1878017

Sherin, B. 2013. "A Computational Study of Commonsense Science: An Exploration in the Automated Analysis of Clinical Interview Data." *Journal of the Learning Sciences* 22, no. 4: 600–38. https://doi.org/10.1080/10508406.2013.836654

Shulman, L. S. 1986. "Those Who Understand: A Conception of Teacher Knowledge." *American Educator* 10, no. 1: 4–14.

Sung, S. H., Li, C., Chen, G., Huang, X., Xie, C., Massicotte, J., and Shen, J. 2021. "How Does Augmented Observation Facilitate Multimodal Representational Thinking? Applying Deep Learning to Decode Complex Student Construct." *Journal of Science Education and Technology* 30, no. 2: 210–26. https://doi.org/10.1007/s10956-020-09856-2

Windzio, M., and Heiberger, R. 2022. "Talking about Education: How Topics Vary Between International Organizations." In *Global Pathways to Education. Cultural Spheres, Networks, and International Organizations*, edited by K. Martens and M. Windzio, 239–66. Cham: Palgrave Macmillan. https://doi.org/10.1007/978-3-030-78885-8_9

Wulff, P., Buschhüter, D., Westphal, A., Nowak, A., Becker, L., Robalino, H., Stede, M., and Borowski, A. 2021. "Computer-Based Classification of Preservice Physics Teachers' Written Reflections." *Journal of Science Education and Technology* 30, 1–15. https://doi.org/10.1007/s10956-020-09865-1

Zehner, F., Sälzer, C., and Goldhammer, F. 2016. "Automatic Coding of Short Text Responses via Clustering in Educational Assessment." *Educational and Psychological Measurement* 76, no. 2: 280–303. https://doi.org/10.1177/0013164415590022

Zhai, X. 2021. "Practices and Theories: How Can Machine Learning Assist in Innovative Assessment Practices in Science Education." *Journal of Science Education and Technology* 30, no. 2: 139–49. https://doi.org/10.1007/s10956-021-09901-8

Zhai, X., Haudek, K. C., Shi, L., Nehm, R. H., and Urban-Lurain, M. 2020. "From Substitution to Redefinition: A Framework of Machine Learning-Based Science Assessment." *Journal of Research in Science Teaching* 57, no. 9: 1430–59. https://doi.org/10.1002/tea.21658

Zhai, X., Krajcik, J., and Pellegrino, J. W. 2021. "On the Validity of Machine Learning-based Next Generation Science Assessments: A Validity Inferential Network." *Journal of Science Education and Technology* 30, no. 2: 298–312. https://doi.org/10.1007/s10956-020-09879-9

Zhai, X., Shi, L., and Nehm, R. H. 2021. "A Meta-Analysis of Machine Learning-Based Science Assessments: Factors Impacting Machine-Human Score Agreements." *Journal of Science Education and Technology* 30, no. 3: 361–79. https://doi.org/10.1007/s10956-020-09875-z

Zhai, X., Yin, Y., Pellegrino, J. W., Haudek, K. C., and Shi, L. 2020. "Applying Machine Learning in Science Assessment: A Systematic Review." *Studies in Science Education* 56, no. 1: 111–51. https://doi.org/10.1080/03057267.2020.1735757

20

Classification of Instructional Activities in Classroom Videos Using Neural Networks

Jonathan K. Foster, Matthew Korban, Peter Youngs, Ginger S. Watson and Scott T. Acton

Introduction

There are several objectives for using classroom videos in teacher education and educational research. In their review of the literature, Gaudin and Chaliès (2015) distinguished six objectives for videos in teacher education and professional development: (a) show examples of good teaching practices, (b) show characteristic professional situations, (c) analyze the diversity of classroom practices from different perspectives, (d) stimulate personal reflection, (e) guide/coach teaching, and (f) evaluate competencies. In educational research, classroom videos are a common data source for examining student learning and teacher practice (Brophy 2004; de Freitas 2016; de Freitas, Lerman, and Parks 2017; Janík and Seidel 2009). For example, video recordings of classrooms have supported the examination of teaching practices across international contexts (e.g., Hiebert et al. 2003; Klette, Blikstad-Balas, and Roe 2017; Pons 2018; Stigler et al. 1999).

Due to the accessibility and low costs of video-capturing technologies, many educational researchers and teacher educators are collecting vast amounts of classroom video data and facing the challenge of storing, cataloguing, and analyzing the data with efficiency. For instance, educational researchers using classroom videos for assessing teaching quality at a large scale with classroom observation protocols encounter considerable financial and time-consuming costs for amassing human raters to analyze hundreds of hours of videos. Even analyzing fine-grained measures of instruction (e.g., turns of talk or questions) in classroom videos can be laborious (Kelly et al. 2020). Recent advances with artificial intelligence (AI) technologies, however, may offset some of these costs by automating some of the cataloging and analysis of large classroom video datasets (Roschelle, Lester, and Fusco 2020). For example, computers with these technologies could identify certain instructional activities (e.g., a teacher facilitating discussions) occurring within videos (Wang et al. 2014).

Within the past twenty-five years, the design and implementation of AI technologies in education have become an emerging area of research (Celik et al. 2022; L. Chen et al. 2020; X. Chen et al. 2020; Roll and Wylie 2016). In science, technology, engineering, and mathematics (STEM) education, these AI technologies have (a) augmented the delivery and content of (personalized) instruction, (b) automated

Jonathan K. Foster et al., *Classification of Instructional Activities in Classroom Videos Using Neural Networks.* In: *Uses of Artificial Intelligence in STEM Education.* Edited by: Xiaoming Zhai and Joseph Krajcik, Oxford University Press.
 DOI: 10.1093/oso/9780198882077.003.0020

the detection or assessment of performance, and (c) offered feedback for or assistance with decision-making (Alavi et al. 2022; Hwang and Tu 2021; Xu and Ouyang 2022). The study presented in this chapter builds on prior work in the application of AI in education for automated detection of instructional activities. More specifically, our purpose is to report on the application of neural networks to detect instructional activities in videos recorded in elementary classrooms.

Previous research analyzing the use of AI to detect instructional activities has primarily focused on one modality, but there is promising research using multiple modalities. Classroom transcripts and acoustic features are common modalities. Most of these applications are able to detect features of classroom talk in transcripts or audio recordings at the utterance level such as teacher questioning (Kelly et al. 2018) and uptake of students' ideas (Demszky et al. 2021). Other applications can detect structured discourse. For example, Wang et al. (2014) developed a system that was able to discriminate among classroom discourse structures (e.g., teacher-led lecture, whole-class discussion, and group work) from audio recordings. Images from video are another modality for developing systems to detect instructional activities. For example, Gang et al. (2021) applied a neural network to detect teacher actions such as writing on the board.

Unlike the AI applications for analyzing classroom transcripts and acoustic features, the applications for analyzing classroom videos have not been designed to detect more complex activities (e.g., teacher supporting a group of students) or classroom discourse structures (e.g., whole-class discussions). This is in part due to a lack of high-quality datasets needed for training AI (Sharma et al. 2021; Sun et al. 2021). Furthermore, multimodal approaches for detecting instructional activities are emerging as well. The Teacher Activity Recognizer from Transcriptions and Audio (TARTA) is one application designed to detect instructional forms of presenting, administration, and guiding based on the Classroom Observation Protocol for Undergraduate STEM (COPUS; Schlotterbeck et al. 2021).

Even though there is potentiality for applying AI to assist with the tasks of processing, cataloging, and analyzing classroom videos, there are also unique challenges with automating these complicated tasks traditionally done by humans. In this chapter, our intent is to illustrate the opportunities and challenges in our ongoing research using AI for detecting features of ambitious instruction in elementary mathematics and ELA instruction. More specifically, we take some steps toward examining whether some machine-learning techniques (i.e., neural networks) can recognize common instructional activities (i.e., small group activity) in videos of elementary classrooms. Because of the promising research detecting instructional activities using transcriptions or audio recordings of classroom talk, we focused our initial efforts on developing an AI system for automatically detecting instructional activities from video signals. Therefore, the study in this chapter only contains results of our efforts to train neural networks using one modality (i.e., videoframes) to detect instructional activities.

For our study, we selected three state-of-the-art deep-learning neural networks: Background Suppression Network (BaS-Net; Lee, Uh, and Byun 2020), Multi-label Action Dependencies (MLAD; Tirupattur et al. 2021), and Long Short-Term Transformer (LSTR; Xu et al. 2021). We address the following research question:

How accurate is each neural network at classifying instructional activities in classroom video?

We first provide a broad technical overview of computer vision-based human activity recognition systems and neural networks. We then discuss our prospective on ambitious instruction in mathematics and ELA for the elementary grades in the United States. Next, we share initial evidence that neural networks are capable of detecting various instructional activities in elementary classroom videos. The outcomes of this study demonstrate our initial efforts in developing a human activity recognition system, as related to some low-inference features of instruction, using videos collected from elementary classrooms. In closing, we discuss potential future design directions for human activity recognition systems by considering the challenges and opportunities for classroom observation.

Background and Perspective

Human Activity Recognition

The goal of human activity recognition systems is to identify an activity despite variability of persons and conditions. Human activity recognition is the process of detecting and identifying human activities by applying AI techniques to sensory data (Gupta et al. 2022). These sensory data may be collected from data sources such as accelerometers, touch screens, wearable sensors, and videoframe sequences. Vision-based human activity recognition systems use videoframe sequences, and these sequences can be captured from single or multiple cameras. Another way to differentiate human activity recognition systems is to consider the complexity of the human activities being detected (Beddiar et al. 2020). These actions could be simple actions (e.g., walking), gestures (e.g., pointing), behaviors (e.g., displays of frustration or concentration), interactions (e.g., hugging or reading a book), group actions (e.g., playing a game), or events (e.g., lecture).

Our approach focuses on vision-based human activity recognition where recorded videoframe sequences from a single viewpoint within a classroom are used to detect instructional activities. Our instructional activities include a range of human activities from simple actions (e.g., raising hand) to interactions with objects (e.g., using or holding book) and more complex actions like group actions (e.g., teacher supporting multiple students with interaction) and event actions (e.g., small group activity).

Developing a vision-based human activity recognition system for education presents several challenges. First, the development of vision-based human activity recognition systems using machine learning requires large video datasets with reliable and valid activity annotations for training. Publicly available human activity recognition datasets allow researchers to benchmark and compare algorithm performance. Unfortunately, most public datasets for developing vision-based human activity recognition systems contain activities that are outside the context of education and thus too general or outside the scope of instructional activities (e.g., running or cooking). The *EduNet* dataset is one exception that includes twelve hours of video from elementary and secondary classrooms sourced from YouTube and actual video recordings collected by developers in classrooms (Sharma et al. 2021). Second, there is the concern for the privacy of students and teachers. Many large-scale classroom-based video studies limit video access and only publicly share the video data with strict usage restrictions. If large-scale classroom-based video studies do make videos publicly available without restrictions, they typically make available only a very limited subset to safeguard the privacy of students and teachers (e.g., the TIMSS 1999 Video Study publicly released fifty-three video lessons: https://www.timssvideo.com). Researchers developing vision-based human activity recognition systems need to be able to download and process hundreds or more video files for training neural networks.

Third, there are many variations of video quality when collecting video in classrooms. The quality may differ based on recording capabilities (e.g., resolution or framerate), environmental factors (e.g., lighting conditions or cluttered visual scenes), or other factors such as movements of the camera, missing segments of video, multiple occlusions, and demographics of subjects. Finally, many instructional activities in classroom videos co-occur and sometimes these activities are performed by the same person. For example, a teacher may be writing while supporting multiple students during a small group activity. A teacher writing would be considered a simple action and supporting multiple students would be an interaction action. Writing and supporting students could also be occurring during a small group activity, which is best categorized as an event action. The complexity of co-occurring actions (i.e., writing and supporting students) and events (i.e., small group activity) creates challenges for detecting instructional activities from video.

Deep-Learning Neural Network

Deep-learning methods for vision-based human activity recognition systems are promising, especially for complex activities (Beddiar et al. 2020). We applied deep-learning neural networks to detect instructional activities. A deep-learning neural network is a hierarchical structure that can approximate complicated decision functions by directly mapping input features (e.g., raw video signals) to output labels (e.g., teacher walking). Input features pass through multiple layers and these layers detect certain features. For example, one input layer may detect edges between light and dark pixels from the video signal and a deeper layer processes these edges to detect higher level information such as the surface of a desk. Subsequently, the detected surfaces in the deeper layers may be useful for distinguishing whether students are sitting at desks or on the floor. To learn the aforementioned features, a deep-learning neural network is trained iteratively. In each learning iteration, the deep-learning neural network assigns labels to the videoframes based on the previously learned label assignment. If the network assigns an incorrect label to the videoframe, it decreases the weights of the pathways leading to the incorrect label. Otherwise, the network increases the weights to preserve the correct pathway.

Ambitious Instruction

In the United States, the goal of many teacher education and professional development programs is to prepare teachers for ambitious instruction. Broadly, ambitious instruction includes a set of teaching practices that foster rich, conceptual understanding of disciplinary content (Franke, Kazemi, and Battey 2007; Newmann and Associates 1996; Thompson, Windschitl, and Braaten 2013). These teaching practices may include, but are not limited to, establishing clear goals for student learning, engaging students in academic tasks that promote deep discussion and reasoning, supporting students in connecting representations of content, and promoting students' sense making of important discipline concepts (Grossman et al. 2013; National Council of Teachers of Mathematics 2014). Teaching practices aligned with ambitious instruction have been shown to promote student achievement (Carlisle et al. 2011; Grossman et al. 2013; Hiebert and Grouws 2007; National Mathematics Advisory Panel 2008; Newmannk, Bryk, and Nagaoka 2001). Even though the Common Core State Standards and other state standards call for teachers to engage in ambitious instruction, evidence suggest that it is not the norm in U.S. classrooms (Grossman et al. 2014; Kane and Staiger 2012).

One approach teacher educators have taken to support teachers in developing ambitious instruction is using classroom video examples of such instruction (van Es et al. 2017). Classroom videos have become a hallmark for preparing teachers in teacher education and professional development globally (Gaudin and Chaliès 2015). These videos allow teacher educators to develop teachers' professional vision and understanding of ambitious instruction (Sherin and van Es 2008). Furthermore, the use of video in teacher education have been used in ways aligned with Grossman and colleagues' (2009) pedagogies of practice: representation, decomposition, and approximation of practice. For example, videos have been used to provide representations of ambitious instruction and to decompose those teaching practices aligned with it. In addition, teacher candidates are sometimes asked to video record their approximations of ambitious instruction to receive feedback from teacher educators.

Education researchers have developed and used observation protocols to evaluate features of ambitious instruction. The Mathematics Scan (M-Scan) and the Protocol for Language Arts Teaching Observation (PLATO) are two observation protocols aligned with ambitious instruction (Berry et al. 2013; Cohen 2015; Grossman et al. 2013; Walkowiak et al. 2018). M-Scan includes nine features of ambitious instruction organized around four domains: mathematical tasks, discourse, representations, and coherence (Berry et al. 2013; Walkowiak et al. 2014). PLATO includes eleven features of instruction organized around four factors: instructional scaffolding, the representation and organization of content, disciplinary demand, and classroom environment (Cohen 2015; Grossman et al. 2013). PLATO was first created for use in analyzing secondary ELA instruction. It was later adapted in order to assess mathematics instruction from the Measures of Effective Teaching (MET) study (Cohen 2015). Others have also used PLATO to assess mathematics instruction (e.g., Luoto, Klette, and Blikstad-Balas 2023).

Methods

Video Data

The videos of elementary instruction used in the study reported here were collected as part of a previous research study known as the Developing Ambitious Instruction (DAI) project (Youngs et al. 2022). The DAI study focused on eighty-three beginning elementary teachers who graduated from teacher preparation programs at five universities in the United States in either 2015–16 or 2016–17. After graduation, these individuals started teaching full-time in grades K–5 in general education settings. The DAI project team observed each teacher as they taught mathematics and ELA up to six times each during their first two years of full-time teaching (i.e., up to three times each for mathematics and ELA per school year).

Each video-recorded lesson was about forty-five minutes to an hour in length. The camera was primarily focused on the teacher in the center of the frame. During whole-class activities, the videoframe is zoomed out to record as much of the entire class interactions. During small group activities, the camera remains primarily focused on the group of students that the teacher is instructing. If the instructional format is individual seatwork or transition, then the camera follows the teacher while trying to cover as much detail of the classroom.

Development of Instructional Activity Labels

Our team developed a set of instructional activity labels using features from two classroom observation instruments: M-Scan (Berry et al. 2013) and PLATO (Grossman et al. 2013). See Table 20.1 for a full list of the twenty-four child-level activity labels (e.g., teacher sitting or teacher walking) that are organized under six parent-level labels: activity type, discourse, teacher location, student location, teacher supporting, and representing content. The detection of the child-level labels for activity type (i.e., whole-class activity, individual activity, small group activity, and transition) became a priority in this study because previous research had suggested that some instructional activity types were linked with certain ratings for some dimensions in PLATO (Luoto, Klette, and Blikstad-Balas 2023) and previous video-based approaches have not evaluated whether neural networks could detect activity types in the classroom (Ahuja et al. 2019; Sharma et al. 2021; Sun et al. 2021).

To facilitate the differentiation of the child labels under activity type (i.e., whole-class activity versus individual activity), we included the child-level labels under discourse, teacher location, student location, teacher supporting, and representing content. For instance, if students are sitting on the floor and the teacher is standing and writing on the board, then it may be assumed with some confidence that this is occurring during a whole-class activity. Even though many of the child-level labels are low-inference activities, detecting the presence or absence of some of these activities is also important for using the classroom observation instruments to rate aspects of ambitious instruction. For example, one dimension of M-Scan assesses whether there

Table 20.1 List of Instructional Activities

Instructional activity	Definition	Action complexity
Activity type		
Whole-class activity	All students involved in one activity, with teacher leading the learning (e.g., lecture, presentation, carpet time).	Event
Individual activity	All students are privately working (e.g., independent practice, reading) alone at a separated desk or small groups with no interaction between students.	Event
Small group activity	Students are working together with peers (e.g., think-pair-share, book club); this is prioritized when there are students interacting or somewhat interacting near one another.	Event
Transition	The students and teacher are transitioning from one instructional activity to another (e.g., whole class to small group). The teacher and students are moving from one spot of the room to another (e.g., from the carpet to desks). Other than specific behavioral directions, no instruction or meaningful instructional activity is occurring during the transition.	Event
Discourse		
On task student talking with student	Students are conversing together; can overlap with "small group activity"; this is specific to mouth movements within the parent code time interval; without teacher support.	Group
Student raising hand	Hand is up for more than one second; clearly and purposefully raising hand.	Simple
Teacher location		
Sitting	Teacher is sitting (chair, stool, floor, crouching, on desk, kneeling).	Simple
Standing	Teacher is standing (in generally the same spot to maintain the same orientation to students).	Simple
Walking	Teacher is walking with purpose to change orientation to students.	Simple
Student location		
Sitting on carpet or floor	Students is sitting on floor/carpet.	Simple
Sitting at group tables	Students is sitting at tables.	Simple
Sitting at desks	Students is at individual desks.	Simple
Student(s) standing or walking	Student is standing up or walking around the room; can be one or multiple students.	Simple
Teacher supporting		
One student	Teacher uses proximity to offer assistance to one student, can be verbal or nonverbal.	Group

Continued

Table 20.1 *Continued*

Instructional activity	Definition	Action complexity
Multiple students with student interaction	Teacher uses proximity to offer assistance to multiple students, can be verbal or nonverbal; individual students are also interacting with one another.	Group
Multiple students without student interaction	Teacher uses proximity to offer assistance to multiple students who are engaged in an activity, can be verbal or nonverbal; students are sitting close to one another or in a small group but are not interacting with one another.	Group
Representing content		
Using or holding book	A book is used or held by teacher or student.	Interaction
Using or holding worksheet	A worksheet is used or held by teacher or student.	Interaction
Presentation with technology	An interactive whiteboard, document camera, or projector is used to show content.	Interaction
Using or holding instructional tool	A tangible object (e.g., ruler, math manipulative; anything in someone's hand other than what is already listed; does not include pencil/pen) is used or held by teacher or student for instructional purposes.	Interaction
Using or holding notebook	A notebook is used or held by teacher or student.	Interaction
Individual technology	Student or teacher is using a laptop, tablet, etc.	Interaction
Teacher writing	Teacher is inscribing on paper or on a board; includes erasing.	Interaction
Student writing	Student is inscribing on paper or on a board; includes erasing.	Interaction

are opportunities to use mathematical tools to represent mathematical content; thus, the team developed the label *using or holding instructional tool* to indicate whether the teacher or students were using an instructional tool (e.g., pattern blocks, fraction strips, or card sorts) for instructional purposes.

Annotation of the Video Data

Six annotators labeled the forty-six hours of video from the dataset using the instructional activity labels developed. Three master annotators, a post-doctoral researcher and two curriculum and instruction PhD students, trained three undergraduate students to become annotators to apply the labels to the dataset. All annotators went through an initial training with the instructional activity labels and then the team established and maintained inter-rater reliability while labeling the dataset (Youngs et al. under review). The annotators' average raw agreement ranged from 0.89 to 0.99 and kappa scores ranged from 0.38 to 0.88 across all instructional activity labels.

Annotators used a free and open-source computer software ELAN (2021) to label all of the activities evident in a videoframe. ELAN has been used in several disciplines, including education, psychology, and medicine (de Freitas, Lerman, and Parks 2017; Wittenburg et al. 2006); it has been applied to topics such as human–computer interaction and nonverbal communication and gesture analysis (e.g., Giuliani et al. 2015; Kong et al. 2015). ELAN allows multilabel and multiannotator labeling of videos. Figure 20.1 is an example of the ELAN interface. In the upper left of ELAN, a video player displays the video. Annotators were able to adjust the video playback speed and volume with controls functions in the upper right. In the lower half of ELAN, a video timeline with annotations for instructional activities. To annotate, annotators selected start and end times for an instructional activity and entered "y" as the annotation value to indicate the presence of the instructional activity. All annotations were at least one second in duration and completed without sound playback from the video by using the mute function in ELAN. No sound was used during annotation so that the comparison of the neural network outputs to the ground truth of the human annotation would be comparable. The neural network only received video signal during training; no audio features from the video were used during training. Therefore, annotators had to use visual cues for some labels. For instance, for the discourse label of *on task student talking to student*, annotators had to clearly see students' mouths moving when engaging in a content-based activity.

Annotated Video Data

In the video dataset, there were fifty distinct lesson videos (twenty-four mathematics and twenty-six ELA) from forty-three teachers' classrooms. Figure 20.2 displays a comparison of the presence of the instructional activities as identified by human annotators across mathematics and ELA lesson videos. As shown in Figure 20.2, the instructional activities were present across many lesson videos. These lesson videos included variety in instructional content (i.e., mathematics or ELA), but also other conditions such as the demographics of the teacher and students and the classroom scene. Recall, a diverse classroom video dataset is important as our goal is to develop a system capable of identifying instructional activities despite variability of persons and conditions.

Figure 20.3 displays a summary of the duration of instructional activities across the annotated dataset as labeled by human annotators with respect to the mathematics and ELA lesson videos. All durations are represented in a duration time format separating hours, minutes, and seconds (HH:MM:SS), which are cumulative across the video dataset. As shown in Figure 20.3, our dataset was imbalanced with certain

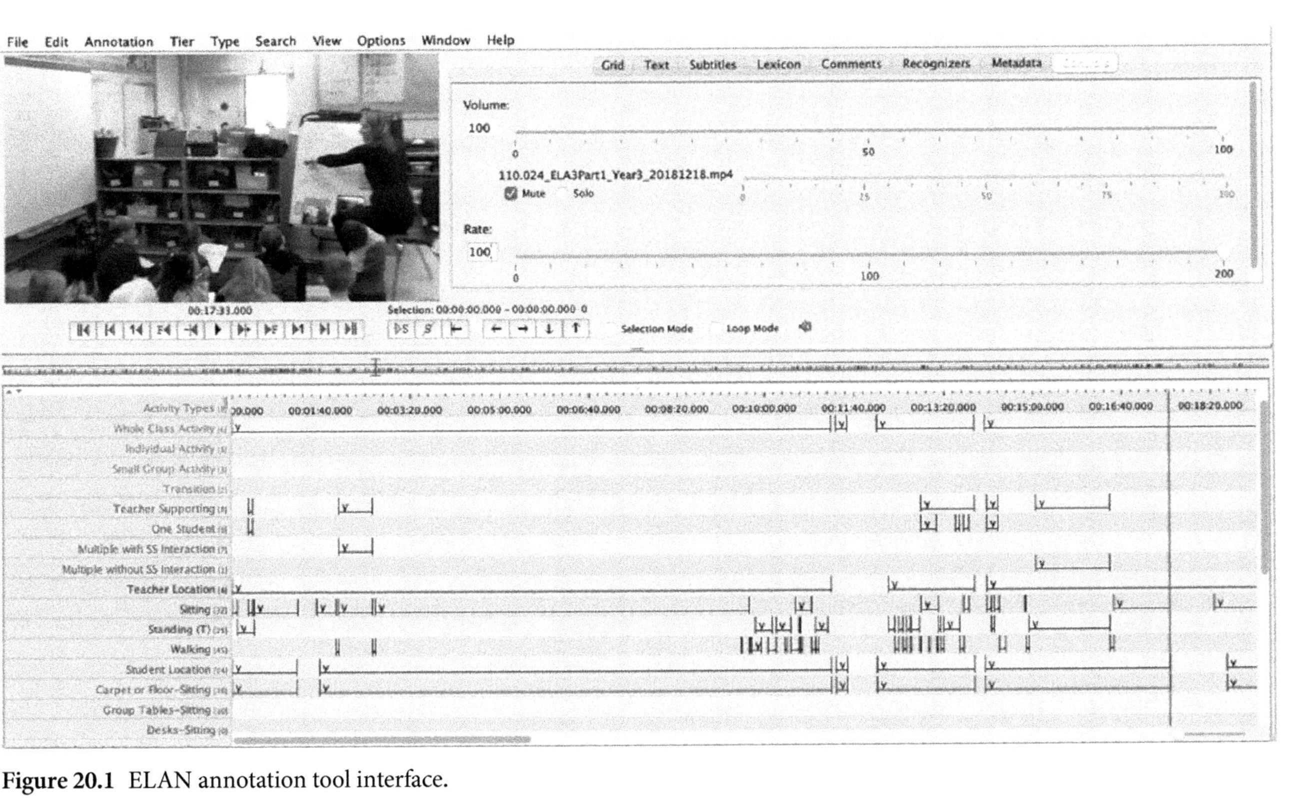

Figure 20.1 ELAN annotation tool interface.

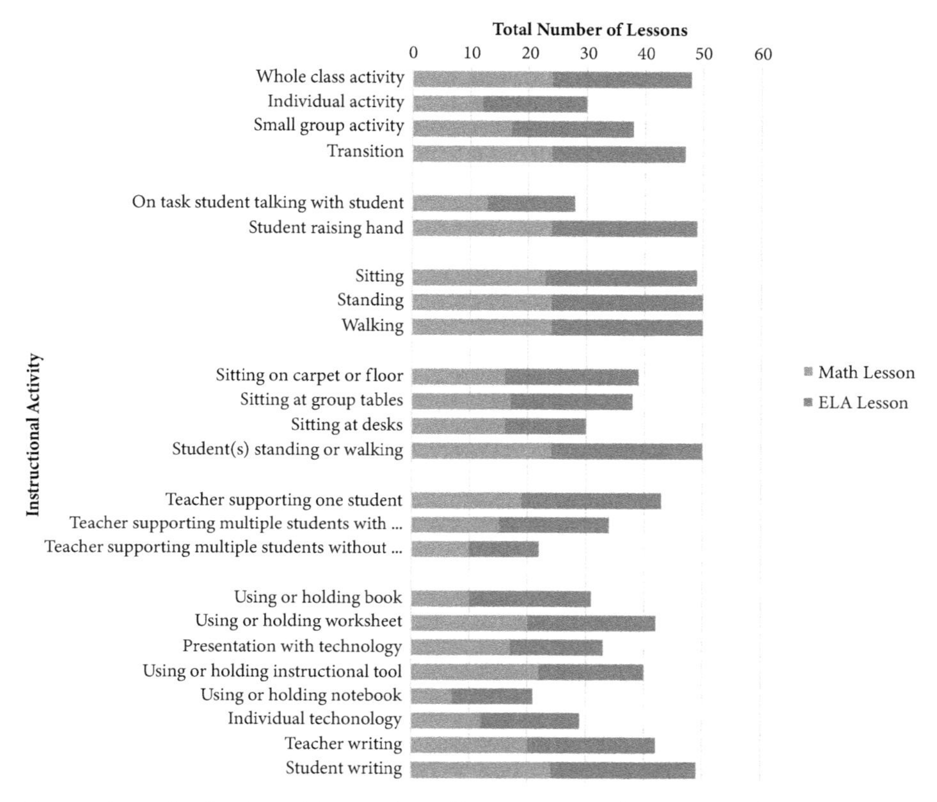

Figure 20.2 Distribution of the number of lessons across all instructional activity classes.

activities appearing for much longer in duration across videos than other activities (e.g., *sitting* versus *raising hand*), which is a challenging problem for machine learning (Yang and Wu 2006).

Neural Network Models

For our study, we selected three state-of-the-art networks: BaS-Net, MLAD, and LSTR. We chose to apply these neural networks in our study for two reasons. First, these neural networks achieved leading performance in two well-known long video activity datasets, THUMOUS (Idrees et al. 2017) and ActivityNet (Heilbron et al. 2015). These two datasets have several similarities to our classroom video dataset, including (1) they consist of long videos; (2) the videos are continuous-streaming, meaning without being segmented; (3) the annotation data include multiple co-occurring labels. Second, each neural network has unique advantages for handling the

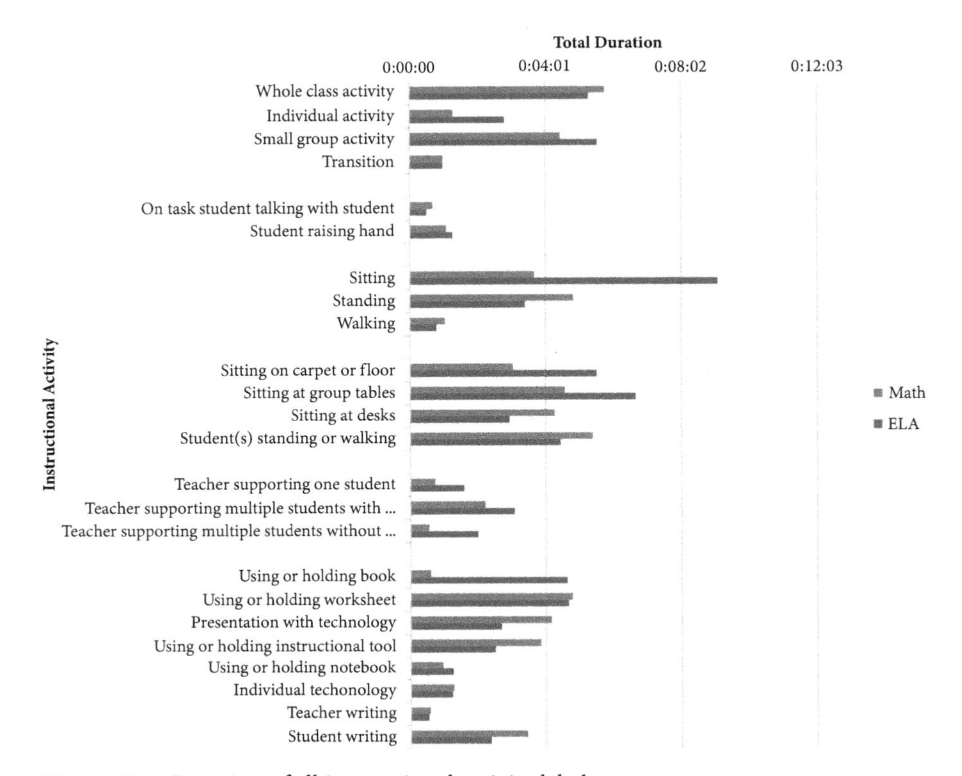

Figure 20.3 Duration of all instructional activity labels.

complexities found within classroom video. We highlight these specific advantages in the following sections for each neural network.

Background Suppression Network

BaS-Net is advantageous for handling crowded background scenes in classroom videos; it segments the background and foreground for each videoframe (Lee, Uh, and Byun 2020). Although the foreground provides critical information about classroom activities, the background often includes nonessential information that sometimes negatively impacts the network's performance. An example is shown in Figure 20.4 where the foreground includes the teacher and students sitting at a group table, whereas the background includes less informative details such as the wall, hung clothes, and objects on the shelf. Distinguishing between the background and foreground in videoframes may be necessary for detecting instructional activities in classroom videos which are often crowded with so much peripheral details.

Multi-label Action Dependencies

An asset of the MLAD is the ability to accommodate reliances between activities (Tirupattur et al. 2021). Many instructional activities might occur simultaneously, such as in Figure 20.5 where the teacher is *writing* and *standing* during a *whole-class*

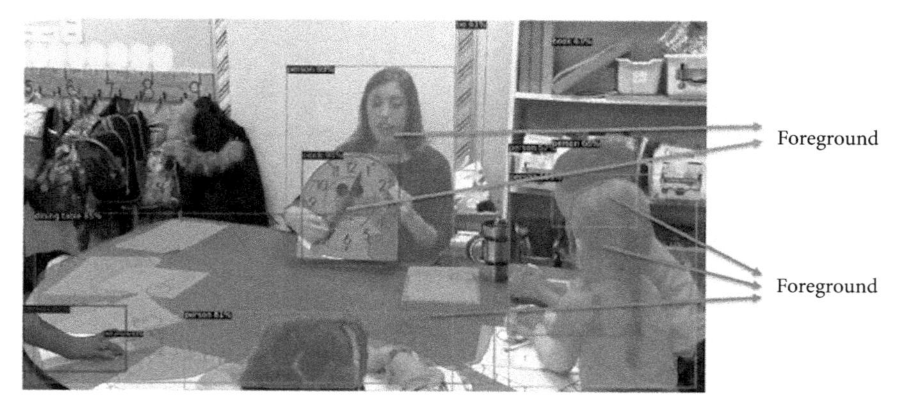

Figure 20.4 Highlighted regions of foreground in a videoframe.

Figure 20.5 Multiple activities co-occurring in a videoframe.

activity part of a lesson. The co-occurrence and dependencies among instructional activities (e.g., *teacher writing* and *standing*) are useful in detecting instructional activities where multiple actions might happen simultaneously (e.g., *whole-class activity*). So, MLAD network aims to find these dependencies among activities effectively.

Long Short-Term Transformer

The salient characteristic of LSTR is the ability to learn sequence-based tasks (Xu et al. 2021). LSTR can maintain temporal information and make decisions based on long-term motion features by finding the long- and short-term correlations among videoframes. These correlations may be useful for recognizing certain instructional

Figure 20.6 Long- and short-term motion features across videoframes.

activities. For example, in Figure 20.6, we show a teacher holding a book, where the short-term correlations are between the frames when the teacher moves the book away from her, and the long-term correlations are between the frames when the teacher moves the book toward her.

Performance Analysis of Neural Networks

We used a standard 80–20 train-test split procedure for the training and validation sets to analyze the performance of the neural networks. There are multiple performance measures currently in use for human activity recognition systems (Beddiar et al. 2020; Santafe, Inza, and Lozano 2015). We used the metrics of accuracy and F_1-score to compare the performance of the neural networks. Accuracy is the percentage of correct predictions relative to the total number of predictions. The F_1-score is one of the most popular metrics to evaluate machine-learning performance (Santafe, Inza, and Lozano 2015). It is the harmonic mean of precision (i.e., positive prediction rate, also sometimes referred to as positive prediction value, is the proportion of videoframes a network labeled with an activity that was actually correct) and recall (i.e., true positive rate or the proportion of all videoframes for a particular activity the network accurately detected). Accuracy and F_1-score report values between 0 and 1 with outputs closer to 1 reflecting better performance. Due to F_1-scores dropping exponentially when the skew ratio is greater than 1 (Jeni et al. 2013), we interpreted the networks performing well when $F_1 \geqslant 0.6$, moderately well when $0.4 \leqslant F_1 < 0.6$, and poor if $F_1 < 0.4$.

Results

Of the three neural networks, BaS-Net performed the best with an overall F_1-score of 0.49 and unweighted average accuracy of 85.6%. Comparing the overall performance of the other two neural networks, however, reveals that they performed somewhat similar to BaS. The overall F_1-scores for MLAD and LTSR were 0.48 and 0.46, respectively. The unweighted average accuracies were 83.1 and 84.1% for MLAD and LSTR, respectively. Looking at the overall performance, each neural network performed moderately well in detecting the instructional activities collectively in classroom videos of elementary instruction. Next, we more closely examine the performance of the neural networks across the instructional activities.

BaS-Net performed the best for most of the instructional activity labels when comparing F_1-scores. It outperformed MLAD and LTSR for ten of the twenty-four instructional activity labels. MLAD was a close second by outperforming BaS-Net and LTSR on seven instructional activity labels and LSTR performed the best on only four instructional activities. The performance of the three neural networks is shown in Figure 20.7. The Appendix lists the accuracy and F_1-scores for each of the instructional activities across the three neural networks. We further explicate the results on the neural networks' performance by instructional activity organized by parent level: activity type, discourse, teacher and student location, teacher supporting, and representing content.

Activity Type

BaS-Net and LSTR are useful neural networks for detecting activity type, which are event actions, in classroom videos. BaS-Net and LSTR performed well for detecting certain activity types but not necessarily for the same activity type. BaS-Net performed well for individual activity and transition with F_1-scores of 0.62 and 0.63, respectively. However, BaS-Net only made slight improvements for detecting individual activity and transition in comparison to the other neural networks. LSTR performed well for whole-class activity and small group activity with F_1-scores of 0.78 and 0.68, respectively. LSTR provided modest improvements for detecting whole-class activity and small group activity over the other neural networks. MLAD performed moderately well for detecting each activity type but did not outperform either BaS-Net or LSTR.

Discourse

MLAD was superior to BaS-Net and LSTR at detecting discourse labels: on task student talking with student and raising hand. BaS-Net and LSTR performed poorly at detecting on task student talking with student and raising hand. In comparison, MLAD performed moderately well in detecting those discourse labels with F_1-scores of 0.55 and 0.57, which were generally two to three times more than the other neural networks.

Teacher and Student Location

For detecting the simple actions of teacher and student location, BaS-Net was the best neural network. For most of the teacher and student location activities, BaS-Net

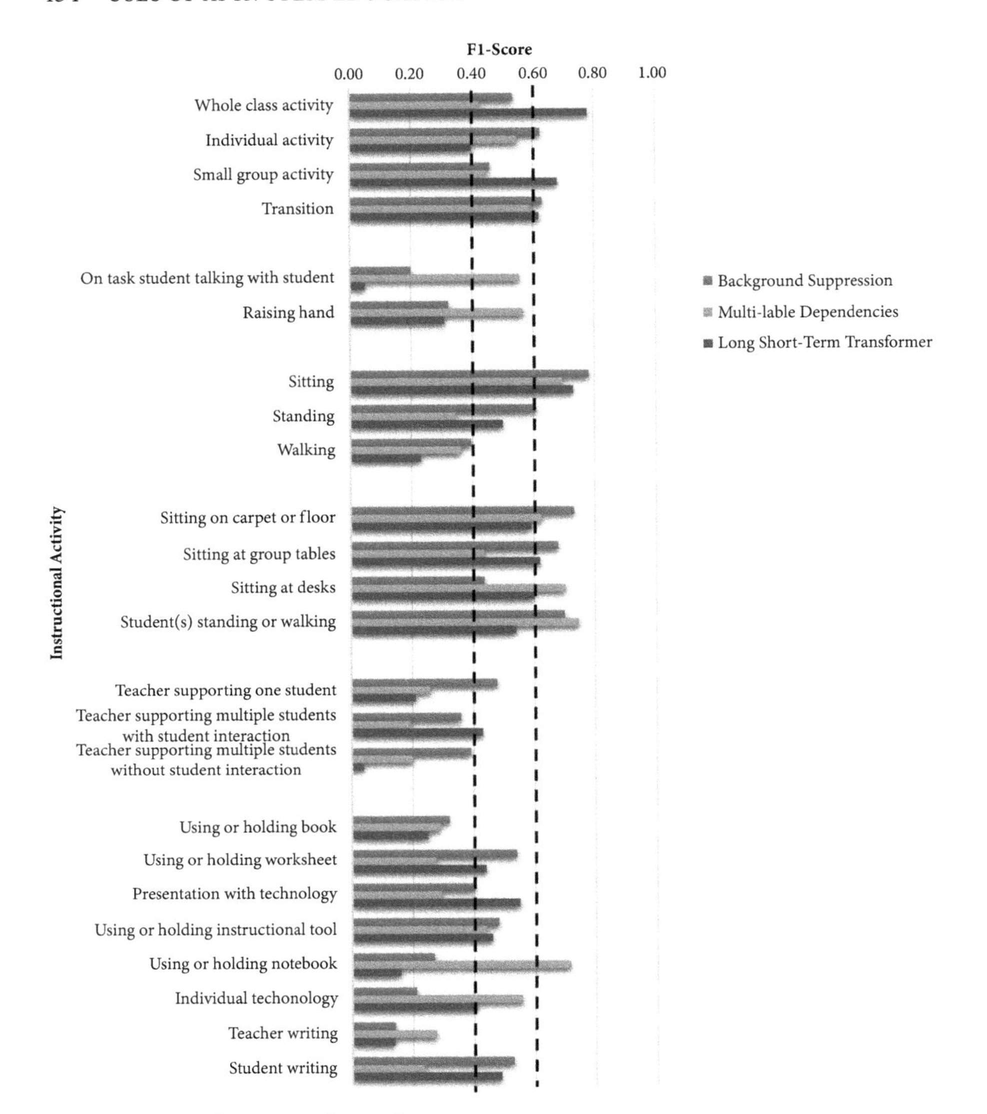

Figure 20.7 Performance of neural networks.

outperformed the other neural networks with higher F_1-scores. All three networks performed well for detecting teacher sitting but poorly for teacher walking. For teacher sitting and teacher walking, BaS-Net performed better than the other neural networks. BaS-Net made only slight gains in performance, however, for detecting teacher sitting and teacher walking over MLAD and LSTR. Only BaS-Net performed well for detecting teacher standing. There were modest gains in performance by BaS-Net over the two other neural networks for teacher standing.

BaS-Net performed well for detecting all student location activities except for sitting at desks. MLAD performed well for detecting all student location activities except for sitting at group tables. LSTR performed well for detecting sitting at group tables and sitting at desks. These were modest gains in performance by BaS-Net, in comparison to either of the two other neural networks, for student sitting on carpet or floor. BaS-Net made only slight gains in performance for detecting student sitting at group tables. In comparison to the two other neural networks, there were modest gains in performance by MLAD in recognizing sitting at desks and only slight gains in performance for recognizing student(s) standing or walking.

Teacher Supporting

The neural networks generally struggled to detect teacher supporting activities, but BaS-Net may be the most promising neural network for detecting these complex group actions. BaS-Net performed poor to moderately well: poor for teacher supporting multiple students with (and without) student interactions and moderate for teacher supporting one student. Even though BaS-Net performed poor to moderately well for these activities, it was mostly superior to MLAD and LSTR with F_1-scores at least double. However, LSTR did outperform BaS-Net in detecting multiple students with student interaction with modest gains in performance.

Representing Content

Overall, BaS-Net only slightly outperforms MLAD and LSTR in detecting the representing content activities, which are at the action complexity level of interactions. All three neural networks performed moderately well for detecting using or holding an instructional tool with BaS-Net slightly outperforming the other neural networks. BaS-Net and LSTR performed moderately well for detecting using or holding worksheet, presentation with technology, and student writing. MLAD and LSTR performed moderately well for detecting individual technology. MLAD performed well for detecting using or holding notebook. All three neural networks performed poorly when detecting using or holding book and teacher writing.

There were modest gains in performance by applying BaS-Net in comparison to the two other neural networks for using or holding worksheet but only slight gains in performance for using or holding book, using or holding instructional tool, and student writing. The performance of MLAD was superior in recognizing using or holding notebook and teacher writing with F_1-scores at least double in comparison to those of BaS-Net and LSTR. There were also modest gains in performance with MLAD in detecting individual technology and with LSTR in detecting presentation with technology.

Discussion and Implications

This study set out with the aim of evaluating and comparing the performance of three neural networks (BaS-Net, MLAD, and LSTR) in detecting instructional activities in classroom videos of elementary mathematics and ELA instruction. These instructional activities were based on some low-inference instructional activities that have implications for assessing instructional quality with classroom observation rubrics (i.e., M-Scan and PLATO) aligned with ambitious instruction. The results indicated that, when examining the average accuracy and overall F_1-scores, all three of the neural networks performed moderately well. When examining the performance by instructional activity, however, we found BaS-Net outperformed MLAD and LSTR on most of the instructional activity labels. In particular, BaS-Net detected with moderate success individual activity, teacher sitting and standing, and students sitting on floor or carpet and sitting at group tables. However, LSTR did outperform BaS-Net when detecting whole-class activity and small group activity and MLAD outperformed BaS-Net when detecting discourse activities (e.g., student raising hand) and teacher writing.

The performance of three neural network models may not seem too surprising given the success of previous research (e.g., Gang et al. 2021; Rafique et al. 2022; Sharma et al. 2021; Sun et al. 2021) in detecting similar instructional activities. For example, Gang et al. (2021) achieved an overall accuracy of 81% using the 3D-BP-TBR neural network on a set of teacher-centric actions (e.g., writing on board, walking around classroom, and operating a model or object). Similarly, Sharma et al. (2021) found an overall accuracy of 72.3% using the I3D-ResNet-50 neural network model for a set of student- and teacher-centric actions (e.g., hand raise, standing, and writing on board). Our evaluation suggests BaS-Net, MLAD, and LSTR would perform similarly to these other neural networks for detecting simple and interaction actions in classrooms (e.g., standing and student writing). However, the instructional activities in these prior studies did not examine more complex actions like group actions and events (e.g., a teacher supporting students during a small group activity). Activities of this complexity are known to be more difficult to detect (Beddiar et al. 2020).

Our results add to the expanding application of computer vision-based human activity recognition technologies for automated classroom observation by illustrating the potential for neural networks to detect activities of higher complexity (i.e., group and event). These complex activities may contribute towards the ratings of instructional quality in research-based classroom observation protocols. For instance, some teachers received lower scores on PLATO for responsiveness to students' ideas when the dominant activity was individual activity (Luoto, Klette, and Blikstad-Balas 2023). Therefore, detecting the activity type (e.g., whole-class activity versus individual seatwork) may be useful for automating the scoring of instructional videos with research-based observation protocols (i.e., M-Scan and PLATO).

Additionally, the results in this chapter establish benchmarks for detecting instructional activities of varying complexity across three neural networks (i.e., BaS-Net, MLAD, and LSTR). As more public datasets become available, others may compare the performance of future neural networks to the neural networks that we have evaluated in this chapter or those of others (e.g., Gang et al. 2021; Sharma et al. 2021) to assess any improvements in detection or computational performance.

Given the performance of BaS-Net to detect our instructional activity labels, we plan to further explore ways to extend BaS-Net for application in classroom-based contexts. One area that we are exploring is incorporating methods to distinguish between individuals and objects within a videoframe. For instance, after suppressing the background, developing techniques to augment the detection of the individuals or objects in the foreground by bounding their location in the frame. These methods could potentially improve the performance.

Challenges for Automated Instructional Activity Recognition

As previously mentioned, there are various methodological challenges to detecting classroom-based activities in videos due to, but not limited to, variation in lighting conditions, movements of the camera, duration of missing segments of video, multiple occlusions, and cluttered visual scenes. Challenges such as these are often highlighted in video-based human activity recognition research (e.g., Beddiar et al. 2020) and by researchers developing detection methods for classroom videos (e.g., Rafique et al. 2022; Sharma et al. 2021; Sun et al. 2021). Rather than restate these common challenges from human activity recognition research, we highlight two important methodological issues from video studies research in the social sciences that are typically unstated in research on human activity recognition in classroom videos. These methodological issues affect the potential for automating the assessment of instructional quality in classroom videos.

First, most videos of classroom instruction are unable to capture the entire classroom scene, although some researchers are exploring the uses and implications of 360-degree video for classroom research (e.g., Gold and Windscheid 2020; Kosko et al. 2021; Walshe and Driver 2019). As such, the perspective of a typical, single-camera classroom video is not completely phenomenologically neutral (Erickson 2006). For instance, placing the camera in the corner of the classroom and focusing on the teacher in center of frame places the teacher's instructional activities as central. Some classroom-based activity recognition studies are explicit about the perspective of the camera used to capture the video data for training neural networks (e.g., Rafique et al. 2022; Sun et al. 2021) but others, such as EduNet, do not explicitly discuss the issue of the perspective of the camera (e.g., Gang et al. 2021; Sharma et al. 2021). We believe the perspective of the camera is especially important if automated video analysis techniques will be used to detect and evaluate features of instruction. Therefore, we did not use EduNet dataset to compare the performance of our models as the developers were not explicit in how they took the perspective of the camera into the development of the dataset. Furthermore, there are still open questions as to whether the perspective of the camera may affect classroom observation measurements. The evaluation of the instruction by the neural network may reflect the perspective of the camera rather than features of instruction occurring in the classroom. We recommend that future research investigate the implications of the camera perspective in classroom-based recognition systems, especially if these systems will be used for evaluative purposes. In the meantime, researchers should develop and document standard procedures for recording or selecting classroom videos for human activity recognition applications for education research.

Second, if researchers are interested in applying neural networks to automate the measuring of the instructional quality across teachers and contexts, then they will need to make some considerations regarding the specifications on the data as stated in the observation protocols. One consideration is whether there is a standardized protocol for collecting the video data. Some video studies analyzing instructional quality are explicit about standardized protocols for video data (e.g., Stigler et al. 1999). If standard protocols are not available, researchers will need to set clear guidelines for the quality of videos that are acceptable and specify standardized methods for video data collection so as not to potentially bias ratings of instructional quality by the neural networks. Relatedly, the complexity of developing automated methods for scoring classroom videos increases if researchers use multimodal data with the neural networks to access instructional quality. For instance, the M-Scan protocol specifies using video as the only data source for scoring (Walkowiak et al. 2014). Whether having access to video and lesson transcripts or just video impacts human raters' assessments of instructional quality using M-Scan is an open question. Therefore, adding labeled text data from the lesson transcripts for training the neural network may impact the outcome of automated ratings when compared to human raters of M-Scan. As such, researchers should consider the specifications for the data as outlined in observation protocols and how those specifications may interact with automation efforts.

Opportunities for Automated Instructional Activity Recognition

Despite the challenges for automating instructional activity recognition in classroom videos, there are also some opportunities for education research and practice. For research, this study offers some perspective on neural networks' ability to detect some low-inference instructional activities. We now turn to opportunities for research more broadly. First, neural networks may support video studies in education by efficiently and consistently cataloguing or indexing classroom videos based on the instructional activities featured in videos. This cataloguing would help researchers to quickly identify moments in instruction for further analysis. Second, it is tedious to detect low-inference instructional activities, such as those in this study, without students and the teacher wearing sensors, but these activities may be useful for researchers in learning analytics. Neural networks could learn and analyze data on multiple activities as they co-occur and extend the field's understanding of how the learning environment is shaping student learning. Third, neural networks may also assist in ensuring rater quality through certification and periodic calibration. For instance, neural networks could identify potential raters that are beginning to drift and provide just-in-time interventions.

Another area of opportunity for automating instructional activity recognition is teacher practice. Quality feedback for instructional improvement require extensive resources such as staff for observation training and time to complete the observation for one teacher. Scaling quality feedback for a large group of teachers is even more challenging. Neural networks could provide timely lesson-level insights to teachers and instructional coaches for planning future instruction. Demszky et al. (2021) found that providing consistent feedback to teachers with an application with AI technologies increased teachers' uptake of students' ideas by 24%. Similarly, Jacobs et al. (2022) piloted the TalkMoves application to provide teachers with automated feedback on their use of talk moves (Chapin, O'Connor, and Anderson 2009). Teachers thought the application provided valuable feedback of their instruction and there was an overall increase in teachers' use of talk moves over the course of their use of the automated feedback. Some of the instructional activity labels from this study may also be valuable for teachers and instructional coaches as automated feedback. For instance, an interactive automated dashboard could provide teachers with quantifiable and non-evaluative feedback on the duration of activity types (i.e., whole group, small group, independent work, and transition) of a lesson. The application of neural networks to give automated feedback to teachers for growing their instructional practice is promising.

Beyond the scope of this chapter, our ultimate goal is to develop and evaluate automated multimodal analysis for classroom videos aligned with research-based observation protocols. Future directions for our work include incorporating features of classroom discourse (based on audio transcripts from the videorecorded lessons) aligned with ambitious instruction. Some researchers have successfully used audio features and natural language processing technologies to detect or evaluate features of classroom discourse (e.g., Chen, Clare, and Resnick 2015; Dale et al. 2022; Jacobs et al. 2022; Kelly et al. 2018; Wang et al. 2014). For example, Kelly et al. (2018) reported high correlations between human raters and computer ratings of the frequency of authentic questions asked by secondary ELA teachers at the classroom level. Our project is in the early stages of conducting experiments on detecting features of classroom discourse in elementary mathematics and ELA instruction. It is still an open question whether multimodal methods for automated analysis of classroom videos aligned with research-based observation protocols M-Scan and PLATO will produce comparable results to those of human raters. Given that researchers have been able to use multimodal machine learning to detect features of instruction consistent with human raters using the COPUS observation protocol (Schlotterbeck et al. 2021), we are optimistic that similar technologies may be adapted for evaluating features of ambitious instruction in elementary classroom videos.

Conclusion

This study demonstrates the potential of neural networks to detect teacher- and student-centric instructional activities at multiple levels of complexity in classroom videos of elementary mathematics and ELA instruction. Of the three neural networks (BaS-Net, MLAD, and LSTR) examined, BaS-Net performed the best on almost half of the instructional activity labels. BaS-Net has potential for accurately detecting instructional activities at scale and may help human raters in the task of evaluating instruction in the future. We expect noticeable improvements in the performance of BaS-Net with more annotated video data for training and making further modifications to BaS-Net specifically for elementary classroom videos.

Acknowledgments

This material is based upon work supported by the Robertson Foundation under Grant 9909875 and the National Science Foundation under Grant 2000487. Any opinions, findings, and conclusions or recommendations expressed in this material are those of the author(s) and do not necessarily reflect the views of the funders.

References

Ahuja, K., Kim, D., Xhakaj, F., Varga, V., Xie, A., Zhang, S., Townsend, J. E., Harrison, C., Ogan, A., and Agarwal, Y. 2019. "EduSense: Practical Classroom Sensing at Scale." Proceedings of the ACM on Interactive, Mobile, Wearable and Ubiquitous Technologies 3, no. 3: 1–26. https://doi.org/10.1145/3351229

Alavi, A. H., Ouyang, F., Jiao, P., and McLaren, B. M. 2022. *Artificial Intelligence in STEM Education: The Paradigmatic Shifts in Research, Education, and Technology*, 1st ed. Boca Raton, FL: CRC Press. https://doi.org/10.1201/9781003181187

Beddiar, D. R., Nini, B., Sabokrou, M., and Hadid, A. 2020. "Vision-Based Human Activity Recognition: A Survey." *Multimedia Tools and Applications* 79, no. 41: 30509–55. https://doi.org/10.1007/s11042-020-09004-3

Berry, R. Q., Rimm-Kaufman, S. E., Ottmar, E. M., Walkowiak, T. A., Merritt, E. G., and Pinter, H. H. 2013. *The Mathematics Scan (M-Scan): A Measure of Standards-Based Mathematics Teaching Practices.* University of Virginia.

Brophy, J. E., ed. 2004. *Using Video in Teacher Education*, 1st ed. Amsterdam: Elsevier/JAI.

Carlisle, J. F., Kelcey, B., Rowan, B., and Phelps, G. 2011. "Teachers' Knowledge about Early Reading: Effects on Students' Gains in Reading Achievement." *Journal of Research on Educational Effectiveness* 4, no. 4: 289–321. https://doi.org/10.1080/19345747.2010.539297

Celik, I., Dindar, M., Muukkonen, H., and Järvelä, S. 2022. "The Promises and Challenges of Artificial Intelligence for Teachers: A Systematic Review of Research." *TechTrends* 66, no. 4: 616–30. https://doi.org/10.1007/s11528-022-00715-y

Chapin, S. H., O'Connor, M. C., and Anderson, N. C. 2009. *Classroom Discussions: Using Math Talk to Help Students Learn*, 2nd ed. Math Solutions.

Chen, G., Clarke, S. N., and Resnick, L. B. 2015. "Classroom Discourse Analyzer (CDA): A Discourse Analytic Tool for Teachers." *Technology, Instruction, Cognition and Learning* 10, no. 2: 85–105.

Chen, L., Chen, P., and Lin, Z. 2020. "Artificial Intelligence in Education: A Review." *IEEE Access* 8: 75264–78. https://doi.org/10.1109/ACCESS.2020.2988510

Chen, X., Xie, H., and Hwang, G.-J. 2020. "A Multi-perspective Study on Artificial Intelligence in Education: Grants, Conferences, Journals, Software Tools, Institutions, and Researchers." Computers and Education: Artificial Intelligence 1: 100005. https://doi.org/10.1016/j.caeai.2020.100005

Cohen, J. 2015. "Challenges in Identifying High-Leverage Practices." *Teachers College Record* 117, no. 7: 1–41. https://doi.org/10.1177/016146811511700702

Dale, M. E., Godley, A. J., Capello, S. A., Donnelly, P. J., D'Mello, S. K., and Kelly, S. P. 2022. "Toward the Automated Analysis of Teacher Talk in Secondary ELA Classrooms." *Teaching and Teacher Education* 110: 103584. https://doi.org/10.1016/j.tate.2021.103584

de Freitas, E. 2016. "The Moving Image in Education Research: Reassembling the Body in Classroom Video Data." *International Journal of Qualitative Studies in Education* 29, no. 4: 553–72. https://doi.org/10.1080/09518398.2015.1077402

de Freitas, E., Lerman, S., and Parks, A. N. 2017. "Qualitative Methods." In *Compendium for Research in Mathematics Education*, edited by J. Cai, 159–82. National Council of Teachers of Mathematics.

Demszky, D., Jing, L., Hill, H. C., Jurafsky, D., and Piech, C. 2021. *Can Automated Feedback Improve Teachers' Uptake of Student Ideas? Evidence From a Randomized Controlled Trial In a Large-Scale Online Course.* Annenberg Institute at Brown University. https://www.edworkingpapers.com/ai21-483

ELAN [computer software]. 2021. Nijmegen: Max Planck Institute for Psycholinguistics, The Language Archive. Retrieved from https://archive.mpi.nl/tla/elan

Erickson, F. 2006. "Definition and Analysis of Data from Videotape: Some Research Procedures and Their Rationales." In *Handbook of Complementary Methods in Education Research*, edited by J. L. Green, G. Camilli, and P. B. Elmore, 177–191. Mahwah, NJ: Lawrence Erlbaum Associates.

Franke, M. L., Kazemi, E., and Battey, D. 2007. "Mathematics Teaching and Classroom Practice." In *Second Handbook of Research on Mathematics Teaching and Learning*, edited by F. K. Lester, 225–56. Charlotte, NC: Information Age Publishing.

Gang, Z., Wenjuan, Z., Biling, H., Jie, C., Hui, H., and Qing, X. 2021. "A Simple Teacher Behavior Recognition Method for Massive Teaching Videos Based on Teacher Set." *Applied Intelligence* 51, no. 12: 8828–49. https://doi.org/10.1007/s10489-021-02329-y

Gaudin, C., and Chaliès, S. 2015. "Video Viewing in Teacher Education and Professional Development: A Literature Review." *Educational Research Review* 16: 41–67. https://doi.org/10.1016/j.edurev.2015.06.001

Giuliani, M., Mirnig, N., Stollnberger, G., Stadler, S., Buchner, R., and Tscheligi, M. 2015. "Systematic Analysis of Video Data from Different Human–Robot Interaction Studies: A Categorization of Social Signals during Error Situations." *Frontiers in Psychology* 6. https://www.frontiersin.org/articles/10.3389/fpsyg.2015.00931

Gold, B., and Windscheid, J. 2020. "Observing 360-Degree Classroom Videos—Effects of Video Type on Presence, Emotions, Workload, Classroom Observations, and Ratings of Teaching Quality." *Computers & Education* 156: 103960. https://doi.org/10.1016/j.compedu.2020.103960

Grossman, P., Cohen, J., Ronfeldt, M., and Brown, L. 2014. "The Test Matters: The Relationship between Classroom Observation Scores and Teacher Value Added on Multiple Types of Assessment." *Educational Researcher* 43, no. 6: 293–303. https://doi.org/10.3102/0013189X14544542

Grossman, P., Compton, C., Igra, D., Ronfeldt, M., Shahan, E., and Williamson, P. 2009. "Teaching Practice: A Cross-professional Perspective." *Teachers College Record* 111, no. 9: 2055–100.

Grossman, P., Loeb, S., Cohen, J., and Wyckoff, J. 2013. "Measure for Measure: The Relationship between Measures of Instructional Practice in Middle School English Language Arts and Teachers' Value-Added Scores." *American Journal of Education* 119, no. 3: 445–70. https://doi.org/10.1086/669901

Gupta, N., Gupta, S. K., Pathak, R. K., Jain, V., Rashidi, P., and Suri, J. S. 2022. "Human Activity Recognition in Artificial Intelligence Framework: A Narrative Review." *Artificial Intelligence Review* 55, no. 6: 4755–808. https://doi.org/10.1007/s10462-021-10116-x

Heilbron, F. C., Escorcia, V., Ghanem, B., and Niebles, J. C. 2015. "ActivityNet: A Large-Scale Video Benchmark for Human Activity Understanding." In *2015 IEEE Conference on Computer Vision and Pattern Recognition (CVPR)*, 961–70. https://doi.org/10.1109/CVPR.2015.7298698

Hiebert, J., Gallimore, R., Garnier, H., Givvin, K. B., Hollingsworth, H., Jacobs, J., Chui, A. M.-Y., et al. 2003. *Teaching Mathematics in Seven Countries: Results from the TIMSS 1999 Video Study.* National Center for Education Statistics.

Hiebert, J., and Grouws, D. A. 2007. "The Effects of Classroom Mathematics Teaching on Students' Learning." In *Second Handbook of Research on Mathematics Teaching and Learning*, edited by F. K. Lester, Jr., 371–404. Information Age Publishing.

Hwang, G.-J., and Tu, Y.-F. 2021. "Roles and Research Trends of Artificial Intelligence in Mathematics Education: A Bibliometric Mapping Analysis and Systematic Review." *Mathematics* 9, 6: Article 6. https://doi.org/10.3390/math9060584

Idrees, H., Zamir, A. R., Jiang, Y.-G., Gorban, A., Laptev, I., Sukthankar, R., and Shah, M. 2017. "The THUMOS Challenge on Action Recognition for Videos 'in the Wild.'" *Computer Vision and Image Understanding* 155: 1–23. https://doi.org/10.1016/j.cviu.2016.10.018

Jacobs, J. K., Scornavacco, K., Harty, C., Suresh, A., Lai, V., and Sumner, T. 2022. "Promoting Rich Discussions in Mathematics Classrooms: Using Personalized, Automated Feedback to Support Reflection and Instructional Change." *Teaching and Teacher Education* 112: 103631. https://doi.org/10.1016/j.tate.2022.103631

Janík, T., and Seidel, T., eds. 2009. *The Power of Video Studies in Investigating Teaching and Learning in the Classroom.* Münster, Germany: Waxmann.

Jeni, L. A., Cohn, J. F., and De La Torre, F. 2013. "Facing Imbalanced Data—Recommendations for the Use of Performance Metrics." In 2013 Humaine Association Conference on Affective Computing and Intelligent Interaction, 245–51. https://doi.org/10.1109/ACII.2013.47

Kane, T. J., and Staiger, D. O. 2012. "Gathering Feedback for Teaching: Combining High-Quality Observations with Student Surveys and Achievement Gains." Research Paper. MET Project. Bill and Melinda Gates Foundation.

Kelly, S., Bringe, R., Aucejo, E., and Cooley Fruehwirth, J. 2020. "Using Global Observation Protocols to Inform Research on Teaching Effectiveness and School Improvement: Strengths and Emerging Limitations." *Education Policy Analysis Archives* 28: 62. https://doi.org/10.14507/epaa.28.5012

Kelly, S., Olney, A. M., Donnelly, P., Nystrand, M., and D'Mello, S. K. 2018. "Automatically Measuring Question Authenticity in Real-World Classrooms." *Educational Researcher* 47, no. 7: 451–64. https://doi.org/10.3102/0013189X18785613

Klette, K., Blikstad-Balas, M., and Roe, A. 2017. "Linking Instruction and Student Achievement: A Research Design for a New Generation of Classroom Studies." *Acta Didactica Norge* 11, no. 3: Article 3. https://doi.org/10.5617/adno.4729

Kong, A. P.-H., Law, S.-P., Kwan, C. C.-Y., Lai, C., and Lam, V. 2015. "A Coding System with Independent Annotations of Gesture Forms and Functions during Verbal Communication: Development of a Database of Speech and Gesture (DoSaGE)." *Journal of Nonverbal Behavior* 39, no. 1: 93–111. https://doi.org/10.1007/s10919-014-0200-6

Kosko, K., Yang, Y., Austin, C., Guan, Q., Gandolfi, E., and Gu, Z. 2021. "Examining Preservice Teachers' Professional Noticing of Students' Mathematics through 360 Video and Machine Learning." In *Proceedings of the Forty-third Annual Meeting of the North American Chapter of the International Group of the Psychology of Mathematics Education*, edited by D. Olanoff, K. Johnson, and S. M. Spitzer, 1649–58.

Lee, P., Uh, Y., and Byun, H. 2020. "Background Suppression Network for Weakly-Supervised Temporal Action Localization." *Proceedings of the AAAI Conference on Artificial Intelligence* 34, no. 7: Article 07. https://doi.org/10.1609/aaai.v34i07.6793

Luoto, J., Klette, K., and Blikstad-Balas, M. 2023. "Possible Biases in Observation Systems When Applied across Contexts: Conceptualizing, Operationalizing, and Sequencing Instructional Quality." *Educational Assessment, Evaluation and Accountability* 35, no. 1: 105–28. https://doi.org/10.1007/s11092-022-09394-y

National Council of Teachers of Mathematics (Ed.). 2014. *Principles to Actions: Ensuring Mathematical Success for All.* National Council of Teachers of Mathematics.

National Mathematics Advisory Panel. 2008. *Foundation for Success: The Final Report of the National Mathematics Advisory Panel.* US Department of Education.

Newmann, F. M., and Associates. 1996. *Authentic Achievement: Restructuring Schools for Intellectual Quality.* Hoboken, NJ: Jossey-Bass.

Newmann, F. M., Bryk, A. S., and Nagaoka, J. K. 2001. Authentic Intellectual Work and Standardized Tests: Conflict or Coexistence? Improving Chicago's Schools. https://eric.ed.gov/?id=ED470299

Pons, A. 2018. "What Does Teaching Look Like? A New Video Study." OECD Education and Skills Today. http://oecdedutoday.com/what-does-teaching-look-like-a-new-video-study/

Rafique, M. A., Khaskheli, F., Hassan, M. T., Naseer, S., and Jeon, M. 2022. "Employing Automatic Content Recognition for Teaching Methodology Analysis in Classroom Videos." *PLOS ONE* 17, no. 2: e0263448. https://doi.org/10.1371/journal.pone.0263448

Roll, I., and Wylie, R. 2016. "Evolution and Revolution in Artificial Intelligence in Education." *International Journal of Artificial Intelligence in Education* 26, no. 2: 582–99. https://doi.org/10.1007/s40593-016-0110-3

Roschelle, J., Lester, J., and Fusco, J., eds. 2020. *AI and the Future of Learning: Expert Panel Report*. Digital Promise. https://doi.org/10.51388/20.500.12265/106

Santafe, G., Inza, I., and Lozano, J. A. 2015. "Dealing with the Evaluation of Supervised Classification Algorithms." *Artificial Intelligence Review* 44, no. 4: 467–508. https://doi.org/10.1007/s10462-015-9433-y

Schlotterbeck, D., Uribe, P., Jiménez, A., Araya, R., van der Molen Moris, J., and Caballero, D. 2021. "TARTA: Teacher Activity Recognizer from Transcriptions and Audio." In *Artificial Intelligence in Education*, edited by I. Roll, D. McNamara, S. Sosnovsky, R. Luckin, and V. Dimitrova, 369–80. Cham, Switzerland: Springer International. https://doi.org/10.1007/978-3-030-78292-4_30

Sharma, V., Gupta, M., Kumar, A., and Mishra, D. 2021. "EduNet: A New Video Dataset for Understanding Human Activity in the Classroom Environment." *Sensors* 21, no. 17: 5699. https://doi.org/10.3390/s21175699

Sherin, M. G., and van Es, E. A. 2008. "Effects of Video Club Participation on Teachers' Professional Vision." *Journal of Teacher Education* 60, no. 1: 20–37. https://doi.org/10.1177/0022487108328155

Stigler, J. W., Gonzales, P., Kawanaka, T., Knoll, S., and Serrano, A. 1999. *The TIMSS Videotape Classroom Study: Methods and Findings from an Exploratory Research Project on Eighth-Grade Mathematics Instruction in Germany, Japan, and the United States*. National Center for Education Statistics.

Sun, B., Wu, Y., Zhao, K., He, J., Yu, L., Yan, H., and Luo, A. 2021. "Student Class Behavior Dataset: A Video Dataset for Recognizing, Detecting, and Captioning Students' Behaviors in Classroom Scenes." *Neural Computing and Applications* 33, no. 14: 8335–54. https://doi.org/10.1007/s00521-020-05587-y

Thompson, J., Windschitl, M., and Braaten, M. 2013. "Developing a Theory of Ambitious Early-Career Teacher Practice." *American Educational Research Journal* 50, no. 3: 574–615. https://doi.org/10.3102/0002831213476334

Tirupattur, P., Duarte, K., Rawat, Y. S., and Shah, M. 2021. "Modeling Multi-label Action Dependencies for Temporal Action Localization." In *2021 IEEE/CVF Conference on Computer Vision and Pattern Recognition* (CVPR), 1460–1470. https://doi.org/10.1109/CVPR46437.2021.00151

van Es, E. A., Cashen, M., Barnhart, T., and Auger, A. 2017. "Learning to Notice Mathematics Instruction: Using Video to Develop Preservice Teachers' Vision of Ambitious Pedagogy." *Cognition and Instruction* 35, no. 3: 165–87. https://doi.org/10.1080/07370008.2017.1317125

Walkowiak, T. A., Berry, R. Q., Meyer, J. P., Rimm-Kaufman, S. E., and Ottmar, E. R. 2014. "Introducing an Observational Measure of Standards-Based Mathematics Teaching Practices: Evidence of Validity and Score Reliability." *Educational Studies in Mathematics* 85, no. 1: 109–28. https://doi.org/10.1007/s10649-013-9499-x

Walkowiak, T. A., Berry, R. Q., Pinter, H. H., and Jacobson, E. D. 2018. "Utilizing the M-Scan to Measure Standards-Based Mathematics Teaching Practices: Affordances and Limitations." *ZDM* 50, no. 3: 461–74. https://doi.org/10.1007/s11858-018-0931-7

Walshe, N., and Driver, P. 2019. "Developing Reflective Trainee Teacher Practice with 360-Degree Video." *Teaching and Teacher Education* 78: 97–105. https://doi.org/10.1016/j.tate.2018.11.009

Wang, Z., Pan, X., Miller, K. F., and Cortina, K. S. 2014. "Automatic Classification of Activities in Classroom Discourse." *Computers & Education* 78: 115–23. https://doi.org/10.1016/j.compedu.2014.05.010

Wittenburg, P., Brugman, H., Russel, A., Klassmann, A., and Sloetjes, H. 2006. "ELAN: A Professional Framework for Multimodality Research." *Proceedings of the Fifth International Conference on Language Resources and Evaluation*. LREC 2006, Genoa, Italy. http://www.lrec-conf.org/proceedings/lrec2006/pdf/153_pdf.pdf

Xu, M., Xiong, Y., Chen, H., Li, X., Xia, W., Tu, Z., and Soatto, S. 2021. "Long Short-Term Transformer for Online Action Detection." *Advances in Neural Information Processing Systems* 34: 1086–99.

Xu, W., and Ouyang, F. 2022. "The Application of AI Technologies in STEM Education: A Systematic Review from 2011 to 2021." *International Journal of STEM Education* 9, no. 1: 59. https://doi.org/10.1186/s40594-022-00377-5

Yang, Q., and Wu, X. 2006. "Challenging Problems in Data Mining Research." *International Journal of Information Technology and Decision Making* 5, no. 4: 597–604. https://doi.org/10.1142/S0219622006002258

Youngs, P., Elreda, L. M., Anagnostopoulos, D., Cohen, J., Drake, C., and Konstantopoulos, S. 2022. "The Development of Ambitious Instruction: How Beginning Elementary Teachers' Preparation Experiences Are Associated with Their Mathematics and English Language Arts Instructional Practices." *Teaching and Teacher Education* 110: 103576. https://doi.org/10.1016/j.tate.2021.103576

Youngs, P., Foster, J. K., van Aswegen, R., Singh, S., Watson, G.S., and Acton, S.T. (under review). "Automated Classification of Elementary Instructional Activities: Analyzing Consistency of Human Annotations."

Appendix

Occurrences and Duration of Each Instructional Activity across Classroom Video Lessons and Evaluation Metrics

Instructional activity	BaS		MLAD		LSTR		Total		Action
	Accuracy (%)	F_1-score	Accuracy (%)	F_1-score	Accuracy (%)	F_1-score	Lessons	Duration	
Activity type									
Whole-class activity	80.5	0.54	75.2	0.43	96.6	**0.78**	48	18:28:24	Event
Individual activity	83.6	**0.62**	81.0	0.55	80.0	0.40	30	6:50:21	Event
Small group activity	88.9	0.46	70.5	0.45	91.1	**0.68**	38	16:41:53	Event
Transition	78.6	**0.63**	78.0	0.59	79.4	0.62	47	3:18:38	Event
Discourse									
On task student talking with student	93.3	0.20	95.2	**0.55**	84.8	0.05	28	1:59:05	Group
Student raising hand	89.0	0.32	92.4	**0.57**	89.0	0.31	49	3:58:34	Simple
Teacher location									
Sitting	75.8	**0.78**	71.7	0.69	72.6	0.73	49	21:22:22	Simple
Standing	86.2	**0.61**	83.5	0.34	84.2	0.50	50	13:45:14	Simple
Walking	93.5	**0.40**	93.4	0.36	92.9	0.23	50	3:04:38	Simple
Student location									
Sitting on carpet or floor	77.0	**0.73**	76.1	0.62	75.9	0.59	39	14:19:27	Simple
Sitting at group tables	86.0	**0.68**	82.2	0.44	85.5	0.62	38	18:45:50	Simple
Sitting at desks	86.4	0.44	89.9	**0.70**	88.8	0.60	30	12:02:11	Simple
Student(s) standing or walking	82.9	0.70	83.3	**0.75**	82.9	0.54	50	16:26:44	Simple

Continued

Continued

Instructional activity	BaS		MLAD		LSTR		Total		Action
	Accuracy (%)	F_1-score	Accuracy (%)	F_1-score	Accuracy (%)	F_1-score	Lessons	Duration	
Teacher supporting									
One student	88.5	**0.48**	85.6	0.26	85.5	0.21	43	3:54:47	Group
Multiple students with student interaction	91.9	0.36	89.8	0.19	92.0	**0.43**	40	10:38:04	Group
Multiple students without student interaction	86.6	**0.39**	82.4	0.20	79.8	0.04	22	4:17:45	Group
Representing content									
Using or holding book	80.3	**0.32**	78.5	0.29	74.4	0.25	31	8:47:23	Interaction
Using or holding worksheet	80.3	**0.54**	76.3	0.28	78.8	0.44	42	15:50:28	Interaction
Presentation with technology	90.9	0.40	83.4	0.29	92.5	**0.55**	33	11:27:59	Interaction
Using or holding instructional tool	79.9	**0.48**	70.7	0.44	78.0	0.46	40	10:38:04	Interaction
Using or holding notebook	87.9	0.27	92.0	**0.72**	73.2	0.16	21	3:43:58	Interaction
Individual technology	91.6	0.21	94.8	**0.56**	92.5	0.41	29	4:15:15	Interaction
Teacher writing	90.1	0.14	92.5	**0.28**	91.8	0.14	42	1:55:08	Interaction
Student writing	84.2	**0.53**	75.9	0.24	77.3	0.49	49	9:46:07	Interaction

PART IV
ETHICS, FAIRNESS, AND INCLUSIVENESS OF AI-BASED STEM EDUCATION

21

AI for Students with Learning Disabilities

A Systematic Review

Sahrish Panjwani-Charania and Xiaoming Zhai

Introduction

The number of individuals with learning disabilities worldwide has reached 79.2 million and is increasing steadily (UNICEF 2021). Learning disability impacts children's listening, thinking, speaking, scientific reasoning, reading, writing, spelling, or math and has created substantial needs for special education. In the United States, more than 15% of public school students (approximately 2.3 million) receive special education services due to learning disabilities; in countries with lower socioeconomic developments, this need is even more substantial due to the limited resources available (National Center for Education Statistics 2022). Challenges with reading, writing, or math reasoning caused this group of students to receive fewer opportunities to succeed in learning than their peers, as evidenced by their consistently lower scores on reading, science, math, and other subjects (Asghar et al. 2017).

Learning disabilities impact students in a wide range of academic skills but can also impact their emotions and social abilities (Ouherrou et al. 2019). Research has shown that students with learning disabilities (SWLDs) experience more negative emotions, such as depression and loneliness, than their counterparts without learning disabilities. Thus, supporting SWLDs in overcoming their academic needs will also support their social and emotional development. Additionally, the impact of learning disabilities on students is particularly profound in STEM areas. This is because learning in these disciplines demands students' multimodal cognitive processing capacity, including acquiring, retaining, and recalling information presented in class (Asghar et al. 2017). While teachers support SWLDs in the classroom, it can be challenging to meet the needs of every single SWLD in their classrooms, as a learning disability manifests itself in unique ways for each student. Thus, teachers need advanced tools, such as artificial intelligence (AI) applications, to help them identify students' unique needs and strategies to meet them. Furthermore, the importance of supporting SWLDs cannot be stressed more as their academic failures also impact their emotional status, and using AI to support them academically can help reduce the likelihood of these students being depressed or lonely.

AI has been used to support SWLDs for many years for diagnosis and intervention purposes (Drigas and Ioannidou 2013). Drigas and Ioannidou (2013) report that AI

Sahrish Panjwani-Charania and Xiaoming Zhai, *AI for Students with Learning Disabilities*. In: *Uses of Artificial Intelligence in STEM Education*. Edited by: Xiaoming Zhai and Joseph Krajcik, Oxford University Press.
DOI: 10.1093/oso/9780198882077.003.0021

could be used to diagnose or screen for dyslexia and also for symptoms of disabilities such as lower attention levels. Drigas and Ioannidou (2012) suggest that AI has the potential to automate the scoring of essays, identify SWLDs' reading and writing difficulties, create psychological profiles for SWLDs, and estimate their spelling difficulties. However, these studies primarily focus on screening and diagnosis of learning disability (Rauschenberger et al. 2019; Rello et al. 2018; Zvoncak et al. 2019). While diagnosis and screening are critical, they are insufficient for teachers to support SWLDs and provide customized guidelines for SWLD learning. There is potential to develop AI learning interventions for SWLDs (Drigas and Ioannidou 2012, 2013). In the literature, a few applications, such as intelligent tutoring systems, could provide speech therapy, personalized feedback, and social skills development (Drigas and Ioannidou 2012, 2013). Looking more in-depth into existing AI applications for SWLDs and uncovering what AI applications are used and how those AI technologies have been integrated to support SWLDs in terms of learning and intervention is critical to fill the existing gaps. The focus of this study thus is on the "use of AI" instead of AI itself, which is of critical importance (Zhai and Nehm 2023).

The purpose of this study was to systematically examine the literature and promote an understanding of how AI has been used to support SWLDs, apart from it being used only for screening or diagnostic purposes. Specifically, this study identified ways teachers or students could use AI to provide individualized support for students who have already been identified as having a learning disability. This study answered the following research questions:

1. What AI applications have been developed in the past fifteen years to support students with learning disabilities?
2. How have these AI technologies been integrated into supporting students with learning disabilities in the classroom?

Students with Learning Disabilities

Learning disabilities, also known as neurodevelopmental disorders, are due to genetic or neurobiological factors that alter brain functions; thus, learning disabilities do not include any learning problems that may be due to visual, hearing, emotional, or motor disabilities, and it does not include any learning problems that may be due to environmental, cultural, or economic disadvantages (Learning Disabilities Association of America n.d.; US Department of Education 2007). The Individuals with Disabilities Education Act, a crucial piece of legislation in the United States, provides a specific definition for learning disability:

> a disorder in one or more of the basic psychological processes involved in understanding or in using language, spoken or written, that may manifest itself in the imperfect ability to listen, think, speak, read, write, spell, or to do mathematical calculations, including conditions such as perceptual disabilities, brain injury, minimal brain dysfunction, dyslexia, and developmental aphasia. (US Department of Education 2007, para. 10)

Learning disabilities involve processing problems that interfere with basic learning skills such as reading, writing, and math and other skills such as organization, scientific reasoning, attention, and long or short-term memory (Learning Disabilities Association of America n.d.). Learning disabilities impacting different areas of learning have also been categorized based on domains, including dyslexia (i.e., affects reading and related language-based processing skills), dysgraphia (i.e., affects handwriting ability and fine motor skills), dyscalculia (i.e., affects the ability to understand numbers and learn math facts), and nonverbal learning disabilities (i.e., affects the interpretation of nonverbal cues) (Learning Disabilities Association of America n.d.). A learning disability can be highly associated with students' reading, writing, or math performance. Additionally, students may be impacted socially and emotionally by having lower self-esteem, behavior challenges, or social difficulties due to their academic struggles. Supporting SWLDs in managing and coping with their academic challenges can help them achieve academically and improve their social and emotional growth. Büttner and Hasselhorn (2011) found that external factors cannot explain these learning disability-related performances. In addition, researchers found that learning disabilities can result from other types of disorders. For example, autism spectrum disorder (ASD), attention deficit disorder (ADD), and attention deficit hyperactivity disorder (ADHD) are not included in the learning disabilities category. However, students with these disabilities can also have a learning disability, thus falling into both categories.

There is a clear impact on academic performance for SWLDs, which is not explainable by external factors such as a physical disability or lack of adequate instruction. This implies that SWLDs neither need a physical accommodation nor can their academic struggles be blamed on inadequate instruction. Instead, SWLDs need individualized supports that can be provided most efficiently through high-intelligence technology such as AI or a teacher. A teacher would need to sit with each student one-on-one to identify their needs, determine the best-suited strategies, and then adapt the content to their needs and learning styles. This task would be time-consuming, but AI could reduce the time and effort a teacher needs. For example, an AI-based software could be used to collect data on students' needs which is then used to identify the most helpful tools and strategies for that student (Zingoni et al. 2021). While a teacher would need to take time with each student to determine that, not to mention the expertise the teacher would need to have, an AI-based software could do this for multiple students simultaneously and more efficiently. Similarly, if students need materials adapted for their different needs, a teacher would require time to adapt the material for each student, but an AI-based mobile application could quickly adapt the material for students' needs by capturing the text via camera and allowing students access to different tools to adapt the text. This AI-based application would again be more efficient regarding the number of students that AI could support and the amount of time needed.

Artificial Intelligence for Learning Disabilities

AI has been proposed for decades, but the field has not reached a consensus regarding what AI is. Consequently, there is a multitude of definitions of AI, and they vary based on the field. To clarify the understanding of AI, Samoili et al. (2020) conducted a qualitative analysis of over fifty documents defining AI, which were then used to develop an operational definition for AI by a high-level expert group. They concluded that AI is software and hardware designed by humans that act in the physical or digital dimension by perceiving the environment through data acquisition, interpretation, reasoning, or processing of information and then deciding the best action to take to achieve the given goal (Samoili et al. 2020). The popularity of AI has fluctuated in the past decades, and the recent high attention drawn in academia and industry is due to the development of a subcategory—machine learning (Thompson, Li, and Bolen n.d.), a milestone development, as it enables the machine to "learn" from "experience" and apply what it learned to solve new problems—similar to how humans usually do. This new feature has drawn enormous attention, and thus different AI technologies (e.g., natural language processing, computer vision) and applications are being developed and applied in every sector of society, including in the field of education (Zhai et al. 2020). These formats include chat robots, communication assistants, adaptive learning devices, facial expression recognition, intelligent tutors, interactive robots, and mastery learning devices. The variation in the type and intensity of AI applications in education makes AI a powerful tool for identifying and addressing the unique challenges SWLDs face with corresponding support.

In recent years, the literature has seen more publications regarding using AI to improve outcomes for students with learning disabilities. Poornappriya and Gopinath (2020) published a review study looking at machine-learning applications for dyslexia prediction and e-learning for learning and cognitive disorders. Among twenty-four reviewed studies, six employed external AI-based appearances to improve learning. Specifically, four were focused on providing customized or personalized learning, one was focused on the influence of online learning activities, and one was on general machine-learning intervention. The majority of the reviewed studies (n = 13) focused on screening, predicting, or diagnosing a learning disability or learning difficulty. Poornappriya and Gopinath's (2020) work shows an intense concentration of research in AI for SWLDs being focused on either predicting, screening for, or diagnosing a learning disability, while less attention was paid to improving SWLDs' learning, which is of most importance, yet complex.

This literature review shifted from Poornappriya and Gopinath's (2020) work by looking specifically at studies using AI to support SWLDs in aspects other than predicting, screening for, or diagnosing a learning disability. Three of the studies that Poornappriya and Gopinath (2020) reviewed are also included in this literature review as they met the inclusion criteria for this review (see Table 21.1). Additionally, the level of integration or depth of intensity of the AI technology also varies. The literature reviewed in this study shows multiple AI applications and levels of integration identified by Puentedura's (2006) SAMR model.

Technology Integration Model for Learning Disabilities

Technology cannot improve learning by itself—it is the users and the ways of using technology that make a change for learners. If used purposefully and meaningfully, technology can support students with and without disabilities to achieve greater academic achievement in the classroom. However, if technology is not integrated or incorporated correctly into a lesson or the classroom, it does not enhance or support learning (Zhai 2021). Therefore, uncovering how AI technologies are integrated into specific learning activities to support SWLDs is critical. Puentedura (2006) proposed the SAMR (i.e., substitute, augment, modify, and redefine) model as a powerful tool for understanding technology integration in learning. The SAMR model was initially laid out to look at the transformative nature of online learning and has since been found powerful in analyzing technology integration with other technologies, such as mobile learning (Zhai, Zhang, and Zhang 2019). With its clear definitions of technology integration, the SAMR model can be used to identify how much technology can transform and enhance learning rather than just repeating a teacher's action (Terada 2020).

The model assumes that a higher level of technology integration leads to increased student achievements. With the SAMR model, Puentedura (2006) divides technology integration into four successive levels: substitution, augmentation, modification, and redefinition. With *substitution*, technology is a direct substitute for a learning practice without any functional improvement, while with *augmentation*, technology is a direct substitute for a learning practice with functional improvement. *Modification* is when technology provides a significant redesign for a learning practice. *Redefinition* is the highest level of integration, and this is when technology allows for the creation of new learning tasks that were impossible in a traditional setting without the technology. The modification and redefinition levels are where one sees learning being transformed with technology; at these levels, technology is not just replacing a traditional learning task but also allowing for a novel and more integrated use of technology in the classroom.

The SAMR model was adapted as the framework for this study to understand how technology, specifically AI technology, was integrated with learning activities in supporting and enhancing the learning of SWLDs. Specifically, we adapted the SAMR model by incorporating the uses of AI technologies with the learning activities of SWLDs (SAMR-LD). Unlike the SAMR model, the SAMR-LD model looks explicitly at how technology is integrated to transform learning for SWLD. A technology integrated for learning can vary between students with and without learning disabilities, and SAMR-LD is used specifically for the latter. We used the same level names of SAMR for the new model, but the connotations of levels have changed. These levels allowed us to categorize the different AI technologies based on how the content and learning activities were changed or enhanced to support SWLDs:

The *substitution* level of integration for AI could involve AI being used in place of an existing learning practice without providing any functional improvement in support of SWLDs. For example, this may involve using facial expression data of SWLDs to provide teachers with surface-level information such as engagement (Abdul Hamid et al. 2018b).

The *augmentation* level of integration could involve AI being used as a substitute, but at this level, there would be some functional improvement in how SWLDs are supported. For example, AI can allow SWLDs to change the format of the text, such as having it chunked or read aloud (Rajapakse et al. 2018). While this example may seem like a *substitution*, it is important to note the needs of SWLDs; for students without learning disabilities, having the text read aloud may be simply substitution, but for SWLDs who may struggle with reading decoding or comprehension, having the text read aloud would be augmentation as it provides additional functions that are especially useful for SWLDs' learning. The substitution and augmentation levels of the SAMR model are considered an enhancement of learning (Terada 2020).

Modification, regarding AI, would involve using AI to redesign a learning activity with significant functional improvement in supporting SWLDs. For instance, AI can be used to understand the type of disability a SWLD has and then recommend personalized learning strategies (Sharif and Elmedany 2022). This could involve the AI technology providing a report of strategies that the teacher or student could utilize to support learning. This would be a significant improvement to a learning activity as without this technology; the student would need intensive support and time from a teacher to understand their disability and then to identify personalized learning strategies.

Lastly, *redefinition*, which is the highest level of integration, would involve using AI to not only redesign a learning activity but to redesign it in a way that would not be possible in a traditional learning environment to support SWLDs. An example of AI at the redefinition level involves using AI to identify a SWLD's personalized learning style and adapt the material accordingly as an output to the SWLD (Zingoni et al. 2021). AI at both the modification and redefinition levels identifies the personalized learning style and sometimes even the disability of the user, but the difference between the two levels is that AI that falls at the modification level provides strategies that the user or the teacher will need to implement, whereas AI at the redefinition level adapts the material accordingly and provides the user with content and activities that have been adapted to match their needs. For example, modification may involve suggesting the use of visuals to support student learning, whereas redefinition would adapt the content material to include the visual support. Modification and redefinition are considered transformations of learning (Terada 2020). As one moves through the levels of integration on the SAMR and the modified SAMR-LD models, the technology becomes increasingly integrated with the learning process in a transformative way, with the highest level being a total transformation of learning in a manner that would not be possible without technology.

Methods

We employed a three-stage procedure to conduct this systematic literature review: (a) identifying literature based on the title and abstract, (b) reading the selected literature thoroughly, and (c) analyzing the literature using the defined coding scheme.

Literature Collection

To identify the qualified literature, we first collected the relevant literature from three databases, Web of Science, ProQuest, and Google Scholar. The search terms used for the study were ("artificial intelligence" OR "AI" OR "machine learning" OR "deep learning") AND ("learning disabilit*" OR "learning disorder" OR "learning difficult*" OR "dyslexia" OR "dyscalculia" OR "dysgraphia"). Our preliminary review suggests that AI was rarely involved in supporting SWLDs until the past ten years, so we limited the search to the past fifteen years and slightly extended the period to ensure all substantial studies were included in the review. The search was completed in June 2022. Web of Science and ProQuest returned n_1 = 375 and n_2= 6,246 articles, respectively. Given the relatively large grain size of the search criteria and the significant overlapping between Google Scholar and the other two datasets, we only included the first n_3 = 100 results from Google Scholar, sorted by relevance. Therefore, 6,721 articles, including titles and abstracts, were included in the first round of screening.

Identify Qualified Literature

To answer our research questions, we developed a set of seven inclusion and exclusion criteria to narrow the scope further and identify targeted research (see Table 21.1). We only reviewed journal articles and conference proceedings to ensure the most substantial work in the field was being reviewed. This review only looked at articles being published in English for accessibility to the authors, as well as the technology being used in the study should incorporate AI. The studies were also limited to those focused on supporting students with learning disabilities rather than other disabilities. The inclusion criteria also required that the reading, writing, or math content being supported for students in the study be in English, as the issues SWLDs face in these areas can change considerably from one language to another (Zingoni et al. 2021). Compared to many other languages, English has an orthography with many more inconsistencies and complexities, leading to a much slower learning rate (Seymour, Aro, and Erskine 2003).

Further, words in the English language are spelled according to phonemes, or sounds, and morphemes, or meaningful roots, whereas some languages, such as Spanish and Finnish, only use phonemes (Moats 2006). Thus, limiting studies in which the content being supported was in English allowed for more accurate comparisons among studies because the signs and symptoms of a learning disability depend on the language being used, so it is crucial to take language-based classification into account (Poornappriya and Gopinath 2020). We also excluded literature related to the field of medicine, that took place in a medical or clinical setting, or that required medical equipment or personnel, because this study aimed to find research that could be used by teachers or students with learning disabilities in a classroom setting. And lastly, any literature that focused solely on screening, diagnosing, or predicting a learning disability was excluded for two reasons: (1) a review has been conducted looking at how AI is used to screen for or diagnose learning disabilities (Poornappriya and Gopinath

Table 21.1 Inclusion and Exclusion Criteria

Inclusion criteria	Exclusion criteria
The source is a journal article or conference proceeding.	The source is something other than a journal article or conference proceeding. The source is a review study.
Published in English	Not in the English language
The study involves artificial intelligence.	The study does not involve artificial intelligence.
The study targets students with learning disabilities, which includes dyslexia, dyscalculia, and dysgraphia.	The study is targeting students without disabilities or with other disabilities.
Content being looked at is reading, writing, or math in the English language.	Content being looked at is reading, writing, or math in a language other than English.
The study is related or conducted to the field of education or oriented towards supporting students' education.	The study is related to the field of medicine, taking place in a clinical or medical setting, or requiring medical equipment or personnel.
The study provides information on supporting, instructing, or assessing students with learning disabilities.	The study is focused solely on screening, diagnosing, identifying, predicting, or classifying a learning disability.

2020) and (2) the goal of this study was to support learning and teaching for students already diagnosed with learning disabilities, so identifying or diagnosing a student's disability would not be helpful.

Based on these inclusion and exclusion criteria, the lead author screened the titles and abstracts of the 6,721 sources, which resulted in an initial amount of forty-five sources. These forty-five studies were then read in-depth, leading to sixteen

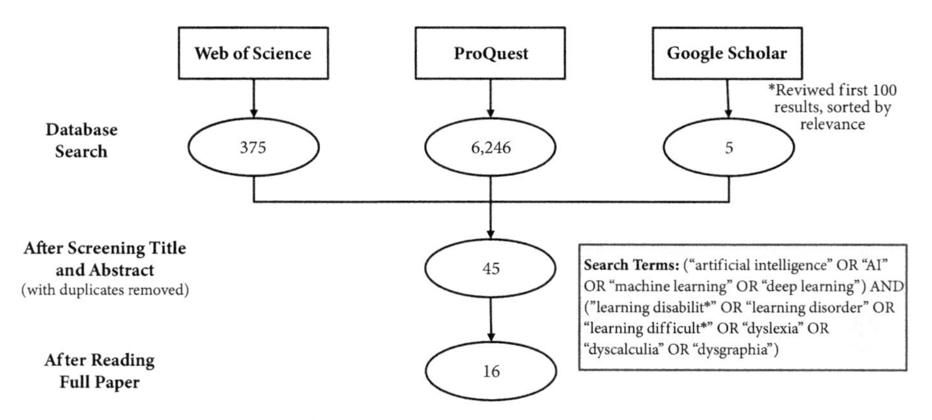

Figure 21.1 Literature search procedures.

studies that met this literature review's inclusion and exclusion criteria. Figure 21.1 summarizes the search procedure.

Analysis of the Literature

Both inductive and deductive approaches were used to analyze the literature in this review to answer the two research questions. For the first research question, an inductive approach was used to determine what AI applications have been developed in the past fifteen years to support SWLDs. The codes were determined by the two authors collaboratively, who have expertise in special education and AI and portrayed the AI applications or the uses of AI. The codes were derived based on the literature reviewed for seven different codes. These AI applications, or codes, can be seen in Table 21.2, including adaptive learning, communication assistant, chat robot, mastery learning, facial expression, interactive robot, and intelligent tutor. Given that different papers may name the same AI applications differently, the authors derived the AI application names. These AI applications may not have been referred to specifically as such in every relevant article reviewed but were based on how the AI technology was described.

A deductive approach was employed to answer the second research question, which focused on integrating these AI technologies, and codes were assigned using the adapted SAMR Model of Technology Integration (Puentedura 2006). Each study was assigned a level of integration from the SAMR model based on the description of the AI technology used. The codes were assigned by both authors collaboratively. Examples of literature coded for each of the different levels of AI integration can also be seen in Table 21.2. As the examples of literature coded for the four different levels of AI integration will demonstrate, the reliance and need for AI technology for the teaching practice increases as one moves up the four levels; thus, a practice at the substitution level of integration does not need the AI technology and can be done by a classroom teacher with ease. In contrast, a practice at the redefinition level of integration relies on AI technology and is almost impossible without it.

Results

Ten out of the sixteen studies that met the inclusion and exclusion criteria for this review focused specifically on dyslexia, a learning disability that involves difficulty with reading, such as decoding or comprehension. Only one of the studies was focused specifically on dyscalculia, a learning disability in math. Moreover, the remaining five studies were focused on learning disabilities in general. The majority, 50%, of the studies reviewed focused on school-age children, with the remaining focused on individuals above eighteen, such as university students, or did not provide the age segment. The studies ranged geographically, including the United States, Malaysia, Pakistan, Italy, China, Greece, India, Morocco, Slovenia, Saudi Arabia, South Africa, Sri Lanka, the United Kingdom, and Switzerland. Appendix Table A1 provides a summary of all the literature reviewed.

Table 21.2 AI Applications in Supporting Students with Learning Disabilities

AI applications	No. of studies	AI technologies	Type(s) of learning disability supported	How the AI supported SWLDs	Studies
Adaptive learning	5	Naive Bayes classifier; machine learning; Bayesian network	Dyslexia, dyscalculia, and learning disabilities in general	AI technology involved adapting the material to meet the user's learning style or needs.	Käser et al. (2013) Gupta (2019) Yaquob and Hamed (2019) Flogie et al. (2020) Zingoni et al. (2021)
Facial expression	3	Bag of features (BOG) image classification; Speed-up robust features (SURF); Support vector machines (SVM)	Dyslexia and learning disabilities in general	AI technology utilized facial expression data to provide information on student engagement.	Abdul Hamid et al. (2018a) Abdul Hamid et al. (2018b) Ouherrou et al. (2019)
Chat robot	2	Machine learning	Dyslexia and learning disabilities in general	AI technology involved using a smart robot via a chat feature to support users.	Rajapakse et al. (2018) Gupta and Chen (2022)
Communication assistant	2	Neural machine translation; natural language Processing; Computer Vision	Dyslexia	This type of AI technology supported users in terms of communication—written or oral.	Wu et al. (2019) Wang, Muthu, and Sivaparthipan (2021)
Mastery learning	2	Machine learning	Dyslexia	This type of AI technology supported the user in mastering a learning concept through repetition or relearning until they have achieved mastery.	Ndombo, Ojo, and Osunmakinde (2013) Latif et al. (2015)
Intelligent tutor	1	Machine learning	Learning disabilities in general	This type of AI technology identified a user's learning style or needs and recommended learning strategies.	Sharif and Elmedany (2022)
Interactive robot	1	Multimodal machine learning	Learning disabilities in general	This type of AI technology involved a physical robot that can interact with a user.	Papakostas et al. (2021)

AI Technologies for Students with Disabilities

Seven types of AI applications were identified from the literature: adaptive learning, facial expression, chat robot, communication assistant, mastery learning, intelligent tutor, and interactive robot. This section introduces the seven types of applications.

Adaptive Learning

SWLDs' learning needs are more diverse than those of students without learning disabilities, which creates additional challenges in supporting them in learning. The best instructional strategy to meet this challenge is to provide customized learning support or adapt the learning materials according to their needs. Five of the sixteen studies in this review included an adaptive learning type of AI technology targeting a diverse range of ages (from under the age of five to adulthood) and disabilities (e.g., dyslexia, dysgraphia). Researchers have developed adaptive learning strategies using AI to supply learning support based on individual SWLD's learning needs in the form of intelligent, serious learning games (Flogie et al. 2020), intelligent tutoring systems (Käser et al. 2013), or e-learning management system (Yaqoub and Hamed 2019). In an example study, Zingoni et al. (2021) developed a BESPECIAL software platform, which is based on AI capable of understanding the issues experienced by a dyslexic student and provides ad hoc digital support methodologies and adapted study materials. BESPECIAL uses students' clinical reports of dyslexia, survey results, and psychometric test results as inputs to train AI algorithms. Using the trained AI algorithms, the system can predict SWLDs' individual needs (e.g., concentration when alone, memory impairments) and provide supporting and adaptive strategies (e.g., concept maps, schemes, highlighted keywords) to meet individual students' needs. It also provides their teachers with strategies and best practices specific to that student.

Facial Expression

Engaging students in the classroom is an essential first step in supporting their learning, including the learning of SWLDs. Facial expression is one-way researchers have predicted student engagement with the content. Three of the sixteen studies used AI technologies for facial expression, and all three used facial expression data to predict student engagement with the content. In these studies, where students ranged in age between seven and twelve, researchers analyzed facial expressions through AI technologies such as the bag of features (BOF) (Abdul Hamid et al. 2018b), speed-up robust features (SURF) and support vector machines (Abdul Hamid et al. 2018a), and convolutional neural networks (CNN) (Ouherrou et al. 2019). All the studies using computer vision for facial expression looked at frontal face detection to predict the engagement of SWLDs towards the content, while the latter employed deep learning to identify subtle changes in students' faces. These applications with facial expressions provide useful information for teachers in ensuring whether SWLDs are engaged in the lesson and determining which activities increase student engagement compared to others.

Chat Robot

As chat robots are increasingly used in digital platforms related to students' lives, many students worldwide have gotten familiar with the use of chat robots or smart assistants through the advancement of technology. The AI technology of chat robots has been utilized by large companies to provide customer support and to troubleshoot their products, which inspired the application in education. Specifically, two studies in this review used the chat robot to support SWLDs. One used a smart assistant, Sammy, who interacted with students via chat to provide accessibility and resources or feedback based on student needs (Gupta and Chen 2022). Another study used a mobile application called ALEXZA to support individuals with dyslexia by reading aloud, chunking, highlighting, and manipulating the text in other ways (Rajapakse et al. 2018). This smart assistant on the app could also answer user questions directly. Both studies utilized a chat assistant with AI technology to provide accessibility support for students with reading-based learning disabilities.

Communication Assistant

SWLDs have difficulty communicating due to their struggles with being unable to express themselves in a verbal or written manner due to a lack of confidence stemming from their language-based disabilities. Communication assistants can be a helpful tool in supporting SWLDs in communicating with their peers and adults. Two of the sixteen studies in this review used AI technology as a communication assistant to support students, specifically with dyslexia. Wang, Muthu, and Sivaparthipan (2021) added AI to an Augmentative and Alternative Communication (AAC) device to increase the ease of verbal communication for students. Another study used Neural Machine Translation (NMT) to develop a tool called Additional Writing Help (AWH) which "translated" text with common dyslexia writing issues to text without it while preserving the slang abbreviations, hashtags, mentions, and other elements that are common among social media platforms (Wu et al. 2019).

Mastery Learning

AI technology focused on mastery learning uses machine learning to understand the user's progress and support the user in achieving mastery through relearning and frequent evaluation. Two of the sixteen studies utilized mastery learning to support students with dyslexia. Latif et al. (2015) used machine learning to implement the relearning process for writing and allowed learners to practice similar skills until they reached mastery before moving on to the next learning segment. Similarly, Ndombo, Ojo, and Osunmakinde (2013) proposed using machine learning in their model called the Intelligent Assistive Dyslexia System (IADS). IADS was proposed to support reading and writing skills among students with dyslexia by evaluating their learning throughout the process. Machine learning is a way to improve targeted skills among SWLDs through the repetition or the relearning process supported by continuous evaluation.

Intelligent Tutor

An intelligent tutor technology uses dynamic machine-learning models to identify an individual's learning difficulties and their level and to recommend a personalized learning strategy. Only one of the sixteen studies utilized this technology, and that study (Sharif and Elmedany 2022) is centered around a proposed approach that is not yet fully studied. Sharif and Elmedany (2022) proposed utilizing machine learning to identify patterns in the learner's reading, writing, typing, and other areas to provide feedback on their progress and specific strategies to support the students. While the study is still in the proposal stage and the strategies to be provided by the technology are still in development, the study is promising in supporting educators and providing individualized support for SWLDs.

Interactive Robot

The interactive robot also utilizes a machine learning-based methodology that allows a social robot to interact with students physically. Only one out of the sixteen studies utilized an interactive robot as an AI technology to support SWLDs, and this study focused specifically on understanding student engagement using the interactive robot (Papakostas et al. 2021). Unlike the chat robot, the social robot interacted with SWLDs and utilized multimodal machine learning to predict the engagement of SWLDs in the classroom (Papakostas et al. 2021).

AI Technology Integration for Students with Disabilities

Based on Puentedura's (2006) SAMR model, our analysis suggests that AI applications have been used to enhance and transform learning for SWLDs. In this review, four studies were found to be at the substitution level, six at the augmentation level, two at the modification level, and four at the redefinition level. The model suggests that a higher level of technology integration leads to increased student achievements (see Zhai, Zhang, and Zhang 2019); thus, it is expected that a higher level of AI integration would be beneficial for student achievement. This section looks at each of the levels of integration and the studies categorized into those levels. Table 21.3 summarizes the four levels of integration and provides an example.

Of the four studies at the substitution level, AI was used to substitute or replace an existing learning activity with human assistance using AI technologies such as facial expressions or an interactive robot to predict student engagement (Abdul Hamid et al. 2018a, 2018b; Ouherrou et al. 2019; Papakostas et al. 2021). Though this information is vital for teachers in keeping SWLDs engaged in the lesson, they provide limited functional improvement to the traditional learning activities. For example, Papakostas et al. (2021) engaged ten elementary SWLDs in learning activities using a social chat robot NAO. They developed ten scenarios (e.g., meet/greet, story listening and telling, and sentence structuring) to engage SWLDs to experience the relevant activities in each scenario. The scenarios include eight types of activities: (a) meet/greet; (b) text decoding, comprehension, and reading; (c) phonology composition, decomposition, discrimination, and addition; (d) memory; (e) robot–child relaxation game; (f) story listening and telling; (g) sentence structuring; and (h) strategic visual representation. Students spent an average of thirty-five minutes on each scenario. Researchers collected students' multimodal data (e.g., visual sensing, audio sensing, and feature extraction) and examined the ten SWLDs' engagement

Table 21.3 Technology Integration Levels of AI Applications in Supporting Students with Learning Disabilities

Integration level	No. of studies	Description	Example
Substitution	4	Technology is substituted for an existing learning activity without any functional improvement compared to human assistance for SWLDs.	The AI technology provides the teacher with surface-level information about SWLDs, such as engagement (Papakostas et al. 2021).
Augmentation	6	Technology is used to support learning activities with functional improvement compared to human assistance for SWLDs.	The AI technology acts as a writing assistant for individuals with dyslexia, helping to replace word errors commonly made by individuals with dyslexia while preserving slang, abbreviations, and other content features commonly used in social media (Wu et al. 2019).
Modification	2	Technology is used to redesign learning activities with significant functional improvement compared to human assistance for SWLDs.	The AI technology generates new levels of practice for SWLDs through adaptive tests that understand their needs and support mastery through practice (Gupta 2019).
Redefinition	4	This is the highest level of integration. Technology is used to redesign a learning activity that is impossible in a traditional human-assisted learning environment for SWLDs.	The AI technology identifies the user's dyslexia type, detects the preferred learning style associated with that type of dyslexia, and adapts the material or content presented in accordance with the user's learning style (Yaquob and Hamed 2019).

levels during learning. Figure 21.2 summarizes the methodology the researchers in this study used. The researchers could predict student engagement with 93% accuracy but also found that the study brought to light the variability in definitions for engagement. This study used AI to collect data on and predict student engagement. While this is valuable information for teachers supporting SWLDs, it did not provide any functional improvement specifically for SWLDs nor for the teachers supporting them, such as providing specific ways to increase engagement for SWLD. Therefore, according to the SAMR-LD model, this level of AI application is at the substitution level.

Augmentation, on the other hand, involves the substitution of an existing learning activity with human assistance but with functional improvement. Six studies in this review were categorized to be at the augmentation level, and the studies involved

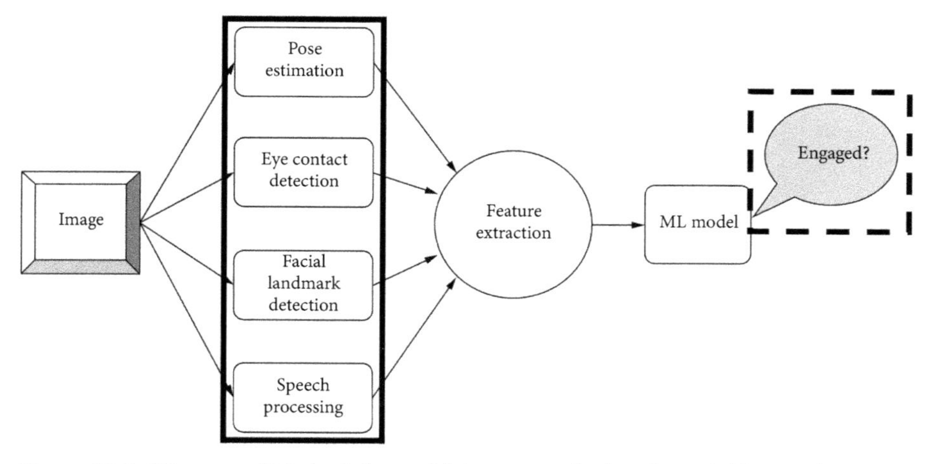

Figure 21.2 Diagram of Methodology with inputs marked with a solid box and outputs marked with a dashed box. Adapted with permission from Papakostas et al. (2021) "Estimating children engagement interacting with robots in special education using machine learning," *Mathematical Problems in Engineering.* https://doi.org/10.1155/2021/9955212.

the use of AI to enhance the support an individual with a learning disability would receive from a teacher or another adult. Rajapakse et al. (2018) found that despite many applications existing to support individuals with dyslexia, those applications focused on identifying dyslexia and provided long-term solutions rather than more immediate day-to-day support that those individuals needed. Thus, they developed an application, ALEXZA, that utilizes AI to adapt the learning content to the learning preferences of the individual with dyslexia using the application. ALEXZA utilized an image pre-processing algorithm to enhance the quality of the text and images that the camera captured; the user was then able to manipulate and enhance the text using different features. These features included (a) chunking or segmenting the captured text, (b) changing the text format (e.g., color, font), (c) text-to-speech, (d) text highlighting, (e) dictionary integration, (f) word replacement using machine learning, and (g) a Smart AI Assistant. Figure 21.3 provides screenshots of the prototype application and shows how scanned text can be manipulated through the application. While the manipulation of a text, such as changing the text format or having it read aloud, may seem to be simply a substitution for printed text, when it comes to students with learning disabilities, specifically a language-based one such as dyslexia, these features support the learning of SWLDs (i.e., fall within the augmentation level of the SAMR-LD model). For a student with a reading learning disability, the features of the ALEXZA application allow them to access the previously challenging content.

Another example of AI technology at the augmentation level of the SAMR-LD is the Additional Writing Help (AWH), a writing assistant for individuals with dyslexia which proofreads text prior to posting on social media and focuses on word errors commonly made by individuals with dyslexia while preserving slang, abbreviations,

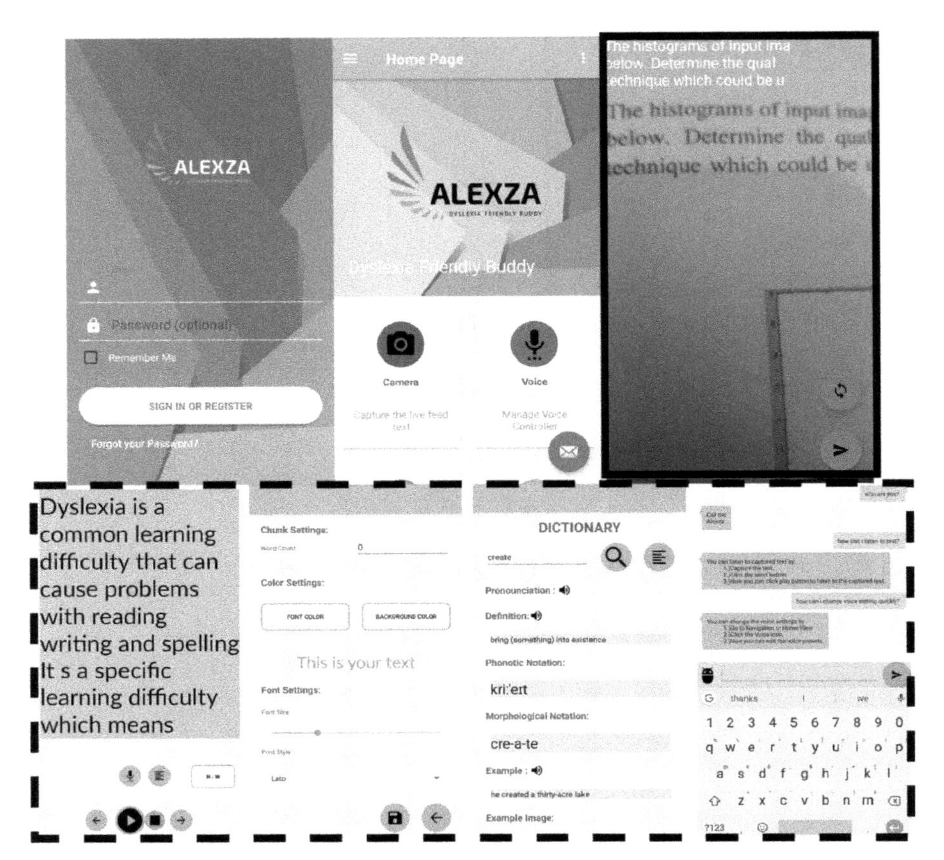

Figure 21.3 ALEXZA Application Prototype with inputs marked with a solid box and outputs marked with a dashed box. Adapted with permission from Rajapakse et al. (2018), "ALEXZA: A mobile application for dyslexics utilizing artificial intelligence and machine learning Concepts," *2018 3rd International Conference on Information Technology Research* (ICITR). https://doi.org/10.1109/ICITR.2018.8736130.

and other content features commonly used in social media (Wu et al. 2019). AWH "translates" text with common writing issues that individuals with dyslexia make to writing without those mistakes. This is another example of a tool that supports SWLDs in a manner that goes beyond the typical support a classroom teacher could provide. While a teacher can support students with dyslexia in replacing word errors, the writing assistant increases the number of individuals that can be supported and the speed and depth of the support, thus bringing a functional improvement to a teacher's practice.

Modification is the third level of AI integration, and this level involves using AI to redesign a learning activity with human assistance with significant functional improvement. Only two studies included in this review were categorized on this level. Sharif and Elmedany (2022) proposed a model that would use a dynamic machine-learning model to identify the learning difficulties of the individual and then recommend a personalized learning strategy based on the data collected and predictions. Figure 21.4 shows their proposed model. The proposed approach utilizes quantitative data, such as electroencephalogram (EEG) data, and qualitative data, such as behavioral data from psychologists' interactions with the user.

Furthermore, the process of identifying learning difficulties and suggesting personalized strategies continues weekly or monthly based on the severity of the

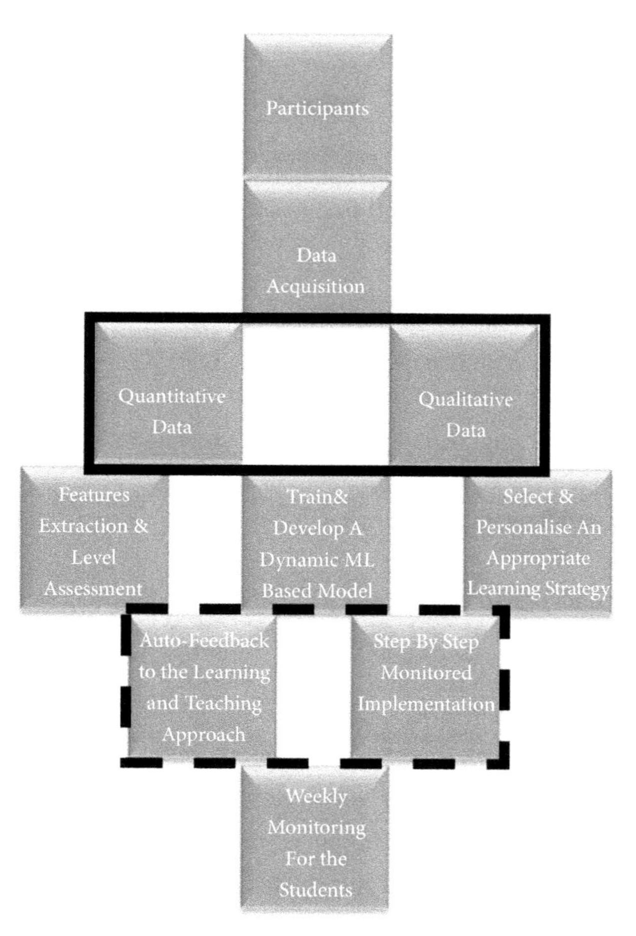

Figure 21.4 Proposed Model to Support SWLD with inputs marked with a solid box and outputs marked with a dashed box. Adapted with permission from Sharif and Elmedany (2022), "A proposed machine learning based approach to support students with learning difficulties in the post-pandemic norm," *2022 IEEE Global Engineering Education Conference* (EDUCON). https://doi.org/10.1109/EDUCON52537.2022.9766690.

individual needs. Sharif and Elmedany's (2022) proposed model is an example of the modification level, as it involves using AI to redesign a teaching practice with significant functional improvement. A key feature of their proposed model is the output of individualized, personalized strategies for the user's needs; this is a difficult task for classroom teachers. While teachers can identify individualized strategies for each student, it is a timely process and requires teachers to not only collect multiple forms of data but also have a wide array of strategies to support students.

The final level and highest level of AI integration is redefinition, which involves redesigning a learning activity with human assistance to such an extent that it would not be possible in the absence of that AI technology. Four of the studies included in this review were identified as being at the redefinition level of integration. An example of AI technology at the redefinition level was presented by Zingoni et al. (2021) with their software platform BESPECIAL. For each user, the BESPECIAL software utilizes clinical reports from experts and self-evaluation questionnaires from the users about the problems they face while studying and helpful solutions. The results from these assessments drive the identification of those tools and strategies that would be most helpful for the user. Up to this stage of the software, this AI technology would be considered at the modification level of integration as it identifies the user's learning needs and matches the tools and strategies to those needs. The component of the software that takes it from the modification to the redefinition level of integration is the digitization of the content. The BESPECIAL software identifies the needs and individualized strategies and adapts the material according to the individual's needs and preferred learning style. Additionally, the gathered information is also passed onto the teachers of the users to enable the teachers to support the students better. Figure 21.5 shows a diagram of the process whereby multiple input sources gather information followed by an output that is teacher facing, the strategies, and an output that is student facing, the digitized supporting materials. This software falls in the

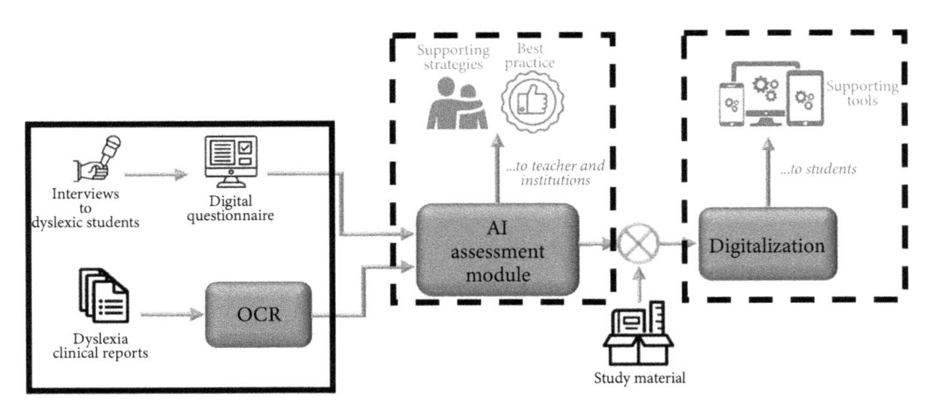

Figure 21.5 BESPECIAL Diagram with inputs marked with a solid box and outputs marked with a dashed boxes. Adapted with permission from Zingoni et al. (2021) "Investigating issues and needs of dyslexic students at university: proof of concept of an artificial intelligence and virtual reality-based supporting platform and preliminary results," *Applied Sciences*, 11(10). https://doi.org/10.3390/app11104624.

highest level of integration as the AI technology is used to redesign learning in a way that would not be possible in a traditional human-assisted learning environment.

Conclusion and Discussion

We found that various AI applications are applied in supporting learning for SWLDs, and the ways the technologies are integrated to support their learning are diverse. With the focus of this review study being specifically to identify research on how AI can be used to support the learning process of SWLDs, rather than the diagnosis or identification of a learning disability, this study's findings have revealed the potential of AI in supporting SWLDs' learning. However, the small number of empirical studies in this area also implies significant research gaps and the need for more research on how AI can support SWLDs beyond just identifying and diagnosing a learning disability. More design and development research is needed to leverage AI to support SWLDs in their learning, and more empirical evidence is needed to advance our knowledge about AI's potential for SWLDs. This review's findings contribute to the literature in several ways.

Firstly, the focus on AI applications for SWLDs, specifically dyslexia, provides a valuable understanding of the current research in this field. The findings of this review add valuable insight into the use of AI in supporting SWLDs. It revealed that ten out of the sixteen studies focused specifically on dyslexia, with only one focused on dyscalculia, and the remaining five studies focused on learning disabilities in general. This highlights the growing interest in using AI to support individuals with learning disabilities and the simultaneous need for more research in this area.

The fact that many of the studies, 50%, focused on school-age children ranging from seven to twelve years highlights the importance of addressing the needs of this population and the potential for AI to impact their learning experiences significantly. With the aim of this study being to identify how AI has been used to support the learning of SWLDs, it is promising to see that most of the studies focused on school-age children. However, it is also noted that some studies included individuals above eighteen or did not specify the age segment, indicating the need for a broader range of age groups to be studied to fully understand the potential impact of AI on the learning of individuals with LDs.

The identification of seven types of AI applications that have been used to support SWLDs, including adaptive learning, facial expression, chat robot, communication assistant, mastery learning, intelligent tutor, and interactive robot, provides a comprehensive overview of the AI technologies being used in this field. The adaptive learning type of AI technology was the most widely used, with five out of the sixteen studies including it as part of their research. This highlights the potential for AI to provide personalized learning experiences for SWLDs, which is critical for their academic success.

The variety of countries represented in the studies, such as the United States, Malaysia, Pakistan, Italy, China, Greece, India, Morocco, Slovenia, Saudi Arabia, South Africa, Sri Lanka, United Kingdom, and Switzerland, suggests a growing interest in the use of AI to support individuals with learning disabilities. Additionally, identifying the different types of AI applications used to support SWLDs highlights the diverse ways AI is being used to support this population.

Furthermore, using the SAMR-LD, an adapted version of Puentedura's (2006) SAMR model, to analyze how AI was integrated into the learning activities for SWLDs provides a framework for understanding the various levels of technology integration and the impact on student achievement. The analysis revealed that AI applications were used in various ways to support the learning of SWLDs, with four studies categorized at the substitution level, six at the augmentation level, two at the modification level, and four at the redefinition level. This finding highlights the potential for AI to enhance and transform the learning experiences of SWLDs and suggests that a higher level of AI integration may lead to increased student achievements.

Overall, this review adds significant insights into the use of AI in supporting the reading, writing, and math education of SWLDs and highlights the need for further research in this area. The diversity of countries represented and the range of AI applications used demonstrates a growing interest in using AI technology to support this population. The analysis using the adapted SAMR-LD model provides a framework for understanding the impact of AI on student achievement in reading, writing, and math. Future research should further investigate the usability, feasibility, and efficiency of the AI tools for SWLDs. A synthesis of the knowledge in these regards will help us better understand how to take advantage of AI in supporting SWLDs.

Acknowledgement

This material is based upon work supported by the National Science Foundation (NSF) under Grants 2101104 and 2138854. Any opinions, findings, conclusions, or recommendations expressed in this material are those of the author and do not necessarily reflect the views of the NSF.

References

Abdul Hamid, S. S., Admodisastro, N., Manshor, N., Ghani, A. A. A., and Kamaruddin, A. 2018a. "Engagement Prediction in the Adaptive Learning Model for Students with Dyslexia." In *Proceedings of the 4th International Conference on Human-Computer Interaction and User Experience in Indonesia, CHIuXiD '18*, 66–73.

Abdul Hamid, S. S., Admodisastro, N., Manshor, N., Kamaruddin, A., and Ghani, A. A. A. 2018b. "Dyslexia Adaptive Learning Model: Student Engagement Prediction Using Machine Learning Approach." In *Recent Advances on Soft Computing and Data Mining*, edited by R. Ghazali, M. M. Deris, N. M. Nawi, and J. H. Abawajy, 372–84. Cham: Springer. https://link.springer.com/chapter/10.1007/978-3-319-72550-5_36#citeas

Asghar, A., Sladeczek, I. E., Mercier, J., and Beaudoin, E. 2017. "Learning in Science, Technology, Engineering, and Mathematics: Supporting Students with Learning Disabilities." *Canadian Psychology/Psychologie Canadienne* 58, no. 3: 238–49.

Büttner, G., and Hasselhorn, M. 2011. "Learning Disabilities: Debates on Definitions, Causes, Subtypes, and Responses." *International Journal of Disability, Development and Education* 58, no. 1: 75–87.

Drigas, A., and Ioannidou, R.-E. 2012. "Artificial Intelligence in Special Education: A Decade Review." *International Journal of Engineering Education* 28, no. 6: 1366–72.

Drigas, A., and Ioannidou, R.-E. 2013. "A Review on Artificial Intelligence in Special Education." In *Communications in Computer and Information Science*, edited by M. D. Lytras, D. Ruan, R. D. Tennyson, P. O. De Pablos, F. J. García Peñalvo, and L. Rusu, 385–91.

Flogie, A., Aberšek, B., Kordigel Aberšek, M., Sik Lanyi, C., and Pesek, I. 2020. "Development and Evaluation of Intelligent Serious Games for Children with Learning Difficulties: Observational Study." *JMIR Serious Games* 8, no. 2: e13190.

Gupta, R. 2019. "Adaptive Testing Tool for Students with Dyslexia." In *2019 China-Qatar International Workshop on Artificial Intelligence and Applications to Intelligent Manufacturing (AIAIM), Doha, Qatar*, 11–16. https://doi.org/10.1109/aiaim.2019.8632775

Gupta, S., and Chen, Y. 2022. "Supporting Inclusive Learning Using Chatbots? A Chatbot-Led Interview Study." *Journal of Information Systems Education* 33, no. 1: 98–108.

Käser, T., Busetto, A. G., Solenthaler, B., Baschera, G.-M., Kohn, J., Kucian, K., von Aster, M., and Gross, M. 2013. "Modelling and Optimizing Mathematics Learning in Children." *International Journal of Artificial Intelligence in Education* 23, no. 1: 115–35.

Latif, S., Tariq, R., Tariq, S., and Latif, R. 2015. "Designing an Assistive Learning Aid for Writing Acquisition: A Challenge for Children with Dyslexia." *Studies in Health Technology and Informatics* 217: 180–88.

Learning Disabilities Association of America. n.d. "Types of Learning Disabilities." Learning Disabilities Association of America. https://ldaamerica.org/types-of-learning-disabilities/

Moats, L. C. 2006. "How Spelling Supports Reading and Why It Is More Regular and Predictable Than You May Think." *American Educator* 12–43.

National Center for Education Statistics. 2022. *Students with Disabilities.* U.S. Department of Education, Institute of Education Sciences. https://nces.ed.gov/programs/coe/indicator/cgg/students-with-disabilities#suggested-citation

Ndombo, D. M., Ojo, S., and Osunmakinde, I. O. 2013. "An Intelligent Integrative Assistive System for Dyslexic Learners." *Journal of Assistive Technologies* 7, no. 3: 172–87.

Ouherrou, N., Elhammoumi, O., Benmarrakchi, F., and El Kafi, J. 2019. "Comparative Study on Emotions Analysis from Facial Expressions in Children with and without Learning Disabilities in Virtual Learning Environment." *Education and Information Technologies* 24, no. 2: 1777–92.

Papakostas, G. A., Sidiropoulos, G. K., Lytridis, C., Bazinas, C., Kaburlasos, V. G., Kourampa, E., Karageorgiou, E., Kechayas, P., and Papadopoulou, M. T. 2021. "Estimating Children Engagement Interacting with Robots in Special Education Using Machine Learning." *Mathematical Problems in Engineering* 2021: article 9955212. https://doi.org/10.1155/2021/9955212

Poornappriya, T. S., and Gopinath, R. 2020. "Application of Machine Learning Techniques for Improving Learning Disabilities." *International Journal of Electrical Engineering and Technology* 11, no. 10: 403–11.

Puentedura, R. R. 2006. "Transformation, Technology, and Education." http://hippasus.com/resources/tte/puentedura_tte.pdf

Rajapakse, S., Polwattage, D., Guruge, U., Jayathilaka, I., Edirisinghe, T., and Thelijjagoda, S. 2018. "ALEXZA: A Mobile Application for Dyslexics Utilizing Artificial Intelligence and Machine Learning Concepts." In *2018 3rd International Conference on Information Technology Research (ICITR), Moratuwa, Sri Lanka, 2018*, 1–6. https://doi.org/10.1109/icitr.2018.8736130

Rauschenberger, M., Lins, C., Rousselle, N., Hein, A., and Fudickar, S. 2019. "Designing a New Puzzle App to Target Dyslexia Screening in Pre-readers." In *Proceedings of the 5th EAI International Conference on Smart Objects and Technologies for Social Good*, 155–59.

Rello, L., Romero, E., Rauschenberger, M., Ali, A., Williams, K., Bigham, J. P., and White, N. C. 2018. "Screening Dyslexia for English Using HCI Measures and Machine Learning." In *Proceedings of the 2018 International Conference on Digital Health*, 80–84.

Samoili, S., López Cobo, M., Gómez, E., De Prato, G., Martínez-Plumed, F., and Delipetrev, B. 2020. *AI Watch Defining Artificial Intelligence towards an Operational Definition and Taxonomy of Artificial Intelligence.* Joint Research Centre (JRC).

Seymour, P. H. K., Aro, M., and Erskine, J. M. 2003. "Foundation Literacy Acquisition in European Orthographies." *British Journal of Psychology* 94, no. 2: 143–74.

Sharif, M. S., and Elmedany, W. 2022. "A Proposed Machine Learning Based Approach to Support Students with Learning Difficulties in the Post-Pandemic Norm." In *2022 IEEE Global Engineering Education Conference (EDUCON), 1988–1993.*

Terada, Y. 2020, May 4. "A Powerful Model for Understanding Good Tech Integration." Edutopia. https://www.edutopia.org/article/powerful-model-understanding-good-tech-integration

Thompson, W., Li, H., and Bolen, A. n.d. "Artificial Intelligence, Machine Learning, Deep Learning and Beyond." SAS Institute. https://www.sas.com/en_us/insights/articles/big-data/artificial-intelligence-machine-learning-deep-learning-and-beyond.html

UNICEF. 2021, November. "Nearly 240 Million Children with Disabilities around the World, UNICEF's Most Comprehensive Statistical Analysis Finds." UNICEF. https://www.unicef.org/rosa/press-releases/nearly-240-million-children-disabilities-around-world-unicefs-most-comprehensive

US Department of Education. 2007. Individuals with Disabilities Education Act, 20 U.S.C. § 300.8

Wang, M., Muthu, B., and Sivaparthipan, C. B. 2021. "Smart Assistance to Dyslexia Students Using Artificial Intelligence Based Augmentative Alternative Communication." *International Journal of Speech Technology* 25: 343–53. https://doi.org/10.1007/s10772-021-09921-0

Wu, S., Reynolds, L., Li, X., and Guzmán, F. 2019. "Design and Evaluation of a Social Media Writing Support Tool for People with Dyslexia." In *Proceedings of the 2019 CHI Conference on Human Factors in Computing Systems*, 1–14.

Yaquob, A. A., and Hamed, A. K. 2019. "Adaptation Algorithms for Selecting Personalised Learning Experience Based on Learning Style and Dyslexia Type." *Data Technologies and Applications* 53, no. 2: 189–200.

Zhai, X. 2021. "Practices and Theories: How Can Machine Learning Assist in Innovative Assessment Practices in Science Education." *Journal of Science Education and Technology* 30, no. 2: 1–11.

Zhai, X., and Nehm, R. 2023. "AI and Formative Assessment: The Train Has Left the Station." Journal of Research in Science Teaching 60, no. 6: 1390–98. https://doi.org/DOI:10.1002/tea.21885

Zhai, X., Yin, Y., Pellegrino, J. W., Haudek, K. C., and Shi, L. 2020. "Applying Machine Learning in Science Assessment: A Systematic Review." *Studies in Science Education* 56, no. 1: 111–51.

Zhai, X., Zhang, M., Li, M., and Zhang, X. 2019. "Understanding the Relationship between Levels of Mobile Technology Use in High School Physics Classrooms and the Learning Outcome." *British Journal of Educational Technology: Journal of the Council for Educational Technology* 50, no. 2: 750–66.

Zingoni, A., Taborri, J., Panetti, V., Bonechi, S., Aparicio-Martínez, P., Pinzi, S., and Calabrò, G. 2021. "Investigating Issues and Needs of Dyslexic Students at University: Proof of Concept of an Artificial Intelligence and Virtual Reality-Based Supporting Platform and Preliminary Results." *Applied Sciences* 11, no. 10: 4624. https://doi.org/10.3390/app11104624

Zvoncak, V., Mekyska, J., Safarova, K., Smekal, Z., and Brezany, P. 2019. "New Approach of Dysgraphic Handwriting Analysis Based on the Tunable q-Factor Wavelet Transform." In *2019 42nd International Convention on Information and Communication Technology, Electronics and Microelectronics (MIPRO)*, Opatija, Croatia, 2019, 289–94. https://doi.org/10.23919/mipro.2019.8756872

Appendix

Table A1 Summary of Literature Reviewed

Year	Title	Author(s)	Country	Journal or conference title	Sample size	Age focus	Disability focus
2013	"An Intelligent Integrative Assistive System for Dyslexic Learners"	Ndombo, Ojo, and Osun-makinde	South Africa	*Journal of Assistive Technologies*	0	N/A	Dyslexia
2013	"Modeling and Optimizing Mathematics Learning in Children"	Kaser et al.	Switzerland	*International Journal of Artificial Intelligence in Education*	63	Grades 2–5	Dyscalculia
2015	"Designing an Assistive Learning Aid for Writing Acquisition: A Challenge for Children with Dyslexia"	Latif et al.	Pakistan	*13th European Conference on the Advancement of Assistive Technology (AAATE)*	20 (but includes students and teachers)	Five and under	Dyslexia
2018	"ALEXZA: A Mobile Application for Dyslexics Utilizing Artificial Intelligence and Machine Learning Concepts"	Rajapakse et al.	Sri Lanka	*International Conference on Information Technology Research (ICITR)*	5	No age or disease limitation; none identified	Dyslexia
2018	"Engagement Prediction in the Adaptive Learning Model for Students with Dyslexia"	Abdul Hamid et al.	Malaysia	*International Conference on Human-Computer Interaction and User Experience in Indonesia*	30	7–12 -year-olds	Dyslexia

Continued

Table A1 *Continued*

Year	Title	Author(s)	Country	Journal or conference title	Sample size	Age focus	Disability focus
2018	"Dyslexia Adaptive Learning Model: Student Engagement Prediction Using Machine Learning Approach"	Abdul Hamid et al.	Malaysia	*International Conference on Soft Computing and Data Mining (SCDM 2020)*	30	7–12 -year-olds	Dyslexia
2019	"Design and Evaluation of a Social Media Writing Support Tool for People with Dyslexia"	Wu et al.	United States	*CHI Conference on Human Factors in Computing Systems*	19	Adults	Dyslexia
2019	"Adaptive Testing Tool for Students with Dyslexia"	Gupta	India	*International Workshop on Artificial Intelligence and Applications to Intelligent Manufacturing (AIAIM)*	0	N/A	Dyslexia
2019	"Adaptation Algorithms for Selecting Personalised Learning Experience Based on Learning Style and Dyslexia Type"	Yaqoub and Hamed	Saudi Arabia	*Data Technologies and Applications*	48 (11 with dyslexia, 28 with symptoms of dyslexia, 14 without dyslexia)	Over 18 yrs old	Dyslexia
2019	"Comparative Study on Emotions Analysis from Facial Expressions in Children with and without Learning Disabilities in Virtual Learning Environment"	Ouherrou et al.	Morocco	*Education and Information Technologies*	42 (14 with LD and 28 without LD)	7–11 -year-olds	Learning disabilities

2020	"Development and Evaluation of Intelligent Serious Games for Children with Learning Difficulties: Observational Study"	Flogie et al.	Slovenia	*JMIR Serious Games*	51 (Initial Eval) 93 (Pilot Eval)	11–12 -year-olds	Learning disabilities
2021	"Smart Assistance to Dyslexia Students Using Artificial Intelligence-Based Augmentative Alternative Communication"	Wang, Muthu, and Siva-parthipan	China	*International Journal of Speech Technology*	20	School- and university-age students	Dyslexia
2021	"Investigating Issues and Needs of Dyslexic Students at University: Proof of Concept of an Artificial Intelligence and Virtual Reality-Based Supporting Platform and Preliminary Results"	Zingoni et al.	Italy	*Applied Sciences—Basel*	693	University level	Dyslexia
2021	"Estimating Children Engagement Interacting with Robots in Special Education Using Machine Learning"	Papakostas et al.	Greece	*Mathematical Problems in Engineering*	10	9 to 10 year olds	Learning disabilities
2022	"Supporting Inclusive Learning Using Chatbots? A Chatbot-Led Interview Study"	Gupta and Chen	United States	*Journal of Information Systems Education*	215 (none specifically identified as having a learning disability)	University students	Learning disabilities
2022	"A Proposed Machine Learning-Based Approach to Support Students with Learning Difficulties in the Post-Pandemic Norm"	Sharif and Elmedany	UK	*IEEE Global Engineering Education Conference (EDUCON)*	0	N/A	Learning disabilities

22

Artificial Intelligence (AI) as the Growing Actor in Education

Raising Critical Consciousness towards Power and Ethics of AI in K–12 STEM Classrooms

Selin Akgün and Joseph Krajcik

Introduction

Artificial intelligence (AI) has brought drastic change to various fields of technology, engineering, health care, manufacturing, and education (Druga et al. 2018; Su and Yang 2022). Investors and companies are pouring money into this area to test AI's ability to support human power for all people worldwide. Similar to the other fields, education became one of the biggest venues that AI has consistently entered through various machine-learning (ML) applications in elementary- to tertiary-level classrooms (Druga et al. 2018; Lin and Brummelen 2021; Yang 2022). Personalized or intelligent tutoring systems, automated assessment systems, face recognition, and predictive analytics are increasingly being deployed in educational contexts (Hemachandran et al. 2022; Krueger 2017; Li and Wong 2021). These AI applications have their affordances in education, such as giving students individualized, timely, and detailed feedback, reducing teachers' workload, and supporting students to find future career paths.

Although AI holds considerable promise in an educational context, scholarly and public discussion raises questions of ethics, power, race, and technology (Benjamin 2019; Cheuk 2021). The concerns surrounding AI use in terms of privacy, autonomy, surveillance, bias, and discrimination, as well as how, what, and for whom technologies are designed, are vital considerations (Akgün and Greenhow 2021; Kizilcec and Lee 2022; Sharma, Kawachi, and Bozkurt 2019; Vakil, Marshall, and Ibrahimovic 2020). These concerns stem from how AI learns from existing historical data from a variety of sources without necessarily accounting for any inherent biases in the data training sets, which occasionally perpetuate inequalities and injustices, mostly towards disadvantaged and marginalized groups (Broussard 2018; Crawford 2021; Eubanks 2018). In other words, the problem stems from how the use and consequences of AI technologies are considered as objective and neutral; however, AI systems shape and are shaped by the social, cultural, institutional, and political structures and biases of the society (Benjamin 2019; Cheuk 2021; O'Neil 2016).

Selin Akgün and Joseph Krajcik, *Artificial Intelligence (AI) as the Growing Actor in Education*. In: *Uses of Artificial Intelligence in STEM Education*. Edited by: Xiaoming Zhai and Joseph Krajcik, Oxford University Press. © Oxford University Press (2024). DOI: 10.1093/oso/9780198882077.003.0022

Considering the critical nature of the issue, science, technology, engineering, and mathematics (STEM) education researchers, learning and computer scientists, and practitioners have engaged in debates, narratives, and research on ethical AI usage in education (e.g., Boddington 2017; Whittaker et al. 2018; Winfield and Jirotka 2018; Zhai, Yin et al. 2020). They generate a growing body of research on (a) supporting K–12 students and teachers' understanding of social, cultural, and ethical implications of AI (e.g., Ali et al. 2019; Han 2021; Li et al. 2023; Wilson et al. 2021) and (b) university students' engagement with ethical ideas about algorithmic bias and fairness (e.g., Bogina et al. 2022; Holmes et al. 2022).

Yet, despite the critical importance of the issues of ethics and power of AI, they are largely absent from discussions of formal or informal STEM education (Vakil, Marshall, and Ibrahimovic 2020). Therefore, as educators and researchers, we have a critical responsibility to support teachers and students to both embrace the affordances of AI and promote the critical AI literacy by helping students to recognize the ethical and societal challenges and implications of AI use in K–12 STEM classrooms. To build a future generation where a diverse, critical, and inclusive citizenry can participate in the development of future AI, we have to develop opportunities for K–12 teachers and students to learn about AI by highlighting its ethical dimension (Akgün and Greenhow 2021; Holstein and Doroudi 2021). Therefore, the existing research needs to reflect more on (a) what counts as ethical AI and what makes AI unethical; and (b) what pedagogical content, tools, and platforms can teachers and students use to support them to identify and critique ethical implications of AI use for K–12 students and teachers.

This chapter will address the following research questions to contribute to the growing AI and ethics research in STEM education: (a) How can we define and unpack the benefits and affordances of AI systems in education? (b) What counts as an ethical AI system and how can we synthesize the macro-ethical issues surrounding AI in STEM education? and (c) What pedagogical approaches can we offer for educators to teach about macro-ethical issues in K–12 STEM education?

What Do We Mean by Artificial Intelligence?

When John McCarthy coined the term artificial intelligence in 1955, he defined AI as "the science and engineering of making intelligent machines." Since then, McCarthy's core idea remains the same; the latest innovations in computer science have led to various working definitions of AI: "creating intelligent machines which can replicate human behavior," and "the ability of a digital computer-controlled robot to perform tasks commonly associated with intelligent beings" (Naqvi 2020; Remian 2019). Focusing on the mimicry of human consciousness and behavior, AI also has been defined within its methodologies and applications (Manning et al. 2020; Naqvi 2020; Remian 2019; UNESCO 2019). AI systems can be defined through algorithmic models or systems that rely on mountains of data to train algorithms to recognize patterns and make decisions (Gaskins 2023). Considering the algorithms as a core element of any AI system, it is important to highlight that algorithms are human-made sets of instructions. They reflect the values and mindset of their developers who hold positions of power. Whenever people create algorithms, they also build a set of data that represents society's historical and systemic biases, which ultimately transform into algorithmic bias intentionally or not intentionally (Benjamin 2019; O'Neil 2016).

To explain how algorithms are the reflections of human decision, choice, and values, we will refer to a visualization of avocados created by a group of researchers at Harvard's Kennedy School of Government (Automating NYC n.d.). The avocado representation explains how an algorithm works in the easiest possible terms that everyone can relate to from their daily lives. Let's think of how we would buy an avocado. What kind of factors would we consider picking "the best" avocado for our purpose? For example, our options might be towards finding (a) the most affordable avocado, which is less than $1, (b) an organic avocado, or (c) the ripest avocado that we can use to make a delicious guacamole.

Considering the four avocados in Figure 22.1, we might prioritize some of their characteristics to define "the best" avocado based on our needs, values, and choices. When we set some variables (such as the cost, ripeness, and being organic or not), these variables lead us and impact our decision making. For example, buying a cheaper and ripest avocado would be preferable for most people than buying an organic avocado. Therefore, to reach a decision of buying Avocado #3, we initially analyze the full set of data points (the group of avocados) we have.

Here, the avocado visualization represents how the set of variables of the data points are used to create a set of instructions (what we refer to as "algorithms") based on our personal choices, preferences, and so biases. In other words, when we create "the best" algorithm for a problem, our choices reflect our social and cultural backgrounds, critical personal experiences, values, and priorities. Therefore, once the criteria are set to form definitions, we create patterns in the data to decide which variables matter the most to us. The automated decision making might work in a similar way since the algorithm would try to rank each of these fictional avocados based on how well it fits into the provided rules to decide what data to use and, often, which variables are important.

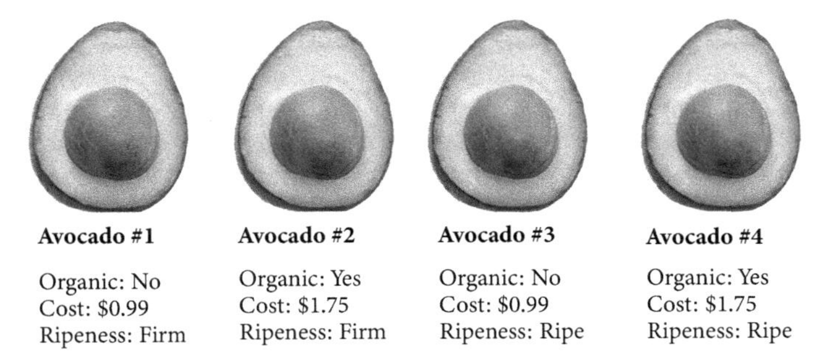

Figure 22.1 Avocado representation/analogy to define the working mechanism of algorithms.

Benefits and Applications of AI in K–12 STEM Education

Artificial intelligence is increasingly becoming a part of our everyday lives as it integrates innovations and solutions in a constantly changing and developing world, such as in the fields of healthcare, environment, agriculture, engineering, and education (Brooks 2019; McNemar 2021; O'Grady, Langton, and O'Hare 2019). As AI evolves and becomes more widespread in various areas and aspects in our lives, it also has become a significant assistant and tool for students, teachers, and institutions in the field of STEM education. There are various ways that AI is being integrated into educational contexts from elementary to higher level education. Powered by algorithms, the most common applications in education include (a) intelligent (personalized) tutoring systems, (b) automated assessment and evaluation systems, and (c) predictive analytics and chatbots (Holmes et al. 2022; Ungerer and Slade 2022; Zawacki-Richter et al. 2019). These applications hold numerous affordances at the individual (students and teachers) and systems levels (administrations and institutions). More specifically, the applications of AI have shown promise in (a) giving students an individualized, timely, and detailed feedback based on their learning needs; (b) reducing teachers' workload and helping them to support their students by gathering information in their collaborative knowledge-building processes; and (c) supporting students to find their future majors and universities, as well as their future career paths by optimizing educational administration and planning.

AI Systems to Support Students

AI-based learner tools provide software that students can use to learn multiple subject areas through intelligent (personalized) tutoring systems (ITS) (Baker and Smith 2019; Cevikbas and Kaiser 2022; Condor, Pardos, and Linn 2022; Gobert, Sao Pedro, and Betts 2023). More specifically, ITS aims to support students in K–12 STEM education by providing them access to various resources to learn in a particular area. The goal of ITS is to identify students' individual learning needs, strengths, and gaps as they are learning. The main benefits of these systems include providing feedback and suggestions to address content-related questions, offering learning materials based on students' needs and behaviors, and fostering collaborative learning environments between students (Humble and Mozelius 2019). For example, Gobert and colleagues (2023) developed an Inquiry-Intelligent Tutoring System (Inq-ITS) based on the expected science competencies for students using the reform documents of K–12 science education (NGSS 2013). Through Inq-ITS, they integrate these reform documents into an AI system by designing and developing valid, reliable, fine-grained AI-based learning and assessment resources to support both teachers' pedagogical practices and students' science learning (Gobert, Sao Pedro, and Betts 2023). Inq- ITS support students in (a) assessing their competencies in real time, (b) scaffolding their science inquiry, and (c) generating tips and suggestions to support science instruction (Gobert 2023; Gobert, Sao Pedro, and Betts 2023). Therefore, the appropriate use of ITS can promote convenient, easy, and equitable access to learning materials in online learning settings and enables the learners' individual characteristics to be efficiently addressed (Cevikbas and Kaiser 2022).

AI Systems to Support Teaching/Teachers

There are multiple forms of AI tools to support STEM educators in reducing their workload and performing their tasks on assessing and evaluating student work, and providing them feedback (Perin and Lauterbach 2018; Ungerer and Slade 2022). Specifically, automated scoring/assessment systems have become one of the main tools for combining human oversight and ML automation for evaluating and providing feedback for students' assignments in K–12 STEM education (e.g., Gerard, Kidron, and Linn 2019; Ha and Nehm 2016; Lee et al. 2021; Zhai, Yin et al. 2020; Zhai, Haudek et al. 2020; Zhai and Nehm 2023). In the past decades, researchers of science education have worked on students' written and drawn responses (such as models) to train AI to assign scores to new student responses (Haudek et al. 2011; Zhai, Yin et al. 2020). Machine learning has been applied to automatically score students' understanding, explanations, and arguments in fields of STEM (Wilson et al. 2024; Zhai, Haudek et al. 2020). More specifically, the growing body of research suggests that ML-based science assessments have potential to support students in (a) building and revising scientific explanations, (b) constructing arguments to back up their claims and explanations, (c) finding solutions to the problems they engage, and (d) fostering their active participation in science learning (Zhai, Yin et al. 2020). For example, Lee and colleagues (2021) designed a study to test a ML-enabled automated feedback system developed to support students' revision of scientific arguments using data from published sources and simulations (such as Trap, Aquifer, and Supply). Their study suggests that ML was used to develop automated scoring models for students' argumentation texts as well as to explore emerging patterns between students' simulation interactions and argumentation scores.

Considering the affordances and benefits of automated scoring systems in K–12 STEM settings, we argue that it is critical to focus on how to integrate AI more effectively, relevantly, and meaningfully in classrooms, how to train teachers to understand and use AI applications, and how to develop ethical AI that can be used in diverse teaching and learning settings.

AI Systems to Support Educational Administrations/Institutions

AI can provide several institutional tools using predictive analytics to support administrators to generate information in relation to finding marketing strategies for prospective students, planning curricula, estimating class sizes, or allocating financial resources and facilities for students (Luckin et al. 2022; Ungerer and Slade 2022). These administrative AI tools also can support K–12 students' interactions with the different aspects of an educational institution, such as students scheduling course loads, receiving recommendations for their courses and career paths, and using the guidance to find counselors and career services as they transition from K–12 education to tertiary level. In a way, predictive analytics in education assists students to determine their future university major and career path (Phani Krishna, Mani Kumar, and Aruna Sri 2018).

On the other hand, even though AI holds considerable promise in K–12 STEM education, scholars raise critical perspectives and challenge these proposed benefits of AI in education. There are numerous concerns surrounding AI use in terms of the issues of privacy, autonomy, surveillance, bias, and discrimination especially for minoritized and underserved people in the community (Akgün and Greenhow 2021; Broussard 2018; Crawford 2021; Eubanks 2018; Li et al. 2023; Sharma, Kawachi, and Bozkurt 2019). Therefore, we will next address the challenges and problematic nature of AI by discussing different philosophical and empirical standpoints on what counts as ethical and unethical AI and how the issues of power, bias, and fairness inform the affects and implications of unethical AI.

What Counts as an Ethical AI in the Context of Education?

While the benefits of using AI systems in education are visible, many members of the education research community raise ethical concerns and implications (Dignum 2018; Holmes et al. 2022). The field currently engages with the questions of what constitutes the ethics of AI in the context of education and what does "being ethical" mean in designing, using, and teaching about AI in education.

In line with these questions, the discussion of ethics and ethical policies in education tends to focus on micro-ethical concerns. The micro-ethical lens to education deals with the interpersonal decision-making processes and brings a more individual perspective to discuss the issue of trust, such as in assessments. Issues concerning the ethics of educational technology and AI are no different (Lachney et al. 2018). However, apart from the micro-ethics lens, the concept of macro-ethics goes beyond the individual levels of ethical concerns, and it centers the systemic and critical economic, political, and environmental issues in education to promote critical consciousness and collective action (Hudspith 1991, 1993; Lachney et al. 2018). Therefore, we navigate the critical discussion around ethical AI by using the concept and concerns of macro-ethics. Since we aim to move away from the traditional sense of ethics (which aligns with following the set of ethical guidelines to make hard choices) to larger and critical macro-issues, we engage with the conversation on more complicated issues, such as structural racism and discrimination, and environmental injustices to raise commitment towards ethical AI.

Even though unpacking the array of different philosophical standpoints (such as consequentialist, utilitarian, Kantian views) are beyond the scope of this chapter, we argue that it is critical to address macro-ethical issues (a) to prepare teachers and students to grasp and confront the educational dilemmas of AI, and (b) to make critical judgments and reflections about large-scale macro-ethical issues and take conscious and proactive actions (Bielefeldt 2016).

In line with the concept of macro-ethics, many scholars have defined and discussed the core ethical concerns that AI systems raise by capitalizing on the issues of bias and discrimination (especially through algorithmic bias), surveillance, privacy, and autonomy (Akgün and Greenhow 2021; Almeida, Shmarko, and Lomas 2022; Ko et al. 2020; Stahl and Wright 2018).

Figure 22.2 represents the main ethical issues raised in AI use in education for teachers and students (Akgün and Greenhow 2021). As people are exposed to an intensive amount of personal data (e.g., their location, language, biographical data, racial identity) in different online platforms, *privacy violations* could potentially occur. Although legislation exists to protect sensitive personal information, tech companies' violations with respect to security and data access increase concerns about privacy and human agency (McMurtrie 2018). *Surveillance* becomes another ethical concern which relates to tracking preferences and actions of students and teachers. AI-based surveillance or tracking systems not only monitor activities but also determine the future actions of their users (Regan and Jesse 2019). In addition to these surveillance concerns, concerns about *autonomy* stem from diminishing people's ability and freedom to act based on their own values and interests. For instance, predictive algorithms' assumptions in relation to people's future actions based on their metadata raise serious ethical questions about amplifying existing bias and prejudices of social stratification (Herodotou et al. 2020; Murphy 2019). Finally, *bias and discrimination* concerns raise another critical issue for AI ethics in K–12 education (Stahl and Wright 2018). For instance, gender bias and race- and ethnicity-specific

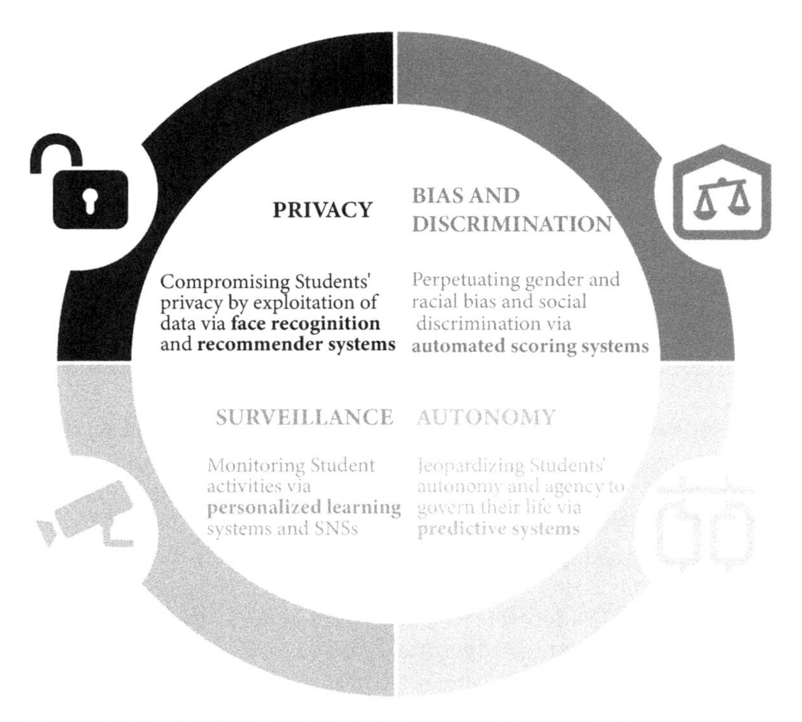

Figure 22.2 Ethical and societal challenges and issues with AI systems (Akgün and Greenhow 2021, 435).

stereotypes become one of the visible forms of this problem. Racial bias is visible in facial recognition systems towards darker skinned people that has even led to wrongful arrests (Benjamin 2019; Murphy 2019).

While these macro-ethical issues shape how we define and discuss the ethics of AI, it is also critical to reflect on and delve more into what causes these ethical issues to arise in the first place. Therefore, we will continue to discuss the underlying reasons and implications of unethical AI.

Perpetuation of Macro-ethical Issues within AI Systems: A Closer Look at the Issues of Power and Power Imbalances

To understand the underlying causes of ethical problems with AI systems, it is essential to address how AI has become one of the new "power" tools in education governance and policy through automated decision-making systems at the school and systems levels (Feathers 2019; Gulson and Witzenberger 2022). AI is already being built into everything from business intelligence platforms to schools by integrating both human and machine components and using data to model the world in K–12 education (Gulson and Sellar 2019; Gulson and Witzenberger 2022). As tech companies have already established themselves as the new players in education policies, their emergent governance assemblage may promote new forms of expertise, power, and authority within the capitalistic mindset and actions in education (Kizilcec and Lee 2022). Like all power tools, AI can provide great efficiency and productivity; however, it can also bring serious harm if not critically understood and applied safely. In doing so, the issue of power duality for human versus machine also leads to concerns for AI systems. As it is routinely portrayed in dystopian and utopian imaginings and projections, the powerful influence of algorithms manifests our worst fears and best hopes in the changing world.

Utopian and Dystopian Discourses to Tackle with the Notion of Power

On the utopian side, AI could profoundly change our world by ultimately taking over our mundane tasks, leaving us free to engage in visionary and creative tasks and pursuits, and most importantly create more just and fair living, learning, and teaching environments where social, cultural, and political biases and discrimination would be resolved. The practice of utopian thinking can be considered as "social design-based experimentation" or "informed or educated hope" that moves us from abstract notions of the ideal to concrete processes (Gutiérrez, Jurow, and Vakil 2020; Levitas 2013). Thus, utopian methodology and thinking lead us to make commitments to achieve social transformation by harmoniously bringing together AI and education. Such futuristic social imagination would cause a meaningful change by promoting equitable, resilient, sustainable, future-oriented, and contextualized learning spaces by bringing about new forms of participatory and transformative inquiry potential for vulnerable communities (Gutiérrez et al. 2017). Therefore, AI would become an essential tool for such a utopia, since it can provide more affordances for students, teachers, and educational institutions in terms of accessible, equitable, and affordable learning resources and experiences by addressing the needs, values, and personal characteristics of each community (VanLehn, Banerjee, Milner, and Wetzel 2020).

On the dystopian side, the main fear stems from humans seeking power, authority, and superiority over machine systems, and AI robots eclipsing human intelligence by dominating the human race. Various dystopian scenarios show humans' desperate search for power and fear of losing their control over AI. For example, the show *Westworld* masterfully incites us to think about where the advancement of technology will take us, and how people will continually live with an AI close in intelligence to the human mind while gaining free will and consciousness. Similarly, a famous cartoon, *The Jetsons*, portrays a universe where humans are surrounded by sophisticated AI while themselves remaining unadvanced (Schneider 2019). The historian Michael Bess has called this phenomenon "The Jetsons Fallacy." In reality, AI will not just transform the world; it will also transform us. Today's AI technology, such as the artificial hippocampus, neural lace, and brain chips for treating mood disorders, is already developing mind-altering techniques. These advancements have also created another philosophical and cultural movement and research area known as *transhumanism* (Schneider 2019). Transhumanism holds the argument that the human species is now in a comparatively early phase and its evolution will be altered through developing technologies by merging humans with machines. While there is a camp that sees transhumanist arguments and developments as technology overpowering and potentially ending the human species, another camp hopes to use AI to help end diseases and even enhance our mental lives (Schneider 2019).

The reason for us to discuss the issues of power and ethics through utopias and especially dystopias (as forms of speculative fiction) is to raise a real debate about systems using AI, their limitations, affordances, and evolution. They also show us how these imaginative alternatives connect with the realities of the real world when the discussion becomes about people seeking power and authority and transforming their own biases into discriminative AI systems. However, whatever view we take about the power of AI, it is clear that AI is changing the way we live and work, and it is our responsibility to understand the complexity of the landscape facing both developers and educators (Posner and Fei-Fei 2020).

From Dystopias to Reality: Delving into the Definition, Affect, and Implications of "Bias"

Earlier in the chapter, the avocado illustration helped us to think about how AI learns from the data, who designs and develops the AI, and how the use of misleading data would feed more biased algorithms. Transitioning to reality, the critical questions to unpack become the following: What student data are used to inform AI? How do the data (such as standardized test scores) lead to injustices and unethical results and experiences for students in the context of education?

The answers lie in the fact that AI systems offer vast amounts of information precisely because they have access to massive amounts of personal data. These data are collected, classified, grouped, analyzed, and repurposed at an unprecedented speed, scale, and frequency (Vakil, Marshall, and Ibrahimovic 2020). Typically, the data that navigate the computational operations in AI systems are categorical and numerical data that represent values that have words, while numerical variables represent values that have numbers (e.g., "Gender" could have values 0 and 1, where 0 = Male and 1 = Female) (Lee and Delaney 2022). Therefore, in nature, categorical and numerical data are used to classify, not to measure. Such classification makes individuals vulnerable to a variety of risks (e.g., surveillance, exclusion from critical material opportunities). Moreover, these risks are visible and real, are difficult to reason about, and impact social groups who are already vulnerable (Eubanks 2018; Vakil and Higgs 2019).

As a result of the types of data that AI systems use, discussions of algorithmic bias in education have been growing with the various definitions of the term "bias" (Baker and Hawn 2022; Blodgett et al. 2020; Crawford 2021; Gaskins 2023). The notion of "algorithmic bias" has been unpacked through an array of examples of unfairness in automated assessment systems, which seem to fit technical or statistical meanings of bias (Polonski 2018; Raji et al. 2020). In response, researchers working at the intersection of social sciences and computer science have attempted to widen the criteria to define bias (Baker and Hawn 2022). They have expanded the societal and statistical distinction of the kinds of bias that can be formed in ML systems, and they categorize the potential harms and implications that stem from that bias.

For example, Mitchell, Finn, and Manning (2021) made an important distinction between the societal and statistical forms of bias. They described societal bias as "concerns about objectionable social structures that are represented in the data" (p. 4), and "a model's predictive performance unjustifiably differs across disadvantaged groups along social axes such as race, gender, and class" (p. 1). The authors claim that statistical bias reflects the sampling bias and measurement error in the data. Suresh and Guttag (2021) expand the definition by referring to bias as potential sources of unwanted or societally unfavorable outcomes which algorithms that we create reinforce. Similarly, scholars such as O'Neil (2016), Noble (2018), and Benjamin (2019) have described the impacts of AI bias in social systems and how AI could become a major human rights issue. Noble (2018) focuses on how data use in AI is often biased due to historical perceptions of minorities (such as race and gender) that inform and influence how developers prioritize the needs of majorities or justify discriminatory attitudes through historical biased data. Building on that, Benjamin (2019) dismantles the idea of "technology is objective and neutral" by explaining how data, algorithms, and AI privilege Whiteness and other forms of power. Benjamin considers how algorithms act as narratives that reaffirm existing inequalities and operate within powerful systems, which eventually amplifies the racial hierarchies and replicates social divisions.

On the other hand, other authors prefer to use the term "unfair" over biased, to highlight bias for its statistical meaning and preserve fairness for its moral and societal implications (Barocas, Hardt, and Narayanan 2019; Kizilcec and Lee 2022; Mehrabi et al. 2021). For example, Mehrabi et al. (2021) described fairness in the context of algorithmic decision-making as "the absence of any prejudice or favoritism toward an individual or a group based on their inherent or acquired characteristics. An unfair algorithm is one whose decisions are skewed towards a particular group of people" (p. 1). Instead of using demographic disparity and discrimination to refer to the negative impacts of applying some models, Barocas, Hardt, and Narayanan (2019) maintain the meaning of bias in its statistical sense as systematic error in either data or model estimates. Overall, from statistical biases of measurement and error to unwanted societal impacts and discrimination of algorithmic models, there are a range of biases. Even though the descriptions and sources of the bias seem various, its impact and implications bring some consensus on how harmful they are for society.

In education, the examples of AI bias can perpetuate the harm in standardized testing and automated assessment which impact high-stakes admission decisions (Dorans, Moses, and Eignor 2010; Gaskins 2023) and the biased systematic representations of underserved groups (Crawford 2021). For example, a college admissions office is using a software program to identify applicants likely to succeed at the college; since the algorithm is "learning" from that institution's previous admissions data, it will tend to make recommendations that resemble past biases. England's A-level and GCSE secondary-level examinations from 2020 is one of the critical examples of such bias. When the examinations were canceled due to the pandemic, the alternative assessment method was implemented to determine the qualification grades of students. The grade standardization algorithm worked based on schools' previous examination results; therefore thousands of students were shocked to receive unexpectedly low grades. Algorithms created a score distribution favored by students who attended private or independent schools, while students from under-represented groups were hit hardest. Unfortunately, automated assessment algorithms have the potential to reconstruct unfair and inconsistent results by disrupting student's final scores and future careers. Similarly, algorithmic bias in higher education is showing up in similar ways. In 2020, the computer science department at the University of Texas at Austin abandoned a ML program which evaluated prospective applicants to their PhD program (Burke 2020). The program's database used past admission decisions in its algorithm, which critics contended reduced opportunities for students from diverse backgrounds. They found that Black students were identified as "high risk" to not graduate in their selected major at four times the rate of White peers, which illustrates the race as a social construct took precedence over other social markers. These cases illustrate that use of facial recognition and surveillance systems have a potential to specifically harm students from under-represented groups. That's why educators, researchers, and administrators also need to think about the risk of structural inequities informing the software's recommendations, a phenomenon known as algorithmic bias.

Ethical Concerns of AI Integration in Classrooms: Amplifying the Existing Educational Inequities

Previously, we focused on the types and underlying reasons of increasing macro-ethical concerns of using historical data to train AI. Here, we want to specifically zoom in on the pedagogical and instructional challenges and implications of AI integration in K–12 STEM classrooms. We argue that macro-ethical concerns towards AI might potentially exacerbate the existing inequalities and create new forms of inequities in education by diminishing human agency, teacher–student relationship, and educational equity. Addressing these educational challenges is particularly important, because without introducing and connecting the issues of macro-ethics of AI to STEM education, it's hard to propose critical and relevant pedagogies and practices on how to raise critical consciousness towards ethical AI.

First, we argue that learning, at its core, is about exercising choice and agency with the sense of ownership and responsibility (Bu 2022; Louie 2020; McDonald, Kazemi, and Kavanagh 2013). This mindset leads us to think about what happens to human choice, rights, and more importantly human agency as AI enters the schools and classrooms. This is a critical question because these value judgments can inform the experiences and agency of students in terms of having or not having a choice, and collective responsibility in their own learning experiences (Berendt, Littlejohn, and Blakemore 2020; Bu 2022). This concern calls for serious considerations around transparency, data ownership, and privacy resulting from algorithmic biases associated with education that should be addressed (Slade and Prinsloo 2013).

Second, with the integration of AI into education, the traditional educational environment has started to shift from "teachers as the main facilitators" to "teachers and AI as the collaborative helpers" to support students in classrooms. On the one hand, such collaboration may help teachers to lessen their duties and repetitive tasks and allow them to focus more on how to support students' learning experiences more meaningfully (Wilson et al. 2021). On the other hand, the concern becomes whether the "human-like AI" is capable of supporting social, emotional, and cultural components of learning and supporting students' complex and higher-order thinking skills. Considering human interaction and learning as a sociocultural process, teacher expertise and involvement becomes crucial for fostering situated and bounded learning experiences for students (Lave and Wenger, 1991; Peressini et al. 2004). Therefore, the concern becomes how AI remains limited in integrating students' backgrounds, communities, and personal experiences in a learning context. Another critique is that AI does not demonstrate social and emotional skills to prepare students for future social integration (Bu 2022). Teacher–student and interstudent interaction are limited within the AI system, especially in terms of cultivating collaboration and self-reflection (Baines et al. 2017). Therefore, we also need to consider how the integration of AI systems might and to what extent challenge the healthy ecology of teacher–student relationship in a learning environment.

Finally, AI systems' risk of amplifying educational inequities by mitigating exclusion (based on students' racial, ethnic, gender backgrounds) in social networks, curriculum, pedagogy, and course participation is worth considering. As mentioned earlier, personalized learning systems remain limited with respect to integrating students' sociocultural backgrounds and cultural resources and experiences into the learning process. Similarly, automated assessment systems might amplify inequities especially for the under-represented group of students (as seen in England's A-level and GCSE exams in 2020). Beyond resolving the material access issue to AI systems for students, AI instruction should also provide students with cultural resources to integrate their own personal, social, and cultural backgrounds into the learning process. It should also help them realize and critique existing power structures in AI systems and help them cultivate social awareness about the injustices and inequities AI creates (and for whom) in society.

Strategies for Researchers and Educators to Address and Raise Critical Consciousness towards Ethical AI in Education

Considering the benefits and growing challenges of AI, the core question for STEM educators become the following: What proactive pedagogical and instructional strategies can we provide for teachers and students, so that they can identify, critique, and take actions on the ethical challenges of AI?

Previously, we argued that the core ethical issues of AI stem from issues of power, power imbalances, and the data used in AI systems. Therefore, to support students' AI literacy and help them develop critical consciousness towards designing ethical future AI, we now introduce various pedagogical tools, frameworks, and strategies for STEM educators (see Figure 22.3).

Figure 22.3 reflects on interdisciplinary, asset-based, creative, and justice-oriented strategies and tools to teach students about ethical AI within the issues of bias, power imbalances, and inequities that AI systems cause. We argue that these strategies are interconnected and work with each other. In other words, they reinforce each other recursively with an equal amount of significance to be able to support students to critique AI's ethical challenges and to become its critical consumers and future designers.

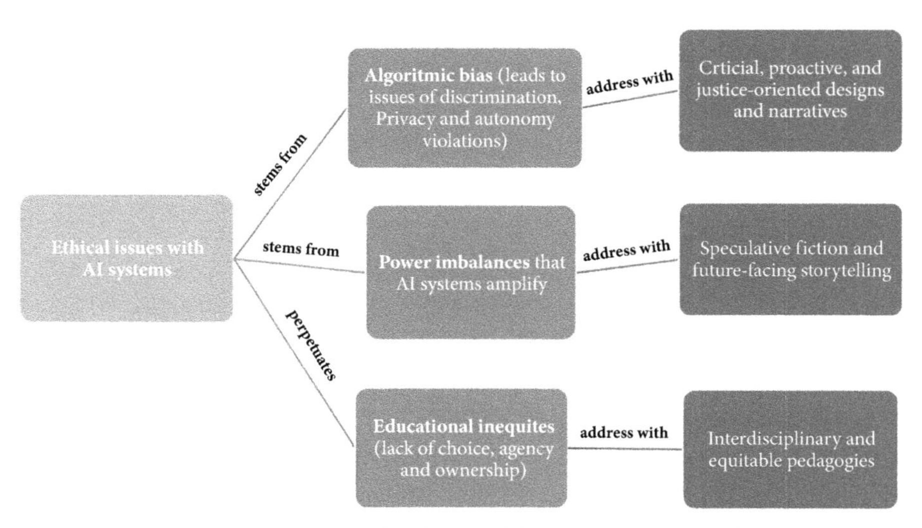

Figure 22.3 Potential causes of unethical AI and future actions to be taken to address them in education.

Strategy 1: Critical, Proactive, and Justice-Oriented Designs and Narratives to Critique and Dismantle Algorithmic Bias in Education

In the following, we introduce quality pedagogical tools and resources to enable a critical and justice-oriented perspective. These resources can be instrumental in introducing and discussing algorithmic bias and ways to dismantle the macro-ethical challenges of AI.

Introducing Students to the "Gender Shades" Project: Highlighting Gender and Racial Algorithmic Biases

Researchers Joy Buolamwini and Timnit Gebru (2018) illustrated that algorithms can discriminate based on social markers like race and gender. Buolamwini and Gebru examined bias in automated facial analysis algorithms with respect to phenotypic subgroups. Their analysis showed that darker-skinned females are the most misclassified group and facial recognition systems performed better on male than female faces, and better on lighter-skin than darker-skin faces. Using this research, MIT Media Lab's elementary curricula of "AI and Ethics" and "DAILy AI" introduced the findings from their Gender Shades project as a case study for addressing the concept of algorithmic bias through what Buolamwini calls "coded gaze" in data, which reflects the priorities, preferences, and prejudices of those who have the power to shape technology. Engaging with the ideas, students can discuss what might cause the biased results towards people from certain gender and racial backgrounds, and what can be done to make those AI systems (i.e., facial recognition) perform better.

Integrating the critical work of the Gender Shades project is critical for STEM learning environments for several reasons. First, as students actively work with facial recognition software, they will engage with the topics of racial and gender discrimination more and identify how these ethical implications present within the production of data (algorithms) in society (Noble 2018). Second, teaching about these issues will help students develop critical consciousness towards how data are inherently socially constructed in ways that can exclude marginalized individuals and populations (Cheuk 2021). We argue that without a critical lens on data and AI literacy, students might develop problematic assumptions, such as that data are objective and independent of the thought systems that create them (Kitchin 2014; Vakil and Higgs 2019). Therefore, such a lesson on the creation of unethical AI systems would be complemented by highlighting how people who developed those algorithms carry and transform certain biases into the ML algorithms.

"Essay Auto-grader": Introducing Algorithmic Biases in Automated Assessment Systems

Essay auto-graders are automated grading tools that can "read" and assess essays, which requires the computer to make decisions about what the essay is about, and how good it is. It is important (a) to help students understand why automated essay graders exist and why they are becoming one of the most common forms of AI in education, and (b) to allow students to directly work with these auto grader tools, so that they can reflect on the critical and meaningful ways of implementing instructions. As one of the US-based nonprofits in AI education, AI4ALL's "Bytes of AI" curriculum provides quality resources in teaching about AI and ethics. The Bytes of AI curriculum grounds the conversation for students around the need and affordances of automated essay graders. It leads students to discuss how AI saves time for teachers, and how they can also get individualized feedback to their written work. Students can work with a sample essay grader (https://www.paperrater.com), add one of their essays into the system, and analyze how the auto-grader grades the essay and whether it's similar to how their teacher assessed the essay. Most importantly, students can attempt to trick the grader by uploading two essays for which (a) they received a good grade but don't think the auto-grader will grade them well and (b) they think is bad but believe the auto-grader will grade them well. In that way, they imitate BABEL Generator team's earlier experiment on trying to fool automated essay scoring machines which are unsystematic (AI4ALL 2023). Such investigations and discourse have the potential to allow students to take part in a critical discussion about what biases automated grading systems have, where those biases might have come from, and how those biases might be mitigated.

Google's Teachable Machine and ChatGPT

Google's Teachable Machine is a powerful tool for supporting students in exploring and designing their own AI systems to experience how these systems are created by using classification and lead programmers to transform their biases into algorithms. More specifically, Google's Teachable Machine, a Web tool, makes it fast and easy to create ML models for people's individual projects. Bytes of AI and DAILy AI curricula offer lessons for students to train their own AI (facial recognition) systems to recognize their images (AI4ALL 2023; MIT RAISE 2023). In one of these investigations, students create a cat-and-dog classifier by initially designing a training dataset that includes several different cat and dog images based on their color, posture, and types (MIT RAISE 2023). Then, to test their dataset, students show the same and different image sets to their model and record whether their classifier can predict the image. Finally, they rearrange their dataset with an assortment of images to make their training dataset of cats and dogs larger and more diverse. In that way, students have first-hand experiences of creating their own datasets, testing whether their AI classifies each image correctly (within a good confidence score), and testing whether their AI is better with dogs or cats and explaining why they think so. As the students explore how their AI makes decisions and judgements, they explore the idea of how bias towards cats or dogs occurs in their AI system.

Another critical and timely tool for engaging with in K–12 classrooms is ChatGPT. OpenAI's essay-writing, test-taking chatbot has raised a variety of questions, concerns, and promises about the future of STEM learning and teaching for practitioners and educators (Heaven 2023; Zhai; 2023). As a tool, ChatGPT is able to provide quick, easy, and meaningful responses to questions, especially when well-constructed prompts are provided. On the other hand, many people push back in terms of raising ethical issues on cheating and misinformation, as well as the tool limiting students' critical-thinking and problem-solving skills in classrooms (Heaven 2023). We argue that STEM educators and researchers need to critically consider the challenges and affordances of ChatGPT in K–12 settings. First, ChatGPT can be seen as a meaningful teaching and learning scaffold with the use of critical mindset and approach. In other words, teachers can guide students not only on how to just find responses and solutions to their questions and problems but on how to use the tool as a guide to write better, research better, find relevant learning sources better, and determine better which information to trust and criticize (Roose 2023). The tool can be extremely helpful for students in developing their writing skills (especially for English language learners), as well as their critical science and language literacies. For example, students can use ChatGPT during class to create outlines for their models, artifacts, or essays, comparing and contrasting different arguments about critical science phenomena and driving question. Once the outlines are generated based on the students' meaningful prompts, students can put their laptops away and start writing their positions, arguments, and essays in a contextualized and detail way. In that way, students can learn how to interact with AI models and how to use them ethically to ground their learning experiences as a tool for in-class activities. In addition, instead of feeling threatened and banning the tool itself, an alternative critical perspective can be leveraged by having students work with ChatGPT and discuss what ethical questions and concerns are raised in using the tool. From this first-hand experience, students can spot cases where the tool amplifies issues of privacy, misinformation, bias, and discrimination (Roose 2023). We argue that students will need hands-on experiences with these tools to figure out how this type of AI works, what types of bias it contains and perpetuates, and how it can be misused in different fields (Roose 2023).

Strategy 2: Speculative Fiction to Critique Power Imbalances and Problematic Implications of AI

Speculative fiction is a powerful medium and future-thinking tool for supporting students' creative and critical narratives on equitable and sustainable use of AI in their communities (Dunne and Raby 2013; Gaskins 2023). As a genre of speculative fiction, utopian and dystopian narratives invite students to think of the most extreme cases and to see how we choose to respond to a moment of systemic and structural bias and discrimination formed through power imbalances in reality (Atwood 2014; Huddleston 2016). In other words, using fictional narratives and future-facing storytelling with students has the potential to guide researchers and teachers in bringing up critical conversations about (a) how the implementation of AI causes equity and power issues, as well as the social reproduction of injustices across different systems and contexts, and (b) how ethical AI also might ameliorate existing inequities by ensuring transparent and fair results for underserved students (Gaskins 2023; Noble 2018; Reich and Ito 2017; Watkins and Cho 2018). Therefore, we argue that speculative fiction in STEM education (such as utopias and dystopias) might be a powerful, engaging, and creative tool for centering and reflecting on how power imbalances lead to our fears and/or hopes concerning AI.

For example, using the lenses of speculative fiction Gaskins (2023) discusses how algorithmic bias manifests in under-represented communities through educational technology. Focusing on various artists and activists' creative work (such as films, physical artifacts, toolkits, and prototypes), Gaskins (2023) explores both fictional and real-life visions of AI in education. Through the near-future speculative fiction film *#tresdancing*, Gaskins emphasizes the harms of algorithmic bias and surveillance systems, and how AI tools and applications are used to monitor, track, and assess students (Attewell, Kasinitz, and Dunn 2010). In the short film, students are increasingly being required to use distance learning and online assessment tools, as well as tools of virtual and augmented reality. The film illustrates how students in real life have become more vulnerable to bias and surveillance and alienated from real-life learning settings. The film also becomes a multimodal learning tool that portrays how market mechanisms and capitalism in education has led to the perception of students as consumers or passive learners (Harrison and Risler 2015; Naidoo and Whitty 2013).

In addition to future-facing films, different forms of speculative fiction are being used in various curricula. For example, MIT Media Lab's AI and ethics curriculum provides students with an opportunity to interact with various technologies, such as emotion detection software called *AlterEgo*. AlterEgo is a wearable headset that allows people to "talk" to their devices, such as the search engine on their phone, or simply by thinking (MIT RAISE 2023). From interacting with how AlterEgo works, students have a discourse using the prompt "In 50 years this technology could do the most *good* and *harm* by . . . ." This potentially leads to critical conversation about the technology's ethical ramifications, because it helps students think about who could be helped by this technology, and what hopes or fears we might have about it. Students use creative writing prompts to respond to such questions as who might be affected by the technology and how it might produce benefit or harm in the future.

Strategy 3: Interdisciplinary and Equitable Pedagogies to Address the Ethical Issues and Eliminate Educational Inequities

Besides discussing its benefits, we previously argued that AI in education can amplify existing educational inequities by (a) decreasing student agency, choice, and ownership in learning process; (b) limiting their access to quality educational resources (especially the newest AI technologies in classrooms) and critical learning moments; and (c) interrupting their meaningful cultural, social-emotional, and academic experiences and interactions. To design more equitable experiences within the context of AI and STEM education, learning scientists and teacher educators should consider, adopt, and promote critical pedagogies that are embodied, relevant, and socially and culturally responsive. In the following, we discuss potential pathways for leveraging more equitable and justice-oriented learning experiences for students in both learning about and designing ethical AI in K–12 STEM classrooms.

Cultivating Critical AI Literacy through Culturally Relevant Pedagogies

AI literacy is an essential part of digital literacy for all students, as it helps them understand how computers perceive, learn, make decisions, act, and create (Williams, Park, and Breazeal 2019). As a part of fostering digital literacy, AI literacy has an increasingly important role for students to understand and discuss the foundational knowledge of AI and how to design future ethical AI (Druga et al. 2018; Villegas, 1991).

Across the education literature, *culturally relevant and culturally responsive pedagogies* have set the tone for incorporating cultural relevance into education through a social justice lens. By using equitable and culturally responsive pedagogies (CRP) to teach about ethical AI in STEM learning environments, students can develop AI literacy from a critical perspective. Considering CRP originated from Ladson-Billings' (1995) seminal work of culturally relevant pedagogy and Gay's (2018) work on culturally responsive teaching, CRP prioritize addressing student academic success, cultural competence, community connection, raising sociopolitical consciousness, and challenging deficit perspectives about students of color (particularly African American students in the US context).

Since CRP prioritizes using cultural knowledge and relevant prior experiences for ethnically diverse students, it is critical for us to integrate CRP as a pedagogical perspective to help students (a) gain an understanding of how algorithms reflect society's social, political, and historical knowledge and biases, and (b) work collaboratively with peers to challenge and solve problems and design ethical and just AI systems while considering the needs of their local communities. With its affordances, CRP is already one of the critical teaching perspectives in the field of STEM education (via computing). CRP has mainly emerged by including *ethnocomputing* (e.g., Babbit, Lyles, and Eglash 2012; Tedre et al. 2006), *culturally responsive computing* (e.g., Morales et al. 2019; Scott, Sheridan, and Clark 2015), and *culturally situated design tools* (Allen Kuyenga, Lachney, and Green 2022; Eglash et al. 2020; Lachney 2017) in STEM education.

For example, Scott, Sheridan, and Clark (2015) offer a nuanced vision of culturally responsive computing (CRC) to guide researchers and educators of digital media and computer education. Creating a program called COMPUGIRLS, Scott and colleagues taught computational skills using culturally relevant practice. The program centers intersectionality and techno-social activism to address the inequities in computer education, especially the injustices that result from the lack of opportunities that historically marginalized groups face. They define these marginalized groups as (a) women, who tend not to enter information technology as much as men; (b) racialized minority groups (e.g., African American, Native American, and Latinos); and (c) economically underserved districts that have less access to advanced computer science courses. Similarly, Pinkard and colleagues (2020) investigate how *Digital Youth Divas* (DYD), which is an out-of-school program for middle school girls from non-dominant communities, engage participants in computational thinking by linking to their broader interests, home networks, and continuing opportunities.

Together, ethno-computing and CRP can help STEM educators move the needle towards equity and justice in computing and learning about ethical technology and AI systems by considering many forms of students' cultural wealth. These theories and tools, therefore, will help STEM educators and students outline the novel and critical ways to engage with the digital divide, ethics of AI, and AI literacy (Hammond 2014; Madaio et al. 2022).

Broadening Meaningful Participation: Holistic and Interdisciplinary AI Education

It is vital to use an interdisciplinary and inquiry-based approach in STEM education where learners can bring their own questions, interests, prior experiences, and knowledge to the newly introduced AI ideas using multiple literacies (Su and Yang 2022). Integrated with language, math, and/or science literacy, it is critical to provide engaging, playful, and hands-on learning experiences for students to deepen their understanding of AI concepts and their societal, cultural, and ethical aspects. For instance, Sakulkueakulsuk et al. (2018) and DiPaola, Payne, and Breazeal (2020) connected AI with STEM to promote wonderment and collaboration in learning an AI-based activity. These studies discuss the design principle of "embedded ethics" and how educators can incorporate ethical thinking activities into project-based ML curricula on emerging AI topics, such as generative adversarial networks, affective perception, and supervised ML. Using real-world ML demos, conceptual discussions, and open-ended artifact creation, students learn to anticipate potential beneficial and harmful uses of various generative AI tools. Similarly, Williams, Park, and Breazeal (2019) designed a social robot called "PopBots" to make AI concepts accessible and to help elementary students to interact with AI technology through hands-on experiences. The social robot was an intelligent agent and used by students in three hands-on activities. As students engage with the social robot, they focus on knowledge-based systems, generative algorithms, and supervised ML, respectively. Informed by the views of sociocultural and constructionist learning, PopBots promotes students learning by experiencing (Williams, Park, and Breazeal 2019).

Additionally, to have meaningful learning experiences about ethical AI systems, students need agency to figure out, use, and evaluate AI with purposeful guidance within the context of interdisciplinary knowledge. A study conducted in Finland investigated how the digital *Poetry Machine* influences students' poetry writing and improves their linguistic skills and creative thinking by applying AI techniques (Kangasharju et al. 2022). Poetry Machine is an AI-based co-creative tool designed at the University of Helsinki in the Department of Computer Science to investigate students' computational linguistic creativity. More specifically, this digital AI-based tool produces poems and helps students to revise their poems. The tool pays particular attention to phonological features and semantics of poems (rhymes, alliteration, assonances, and free mimetic repetition) which are key elements of poetic language while supporting students (Wilson and Dymoke 2017). As students engaged with the Poetry Machine, they had more motivation to compose poems and also develop their writing competencies, including poetry writing, by experimenting with various poetic features and structures (Kangasharju et al. 2022). Poetry Machine inspired students who engaged in the writing process and supported their literacy skills by narrowing the gap between students' digital writing practices outside of school and writing practices in school (Kangasharju et al. 2022). Students need more and varied opportunities like this to develop their multiple literacies and competencies by using the various features and structures with AI-based and other digital tools.

Enhancing Relevance, Interest, and Critical Thinking

To enrich equitable and critical AI instruction, increasing learning opportunities that are relevant and important to students and their communities' lives is critical.

Such learning space also should support and foreground students' linguistic, cultural, and intellectual interest and resources. One way to achieve such a goal is to offer investigations where students can design and create their own AI systems that would support their community's values and needs. In that way, students can figure out what kind of design might be ideal for helping people or be harmful to their local communities. In addition, when students see the relevance and connection between what they learn and how they can connect this new knowledge to their own lives, it might motivate them to resolve the dilemmas and problems that AI systems might pose (Brown 2017; Gutiérrez and Rogoff 2003; Rodriguez 2015).

As an example, the Bytes of AI curriculum offers a lesson on AI and environmental activism which brings AI and science literacy together by centering justice-oriented and experiential approach. Through these lessons, students can think further about how environmentalists use AI to analyze and work with graphical data (Cho 2018; Oconnor 2017). More specifically, students initially identify pictures of animals from close up and far away to mimic the way environmentalists look at data. Then, they start analyzing satellite data by focusing on how AI can look at millions of pictures in an hour, freeing researchers and environmentalists to make inferences and plans. Finally, students watch a video of how an AI classifies images, so they can interpret how data helps models to classify pictures more accurately and analyze graphical data. Most importantly, these lessons also bring a critical community connection to AI and STEM education. They specifically critique how poor and marginalized populations are more likely to be victims of poor environmental care and how pollution affects marginalized communities in a broader spectrum.

Conclusion and Future Directions in Practice and Research

There is a growing interest in how to better prepare and support K–12 students to work with AI and raise their critical consciousness towards ethical aspects of AI in STEM education. In this chapter, we first discuss the benefits and affordances of AI in education by supporting students' learning experiences, teachers' instruction and workload, and schools' administrative and institutional roles (Holmes, Bialik, and Fadel 2019; Ungerer and Slade 2022; Remian 2019). Then, we unpack how the increasing algorithmically driven world raises significant ethical and pedagogical questions in relation to (a) amplifying power imbalances, bias, and discrimination against members of underserved communities, and (b) perpetuating educational inequities by diminishing students' agency and choice and limiting students' opportunities to engage with meaningful and equitable social, emotional, and cultural learning experiences. Therefore, while reaping the benefits of AI, STEM educators and researchers also need to support students in identifying and evaluating the risks of AI to provide solutions and remedies. Teachers and students should also embrace their roles in education, adapt to new teaching ecology integrated with AI, and develop a critical AI literacy by becoming critical consumers of advanced AI technologies and knowledge by addressing AI's potential ethical risks. To enhance this goal, we offer a set of pedagogical and instructional strategies and tools based on various works from the interdisciplinary literature and multiple bodies of educational research to inform more effective, responsible, and inclusive teaching and research opportunities for students in STEM.

Therefore, this chapter adds to the field in two important ways. First, it defines and explores the existing macro-ethical issues that AI raises in education. Second, it discusses how to teach these macro-ethical challenges (such as bias, discrimination, and privacy) and what pedagogical strategies to use to promote students' critical consciousness and AI literacy in STEM education. In other words, this chapter contributes to the understanding of how opportunities to learn about the ethics of advanced AI technologies emerge and are negotiated through interactions between students and teachers in STEM-learning environments.

Considering that existing research on how best to support researchers and practitioners in teaching AI and ethics is still in its infancy, there are a number of critical future implications of this chapter for curriculum developers, teacher educators, and researchers in this growing field. First, in terms of the implications for STEM teacher educators, it is critical to conduct future research on designing quality and relevant professional learning opportunities for in-service and pre-service teachers.

Second, further research is needed in terms of curriculum development. There is an urgent need for designing more critical, relevant, and quality curriculum materials for K–12 STEM educators where equity and justice-oriented AI and data literacy can be leveraged. In other words, it is critical to center the systemic injustices, racial and gendered hierarchies, and power dynamics of AI systems to address the concerns of surveillance, privacy, autonomy, and bias in STEM classrooms (Greener 2019). Such curriculum resources and materials can provide students more opportunities to voice their own contextual and cultural experiences while trying to critique and disrupt existing power structures that AI systems pose.

Finally for STEM education researchers who study AI and ethics instruction, it is critical to conduct future research that considers students' humanistic entanglements with data and AI systems. With the field of computing only recently re-emerging in education, studies on how to embed culturally relevant pedagogies in AI and ethics teaching in STEM are still budding. Therefore, to improve future studies where CRP occurs to raise sociopolitical consciousness, researchers should consider studying larger and more diverse samples with various curriculum resources. In other words, future research that investigates the implementation of CRP-oriented AI and ethics curriculum could benefit from and longitudinal intervention studies.

There is much at stake, because AI systems can be trained to advocate or discriminate, appreciate or reject, or make visible or invisible. Therefore, AI systems must be introduced to students with its affordances and challenges and as educators, we need to help students have wider discussions about their consequences. By learning from past mistakes, we can move forward to a future where more people feel liberated to reimagine constructions of different social markers in the constructions of AI. Looking ahead, we must promote honest, caring, and critical conversations around the many challenges that lie in creating fair and ethical AI. We hope this chapter serves to further discussion to bring new ideas, strategies, and discourses into the area of AI-supported education.

Acknowledgments

The intellectual work and writing process of this chapter was done and completed at CREATE for STEM Institute, Michigan State University.

References

Akgün, S., and Greenhow, C. 2021. "Artificial Intelligence in Education: Addressing Ethical Challenges in K–12 Settings." *AI and Ethics* 2, no. 10: 431–40.

AI4ALL. 2023. https://ai-4-all.org/open-learning/resources/

Ali, S., Payne, B. H., Williams, R., Park, H. W., and Breazeal, C. 2019, June. "Constructionism, Ethics, and Creativity: Developing Primary and Middle School Artificial Intelligence Education." In *International Workshop on Education in Artificial Intelligence k–12 (eduai'19)*, 1–4.

Allen Kuyenga, M. C., Lachney, M., and Green, B. 2022. "Race-Positive Career and Technical Education: Techno-Social Agency Beyond the Vocational-Liberal Divide." *TechTrends* 67: 446–55.

Almeida, D., Shmarko, K., and Lomas, E. 2022. "The Ethics of Facial Recognition Technologies, Surveillance, and Accountability in an Age of Artificial Intelligence: A Comparative Analysis of US, EU, and UK Regulatory Frameworks." *AI and Ethics* 2, no. 3: 377–87.

Attewell, P., Kasinitz, P., and Dunn, K. 2010. "Black Canadians and black Americans: Racial Income Inequality in Comparative Perspective." *Ethnic and Racial Studies* 33, no. 3: 473–95. https://doi.org/10.1080/01419870903085883

Atwood, M. 2014. *In Other Worlds: SF and the Human Imagination*. London: Virago.

Automating NYC. n.d. "Automating NYC and (En)coding Inequality?" https://automating.nyc/#introduction

Babbit, B., Lyles, D., and Eglash, R. 2012. "From Ethnomathematics to Ethnocomputing." *Alternative Forms of Knowing (in) Mathematics*. Rotterdam: Sense Publishers.

Baines, A., DeBarger, A., De Vivo, K., and Warner, N. 2017. "Why is Social and Emotional Learning Essential to Project-Based Learning." LER position paper, *2*.

Baker, R. S., and Hawn, A. 2022. "Algorithmic Bias in Education." *International Journal of Artificial Intelligence in Education* 32, no. 4: 1052–92.

Baker, T., and Smith, L. 2019. *Educ-AI-tion Rebooted? Exploring the Future of Artificial Intelligence in Schools and Colleges*. London: nesta. https://media.nesta.org.uk/documents/Future_of_AI_and_education_v5_WEB.pdf

Barocas, S., Hardt, M. and Narayanan, A. 2019. *Fairness and Machine Learning: Limitations and Opportunities*. https://fairmlbook.org.

Benjamin, R. 2019. "Race after Technology: Abolitionist Tools for the New Jim Code." New York: Wiley.

Berendt, B., Littlejohn, A., and Blakemore, M. 2020. "AI in Education: Learner Choice and Fundamental Rights." *Learning, Media, and Technology* 45, no. 3: 312–24.

Bielefeldt, A. R., Canney, N., Swan, C., and Knight, D. W. 2016. "Contributions of Learning through Service to the Ethics Education of Engineering Students." International Journal for Service Learning in Engineering, Humanitarian Engineering and Social Entrepreneurship 11, no. 2: 1–17.

Blodgett, S. L., Barocas, S., Daumé III, H., and Wallach, H. 2020. "Language (Technology) is Power: A Critical Survey of 'Bias' in NLP." *arXiv preprint arXiv:2005.14050.*

Boddington, P. 2017. *Towards a Code of Ethics for Artificial Intelligence*, 27–37. Cham: Springer.

Bogina, V., Hartman, A., Kuflik, T., and Shulner-Tal, A. 2022. "Educating Software and AI Stakeholders about Algorithmic Fairness, Accountability, Transparency, and Ethics." *International Journal of Artificial Intelligence in Education* 32, no. 3: 808–33.

Brooks, A. 2019, November 4. *The Benefits of AI: 6 Societal Advantages of Automation*. Rasmussen University. https://www.rasmussen.edu/degrees/technology/blog/benefits-of-ai/

Broussard, M. 2018. *Artificial Unintelligence: How Computers Misunderstand the World.* Cambridge, MA: MIT Press.

Brown, J. C. 2017. "A Metasynthesis of the Complementarity of Culturally Responsive and Inquiry-Based Science Education in K-12 Settings: Implications for Advancing Equitable Science Teaching and Learning." *Journal of Research in Science Teaching* 54, no. 9: 1143–73.

Bu, Q. 2022. "Ethical Risks in Integrating Artificial Intelligence into Education and Potential Countermeasures." *Science Insights* 41, no. 1: 561–66.

Buolamwini, J., and Gebru, T. 2018, January. "Gender Shades: Intersectional Accuracy Disparities in Commercial Gender Classification." In *Conference on Fairness, Accountability, and Transparency*, 77–91. PMLR.

Burke, L. 2020, December 13. "The Death and Life of an Admissions Algorithm." Inside Higher Ed. https://www.insidehighered.com/admissions/article/2020/12/14/u-texas-will-stop-using-controversial-algorithm-evaluate-phd

Cevikbas, M., and Kaiser, G. 2022. "Promoting Personalized Learning in Flipped Classrooms: A Systematic Review Study." *Sustainability* 14, no. 18: 11393.

Cheuk, T. 2021. "Can AI Be Racist? Color-Evasiveness in the Application of Machine Learning to Science Assessments." Science Education 105, no. 5: 825–36.

Cho, R. 2018, June 5. *Artificial Intelligence—A Game Changer for Climate Change and the Environment.* Columbia Climate School. https://news.climate.columbia.edu/2018/06/05/artificial-intelligence-climate-environment/

Condor, A., Pardos, Z., and Linn, M. 2022, July. "Representing Scoring Rubrics as Graphs for Automatic Short Answer Grading." In *International Conference on Artificial Intelligence in Education*, 354–65. Cham: Springer International Publishing.

Crawford, K. 2021. *Atlas of AI.* New Haven, CT: Yale University Press.

Dignum, V. 2018. "Ethics in Artificial Intelligence: Introduction to the Special Issue." *Ethics and Information Technology* 20, no. 1: 1–3.

DiPaola, D., Payne, B. H., and Breazeal, C. 2020, June. "Decoding Design Agendas: An Ethical Design Activity for Middle School Students." In *Proceedings of the Interaction Design and Children Conference*, 1–10.

Dorans, N. J., Moses, T. P., and Eignor, D. R. 2010. "Principles and Practices of Test Score Equating." *ETS Research Report Series* 2010, no. 2: 1–41.

Druga, S., Williams, R., Park, H. W., and Breazeal, C. 2018, June. "How Smart Are the Smart Toys? Children and Parents' Agent Interaction and Intelligence Attribution." In *Proceedings of the 17th ACM Conference on Interaction Design and Children*, 231–40.

Dunne, A., and Raby, F. 2013. *Speculative Everything: Design, Fiction, and Social Dreaming.* Cambridge, MA: MIT Press.

Eglash, R., Lachney, M., Babbitt, W., Bennett, A., Reinhardt, M., and Davis, J. 2020. "Decolonizing Education with Anishinaabe Arcs: Generative STEM as a Path to Indigenous Futurity." *Educational Technology Research and Development* 68, no. 3: 1569–93.

Eubanks, V. 2018. *Automating Inequality: How High-Tech Tools Profile, Police, and Punish the Poor.* London: St Martins.

Feathers, T. 2019, August 20. "Flawed Algorithms Are Grading Millions of Students' Essays." Vice. https://www.vice.com/en/article/pa7dj9/flawed-algorithms-are-grading-millions-of-students-essays

Gaskins, N. 2023. "Interrogating Algorithmic Bias: From Speculative Fiction to Liberatory Design." *TechTrends* 67: 417–25.

Gay, G. 2018. *Culturally Responsive Teaching: Theory, Research, and Practice.* New York: Teachers College Press.

Gerard, L., Kidron, A., and Linn, M. C. 2019. "Guiding Collaborative Revision of Science Explanations." *International Journal of Computer-Supported Collaborative Learning* 14: 1–34.

Gobert, J. D. 2023. "Inq-ITS: Creating Rigorous Assessment and Real-Time Support of Science Learning." *XRDS: Crossroads, The ACM Magazine for Students* 29, no. 3: 36–40.

Gobert, J. D., Sao Pedro, M. A., and Betts, C. G. 2023. "An AI-Based Teacher Dashboard to Support Students' Inquiry: Design Principles, Features, and Technological Specifications." In *Handbook of Research on Science Education*, edited by N. G. Lederman, D. L. Zeidler, and J. S. Lederman, 1011–44. London: Routledge.

Greener, S. 2019. "Supervision or Surveillance: The Tension of Learning Analytics." *Interactive Learning Environments* 27, no. 2: 135–36. https://doi.org/10.1080/10494820.2019.1575631

Gulson, K. N., and Sellar, S. 2019. "Emerging Data Infrastructures and the New Topologies of Education Policy." *Environment and Planning D: Society and Space* 37, no. 2: 350–66.

Gulson, K. N., and Witzenberger, K. 2022. "Repackaging Authority: Artificial Intelligence, Automated Governance, and Education Trade Shows." *Journal of Education Policy* 37, no. 1: 145–60.

Gutiérrez, K. D., Cortes, K., Cortez, A., DiGiacomo, D., Higgs, J., Johnson, P., Lizárraga, J. R., Mendoza, E., Tien, J., and Vakil, S. 2017. "Replacing Representation with Imagination: Finding Ingenuity in Everyday Practices." Review of Research in Education 41, no. 1: 30–60.

Gutiérrez, K. D., Jurow, A. S., and Vakil, S. 2020. "Social Design-Based Experiments: A Utopian Methodology for Understanding New Possibilities for Learning." In *Handbook of the Cultural Foundations of Learning*, edited by N. S. Nasir, C. D. Lee, R. Pea, and M. McKinney de Royston, 330–47. London: Taylor and Francis.

Gutiérrez, K. D., and Rogoff, B. 2003. "Cultural Ways of Learning: Individual Traits or Repertoires of Practice." *Educational Researcher* 32, no. 5: 19–25.

Ha, M., and Nehm, R. 2016. "The Impact of Misspelled Words on Automated Computer Scoring: A Case Study of Scientific Explanations." *Journal of Science Education and Technology* 25, no. 3: 358–74.

Hammond, Z. 2014. *Culturally Responsive Teaching and the Brain: Promoting Authentic Engagement and Rigor among Culturally and Linguistically Diverse Students.* Thousand Oaks, CA: Corwin Press.

Han, X. 2021, December. "How Does AI Engage in Education? A Quantitative Research on AI Curriculum and Instruction in Public Primary Schools." In *2021 4th International Conference on Education Technology Management*, 15–19.

Harrison, L. M., and Risler, L. 2015. "The Role Consumerism Plays in Student Learning." *Act Learn High Educ* 16, no. 1: 67–76.

Haudek, K. C., Kaplan, J. J., Knight, J., Long, T., Merrill, J., Munn, A., Nehm, R., Smith, M., and Urban-Lurain, M. 2011. "Harnessing Technology to Improve Formative Assessment of Student Conceptions in STEM: Forging a National Network." *CBE Life Sciences Education* 10, no. 2: 149–55. https://doi.org/10.1187/cbe.11-03-0019

Heaven, W. D. 2023, April 6. "ChatGPT is Going to Change Education, Not Destroy It." https://www.technologyreview.com/2023/04/06/1071059/chatgpt-change-not-destroy-education-openai/

Hemachandran, K., Verma, P., Pareek, P., Arora, N., Rajesh Kumar, K. V., Ahanger, T. A., Pise, A. A. and Ratna, R. 2022. "Artificial Intelligence: A Universal Virtual Tool to Augment Tutoring in Higher Education." *Computational Intelligence and Neuroscience* 2022: article 1410448.

Herodotou, C., Naydenova, G., Boroowa, A., Gilmour, A., and Rienties, B. 2020. "How Can Predictive Learning Analytics and Motivational Interventions Increase Student Retention and Enhance Administrative Support in Distance Education?" *Journal of Learning Analytics* 7, no. 2: 72–83.

Holmes, W., Bialik, M., and Fadel, C. 2019. *Artificial Intelligence in Education: Promises and Implications for Teaching and Learning.* Boston: Center for Curriculum Redesign.

Holmes, W., Porayska-Pomsta, K., Holstein, K., Sutherland, E., Baker, T., Shum, S. B., Santos, O. C., et al. 2022. "Ethics of AI in Education: Towards a Community-Wide Framework." *International Journal of Artificial Intelligence in Education* 32, no. 3: 504–26.

Holstein, K., and Doroudi, S. 2021. "Equity and Artificial Intelligence in Education: Will 'AIEd' Amplify or Alleviate Inequities in Education?" *arXiv preprint* . arXiv:2104.12920.

Huddleston, G. 2016. "The Zombie in the Room: Using Popular Culture as an Apparatus." *Counterpoints* 501: 109–22.

Hudspith, R. 1991. "Broadening the Scope of Engineering Ethics: From Micro-ethics to Macro-ethics." *Bulletin of Science, Technology and Society* 11, nos. 4–5: 208–11.

Hudspith, R. C. 1993. "Macro-ethics in an Engineering Program." *Bulletin of Science, Technology and Society* 13, no. 5: 268–72.

Humble, N., and Mozelius, P. 2019, October. "Artificial Intelligence in Education—A Promise, a Threat or a Hype." In *Proceedings of the European Conference on the Impact of Artificial Intelligence and Robotics*, 149–56.

Kangasharju, A., Ilomäki, L., Lakkala, M., and Toom, A. 2022. "Lower Secondary Students' Poetry Writing with the AI-Based Poetry Machine." *Computers and Education: Artificial Intelligence* 3, 100048.

Kitchin, R. 2014. "Big Data, New Epistemologies, and Paradigm Shifts." Big Data and Society 1, no. 1.

Kizilcec, R. F., and Lee, H. 2022. "Algorithmic Fairness in Education." In *The Ethics of Artificial Intelligence in Education*, edited by W. Holmes and K. Porayska-Pomsta, 174–203. London: Routledge.

Ko, A. J., Oleson, A., Ryan, N., Register, Y., Xie, B., Tari, M., Davidson, M., Druga, S., and Loksa, D. 2020. "It Is Time for More Critical CS Education." *Communications of the ACM* 63, no. 11: 31–33.

Krueger, N. 2017. "Artificial Intelligence Has Infiltrated Our Lives. Can It Improve Learning?" International Society for Technology in Education (ISTE). https://www.iste.org/explore/Empowered-Learner/Artificial-intelligence-has-infiltrated-our-lives-Can-it-improve-learning

Lachney, M. 2017. "Culturally Responsive Computing as Brokerage: Toward Asset Building with Education-Based Social Movements." *Learning, Media and Technology* 42, no. 4: 420–39.

Lachney, M., Boltz, L. O., Dillman, B., Robertson, C., and Yadav, A. 2018. "Local Classrooms, Global Technologies: Toward the Integration of Sociotechnical Macroethical Issues into Teacher Education." *Bulletin of Science, Technology and Society 38*, nos. 1–2: 13–22.

Ladson-Billings, G. 1995. "Toward a Theory of Culturally Relevant Pedagogy." *American Educational Research Journal* 32, no. 3: 465–91.

Laru, J., and Järvelä, S. 2015. "Integrated Use of Multiple Social Software Tools and Face-to-Face Activities to Support Self-regulated Learning: A Case Study in a Higher Education Context." In *Seamless Learning in the Age of Mobile Connectivity*, edited by L. H. Wong, M. Mirad, and M. Specht, 471–84. Singapore: Springer.

Lave, J., and Wenger, E. 1991. *Situated Learning: Legitimate Peripheral Participation*. Cambridge, MA: Cambridge University Press.

Lee, H. S., Gweon, G. H., Lord, T., Paessel, N., Pallant, A., and Pryputniewicz, S. 2021. "Machine Learning-Enabled Automated Feedback: Supporting Students' Revision of Scientific Arguments Based on Data Drawn from Simulation." *Journal of Science Education and Technology* 30: 168–92.

Lee, V. R., and Delaney, V. 2022. "Identifying the Content, Lesson Structure, and Data Use within Pre-collegiate Data Science Curricula." *Journal of Science Education and Technology* 31, no. 1: 81–98.

Levin, S. 2016. "A Beauty Contest Was Judged by AI and the Robots Didn't Like Dark Skin." The Guardian 11, no. 8.

Levitas, R. 2013. *Utopia as Method: The Imaginary Reconstitution of Society*. Cham: Springer.

Li, K. C., and Wong, B. T. M. 2021. "Features and Trends of Personalised Learning: A Review of Journal Publications from 2001 to 2018." *Interactive Learning Environments* 29, no. 2: 182–95.

Li, T., Reigh, E., He, P., and Adah Miller, E. 2023. "Can We and Should We Use Artificial Intelligence for Formative Assessment in Science?" Journal of Research in Science Teaching 60, no. 6: 1385–9. https://doi.org/10.1002/tea.21867

Lin, P., and Van Brummelen, J. 2021, May. "Engaging Teachers to Co-design Integrated AI Curriculum for K–12 Classrooms." In *Proceedings of the 2021 CHI Conference on Human Factors in Computing Systems*, 1–12.

Louie, N. 2020. "Agency Discourse and the Reproduction of Hierarchy in Mathematics Instruction." Cognition and Instruction 38, no. 1: 1–26.

Luckin, R., Cukurova, M., Kent, C., and du Boulay, B. 2022. "Empowering Educators to be AI-Ready." *Computers and Education: Artificial Intelligence* 3: 100076.

Madaio, M., Egede, L., Subramonyam, H., Wortman Vaughan, J., and Wallach, H. 2022. "Assessing the Fairness of AI Systems: AI Practitioners' Processes, Challenges, and Needs for Support." *Proceedings of the ACM on Human-Computer Interaction* 6(CSCW1): 1–26.

Manning, C. D., Clark, K., Hewitt, J., Khandelwal, U., and Levy, O. 2020. "Emergent Linguistic Structure in Artificial Neural Networks Trained by Self-supervision." *Proceedings of the National Academy of Sciences* 117, no. 48: 30046–54.

McDonald, M., Kazemi, E., and Kavanagh, S. S. 2013. "Core Practices and Pedagogies of Teacher Education: A Call for a Common Language and Collective Activity." *Journal of Teacher Education* 64, no. 5: 378–86.

McMurtrie, B. 2018. "How Artificial Intelligence Is Changing Teaching." *The Chronicle of Higher Education*, 1–7.

McNemar, E. 2021, August 13. "How to Use Predictive Analytics in Chronic Disease Prevention." *Health IT Analytics*. https://healthitanalytics.com/news/how-to-use-predictive-analytics-in-chronic-disease-prevention

Mehrabi, N., Morstatter, F., Saxena, N., Lerman, K., and Galstyan, A. 2021. "A Survey on Bias and Fairness in Machine Learning." *ACM Computing Surveys (CSUR)* 54, no. 6: 1–35.

Meltzer, A. 2017, June 4. "M-Write Expands to Include Computer Analysis in Grading Student Essays." *The Michigan Daily*. https://www.michigandaily.com/news/academics/university-introduce-automated-writing-analysis-fall-classes/

MIT RAISE. 2023. "DAILy Curriculum." https://raise.mit.edu/daily/index.html

Mitchell, E., Finn, C., and Manning, C. 2021, August. "Challenges of Acquiring Compositional Inductive Biases via Meta-learning." In *AAAI Workshop on Meta-Learning and Meta DL Challenge*, 138–48. PMLR.

Morales-Chicas, J., Castillo, M., Bernal, I., Ramos, P., and Guzman, B. L. 2019. "Computing with Relevance and Purpose: A Review of Culturally Relevant Education in Computing." *International Journal of Multicultural Education* 21, 1: 125–55.

Murphy, R. F. 2019. "Artificial Intelligence Applications to Support K–12 Teachers and Teaching: A Review of Promising Applications, Opportunities, and Challenges." Santa Monica, CA: Rand Corporation. https://www.rand.org/pubs/perspectives/PE315.html.

Naidoo, R., and Whitty, G. 2013. "Students as Consumers: Commodifying or Democratising Learning?" *International Journal of Chinese Education* 2, no. 2: 212–40.

Naqvi, A. 2020. *Artificial Intelligence for Audit, Forensic Accounting, and Valuation: A Strategic Perspective*. Chichester: John Wiley and Sons.

NGSS Lead State Partners. 2013. *Next Generation Science Standards: For States, by States*. Washington, DC: National Academies Press.

Noble, S. U. 2018. "Algorithms of Oppression." In *Algorithms of Oppression*. New York: New York University Press.

Oconnor, M. C. 2017, July 11. *Dumpster Diving Robots: Using AI for Smart Recycling*. GE Vernova, https://www.ge.com/news/reports/dumpster-diving-robots-using-ai-smart-recycling

O'Grady, M. J., Langton, D., and O'Hare, G. M. P. 2019. "Edge Computing: A Tractable Model for Smart Agriculture?" *Artificial Intelligence in Agriculture* 3: 42–51.

O'Neil, C. 2016. *Weapons of Math Destruction: How Big Data Increases Inequality and Threatens* Democracy. New York: Broadway Books.

Patrick, M. E., Parks, M. J., Fairlie, A. M., Kreski, N. T., Keyes, K. M., and Miech, R. 2022. "Using Substances to Cope with the COVID-19 Pandemic: US National Data at Age 19 Years." *Journal of Adolescent Health* 70, no. 2: 340–44.

Peressini, D., Borko, H., Romagnano, L., Knuth, E., and Willis, C. 2004. "A Conceptual Framework for Learning to Teach Secondary Mathematics: A Situative Perspective." *Educational Studies in Mathematics* 56, no. 1: 67–96.

Perin, D., and Lauterbach, M. 2018. "Assessing Text-Based Writing of Low-Skilled College Students." *International Journal of Artificial Intelligence in Education* 28, no. 1: 56–78.

Phani Krishna, K. V., Mani Kumar, M., and Aruna Sri, P. S. G. 2018. "Student Information System and Performance Retrieval through Dashboard." *International Journal of Engineering and Technology (UAE)* 7: 682–85.

Pinkard, N., Martin, C. K., and Erete, S. 2020. "Equitable Approaches: Opportunities for Computational Thinking with Emphasis on Creative Production and Connections to Community." *Interactive Learning Environments* 28, no. 3: 347–61.

Polonski, S. 2018, November 23. "Mitigating Algorithmic Bias in Predictive Justice: 4 Design Principles for AI Fairness." *Towards Data Science.* https://towardsdatascience.com/mitigating-algorithmic-bias-in-predictive-justice-ux-design-principles-for-ai-fairness-machine-learning-d2227ce28099

Posner, T., and Fei-Fei, L. 2020. "AI Will Change the World, So It's Time to Change AI." *Nature 588,* no. 7837: S118.

Raji, I. D., Smart, A., White, R. N., Mitchell, M., Gebru, T., Hutchinson, B., Smith-Loud, J., Theron, D., and Barnes, P. 2020, January. "Closing the AI Accountability Gap: Defining an End-to-End Framework for Internal Algorithmic Auditing." In *Proceedings of the 2020 Conference on Fairness, Accountability, and Transparency,* 33–44.

Regan, P. M., and Jesse, J. 2019. "Ethical Challenges of Edtech, Big Data and Personalized Learning: Twenty-first Century Student Sorting and Tracking." *Ethics and Information Technology* 21, no. 3: 167–79.

Reich, J., and Ito, M. 2017. *From good intentions to real outcomes: Equity by design in learning technologies.* Irvine, CA: Digital Media and Learning Research Hub.

Remian, D. 2019. "Augmenting Education: Ethical Considerations for Incorporating Artificial Intelligence in Education." *Instructional Design Capstones Collection,* 52.

Rodriguez, A. J. 2015. "What about a Dimension of Engagement, Equity, and Diversity Practices? A Critique of the Next Generation Science Standards." *Journal of Research in Science Teaching* 52, no. 7: 1031–51.

Roose, K. 2023, January 12. "Don't Ban ChatGPT in Schools. Teach with It." The New York Times. https://www.nytimes.com/2023/01/12/technology/chatgpt-schools-teachers.html

Sakulkueakulsuk, B., Witoon, S., Ngarmkajornwiwat, P., Pataranutaporn, P., Surareungchai, W., Pataranutaporn, P., and Subsoontorn, P. 2018, December. "Kids Making AI: Integrating Machine Learning, Gamification, and Social Context in STEM Education." In 2018 IEEE international conference on teaching, assessment, and learning for engineering (TALE), 1005–10. IEEE.

Schneider, S. 2019. *Artificial You: AI and the Future of Your Mind.* Princeton, NJ: Princeton University Press.

Scott, K. A., Sheridan, K. M., and Clark, K. 2015. "Culturally Responsive Computing: A Theory Revisited." *Learning, Media and Technology* 40, no. 4: 412–36.

Sharma, R. C., Kawachi, P., and Bozkurt, A. 2019. "The Landscape of Artificial Intelligence in Open, Online and Distance Education: Promises and Concerns." *Asian Journal of Distance Education* 14, no. 2: 1–2.

Slade, S., and Prinsloo, P. 2013. "Learning Analytics: Ethical Issues and Dilemmas." *American Behavioral Scientist* 57, no. 10: 1509–28.

Stahl, B. C., and Wright, D. 2018. "Ethics and Privacy in AI and Big Data: Implementing Responsible Research and Innovation". *IEEE Security and Privacy* 16, no. 3: 26–33.

Su, J., and Yang, W. 2022. "Artificial Intelligence in Early Childhood Education: A Scoping Review." *Computers and Education: Artificial Intelligence* 3: 100049.

Suresh, H., and Guttag, J. 2021. "A Framework for Understanding Sources of Harm throughout the Machine Learning Life Cycle." In *EAAMO'21: Equity and Access in Algorithms, Mechanisms, and Optimization,* 1–9.

Tedre, M., Sutinen, E., Kähkönen, E., and Kommers, P. 2006. "Ethnocomputing: ICT in Cultural and Social Context." *Communications of the ACM* 49, 1: 126–30.

UNESCO. 2019. "How Can Artificial Intelligence Enhance Education?" https://en.unesco.org/news/how-can-artificial-intelligence-enhance-education

Ungerer, L., and Slade, S. 2022. "Ethical Considerations of Artificial Intelligence in Learning Analytics in Distance Education Contexts." In *Learning Analytics in Open and Distributed Learning,* edited by P. Prinsloo, S. Slade, and M. Khalil, 105–20. Singapore: Springer.

Vakil, S., and Higgs, J. 2019. "It's about Power." *Communications of the ACM* 62, 3: 31–33.

Vakil, S., Marshall, J., and Ibrahimovic, S. 2020. "'That's Bogus as Hell!': Getting Under the Hood of Surveillance Technologies in an Out of School STEM Learning Environment." In *The Interdisciplinarity of the Learning Sciences, 14th International Conference of the Learning Sciences (ICLS) 2020,* edited by M. Gresalfi and I. S. Horn, Vol. 3, 1301–8.

VanLehn, K., Banerjee, C., Milner, F., and Wetzel, J. 2020. "Teaching Algebraic Model Construction: A Tutoring System, Lessons Learned and an Evaluation." *International Journal of Artificial Intelligence in Education* 30: 459–80.
Villegas, A. M. 1991. "Culturally Responsive Pedagogy for the 1990s and Beyond.". Trends and Issues Paper No. 6. Washington, DC: ERIC Clearinghouse on Teacher Education.
Watkins, S. C., and Cho, A. 2018. "The Digital Edge." In *The Digital Edge*. New York: New York University Press.
Whittaker, M., Crawford, K., Dobbe, R., Fried, G., Kaziunas, E., Mathur, V., West, S. M., Richardson, R., Schultz, J., and Schwartz, O. 2018. *AI Now Report 2018*, 1–62. New York: AI Now Institute at New York University.
Williams, R., Park, H. W., and Breazeal, C. 2019, May. "A is for Artificial Intelligence: The Impact of Artificial Intelligence Activities on Young Children's Perceptions of Robots." In *Proceedings of the 2019 CHI Conference on Human Factors in Computing Systems*, 1–11.
Wilson, A., and Dymoke, S. 2017. "Towards a Model of Poetry Writing Development as a Socially Contextualised Process." *Journal of Writing Research* 9, no. 2: 127–50.
Wilson, C., Haudek, K., Osborne, J., Stuhlsatz, M., Cheuk, T., Donovan, B., Bracey, Z., Mercado, M., and Zhai, X. 2024. "Using Automated Analysis to Assess Middle School Students' Competence with Scientific Argumentation." Journal of Research in Science Teaching 61, no. 1: 38–69.
Wilson, J., Huang, Y., Palermo, C., Beard, G., and MacArthur, C. A. 2021. "Automated Feedback and Automated Scoring in the Elementary Grades: Usage, Attitudes, and Associations with Writing Outcomes in a Districtwide Implementation of MI Write." *International Journal of Artificial Intelligence in Education* 31, no. 2: 234–76.
Winfield, A. F., and Jirotka, M. 2018. "Ethical Governance Is Essential to Building Trust in Robotics and Artificial Intelligence Systems." *Philosophical Transactions of the Royal Society A: Mathematical, Physical and Engineering Sciences* 376, no. 2133: 20180085.
Yang, W. 2022. "Artificial Intelligence Education for Young Children: Why, What, and How in Curriculum Design and Implementation." *Computers and Education: Artificial Intelligence* 3: 100061.
Zawacki-Richter, O., Marín, V. I., Bond, M., and Gouverneur, F. 2019. "Systematic Review of Research on Artificial Intelligence Applications in Higher Education—Where Are the Educators?" *International Journal of Educational Technology in Higher Education* 16, no. 1: 39.
Zhai, X. 2023. "ChatGPT for Next Generation Science Learning. XRDS: Crossroads." *ACM Magazine for Students* 29: 42–46. https://doi.org/10.1145/3589649
Zhai, X., Haudek, K. C., Shi, L., Nehm, R., and Urban-Lurain, M. 2020. "From Substitution to Redefinition: A Framework of Machine Learning-Based Science Assessment." *Journal of Research in Science Teaching* 57, no. 9: 1430–59.
Zhai, X., and Nehm, R. 2023. "AI and Formative Assessment: The Train Has Left the Station." *Journal of Research in Science Teaching* 60, no. 6: 1390–98. https://doi.org/DOI:10.1002/tea.21885
Zhai, X., Yin, Y., Pellegrino, J. W., Haudek, K. C., and Shi, L. 2020. "Applying Machine Learning in Science Assessment: A Systematic Review." *Studies in Science Education* 56, no.1: 111–51.

23

Fair Artificial Intelligence to Support STEM Education

A Hitchhiker's Guide

Wanli Xing and Chenglu Li

Introduction

There are increasing adoptions and deployments of artificial intelligence (AI) techniques in both K–12 and higher education contexts to provide teachers and students with actionable intelligence for interventions and optimal assignment of learning resources (Dawson et al. 2017). The burgeoning development of AI in education can be partly attributed to access to powerful data infrastructure and the advancement of automatic data analysis techniques such as machine learning (ML). The former offers educational researchers an abundance of data (e.g., educational big data) to support the identification and prediction of students' learning profiles (Li et al. 2020), emotions (Xing, Tang, and Pei 2019), and academic achievements (Leite et al. 2019). The latter provides essential tools to power studies with accurate insights (e.g., precise prediction of students' future test scores based on their prior experience).

Such transformative technologies have also enabled science, technology, engineering, and mathematics (STEM) education researchers to automatically investigate, assess, and scaffold students' learning inquiries. For example, Sung et al. (2021) utilized natural language processing (NLP) models to automate the decoding of students' multimodal representational thinking to understand the affordances of a mobile thermodynamics lab using augmented reality. Their results suggested that NLP could effectively capture students' representational thinking in multiple dimensions when learning thermodynamics. Zhai, He, and Krajcik (2022) adopted computer vision (CV) and NLP models to evaluate middle students' modeling (both in graphic and textual formats) of thermal energy questions. These researchers showed that CV and NLP models could achieve highly consistent scoring on students' science learning artifacts with human evaluators. Finally, Marwan, Williams, and Price (2019) used a data-driven approach, utilizing similarities between students' codes and possible solutions, to provide hints to help students solve programming quests in real time. They then conducted a randomized experiment with Amazon Mechanical Turk (MTurk) to investigate the effects of providing automatic hints. Their results showed that having access to data-driven programming hints could statistically significantly improve participants' performance.

Wanli Xing and Chenglu Li, *Fair Artificial Intelligence to Support STEM Education*. In: *Uses of Artificial Intelligence in STEM Education*. Edited by: Xiaoming Zhai and Joseph Krajcik, Oxford University Press.
DOI: 10.1093/oso/9780198882077.003.0023

Regardless of the many benefits of AI in education, there are ethical concerns about its fairness. Numerous studies have found that AI can biasedly treat people with specific attributes across domains (see the review of Zou and Schiebinger 2018), including education, business, and medicine. This chapter aims to guide the building of fair and ethical AI in STEM education. Specifically, we provided an overview of fair AI to operationalize AI fairness, investigate its importance, and discuss current attempts to enhance AI fairness in education. We then selected three case studies of fair AI in online supporting math learning to illustrate their rationales, methods, and implications. Finally, we discussed the limitations of current studies on fair AI in the hope of inspiring future studies.

Background

Working Definition of AI Fairness

AI fairness and bias are mutually exclusive. That is, AI fairness is achieved, to a large extent, with the absence of AI bias. However, what does one mean when claiming an AI model is biased? Researchers in AI in education often refer to bias as algorithmic bias (Baker and Hawn 2021), which leaves one to wonder further what algorithmic bias stands for. While the research community has yet to come to an agreement on a single definition of algorithmic bias, researchers have shown a few consistent interpretations. In the study of Mitchell et al. (2021), researchers deemed that algorithmic bias showed asymmetric prediction performance between privileged and underprivileged students, favoring those with advantages. Likewise, Gardner, Brooks, and Baker (2019) held that "inequitable prediction" (p. 228) based on students' demographic attributes was algorithmic bias. A more general definition was given by Suresh and Guttag (2021), where they operationalized algorithmic bias as different forms of harm caused in AI building and deployment phases, including but not limited to unintentional, intentional, or subtle actions of AI that yielded undesirable results. In this chapter, algorithmic bias is operationalized as the decisions of automatic models that systematically favor for or against individuals or groups of certain attributes (e.g., gender, race, learning profile) (Baker and Hawn 2021; Li, Xing, and Leite 2022c; Zhai and Krajcik 2022). An example of such systematic mistreatment is the imbalanced predictive correction and false alarm rates of automatic models regarding demographic groups. Given the operationalization of algorithmic bias, algorithmic fairness is thus defined as the result of minimizing or eliminating algorithmic bias in AI models. However, why can AI models have an algorithmic bias? In the next section, we discuss possible sources of bias in AI.

Origins of Bias

Baker and Hawn (2021) thoroughly review the origins of algorithmic bias. Table 23.1 summarizes and synthesizes six common sources that could lead to algorithmic bias in AI in education and their corresponding stages in AI development. From the different sources of algorithmic bias, one can see that bias is contextual and cultural. For example, what is deemed fair in our days might be biased in the future, similar to

Table 23.1 Origins of Algorithmic Bias

Stage	Name	Definition	Example
Data collection	Historical bias	Biased model decisions based on outdated opinions caused by the conflicts between the real world and the ideal world.	An algebra assessment predictor constantly predicts lower grades for African American students than for Caucasian or Asian students because the dataset contains longitudinal data on students' algebra performance, where there was discrimination against African American students and educational resources were extremely imbalanced.
	Representation bias	Model bias caused by the under-representation of certain groups in the training data.	A facial detector to capture students' sentiments made more errors on people with dark skin due to the fact that the training data mainly consisted of light-skinned samples.
	Measurement bias	Biased model decisions caused by poor construct validity that can lead to biased predictions across groups.	A model predicting students' attention in classrooms can be problematic depending on whether prejudice exists when rating students' attention levels to construct training data. For example, chit-chatting during class was rated as poor attention for one group of students while being fair attention level for another group.
Data preparation	Aggregation bias	Model bias caused by aggregating/merging data of different populations, which can lead to a model yielding poorer performance for certain groups.	A sentiment predictor tended to predict less accurately if urban, rural, and suburban students were merged as one dataset than when individual predictors trained on each of the groups.

Stage	Name	Definition	Example
Model evaluation	Evaluation bias	Model bias caused by using data from nonrepresentative populations to evaluate models.	An automatic text classifier was constructed to detect high school students' socioemotional support in online learning. However, the model was trained and evaluated with text data whose population was online learners that have taken a course with Khan Academy, ranging from primary school students to adults.
Model deploy-ment	Deployment bias	Model bias caused by the misalignment between a model's purpose and how it is actually applied.	A prediction model was designed to predict students' motivation levels in a problem-solving environment but was solely used to predict students' final performance.

Note. Information in the table was adapted from the study of Baker and Hawn (2021) and Suresh and Guttag (2021).

people's opinions on gender and race that have developed since the twentieth century (e.g., historical bias). Therefore, how to validly define attention is culturally relevant (see the example of measurement bias on attention in Table 23.1). For instance, some international students from Asia might not as proactively participate in classroom discussions as their US counterparts (Lee 2007); as a consequence, they are shown to have lower attention in some measurement results. This result may be biased as it does not necessarily mean that these Asian students have lower attention; instead, it is just a cultural difference. The culture can partly explain the low participation in Asian countries where students are not encouraged to speak unless invited. Furthermore, bias can be volatile. For instance, data-mining strategies such as merging or transforming data can help construct more robust models. However, it is possible that they can also undermine the fairness of models (e.g., aggregation bias). Finally, though challenging, bias is preventable. The fact that there are taxonomies on different sources of algorithmic bias suggests that researchers can create a checklist along with diagnostic tools to help them identify and mitigate bias. The following section, "Types of Fairness," discusses existing popular tools for diagnosing algorithmic bias.

Types of Fairness

Algorithmic Fairness and Perceived Fairness

Before we discuss the evaluation of fairness and bias, it is worth noting that the operationalization of fairness is based on algorithmic bias, the use of which should stay in the algorithmic contexts. Perceived fairness of individuals is another type of fairness in AI that is equally important to examine (Marcinkowski et al. 2020). Perceived fairness in AI describes "students' emotional (e.g., fear), cognitive (e.g., trust), and behavioral (e.g., protest) responses towards the justice of AI systems" (Li and Xing 2022, 409). Perceived fairness can be further distilled down to distributive, procedural, and interactional fairness (Colquitt et al. 2013). Distributive fairness in AI focuses on AI systems' results (e.g., predictions), describing the consistency between students' received and expected resource allocations (e.g., automatic assessment feedback, learning material recommendations). Procedural fairness in AI, as the term suggests, describes students' perceptions of the decision-making process of an AI system, focusing on students' access to voice their opinions in the process. Finally, interactional fairness in AI focuses on the human–AI symbiosis, describing students' opinions towards how AI decisions are applied (e.g., fully automated vs semi-automated with instructors' inputs) and explained (e.g., black box vs transparent models) in the educational contexts.

Many factors can influence participants' perceived fairness regardless of whether an AI system adopts fairness-aware algorithms. A fairness-aware algorithm proactively counters algorithmic bias through pre-processing (e.g., sensitive information removal through data transformation by Calmon et al. 2017), algorithm modification (e.g., loss function modification by Li, Xing, and Leite 2022c), and post-processing techniques (e.g., model prediction modification by Pleiss et al. 2017). For example, Wang, Harper, and Zhu (2020) conducted an experimental study to examine participants' perceived fairness towards a predictive system on their qualifications to conduct tasks on MTurk. Their results showed that participants tended to report higher perceived fairness in the system when the prediction decision was favorable (e.g., they were qualified). The degree of effects of prediction favorability on perceived fairness interacted with other variables such as educational level and gender. However, the effects of prediction favorability can be affected by contexts. In an experiment by Li and Xing (2022) with undergraduate and graduate students, the researchers found that prediction favorability did not influence students' perceived fairness towards a pass/fail predictive system for math learning. Instead, students 'math anxiety and academic background (e.g., major) could significantly influence their perceptions of fairness. The differences in cognitive involvement and participants' demographics might explain the conflicting findings between Wang, Harper, and Zhu (2020) and Li and Xing (2022). However, there is a need for more studies to investigate students' perceived fairness to establish better and explain the mechanism of those factors.

Group Fairness and Individual Fairness

There are also nuances in algorithmic fairness. Research communities usually examine algorithmic fairness from two perspectives, group fairness and individual fairness (see the review of Deho et al. 2022). Group fairness focuses on statistical parity across demographic groups. That is, researchers evaluate group fairness of AI models by examining how correct predictions and false alarms distribute in binary groups such as race (White vs non-White) and gender (female vs male). Popular metrics for evaluating group fairness include equalized odds (EO; Hardt, Price, and Srebro 2016) and absolute between-ROC area (ABROCA; Gardner, Brooks, and Baker 2019). Conceptually, EO examines the differences of true positive and false positive rates between two subgroups, respectively, when 0.5 is used by a predictive model as the threshold to differentiate positive and negative labels. ABROCA evaluates the difference of the area under the ROC curve (AUC) between two subgroups. Both EO and ABROCA seek to achieve smaller values to indicate fairer prediction results. On the other hand, individual fairness evaluates whether students with a similar background will receive similar predictions. One of the most commonly used metrics is the consistency measure proposed by Zemel et al. (2013). Conceptually, consistency examines a prediction outcome of an individual compared to the outcomes of similar individuals. Similar individuals are identified with a *k*-nearest neighbors model that treats attributes (e.g., no. assessment attempts and no. modules learned) of the specific individual as the center and draws a circle with an optimized radius to capture neighboring individuals. However, the criteria for similarity can be oversimplified, and it is challenging to determine what individual characteristics to include when selecting similar students. Therefore, most studies evaluate algorithmic fairness at the group level (Kizilcec and Lee 2022).

Roles of Algorithmic Fairness in AI in Education

After operationalizing algorithmic fairness and bias in AI, we intend to discuss why it is crucial for educational researchers to enhance fairness and mitigate bias in AI. First, sustainable AI in education demands algorithmic fairness. Although the potential benefits of AI in education can be transformative, ignoring fairness can cause unexpected consequences, as biased AI can give those privileged even more advantages (Pedro et al. 2019). Vincent-Lancrin and Van der Vlies (2020) share this viewpoint as well and believe that unfair AI could greatly threaten its adoption in education and even exacerbate social divisions. Moreover, student–AI symbiosis needs algorithmic fairness to serve as the bridge of trust. Tsai, Perrotta, and Gašević (2020) conducted interviews with students to get their thoughts on AI-based educational systems. Their findings suggested that one of the primary factors contributing to students' mistrust of AI was the lack of transparency surrounding its fairness. Those working in educational research ought to incorporate the procedures of fair AI into their investigation and deployment of AI systems to build trustworthy systems. Finally, algorithmic fairness is important to achieving equity in AI (Kizilcec and Lee 2022). For example, an AI system achieves equality and equity in its impact by promoting equal resource allocations and creating inclusive learning environments regardless of students' group membership, which is only possible by enhancing the fairness of AI systems.

Related Work on Fair AI in Education

Current educational investigation into fair AI focuses on two strands: conceptual discussions on AI fairness and bias and empirical evaluations of AI fairness. For example, Kizilcec and Lee (2022) introduce existing statistical measures of algorithmic bias and discuss the relationship between algorithmic bias and learning equity with AI. Baker and Hawn (2021) further discuss possible sources of algorithmic bias, concerns regarding the current evaluation of algorithmic bias (e.g., protected attributes were selected more from a political instead of a learning standpoint), and challenges in mitigating algorithmic bias (e.g., the lack of established tools). Utilizing slicing analysis, Gardner, Brooks, and Baker (2019) formulate a new measurement of algorithmic bias designated in educational contexts to support the evaluation of AI fairness. Another strand—fairness evaluation—adopts existing metrics to understand whether algorithmic bias exists in AI models to support learning. For example, Riazy and Simbeck (2019) adopt equalized odds to examine their models to predict students' academic achievement. Their results show that one of the competitive models yielded great bias against students with physical or mental conditions. Such bias against disadvantaged students can also be found in Sha et al. (2021), where the researchers found that automatic text classifiers could show higher rates for students whose primary language was not English. Finally, Hutt et al. (2019) adopt ABROCA to evaluate whether their predictive models on students' graduation time are biased. In their study, no bias was found in AI models. However, the researchers emphasize that fairness evaluation of AI models is necessary even though algorithmic bias is not always present.

Case Studies

There are a few educational efforts to investigate algorithmic strategies beyond fairness evaluation to enhance the fairness of AI models. For example, Li, Xing, and Leite (2022c) propose a model in the context of an early warning system using a fair AI framework. The proposed model by Li, Xing, and Leite allows researchers to define custom fairness constraints, with which the model would adjust its parameters to satisfy. In another study, Li, Xing, and Leite (2022a) use a Bayesian method to construct a peer recommender that can fairly suggest potentially helpful peers to support learners' help-seeking activities. Finally, Li, Xing, and Leite (2022b) extend the typical notion of algorithmic fairness and mitigated safety issues in language generation models to responsibly and socioemotionally support algebra learners. The following sections take the three studies mentioned above as case studies to demonstrate what strategies researchers can take to build fair AI models in education.

Case 1: Fair Logistic Regression for Early Warning Prediction

Overview

The potential of early warning systems (EWS) that utilize AI to predict students' learning status has been theoretically and empirically supported. On the one hand, EWS provides students with the tool for goal-setting and helps teachers identify students' self-regulated learning (SRL) phases for interventions. Both are essential for supporting and evaluating students' SRL, especially in online learning environments where means of observation and classroom orchestration are limited

(Drijvers et al. 2010; Harkin et al. 2016; Lodge, Horvath, and Corrin 2018). On the other hand, there have been successful adoptions of EWS in learning contexts. The most famous example might be Purdue's Signals system, which has been integrated into colleges to assist with students' progress examinations. It has been reported that students using Signals tended to achieve better end-of-course performance than those who did not, yielding 10% more A's and B's (Sclater, Peasgood, and Mullan 2016).

However, Li, Xing, and Leite (2022c) are concerned about the algorithmic fairness of such systems, which could favor historically advantaged groups such as Caucasian students due to implicit data bias. Therefore, the researchers propose a fairness-aware logistic regression (Fair-LR) model by adopting a state-of-the-art fair AI framework to support fair EWS. Specifically, the researchers examined the Fair-LR's ability to fairly and accurately predict 484 high students' future assessment-taking (pass/fail) in an online math-learning platform called Algebra Nation. Demographic attributes, race, and gender were used in their study to examine algorithmic fairness. The researchers compared Fair-LR with other fairness-unaware models: Regular Logistic Regression (LR), Support Vector Machine (SVM), and Random Forest (RF). To find more details on model selection, please refer to Li, Xing, and Leite (2022c). The researchers found that Fair-LR could effectively reduce algorithmic bias while retaining competitive predictive accuracy compared to the benchmarked models.

Approaches and Models

Two components were needed to construct Fair-LR: a fairness evaluation metric and a ML algorithm that can adjust its learning based on the metric. The researchers selected equalized odds (EO by Hardt, Price, and Srebro 2016) to control the difference in correction rates and error rates between race (non-White vs White) and gender (female vs male). EO is defined in Equations 1 (equal true positive rates) and 2 (equal false positive rates). The researchers then developed Fair-LR using the Seldonian framework (Thomas et al. 2019). The Seldonian framework mathematically illustrates how researchers can estimate optimization for predictive accuracy and fairness during model learning. Figure 23.1 demonstrates the algorithmic steps of implementing Fair-LR. There are four essential steps in Fair-LR:

1. Define fairness constraints and threshold fairness values that the model will learn from and try to stay within, as lower values indicate better fairness.
2. Split training data for learning and fairness robustness evaluation.
3. Enhance the loss function to reward or punish models for fairness and accuracy.
4. Adopt a safety net to examine whether the model can achieve the desired fairness level with unseen data.

The study used students' log data (n = 717,402) to predict whether students would pass incoming assessments (n = 2,761). Fair-LR and its three benchmarks were trained with the data and evaluated on their predictive fairness and accuracy.

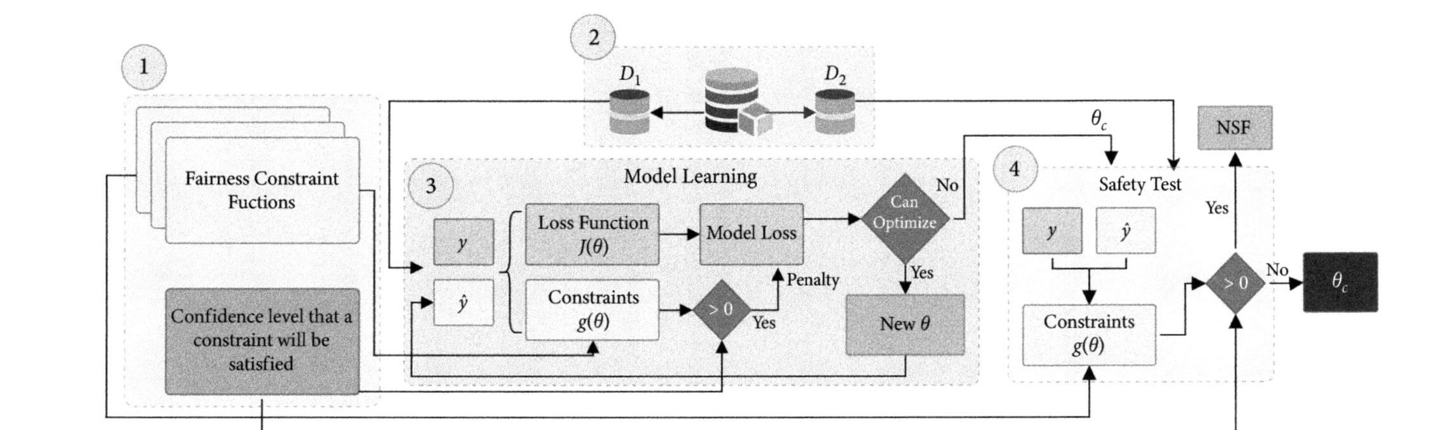

Figure 23.1 Algorithmic illustration of Fair-LR.

$$\text{P}\,(\text{Prediction} = 1|\text{Group} = 0, \text{Y} = 1) = \text{P}\,(\text{Prediction} = 1|\text{Group} = 1, \text{Y} = 1) \quad (1)$$

$$\text{P}\,(\text{Prediction} = 1|\text{Group} = 0, \text{Y} = 0) = \text{P}\,(\text{Prediction} = 1|\text{Group} = 1, \text{Y} = 0). \quad (2)$$

Results and Implications

Li, Xing, and Leite (2022c) adopt accuracy (percentage of correct predictions), F_1 (accuracy taking into account of true positives and false negatives), and AUC (rank-based accuracy on the probability of ranking positive cases higher than negative ones with predictive values). Table 23.2 shows the accuracy, F_1, and AUC scores of Fair-LR, LR, SVM, and RF. Since LR, RF, and SVM are fairness-unaware, their performance did not change with protective attributes (race or gender). For Fair-LR, the performance changed depending on the protective attribute and threshold values of EO. Fair-LR's performance generally decreased as the researchers adopted stricter threshold EO values. However, Fair-LR could achieve comparable predictive performance with its benchmarks. Figure 23.2 demonstrates the fairness evaluation of the models using EO. When using race as the protective attribute, Fair-LR consistently showed fairer results than its benchmarks, especially compared to its direct counterpart, LR. For gender, Fair-LR could still achieve fair results, showing low EO scores. However, RF achieved the fairest result among the models.

There were three key takeaways from the study. First, AI models can be enhanced to be fairness-aware while retaining competitive predictive accuracy. Li, Xing, and Leite (2022c) make Fair-LR fairness-aware by allowing the algorithm to take fairness constraints and dynamically adjust its parameters based on these constraints during learning. Conceptually, a penalty in the loss function was given to inform

Table 23.2 Predictive Accuracy of Fair-LR and Benchmarks

Model	Accuracy	F1	AUC
SVM	0.81	0.79	0.81
RF	**0.82**	**0.81**	**0.82**
LR	0.81	0.79	0.74
$FairLR_{\text{race@0.25}}$	0.81	0.78	0.79
$FairLR_{\text{race@0.2}}$	0.80	0.77	0.76
$FairLR_{\text{race@0.15}}$	0.78	0.72	0.78
$FairLR_{\text{race@0.1}}$	0.77	0.69	0.74
$FairLR_{\text{gender@0.05}}$	0.79	0.78	0.77
$FairLR_{\text{gender@0.01}}$	0.79	0.79	0.77

Note: Best-performed model is in bolded texts. The race and gender tags of Fair-LR suggest the protective attribute to mitigate bias. The values after @ suggest the threshold EO values that Fair-LR tried to stay within. The researchers selected threshold values based on benchmark models' EO scores, aiming to achieve fairer results with Fair-LR. Fewer threshold values were examined with gender, as Fair-LR did not converge when using lower threshold values.

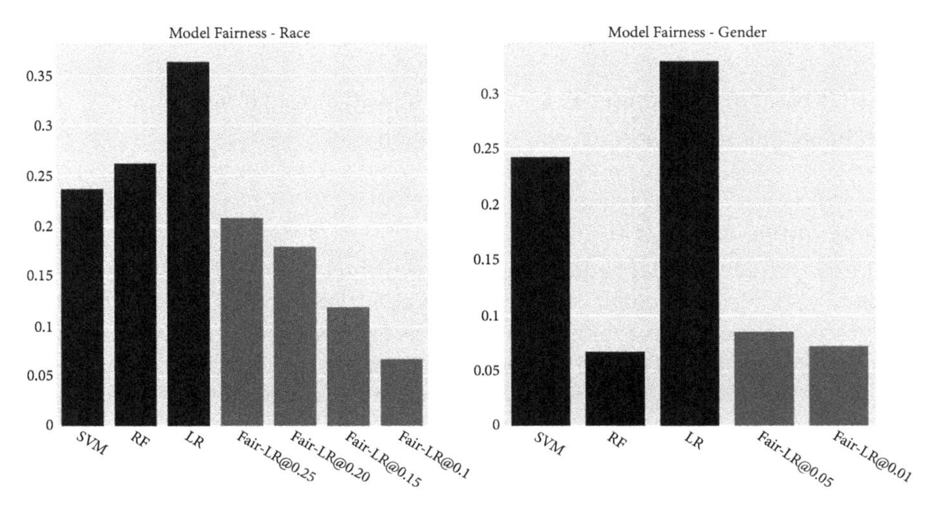

Figure 23.2 Predictive fairness of models.

Note: Lower values indicate fairer results.

Fair-LR of its fairness. The size of the penalty, ranging from 0 to 1000, depended on the satisfaction of the fairness constraints. Their findings showed that Fair-LR could achieve almost the same predictive performance as its benchmarks with relatively loose constraints on fairness. It is worth noting that Fair-LR could outperform fairness-unaware LR, indicating the opportunity to utilize the Seldonian framework to enhance other models (e.g., RF) without sacrificing predictive accuracy. Second, although fairness-unaware models can yield fair results (e.g., RF when using gender as the protective attribute), their fairness is not guaranteed (Metevier et al. 2019). Therefore, researchers should actively evaluate their models' predictive fairness if strategies to enhance fairness were not taken. Finally, while Fair-LR can, to an extent, mitigate bias originating from the data collection phase (e.g., historical bias), other non-algorithmic approaches can be considered. One of the approaches is to utilize data preprocessing techniques to identify and remove potential bias in data through oversampling under-represented groups (e.g., Chawla et al. 2002) or downsampling over-represented groups (e.g., Le Bras et al. 2020).

Case 2: Fair Peer Recommender for Inclusive Help Seeking in Online Discussion Forums

Overview

Online discussion forums have been found to be an important tool to support students' help-seeking (Chao et al. 2018). However, there is sparse participation in online discussion forums due to various factors, such as a lack of motivation to participate and information overload (Shaw 2019). AI-based peer recommenders that can effectively connect help-seekers with potential help-providers have attracted wide attention in the research community (Labarthe et al. 2016; Potts et al. 2018; Sunar et al. 2016). A peer recommender in education is an automatic system that provides students with outreach suggestions. The social outreaches can extend their networking for learning based on students' data (e.g., behavioral logs, prior interactions in discussion forums, and learning profiles) (Garcia-Martinez and Hamou-Lhadj 2013). However, AI-based peer recommenders can also suffer from algorithmic bias. For example, peer recommenders can unintentionally promote non-inclusive learning environments by dominantly suggesting peers from the same demographic group while ignoring students of different backgrounds who can also be helpful. Promoting non-inclusiveness is possible as AI-based peer recommenders learn to make recommendations from existing data. The data can have formed subcommunities with the same demographics (e.g., being dominantly male students in a subcommunity, see Figure 23.3).

Attempting to address the potential issue, Li, Xing, and Leite (2022a) proposed a model to construct peer recommenders that could provide inclusive and precise insights to help students' help-seeking. The researchers sampled 10,182 Algebra I learners and their discussion forum interactions (n = 187,450) from Algebra Nation. Using the data, the researchers experimented with the proposed model (Fair-NE) to construct a peer recommender. Fair-NE aimed to minimize the effects of students' race and gender when inferencing. The researchers compared Fair-NE to two other popular fairness-unaware models for recommender systems: Node2Vec (Grover and Leskovec 2016) and FairWalk (Rahman et al. 2019). The researchers evaluated these models based on representation bias, predictive fairness, and accuracy.

Approaches and Models

Fair-NE, Node2Vec, and FairWalk are network embeddings that utilize neural network models to encode information in a social network (e.g., students' discussion forum interactions) with high-dimensional vectors (e.g., 512 dimensions). These dimensions can capture information such as popularity, interaction frequency, and tendency on whom to connect. Students with a similar interaction focus (e.g., asking questions on quadratic functions) are expected to have similar encoded vectors. Studies have shown that building recommenders with network embedding models can greatly outperform traditional social network-based algorithms (Nelson et al. 2019; Z. Xu et al. 2020). Figure 23.4 illustrates the typical mechanism of network embedding models such as Node2Vec and FairWalk, where sequences of connections are randomly drawn from a social network and are fed to a neural network to get

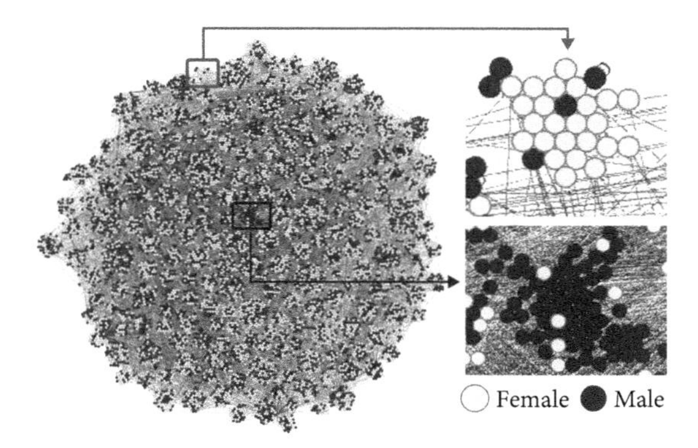

Figure 23.3 Example of non-inclusive subcommunities in a discussion forum.

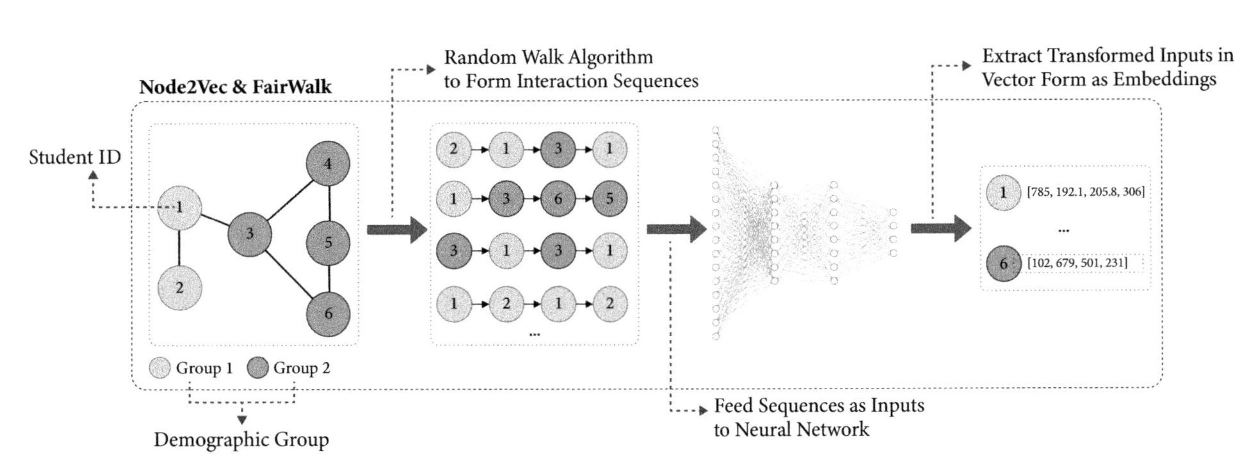

Figure 23.4 Encoding procedures of Node2Vec and FairWalk.

high-dimensional vectors. FairWalk is improved upon Node2Vec by modifying its sequence drawing procedure to ensure that nodes of different attributes (e.g., demographics) have an equal chance of being drawn. Fair-NE, on the other hand, utilized a different encoding mechanism. Inspired by Buyl and De Bie (2020), the researchers developed Fair-NE using a Bayesian inference approach. Conceptually, the Fair-NE model stores students' demographic information in a separate component from the actual encoding component. In this way, Fair-NE will not learn to represent students' demographics in the encoding component, as such information has already been handled. The demographic-agnostic encoder can then be used to make peer recommendations that tend to be more inclusive (please refer to Li, Xing, and Leite 2022a for more technical details).

To evaluate the models, the researchers adopted metrics such as representation bias (RB), ABROCA, and accuracy. RB is proposed to examine algorithmic bias in embedding models (Zemel et al. 2013). Conceptually, RB is the AUC score using embedding vectors to predict students' demographics (e.g., race, gender). An RB less than or equal to 0.5 suggests a fair representation, as it indicates that only random guesses on demographics can be made based on embedding vectors. ABROCA evaluates the prediction fairness of making peer recommendations on whether a target student has eventually connected to the recommended peers. We explained the details of ABROCA in the section "Group Fairness and Individual Fairness."

Results and Implications

Figure 23.5 shows the evaluation results of representations. For both gender and race, Fair-NE could consistently achieve the fairest representation of students' interactions. Another fairness-aware model FairWalk, in contrast, could encode students' interactions fairly in terms of gender while showing the most biased representations among the three models regarding race. It is not surprising as FairWalk's end goal is to improve prediction fairness using the embeddings. However, encoding students' information fairly might not always contribute to prediction fairness (Buyl and De Bie 2020). Figures 23.6 and 23.7 present the prediction fairness of the three models using their embeddings to make peer recommendations. The results showed that both

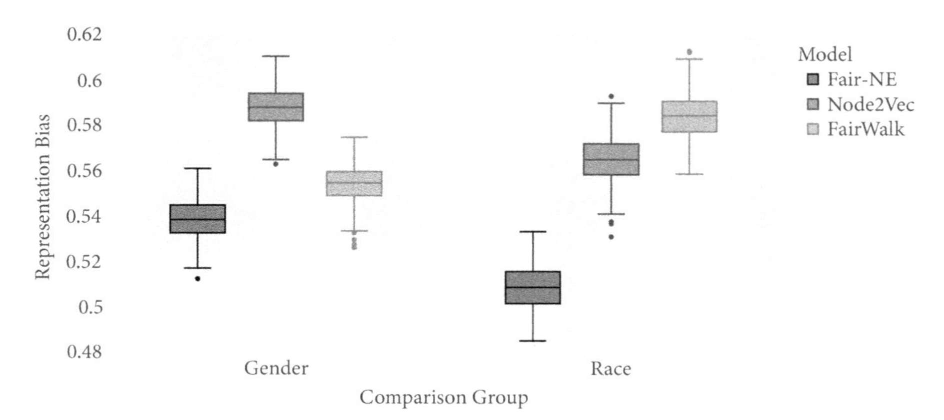

Figure 23.5 Results of representation bias of Fair-NE, Node2Vec, and FairWalk

Note: Values closer to 0.5 are fairer.

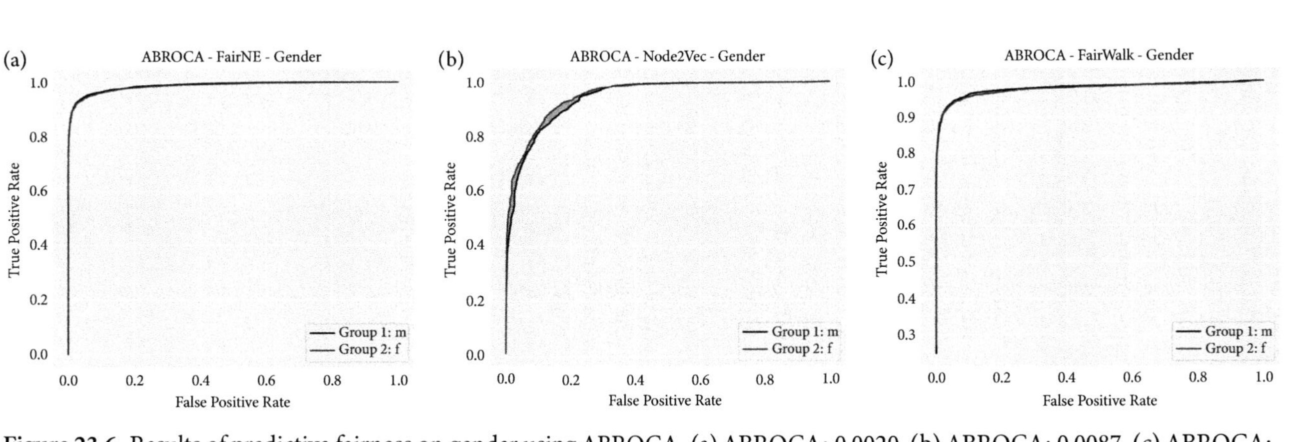

Figure 23.6 Results of predictive fairness on gender using ABROCA. (a) ABROCA: 0.0020. (b) ABROCA: 0.0087. (c) ABROCA: 0.0027.

Note: Lower values are fairer.

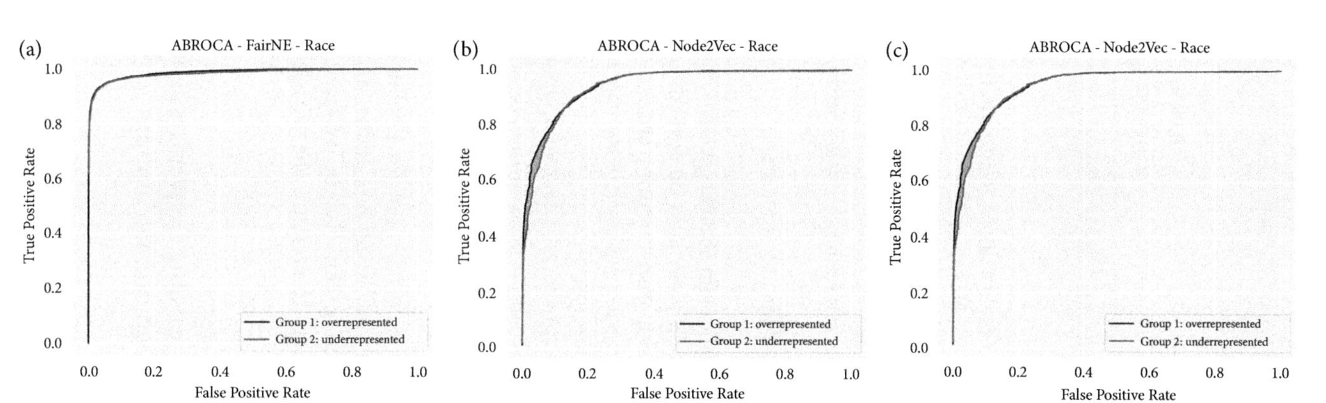

Figure 23.7 Results of predictive fairness on race using ABROCA. (a) ABROCA: 0.0040. (b) ABROCA: 0.0075. (c) ABROCA: 0.0020.

Note: Lower values are fairer.

Table 23.3 Results of Recommendation Accuracy

Models	AUC
Fair-NE	0.9821
Node2Vec	**0.9866**
FairWalk	0.9464

Note: The most accurate model is in bolded texts.

Fair-NE and FairWalk could yield notably fairer results than the fairness-unaware Node2Vec, with Fair-NE being the fairest for gender and FairWalk being the fairest for race. Finally, Table 23.3 shows that all three models could accurately predict whom a target student would connect to, with Fair-NE showing a competitive performance with the best-performed model, Node2Vec. Their results showed that Fair-NE could encode students' information and make predictions more fairly. Meanwhile, Fair-NE can achieve desirable accuracy.

We summarized three implications for practitioners:

1. It is essential to investigate data from the perspective of group memberships. As shown in Figure 23.3, subtle bias could be embedded in data even when students' aggregated membership distributions were similar (n_{female} = 4,909 vs. n_{male} = 5,273). Without investigating the issue, researchers can omit the subtlety and assume that the data are bias-proof.
2. Network embedding models can be an effective approach for building recommender systems. The applications of such models are not bound to peer recommenders. Researchers can extend the technique to other applications, such as video or learning material recommenders (e.g., Ting, Bowles, and Idewu 2022).
3. Bayesian modeling can be a powerful tool for enhancing algorithmic fairness. Besides the advantages of being updatable and explainable (Xing et al. 2021), Bayesian modeling can also be adopted to model potential bias information with its priors to enhance the fairness of its posterior for predictions.

Case 3: Socially Responsible Conversational Agents for Socioemotional Support

Overview

Apart from peer recommenders in Case 2 to revive online discussion participation, using conversational agents to generate supportive responses to students automatically has also attracted increasing attention. The feasibility of using natural language generation to support teaching and learning has been dramatically improved due to the advancement of Transformer models to generate human-like responses (Vaswani et al. 2017). A Transformer is a deep neural network architecture that can efficiently and effectively capture semantic and contextual meanings in text data. A previous study by Li and Xing (2021) has shown that conversational agents using Transformer models can provide informational, emotional, and community support comparable to human beings. However, a concern with using such agents in education is the lack of control over generated content's safety. Content safety is operationalized as "the evaluation of content appropriateness (e.g., offensiveness) in generated texts" (Li, Xing, and Leite 2022b, 778). Dinan et al. (2021) found that automatic conversational agents could initiate unsafe conversations spontaneously (instigator effect) and respond inappropriately to unsafe content (yea-sayer effect). Studies have shown that students can have learning issues such as demotivation and disengagement when experiencing unsafe online discourses (Duggan 2017).

Li, Xing, and Leite (2022b) proposed using generation-style control to address the potential safety issues in conversational agents. To be specific, the researchers developed SafeMathBot by using 2,097,139 Q&A discussion posts from 2015 to 2021 in Algebra Nation. The goal of the study was to automatically generate safe responses regardless of how human inputs were. The researchers compared SafeMathBot with two other safety-unaware conversational models that have shown superior performance in generating human-like content: BlenderBot (Roller et al. 2020) and DialoGPT (Zhang et al. 2019). The researchers evaluated the conversational models with an open-sourced while robust safety classifier, Perspective API, to examine the models' safety (instigator and yea-sayer effects). Their results showed that SafeMathBot could be controlled to generate significantly safer content than its benchmarks.

Approaches and Models

Figure 23.8 demonstrates the architecture of SafeMathBot. SafeMathBot was developed based on generated pretrained transformer 2 (GPT-2; Radford et al. 2019)

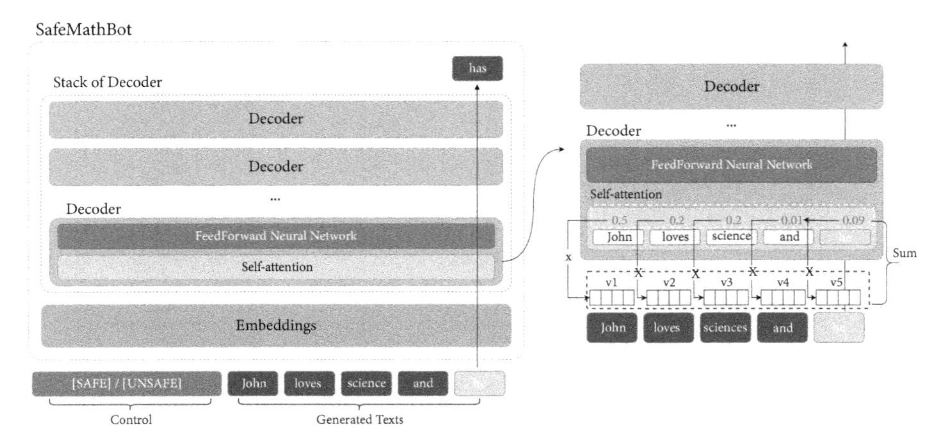

Figure 23.8 Explanation of how SafeMathBot used generation-style control for safety generation.

and generation style control influenced by J. Xu et al. (2020). Conceptually, GPT-2 utilized a stack of decoders, each consisting of a self-attention layer to determine which part in a sentence to focus on and a feedforward neural network for feature extraction to assist content generation. Using word embeddings, position embeddings, and decoders empowers GPT-2 to contextually and semantically understand inputs and generate human-like responses. Generation-style control describes the technique of using special words to influence the generation probabilities of words. The technique of generation-style control has been successfully adopted in the AI research community for generation enhancement to address repetitiveness and embed persona (Chen et al. 2020). In the context of generation safety, researchers can associate appropriate content with the special word [SAFE] when training the model. When generating with the [SAFE] command, SafeMathBot will adjust its word probability distributions to prefer safe content. For the safety evaluation, the researchers randomly sampled 5,000 unsafe and safe initiating posts, respectively. The researchers then used the models to generate responses to the 10,000 posts. To automatically evaluate the response safety, the researchers used Google's Perspective API (see Table 23.4).

Results and Implications

Figure 23.9 presents the safety evaluation results of the conversational models and the original human-generated responses. The researchers conducted a chi-squared test to examine whether content safety is subject to creators. The results not only showed a statistically significant association (χ^2 (4,49,828) = 3744.4, $p < 0.000$) but also indicated a large effect size (Cramer's V = 0.27), demonstrating the effectiveness of SafeMathBot generating safe responses. When controlling SafeMathBot with

Table 23.4 Perspective API's Safety Evaluation and Examples

Safety dimensions	**Descriptions**	**Examples**
Toxicity	Texts of rudeness and disrespectfulness	Don't bother learning it! It is useless.
Identity attack	Texts of negativity or hatred on identity	Girls can't do math.
Threat	Texts that imply or express physical or mental abuse	You don't wanna mess with me!
Profanity	Texts of cursing and obscene language	How the f**k did it make sense?
Insult	Texts of insults and aggravation	The answer should be B, you idiot.
Sexually explicit	Texts of lewdness or references to sexual acts	S**k it!

Note: The table was adapted from Li, Xi, and Leite (2022a).

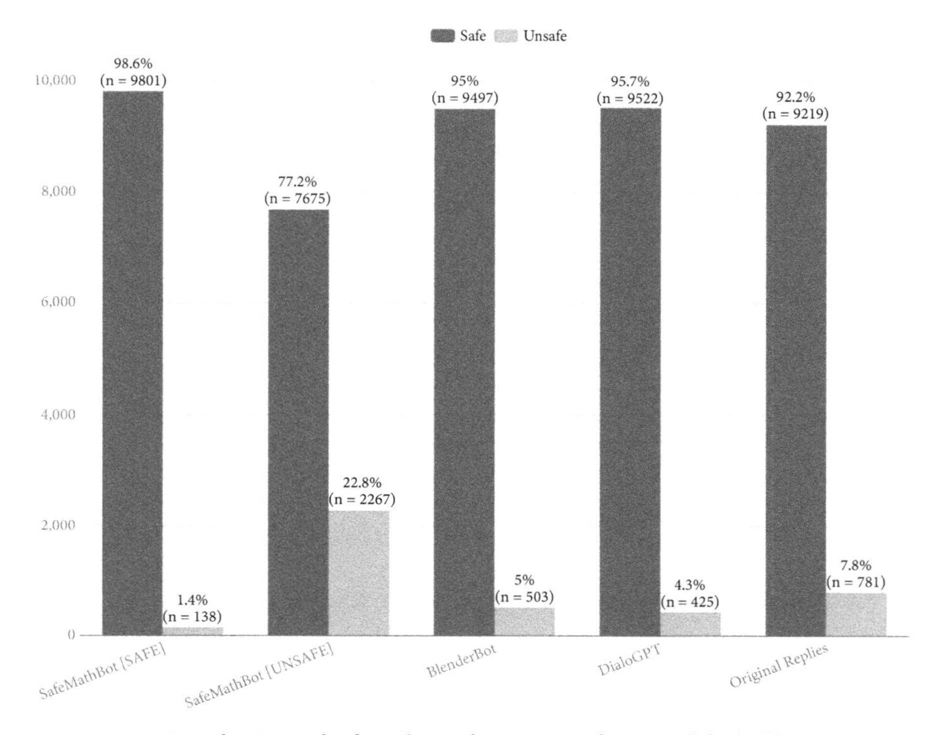

Figure 23.9 Distributions of safe and unsafe responses from models and humans.
Note: Conversational models can generate empty responses, which were removed in the analysis.

[SAFE], significantly fewer unsafe responses were generated. In contrast, the percentage of unsafe responses increased when applying the [UNSAFE] command to SafeMathBot. The change in the percentage of unsafe responses using different commands suggested that SafeMathBot could well differentiate the boundary between appropriate and inappropriate content when generating responses.

There are two major considerations for future practice. First, generation-style control is a powerful yet straightforward technique for language models. Meanwhile, generation-style control can be applied to a series of issues to address fairness and ethics in AI in education. For example, future researchers can use this technique to construct culturally responsive conversational agents. Researchers also can consider addressing the feminine and masculine issues in language models. Online discourses have been found to have more masculine stances than feminine ones (Liu et al. 2019), which can affect language models' tendency towards sexism. Second, researchers and instructional designers can use open-sourced AI models to enhance the evaluation of AI fairness. In the study, the researchers used Perspective API to automate the investigation of content safety. Perspective API has been shown to be a reliable and free service for text safety examination (Obadimu et al. 2019; Rieder and Skop 2021). The researchers also suggested its robustness by manually examining the results from Perspective API.

Current Gaps of Fair AI in Education

There are several technical and empirical gaps in fair AI research in education. From a technical standpoint, there is no established statistical test for gaining inferential insights into AI models' fairness. Most studies stopped at calculating and comparing fairness values of different AI models based on algorithmic fairness metrics. However, without essential statistical tools, it is challenging for researchers to conclude whether a model is meaningfully fairer than the other simply because that model achieved better fairness metrics in a limited dataset. Meanwhile, most algorithmic fairness metrics demand a dichotomous grouping (e.g., over-represented vs under-represented). However, such a binarization might not contribute to meaningful conclusions as it tends to mask the complexities of different categories (Gillborn et al. 2018). The typical White versus Others schema in race signals a pre-existing fixed quality, assuming White students are always privileged. Some preliminary studies aim to create statistical tools and metrics to test algorithmic fairness and embrace a paradigm of non-binary grouping (e.g., Kang et al. 2022; Taskesen et al. 2021). These tools have not been widely examined and await the AI community to understand their affordances in education.

Empirically, the fairness of AI systems is mainly measured with fairness metrics. However, satisfying fairness metrics cannot guarantee the achievement of equity in AI for education (Kizilcec and Lee 2022). A fairness-aware AI system might produce similar correct and error predictions, while students with individual differences can benefit differently from such a system. Studies have suggested that students with higher metacognition or motivation tend to orchestrate learning systems better and improve learning effects (Yokoyama 2019). Therefore, the adoption of fairness-aware AI systems can contribute to the widening of the knowledge gap among students. However, this does not suggest a pessimistic view that algorithmic fairness does not matter. Instead, understanding and enhancing algorithmic fairness might be the first step from equality to equity. There is a need for research to investigate further the effectiveness of using fairness-aware models to support students. Future studies can understand the affordances of equity between fairness-aware and fairness-unaware models. Moreover, more studies are needed to go beyond algorithmic fairness to perceived fairness. For example, little is known about the association between algorithmic fairness and perceived fairness. Future studies may empirically investigate the affordances of algorithmic fairness on students' perceptions of fairness.

Conclusions

The advancements in AI in education have provided educational researchers with a potential methodological shift to investigate, evaluate, and support teaching and learning. However, the power of AI in education can be compromised when algorithmic fairness is not carefully examined. To unleash the full potential of AI in education, educational researchers need to take a paradigm shift from current studies of using AI. Researchers need to investigate beyond AI's predictive accuracy and emphasize the evaluation and enhancement of predictive fairness and accuracy. Previous studies on fair AI in education show that there are strategies for evaluating AI models' fairness and, more importantly, proactively enhancing their fairness. This chapter presents three cases of using fair AI to support math learning in an online environment. Cases one and two utilized an algorithm modification approach to address group fairness. The main difference between these two cases is that case one adopted a reinforcement learning approach while case two adopted a Bayesian approach to counter bias during model training. In contrast, case three aimed to address a broader scope of fairness by using the generation-style control technique to create socially responsible conversational AI, providing students with both supportive and safe content. The developed AI models from the three cases show that they can provide fair, responsible, and accurate insights. We aimed to share the algorithmic strategies (loss function modification, Bayesian approach, and generation-style control) used in these studies to inspire future research using AI for STEM learning. Fair AI is a nascent community in computer science, and so is fair AI in education. More endeavors in the community are needed to build fair, accountable, and transparent AI in education.

References

Baker, R. S., and Hawn, A. 2021. "Algorithmic Bias in Education." *International Journal of Artificial Intelligence in Education* 32: 1052–92. https://doi.org/10.1007/s40593-021-00285-9

Buyl, M., and De Bie, T. 2020. "DeBayes: A Bayesian Method for Debiasing Network Embeddings." Proceedings of Machine Learning Research 119: 1220–29. http://proceedings.mlr.press/v119/buyl20a/buyl20a.pdf

Calmon, F., Wei, D., Vinzamuri, B., Natesan Ramamurthy, K., and Varshney, K. R. 2017. "Optimized Pre-processing for Discrimination Prevention." *Advances in Neural Information Processing Systems* 30: 1–10.

Chao, P.-Y., Lai, K. R., Liu, C.-C., and Lin, H.-M. 2018. "Strengthening Social Networks in Online Discussion Forums to Facilitate Help Seeking for Solving Problems." *Journal of Educational Technology and Society* 21, no. 4: 39–50.

Chawla, N. V., Bowyer, K. W., Hall, L. O., and Kegelmeyer, W. P. 2002. "SMOTE: Synthetic Minority Over-sampling Technique." *Journal of Artificial Intelligence Research* 16: 321–57. https://doi.org/10.1613/jair.953

Chen, Z., Lu, Y., Nieminen, M. P., and Lucero, A. 2020. "Creating a Chatbot for and with Migrants: Chatbot Personality Drives Co-design Activities." In *Proceedings of the 2020 ACM Designing Interactive Systems Conference*, 219–30. https://doi.org/10.1145/3357236.3395495

Colquitt, J. A., Scott, B. A., Rodell, J. B., Long, D. M., Zapata, C. P., Conlon, D. E., and Wesson, M. J. 2013. "Justice at the Millennium, a Decade Later: A Meta-analytic Test of Social Exchange and Affect-Based Perspectives." *Journal of Applied Psychology* 98, no. 2: 199–236. https://doi.org/10.1037/a0031757

Dawson, S., Jovanovic, J., Gašević, D., and Pardo, A. 2017. "From Prediction to Impact: Evaluation of a Learning Analytics Retention Program." In *Proceedings of the Seventh International Learning Analytics and Knowledge Conference*, 474–78. https://doi.org/10.1145/3027385.3027405

Deho, O. B., Zhan, C., Li, J., Liu, J., Liu, L., and Duy Le, T. 2022. "How Do the Existing Fairness Metrics and Unfairness Mitigation Algorithms Contribute to Ethical Learning Analytics?" *British Journal of Educational Technology* 53, no. 4: 822–43. https://doi.org/10.1111/bjet.13217

Dinan, E., Abercrombie, G., Bergman, A. S., Spruit, S., Hovy, D., Boureau, Y.-L., and Rieser, V. 021. "Anticipating Safety Issues in E2E Conversational AI: Framework and Tooling." *ArXiv Preprint ArXiv:2107.03451.*

Drijvers, P., Doorman, M., Boon, P., Reed, H., and Gravemeijer, K. 2010. "The Teacher and the Tool: Instrumental Orchestrations in the Technology-Rich Mathematics Classroom." *Educational Studies in Mathematics* 75, no. 2: 213–34. https://doi.org/10.1007/s10649-010-9254-5

Duggan, M. 2017. *Online Harassment 2017*. Pew Research Center.

Garcia-Martinez, S., and Hamou-Lhadj, A. 2013. "Educational Recommender Systems: A Pedagogical-Focused Perspective." In *Multimedia Services in Intelligent Environments*, edited by G. Tsihrintzis, M. Virvou, and L. Jain, 113–24. https://doi.org/10.1007/978-3-319-00375-7_8

Gardner, J., Brooks, C., and Baker, R. 2019. "Evaluating the Fairness of Predictive Student Models through Slicing Analysis." In *Proceedings of the 9th International Conference on Learning Analytics and Knowledge*, 225–34. https://doi.org/10.1145/3303772.3303791

Gillborn, D., Dixson, A., Ladson-Billings, G., Parker, L., Rollock, N., and Warmington, P. 2018. *Critical Race Theory in Education*. London: Routledge.

Grover, A., and Leskovec, J. 2016. "node2vec: Scalable feature learning for networks." In *Proceedings of the 22nd ACM SIGKDD International Conference on Knowledge Discovery and Data Mining*, 855–64. https://doi.org/10.1145/2939672.2939754

Hardt, M., Price, E., and Srebro, N. 2016. "Equality of Opportunity in Supervised Learning." *Advances in Neural Information Processing Systems* 29: 3315–23.

Harkin, B., Webb, T. L., Chang, B. P., Prestwich, A., Conner, M., Kellar, I., Benn, Y., and Sheeran, P. 2016. "Does Monitoring Goal Progress Promote Goal Attainment? A Meta-analysis of the Experimental Evidence." *Psychological Bulletin* 142, no. 2: 198–229. https://doi.org/10.1037/bul0000025

Hutt, S., Gardner, M., Duckworth, A. L., and D'Mello, S. K. 2019. "Evaluating Fairness and Generalizability in Models Predicting on-time Graduation from College Applications." In Proceedings of the 12th International Conference on Educational Data Mining, edited by M. Desmarais, C. Lynch, A. Merceron, and R. Nkambou, 79–88. International Educational Data Mining Society.

Kang, M., Li, L., Weber, M., Liu, Y., Zhang, C., and Li, B. 2022. "Certifying Some Distributional Fairness with Subpopulation Decomposition." *Advances in Neural Information Processing Systems* 35: 31045–58.

Kizilcec, R. F., and Lee, H. 2022. "Algorithmic Fairness in Education." In *Ethics of Artificial Intelligence in Education*, edited by W. Holmes and K. Porayska-Pomsta, 174–202. London: Routledge.

Labarthe, H., Bouchet, F., Bachelet, R., and Yacef, K. 2016. "Does a Peer Recommender Foster Students' Engagement in MOOCs?" In *Proceedings of the 9th International Conference on Educational Data Mining*, 418–23.

Le Bras, R., Swayamdipta, S., Bhagavatula, C., Zellers, R., Peters, M., Sabharwal, A., and Choi, Y. 2020. "Adversarial Filters of Dataset Biases." *Proceedings of International Conference on Machine Learning* 119: 1078–88.

Lee, E. L. 2007. "Linguistic and Cultural Factors in East Asian Students' Oral Participation in U.S. University Classrooms." *International Education* 36, no. 2: 29–47.

Leite, W. L., Cetin-Berber, D. D., Huggins-Manley, A. C., Collier, Z. K., and Beal, C. R. 2019. "The Relationship between Algebra Nation Usage and High-Stakes Test Performance for Struggling Students." *Journal of Computer Assisted Learning* 35, no. 5: 569–81. https://doi.org/10.1111/jcal.12360

Li, C., and Xing, W. 2021. "Natural Language Generation Using Deep Learning to Support MOOC Learners." *International Journal of Artificial Intelligence in Education* 31, no. 2: 186–214. https://doi.org/10.1007/s40593-020-00235-x

Li, C., and Xing, W. 2022. "Revealing Factors Influencing Students' Perceived Fairness: A Case with a Predictive System for Math Learning." In *Proceedings of the Ninth ACM Conference on Learning@ Scale*, 409–12. https://doi.org/10.1145/3491140.3528293

Li, C., Xing, W., and Leite, W. 2022a. "Building Socially Responsible Conversational Agents Using Big Data to Support Online Learning: A Case with Algebra Nation." *British Journal of Educational Technology* 53, no. 4: 776–803. https://doi.org/10.1111/bjet.13227

Li, C., Xing, W., and Leite, W. L. 2022b. "Toward Building a Fair Peer Recommender to Support Help-Seeking in Online Learning." *Distance Education* 43, no. 1: 30–55. https://doi.org/10.1080/01587919.2021.2020619

Li, C., Xing, W., and Leite, W. 2022c. "Using Fair AI to Predict Students' Math Learning Outcomes in an Online Platform." *Interactive Learning Environments* 1–20. https://doi.org/10.1080/10494820.2022.2115076

Li, S., Chen, G., Xing, W., Zheng, J., and Xie, C. 2020. "Longitudinal Clustering of Students' Self-regulated Learning Behaviors in Engineering Design." *Computers and Education* 153: 103899. https://doi.org/10.1016/j.compedu.2020.103899

Liu, H., Dacon, J., Fan, W., Liu, H., Liu, Z., and Tang, J. 2019. "Does Gender Matter? Towards Fairness in Dialogue Systems." *ArXiv Preprint ArXiv:1910.10486.*

Lodge, J. M., Horvath, J. C., and Corrin, L., eds. 2018. *Learning Analytics in the Classroom: Translating Learning Analytics Research for Teachers.* London: Routledge.

Marcinkowski, F., Kieslich, K., Starke, C., and Lünich, M. 2020. "Implications of AI (Un-)Fairness in Higher Education Admissions: The Effects of Perceived AI (Un-)Fairness on Exit, Voice and Organizational Reputation." In *Proceedings of the 2020 Conference on Fairness, Accountability, and Transparency*, 122–30.

Marwan, S., Williams, J. J., and Price, T. 2019. "An Evaluation of the Impact of Automated Programming Hints on Performance and Learning." In *Proceedings of the 2019 ACM Conference on International Computing Education Research*, 61–70.

Metevier, B., Giguere, S., Brockman, S., Kobren, A., Brun, Y., Brunskill, E., and Thomas, P. S. 2019. "Offline Contextual Bandits with High Probability Fairness Guarantees." *Advances in Neural Information Processing Systems* 32: 14922–33.

Mitchell, S., Potash, E., Barocas, S., D'Amour, A., and Lum, K. 2021. "Algorithmic Fairness: Choices, Assumptions, and Definitions." *Annual Review of Statistics and Its Application* 8: 141–63. https://doi.org/10.1146/annurev-statistics-042720-125902

Nelson, W., Zitnik, M., Wang, B., Leskovec, J., Goldenberg, A., and Sharan, R. 2019. "To Embed or Not: Network Embedding as a Paradigm in Computational Biology." *Frontiers in Genetics* 10: 381. https://doi.org/10.3389/fgene.2019.00381

Obadimu, A., Mead, E., Hussain, M. N., and Agarwal, N. 2019. "Identifying Toxicity within YouTube Video Comment." In *Social, Cultural, and Behavioral Modeling, SBP-BRiMS 2019*, edited by R. Thomson, H. Bisgin, C. Dancy, and A. Hyder, Lecture Notes in Computer Science, vol. 11549, 214–23.

Pedro, F., Subosa, M., Rivas, A., and Valverde, P. 2019. "Artificial Intelligence in Education: Challenges and Opportunities for Sustainable Development." In *International Conference on Social Computing, Behavioral-Cultural Modeling and Prediction and Behavior Representation in Modeling and Simulation*, 214–23. Cham: Springer.

Pleiss, G., Raghavan, M., Wu, F., Kleinberg, J., and Weinberger, K. Q. 2017. "On Fairness and Calibration." *Advances in Neural Information Processing Systems* 30: 5680–89.

Potts, B. A., Khosravi, H., Reidsema, C., Bakharia, A., Belonogoff, M., and Fleming, M. 2018. "Reciprocal Peer Recommendation for Learning Purposes." In *Proceedings of the 8th International Conference on Learning Analytics and Knowledge*, 226–235. https://doi.org/10.1145/3170358.3170400

Radford, A., Wu, J., Child, R., Luan, D., Amodei, D., and Sutskever, I. 2019. "Language Models Are Unsupervised Multitask Learners." *OpenAI Blog* 1, no. 8.

Rahman, M. H., Schimpf, C., Xie, C., and Sha, Z. 2019. "A Computer-Aided Design Based Research Platform for Design Thinking Studies." *Journal of Mechanical Design* 141, no. 12: 121102. https://doi.org/10.1115/1.4044395

Riazy, S., and Simbeck, K. 2019. "Predictive Algorithms in Learning Analytics and their Fairness." *DELFI 2019.*

Rieder, B., and Skop, Y. 2021. "The Fabrics of Machine Moderation: Studying the Technical, Normative, and Organizational Structure of Perspective API." *Big Data and Society* 8, no. 2: Article 20539517211046180.

Roller, S., Dinan, E., Goyal, N., Ju, D., Williamson, M., Liu, Y., Xu, J., Ott, M., Shuster, K., and Smith, E. M. 2020. "Recipes for Building an Open-Domain Chatbot." *ArXiv Preprint ArXiv:2004.13637.*

Sclater, N., Peasgood, A., and Mullan, J. 2016. "Learning Analytics in Higher Education." *London: Jisc. Accessed February* 8, no. 2017: 176.

Sha, L., Rakovic, M., Whitelock-Wainwright, A., Carroll, D., Yew, V. M., Gasevic, D., and Chen, G. 2021. "Assessing Algorithmic Fairness in Automatic Classifiers of Educational Forum Posts." In Artificial Intelligence in Education, edited by I. Roll, D. McNamara, S. Sosnovsky, R. Luckin, and V. Dimitrova, 381–94. New York: Springer. https://doi.org/10.1007/978-3-030-78292-4_31

Shaw, E. 2019. *A Study of Factors and Perceptions that Mediate Student Participation in Supplementary Discussion Forums.* EdD thesis, the Open University.

Sunar, A. S., White, S., Abdullah, N. A., and Davis, H. C. 2016. "How Learners' Interactions Sustain Engagement: A MOOC Case Study." *IEEE Transactions on Learning Technologies* 10, no. 4: 475–87. https://doi.org/10.1109/tlt.2016.2633268

Sung, S. H., Li, C., Chen, G., Huang, X., Xie, C., Massicotte, J., and Shen, J. 2021. "How Does Augmented Observation Facilitate Multimodal Representational Thinking? Applying Deep Learning to Decode Complex Student Construct." *Journal of Science Education and Technology* 30, no. 2: 210–26. https://doi.org/10.1007/s10956-020-09856-2

Suresh, H., and Guttag, J. 2021. "A Framework for Understanding Sources of Harm throughout the Machine Learning Life Cycle." In *Equity and Access in Algorithms, Mechanisms, and Optimization (EAAMO '21), October 5–9, 2021—NY, USA*, 1–9. New York: Association for Computing Machinery.

Taskesen, B., Blanchet, J., Kuhn, D., and Nguyen, V. A. 2021. "A Statistical Test for Probabilistic Fairness." In *Proceedings of the 2021 ACM Conference on Fairness, Accountability, and Transparency*, 648–65. https://doi.org/10.1145/3442188.3445927

Thomas, P. S., da Silva, B. C., Barto, A. G., Giguere, S., Brun, Y., and Brunskill, E. 2019. "Preventing Undesirable Behavior of Intelligent Machines." *Science* 366, no. 6468: 999–1004.

Ting, C. C., Bowles, M., and Idewu, I. 2022. "Micro-video Recommendation Model Based on Graph Neural Network and Attention Mechanism." *ArXiv Preprint ArXiv:2205.10588.*

Tsai, Y.-S., Perrotta, C., and Gašević, D. 2020. "Empowering Learners with Personalised Learning Approaches? Agency, Equity and Transparency in the Context of Learning Analytics." *Assessment and Evaluation in Higher Education* 45, no. 4: 554–67. https://doi.org/10.1080/02602938.2019.1676396

Vaswani, A., Shazeer, N., Parmar, N., Uszkoreit, J., Jones, L., Gomez, A. N., Kaiser, Ł., and Polosukhin, I. 2017. "Attention Is All You Need." *Advances in Neural Information Processing Systems* 30: 5998–6008.

Vincent-Lancrin, S., and Van der Vlies, R. 2020. "Trustworthy Artificial Intelligence (AI) in Education: Promises and Challenges." *OECD Education Working Papers* 218: 1–13. https://doi.org/10.1787/a6c90fa9-en.

Wang, R., Harper, F. M., and Zhu, H. 2020. "Factors Influencing Perceived Fairness in Algorithmic Decision-Making: Algorithm Outcomes, Development Procedures, and Individual Differences." In *Proceedings of the 2020 CHI Conference on Human Factors in Computing Systems*, 1–14. https://doi.org/10.1145/3313831.3376813

Xing, W., Li, C., Chen, G., Huang, X., Chao, J., Massicotte, J., and Xie, C. 2021. "Automatic Assessment of Students' Engineering Design Performance Using a Bayesian Network Model." *Journal of Educational Computing Research* 59, no. 2: 230–56. https://doi.org/10.1177/0735633120960422

Xing, W., Tang, H., and Pei, B. 2019. "Beyond Positive and Negative Emotions: Looking into the Role of Achievement Emotions in Discussion Forums of MOOCs." *The Internet and Higher Education* 43: Article 100690. https://doi.org/10.1016/j.iheduc.2019.100690

Xu, J., Ju, D., Li, M., Boureau, Y.-L., Weston, J., and Dinan, E. 2020. "Recipes for Safety in Open-Domain Chatbots." *ArXiv Preprint ArXiv:2010.07079.*

Xu, Z., Ou, Z., Su, Q., Yu, J., Quan, X., and Lin, Z. 2020. "Embedding Dynamic Attributed Networks by Modeling the Evolution Processes." In *Proceedings of the 28th International Conference on Computational Linguistics*, 6809–19. http://dx.doi.org/10.18653/v1/2020.coling-main.600

Yokoyama, S. 2019. "Academic Self-efficacy and Academic Performance in Online Learning: A Mini Review." *Frontiers in Psychology* 9: 2794. https://doi.org/10.3389/fpsyg.2018.02794

Zemel, R., Wu, Y., Swersky, K., Pitassi, T., and Dwork, C. 2013. "Learning Fair Representations." In *Proceedings of the 30th International Conference on Machine Learning, 28*, 325–33.

Zhai, X., He, P., and Krajcik, J. 2022. "Applying Machine Learning to Automatically Assess Scientific Models." *Journal of Research in Science Teaching* 59, no. 10: 1765–94.

Zhai, X., and Krajcik, J. 2022. "*Pseudo AI Bias.*" ArXiv. https://doi.org/10.48550/arXiv.2210.08141

Zhang, Y., Sun, S., Galley, M., Chen, Y.-C., Brockett, C., Gao, X., Gao, J., Liu, J., and Dolan, B. 2019. "DialoGPT: Large-Scale Generative Pre-training for Conversational Response Generation." *ArXiv Preprint ArXiv:1911.00536.*

Zou, J., and Schiebinger, L. 2018. "AI Can Be Sexist and Racist—It's Time to Make it Fair." *Nature* 559: 324–26. https://doi.org/10.1038/d41586-018-05707-8

24

Supporting Inclusive Science Learning through Machine Learning

The AIISE Framework

Marvin Roski, Anett Hoppe and Andreas Nehring

With the integration of artificial intelligence (AI) and machine learning (ML) in (science) education, a unique potential to assess and enhance teaching and learning processes has become available (e.g., Zhai et al. 2020; Zhai and Nehm 2023). At the same time, the understanding of inclusion in education has shifted internationally from focusing exclusively on disabilities to a broader understanding that incorporates and values all dimensions of learners. Supporting approaches to access meaningful and equitable science education has become a major field gaining increasingly more interest in chemistry education research (Wilson-Kennedy et al. 2022). Significant progress has been made worldwide in the past twenty years. However, ensuring that every learner receives individualized support for their learning process is far from complete. The United Nations' fourth Sustainable Development Goal (SDG) on quality education aims to ensure access to inclusive education for all by 2030 (UNESCO-IIEP 2017). The *Framework for K–12 Science Education* also addressed this issue to enable educational equity and make diversity visible (National Research Council 2012).

The interplay of the three perspectives ("artificial intelligence in education," "science education," and "inclusive pedagogy") is promising. Through technological progress, individual learning can be realized on a high level, and every learner can be addressed (Humble and Mozelius 2019; Zhai 2021). The organization of individualized learning is challenging for teachers; ML algorithms and learning analytics (LA) can track, analyze, and ultimately individualize learning to automatically provide barrier-reduced learning opportunities (Neumann and Waight 2020). The interplay is also challenging because these three perspectives bring along different concepts, which must be aligned purposefully not to be detrimental to supporting inclusion.

Enabling "inclusive science education" requires merging the two perspectives of "inclusive pedagogy" and "science education." The Network Inclusive Science Education (NinU) has developed the so-called "NinU scheme" for this task. The scheme enables educators and researchers to provide inclusive science education, considering essential concepts of both disciplines (Stinken-Rösner et al. 2020). The unique challenge at this point is to add the perspective of "artificial intelligence in education" to enhance this interplay.

Marvin Roski, Anett Hoppe, and Andreas Nehring, *Supporting Inclusive Science Learning through Machine Learning.* In: *Uses of Artificial Intelligence in STEM Education.* Edited by: Xiaoming Zhai and Joseph Krajcik, Oxford University Press.
 DOI: 10.1093/oso/9780198882077.003.0024

Based on this prior work, this chapter introduces the Artificial Intelligence in Inclusive Science Education (AIISE) framework, designed to help researchers and educators integrate AI into inclusive science education processes. The NinU scheme is used and extended with the perspective of artificial intelligence in education.

The AIISE Framework—General Idea and Structure

AI helps learners with disabilities or special needs participate by reducing learning, hearing, seeing, and mobility barriers. At the same time, learners are pushed into a categorization system when differentiating between disabled and non-disabled, which can be discriminatory. However, it was meant to support these learners. Following this narrow understanding of inclusion might, in the worst case, conclude in binary solutions such as "those with disabilities need AI-based support; others do not" (Garg and Sharma 2020). Suppose this narrow understanding of inclusion is broadened to the point that all learners have different needs and can benefit from AI-based support. A discriminatory system is dismantled in that case, and "education for all" can be fully supported (Ainscow 2007; Garg and Sharma 2020). Baker (2016) describes the potential and vision of educational data mining (EDM) and learning analytics to understand learning better and enable individual learning through intelligent tutor systems or intelligent humans. He describes the symbiosis of the perspectives of artificial intelligence in education and science education. Adding the perspective of inclusive pedagogy increases the complexity of bringing together the different approaches.

The challenges start with the data collection. While innovations from EDM, LA, and AI promise to find patterns to take the analysis of learning to a new level (Kubsch, Krist, and Rosenberg 2023; Neumann and Waight 2020; Zhai et al. 2020), the question arises of how those patterns are generated: The barriers for learners to interact with the system are potentially too high, meaning that failure on a learning task can be detected, but providing hints or other tasks only addresses the symptomatic and not the actual learning barrier. Barriers to achieving different learning goals may arise from the content itself, its representations, or different aspects of learners, such as their socioeconomic or cultural background. They may ensure that learners need different learning activities, such as using a read-aloud feature in addition to a text or watching a video (CAST 2018; Stinken-Rösner et al. 2020). Nevertheless, the assessment can also be barrier-reduced by offering the possibility of writing a text or drawing a diagram (Zhai, He, and Krajcik 2022). These considerations underline the need for a framework guiding teachers and researchers and highlight essential aspects to consider when integrating AI into inclusive science education.

The AIISE framework is a three-step approach designed to help acknowledge diversity with the prior selection of an inclusion definition, recognize barriers with LA, and enable the participation of all learners in the learning process through ML-based support. The framework incorporates multiple facets from inclusive pedagogy, science education, several domains of AI, and the research field of fairness and bias (see Figure 24.1). The basis for the AIISE framework is given by the NinU scheme, which has already set the objective of combining the perspectives of inclusive pedagogy and

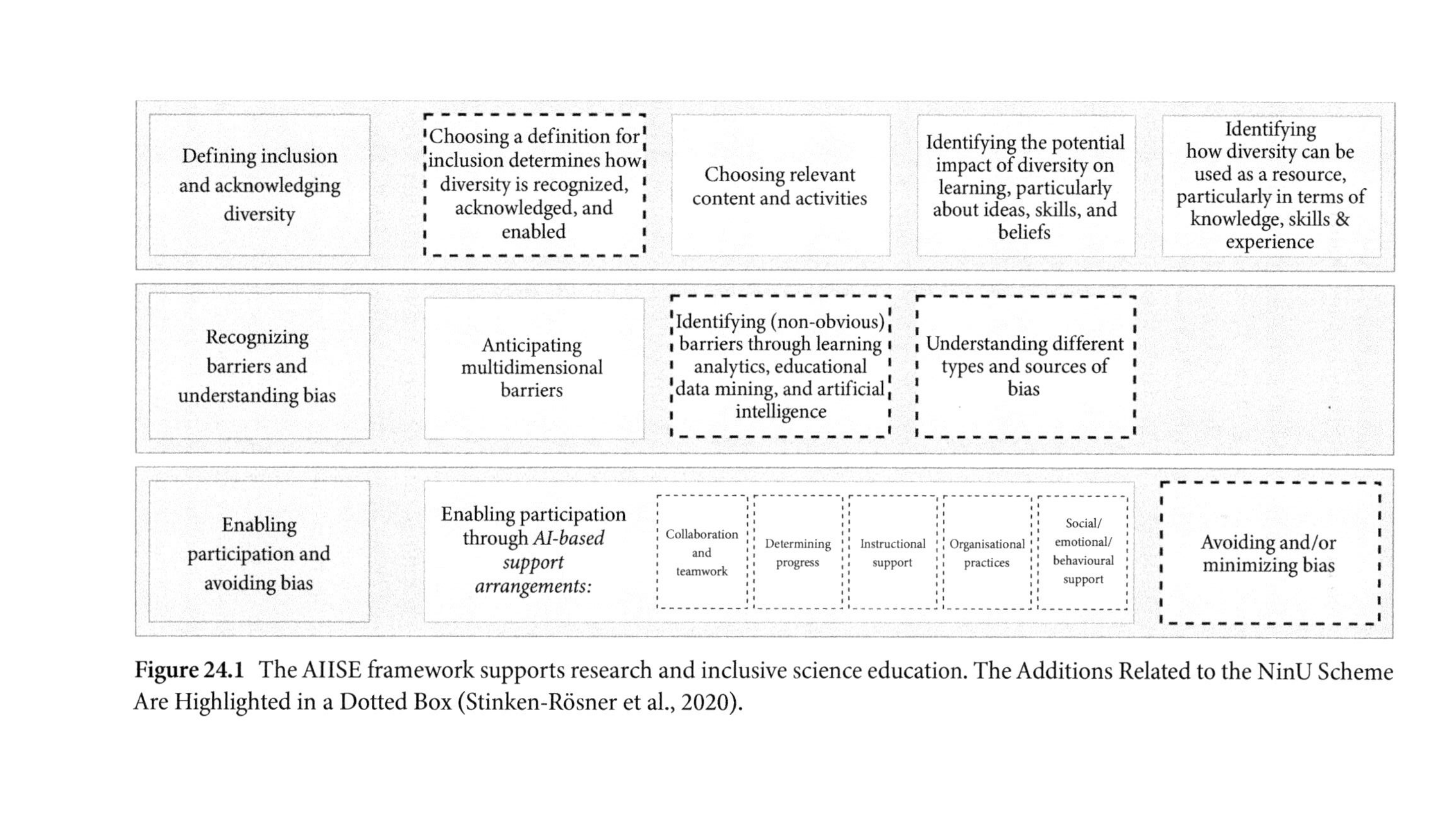

Figure 24.1 The AIISE framework supports research and inclusive science education. The Additions Related to the NinU Scheme Are Highlighted in a Dotted Box (Stinken-Rösner et al., 2020).

science education. AIISE can be understood as an extension that adds aspects from the field of artificial intelligence in education. The AIISE framework is derived from a process of reasoning, combining, and merging existing literature.

The framework follows a chain of reasoning helping to guide the design and the reflection of AI-supported learning opportunities. This chain of argumentation has a reading direction from top to bottom.

The three primary steps are highlighted in orange in the framework. The three primary steps are highlighted in orange in the AIISE framework. These steps are an adaptation from the NinU scheme: The inclusive pedagogy perspective is represented by the three steps acknowledging diversity, recognizing barriers, and enabling participation (Stinken-Rösner et al. 2020). These three steps first acknowledge that all learners have different prerequisites and personalities for encountering a learning opportunity, which can be used as a resource for learning (Florian and Spratt 2013; Taber and Riga 2016). Furthermore, diversity from each learner needs to be recognized if it is to be used beneficially (Florian and Spratt 2013; Goethe and Colina 2018). Finally, the participation of all learners is enabled by minimizing barriers. Participation means providing access to learning resources and social participation in the learning process (Booth 2003). Existing barriers for learners may not only be brought by the learners. They may also be created through interacting with the learning environment (Stinken-Rösner et al. 2020).

The NinU scheme refers to a broader definition of inclusion (Stinken-Rösner et al. 2020). At the same time, we have added to the AIISE framework the selection of a definition of inclusion to include approaches specifically designed to support people with disabilities under the presumption of being sensible about not creating a discriminatory category system (Garg and Sharma 2020; Mikropoulos and Iatraki 2022; Stinken-Rösner et al. 2020). The prior choice of a definition is decisive for the learner's type and extent of analysis and support (Göransson and Nilholm 2014). For this reason, the AIISE framework starts with explicitly defining inclusion. If the goal is to develop an ML-based assessment for people with disabilities (e.g., Zingoni et al. 2021), then the focus and attention will be quite different than if the focus is on individualized learning for all learners (e.g., Zingoni et al. 2021). Focusing on people with disabilities is a narrow definition while acknowledging all people's diversity is a broader definition of inclusion (e.g., Lamb, Neumann, and Linder 2022). In a narrow definition, the ML-based support system tries to identify and specifically support people with disabilities. In a broader definition, other traits are considered, such as reading ability, social background, ethnicity, gender, and even learning relevant preferences, such as choosing a video instead of a text. In this case, the focus is on optimizing the learning process of all learners and not just a vulnerable group.

The yellow boxes on the right in Figure 24.1 illustrate the individual facets of the primary steps. The NinU scheme has used Hodson's (2014) four learning goals of science education (reasoning about scientific issues, learning science content, doing science, and learning about science) for the consideration of the science education perspective to achieve "scientific literacy for all" (Bybee 1997). These aspects of the NinU scheme can also be found in the AIISE framework, however, in a compressed form to ensure clarity.

After clarifying the idea of inclusion for a particular project and considering the four learning goals of science education, ML applications become relevant in the following steps defined by the AIISE framework. Here we focus on two different uses: (a) the use of ML for barrier identification and (b) the use of ML for enabling participation by providing ML-based support systems. In this way, we integrate AI into inclusive science education.

When taking assessment and decision-making processes out of (human) hands, we must consider fairness and bias (Ntoutsi et al. 2020). Biased ML-based decisions might contribute to exclusive practices and be detrimental to inclusion. Consequently, we explicitly integrated a section on fairness and bias in the AIISE framework as a safety mechanism when integrating ML. Finally, we extended and classified the use of ML to enable participation by providing ML-based support systems based on Finkelstein, Sharma, and Furlonger's (2021) five inclusive teaching practices. By doing this, we can better categorize the integration of AI into inclusive science education to enable participation. AI-based support arrangements can be targeted more accurately.

In the AIISE framework (see Figure 24.1) is a colored highlighting to distinguish the original parts from the NinU scheme (no additional highlighting), the added aspects of AI, or the definition of inclusion (red highlighting). The inclusive teaching practice by Finkelstein, Sharma, and Furlonger (2021) helps categorize AI-based support arrangements (green highlighting).

In the further course of this chapter, after the short introduction of the learning platform I_3Learn, we will show how the AIISE framework can guide and reflect the development of learning support systems to foster inclusive science education.

Applying the AIISE Framework on the Learning Platform I_3Learn

I_3Learn is a digital and inclusive learning platform for teaching chemistry in German schools. The learning platform includes several lessons on ion bonding and can be used independently by the students. In addition to developing the learning platform, the project aims to analyze the learners' learning behavior through ML and offer individual learning support to ensure an optimal learning experience for each learner. In the following, we use the learning platform I_3Learn as an example of applying the AIISE framework. The development of I_3Learn and the AIISE framework are closely related. Our intention in developing AIISE frameworks centers on providing a tool to reflect on the development of I_3Learn critically.

In order to enable ML-based assessment and support, the platform records and stores log files for each learner to reconstruct individual learning behavior down to the second. This is noteworthy because the learning platform offers different and freely selectable learning paths. In I_3Lern, learners can choose between different representations for obtaining information, tasks with or without help, tasks with different difficulty levels, and additional information. Learners can choose which content they view first and repeat previous content briefly. Even if learners change their response behavior, this is recorded in the log files (e.g., select a different answer option for multiple-choice questions or add or remove text in open-ended responses).

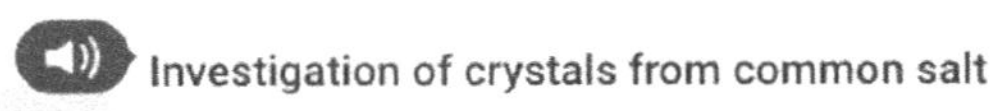

Figure 24.2 Screenshot of the I3Learn learning platform. Learners examine common salt crystals of different sizes.

During remote teaching during the SARS-Cov-2 pandemic (December 2021 to April 2022), the I3Learn learning platform was used by twenty-seven classes (ninth and tenth grade) in German schools, and more than half a million log files were recorded. Figures 24.2 and 24.3 show sections from the learning platform.

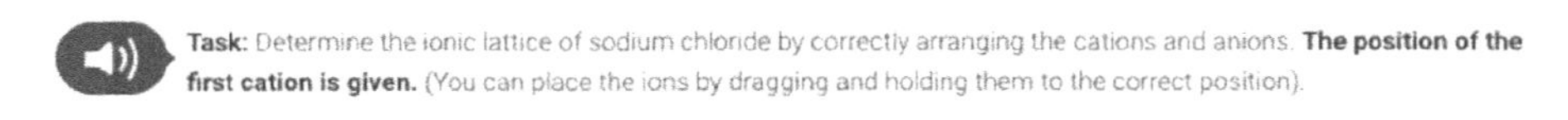

Figure 24.3 Screenshot of the I3Learn learning platform. Learners arrange a two-dimensional ion lattice.

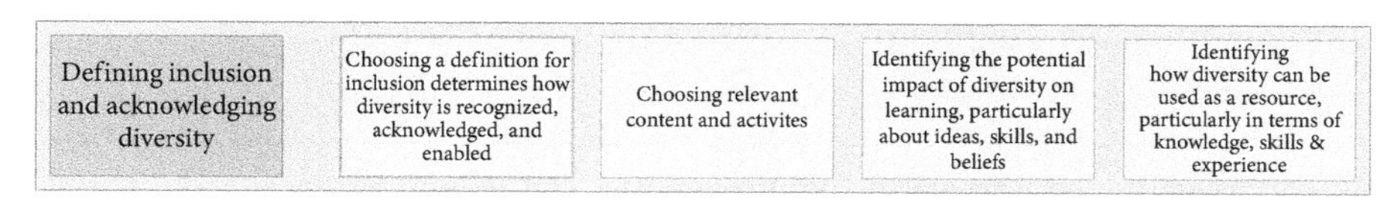

Figure 24.4 The first step in the AIISE framework: defining inclusion and acknowledging diversity.

First Step: Defining Inclusion and Acknowledging Diversity in I3Lern

This section considers aspects of the first step of the AIISE framework, "defining inclusion and acknowledging diversity" (see Figure 24.4).

Choosing a Definition for Inclusion

The definition of inclusion is multifaceted, complex, and highly controversial (Armstrong, Armstrong, and Spandagou 2011). However, clarifying a concrete understanding of inclusion is essential as it impacts how diversity is acknowledged and recognized. A unified definition is missing, significantly impacting inclusive research and practice (Farrell 2004; Florian and Black-Hawkins 2011). The popular understanding is that inclusion is synonymous with integrating learners with "special needs" or disabilities into mainstream schools (Ainscow et al. 2006). This idea dated to the 1990s when the Salamanca Statement called for integrating these vulnerable groups into mainstream schools mainly because special education in many countries suffers from a lack of quality (Artiles et al. 2006; UNESCO 1994) or exclusion of people with disabilities from the education system (Miles and Singal 2010). Since then, many different understandings of "inclusion" can be described, of which UNESCO promotes the "education for all" approach (Ainscow et al. 2006). The focus is on providing education access for all learners, removing all possible barriers to learning, and ensuring that everyone benefits from barrier-free learning (UNESCO 2000; UNESCO-IIEP 2017).

There are different definitions of inclusion, which differ in how vulnerable groups are included. A widely used and unsophisticated distinction is that of Ainscow et al. (2006). A distinction is made between a narrow (only learners with disabilities) and a broad (all learners are included) concept of inclusion (Finkelstein, Sharma, and Furlonger 2021). A more nuanced definition arises from the examination conducted by Göransson and Nilholm (2014; see Table 24.1).

UNESCO's "education for all" approach can be understood as a broad definition according to the classification of Ainscow et al. (2006), or even as a "community definition" following Göransson and Nilholm (2014). The objective of the fourth SDG is to create an inclusive society by 2030 (UNESCO-IIEP 2017). The choice of the definition of inclusion has a significant impact on how diversity is recognized, perceived, and ultimately enabled.

I3Learn was primarily developed for use in German integrated comprehensive schools. Based on a broad inclusion definition, all learners are educated in one class regardless of their prerequisites (Niedersächsiches Kultusministerium 2020). For this reason, a broader concept of inclusion was also used for I3Learn. According to Göransson and Nilholm (2014), the learning platform refers to a "general

Table 24.1 Comparison of Different Definitions of Inclusion According to Finkelstein, Sharma, and Furlonger (2021).

Ainscow et al. (2006)	**Göransson and Nilholm (2014)**	
Narrow	Placement definition	Learners with disabilities are placed in the classroom; no special assistance is provided.
	Specified individualized definition	Special support for learners with disabilities in mainstream schools
Broad	General individualized definition	0049nclusion is fulfilling the individual needs of all learners.
	Community definition	Creating an inclusive community

individualized definition." The diversity of all students is appreciated, and the goal is to provide optimal learning support for everyone.

Choosing Relevant Content and Activities

The NinU scheme sees itself as a holistic framework (Stinken-Rösner et al. 2020). For this reason, selecting content and activities is particularly important for the learning process. Learners come to class with their "personal framework of understanding" (Hodson 1998, 113). They have different facets of experience and construct different conceptions (DiSessa and Sherin 2006), which can be expanded through a scientific understanding as part of a learning process (Hodson 2014). Learners should encounter accessible and relevant content and acquire a scientific understanding through scientific inquiry of phenomena (Stinken-Rösner et al. 2020).

The learning platform I_3Learn focuses on ion bonding, which is challenging for learners (Barke and Pieper 2008). Ion bonding is a very presuppositional topic. Students need a deeper insight into the particle model, the model of electric current, and the Rutherford model to fulfill the prerequisite of gaining a profound understanding of the bonding forces between ions (Hilbing and Barke 2004). Chemical bonds are an elementary component of further science education for learners. Conventional table salt is used to create an everyday life context, and the brittleness of salt crystals is investigated within the framework of virtual experiments to get to ion lattice and ion bonding in this way. Through this structure, learners are guided toward scientific inquiry.

Identifying the Potential Impact of Diversity on Learning

Learner diversity is multifaceted and can significantly impact learning (Gurin et al. 2002). Learners encounter learning processes (in I_3Learn) with different prerequisites. They have different backgrounds, have grown up with different languages and cultures, and have different socioeconomic backgrounds, interests, abilities, and problems (Ainscow 2007; Stinken-Rösner et al. 2020). All of these (and perhaps more) can be considered when integrating AI into the inclusive science classroom, assuming a broader definition of inclusion. With a narrow definition, diversity is more precise, focusing on disabilities as differences between learners (Göransson and Nilholm 2014).

Before starting to learn with I3Learn, learners can provide various information relevant to a broad understanding of the diversity of learners. It starts with the socioeconomic background (Torsheim et al. 2016), which can influence experience with technical devices, access to the Internet or the presence of a quiet workplace in remote learning (Angelico, 2020), reading ability (Mayringer and Wimmer 2014), intelligence (Heller and Perleth 2000), and learners' knowledge and perception of ions and their bonding (adapted version of the bonding representations inventory of Luxford and Bretz 2014).

Identifying How Diversity Can Be Used as a Resource

Using diversity as a resource in the NinU scheme is often based on knowledge skills and experiences that are subsequently shared with the learning group in community learning (González et al. 2021; Stinken-Rösner et al. 2020).

Due to the SARS-Cov-2 pandemic, these advantages cannot be used in I3Learn. The learning platform is designed for remote learning. Each learner can work alone and independently with the learning platform to meet the conditions for emergency remote learning. Collaborative learning is not implemented yet, so diversity, bringing different experiences and skills to work on a common task, cannot be implemented (unfortunately) in the current version of I3Learn. The AIISE framework helps us reflect on potential future directions of using diversity in collaborative learning settings.

Second Step: Recognizing Barriers and Understanding Bias

The second step of the AIISE framework, "recognizing barriers and understanding bias," is discussed in the following (see Figure 24.5).

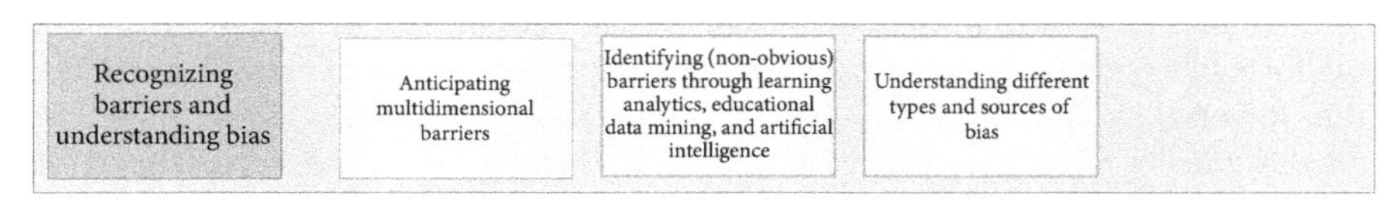

Figure 24.5 The second step in the AIISE framework: recognizing barriers and understanding bias.

Anticipating Multidimensional Barriers

Barriers occur when learners interact with the learning environment. Possible barriers for learners cannot be simply enumerated because every learner and learning group is different, and different barriers occur in particular learning situations. Possible origins of barriers can be social, language (especially about the communication between different stakeholders or the improper use of academic language), cognitive, affective, or physical (Stinken-Rösner et al. 2020). Suppose little is known about the learning group beforehand. In that case, barriers can also be identified while developing a learning environment, such as the I3Learn learning platform.

Social barriers lie with the learning platform itself. It must be accessible to all students. However, this can be problematic if, for example, this is only possible with the end device of a specific producer, which a learner may not be able to use for socioeconomic reasons. Language barriers may also arise: Academic language, especially for chemical topics, is very demanding and complex. Understanding academic language is an essential part of being able to participate fully in the learning platform (Taber 2015). This creates a barrier that not all learners can overcome.

During the development of I3Learn, few details were available about the learning groups that worked with it. There was rather general information available about the learning group that was advised. According to consultations with teachers of the German integrative comprehensive schools, ion bonding is a challenging topic for learners, which aligns with the literature's information (see the section "Choosing Relevant Content and Activities"). For this reason, cognitive barriers were identified: Knowledge assessment allows us to identify prior knowledge and inadequate learner conception (Luxford and Bretz 2014). Furthermore, we anticipate problems in learners' reading ability, allowing the reading ability test to capture this barrier (Becker-Mrotzek et al. 2019). Through emergency remote learning, learners are faced with learning independently using the learning platform. For technical and data security reasons, the teachers do not receive feedback about the learners during the current data collection and can, therefore, intervene in the event of a lack of motivation. This affective barrier can also have a socioeconomic background. In this case, learners may receive little support from home, no quiet workplace may be available, or end devices may have to be shared. Physical barriers may be in the perception of information, such as text, because the font size, font, or background is unsuitable for learners, so the text cannot be perceived.

Of course, this is only a selection of the barriers that can arise with a digital learning platform like I3Learn. A widely used resource to get an overview of possible barriers is the Universal Design for Learning (UDL) guidelines (CAST 2018). These guidelines are designed to minimize barriers; by logic, they belong in the next step of the AIISE framework. However, since these measures are mainly not AI-based, we will not go further into UDL. On the other hand, UDL is a good retrospective instrument for recognizing barriers. For example, multiple representations are offered, i.e., a video in addition to text (CAST 2018).

Identifying (Non-obvious) Barriers through Learning Analytics, Educational Data Mining, and Machine Learning

Technological advances allow researchers to examine extensive data that would be impossible to analyze by hand. LA covers a wide range of data collection methods and types of data that allow for deep insight into learning processes (Li and Lajoie 2022). The possibilities of LA concerning individualized learning highlighted by Baker (2016) give a sense of the opportunities: LA can be used to analyze learning behavior to enable individualized learning or identify examples of "gaming the system" that indicate the presence of motivational barriers. Furthermore, LA can examine learners' interaction with a digital learning platform in real time, identify learning success and critical points of failure, and determine the effectiveness of learning tasks and materials (Ifenthaler, Gibson, and Dobozy 2018). The literature also shows that LA's capabilities are not limited to digital learning environments. However, the data collected by various sensors has great potential in the future (Ferguson 2017).

Li and Lajoie (2022) categorize the applicable data as "behavioral motoric," "behavioral physiological," and "contextual." Behavioral motoric can be defined as the data collection of learners' visible or audible behavior. This includes body movement (e.g., Bosch et al. 2015), facial expression (e.g., Liaw et al. 2020), eye movement (e.g., Merceron, Blikstein, and Siemens 2016; Peterson et al. 2015), and analysis of speech (e.g., Caballero et al. 2017). In behavioral physiological, learners' sensor data are processed: This includes, for example, EEG (Ghali, Ouellet, and Frasson 2015) or fNIRS (Lamb, Neumann, and Linder 2022). The category contextual includes the analysis of log files (Gobert et al. 2013) or texts (Nehm, Ha, and Mayfield 2012).

The current research on identifying barriers in an inclusive classroom is sparse. Nonetheless, existing projects and ideas can identify problems in learning even if inclusivity was not a primary consideration in implementing these systems. In I3Learn, extensive log files of each learner were recorded. This allows for a dedicated reconstruction of the learning behavior, which creates the basis for using LA and ML to identify patterns not obvious to humans and could, for example, indicate barriers among learners. For example, learners look at specific content for an unusually long (or short) time.

Understanding Different Types and Sources of Bias

As described in the previous section, AI systems have significant potential to promote inclusive science education. However, a broad understanding of inclusion involves many learner characteristics, such as gender or socioeconomic background. There is a risk that a trained system based on these characteristics will bias the system and—contrary to actual intentions—lead to more exclusion from learning or other social processes (Porayska-Pomsta and Rajendran 2019). There are numerous examples of bias in systems (Mehrabi et al. 2021). It should also be noted that using AI does not cause all types of suspected bias. Pseudo AI bias (PAIB) refers to human errors and misperceptions falsely attributed to AI (Zhai and Krajcik 2022). Bias is not a new phenomenon that has appeared simultaneously with technological progress. However, AI risks reinforcing existing biases and promoting new types of bias (Ntoutsi et al. 2020).

The first step to preventing bias is to understand bias. The field of AI is primarily a discipline heavily dependent on data. The data collection process also depends on humans, as either the data comes from humans or human-created systems collect the data (Ntoutsi et al. 2020). Bias can occur anywhere where a transformation of information takes place. Information about the user interaction is converted into data. The data are further transformed by training an algorithm, which then provides information to the user and thus influences their behavior: A cycle of information transformation is created. This cycle is susceptible to different bias types at different points and times, for example, when a bias appears only in the second round of the loop (Mehrabi et al. 2021). A selection of possible bias types can be seen in Table 24.2. A complete list can be found in Mehrabi et al. (2021).

In this step of the AIISE framework, it is essential to be aware that different forms of bias can negatively impact vulnerable groups. For I3Learn, we are aware that when training ML models, variables such as gender serve as the basis for gender bias. Alternatively, data from the population are only a snapshot and may not be up to date for future non-pandemic times.

Third Step: Enabling Participation and Avoiding Bias

This section explains the third step, enabling participation and avoiding bias, of the AIISE framework (see Figure 24.6). Enabling the participation of all learners is explicitly based on using AI in the AIISE framework. Besides the AIISE framework, other non-AI-based ways to minimize barriers, such as the UDL guidelines, are not discussed here.

Table 24.2 Selection of Different Bias Types (Mehrabi et al. 2021)

User interaction with data	
Population bias	The population of users interacting with the algorithms has changed compared to those from whom the data originated.
Self-selection bias	People self-select to generate data because, for example, they have a higher-than-average level of interest to participate.
Data to algorithm	
Representation bias	Data to train the algorithm are insufficiently diverse, leaving certain groups under-represented.
Omitted variable bias	Essential variables are omitted or not present in the data.
Algorithm to user interaction	
Algorithmic bias	The design of the algorithm leads to bias.
Emergent bias	Changes in cultural values or anything similar will cause the training data to no longer fit the current population.

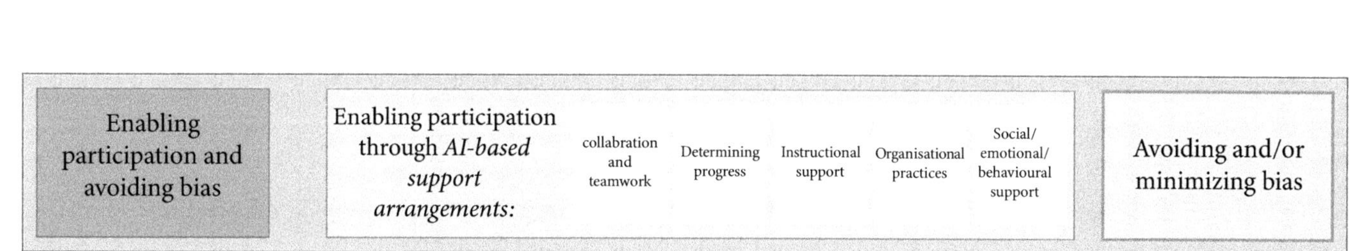

Figure 24.6 The third step in the AIISE framework: enabling participation and avoiding bias.

Enabling Participation through AI-Based Support Arrangements

Inclusive teaching practices are multifaceted and complex (Brauns and Abels 2020). Finkelstein, Sharma, and Furlonger (2021) mapped this complexity into five categories: collaboration and teamwork, determining students' progress, instructional support, organizational practices, and social/emotional/behavioral support (see Table 24.3). These categories are not initially related to integrating AI into inclusive science education but serve as a helpful starting point to categorize existing and upcoming AI-based systems and their purpose.

I3Learn is a learning platform that continuously and automatically assesses learners' performance. In addition to a pre- and post-tests, learners complete tasks at regular intervals, all of which can be assigned to so-called knowledge components (see Table 24.4; VanLehn 2006).

Through these knowledge components, a learner model can be built that highlights the strengths and weaknesses of each learner in terms of domain knowledge, as well as other factors such as reading ability. As a result, the diversity of learners in terms of different levels of knowledge and skills is made tangible.

Table 24.3 Types of Inclusive Teaching Practice (Finkelstein, Sharma, and Furlonger 2021)

Collaboration and teamwork	Interactions between different actors in the classroom, such as teachers or experts in special needs.
Determining the progress of students	Measuring individual learner progress beyond academic goals (depending on the definition of inclusion used). This category includes all types of assessments.
Instructional support	How learning content is provided, and individualized learning can be realized.
Organizational practices	This includes physical access to the classroom, as well as accessibility to materials and sufficient time.
Social/emotional/behavioral support	Provide a positive learning environment where learners receive social, emotional, and behavioral support.

Table 24.4 All Knowledge Components Included in I3Learn

Knowledge components	
KC 1	Structure of atoms and ions
KC 2	Formation of ions during electron transfer
KC 3	Characteristics of salts
KC 4	Ratio formulas of salts
KC 5	Bonding as an attraction between ions
KC 6	Lattice structure of salts
KC 7	Differentiation between macroscopic and submicroscopic levels

Each learner's performance can be predicted using ML and Bayesian knowledge tracing. If necessary, an intervention in the learning process can take place to optimize each learner's learning (Mao, Lin, and Chi 2018). Another non-I3Learn example of an ML-based implementation of determining the progress of students is the assessment of Zhai, He, and Krajcik (2022). Learners benefit from being able to draw in addition to a text-based answer, both of which are evaluated automatically. Answering a task with a text challenges a learner differently than drawing. Individual characteristics depend on whether a learner is more comfortable writing text or drawing.

One way to provide ML-based instructional support is a recommendation system. For this purpose, a small part of the learning platform is considered an example. I3Learn contains possibilities of repeating previous contents, namely the definition of ions. By doing so, the cognitive barrier created by the challenging topic of ion binding can be minimized. The architecture of this part of I3Learn can be seen in Figure 24.7.

ML-based instructional support can be provided through a recommendation system that helps learners select the best learning path for each individual. In I3Learn, the learners can choose among three chapters to repeat prerequisite content (ions (see Figure 24.7), electron transfer, and noble gas configuration). Learners can choose whether to repeat a topic and which chapters they want to repeat.

After selecting one of these chapters, learners have several choices to shape their learning path: First, they can choose whether to perceive the content as text or video. After that, the possibilities include the read-aloud function and customizing the interface (font size, font type, and background). On the one hand, these decisions are a powerful way for learners to minimize barriers. On the other hand, these choices also create a cognitive barrier when learners have trouble choosing a suitable representation or do not choose the learning path best suited for their learning process but one that seems easiest. This barrier can be reduced by an individual and ML-based recommendation, in which characteristics and preferences are included in the recommendation process. Preferences are queried after working through the relevant section. Learners can self-assess how they cope with a task, text, or video and serve as features to train the recommended system besides log files. This ML-based support arrangement can be categorized as "instructional support" of inclusive teaching practice (Finkelstein, Sharma, and Furlonger 2021). Appropriate choices offered in I3Learn are consistent with the UDL guidelines (CAST 2018). The UDL principle of

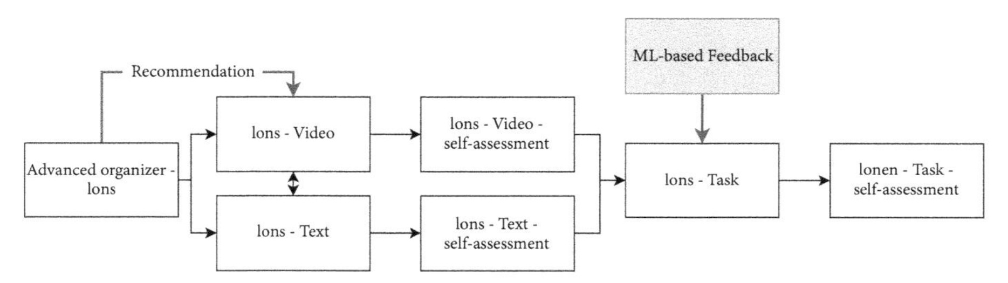

Figure 24.7 Exemplary architecture from the learning platform I3Learn. The learners can repeat the chapter "Ions."

"multiple means of representations" minimizes cognitive barriers by offering learning content in different auditory and visual ways (Hall et al. 2015).

The log files in I3Learn reveal a detailed insight into the learning behavior, i.e., whether the learners lack motivation or try to game the system. Indicators of such behavior could be unusual clicking behavior, random guessing when giving answers, or open-ended answers when learners express their lack of motivation. AI-based detection and support of such phenomena belong to the category "social/emotional/behavioral support teacher."

Avoiding and Minimizing Bias

There are several approaches for keeping the influence of bias as slight as possible: pre-processing, in-processing, and post-processing (Mehrabi et al. 2021; Ntoutsi et al. 2020). In pre-processing, several methods are used to minimize the potential of bias already in the dataset. In-processing focuses on sensitizing the algorithm during training to reduce bias (Mehrabi et al. 2021). In the post-processing approach, the trained algorithm is focused. A distinction can be made between a white-box approach and a black-box approach. In the white-box approach, the internal possibilities of the model are varied, such as the probabilities in a naïve Bayes model. For the black-box approach, the prediction results are examined in more detail. For example, the outcomes at the decision boundaries are examined more closely (Ntoutsi et al. 2020). Currently, there is no state-of-the-art on the best and most effective way to minimize bias (Ntoutsi et al. 2020). Separate studies will be necessary to evaluate trained systems.

Summary and Future Work

In this chapter, the AIISE framework has been presented as a tool to support inclusive learning processes in STEM education with the help of AI. For this purpose, important steps that are necessary or at least recommended have been highlighted. The AIISE framework supports researchers and educators in implementing AI in inclusive STEM education. The AIISE framework can be seen as an extension of the NinU scheme, which has already been used and evaluated in undergraduate teacher education (Föhner et al. 2022).

We designed the AIISE framework to accompany the development of the digital and inclusive learning platform I3Learn to be able to reflect on the development critically. A particular focus is to have a comprehensive approach that starts with the definition of inclusion and ends with the minimization of bias. Unlike the original NinU scheme, the AIISE framework is not intended for teachers but researchers and developers who want to establish AI-based support in inclusive science education learning processes. The framework is intended to serve as a support so that essential aspects can be considered. It can thus be seen as a development tool, a research tool, a reflection tool, and an improvement tool for existing implementations. The AIISE framework was developed and piloted during the development of the I3Lern digital learning platform. Extensive data have been collected, and initial AI implementations are being tested (e.g., Roski, Hoppe, and Nehring 2023; Roski, Sebastian et al. 2023). Further evaluations are planned.

The framework varies in its precision, which is critical. However, it partly gives no other option because the current research does not offer state-of-the-art solutions. While bias is not a new phenomenon and existed long before the first computers, it is an individual problem that cannot be fully captured by a universally applicable framework (Ntoutsi et al. 2020). This work has included a narrow and broader understanding of inclusion. Looking at the definitions of Göransson and Nilholm (2014), the AIISE framework can still be improved in creating an inclusive community and integrating corresponding social constructs that influence inclusion and exclusion more strongly. This includes, for example, how science identities are reconstructed within AI-based teaching and learning (Hazari et al. 2020), but also opening frameworks and learning activities towards non-Western perspectives, worldviews, and researcher and participant voices (Hunter and Richmond 2022), or how the failure to recognize barriers is due to implicit but systemic racism framing (Russo-Tait 2022).

At these points, AIISE serves not as a guide but as a reminder for researchers to think through appropriate problems when implementing AI in inclusive science education. AIISE is not intended to be a holistic framework that provides universal answers to future research and development processes but is explicitly left open to allow freedom of exploration, innovation, and creativity to meet the evolving challenges and opportunities of inclusive science education using AI. At the same time, it is defined as providing concrete steps for thinking and working.

References

Ainscow, M. 2007. “Taking an Inclusive Turn.” *Journal of Research in Special Educational Needs* 7, no. 1: 3–7. https://doi.org/10.1111/j.1471-3802.2007.00075.x

Ainscow, M., Booth, T., Dyson, A., Farrell, P., Frankham, J., and Gallannaugh, F. 2006. *Improving Schools, Developing Inclusion*. London: Routledge.

Angelico, T. 2020. “Educational Inequality and the Pandemic in Australia: Time to Shift the Educational Paradigm.” *International Studies in Educational Administration* 48, no. 1: 39–45. http://www.cceam.org.

Armstrong, D., Armstrong, A. C., and Spandagou, I. 2011. “Inclusion: By Choice or by Chance?” *International Journal of Inclusive Education* 15, no. 1: 29–39. https://doi.org/10.1080/13603116.2010.496192

Artiles, A. J., Kozleski, E. B., Dorn, S., and Christensen, C. 2006. “Chapter 3: Learning in Inclusive Education Research: Re-mediating Theory and Methods with a Transformative Agenda.” *Review of Research in Education* 30, no. 1: 65–108. https://doi.org/10.3102/0091732X030001065

Baker, R. 2016. “Using Learning Analytics in Personalized Learning.” In *Handbook on Personalized Learning for States, Districts, and Schools*, edited by M. Murphy, S. Redding, and J. Twyman, 165–74. Charlotte, NC: Information Age Publishing.

Baker, R. S. 2016. “Stupid Tutoring Systems, Intelligent Humans.” *International Journal of Artificial Intelligence in Education* 26, no. 2: 600–14. https://doi.org/10.1007/s40593-016-0105-0

Barke, H.-D., and Pieper, C. 2008. “Der Ionenbegriff—historischer Spätzünder und gegenwärtiger Außenseiter.” *Chemkon* 15, no. 3: 119–24. https://doi.org/10.1002/ckon.200810075

Becker-Mrotzek, M., Lindauer, T., Pfost, M., Weis, M., Strohmaier, A., and Reiss, K. 2019. “Lesekompetenz heute—eine Schlüsselqualifikation im Wandel.” In *PISA 2018. Grundbildung im internationalen Vergleich. 1. Auflage*. https://doi.org/10.25656/01

Booth, T. 2003. "Inclusion and Exclusion in the City: Concepts and Contexts." In *Inclusion in the City: Selection, Schooling and Community*, 1–14. London: Routledge Falmer.
Bosch, N., D'Mello, S., Baker, R., Ocumpaugh, J., and Shute, V. 2015. "Temporal Generalizability of Face-Based Affect Detection in Noisy Classroom Environments." *Lecture Notes in Computer Science 9112*: 44–53. https://doi.org/10.1007/978-3-319-19773-9_5
Brauns, S., and Abels, S. 2020. "Inclusive Science Education—Framework for Inclusive Science Education." Inclusive Science Education, Working Paper No. 1/2020.
Bybee, R. W. 1997. "Toward an Understanding of Scientific Literacy." In *Scientific Literacy—An International Symposium*, edited by W. Gräber and C. Bolte, 37–68. Kiel: Institüt für die Pädagogik der Naturwissenschaften an der Universität Kiel.
Caballero, D., Araya, R., Kronholm, H., Viiri, J., Mansikkaniemi, A., Lehesvuori, S., Virtanen, T., and Kurimo, M. 2017. "ASR in Classroom Today: Automatic Visualization of Conceptual Network in Science Classrooms." *Lecture Notes in Computer Science (Including Subseries Lecture Notes in Artificial Intelligence and Lecture Notes in Bioinformatics), 10474 LNCS*, 541–544. https://doi.org/10.1007/978-3-319-66610-5_58
CAST. 2018. *Universal Design for Learning Guidelines version 2.2.*
DiSessa, A. A., and Sherin, B. L. 1998. "What Changes in Conceptual Change?" International Journal of Science Education 20, no. 10: 1155–91. https://doi.org/10.1080/0950069980201002
Farrell, P. 2004. "School Psychologists: Making Inclusion a Reality for All." *School Psychology International 25*, no. 1: 5–19. https://doi.org/10.1177/0143034304041500
Ferguson, R. 2017. "Learning Analytics: A Firm Basis for the Future." In *Education and New Technologies: Perils and Promises for Learners*, edited by K. Sheehy and A. Holliman, Vol. 51, no. 6, 162–76. https://doi.org/10.5860/choice.51-2973
Finkelstein, S., Sharma, U., and Furlonger, B. 2021. "The Inclusive Practices of Classroom Teachers: A Scoping Review and Thematic Analysis." *International Journal of Inclusive Education 25*, no. 6: 735–62. https://doi.org/10.1080/13603116.2019.1572232
Florian, L., and Black-Hawkins, K. 2011. "Exploring Inclusive Pedagogy." *British Educational Research Journal* 37, no. 5: 813–28. https://doi.org/10.1080/01411926.2010.501096
Florian, L., and Spratt, J. 2013. "Enacting Inclusion: A Framework for Interrogating Inclusive Practice." *European Journal of Special Needs Education* 28, no. 2: 119–35. https://doi.org/10.1080/08856257.2013.778111
Fühner, L., González, L. F., Weck, H., Pusch, A., and Abels, S. 2022. "Das NinU-Raster zur Planung und Reflexion inklusiven naturwissenschaftlichen Unterrichts für Lehramtsstudierende." In *Inklusion in der Lehramtsausbildung—Lerngegenstände, Interaktionen und Prozesse*, 63–78.
Garg, S., and Sharma, S. 2020. "Impact of Artificial Intelligence in Special Need Education to Promote Inclusive Pedagogy." *International Journal of Information and Education Technology* 10, no. 7: 523–27. https://doi.org/10.18178/ijiet.2020.10.7.1418
Ghali, R., Ouellet, S., and Frasson, C. 2015. "LewiSpace: an Exploratory Study with a Machine Learning Model in an Educational Game." *Journal of Education and Training Studies* 4, no. 1: 192–201. https://doi.org/10.11114/jets.v4i1.1153
Gobert, J. D., Sao Pedro, M., Raziuddin, J., and Baker, R. S. 2013. "From Log Files to Assessment Metrics: Measuring Students' Science Inquiry Skills Using Educational Data Mining." *Journal of the Learning Sciences* 22, no. 4: 521–63. https://doi.org/10.1080/10508406.2013.837391
Goethe, E. v., and Colina, C. M. 2018. "Taking Advantage of Diversity within the Classroom." Journal of Chemical Education 95, no. 2: 189–92. https://doi.org/10.1021/acs.jchemed.7b00510
González, L. F., Fühner, L., Sührig, L., Weck, H., Weirauch, K., and Abels, S. 2021. "Ein Unterstützungsraster zur Planung und Reflexion inklusiven naturwissenschaftlichen Unterrichts." *Naturwissenschaftsdidaktik Und Inklusion, 4. Beiheft Sonderpädagogische Förderung Heute*, 119–215.
Göransson, K., and Nilholm, C. 2014. "Conceptual Diversities and Empirical Shortcomings—A Critical Analysis of Research on Inclusive Education." *European Journal of Special Needs Education* 29, no. 3: 265–80. https://doi.org/10.1080/08856257.2014.933545
Gurin, P., Dey, E. L., Hurtado, S., and Gurin, G. 2002. "Diversity and Higher Education: Theory and Impact on Educational Outcomes." *Harvard Educational Review* 72, no. 3: 330–66. https://doi.org/10.17763/haer.72.3.01151786u134n051

Hall, T. E., Cohen, N., Vue, G., and Ganley, P. 2015. "Addressing Learning Disabilities with UDL and Technology: Strategic Reader." *Learning Disability Quarterly* 38, no. 2: 72–83. https://doi.org/10.1177/0731948714544375

Hazari, Z., Chari, D., Potvin, G., and Brewe, E. 2020. "The Context Dependence of Physics Identity: Examining the Role of Performance/Competence, Recognition, Interest, and Sense of Belonging for Lower and Upper Female Physics Undergraduates." *Journal of Research in Science Teaching* 57, no. 10: 1583–607. https://doi.org/10.1002/tea.21644

Heller, K. A., and Perleth, C. 2000. *Kognitiver Fähigkeitstest für 4. bis 12. Klassen, Revision.*

Hilbing, C., and Barke, H.-D. 2004. "Ionen und Ionenbindung: Fehlvorstellungen hausgemacht! Ergebnisse empirischer Erhebungen und unterrichtliche Konsequenzen." *CHEMKON* 11, no. 3: 115–20. https://doi.org/10.1002/ckon.200410009

Hodson, D. 1998. Teaching and Learning Science: A Personalized Approach. Philadelphia: Open University Press.

Hodson, D. 2014. "Learning Science, Learning about Science, Doing Science: Different Goals Demand Different Learning Methods." *International Journal of Science Education* 36, no. 15: 2534–53. https://doi.org/10.1080/09500693.2014.899722

Humble, N., and Mozelius, P. 2019. "Artificial Intelligence in Education—A Promise, a Threat or a Hype?" In Proceedings of the European Conference on the Impact of Artificial Intelligence and Robotics, edited by P. Griffiths and M. N. Kabir, 149–56.

Hunter, R. H., and Richmond, G. 2022. "Theoretical Diversity and Inclusivity in Science and Environmental Education Research: A Way Forward." *Journal of Research in Science Teaching* 59, no. 6: 1065–85. https://doi.org/10.1002/tea.21752

Ifenthaler, D., Gibson, D., and Dobozy, E. 2018. "Informing Learning Design through Analytics: Applying Network Graph Analysis." *Australasian Journal of Educational Technology* 34, no. 2: 117–32. https://doi.org/10.14742/ajet.3767

Kubsch, M., Krist, C., and Rosenberg, J. M. 2023. "Distributing Epistemic Functions and Tasks—A Framework for Augmenting Human Analytic Power with Machine Learning in Science Education Research." *Journal of Research in Science Teaching* 60, no. 2: 423–47. https://doi.org/10.1002/tea.21803

Lamb, R., Neumann, K., and Linder, K. A. 2022. "Real-Time Prediction of Science Student Learning Outcomes Using Machine Learning Classification of Hemodynamics during Virtual Reality and Online Learning Sessions." *Computers and Education: Artificial Intelligence* 3: 100078. https://doi.org/10.1016/j.caeai.2022.100078

Li, S., and Lajoie, S. P. 2022. "Promoting STEM Education through the Use of Learning Analytics: A Paradigm Shift." In *Artificial Intelligence in STEM Education: The Paradigmatic Shifts in Research, Education, and Technology*, edited by F. Ouyang, P. Jiao, B. McLaren, and A. Alavi, 211–24. Boca Raton, FL: CRC Press.

Liaw, H., Yu, Y. R., Chou, C. C., and Chiu, M. H. 2020. "Relationships between Facial Expressions, Prior Knowledge, and Multiple Representations: A Case of Conceptual Change for Kinematics Instruction." *Journal of Science Education and Technology* 30: 227–238. https://doi.org/10.1007/s10956-020-09863-3

Luxford, C. J., and Bretz, S. L. 2014. "Development of the Bonding Representations Inventory to Identify Student Misconceptions about Covalent and Ionic Bonding Representations." *Journal of Chemical Education* 91, no. 3: 312–20. https://doi.org/10.1021/ed400700q

Mao, Y., Lin, C., and Chi, M. 2018. "Deep Learning vs. Bayesian Knowledge Tracing: Student Models for Interventions." *Journal of Educational Data Mining* 10, no. 2: 28–54. https://jedm.educationaldatamining.org/index.php/JEDM/article/view/318

Mayringer, H., and Wimmer, H. 2014. *Salzburger Lese-Screening für die Schulstufen 2–9 (SLS 2–9).*

Mehrabi, N., Morstatter, F., Saxena, N., Lerman, K., and Galstyan, A. 2021. "A Survey on Bias and Fairness in Machine Learning." *ACM Computing Surveys* 54, no. 6: 1–35. https://doi.org/10.1145/3457607

Merceron, A., Blikstein, P., and Siemens, G. 2016. "Learning Analytics: From Big Data to Meaningful Data." *Journal of Learning Analytics* 2, no. 3: 4–8. https://doi.org/10.18608/jla.2015.23.2

Mikropoulos, T. A., and Iatraki, G. 2022. "Digital Technology Supports Science Education for Students with Disabilities: A Systematic Review." *Education and Information Technologies* 29: 3911–35. https://doi.org/10.1007/s10639-022-11317-9

Miles, S., and Singal, N. 2010. "The Education for All and Inclusive Education Debate: Conflict, Contradiction or Opportunity?" *International Journal of Inclusive Education* 14, no. 1: 1–15. https://doi.org/10.1080/13603110802265125

National Research Council. 2012. *A Framework for K-12 Science Education: Practices, Crosscutting Concepts, and Core Ideas.* Washington, DC: National Academies Pres. https://doi.org/10.17226/13165

Nehm, R. H., Ha, M., and Mayfield, E. 2012. "Transforming Biology Assessment with Machine Learning: Automated Scoring of Written Evolutionary Explanations." *Journal of Science Education and Technology* 21, no. 1: 183–96. https://doi.org/10.1007/s10956-011-9300-9

Neumann, K., and Waight, N. 2020. "The Digitalization of Science Education: Déjà vu All Over Again?" *Journal of Research in Science Teaching* 57, no. 9: 1519–28. https://doi.org/10.1002/tea.21668

Niedersächsiches Kultusministerium. 2020. *Kerncurriculum für die Integrierte Gesamtschule Schuljahrgänge 5-10. Naturwissenschaften.*

Ntoutsi, E., Fafalios, P., Gadiraju, U., Iosifidis, V., Nejdl, W., Vidal, M. E., Ruggieri, S., et al. 2020. "Bias in Data-Driven Artificial Intelligence Systems—An Introductory Survey." *Wiley Interdisciplinary Reviews: Data Mining and Knowledge Discovery* 10, no. 3: e1356. https://doi.org/10.1002/widm.1356

Peterson, J., Pardos, Z., Rau, M., Swigart, A., Gerber, C., and McKinsey, J. 2015. "Understanding Student Success in Chemistry Using Gaze Tracking and Pupillometry." In Artificial Intelligence in Education, AIED 2015, Lecture Notes in Computer Science, edited by C. Conati, N. Heffereman, A. Mitrovic, and M. Verdejo, *9112*, 358–66. Cham: Springer. https://doi.org/10.1007/978-3-319-19773-9_36

Porayska-Pomsta, K., and Rajendran, G. 2019. "Accountability in Human and Artificial Intelligence Decision-Making as the Basis for Diversity and Educational Inclusion." In Artificial Intelligence and Inclusive Education: Perspectives on Rethinking and Reforming Education, edited by J. Knox, Y. Wang, and M. Gallagher, 39–59. Singapore: Springer. https://doi.org/10.1007/978-981-13-8161-4_3

Roski, M., Hoppe, A., and Nehring, A. 2023. Individuelles Lernen durch Bayesian Knowledge Tracing in der webbasierte Lernplattform „I3Lern "analysieren und unterstützen. *Lernen, Lehren Und Forschen in Einer Digital Geprägten Welt.*

Roski, M., Sebastian, R., Ewerth, R., Hoppe, A., and Nehring, A. 2023. "Dropout Prediction in a Web Environment Based on Universal Design for Learning." In *Artificial Intelligence in Education*, AIED2023, Lecture Notes in Computer Science, edited by N. Wang, G. Rebolledo-Mendez, N. Matsuda, O. C. Santos, and V. Dimitrova, vol. 13916, 515–27. Cham: Springer Nature. https://doi.org/10.1007/978-3-031-36272-9_42

Russo-Tait, T. 2022. "Color-blind or Racially Conscious? How College Science Faculty Make Sense of Racial/Ethnic Underrepresentation in STEM." *Journal of Research in Science Teaching* 59, no. 10: 1822–52. https://doi.org/10.1002/tea.21775

Stinken-Rösner, L., Rott, L., Hundertmark, S., Menthe, J., Hoffmann, T., Nehring, A., and Abels, S. 2020. "Thinking Inclusive Science Education from two Perspectives: Inclusive Pedagogy and Science Education." *Ristal* 3: 30–45.

Taber, K. S. 2015. "Exploring the Language(s) of Chemistry Education." *Chemistry Education Research and Practice* 16, no. 2: 193–97. https://doi.org/10.1039/c5rp90003d

Taber, K. S., and Riga, F. 2016. "From each according to her capabilities; to each according to her needs: fully including the gifted in school science education." In *Science Education towards Inclusion*, edited by S. Markic and S. Abels, 195–219. New York: Nova Publishers.

Torsheim, T., Cavallo, F., Levin, K. A., Schnohr, C., Mazur, J., Niclasen, B., and Currie, C. 2016. "Psychometric Validation of the Revised Family Affluence Scale: A Latent Variable Approach." *Child Indicators Research* 9, no. 3: 771–84. https://doi.org/10.1007/s12187-015-9339-x

UNESCO. 1994. "The Salamanca Statement and Framework for Action." *Policy* June: 50.

UNESCO. 2000. "The Dakar Framework for Action." UNESCO April: 26–28. http://unesdoc.unesco.org/images/0012/001211/121147e.pdf

UNESCO-IIEP. 2017. *A Guide For Ensuring Inclusion and Equity in Education.*

VanLehn, K. 2006. "The Behavior of Tutoring Systems." *International Journal of Artificial Intelligence in Education* 16, no. 3: 227–65.

Wilson-Kennedy, Z. S., Winfield, L. L., Nielson, J., Arriaga, E. A., Kimble-Hill, A. C., and Payton-Stewart, F. 2022. "Introducing the *Journal of Chemical Education*'s Special Issue on Diversity, Equity, Inclusion, and Respect in Chemistry Education Research and Practice." *Journal of Chemical Education* 99, no. 1: 1–4. https://doi.org/10.1021/acs.jchemed.1c01219

Zhai, X. 2021. "Practices and Theories: How Can Machine Learning Assist in Innovative Assessment Practices in Science Education." *Journal of Science Education and Technology* 30, no. 2: 139–49. https://doi.org/10.1007/s10956-021-09901-8

Zhai, X., Haudek, K., Shi, L., Nehm, R., and Urban-Lurain, M. 2020. "From Substitution to Redefinition: A Framework of Machine Learning-Based Science Assessment." *Journal of Research in Science Teaching* 57, no. 9: 1430–59. https://doi.org/10.1002/tea.21658

Zhai, X., He, P., and Krajcik, J. 2022. "Applying Machine Learning to Automatically Assess Scientific Models." *Journal of Research in Science Teaching* 59, no. 10: 1765–94. https://doi.org/10.1002/tea.21773

Zhai, X., and Krajcik, J. 2022. "Pseudo AI Bias." https://arxiv.org/abs/2210.08141

Zhai, X., and Nehm, R. H. 2023. "AI and Formative Assessment: The Train Has Left the Station." *Journal of Research in Science Teaching* 60, no. 6: 1390–98. https://doi.org/10.1002/tea.21885

Zingoni, A., Taborri, J., Panetti, V., Bonechi, S., Aparicio-Martínez, P., Pinzi, S., and Calabrò, G. 2021. "Investigating Issues and Needs of Dyslexic Students at University: Proof of Concept of an Artificial Intelligence and Virtual Reality-Based Supporting Platform and Preliminary Results." *Applied Sciences (Switzerland)* 11, no. 10: 4624. https://doi.org/10.3390/app11104624

25
Pseudo Artificial Intelligence Bias

Xiaoming Zhai and Joseph Krajcik

Introduction

As artificial intelligence (AI) is increasingly applied in solving problems in education, the potentially biased decisions that can be made by AI draw significant concerns. AI could assist human beings in scoring students' constructed responses, analyzing processing data, and making administrative decisions (Rosenberg et al. 2022; Zhai et al. 2020). However, researchers realized that AI predictions might systematically deviate from the ground truth, generating results either in favor or against certain groups (Cheuk 2021; Li, Xing, and Leite 2022). Such effects can be detrimental and result in social consequences that have drawn concerns about the use of AI since it was broadly applied in our everyday life (Kapur 2021; Nazaretsky, Cukurova, and Alexandron 2021).

While AI biases may result from deficit design, skewed training data, confounding of the algorithmic models, or the algorithm computational capacity, some do not. Defining AI bias and attributing bias outcomes to AI needs to be cautious. What if AI accurately predicts something unjust by nature? It can be even more complicated if attributions of biases to AI are artificially crafted, which has been seen in the literature (Zou and Schiebinger 2018). This may be particularly detrimental if understudied "biases" are arbitrarily attributed to AI only because users misunderstand the bias, inappropriately operate machine algorithms, misinterpret AI predictions, or have an overexpectation of AI predictions. To conceptualize and study these "biases," we coined the term *pseudo AI bias* (PAIB). Attributing PAIB to AI is unfair and can disadvantage the potential of technologies in education. Moreover, overselling PAIB can result in unnecessary AI fear in society, exacerbate the enduring inequities and disparities in accessing and sharing the benefits of technologies (Rafalow and Puckett 2022), and waste social capital invested in AI research.

In recognizing the potential harmful societal consequences of PIAB, this review study intends to conceptualize PIAB by reviewing the literature. We first review the definition of bias to identify the criteria for conceptualizing PAIBs. We then present three types of PAIBs identified in the literature and discuss the potential impacts of PAIBs on education and society. At last, we present some probable solutions.

Xiaoming Zhai and Joseph Krajcik, *Pseudo Artificial Intelligence Bias*. In: *Uses of Artificial Intelligence in STEM Education*. Edited by: Xiaoming Zhai and Joseph Krajcik, Oxford University Press.
DOI: 10.1093/oso/9780198882077.003.0025

Conceptualization of Pseudo AI Bias

Bias has been broadly referred to in social science and natural science, yet no consensus has been made on the definition. To identify the commonalities of bias across areas, we reviewed the definitions of bias in the literature in both areas, particularly focusing on the authoritative literature in each area (see Table 25.1). Our review yielded three critical properties of bias that are shared across areas: (a) deviation—bias measures the deviation between observations and ground truth (i.e., error); (b) systematic—bias refers to systematic error instead of random error; and (c) tendency—bias is a tendency for or against some ideas or entity over others. These three properties characterize the idea of AI bias and are fundamental to uncovering PAIBs. A review of the literature uncovers three types of PAIBs due to misunderstanding of bias, humans' misoperation of AI, or overexpectation of AI outcomes. In the following sections we present the three types of PAIBs.

Table 25.1 Definitions of Bias in Authoritative Literature of Social Science and Natural Science

Resources	Definition
Oxford English Dictionary	Tendency to favor or dislike a person or thing, especially as a result of a preconceived opinion, partiality, prejudice. (*Statistics*) Distortion of a statistical result arising from the method of sampling, measurement, analysis, etc.
Dictionary of Cognitive Science	A systematic tendency to take irrelevant factors into account while ignoring relevant factors (p. 352). Algorithms make use of additional knowledge (i.e., learning biases; p. 228).
The Science Dictionary	In common terms, bias is a preference for or against one idea, thing, or person. In scientific research, bias is described as any systematic deviation between the results of a study and the "truth."
Wikipedia	Bias is disproportionate weight *in favor of* or *against* an idea or thing, usually in a way that is closed-minded, prejudicial, or unfair. Biases can be innate or learned. People may develop biases for or against an individual, a group, or a belief. In science and engineering, a bias is a systematic error. Statistical bias results from an unfair sampling of a population or from an estimation process that does not give accurate results on average. (Accessed December 20, 2021.)
APA Handbook of Testing and Assessment In Psychology	Systematic inaccuracy of assessment (p. 139).

Category 1: Misunderstanding of Bias

Error versus Bias

Errors can be a bias only if they systematically happen. In scientific research, errors inevitably occur, as it is challenging to reach ground truth in measurement, prediction, classification, etc. (Brown, Kaiser, and Allison 2018). Therefore, instead of attempting to eliminate errors, researchers put efforts into reducing errors using various methods, such as refining measurement tools, averaging observations, or improving prediction algorithms (Kipnis 2011). In contrast, the elimination of bias can occur once its root is identified and correct solutions are implemented (McNutt 2016). Therefore, bias is more troublesome to humans than errors are, particularly when the bias is implicit (Warikoo et al. 2016). It is critical to correctly identify bias and eliminate it. Examples in the literature are broadly cited as evidence of AI bias and demonstrate AI's harmfulness (see Cheuk 2021). However, some of them may provide examples of AI prediction errors instead of bias.

Among such, the most popular is the example of humans being mistaken as Gorillas (Pulliam-Moore 2015). In a 2015 Twitter post, Jacky Alcine shared a screenshot in which a face recognition algorithm tagged him and another African American as gorillas. This case shows evidence of the problem of algorithm prediction, indicating significant work needs to be done to improve prediction accuracy. However, although we find this example deplorable, numerous authors who cited this case as "AI bias" did not provide sufficient evidence that this terrible misidentification resulted from inherent AI bias—a single case is challenging to testify that the errors "systematically" happen for a specific group. Another example includes face recognition software labeling a Taiwanese "blinking" (Rose 2010) and an automated passport system not being able to detect whether an individual from Asia had his eyes open for a passport picture (Griffiths 2016). These cases reported AI errors instead of AI bias, and the errors were caused by human programming of the algorithms, which need to be addressed through in-depth research, because no evidence had shown that these errors occurred systematically when the cases were cited.

Confusing bias with errors could extend the societal fear of AI, particularly towards certain groups. As mentioned above, we see these errors as deploring and we need to work hard to ensure these errors don't happen. However, in the world of programming, "bugs" happen, and we just need to make sure that public announcements such as bias are made with evidence. Currently, society invests trillions of dollars in technology developments every year, while certain groups under-represented in society have been found less likely to benefit from these innovations (Rafalow and Puckett 2022). This consequence can be exacerbated by the fear of inaccurate technological outcomes that result from human errors, instead of some engrained bias in the technology. The unfairness could be even worse if the extended AI fear happens explicitly to the under-represented groups. Therefore, researchers should use these mislabeled alerts to further examine potential bias due to programming and increase the accuracy of AI predictions instead of overselling errors as bias.

Favoriting Percentage versus Ground Truth

Amazon's AI recruiting tool is a broadly cited case for evidence of "AI bias." According to Dastin (2018), this tool favored male applicants compared to females, resulting in the belief that the software was biased towards females and eventually disbanded by Amazon. Although widely citing this case to demonstrate that AI is biased against females, seldom has research referred to the prediction "deviations" from the ground truth—the outcomes based on recruiting criteria. A higher percentage favoring male candidates over females can hardly support a valid conclusion about AI bias before we know the actual numbers of applicants by gender and the false prediction cases. This PAIB results from a lack of information—the gender breakdown of Amazon's technical workforce, according to Dastin (2018), was not even disclosed at that time. Therefore, it is problematic to claim AI bias until more data become available and a deep investigation of gender parity can verify the PAIBs.

This type of PAIB harms people's trust in AI. The predicted favoring percentage towards males is hard to justify discrimination before we know the "deviations." As argued by Howard and Borenstein (2018), favoring a group might also be justified if the evidence supports the facts. For example, charging teenagers more for car insurance seems "discriminating" but arguably justified given that evidence shows a higher risk of accidents for teenage drivers. A higher charge for teenage drivers intends to prevent unnecessary risky driving by teenagers. A key to determining AI bias requires examining the ground truth and comparing it to the then findings instead of seeking the favoriting percentage.

Fairness versus Bias

Accuracy is the primary measure for algorithm predictions, while bias is the extent to which the results are systematically and purposely distorted. Therefore, computer scientists pursue high accuracy and avoid bias. Fairness, however, is beyond measurement. It is a social connotation incorporating factors such as access to social capital and the purpose of fairness (Teresi and Jones 2013). A broadly cited example is equality and equity (see Figure 25.1). When asked which picture represents the best practice of fairness, an educator might point to the right picture without hesitance as it represents the pursuit of equity—everyone has an opportunity to observe the game. Interestingly, when an Asian baseball player was shown this picture, he said he was never given equal opportunity to play in the game. Should athletes be granted equal opportunity? Why do observers deserve equity while athletes who play the game seldom have such considerations? These questions justify that fairness is based on social needs and the purpose of the activities. It is hard to absolutely declare that equity is closer to fairness than equality in every case. With such a complex societal concept, it is difficult to demand an algorithm to achieve fairness goals for every case.

Nevertheless, our research shows that AI was held fully accountable for fairness in some cases. One example is the Correctional Offender Management Profiling for Alternative Sanctions (COMPAS), an algorithm used to predict the risk of recidivism, the tendency of a convicted criminal to reoffend. According to a report (Angwin and Larson 2016), COMPAS achieved equal prediction accuracy for both Black and

Figure 25.1 Fairness: equality (left) and equity (right). Modified from Independent Sector (2022).

White defendants. That is, a risk score that is correct in equal proportion for both groups. However, the report also suggests that Black defendants were twice as likely to be incorrectly labeled as higher risk than White defendants. In reality, nevertheless, White defendants labeled as low risk were more likely to be charged with new offenses than Black defendants with similar scores. According to research from four independent groups (Feller et al. 2016), to satisfy both accuracy and "fairness" is mathematically impossible given that Blacks were re-arrested at a much higher rate than Whites in reality. However, because the purpose of the risk score is to help the judge make decisions in court without considering the defendants' race, COMPAS's performance satisfied the cornerstone criteria (Feller et al. 2016). This case illustrates how we have overly tasked AI algorithms for fairness, which could increase the suspicions of AI applications in societal issues. COMPAS yielded fairness concerns, instead of bias, but the scores predicted were equally accurate for the ethnic groups. Confusing bias with fairness is detrimental to the broad use of AI in solving problems. "Statistics and machine learning are not all-powerful" (Kusner and Loftus 2020). It is the users' responsibility to clearly identify the societal goals of the prediction before using algorithm predictions.

Category 2: Pseudo-Mechanical Bias

In many cases, bias is created because of users' ignorance of critical features of data or inappropriate operations in the algorithm application processes, instead of the capacity of algorithms. This type of bias is not due to the algorithm mechanism but human users' operation and use of AI algorithms, termed *pseudo-mechanical bias*. It is feasible to avoid pseudo-mechanical bias as long as users appropriately apply the

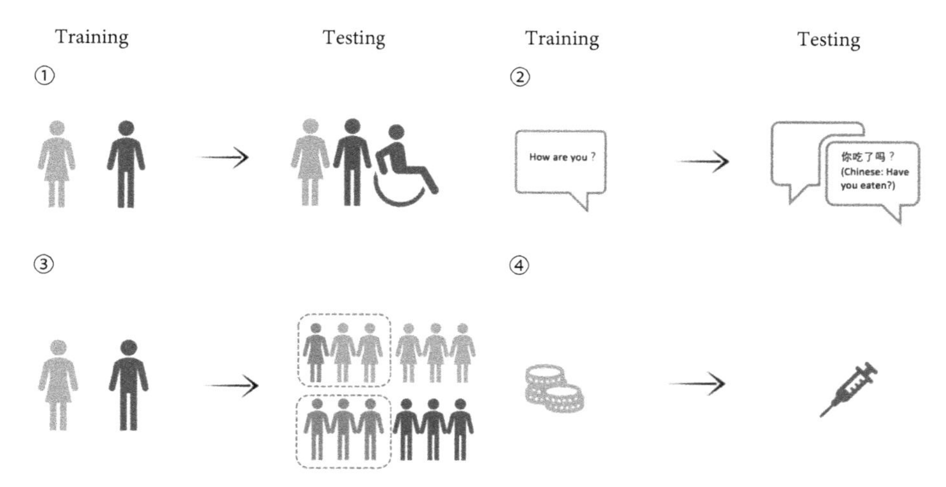

Figure 25.2 Artificial mechanical bias. ① indicates emergent bias, where testing data include samples not included in the training data. ② indicates distinct data for training (e.g., Chinese vs English). ③ indicates distinct samples for training and testing. Samples within the dashed box indicate having an illness, and gray indicates that the illness was predicted by the algorithm. ④ indicates disconnected interpretations of labels.

AI applications. Thus, attributing pseudo-mechanical bias to AI is misleading. In the following, we introduce four categories of pseudo-mechanical bias presented in the literature (see Figure 25.2).

Emergent Error

Emergent error bias results from the out-of-sample input. It is widely assumed that AI algorithms can best predict samples close to the training data. In reality, this is not always the case, as ideal training data are challenging to collect. In this sense, users must be aware of the limitations of AI algorithms to avoid emergent bias. This type of error frequently appears in clinical science, where they are attributed to distributional shifts (Challen et al. 2019). That is, prior experience may not be adequate for new situations because of "out-of-sample" input no matter how experienced the "doctors" are. It is obvious that algorithms are especially weak in dealing with distributional shifts. Therefore, it is critical for users of AI systems to be aware of the limitations and apply AI to appropriate cases to avoid emergent errors.

Distinct Types of Data for Training and Testing

Currently, supervised machine learning requires using the same type of data for training and testing. Cheuk (2021) argues that algorithms would fail to respond to questions in one language if trained using a different language. In the example she raised, an AI trained in English was asked by a Chinese heritage "Have you eaten?" in Chinese (i.e., 你吃了吗). The author suspected that the algorithm would not be able to respond to this question as expected by the Chinese. Instead, the computer might respond intelligently, "No, I haven't eaten," because the computer might interpret the question as to whether the Chinese care about its diet. However, according to Chinese culture, the question "Have you eaten?" equals "How are you?" in English. This example is absolutely correct, but it is almost arbitrary for an English-speaking Chinese to ask AI questions in English (as the machine is trained in English as the author noted) and then expect the machine to answer the question following the Chinese culture. In other words, it is the users' responsibility to be aware that the algorithm was trained in English and expect the response to follow the same conventions in English. These types of situations in which the algorithm is incapable of responding or interpreting could lead to PAIB, only because the AI algorithm was trained in a distinct way from what the users expected.

Distinct Feature Distribution among Groups

In a recent study, Larrazabal and colleagues (2020) examined the gender imbalance of algorithm capacity to diagnose disease based on imaging datasets. They found that for some diseases like pneumothorax, the algorithms consistently performed better on males than on females regardless of how researchers tried to improve the training set. This unintended error was created because patients have unique biological features that prevent algorithms from performing equally based on the gender of the patient. For instance, females' breasts occluded imagining of organs responsible for the disease when using X-ray technology to collect the imaging data of the diseased organs, resulting in poorer performance of algorithms when identifying disease. If users apply the algorithms without being aware of the limitations of the algorithms, it could generate PAIBs.

Disconnected Interpretations of Labels

In practice, if users interpret the meaning of the AI predictions differently from the information encapsulated in the training data, it could generate PAIBs. For example, Obermeyer and colleagues (McClure 2018) examined the most extensive commercial medical risk-prediction system, which is applied to more than 200 million people in the US each year. The system was trained using patients' expenses and was supposed to predict the ideal solutions for high-risk patients. The authors found the "ideal solutions" discriminating—Black patients with the same (predicted) risk scores as White patients tend to be sicker, resulting in unequal solutions provided to patients of color. In this case, the "predicted risk score" was generated based on past medical expenses, which is a combination of both the risk and the affordability of medical service. Suppose doctors interpret this score as an indicator of risk to providing medical care; it would likely put at risk a certain group's life (e.g., Black patients who might generate less medical expense). This assumption is problematic because the assumed bias resulted from doctors' misinterpretation of the risk score—disregarding the fact that the scores reflect not only the severity of illness but also the affordability of the medical service provided to the patients. Obermeyer and colleagues (Obermeyer et al. 2019) attributed the medical bias to label choice—fundamentally reflecting a disconnect between the interpretation of predictions (i.e., the risk of illness) and the information encapsulated in the training samples (i.e., both the risk of illness and the affordability of medical care). They also provided empirical evidence that altering the labels is effective in reducing biased results.

Category 3: Overexpectation

In many cases, overexpectations can result in PAIBs. For example, Levin (2016) reported that in a beauty contest judged by Beauty.AI, forty-four winners were nearly all White, with a limited number of Asian and dark-skinned individuals. Many pinpoint this case as evidence for AI bias. What makes it problematic is that the criteria for beauty are perceptional and vary across people—some care more about color while others concern more about symmetry. It is even challenging to generate a consensus criterion by humans. How could we expect AI to identify the beauty winners to satisfy a diverse population? In this case, AI should be treated as an intelligent individual, equal to a human individual, instead of some intelligence that can overcome diversity dilemmas. In other words, Beauty.AI learned from human-labeled examples and thus is expected to perform as what was learned. The bias does rest in the AI algorithms but in the humans that developed the algorithm. It may be unreasonable to expect the algorithm to perform in a way to satisfy all stakeholders, who might even disagree with each other.

Implications and Solutions

This review by no means argues that AI biases are not worthy of being addressed. Indeed, "the growing scope of AI makes it particularly important to address [biased outcomes]" (Zou and Schiebinger 2018). In this review, however, we contend that understanding the mechanisms and potential bias of AI is essential for educational applications and other societal needs broadly. As the dual use of AI is increasingly recognized in the field, researchers have the responsibility to confirm the ethics before AI becomes mainstream in our society. In this review, our main concern focuses on whether AI biases are correctly identified and appropriately attributed to AI. We focus this review on PAIBs as they have societally consequential (Zhai 2021; Zhai, Krajcik, and Pellegrino 2021). The public needs to realize that PAIBs result from users' or developers' misunderstanding, misoperation, or overexpectations, instead of the fault of the AI. Our position is that humans create algorithms and train machines, and the biases reflect human perspectives and human errors. Realizing the many kinds of PAIBs and how humans are at the center of them could help limit societal fear of AI.

PAIB adds to the existing and enduring human fear of AI. Such fear emerged earlier and faster than the progress in AI research because of numerous science fiction stories that have struck and impacted human thinking about AI. The history of technophobia can be traced back to the 1920s when *Rossum's Universal Robots* proposed scenes of enlarged robots (McClure 2018). However, it did not draw much fear until the recent flood of AI developments, which refreshed humans' fear of AI gleamed from these science fiction stories. Cave and Dihal (2019) analyzed 300 documents and identified four types of AI fears: inhumanity, obsolescence, alienation, and uprising. Because many AI fears are rooted in artificial scenes presented in science fiction books or movies (Bohannon 2015), it is unsurprising that part of the fears might be artificial. Cave and Dihal's (2019) survey of more than 1,000 UK citizens reveals that the common perception of AI is significantly more anxiety than excitement. This evidence, together with the findings from this review, exemplifies the importance of recognizing PAIBs.

The societal consequences can even be worse if research enlarges the factors, such as PAIBs, that yield the fears. The users and developers of AI need to take responsibility to avoid PAIBs by clearly understanding the limitations of machine algorithms and the mechanisms of AI biases. Researchers, on the other side, have the responsibility to guide the use of AI applications and avoid extending PAIBs in academic work. Researchers need to put effort into examining and solving true AI biases instead of PAIBs. To deal with PAIBs, we recommend the following.

Develop Systematic Approaches to Monitor and Reduce Bias

The best approach to clarifying PAIBs will stem from the development of tools and criteria to systematically monitor bias in algorithms. Research is needed especially to collect evidence to realize and eliminate potential AI bias (Zhai and Nehm 2023). Such an approach could ease the public worry about AI applications and prevent biases in the first place. Aligned with this goal, the Center for Data Science and Public Policy created the Aequitas, an open-source bias toolkit to audit machine-learning algorithm biases (Saleiro, Rodolfa, and Ghani 2020). This toolkit could audit two types of biases: (1) biased actions or interventions that are not allocated in a way representative of the population and (2) biased outcomes through actions or interventions that result from the system being wrong about certain groups of people. Besides, methodological efforts are needed to reduce biased results, which can avoid PAIBs. For example, Li, Xing, and Leite (2022) developed a fair logistic regression algorithm and achieved less biased results. Once true AI bias is reduced significantly, the threaten of PAIBs will be limited.

Certify Users for AI Applications to Mitigate AI Fears

PAIBs resulted because of users' unfamiliarity with AI mechanics, as well as misunderstanding of bias that was enriched by both measurement and social connotations. To mitigate AI fears, users need professional education. Osborne, a researcher from the University of Oxford, suggests providing professional certifications to AI users such as doctors and judges (Gent 2015). Such professional education could eliminate most PAIBs and help users mitigate AI fears.

Provide Customized User Guidance for AI Applications

Some PAIBs are developed due to the diverse configurations of the AI algorithms and the complex conditions of applying AI. For example, some algorithms might influence a certain group under a given condition. Unless users know of these constraints, they are not likely to appropriately employ the algorithms for predictions and decision makings. Therefore, customized user guidance, accompanied by professional education, is essential for alleviating the fear of AI and using AI appropriately.

AI has the potential to serve as a viable tool and partner for many professions, including education. However, AI will never reach its potential unless researchers eliminate sources of bias, and the public comes to know that many biases result from human errors in operating algorithms and in misinterpreting the results of AI. Although dealing with AI bias is critical and should draw substantial attention, overselling PAIBs can be detrimental, particularly to those who have fewer opportunities to learn AI, and may exacerbate the enduring inequities and disparities in accessing and sharing the benefits of AI applications.

Acknowledgments

This study was partially funded by National Science Foundation (NSF) (Awards 2101104 and 2100964) and National Academy of Education/Spencer Foundation. Any opinions, findings, conclusions, or recommendations expressed in this material are those of the author(s) and do not necessarily reflect the views of the founders.

References

Angwin, J., and Larson, J. 2016, December 30. "Bias in Criminal Risk Scores Is Mathematically Inevitable, Researchers Say." *ProPublica*. https://www.propublica.org/article/bias-in-criminal-risk-scores-is-mathematically-inevitable-researchers-say

Bohannon, J. 2015. "Fears of an AI Pioneer." *Science* 349, no. 6245: 252.

Brown, A. W., Kaiser, K. A., and Allison, D. B. 2018. "Issues with Data and Analyses: Errors, Underlying Themes, and Potential Solutions." Proceedings of the National Academy of Sciences 115, no. 11: 2563–70.

Cave, S., and Dihal, K. 2019. "Hopes and Fears for Intelligent Machines in Fiction and Reality." *Nature Machine Intelligence* 1, no. 2: 74–78.

Challen, R., Denny, J., Pitt, M., Gompels, L., Edwards, T., and Tsaneva-Atanasova, K. 2019. "Artificial Intelligence, Bias and Clinical Safety." *BMJ Quality and Safety* 28, no. 3: 231–37.

Cheuk, T. 2021. "Can AI Be Racist? Color-Evasiveness in the Application of Machine Learning to Science Assessments." *Science Education* 105, no. 5: 825–36.

Dastin, J. 2018. "Amazon Scraps Secret AI Recruiting Tool That Showed Bias Against Women." San Fransico, CA: Reuters. https://www.reuters.com/article/idUSKCN1MK0AG/

Feller, A., Pierson, E., Corbett-Davies, S., and Goel, S. 2016. "A Computer Program Used for Bail and Sentencing Decisions Was Labeled Biased against Blacks. It's Actually Not That Clear." The Washington Post, 17.

Gent, E. 2015. "AI: Fears of 'Playing God.'" *Engineering and Technology* 10, no. 2: 76–79.

Griffiths, J. 2016. "New Zealand Passport Robot Thinks This Asian Man's Eyes Are Closed." CNN. https://edition.cnn.com/2016/12/07/asia/new-zealand-passport-robot-asian-trnd/index.html

Howard, A., and Borenstein, J. 2018. "The Ugly Truth about Ourselves and Our Robot Creations: The Problem of Bias and Social Inequity." *Science and Engineering Ethics* 24, no. 5: 1521–36. https://link.springer.com/content/pdf/10.1007/s11948-017-9975-2.pdf

Kapur, S. 2021. "Reducing Racial Bias in AI Models for Clinical Use Requires a Top-Down Intervention." *Nature Machine Intelligence* 3, no. 6: 460.

Kipnis, N. 2011. "Errors in Science and Their Treatment in Teaching Science." *Science and Education* 20, no. 7: 655–85.
Kusner, M. J., and Loftus, J. R. 2020. "The Long Road to Fairer Algorithms." *Nature*. https://www.nature.com/articles/d41586-020-00274-3
Larrazabal, A. J., Nieto, N., Peterson, V., Milone, D. H., and Ferrante, E. 2020. "Gender Imbalance in Medical Imaging Datasets Produces Biased Classifiers for Computer-Aided Diagnosis." Proceedings of the National Academy of Sciences 117, no. 23: 12592–94. https://www.pnas.org/content/pnas/117/23/12592.full.pdf
Levin, S. 2016, September 8. "A Beauty Contest Was Judged by AI and the Robots Didn't Like Dark Skin." https://www.theguardian.com/technology/2016/sep/08/artificial-intelligence-beauty-contest-doesnt-like-black-people
Li, C., Xing, W., and Leite, W. 2022. "Using Fair AI to Predict Students' Math Learning Outcomes in an Online Platform." *Interactive Learning Environments*, 1–20.
McClure, P. K. 2018. "'You're fired,' Says the Robot: The Rise of Automation in the Workplace, Technophobes, and Fears of Unemployment." *Social Science Computer Review* 36, no. 2: 139–56.
McNutt, M. 2016. "Implicit Bias." *Science* 352, no. 6289: 1035. https://www.science.org/doi/abs/10.1126/science.aag1695
Nazaretsky, T., Cukurova, M., and Alexandron, G. 2021. "An Instrument for Measuring Teachers' Trust in AI-Based Educational Technology."
Obermeyer, Z., Powers, B., Vogeli, C., and Mullainathan, S. 2019. "Dissecting Racial Bias in an Algorithm Used to Manage the Health of Populations." *Science* 366, no. 6464: 447–53.
Pulliam-Moore, C. 2015. "Google Photos Identified Black People as 'Gorillas,' But Racist Software Isn't New." https://fusion.tv/story/159736/google-photos-identified-black-people-as-gorillas-but-racist-software-isnt-new/amp/
Rafalow, M. H., and Puckett, C. 2022. "Sorting Machines: Digital Technology and Categorical Inequality in Education." *Educational Researcher* 51, no. 4: 274–78.
Rose, A. 2010, January 22. "Are Face-Detection Cameras Racist?" Time. http://content.time.com/time/business/article/0,8599,1954643,00.html
Rosenberg, J. M., Borchers, C., Burchfield, M. A., Anderson, D., Stegenga, S. M., and Fischer, C. 2022. "Posts about Students on Facebook: A Data Ethics Perspective." *Educational Researcher* 51, no. 8: 547–50.
Saleiro, P., Rodolfa, K. T., and Ghani, R. 2020. "Dealing with Bias and Fairness in Data Science Systems: A Practical Hands-on Tutorial." In Proceedings of the 26th ACM SIGKDD International Conference on Knowledge Discovery and Data Mining.
Teresi, J. A., and Jones, R. N. 2013. "Bias in Psychological Assessment and Other Measures." In *APA Handbook of Testing and Assessment in Psychology*, Vol. 1: Test Theory and Testing and Assessment in Industrial and Organizational Psychology, edited by K. F. Geisinger, B. A. Bracken, J. F. Carlson, J.-I. C. Hansen, N. R. Kuncel, S. P. Reise, and M. C. Rodriguez, 139–64. Washington, DC: American Psychological Association. https://doi.org/10.1037/14047-008
Warikoo, N., Sinclair, S., Fei, J., and Jacoby-Senghor, D. 2016. "Examining Racial Bias in Education: A New Approach." *Educational Researcher* 45, no. 9: 508–14.
Zhai, X. 2021. "Practices and Theories: How Can Machine Learning Assist in Innovative Assessment Practices in Science Education." *Journal of Science Education and Technology* 30, no. 2: 139–49. https://link.springer.com/article/10.1007/s10956-021-09901-8
Zhai, X., Haudek, K. C., Shi, L., Nehm, R., and Urban-Lurain, M. 2020. "From Substitution to Redefinition: A Framework of Machine Learning-Based Science Assessment." *Journal of Research in Science Teaching* 57, no. 9: 1430–59.
Zhai, X., Krajcik, J., and Pellegrino, J. 2021. "On the Validity of Machine Learning-Based Next Generation Science Assessments: A Validity Inferential Network." *Journal of Science Education and Technology* 30, no. 2: 298–312.
Zhai, X., and Nehm, R. 2023. "AI and Formative Assessment: The Train Has Left the Station." *Journal of Research in Science Teaching* 60, no. 6: 1390–98.
Zou, J., and Schiebinger, L. 2018. "AI Can Be Sexist and Racist—It's Time to Make It Fair." *Nature*. https://www.nature.com/articles/d41586-018-05707-8

PART V
CONCLUSION

26

Conclusions and Foresight on AI-Based STEM Education

A New Paradigm

Xiaoming Zhai

Introduction

The publication of this book, *Uses of Artificial Intelligence in STEM Education*, occurs within a significant academic context marked by the establishment of a new research community. The formation of this community is highly inspired by the needs of technologies to meet the vision set by the *Framework for K–12 Science Education*—to integrate learning of crosscutting concepts and disciplinary core ideas in science and engineering practices, termed three-dimensional learning (National Research Council 2012). Artificial intelligence (AI) has emerged as a powerful technology that shows substantial potential in pushing forward the field to meet the new vision (Zhai et al. 2020b). Based on more than a decade's effort from predecessors such as Mark Urban-Lurian, Ross Nehm, Marcia Linn, and Kevin Haudek, Kent Crippen and I initiated the Research Interest Group of NARST—RAISE (i.e., Research in AI-based Science Education) in 2022. We held the first hybrid business meeting in Vancouver, CA, during the 2022 (March) NARST annual meeting to celebrate this exciting event. This milestone event serves as a formal acknowledgment of the burgeoning role of AI in shaping educational paradigms within science and STEM disciplines. Since then, RAISE has functioned as a dedicated platform for fostering interdisciplinary dialogues among scholars, educators, and policymakers, offering a forum for sharing research findings and collaboratively addressing the intricate challenges and opportunities that arise from this emergent field. As of October 2023, RAISE has fifty-nine registered members in the NARST community.

To further this effort, Joe Krajcik and I organized the first *International Conference of AI-Based STEM Education* in Athens, Georgia, in May 2022. This conference was funded by the National Science Foundation. Forty-one scholars from around the globe came to Athens to attend the conference and presented their studies. This book is the consequence of the conference, which set forth the general scope of the new community. The publication of this book underscores the growing importance of AI technologies in educational settings and serves to legitimize AI in science, technology, engineering, and mathematics (STEM) education as a distinct and vital field of inquiry within the broader academic community.

Xiaoming Zhai, *Conclusions and Foresight on AI-Based STEM Education*. In: *Uses of Artificial Intelligence in STEM Education*. Edited by: Xiaoming Zhai and Joseph Krajcik, Oxford University Press. © Oxford University Press (2024).
DOI: 10.1093/oso/9780198882077.003.0026

This book offers a comprehensive exploration of the integration of AI into science and STEM education. This multidisciplinary collaborative, extended from the conference, brings together the expertise of sixty-five scholars from around the world, presenting a rich tapestry of perspectives, methodologies, and empirical findings. We organized the volume into four distinct themes, delving into a wide array of topics ranging from AI-driven assessment practices and transformative STEM learning tools to teacher professional development and ethical considerations. The final goal of this book is to inspire STEM educators, researchers, policymakers, and AI scholars, serving as both a guide and a catalyst for future research and practice in this rapidly evolving interdisciplinary field.

The concluding thoughts and foresight offered in this book are of paramount importance, given the rapidly evolving landscape. As AI technologies continue to advance and permeate educational settings (Zhai et al. 2020a), it is crucial for the field to pause and reflect on both the progress made and the challenges that lie ahead. This final chapter serves as a synthesis of the diverse perspectives and empirical findings presented throughout the book, while also projecting into the future to anticipate emerging trends, ethical considerations, and potential areas of research and practice. In a field marked by constant innovation and change, such reflective and forward-looking insights are not just beneficial but essential for educators, researchers, policymakers, and AI scholars who are navigating this complex interdisciplinary domain.

Key Insights from the Book's Sections

The four thematic sections of this volume comprehensively address the prevailing challenges and considerations in STEM education, while also delineating the extant solutions facilitated by AI. This section aims to distill the salient takeaways of the book by providing the audience with a synthesized understanding of the key contributions and implications.

AI-Driven Assessments in STEM Education

The insights of this theme presented in the seven chapters range from the technical advancements facilitated by AI, such as enhanced accuracy of scoring for three-dimensional learning and personalized feedback, to the more complex ethical and pedagogical considerations of AI-based assessment that come into play. In this increasingly diverse area of assessments (Zhai and Wiebe 2023), they collectively offer a nuanced understanding of both the transformative potential and the challenges associated with integrating AI into STEM assessments. Specifically, the major insights that can be found in this section are the following:

- AI-driven assessments have shown significant promise in enhancing the accuracy and efficiency of formative assessment practices in STEM education.

- The integration of machine learning and neural networks in assessments can offer personalized, real-time feedback, thereby promoting deeper understanding and knowledge-in-use among students.
- Despite its potential, AI in STEM assessments raises critical issues related to design, equity, and validity, necessitating a multidisciplinary approach for effective implementation.
- Automated scoring systems, particularly in specialized subjects like biology and chemistry, have demonstrated high levels of accuracy, reinforcing the viability of AI-based assessments across diverse educational contexts.
- The development and validation of AI tools for assessment require careful consideration of technical, pedagogical, and ethical dimensions to ensure equitable and inclusive educational practices.
- The use of AI in assessments has the potential to align closely with the vision of the *Framework for K–12 Science Education* (NRC 2012), offering new avenues for identifying and assessing student thinking, science and engineering practices, and learning progressions.
- AI's role in assessments is not merely technical but extends to influencing educational systems, instructor practices, and student engagement, making its impact multifaceted and complex.
- While AI offers transformative potential in redefining assessment practices, it also necessitates careful navigation of the challenges and complexities inherent in its integration into STEM education.

AI Tools for Transforming STEM Learning

The ensuing section includes six chapters, which present a series of key takeaways that focus on the transformative role of AI in STEM learning. These insights encapsulate the potential of AI tools to revolutionize educational experiences, as exemplified by platforms such as Google Teachable Machine, HASbot, and AI-Scorer. The takeaways also explore the multifaceted challenges of AI integration, including ethical considerations, equity issues, and the need for improved diagnostic models. Together, these points offer a nuanced understanding of the complex landscape of AI in STEM learning, underscoring both its immense potential and the intricate challenges that must be navigated for its effective and ethical implementation.

- AI tools have emerged as a transformative force in STEM learning, enabling more personalized, adaptive, and engaging educational experiences for students.
- AI adds new elements to traditional scientific inquiry, and the uses of AI-enabled tools have demonstrated measurable improvements in students' scientific practices and scientific inquiry skills.
- AI's role in individualized support, particularly in physics learning, has been substantiated through evidence-centered design, offering granular-level assessments that are both valid and unbiased.

- Intelligent tutoring systems have proven effective in providing real-time, automated, and scalable assessment and scaffolding, thereby enhancing authentic science practices in classrooms.
- AI-driven assessment and instructional systems have shown capabilities in immediate, accurate scoring of complex student responses and in providing real-time insights into student performance, respectively.
- While AI tools offer unprecedented opportunities for enhancing STEM learning, they also present challenges in terms of diagnostic model improvement, equity concerns, and the ethical dimensions of automated assessments.
- The integration of AI tools in STEM learning is not merely a technological advancement but a pedagogical shift that requires thoughtful consideration of its impact on teaching strategies and educational outcomes.
- The section concludes that AI tools hold immense potential for revolutionizing STEM education, but their effective and ethical implementation requires a nuanced understanding of both their capabilities and limitations.

AI-Based STEM Instruction and Teacher Professional Development

The third theme of the book provides key insights that illuminate the impact of AI on STEM instruction and teacher professional development. Six chapters focusing on this theme provide the key takeaways that delve into the multifaceted roles that AI technologies are beginning to play in redefining pedagogical strategies and enhancing teaching efficacy. From offering structured frameworks for understanding AI's pedagogical roles to providing actionable insights for effective classroom assessments, these points underscore both the potential and the complexities of AI integration. The section also emphasizes the ethical dimensions and the need for scalability in AI-based educational tools, thereby offering a comprehensive view of the challenges and opportunities in this rapidly evolving field. These key takeaways include the following:

- AI technologies are increasingly playing a transformative role in STEM instruction and teacher professional development, offering dynamic and responsive teaching methods that go beyond traditional pedagogical approaches.
- The three-dimensional framework introduced in Chapter 15 categorizes AI's pedagogical roles into instructional, evaluative, and decision-making partners, providing a structured lens for understanding AI's multifaceted contributions to teaching practices.
- AI-based frameworks, such as the one presented in Chapter 16, offer actionable insights for teachers to utilize AI-driven classroom assessments effectively, particularly in the context of implementing Next Generation Science Standards.
- Tools like the TalkMoves application, discussed in Chapter 17, have shown promise in providing automated, personalized feedback on classroom discourse patterns, enriching teacher–student interactions, and potentially improving teaching and learning outcomes.

- Machine-learning techniques, as explored in Chapter 18, offer innovative methods for scoring teacher observations, revolutionizing traditional educational research methods, and potentially automating classroom observations.
- Ethical considerations, particularly those related to fairness and bias in AI-based assessments, are beginning to be rigorously examined, as evidenced by the focus of Chapter 19 on employing structural topic models to create more equitable educational environments.
- The section highlights the critical need for scalability and automation in teacher assessments and classroom observations, pointing to the potential of neural networks in automating these tasks, as discussed in Chapter 20.
- Overall, the section underscores the intricate ethical and practical challenges that educators, administrators, and policymakers must navigate while integrating AI into STEM instruction and teacher professional development.

Ethics, Fairness, and Inclusiveness of AI-Based STEM Education

The ensuing section with five chapters offers a nuanced exploration of the ethical, fairness, and inclusiveness considerations that are pivotal to the integration of AI in STEM education. These insights underscore the multidimensional nature of ethical challenges, extending from algorithmic fairness to broader societal and educational implications. The section also emphasizes the need for both conceptual and practical frameworks to guide the ethical deployment of AI tools in educational settings. From addressing algorithmic bias to ensuring inclusivity and navigating macro-ethical issues, these points collectively highlight the imperative for a responsible and equitable approach to AI-based STEM education.

- Ethical considerations are integral to the deployment of AI in STEM education, requiring both conceptual and practical frameworks for responsible implementation.
- AI applications in STEM education must be designed with inclusivity in mind, catering not only to a broad range of learning styles but also to various disabilities and diverse demographic backgrounds.
- The ethical dimensions of AI in STEM education extend beyond algorithmic fairness to include broader macro-ethical issues, such as power dynamics and the definition of what constitutes "ethical" technology in educational settings.
- Addressing algorithmic bias is not merely a technical challenge but an ethical imperative, necessitating active strategies for fairness and equity in AI-based educational tools.
- The concept of pseudo artificial intelligence bias (PAIB) emerges as a significant concern, highlighting the need for user education and customized guidance to mitigate misunderstandings and overexpectations of AI applications.
- The development and deployment of AI in STEM education must be guided by ethical frameworks that align with broader educational goals and societal values, emphasizing the need for policy guidelines.

- Inclusivity in AI-based STEM education is not just a matter of ethical importance but also of practical utility, requiring specific criteria and actionable strategies for avoiding discrimination.

Recommendations for Further Research

In light of the diverse and complex issues explored throughout this book, we present a set of comprehensive recommendations that aim to guide future research, policy, and practice in the field of AI-based STEM education. These recommendations are synthesized from insights across all chapters and are designed to address the multifaceted challenges and opportunities that arise from the integration of AI into STEM learning environments. They serve as actionable guidelines for educators, policymakers, AI developers, and researchers, offering a holistic roadmap for the ethical, effective, and equitable deployment of AI in STEM education.

- **Interdisciplinary collaboration**: Foster interdisciplinary research that combines insights from AI, pedagogy, assessment science, and ethics to create a holistic understanding of AI's role in STEM education.
- **Assessment innovation**: Promote the use of AI in creating more dynamic, real-time assessments that can adapt to individual student needs, thereby providing more accurate measures of student thinking and knowledge-in-use.
- **Future citizens preparation in the era of AI.** Integrate AI into core STEM practices to provide students the opportunity to investigate science problems and design solutions using AI, so that students are prepared with the essential competence to thrive in the future when AI is ubiquitous.
- **Inclusive design**: Encourage the development of AI tools that cater to a diverse student population, including those with learning disabilities, and those from varied socioeconomic backgrounds.
- **Algorithmic transparency and fairness**: Establish mechanisms for third-party auditing of AI tools to ensure algorithmic fairness, educational efficacy, and data security.
- **Teacher training and professional development**: Implement comprehensive professional development programs that equip educators with the skills to effectively integrate AI tools into their teaching, assessment, and curriculum planning.
- **User literacy**: Educate both educators and students on the ethical considerations, limitations, and effective use of AI tools in STEM education, perhaps as part of a broader digital literacy initiative.
- **Ethical and inclusive frameworks**: Develop ethical guidelines that are sensitive to issues of inclusivity, fairness, and educational equity, and that can be applied across various AI applications in STEM, from assessments to instructional tools.
- **Policy advocacy**: Advocate for educational policies that mandate the ethical and equitable use of AI in educational settings, including rigorous vetting processes before new AI tools are adopted.

- **Scalability and customization**: Research should focus on how AI tools can be effectively scaled across different educational settings while allowing for customization to meet local educational needs and standards.
- **Ongoing dialogue and review**: Create platforms for continuous dialogue among educators, policymakers, AI developers, and other stakeholders to address emerging challenges, share best practices, and collaboratively review and update guidelines and policies.

These recommendations aim to provide a comprehensive roadmap for various stakeholders, from educators and policymakers to AI developers and researchers, in the rapidly evolving field of AI-based STEM education.

Conclusions

This volume stands as a seminal contribution to the burgeoning field of AI-based STEM education. It brings together a rich tapestry of perspectives, methodologies, and empirical studies, offering a comprehensive overview of the current state of the art. The book serves as a multidimensional lens through which the complexities of integrating AI into STEM education are examined. From AI-driven assessments and transformative learning tools to ethical considerations and teacher professional development, this book not only enriches the academic discourse but also provides actionable insights for practitioners.

The transformative potential of AI in STEM education is both exhilarating and challenging. While AI offers unprecedented opportunities for personalized learning, real-time assessment, and educational equity, it also raises complex ethical and pedagogical questions that require thoughtful consideration (Zhai 2021; Zhai, Neumann, and Krajcik 2023). The chapters in this book collectively argue for a balanced, responsible approach to harnessing AI's potential—one that is rooted in empirical evidence, ethical principles, and a deep understanding of educational contexts.

We extend our heartfelt gratitude to all the contributors who have made this book a rich repository of knowledge and insight. Their expertise and dedication have been invaluable in shaping this volume. We also thank the readers whose engagement with this work completes the knowledge loop and contributes to the ongoing discourse in this dynamic field.

In a rapidly evolving educational landscape, where the integration of technology is no longer a luxury but a necessity (Zhai and Nehm 2023), this book serves as both a guide and a catalyst. It not only addresses the "what" and "how" of AI in STEM education but also delves into the "why," offering a nuanced understanding of the ethical, pedagogical, and societal implications. As such, it is an indispensable resource for educators, policymakers, researchers, and anyone interested in the future of education.

As we look to the future, AI-based STEM education appears poised to become a new paradigm, reshaping how we think about teaching, learning, and educational research. However, this transformation will not be without its challenges. It will require interdisciplinary collaboration, ongoing empirical research, and above all, a commitment to ethical principles. As AI technologies continue to evolve, so too must our strategies for integrating them into educational settings in ways that are both effective and just. This book aims to serve as a roadmap for these critical endeavors, and we are optimistic that the journey ahead, though complex, is filled with promise.

Acknowledgments

This material is based upon work supported by the National Science Foundation (NSF) under Grants 2101104 and 2138854. Any opinions, findings, conclusions, or recommendations expressed in this material are those of the author and do not necessarily reflect the views of the NSF.

References

National Research Council. 2012. *A Framework for K-12 Science Education: Practices, Crosscutting Concepts, and Core Ideas.* Washington, DC: National Academies Press.

Zhai, X. 2021. "Practices and Theories: How Can Machine Learning Assist in Innovative Assessment Practices in Science Education." *Journal of Science Education and Technology* 30, no. 2: 139–49. https://link.springer.com/article/10.1007/s10956-021-09901-8

Zhai, X., Haudek, K. C., Shi, L., Nehm, R., and Urban-Lurain, M. 2020a. "From Substitution to Redefinition: A Framework of Machine Learning-Based Science Assessment." *Journal of Research in Science Teaching* 57, no. 9: 1430–59.

Zhai, X., and Nehm, R. 2023. "AI and Formative Assessment: The Train Has Left the Station." *Journal of Research in Science Teaching* 60, no. 6: 1390–98.

Zhai, X., Neumann, K., and Krajcik, J. 2023. "AI for Tackling STEM Education Challenges." *Frontiers in Education* 8, article no. 1183030. https://www.frontiersin.org/articles/10.3389/feduc.2023.1183030/full

Zhai, X., and Wiebe, E. 2023. "Technology-Based Innovative Assessment." In *Classroom-Based STEM Assessment*, edited by C. J. Harris, E. Wiebe, S. Grover, and J. W. Pellegrino, 99–125. Community for Advancing Discovery Research in Education, Education Development Center.

Zhai, X., Yin, Y., Pellegrino, J. W., Haudek, K. C., and Shi, L. 2020b. "Applying Machine Learning in Science Assessment: A Systematic Review." *Studies in Science Education* 56, no. 1: 111–51.

Index

For the benefit of digital users, indexed terms that span two pages (e.g., 52–53) may, on occasion, appear on only one of those pages.